Sahuarita, Arizona:
Treasured Nuggets From the Past

So much of our future lies in preserving our past.

~ Peter Westbrook ~

Friends of Sahuarita

DEDICATION

This book is dedicated to the many individuals who shared their personal memories, family stories, and community vignettes with a group of tireless and talented volunteers intent on preserving these treasures for future generations.

CONTENTS

PREFACE

When the process of writing this book began, the idea was that it would be a history of the Sahuarita Unified School District (SUSD) of Southern Arizona. But as it took shape, context began creeping in, primarily in the form of stories of the settlers, mines, and farms in the area. How did one school district spring from so many scattered ranch, farm, and mine schools? Who was instrumental in developing the area? Who migrated here and why? How does all of this fit together?

In the spring of 2016, a formal SUSD history committee was launched heralding eager sages with requests to share their stories and memories. Longtime area residents agreed to recount their experiences while a select group of current and retired SUSD team members and community advocates agreed to help compile and edit all of these precious nuggets of history. Rachel Wear, a retired educator and multitalented sage, was instrumental in researching the inceptive data. She also graciously told us about her friend, Mary Kasulaitis, a well-respected, retired librarian and dogged local historian.

The project was later expanded to include the histories of ranches, mines, and schools that were eventually annexed to the Sahuarita Unified School District: Arivaca No. 2, Cerro Colorado No. 25, Helvetia No. 39, Liberty Mine No. 33, Sierrita-McGee Ranch No. 6, Sopori No. 49, Twin Buttes No. 21, and Zinc Mine No. 32. Research led to better knowledge of the towns that had grown alongside the farms, ranches, and mines, clearly providing an understanding that the communities of Green Valley and Sahuarita, while different, were also intertwined.

In the fall of 2018, the focus of the project grew in scope once more. The committee members realized that each time a layer was uncovered, more questions arose. We needed some resolute researchers to unify and expand the body of work. Dayna Burke, an award-winning educator, a new-teacher-induction-tour guide, and our project administrative assistant who needed to complete her National Board Certification, sadly resigned.

It is said that when doors are closed, "God opens a window." Providentially, Monica Christiansen, a hard-working researcher with a can-do attitude and great technological skills, offered to lead the research team. She collaborated closely with Mary and two dedicated oral historians, Oscar Gomez and Amy Millet. As assignments were tweaked and expanded, the project grew to encompass the etymology and background of the name Sahuarita, the early years of Sahuarita from 1820–79, the history of Sahuarita pre- and post-World War II to 1963, and a Sahuarita snapshot that provided personal snippets from the 1930s into the 1980s.

Charles Oldham, a retired principal of Sopori Elementary School and an interim superintendent, provided the committee with a copy of "The Sahuarita Story," written by retired Superintendent Paul S. Frick, which raised the question, "How can a better job be done to maximize the development of [each student's] innate abilities?" The guide provides a fascinating historical sketch of the Sahuarita School District from 1948 to 1973 and how it faced the "challenge of creating and implementing an individualized-curriculum design." After reading "The Sahuarita Story," the reader will have a much clearer view of the District's history and come away with a better understanding of the connectivity of its communities.

Green Valley was home to the interesting and vibrant history of the Continental Elementary School District No. 39, which served grades K–8; unfortunately, there wasn't a local high school to serve our communities, so students were bused to Tucson. That void was addressed on November 18, 1958, when the voters of the Sahuarita School District approved by a vote of thirty to zero the formation of a high school district which to this day serves Green Valley and Sahuarita students.

With the research on the towns and school districts underway, the committee turned to the personal narratives of our local sages and the business community and documented willing individuals' primary-source narratives through a variety of communication mediums. Numerous interviews were conducted to capture the historical diversity of the peoples in the area and their personal stories. Many businesses contributed graciously of their time and talents to retell their beginnings here.

These days, Sahuarita Unified School District hosts an annual New Teachers Induction Program that introduces participants to the school district, and often to the Sahuarita area, through a crash course on local history and lore. New hires have the privilege, via a bus tour, of seeing the pecan groves where vegetables, grains, cotton, peanuts, and even guayule, a natural rubber-producing plant, helped the World War I war effort. They hear about the former gunnery and bombing range located near Walden Grove High School, where locals used to collect spent ammunition. Driving south on Old Nogales Highway toward Continental Road, the new teachers unknowingly pass the site of a fire-razed World War II POW camp on their way to I-19 south to Amado, where their attention is drawn to an eye-catching gigantic longhorn skull that serves as the entrance to the Longhorn Grill and Saloon. On both sides of it is the dry bed of the Kinsley Ranch lake that once attracted tourists to the bar and roping area.

As the bus winds down the two-lane road to rural Arivaca, it passes a shrine dedicated to Santa Rita that perches on a bluff overlooking the Sopori Ranch. A few miles later the teachers pass the playground of the old Sopori School, now completely demolished. As they travel to Arivaca, the teachers find the oldest still-standing adobe brick schoolhouse in Arizona. The Arivaca schoolhouse was built in 1879 and is on the National Historic Registry thanks to one of our writers and preservationists. Heading back north, on the valley's west side, is Twin Buttes, razed and completely buried under miles of mine tailings; this town once touted plans to make Tucson its suburb. Nearby is the McGee Ranch, a small, rural, family community at the base of the Sierritas. Helmet Peak towers over an empty desert where the tiny Zinc School once stood.

New teachers are thus given a small taste of the beautiful diversity in the area and learn to appreciate the sheer size of not only the school district, but the greater Sahuarita community. This brief introductory tour, available only to new teachers for now, serves to barely scratch the surface of the area and leaves each participant with myriad unanswered questions; the desire to answer those questions and to preserve our local history for future generations was the catalyst for this book.

The stories told in this book will undoubtedly make you, the reader smile, laugh, cry, and sigh. Our hope is this book will educate your mind, rejuvenate your heart, and nourish your soul. It might even jump-start positivity in a world deflated by negativity. Wouldn't that be a wonderful by-product?

~ Contributed by Mary Chernoski and Dayna
Burke, with revisions by Monica Lee Elam
Christiansen and Mary N. Kasulaitis

NOTES

Frick, Paul S. Section on "The Story of Sahuarita's Schools" at the end of Part III of this book.

Oldham, Charles. Section on Charles Oldham in Part V.

United States Census: https://www.census.gov/quickfacts/sahuaritatownarizonas

Walenga, Karen. "Days Gone By," interview with R. Grabowski. *Sahuarita Sun*, July 7, 2004.

Walenga, Karen. *The Santa Cruz Valley: a Centennial Celebration*. Sahuarita, AZ: Green Valley News and Sun, 2011.

PART I: INTRODUCTION TO THE ARIZONA EDUCATION SYSTEM

Background on Early Schools in Arizona

When the Territory of Arizona government was established in 1864, schools and a university were planned as a direction to be followed. Prior to that, there had been only Roman Catholic schools. In 1867, a law was passed to establish school districts under each county board of supervisors once a settlement had a resident population of one hundred persons. Many communities could not qualify for lack of size. In 1870 there were fewer than 10,000 persons living in a territory greater than 113,000 square miles. Besides the San Xavier mission school, there were only two schools in Arizona in 1871, both private; one was a Catholic girls' school maintained by the Sisters of St. Joseph of Carondelet in Tucson. Serious effort to provide equitable public schools did not come until the tenure (1869–77) of the third territorial governor, Anson P. K. Safford, whose leadership cannot be overestimated.

An act to establish free public schools in the Territory of Arizona was passed in 1871 at the behest of Governor Safford, who considered the need for public schools to be one of the most important problems in the state during his administration. Estevan B. Ochoa, a legislator from Pima County, introduced the bill. Prior laws had been non-compulsory and not supported by territorial taxes. This act levied a tax of ten cents on each hundred dollars of property value, paid to the territorial treasury in a special fund for school purposes. A county tax not to exceed fifty cents per hundred was also ordered, providing for uniform treatment throughout the territory. In each school district a board of three public school trustees was to be elected that would manage the school. This included constructing and furnishing schoolhouses and taking a school census each year. A uniform series of textbooks was adopted. As soon as the act was passed, and for the next six years, Governor Safford traveled to almost every settlement in Arizona encouraging people to designate trustees, organize districts, and build public schools. New districts could be established upon petition of local residents. Schools were commonly one-room facilities until the population growth of a district warranted larger buildings. In rural areas, schools usually had a short school year because of the difficulty of obtaining teachers, and/or because of harvesting seasons in agricultural areas. In the Territory of Arizona, most of the districts were located in rural areas, which could be defined as sparsely settled, with population centers of 1,000 or less. (Weeks, 1918)

Governor Anson P. K. Safford, "father of the Arizona schools." Courtesy of University of Arizona Special Collections.

The first public school in Pima County under the new law was opened in Tucson in March of 1872. John Spring was the first teacher in a one-room adobe building on the corner of McCormick and Meyer Streets. (This building is no longer in existence.) The floor was dirt and the furniture was rudimentary. Only boys attended this school, and the enrollment reached 138 students at one point. In 1873, Josephine Brawley Hughes opened the first public school for girls. Two pioneer teachers, Maria Wakefield and Harriet Bolton, were persuaded to come from California to teach at this school, which soon included boys as well. With rapid growth of population in Tucson came the opening of more schools to meet the challenge, with citizens raising needed funds on their own. The first school building in Phoenix was constructed of adobe in 1873 on Central Avenue between Monroe and Van Buren, and served thirty-five boys and girls. According to the *Arizona Weekly Miner*, "The new school house is an adobe, 20 by 30 in the clear and 16 feet high, with a good shingle roof. There are three windows on each side (double-hung), one large double door on one end and a fire-place in the other. The floor is of dirt . . ." This building closely resembled the building that would be constructed at Arivaca in 1879. (Wagoner, 1970) The Phoenix building was demolished ten years later when a larger one was needed. During Governor Safford's term, the state school superintendent duties were performed by the governor. After he left office, the new governors were not so focused on this duty, so in 1879 the office of Territorial Superintendent of Public Instruction was established. Moses H. Sherman was the first territorial superintendent, appointed by Governor John C. Fremont.

In the final census taken during Safford's term of office, 2,955 children in the territory were in school and at least 1,450 were able to read and write. He was duly proud of the educational advances made during his administration. Safford was also involved on a personal level. One of the students for whom he served as patron was Ignacio Bonillas, the son of a blacksmith in Tucson. Safford supported Ignacio with books and paper, while Ignacio worked for him and helped him with translations. After his local schooling, Ignacio was able to attend Massachusetts Institute of Technology. Later he became the first ambassador to Mexico from Washington, D.C. Governor Safford had also been involved in mining ventures in the state, including the area around Arivaca and more famously, Tombstone, where he gained a large monetary benefit, and left the Territory in 1882.

~ Contributed by Mary N. Kasulaitis

NOTES

Wagoner, Jay J. *Early Arizona.* Tucson, AZ: The University of Arizona Press, 1975.
Weeks, Stephen. *History of public school education in Arizona.* Bureau of Education. Department of the Interior. Bulletin, 1918, No. 17.

Arizona School District Numbering

If you have ever had reason to take a look at the historic numbering system of Arizona school districts, you will all too quickly find yourself confused and, with minimal effort, will come to the realization that there really was no consistent "system" involved in the process. Neither the Arizona Department of Education nor the Pima County School Superintendent's Office truly has an idea when districts started or stopped carrying the numbers they were assigned. It has been complete mayhem.

In order to start making sense of the number assignments, one must realize that, in the Territory of Arizona, the first county divisions were formed on November 10, 1864, and included only Mohave, Pima, Yavapai, and Yuma Counties. In December of 1865, Pah-Ute County was formed from a piece of

Mohave, but after giving a portion to Nevada in 1866, it was completely disbanded by 1871 when the remaining land was absorbed into Mohave County. In February of 1871, Maricopa was formed from a portion of Yavapai.[1]

In the early 1870s, when the Territory of Arizona first started assigning numbers to schools, there were still only six counties in existence. The Pima County Supervisor Minutes, which will be referenced throughout with dates, illustrate that school district number designations were assigned according to order of formation, so Pima County School District No. 1, created on November 18, 1871, was in Tucson. Pima County District No. 2 was formed in Sanford (also known as Adamsville) on September 21, 1872, and on December 12 of that same year, District No. 2 was split to create District No. 3 of Florence. On March 15, 1873, Mohave County District No. 1 (in Cerbat), Yavapai County District No. 1 (in Prescott), Yuma County District No. 1 (in Arizona City), Yuma County District No. 2 (in Ehrenberg), Maricopa County District No. 1 (south of Phoenix), and Maricopa County District No. 2 (in Phoenix) were created. Pima County District No. 4 was established in San Pedro on July 7, 1873.

The *Arizona Weekly Citizen* reported Pima County School District statistics on July 12, 1873. "In No. 1 there are 540 children between the ages of six and twenty-one years; 263 boys and 277 girls; 138 attend public and 93 private schools, and 183 can read and write. In No. 2 there are 98 between the ages named; 64 boys and 34 girls; 24 attend public and 7 private schools, and 23 can read and write. In No. 3 there are 64 children; 32 boys and 32 girls, and 28 can read and write. In No. 4 there are 49 children; 25 boys and 24 girls, and 9 can read and write."

Pinal County was formed on February 1, 1875, from land taken from Maricopa and Pima. Pima County Districts No. 2 (Sanford) and No. 3 (Florence) were within the boundaries of the new county. When the Safford District was created on April 3, 1876, it became the new Pima County District No. 3 and, at that time, the Board of Supervisors ordered "that the school district at San Pedro shall hereafter be known as school district No. 2."[2] District No. 4 was assigned on December 4, 1876, to "All the Valley of the Santa Cruz lying South of the Canoa."

Over the next few years, Pima County District No. 5 (Arivaca) was formed on April 8, 1879, and District No. 6 (Dos Cabezas) on October 1, 1879. Pima County District No. 7 (Saint Thomas Camp) was named on January 5, 1880, with Districts No. 9 (Contention City) and 10 (Charleston) being established on July 6, 1880. Districts No. 11 (Mormon School), No. 2 (Harshaw, replacing San Pedro), and No. 13 (Solomonville) were created on July 13 of that same year and No. 14 (St. David) was added on November 25.[3]

On the first of February in 1881, Cochise County was created from Pima County, taking Districts No. 4, 6, 9, 10, and 11; when Graham County was formed on March 10, 1881, from portions of Apache and Pima Counties, Districts No. 7 and 13 went with it.

As they had in the past, the Pima County authorities immediately started recycling the district numbers. The Pima County Board of Supervisors assigned Oro Blanco to District No. 5 on July 22, 1881. On October 4, 1881, they assigned Washington Camp the title of District No. 3.

On January 5, 1882, the school superintendent requested that the districts be numbered as follows: Tucson No. 1, Harshaw No. 2, Washington Camp No. 3, Tubac No. 4, Oro Blanco No. 5, and Arivaca No. 6. The Board of Supervisors approved. This session also defined the boundaries for the newly established Tubac District that was replacing the former No. 4, the Santa Cruz Valley south of Canoa. Arivaca had petitioned for creation of a school district and the approval at this same session indicates that the school must have been closed for quite some period of time prior to January of 1882.

Adding to the confusion, many of the small school districts were created in mining camps, which were continually faced with population fluctuations. Market demands, new mine discoveries, and used-up mine closures led to school openings and closures. Others were located in farming or ranching communities and dealt with seasonal highs and lows due to migratory farm workers. To illustrate this, with all of the numbers previously assigned and changed, on January 1, 1882, the only districts included in county funding were Tucson No. 1 (282 students), Harshaw No. 2 (39 students), Washington Camp No. 3 (26 students), Tubac No. 4 (40 students), Oro Blanco No. 5 (33 students), and Arivaca No. 6 (30 students).

Buell's Addition became No. 9 on December 31, 1881, but by December 29, 1882, it had been changed to a Tucson School District along 5th Avenue. Greaterville became No. 7 on July 21, 1882. District No. 8 was, on October 2, 1882, assigned to the Total Wreck Mine, and Buell's Addition No. 9 was reassigned to a Tucson-area school on December 29 of that year.

	Established	#	Change	#	Change	#	Change	#	Annexed	To
Aguirre	1906 Aug 02	24								Closed
Arivaca	1879 Apr 08	5	1882 Jan 05	6	1900 Aug 07	2			1951 Sept 05	Sopori
Canoa	1912 Dec 17	31	1913 Dec 07	21						Closed
Cerro Colorado	Pre-1906	25	1911 Oct 02	25						Closed
Continental	1917 Jul 12	39	1918 Jun 01	39						
Helvetia	1900 Jan 08	38	1900 Aug 07	14	1903 Oct 09	20	1905 Jan 04	14	1926 Jul 18	Closed
Liberty Mine	1897 Jul 24	16								Closed
Sahuarita	1894 Aug 06	29	1900 Aug 07	12	1911 Jul 01	30	1933 Oct 02	30		
Sierrita	1913 Dec 01	6	1930–31	AS*	1939 Jul 01	56			1953 Jul 01	Sahuarita
Sopori	1897 Jul 24	32	1900 Aug 07	15	1916 Jul 01	29	1933 Jul 03	49	1968 Jul 01	Sahuarita
Twin Buttes	1906 Jul 23	21							1948 Jun 30	Sahuarita
Zinc	1913 Oct 06	32							1945 Jul 01	Twin Buttes

Table 1. Organization of Districts
* AS stands for "accommodation school"

On January 14, 1883, the *Tucson Citizen* listed the annual district funding and populations as follows: Tucson No. 1 (229 students), Harshaw No. 2 (14 students), La Noria No. 3 (15 students), Tubac No. 4 (21 students), Oro Blanco No. 5 (31 students), Arivaca No. 6 (25 students), and Greaterville No. 7 (12 students).

Over the next sixteen years, the tradition of "start and stop" districts continued, with numbers being continually recycled. When Santa Cruz County was formed March 15, 1899, it took twelve districts with it. The May 9 Board of Supervisors meeting notes included a discussion about transferring state funds to Santa Cruz County to cover the schools that were now part of that county. Those included on that list were Harshaw No. 2, Lochiel (a.k.a. Luttrell and La Noria) No. 3, Tubac No. 4, Oro Blanco No. 5, Evan's Camp No. 10, Calabasas No. 11, Crittenden No. 13, Nogales No. 14, West Huachuca No. 17, Washington Camp/Duquesne No. 24, Santa Cruz No. 25, and Palo Parado No. 26.

On August 2, 1900, the notes of the Pima County Supervisors state that, "The boundaries of many of the School Districts of Pima County as same now exist of record being conflicting and incorrectly described." On October 4, 1899, the board had ordered the county school superintendent, "to change, harmonize, describe, and renumber said Districts." This was completed on October 30, 1899, and the board approved them. The following list contains the Pima County Districts included in that revision: Tucson No. 1, Arivaca No. 2, Greaterville No. 3, Rincon No. 4, San Xavier No. 5, San Pedro No. 6, Tanque Verde No. 7, Rillito No. 8, Lowell No. 9, Amphitheater No. 10, Buenos Ayres No. 11, Sahuarita No. 12, Rosemont No. 13, Helvetia No. 14, Sopori No. 15, Liberty Mine No. 16, and Laguna No. 17.

With a "new start," of sorts, the County now had an accurate, detailed legal description to go with each of the consecutively numbered districts, but the cyclical nature of district populations continued and the historical naming practices did not change. The chart shown in Table 1, created from the Board of Supervisors Minutes, was an attempt to clarify the post-1900 organization of the districts focused on in this history project.

~ Contributed by Monica Lee Elam Christiansen

NOTES

References

1. https://www.familysearch.org/wiki/en/Arizona_County_Creation_Dates_and_Parent_Counties
2. *Arizona Weekly Citizen*, April 15, 1976.
3. MS 183, F.27, Pima County Collection, Minutes of Board of Supervisors: Organization of School Districts (1872–1933). Arizona State Archives.

Additional resources

Arizona Daily Star, Tucson, Arizona
Tucson Citizen, Tucson, Arizona

1910s-era map of school district boundaries. Courtesy of Monica Lee Elam Christiansen.

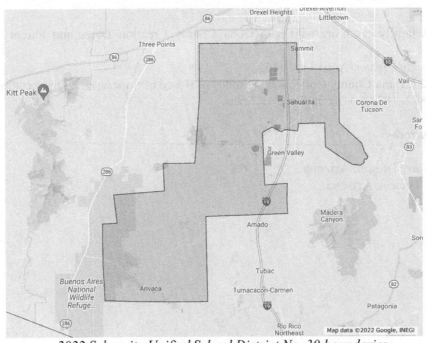

2022 Sahuarita Unified School District No. 30 boundaries.
Courtesy of Sahuarita Unified School District.

PART II: EARLY SCHOOL DISTRICTS

Schools represent the core of their communities, like the hubs of the rusted wheels anchoring spokes to the axle captured in the watercolor painting on this book's cover. Schools are the by-product of the common, vested interest of multiple entities that are focused on advancing local children's knowledge. When the crossbars converge, they form a strong forward-rolling wheel.

Historically, in southern Pima County, small school districts emerged and puttered out like storm cells in an Arizona monsoon. The overview of the Arizona education system presented in the following pages allows readers to now focus on eight of the small "hubs" that welded students, teachers, families, and businesses together into what would someday become Sahuarita Unified School District No. 30.

Arivaca School District, 1879–1953

In the mid-1870s, Arivaca was in a period of rapid growth due to mining activity. As early as 1870, freighter Don Pedro Aguirre had built a stage stop and store there because of proximity to water in the Arivaca *ciénaga*. He also began his Buenos Ayres Ranch in Altar Valley to the west of Arivaca. Pedro's older brother, Epifanio, had married Mary "Mamie" Bernard of Westport, Missouri. Her younger brother, Noah W. Bernard, came to Arivaca and worked in Aguirre's store. Noah became the first postmaster in 1878 and also began to develop a ranch and store of his own. Several well-advertised mining operations attracted prospectors to the area. In 1879, the population had grown to over three hundred. By 1880, the town contained a hotel, customs house, blanket factory, six saloons, two bakeries, two restaurants, one butcher shop, one blacksmith shop, one barbershop, and one brewery. There were three mining mills within three miles of town. Governor Safford had invested in mines in the area and in 1877 ran his sheep herd on Pedro Aguirre's ranch near Arivaca. (Kasulaitis, 2006)

The typical pattern of school development, as outlined previously, transpired in Arivaca. According to Pima County records dated April 8, 1879, Book One, page 345: "The Probate Judge presented a petition of heads of families residing at Aravaca [sic] and vicinity asking for the establishment of a School District at Aravaca. On motion ordered that Aravaca School District No. 5 be formed and established out of all that part of Pima County bounded on the north by a line running east and west one mile north of Sopori Ranch on the east by the range of mountains next east line running north and south through the Baboquivari Peak." Within a few months, on June 7, 1879, the *Arizona Sentinel* (Yuma, Arizona) quoted a report in *El Fronterizo* (Tucson, Arizona) that "Mr. Pedro Aguirre is about establishing a public school at Arivaca at his own expense." By October 9 of that year, the *Arizona Weekly Star* reported that the school building had been constructed. It continued, "Of the half dozen structures which at present constitute the town, the most prominent and neatly finished is the school house." The school that was constructed in 1879 is still in place.

Don Pedro Aguirre, Jr., was from Chihuahua, Mexico, from a family of Spanish heritage that valued the entrepreneurial spirit for which education was necessary. His father and family had moved to Mesilla in the Territory of New Mexico and became American citizens in 1855. They helped him with a freighting business that extended along the Santa Fe Trail from Missouri to Altar, Sonora. Aguirre had maintained a store in Altar, Sonora, where he met his wife, Ana Maria Redondo, who was from a prominent Mexican family. He had a stage line from Tucson through Arivaca to Altar, and it was on this route that he founded his ranch, Buenos Ayres, and built a house in Arivaca. As he prospered, Aguirre built a home in Tucson and was elected to the Pima County Board of Supervisors.

In the early years in Mesilla, Aguirre was involved in a mercantile business with Stephen Ochoa, also from Chihuahua. Ochoa went into the freighting business in Tucson, learned English, and proceeded to become one of the most successful businessmen in the territory. He served as a territorial legislator and in 1875 became mayor of Tucson. In 1871, Ochoa partnered with Governor Safford to promote and provide public schools in Arizona, including the introduction of the 1871 education bill. Ochoa School in Tucson is named for him.

Aguirre's sister, Dolores, married Mariano G. Samaniego, also a freighter. Born in Sonora, Samaniego had been educated at St. Louis University in the United States. He was a successful entrepreneur and was active in politics, having been elected to the Territorial Legislature from Tucson as well as serving on the first Board of Regents. Thus the Aguirres had connections and influence at all levels of public educational development in the Territory of Arizona. Proper education for children was a concern of families who realized its importance. The Aguirre family and their friends and relatives, known as members of the "Mexican elite" of Southern Arizona, recognized the need to speak fluent English as well as Spanish. (Sheridan, 1986) In Arivaca, the school population was predominantly Mexican-American.

The Arivaca school represents a type of school architecture typically used in the early period of education in the Territory of Arizona. Adobe was a common building material. High ceilings and a pyramidal roof combined both Sonoran and Anglo-European types of construction. Although no early photos of the Arivaca School have surfaced, it was likely comparable to the first school building in Phoenix, for which a photo exists. (Wagoner, 1970, 110)

Mary "Mamie" Bernard Aguirre, the first Arivaca teacher. Courtesy of University of Arizona Special Collections.

On January 5, 1882, on the recommendation of School Superintendent John S. Woods, the several school districts of Pima County were renumbered as follows: Tucson District No. 1, Harshaw District No. 2, Washington Camp District No. 3, Tubac District No. 4, Oro Blanco District No. 5, and Arivaca District No. 6. Arivaca District became No. 2 when Santa Cruz County was established in 1899 and the previously mentioned school districts numbered two through five were removed there. It remained No. 2 until the school was closed in 1953.

The first teacher in Arivaca was probably the aforementioned Mary (Mamie) Bernard Aguirre. She had been educated at a private school in Baltimore, Maryland. Her father was a trader on the east end of the Santa Fe Trail in Westport, Missouri. She met her husband, Epifanio Aguirre (Pedro's older brother), on one of his trips to Westport. He spoke no English, so she learned Spanish. After they married, she traveled with him to Arizona. When Epifanio was killed by Native Americans near Sasabe, Arizona, in 1870, Mamie began teaching to support herself and their three boys. In 1878, she left her school at Tres Alamos, near Benson, and went to stay with her brother Noah in Arivaca.

Official records are unavailable for 1879–80, but according to her biographer, Mamie Aguirre was the first teacher at Arivaca. Pima County records report that Mamie taught in Arivaca in 1884, receiving $80 for one month's work. Mrs. Aguirre later became one of the first professors of history and English at the University of Arizona and is a member of the Arizona Women's Hall of Fame. So even though Arivaca was in an isolated area, with a predominantly Mexican population of mine workers, the factors were in place to support construction of a school as well as the territory-wide political forces and personal interests of the Aguirre and Bernard families. Thus it was that the persons most involved in the development of Arivaca were also aligned with the fledgling education movement in the Territory of Arizona. (Gray)

Bell Donnelly and E. K. Anderson taught at Arivaca in 1881 and were paid $75 each. (Mrs. J. T.) Sarah Black was another early teacher, having been there from 1883–84. That year, sixty-five children were enrolled. She moved on to Tubac where she taught for a number of years.

Arivaca School class with teacher Gipsy Clarke in 1912. Courtesy of Chris Clarke.

One of the most interesting sources of information on this school comes from the diary and stories of teacher Gipsy Harper Clarke, who came to Arivaca to teach in 1910. She reported that when she took over the one-room school it was in bad repair, despite the fact that the man who would later become her husband had installed a floor in 1906. She had sixty-five students, most of whom did not speak English. The Arivaca Land and Cattle Company, managed by Noah C. Bernard, the son of Noah W. Bernard, had responsibility for the school. (Arivaca operated more or less as a company town.) Phil Clarke, the store manager, provided repairs and supplies. Only a few months after she arrived, he and Gipsy were married. In those days married women were usually not allowed to teach, but Gipsy continued to teach for several terms. She arranged for the first existing photo of schoolchildren, which was preserved by her family, as was her diary. The latter provides a vivid description of the decrepit conditions she found upon arrival in 1910 and illustrates why, over the years, most teachers lasted only one year. Here is an excerpt from her diary:

> *Near the cemetery was the school. That too was of adobe, which had one time been plastered or white-washed, but now only splotches of white remained around the windows and doors and in odd places on the walls. Many of the window panes were broken; the ones that were not were so grimy we could not see through them. The grounds had never been cleared of brush and rocks except the spot around the door where children's feet had worn it smooth.*

"I have to see Mr. Clarke," I said, "and arrange about getting the school in order. He promised to open the building for me this afternoon . . ."

He unlocked the school door and pushed it open, revealing a filthy floor, upturned desks whittled and ink-stained, a rusty iron stove without a pipe, and the teacher's table and bell.

"Where is the equipment?" I asked lamely.

"What d'you mean, equipment?"

"Doesn't the territory furnish books, charts, paper, and pencils?" I asked.

"Forget it!"

"Do the children buy their own supplies?"

"Of course they don't."

"Perhaps if you'd order them and put them in the store, some of the more ambitious parents would pay for them," I suggested.

"Look here! I've got the whole cattle company and every person for twenty miles tellin' me what to order for that store. I'm not going to have you tellin' me to start a bookstore."

"Really, Mr. Clarke, I've got to wash these windows or this floor, if you're not going to hire it done."

"The kids will clean the school Monday. If they don't, I'll send the constable after them."

Well, Phil didn't do the cleaning—Gipsy and the kids did it. A few months later, Gipsy married him. She later wrote a loosely autobiographical novel, *Out Yonder*. Phil became a prominent cattle rancher and businessman.

According to an attendance report by teacher Mildred Phillips, in 1914 there were ninety-six students, so the additional room must have been constructed about this time. Perhaps this influx of people was the result of the Mexican Revolution, as Arivaca was on one of the main routes from Altar, Sonora, to Tucson. A few years later, in 1919, a photo of the school with an unknown teacher shows at least forty-six students, and about the same number in a 1928 photo.

Arivaca School children in 1930. Courtesy of University of Arizona Special Collections.

Phebe Brink came to Arivaca as a teenager in 1879, when her father came to work for a mining company here. She married A. E. "Beanie" Bogan, brother of prominent rancher and politician John Bogan. She attended school in Tucson and returned to Arivaca in 1901 and 1915–18. Her school records of 1916 are some of the few that have been preserved in the Arizona State Archives. Recently they were instrumental in helping one person prove the Arizona residency of his parents so he could gain U.S. citizenship. Phebe later wrote a book on Yaqui Indians and taught Spanish in the Tucson schools. Other teachers who were there for a number of years were the married couples J. P. and Bertha McDole, and W.

G. and Alice Barnett. (Most teachers were housed in the smaller building across from the store, next to the historic hotel.) Helen Noon (sister of rancher and historian Fred Noon) and Louise Reed Dunlap taught throughout the 1930s. Emma Mae Townsend was the teacher during the final ten years that the school was in operation.

The village of Arivaca was established as a federal town site in 1916, filed by the Arivaca Land and Cattle Company, under the trusteeship of the presiding judge of the Superior Court of Pima County. The only two properties left in the town site still under this trusteeship, unsold to private parties, are the school (town park) block and the cemetery block. They are still federal property. Otherwise, Arivaca is part of unincorporated Pima County. In 2003, the school block was relinquished by Sahuarita School District and became a town park, by action of the presiding judge. Now recognized as the oldest standing schoolhouse in Arizona, the building achieved status on the National Register of Historic Places in 2012. It is maintained by Friends of the Arivaca Schoolhouse and Historic Townsite, Inc.

Arivaca School remained in operation for seventy-four years. It closed its doors in 1953 during a time in Arivaca history when the population was at its lowest. The school building went into use as a community center. What is unique about Arivaca is that its economic development was arrested about the same time it reached its peak growth as a mining boom town in 1880. The boom busted, and many of the miners moved away. However, population remained steady, but below 300, from 1880 to about 1940, dropping when people began moving to Tucson. The need for a larger school building never transpired, so the same one that was constructed in 1879 served its purpose until 1953. In that year the school population was deemed too small to warrant a school and the district was annexed to Sopori School District No. 49, which had a two-room school located fifteen miles northeast of Arivaca. Despite the fact that the population jumped again after 1972 and especially into the 1990s, Sahuarita School District never seriously considered building a school in the Arivaca area.

Arivaca School in the 1940s.
Courtesy of Fred C. Noon.

~ Contributed by Mary N. Kasulaitis

NOTES

Aguirre, Yjinio. *Echoes of the Conquistadores: History of a pioneer family in the Southwest.* 1983.

Bourne, Eulalia. *Nine Months is a Year at Baboquivari School* (1968) and *Ranch Schoolteacher* (1972), both published in Tucson, Arizona, by The University of Arizona Press, give good background on the conditions of schools at the time.

Gray, Annette. *Journey of the heart: a true story of Mamie Aguirre (1844–1906): A southern belle in the "Wild West."* Markerville, AL: 2004.

Kasulaitis, Mary Noon. "A short history of the village of Arivaca." *The Smoke Signal*, No. 75. Fall 2002.

Kasulaitis, Mary Noon. "A Fenian in the Desert: Captain John McCafferty and the 1870s Arivaca Mining Boom." *The Journal of Arizona History.* Spring 2006.

Pima County school records

Sheridan, Thomas E. *Los Tucsonenses: the Mexican Community in Tucson, 1854–1941.* Tucson, AZ: The

University of Arizona Press, 1986
Wagoner, Jay J. *Early Arizona.* Tucson, AZ: The University of Arizona Press, 1975.
Weeks, Stephen. *History of public school education in Arizona.* Bureau of Education. Department of the Interior. Bulletin, 1918, No. 17.
Arizona Daily Star
Tucson Citizen
Arizona Weekly Star

Cerro Colorado School District History

Cerro Colorado School District No. 25 was officially established on October 2, 1911, but several teachers, such as Mary and Mabel Greer, Blanche Walker, Eva Sine, and Arthur Defore, are known to have taught there between 1906 and 1911. The location of any school building is unknown but was probably in the complex of old mine buildings near Arivaca Road and established during the tenure of mine owner Charles Udall. The mine itself was owned by Udall, and his wife was later a school board member. J. F. McDole and Florence Casanega taught between 1912 and 1914, and the latter managed to get new student desks! The last named teacher before the individual district ended in 1917 was Edward Craig in 1914–15. Students subsequently attended Sopori School.

NAMES OF PARENTS OR GUARDIANS	NAMES OF CHILDREN	AGE
Senor Regil Madril	Juan Madril	14
Senor Regil Madril	Pedro Madril	12
Senor Savas Vasquez	Victorino Vasquez	12
Senor Savas Vasquez	Amelia Vasquez	11
Senor Savas Vasquez	Marie Vasquez	7
Senor Savas Vasquez	Jesusita Vasquez	6
Senor Manuel Carrillo	Ramon Carrillo	10
Senor Manuel Carrillo	Mercedes Carrillo	14
Senor Manuel Carrillo	Amelia Carrillo	17
Senor Manuel Carrillo	Josaphina Carrillo	8
Senor Manuel Carrillo	Margarita Carrillo	7
Senor Manuel Carrillo	Manuel Carrillo	6
Senor Jesus Moreno	Mauro Moreno	11
Senor Jesus Moreno	Alberto Moreno	9
Senor Jesus Moreno	Raoul Moreno	7
Senor Jesus Moreno	Manuela Moreno	6
Senor Greg. Sanguetta	Guadalupe Sanguetta	9
Senor Greg. Sanguetta	Alejandro Sanguetta	6
Senor Antonio Lovarino	Rufo Lovarino	11
Senor Antonio Lavorino	Jesus Lavorino	7
Senor E. Monzza	Ramon Monzza	12
Senor E. Monza	Florencio Monza	10
Senor Mau. Mireles	Felipe Mireles	12
Senor Mau. Mireles	Ventura Mireles	6
Senor Mau. Mireles	Rita Mireles	11
Senor Miroles	Pirjirio Miroles	9
Senor Jesus Noriega	Manuel Noriega	9
Senor Jesus Noriega	Jesusita Noriega	7
Senora Lizzy Nelson	Richard Nelson	7
Senor Jesus Piña	Artura Piña	6
Senor Mau. Mindano	Antonio Mindano	8
Senor Jose Lopez	Manuela Lopez	6
Senor Jesus Piña	Millie Piña	10
Senor Jesus Piña	Chona Piña	8
Senor Jesus Redondo	Manuel Redondo	15
Senor Jesus Redondo	Rodolpho Redondo	18
Senor Jesus Marquis	Jose Marquis	18
Senor Yndulesia Aguirre	Yndulesia Aguirre	18

NAMES OF PARENTS OR GUARDIANS	NAMES OF CHILDREN	AGE
Senor Rafael Mendibles	Guadlupe Mendibles	10
Senor Rafael Mendibles	Theresa Mendibles	12
Senor Rafael Mendibles	Jesus Mendibles	15
Senor Jesus Palma	Francisco Palma	18
Senor Jose Uniel	Alejandrio Uniel	19
Senor Y. Aguirre	Patrocinio Aguirre	15
Senor Y. Aguirre	Dolores Aguirre	11
Senor Y. Aguirre	Epifanio Aguirre	8
Senor Y. Aguirre	Demetrio Aguirre	16
Senor Magno Canës	Togosio Canës	11
Senor Magno Canës	Benita Canës	9
Senor Magno Canës	Isabel Canës	8
Senor Magno Canës	Bostesta Canës	6
Senor Jesus Redondo	Patronila Redondo	10
Senor Jesus Redondo	Ramon Redondo	6
Senor Jesus Redondo	Belon Redondo	16
Senor Jesus Redondo	Santiago Redondo	7
Senor Miguel Alcares	Lorita Alcares	12
Senor Miguel Alcares	Pedro Alcares	10
Senor Miguel Alcares	Juan Alcares	7
Senor Miguel Alcares	Isabel Alcares	14

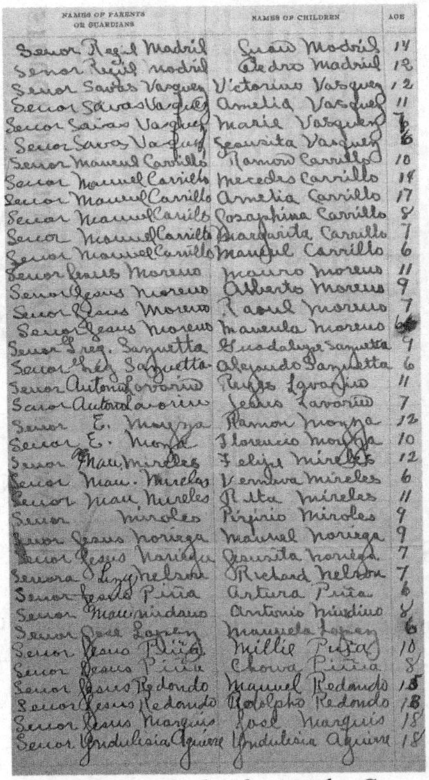

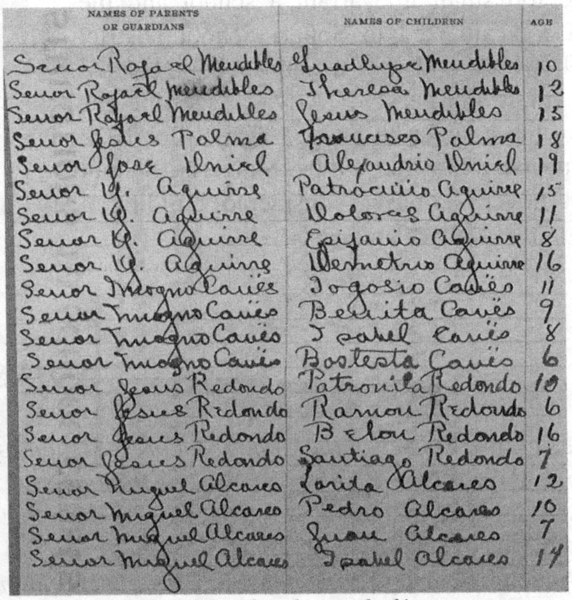

Pima County school records: Cerro Colorado 1906–07 school marshal's census.
Courtesy of Arizona State Archives.

~ Contributed by Mary N. Kasulaitis

Helvetia School District, 1900–23

The Helvetia School operated for a few years in the Helvetia Mining District when several small mining booms brought in enough miners with their families to support a school. In 1878, the Helvetia Mining District was established and named by Ben Hefti, a native of Switzerland. Claims on copper deposits had been staked since 1877 and by 1882, when the Omega Copper Company was formed, there were many claims along the west-side flanks of the Santa Rita Mountains east of Sahuarita. A road from Sahuarito (the J. K. Brown stage line) went over the foothills to Helvetia. Over the ridge from Helvetia, on the eastern slopes, the Rosemont Mining District was also underway. After that, the ups and downs in the price of copper, now in demand for electrical purposes, would determine the fate of the mining companies that followed one after another. In 1899, The Helvetia Copper Company of New Jersey was formed. Due to considerable financial support, the company was able to establish a smelter, assay office, blast furnace, post office, and even an 8,000-foot narrow-gauge railroad. A stage line and road straight north to Vail were

Public school at Helvetia with teacher, Edith Stratton, taken about 1901. Courtesy of Arizona Historical Society.

established to meet the Southern Pacific Railroad. The Harris, Lively, and McGee families that resided at the McGee Ranch on the west side of the valley hauled equipment and ore to and from the mines and Vail. Miners poured in, most of them of Mexican descent. The population was 550 by the end of 1899. In 1900, Helvetia School District No. 39 was established. In 1901–02, Edith Stratton (Kitt) taught at Helvetia. She had thirty students (and later sixty-one) who could be rough. In one case she felt the need to shake a student and gave her a bloody nose. "But all in all, we got along fine," she explained in her autobiography. She enjoyed the life of the mining camp, where there was entertainment, riding, and target shooting, at which she apparently excelled. Edith lasted a year, until one of the mine closures. "One of my last duties at Helvetia, and a sad one, was to shoot all the scrawny stray cats which had been left behind by the departing miners." Apparently teachers had many different duties. In her day, teachers were paid $75 a month and school lasted for periods of from five to eight months, depending on the government allocation. (*Tucson Citizen*, Sep 23, 1908)

At first, the Helvetia School was in a large convenient room, but subsequently a school building was constructed. It was described later as a "gaunt old pioneer schoolhouse with its tall steep roof . . . of lumber, apparently never painted." There were high hopes for a long-term mining operation, but it was not to be. Within a year, the smelter was destroyed by fire and half the workforce was laid off. A drop in the price of copper in 1901 further damaged the mining business. Helvetia was temporarily abandoned in 1902. The school population had dropped from forty-five to eighteen and was closed the next year.

In 1903, the Michigan and Arizona Development Company restarted things and reorganized as the Helvetia Copper Company of Arizona. The school district was reestablished as No. 20. In 1905, once again reorganization was necessary and the smelter was refurbished. The companies knew there was copper under there, but not how to extract it profitably. In 1907, the smelter was closed, but the mines were kept working until they were closed in 1911. All this time there were miners and their families living hopefully nearby, some finding work on ranches or in other mines as need be. The young men from McGee Ranch would work one-month stints hauling freight.

Helvetia mining camp, approximately 1915. Courtesy of U.S. Geological Survey.

The Helvetia mines were working again in 1916 when Eulalia "Sister" Bourne came to teach. World War I had caused a renewed need for copper and other metals such as molybdenum. Four years of Sister's stories form the basis for a wonderful description of life in Helvetia and its school. With one year of teaching under her belt and no family nearby, the people of Helvetia became her family. Her primary problem, in the beginning, was the issue of Spanish-speaking students and her lack of facility in that language.

Sister Bourne and the mine manager, Tom DeVerl, and his bilingual six-year-old daughter Eleanor, were the only English speakers in town. Seventeen children waited on that first day of school. No Spanish was to be spoken in school, and not a word on the school grounds, the rule said, but once school was over, the children taught Spanish to the teacher! Neighbors also helped. It was nothing if not inventive as well as entertaining. Sister learned to teach English as a second language while learning Spanish herself and promoting bilingualism. This would serve her well for most of her subsequent teaching years in Southern Arizona. The school system promoted sewing classes for girls, but no equivalent workshop for the boys. Instituting school parties on the holidays made attendance fun for the children. In the next year or two, Helvetia became the district's "banner school."

Sister taught for four years at Helvetia, leaving in 1920 to go to Tucson where she could get an education degree at the University of Arizona while also teaching. Clara Kistler followed in her footsteps at Helvetia. After World War I ended and demand was reduced, Helvetia was once again failing. Miners and their families moved away. In September, only five people from Helvetia had registered to vote. The post office closed in 1921 and the school in 1923 when attendance fell below ten. The final exercises for the school, under teacher Ellen Harrigan, were held at a picnic in Whitehouse Canyon.

~ Contributed by Mary N. Kasulaitis

NOTES

Bourne, Eulalia. *Ranch schoolteacher*. Tucson, AZ: The University of Arizona Press, 1974.

Briggs, David F. *History of Helvetia-Rosemont Mining District, Pima County, Arizona*. Contributed Report CR-15-D, Arizona Geological Survey.

Buckles, Avi. "A History of Helvetia." *Cultural Resources Report*. Tucson, AZ: Westland Resources, Inc. May 17, 2013. Includes excerpts from an interview of Lynn Harris on file at the Arizona Historical Society Library & Archives.

Feil, Lin B. "Helvetia: Boom town of the Santa Ritas." *The Journal of Arizona History*, Vol. 9, No. 2, Summer 1968.

Kitt, Edith Stratton. *Pioneering in Arizona: The reminiscences of Emerson Oliver Stratton and Edith Stratton Kitt*. Edited by John Alexander Carroll. Tucson, AZ: Arizona Pioneers' Historical Society, 1964.

Articles from the *Tucson Citizen*, *Arizona Daily Star*, and *Arizona Weekly Star*

Eulalia Bourne: "Taken in my doorway—Helvetia at close of school with Eleanor's kittens." Courtesy of Arizona Historical Society.

Liberty Mine School District History

Taken in the school at Liberty Mine in 1899. Composed of the six children of widow May E. Collier Woods Clarke. Edward Woods, Edna Woods, and Mary E. Clarke stand in the back with William, Annabelle, and Cornelius Clarke in the front. Courtesy of Arizona Historical Society.

Liberty Mine District No. 16 (located in the Cerro Colorado Mining District) was organized in 1897 by L. W. Purcell, part owner of mining property in the vicinity and clerk of the probate court in Tucson. Edith Stratton Kitt, who later was well known as the mainstay of the Arizona Historical Society, taught there in 1901, probably for less than one semester. Her name is not on the official register. In her autobiography she reports, "The Liberty Mine was closed and the ranch at that place was run by a widow, Mrs. May M. Clarke [no relation to Phil Clarke]. Her five children and four small Mexican boys, who rode five miles each morning to get to the one-room school, were my pupils. Reading, writing, and arithmetic were about it. I slept in the back of the schoolhouse and boarded with Mrs. Clarke's family." (Kitt, 1964) After Liberty, Edith moved on to Helvetia School.

In 1901–02, Beatriz B. Ferrer and then

Florence M. Taylor are listed as teachers, then Clara Reynolds from 1902–04 when Liberty Mine School District lapsed. The students subsequently attended Sopori School.

~ Contributed by Mary N. Kasulaitis

NOTES

Kitt, Edith Stratton. *Pioneering in Arizona: The reminiscences of Emerson Oliver Stratton and Edith Stratton Kitt*. Edited by John Alexander Carroll. Tucson, AZ: Arizona Pioneers' Historical Society, 1964.

Bill Harris sits in the wagon. Starting from the right, James Riley McGee is second, Fred Harris is third, and Ed Harris is fifth. Courtesy of Lynn Harris.

History of the Sierrita School and McGee Ranch

Nestled against the eastern slopes of the Sierrita Mountains, the families of James Riley McGee, George Harris, Daniel Harris, and David Lively were the original settlers of a rural community today known as McGee Ranch. Prior to their arrival, many miners wandered the mountain foothills, a few even stopping to build small homes in the harsh desert terrain, but none had the tenacity and fortitude to stay.

For many years, the aforementioned families were constantly on the move, spending time in New Mexico, Old Mexico (where Daniel Harris died in 1892), and ultimately, many small towns in Arizona which included Kennelworth, Florence, Helvetia, and Greaterville.

Family tradition tells that in 1895 a wagon driven by James Riley McGee and several of the older Harris boys was headed to California scouting for new opportunities. Once a new settlement location was selected, their intent was to send word for the remaining family members to join them. While meandering toward the Camino del Diablo, which routed them around the south end of the Sierritas, side excursions left them with a broken wagon wheel in the place that would become known as Ezlo Flat. The damage was beyond what they could repair without proper blacksmith tools and equipment, so they were forced to seek assistance in Tucson before they could continue their journey.

While awaiting wagon repairs and hunting for supplies to sustain them, a local prospector told them about "gold in Champurrado Canyon." Always interested in new ideas for profitable ventures, the men decided to try their luck panning for gold. When their initial search yielded a few small flakes of placer gold, they could not resist staying to search for more. It goes without saying that they never made it to California.

On a hunting trip, James Riley McGee and Nephi Bingham stand in the center with mining associates on either side of them. Courtesy of Lynn Harris.

Between 1895 and 1898, a small group of men ran the placer gold operation at Chigger Hill, now called Lobo Peak, high in the Sierrita Mountains. Some families lived in Greaterville, working in the mines, while the remainder of the group farmed several properties and ran a profitable dairy business along the Rillito (Davidson Ranch) and Pantano (Crane and Fraker Ranches) Rivers. In late 1897 or early 1898, the first house was constructed at the base of Keystone Peak in the Sierritas. A number of raised platforms were erected nearby for tent sites, and a blacksmith shop was built. Water was obtained from the shallow Burrow Well, dug in Keystone Canyon.

On a hunting trip, Ono "Matt" McGee, David Lively, James Riley McGee, Arthur Lively, Bill Harris, Alma Harris, Fred Harris, Omeo "George" McGee, and Rero "Robert" McGee pose near their wagon. Courtesy of Lynn Harris.

The families became very close to the Erastus and Susan Green Bingham family that farmed across the river from the Davidson Ranch. In addition to lasting friendships, several marriages took place between the members of the different families. While working at the dairy in April of 1899, Alma "Al" Harris, a son of Daniel Harris, married Florence Mary Holben, a stepdaughter of David Lively's.

The families were extremely focused on the education of their children. On July 14, 1899, the *Arizona Daily Star* reported that the families "propose to have all the educational advantages possible for their children. A county school district to be known as the Davidson district was recently formed, and Mrs. A. J. Nelson, of Columbus, was engaged to teach. The school will open on August 10th, and it is expected that there will be an attendance of thirty children." Another article, dated May 13, 1899, further explained that the Pima County board of supervisors had granted the petition for a new school district, but clarified that, "The parents of the children have offered to furnish the school house and keep it in repair without expense to the county."

At a mining camp in the oaks, James Riley McGee smokes his pipe on the left. Bill Harris stands in the shadow of the tree near the tent corner and Al Harris is in the back near the donkey. Courtesy of Lynn Harris.

While the children were attending classes at their new school, the men were farming and working at a host of new mine sites. Red Boy and Rero, the first mining claims officially filed by James Riley McGee, were recorded on October 26, 1899, in the Sierrita District. Additional Sierrita mining claims—Blue

Horn, Rosenfeld, Napoleon, Garfield, Houston, Lincoln, Blue Belle, Monroe, and Franklin—were filed by James Riley McGee on May 12, 1900.

David Lively and Al Harris at McGee Ranch with a freight wagon
and team of horses. Courtesy of Lynn Harris.

On June 24, 1900, the federal census listed the McGee and Harris families as residing in Pima County Precinct #1, working on the Davidson Ranch as farm laborers, dairymen, house cooks, cattle herders, and a farm foreman. Family records indicate that, although the individuals living at Chigger Hill and Keystone had moved down to the present-day location of McGee Ranch, most family members continued farming along the Rillito River to provide a stable income and allow the children to attend school as the mining activities in the Sierrita Foothills continued to expand. Family members traveled back and forth between the mines and farmland regularly. In January of 1901, they purchased 214 acres of property west of Carrillo's Gardens to expand their dairy business while spending an additional $1,000 to purchase concentrating machinery from the Silverdale Mine near Florence, which they hauled back to the ranch with a team of horses pulling freight wagons.

Rachel Harris making lace.
Courtesy of Lynn Harris.

Florence Holben Harris
repairing shoes for family
members. Courtesy of
Lynn Harris.

Stories of an old English squatter's homesite, nestled in a beautiful cove full of towering oak trees, reached those who were working the placer mining claims at Ezlo Flat. The lonely, industrious man, tired of the difficult life in the mountains, offered his property up to the families if they were interested in taking over his small orchard and garden. He had a shallow well and a small spring at the back of the canyon, providing him sufficient water to survive.

December 29, 1901, found James Riley McGee and his very pregnant wife, Florence "Flora" Sidney Lyon McGee, traveling around the east side of the Sierritas in search of the Englishman's property. When compared to the grassy ridge of Chigger Hill, this beautiful, ready-made homesite so close to the current mining operations was heaven itself and they quickly took him up on his offer. While there in that beautiful, oak-shaded canyon, in the back of the old wooden wagon, Napoleon "Empy" McGee was born—the first birth at what would soon be known as Rero Ranch.

By May 4, 1904, when Lofawn Harris was born, the families had left the farms along the Rillito and Pantano Rivers to move their settlement to the Sierrita Mountains. Life for these early families was not easy. Men tended cattle, farmed, contracted out their freight wagons for hauling, and continued mining operations, which included filing many mining claims in the area. Women worked to process dairy products, including milk, butter, and cheese, while collecting honey from wild bees that nested in trees. The old English settler's fig trees and grapevines were cared for and the fruit harvested by the families. Years of experience using dry farming methods on the Tucson ranches enabled them to raise crops using minimal amounts of water. Surplus was taken by wagon into Nogales, Calabasas, and Tucson to be sold or bartered for needed supplies. By January of 1906, J. R. McGee reported in the *Arizona Daily Star* that they had "500 acres under fence and he intended to plant the entire acreage in corn and beans. A large part of this year's crop had been destroyed by rabbits and gophers. He had succeeded, however, in harvesting something over 1,000 bushels of [early maturing] corn."

Arthur Lively, Robert McGee, Empy McGee and Edward Harris work to build the Cowboy Dam. Courtesy of Lynn Harris.

A *Star* article dated January 23, 1907, reported of Dr. Walter B. Purcell visiting the ranch to care for a number of family members with pneumonia. The doctor "expressed his surprise in finding the work which has been done since locating their new home in the Sierrita Mountains." He proceeded to tell that they had "built a large dam, which is fed by water coming out of two canyons" and that the dam, then full, contained enough water to "irrigate 500 acres of beautiful land fenced and being cultivated—nearly all of which is now planted in wheat, the growth of the same being most luxuriant." The location was "one of the most attractively beautiful anywhere to be found in the Territory—high up in the mountains above the live oak, which is at 4,000 feet in altitude and from which point the S. P. trains can be plainly seen." There were "several very comfortable homes. The people are prosperous and happy. They have located and are developing 100 claims of the most promising mineral ground. McGee and his people are of the kind that make prosperity both by farming and mining, while establishing for themselves a colony of happy and prosperous homes."

The view of McGee Ranch in about 1910 showing the crops and homes. The bean barn is on the right and Mirma's house can be seen on the left. Courtesy of Lynn Harris.

In August of 1910, the *Tombstone Weekly Epitaph* reported that, "Large quantities of tomatoes grown by dry farming methods have been brought to Tucson by J. R. McGee, Fred Harris, and George Harris from Rero Ranch." By November of 1910, after the season's crops were harvested, all of the families left the ranch settlement and moved to the de la Canoa Ranch, a part of the former Spanish land grant that today includes parts of Green Valley and Continental. The Canoa property was very close to the Santa Cruz River and offered a great opportunity to expand their farming and cattle operations, as well as providing an excellent site to raise hogs and other animals to sell to local consumers. The *Star* reported on April 5, 1911, that they had eight hundred acres of barley, wheat, and alfalfa almost ready for harvest, in addition to acres of beets, strawberries, tomatoes, peas, and watermelons.

Family members gather for a photo at Canoa Ranch. Courtesy of Lynn Harris.

The Canoa families had weekly church meetings and immediately started to organize a school. With thirty-eight children and many adults needing education, a private teacher was hired until, on December 17, 1912, the Canoa School District No. 31 was formed by the County supervisors. The September 21, 1913, *Arizona Daily Star* reported that the Canoa School District had hired Edith Cardon to teach.

NAME OF PARENTS OR GUARDIANS		NAME OF CHILDREN	AGE
J. R. McGee	1	O. M. McGee	20
"	2	Rero McGee	18
"	3	Napoleon McGee	12
Zinah Harris	4	Almo Harris	18
"	5	Ceril Harris	12
"	6	Jerome Harris	11
"	7	Numa Harris	9
"	8	Lily Harris	8
"	9	Josephine Harris	6
Jas. & Florence Harris	10	Melrose Harris	14
"	11	Seemore Harris	11
"	12	Lofawn Harris	9
"	13	Rose Harris	8
"	14	Levi Harris	6
Jas. & Annie Lively	15	Orre Lively	20
"	16	Arthur Lively	18
George & Martha Harris	17	Fawnya Harris	17
Edith D. Cardon	18	Edith Cardon	11
"	19	Mary Cardon	8
"	20	Florence Cardon	7

REPORT

— OF —

District School Trustees

— OF —

DISTRICT No. 31

County of Pima, Arizona.

To the County School Superintendent:

We, the undersigned School Trustees of District and County aforesaid, certify that the within Report is a true statement of the condition of the Public Schools of said District.

J. R. McGee
Dave Lively
C. E. Harris
School Trustees.

FILED_____ 19___

County School Superintendent.

The 1913–14 Sierrita District No. 6 school marshal's census record with trustees listed.
Note: Zinah Harris and her children should have been listed with the last name of McGee.
Courtesy of Arizona State Archives.

In November of 1913, not long after the new school opened, the deal to purchase the Canoa Ranch property fell through and the families journeyed the thirty miles to return to their ranch home in the Sierritas. Thankfully, Rachel Thornton Harris and the three young men who had remained at the original ranch had been successful in maintaining the orchards, mining claims, and cattle herds, because the families arrived back at Rero Ranch in the middle of a winter snowstorm. The children's teacher, Mrs. Cardon (Edith Jemima Done Cardon), and her daughters Edith, Mary, and Florence came with them to continue the school year.

On January 26, 1914, the *Tucson Citizen* reported that, "Upon motion a school district was established to be known as Sierrita School District No. 6." A 1914 Rero Ranch School District No. 6 graduation announcement, dated June 26, 1914, lists Edith D. Cardon as teacher, with J. R. McGee and David Lively as school board members, and C. E. Harris as clerk. The school marshal's census report listed students as Ono "Matt" McGee (20), Rero "Robert" McGee (18), Napoleon "Empy" McGee (12), Almo McGee (18), Cyril McGee (12), Jerome McGee (11), Numo McGee (9), Lily McGee (8), Josephine McGee (6), Moroni Harris (14), Seemore Harris (11), Lofawn Harris (9), Rose Harris (8), Levi Harris (6), Ure Lively (20), Arthur Lively (18), Fawnzo Harris (17), and three Cardon girls named Edith (11), Mary (8), and Florence (7). To allow everyone the opportunity to learn, the children would attend classes during the day and adults would have class in the evenings after they finished work.

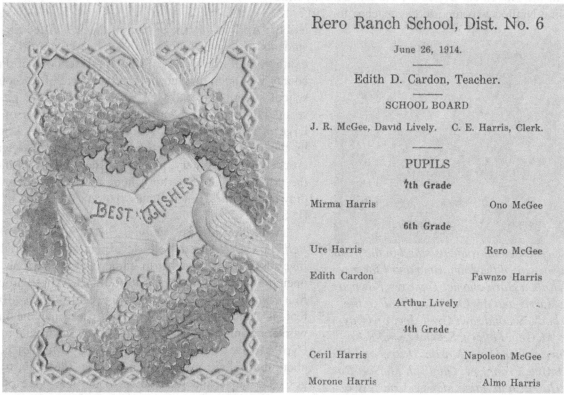

The 1914 Sierrita School graduation announcement illustrates the family use of the name "Rero Ranch." Note that Ceril and Almo Harris should be listed as Cyril and Almo McGee. Courtesy of Lynn Harris.

Edith Cardon moved back to Binghampton, Arizona, where her daughter, Ethel was born in January of 1915. On January 28, 1915, the Sierrita School was apportioned $850 from the school fund and Jennie Ellis Carels Avison was listed as the teacher in March of that same year. At some point during the 1914–15 school year, the first ranch school building was completed. It was a small, wooden structure located southeast of the current community center. Mrs. Avison, a widowed mother of two daughters, taught only one year in the Sierrita School before moving on and eventually living out her life in Hawaii.

The *Arizona Educational Directory* for the 1915–16 school year indicates that Miss Alice E. Marble was the Sierrita School teacher. Born in Michigan, Alice was an experienced teacher who transferred in from Lowell School No. 9. She stayed in the Sierrita School for only one year before moving on to Rillito for a year and then taught for two years in Sahuarita.

On July 19, 1916, the County-funded Sierrita School hired Gladys V. Bowyer. She would have been there when one of the first settlers, James Riley McGee, died of kidney failure on January 24, 1917. He left many children, grandchildren, and trusted friends to mourn him. It was a very difficult time for the families remaining in the community as they found themselves without their main source of leadership.

In the November 27, 1917, *Tucson Citizen*, Miss Pauline Naillon was reported as teacher for 1917–18,

The Sierrita schoolhouse as it looked in 1922, with the flag flying high. Courtesy of University of Arizona Special Collections.

Sierrita School students stand in the front doorway of the John Alma and Florence Holben Harris home. Top row: Fawnzo Harris and Art Lively stand tall in the back. Second row: Cyril, Joe, and Lily McGee; Lofawn, Seemore, and Rose Harris. Third row: Moroni Harris and Bud McGee. Front row: Odeilyah McGee, Roy Harris, and Adina McGee. Courtesy of Lynn Harris.

and the April 19, 1918, edition of the *Star* listed Sierrita students as contributors to a county project. "An exhibition of the work of the rural schools of Pima county will open this morning at the office of the county school superintendent, Miss Vera Zoe Schurtz, on the second floor of the courthouse. The four walls of the large office have been covered with the articles sent in by the rural schools, and they include drawing, sewing, crocheting, embroidery, painting, essays, etc. . . . Among the articles of the Sierrita school district, are excellent drawings of the United States flag and the flags of the [U.S.] allies."

According to *The Personal History of Gale Stanley Bell*, in 1918, Alfred Bell, an expeditor, was hired by investors in Los Angeles to come over to Arizona and open the Cowboy Mine near Rero Ranch. Alfred brought four sons and a daughter with him, and they lived in a tent at the mine. In order to run the mine, he hired workers from the ranch to haul water and work the mine. Cyril McGee (daughter of James Riley McGee) heard about the Bells from the ranch boys, so she and a friend got on a horse and rode down to the tent. One of the sons, Gordon, looked out of a hole in the tent, and all he could see was this pair of ankles while she was on her horse. He came out to see who belonged to those beautiful ankles. Cyril was really gorgeous. Gordon would drive the water truck to the ranch. It would take about an hour to fill up the water tank. Cyril would go out and sit with him while the water filled. They fell in love and were married in Tucson in October 1919.

A *Star* article dated May 17, 1918, says, "The closing exercises of the Sierrita school, which has been taught by Miss Pauline Naillon, were held at 8:30 p.m. May 15th. A very interesting program was rendered by the school and was much appreciated by a large number of visitors. A special feature of the program was the number of patriotic selections delivered and the patriotic spirit which prevailed. . . . At the close of this entertainment, the two eighth-grade students, [Cyril] McGee and [Moroni] Harris, who had very successfully passed their examinations, were awarded their diplomas." Mary Pauline "Polly" Naillon taught approximately seventeen students per year during her two years at the Sierrita School, before moving on to the Davidson School in Tucson. She died of stomach cancer on January 16, 1920, at the age of twenty-nine, in the middle of the 1919–20 school year.

Matt Ono McGee, working as a fireman for the Southern Pacific Railroad, registered for the draft on June 5, 1917, and joined the navy in December of 1919. He attended training school on Goat Island near San Francisco. Though there were not a lot of family members who actually left to serve in the military, World War I and the economic struggles that accompanied it forced many families to leave the settlement looking for work to survive. During this time, a few family members remained at the ranch full-time, with others coming back as they could between jobs.

Students pose in front of the Sierrita School in March of 1931. Beatrice Ann Peters Jones, the teacher, stands on the porch with the hat-wearing donkey. Girls standing in the back are Alice Lopez, Ramona Sandez, Rosa Lopez, and JoAnn and Ruth McGee. Sitting are Robert and Arnulf Lopez; Aurelio, Ramon, and Faustino Sandez, and Jerry McGee. Courtesy of Margaret McGee Elam.

According to the *Arizona Educational Directory*, Alice M. Wilson replaced Pauline Naillon for the 1919–20 school year, but in the February 1920 census, John Freeman McDole was

Walter B. Horton and Ono "Matt" McGee pose for a photo wearing their uniforms in 1918. Courtesy of Lynn Harris.

living in the teacherage. The sixty-three-year-old Ohio native stayed through the 1920–21 school year before moving to the Zinc School for three years. It is said that the elderly man was not a good fit for the lively group of Sierrita students, so his departure after only one year was best for all concerned.

Mrs. S. C. Marshall (Elizabeth Powell Marshall) taught the 1921–22 school year, so we know the school was still in session for the few local families who remained. The latter is substantiated by the April 20, 1922, *Arizona Daily Star* report that, "Miss Evelyn Bently and Miss Mabel de Gomez returned yesterday from Sierrita, where they conducted investigations of the health and nutrition of the children in the public schools there. Fifteen children were examined, ranging in age from four to fifteen years, and of this number only three were found to be underweight. The greater number of children were found to be slightly above the average weight for their age and height."

On April 23, 1922, the *Star* stated, "Gratifying progress in the work of the reading circle at Sierrita school, district No. 6, was reported by Mrs. Kate B. Reynolds, County Superintendent of Schools. The Sierrita school reading circle was established by Mrs. Reynolds last fall. Mrs. Eliza Powell Marshall, the teacher in charge, draws out six or seven books from the Tucson Carnegie Public Library at intervals and these volumes, combined with the circulating library of about 25 or 30 books which is sent to the school from the County Superintendent's Office, forms the reading material that enables the children of the school to employ part of their leisure time in

Empy and Louis McGee guide mules as they drag timbers toward the Upper East Star Shaft. Courtesy of Margaret McGee Elam.

profitable reading."

On the first of June, 1922, the *Star* reported that, "Following the review of the records achieved by the rural schools of Pima county, Mrs. Kate B. Reynolds, county school superintendent, awarded a prize of a beautiful picture to the Sierrita School. The winning school had the highest record for attendance and punctuality for the school year 1921–22. This school had a record of 100 percent in attendance for three months, and 100 percent in punctuality for one month."

The *Tucson Citizen* announced on September 13, 1922, that, "Miss Clara Boyee tendered her resignation as teacher in District No. 6 at the Sierrita School, and following its acceptance the appointment of Miss Beatrice Chamberlain to fill the vacancy was announced." Miss Beatrice Chamberlain was a graduate of Sargent's School of Physical Culture in Boston. She organized and was the guardian of the first group of Camp Fire Girls, known as the Ocotillo Camp for Girls. She completed one year as the Sierrita schoolteacher and then married a Tucson native, Richmond Shaw Smith, over the summer of 1923. She died of tuberculosis in June of 1927 at the age of thirty, having been ill for more than three years.

According to the 1923–24 *Arizona Educational Directory*, Mary Reed was the Sierrita teacher assigned, but the local newspaper indicates that Mary continued teaching in Sunnyside, having opened the new school building there in 1922. The June 23,

Louie McGee, Jerry McGee, Empy McGee, and Arthur Lively strain to help mules pull ore carts uphill to the Upper East Star Shaft. Courtesy of Margaret McGee Elam.

1923, edition of the *Arizona Daily Star* indicated that Mrs. Trussell would be the assigned teacher for the upcoming school year.

Between 1896 and 1925, there were over 313 mining claims filed by the McGee Ranch families in an effort to expand their mining endeavors. On August 14, 1924, the first official homestead deed was assigned to John Alma Harris and was a 636-acre parcel which included a large part of the current McGee Ranch settlement.

In the early '20s, troops stationed at Continental were working on a United States government survey team. Their travels up into the Sierrita Mountains resulted in the marriages of Eldon Bert Heaston to Lura McGee, Fred Allen to Rose Harris, and Leslie Clair Pritchard to Lorena Harris.

Support timbers lie next to the Upper East Star Shaft being worked by Arthur Lively, Empy McGee, and Louie McGee. Courtesy of Margaret McGee Elam.

In spite of progress in the attempt to make financial survival possible for the ranch community, the January 3, 1925, edition of the *Arizona Daily Star* explained that, "Due to lack of [attendance of students within the district boundaries], the Sierrita School

District No. 6 was discontinued upon recommendation of Mrs. Kate Reynolds, retiring county school superintendent." The 1924–25 *Arizona Educational Directory* indicated that there was, "No School This Year," so the closure had taken place in the fall of 1924.

The search for a student population to support the rural school lasted much longer than anticipated. It wasn't until September 4, 1927, that the *Tucson Citizen* reported, "The Sierrita district, which is located 30 miles south and west of Tucson, is to have a rural school again this year, after four years without a school in their district. A school was started there a number of years ago, and was continued for six years, but abandoned when the rural school population decreased materially. Miss Maxine Edith Barnes has been named as teacher of the school, which will be held in a building on the McGee Ranch."

On May 14, 1928, Vivian Irene Cowan married Fawnzo C. Harris, son of George and Martha Thornton Harris. She moved to the ranch with her new husband and taught for the 1928–29 school year. When Fawnzo got a job with

Students and their teacher pose in the doorway of the Sierrita School in the early 1920s. Courtesy of Lynn Harris.

Pima County, the family left the ranch. Vivian taught for many more years at Benson, Pomerene, and Marsh Station. In 1944, widowed at an early age, she eventually moved to Clackamas, Oregon, where she died in 1983.

Helen C. Wood, an Ohio native who came to Arizona in 1927, was hired to teach at the Sierrita School for the 1929–30 school term. Helen was diagnosed with tuberculosis and battled that disease most of her life. She had taught in the Sierrita School for only one school year. On July 16, 1950, she passed away in Tucson, having taught at the Mission View School for six years.

On May 10 and June 29, 1929, Napoleon "Empy" McGee made [the first] Stock-Raising Homestead Entry for property in the McGee Ranch vicinity. In her personal memoir, Empy's wife, Mildred "Mamie" Hopwood Norton McGee writes:

The McGee family poses near the mining operation at the West Star Cabin. Standing are Cyril, Joe, Zinah, Almo "Shorty," and Chad. The four children in front are Socrates "Fudge," Lily, Louis, and Josephine. Courtesy of Lynn Harris.

> *A short time after we came back from Mexico, where Empy took Matt's [Empy's brother, a locomotive fireman, severely burned at work] place to build a clubhouse at Rocky Point, we heard that the "ranch" was going to be lost for the mortgage. Most of the people had moved away—the Harris and Lively families had gone to Nogales. Empy and his brother, Matt, decided to save the ranch and go into the cattle business.*
>
> *The ranch at that time consisted of one section. It was necessary to acquire more land. Most of the land around us was government or state, and land available for home-steading. One section, 640 acres, could be obtained by living on it for five years. Empy and I applied for one and*

Fred Harris, Bud McGee, Arthur Lively, Robert McGee, and Matt McGee pose at the opening of the Washington Shaft. Courtesy of Gary Fox.

Matt did as well. More land was acquired through federal and state leases as we bought more cattle and enlarged the ranch.

It was interesting and exciting when we picked out the spot to build our house. We only expected to be there five years, as it was quite isolated in the hills and hard to get the kids to school, so we didn't need a very large place and planned two large rooms—a kitchen and dining room combined, and a living room and bedroom combined.

In April of 1930, when the census taker made her rounds, the McGee Ranch was pretty much deserted. Bud McGee, Empy's half-brother, was sharing a home with Empy, Mamie, Jerry, JoAnn, and Margaret. Next door, Matt was living with Robert, Faye, and their children Ruth, Donald, and Mickey. Mamie recalls that, "School was a problem. It was about seven and a half miles over a winding, narrow road back to the ranch school. A Mexican family lived further from us so a station wagon school bus, driven by Robert McGee, picked up our kids on the way.

Beatrice Ann Peters Jones was the assigned Sierrita School teacher for the fall of 1930. She stayed through the spring of 1932. Born and raised in Ohio, she had graduated from Ohio Wesleyan University. She taught at the Roskruge School until she was married on November 27, 1929, to Wesley Granville Jones, a telegraph operator for the Southern Pacific Railroad. After leaving the Sierrita school, she moved to several different Arizona towns, including Clarkdale and Cortero, with a long stretch of time in Willcox, Arizona, before she died on February 15, 1996, in Cottonwood, Arizona.

Empy and Matt McGee take a break from roundup in 1940. Courtesy of Margaret McGee Elam.

On January 24, 1931, the *Arizona Daily Star* wrote that a doctor made a report about the conditions of the Pima County schools. Sierrita school's "sanitation was good," and the "water supply was contaminated." On June 6, 1931, Ruby Crawford was the only Sierrita graduate.

Empy helping with laundry at West Star. Courtesy of Margaret McGee Elam.

The next mention of the small school appeared in the *Star* on September 21, 1932: "Sierrita school, a rural district number six, was closed and abandoned yesterday on the order of Mrs. Constance F. Smith, county school superintendent. This school is an accommodation school in an unorganized district. The thirteen children enrolled in the school will be sent to Twin Buttes school, where ample room exists for them." This announcement meant Alicia Lopez (7), Roberto Lopez (10), Rosa Lopez (13), Arnulfo Lopez (15), JoAnn McGee (5), Jerry McGee (6), Ruth McGee (6), Aurelio Sandez (7), Ramona Sandez (11), Ramon Sandez (8), Tino Sandez (10), Rose Crawford (9), and Ruby Crawford (14) would be forced to switch schools for the subsequent school year.

The next few years were busy for the McGee Ranch families. In October of 1932, Matt Ono McGee finalized his claim for 629 acres that included the eastern portion of the current-day settlement, where he had a home. Napoleon "Empy" McGee, in August of 1935, finally received the deed to his 630 acres, referred to as "homestead," where he had built a house for his family almost six years before. Mamie recalled:

Jerry McGee hanging out on the milk truck. Courtesy of Margaret McGee Elam.

Building up a ranch took lots of money, time, and hard work. We continued to live at the homestead year after year. When we sold steers, the money had to go for another reservoir, fence, barn, or more cattle. As time went on, we raised chickens. We sold eggs which had to be candled, cleaned, and packed for the market. We planted fruit trees and, of course, we had milk cows so there was lots of cream, butter, and cheese. We also raised turkeys. We picked turkeys from early morning until late at night when they went to market. I even picked turkeys in my sleep.

JoAnn, Jerry, and Margaret McGee pose in the yard at the ranch. Courtesy of Margaret McGee Elam.

All the water we used was hauled in barrels. Then it had to be siphoned out by buckets full for the house use and all waste water was carried out. Wash day was a hard day, but Empy helped me until we got a washing machine with a gasoline motor. I had so many extras to take care of. Matt sent his brother-in-laws [sic] up to help when they had no work—also some of his friends.

When Norman was born in 1931 and our house seemed to be too small, a large sleeping porch was built. We had lots of company on weekends and summers—mostly kids. Cyril's [Empy's widowed half-sister] boys (James, Gale, and Gordon Bell) came almost every weekend and all summer. I did a lot of cooking and, as no electricity was available, all cooking was done on the woodstove. It was a long trip to town. We had to open five gates before we even got to Twin Buttes.

JoAnn and Jerry pose while Margaret admires her little brother Norman at the homestead. Courtesy of Margaret McGee Elam.

The winters were quite cold. Sometimes we had snow. Our house wasn't built for winter. When the wind blew, the linoleum on the floor would rise up. We had a small wood heater in the living room and we kept it red hot sometimes. Dianne was just learning to walk and when she was on the floor, I barricaded the stove with chairs. One day, I put her down and forgot about the stove. She burned her hand and forehead quite badly and still carries the scar.

Mamie and Empy McGee's home in 1930.
Courtesy of Margaret McGee Elam.

Empy made a cooler by the kitchen window. It was covered with sacks that were kept wet by a constant drip of water. Sometimes it got a little dry and one night, JoAnn and Norry were looking for something in it using matches for a light and set it on fire. Luckily, Empy was there to throw a bucket of water on it. It was a happy day when we finally were able to buy an Electrolux refrigerator powered by kerosene. It was quite a novelty to us to

be able to have ice cubes and make ice cream.

Every night was family night. We spent many evenings playing games and cards. Some nights we went to Empy's mother's and played music. Lee [Leander Harris] played the violin sometimes. Norry was a baby and when Lee played, I would have to take him home. He couldn't take violin music and cried all the time that Lee played.

We had a radio powered by batteries and a wind charger nearby to keep the batteries charged. Sometimes, when the wind didn't blow, the batteries got low and it was hard to hear. One of our favorites was Lydia Mendoza, a Spanish singer, and of course, the boxing matches. Everyone grouped around the radio for the championship matches and prayed for wind.

Ruth, Robert, Don, and Faye McGee pose for a photo. Courtesy of Margaret McGee Elam.

The McGee Ranch slowly came back to life. In 1937, Edward Royal Harris, Leander M. Harris, and Mirma (McGee) Harris Lively received title to an additional 1,915 acres. In March of 1938, Fawnzo Harris added 598 acres, in a claim located southeast of the McGee Ranch, closer to Tinaja, but that ultimately resulted in a land swap between Empy McGee, who purchased the property from Fawnzo, and the Manning Ranch for government lease land adjacent to the existing ranch property. All combined, the families worked together to accumulate over 4,408 acres of deeded property, in addition to thousands of acres of leased state and federal land. While new homes were being built, the industrious families constructed numerous wells, dams, and spillways to harvest water for humans and cattle.

Still, the children were transported to the Twin Buttes School where Mrs. Catherine Foy was their teacher. Mamie recalled that "the kids got along fine with the Mexican children who learned to speak and sing in broken English. "Up on the housetop, cleek, cleek, cleek. Down through the cheemney with good Saint Neek." Robert McGee drove the students to and from

Raymond Kiddoo hoisting Leander Harris out of the shaft. Courtesy of Gary Fox.

school in his Model A station wagon, often traveling through washes as there were no direct roads connecting the ranch, via Tinaja mining camp, to Twin Buttes.

An extensive legal land dispute started that affected the travel route the children took to school. In early 1936, William Choate, a Twin Buttes rancher, removed gates and fenced off the road, a right-of-way that had been in use for over forty years and that traveled through property he leased from the State of Arizona, claiming his cattle were being let out of his property by motorists using the road and that the road was not legal.

While the courts were working through the tangled allegations, purportedly accompanied by some very heated arguments that hindered any form of compromise, on April 6, 1937, the Ramon Sandez

Edward "Ed" R. Harris with his pack mule hauling wood to the homestead. Courtesy of Lynn Harris.

(Sanders) family added chaos to the situation. According to the April 7 edition of the *Arizona Republic*, "The Twin Buttes-McGee road feud, which long has had one section of Pima County in turmoil, celebrated its first birthday today with a sit-down strike by the seven Sandez children, which isolated one community and threatened to close a school. The children refused to walk half a mile. The situation was referred to Governor Stanford tonight by the Pima County Board of Supervisors with a plea to "do something quick." A temporary road over the land of Ramon Sandez, in use while the regular road's fate was being deliberated upon by the state land board, was closed by Sandez this morning in protest against the ruling of Marvin L. Burton, county school superintendent, that the seven Sandez children should walk a half mile between their home and the school bus line. Sandez contended that the bus, using the road on his land, should pick up and deliver his seven offspring to their door. Burton said the walk was not unreasonable. Sandez countered that his flock physically is unable to walk the half mile. Burton took Dr. L. H. Howard, county health director, to the Sandez ranch and had the children examined. The physician reported they physically are able to walk a half mile. So Sandez had the last word by fencing up the road. As a consequence, only five of the twenty-three children due to appear at the Twin Buttes school from the west arrived this morning. Loss of attendance might close the school."

The following week, the Sandez children showed up at the Zinc School near Helmet Peak. On April 11, the *Republic* reported that Dr. George F. Herrick and James N. Pemberton, trustees of the Zinc School, ruled that "the seven little Sandez' removal to the Zinc Community was not bona fide," and that they were "Twin Buttes problem children."

Empy McGee, Leander Harris, Louis McGee, and Arthur Lively use pulleys to install the pump at the ranch well. Courtesy of Lynn Harris.

Finally, in the April 13 edition of the *Star*, news broke that the Sandez road issue had been resolved. "After much palaver with Marvin L. Burton, Mama Sandez won a pair of shoes for each of the muchachas, while Pima County won at least a moral victory in the school bus obstruction matter. It seemed that, way down deep, the reason for

Family gathers to repaint the schoolhouse after the move. Courtesy of Margaret McGee Elam.

fencing off the school bus, after Burton had refused to provide a store-door delivery for the six Sandez children attending the Twin Buttes school, was that the walk of 300 feet (or yards depending on who was disputing) would and had worn out the 12 shoes of the six Sandez children. When that was all settled, the Sandez family agreed to permit the school bus over the private road. Also, the family had agreed to herd the children to within a short distance of where the bus passes by." The Sandez children's new shoes were to be purchased from the governor's fund monies that were allocated for school relief purchases.

The Sandez resolution did little to help the McGee Ranch children make their way to school. On July 8, 1937, an *Arizona Daily Star* article entitled "McGee School is Plan of Burton" reported that "the establishment of an accommodation school in the McGee-Harris neighborhood in the Sierrita mountains was announced yesterday by Marvin L. Burton, county school superintendent. As a consequence of the still untangled row featuring the Twin Buttes-McGee Road for the past 15 months, Burton yesterday stated that, in order to assure uninterrupted school facilities for the children of the McGee community, he would establish an accommodation school. Throughout the last year, Burton reported, as the result of the constant wrangling over the county's attempt to rededicate the Twin-Buttes-McGee Road, the 10 children residing 9 miles from Twin Buttes school were frequently prevented from reaching school. Closures of the road were largely responsible, the school superintendent added. Formerly an accommodation

Arizona Republic, October 3, 1937.

school, there are sufficient children of school age in the community to warrant the re-establishment, Burton said. Under school laws, there must be ten children attending school and an average attendance of eight."

For reasons unknown, the lot where the one-room McGee accommodation schoolhouse had been built was not acceptable to Pima County, so the building had to be moved to a new location, donated by Napoleon "Empy" McGee. It was loaded onto a frame built on axles with four large wheels. The

Chad McGee paints while Jim Bell works on the roof. Courtesy of Margaret McGee Elam.

enormous "trailer" was laid across the bed of a large truck and very slowly driven a quarter of a mile down the road to the new site. With that precarious move completed, Pima County finally gave their "stamp of approval."

At the final location, there was a classroom with a small one-room teacherage in the back. Mamie shared that, "Jerry, JoAnn, and Margaret rode horseback to school by the trail. It was shorter than the road. They rode one horse, Little Bay, and took turns being in front. Poor Little Bay did pretty much his own thing with them. He trotted down the same hills and slowly walked back up them every day."

In the September 28, 1937, edition of the

Arizona Daily Star, the headline read, "Any McGees? Yes, School is Full." The article continued with, "When Mrs. Louise Mae Squire, teacher at the McGee school, calls the roll, all the last names of her flock are McGee. The present enrollment at this accommodation school, nestling on the east slope of the Sierrita mountains, as reported to Marvin K. Burton, county school superintendent yesterday, follow: Donald McGee, Lawrence McGee, Joann McGee, Frank McGee, Peggy McGee, Patricia McGee, Norman McGee, Ruth McGee, Margaret McGee, and Keith McGee. It's the McGee school, in the McGee neighborhood, and all the ten pupils are named McGee."

This same edition stated, "The new McGee school has opened with ten pupils, all with the last name of McGee. Mrs. Louise Mae Squire is the teacher." Louise Mae Stoll Squire was the teacher for the 1937–38 school year. Born in Tonopah, Nevada, she taught in Miami, Arizona, before marrying Frank Squire and accepting the assignment in the Sierrita School. She stayed for only one school year before moving to the Wrightstown School.

The William Choate easement debacle went on. In May of 1937, the State Land Board ruled that the road across state lease land was valid. Immediately thereafter, Choate filed a superior court petition alleging that the land board had overstepped its reach. A Santa Cruz County judge agreed with Choate and the case was off to the Arizona Supreme Court. Finally, on February 8, 1938, the *Star* announced that the Arizona Supreme court had released a decision, written

Chad McGee holds the ladder for Norman McGee while Empy McGee refills his paintbrush and Jim Bell huddles on the roof. Courtesy of Margaret McGee Elam.

by Justice Henry D. Ross, reversing a former Thurman ruling, thereby supporting the State Land Board's authority to grant rights-of-way across leased state land. This cleared the way for the Pima County Board of Supervisors and County Attorney Joseph B. Judge to, "notify the county engineer that he could proceed immediately with the task of improving the Twin Buttes-McGee road." The Supreme Court denied Choate's petition to rehear the case in March of 1938.

County Engineer George T. Grove immediately set county crews to work. Initial steps were taken to fence the roadway and add cattle guards at property boundaries. An official easement to establish the current-day McGee Ranch Road was granted and men from the ranch contracted with Pima County to cut trees and dig stumps out by hand before a grader was used to cut the path. Luther Harris vividly remembered how much work was involved with digging out those tree stumps to prepare the path. For the first time ever, families had a county-maintained road to travel on.

Grading the road near homestead. Courtesy of Margaret McGee Elam.

Back at the school, Alice Ewell Mullins was busy teaching [*Arizona Educational Directory*, 1938–39]. Born and raised in Kentucky, Mary Alice Ewell Mullins Halterman lived for a time in Tucson with her sister before moving to California. During her

Margaret, JoAnn, and Norman McGee stand in front of the cornfields prepared for an adventure. Courtesy of Margaret McGee Elam.

tenure, on February 26, 1939, an *Arizona Daily Star* article discussed school funding concerns. Former county school superintendent, Marvin L. Burton, had committed monies from a reserve fund to provide for "transportation of school pupils living in inaccessible areas and for instruction in unorganized school districts, of which the county school system had two, the McGee accommodation school and the preventorium." Burton defended his use of funds by stating, "The increased expenditure from the reserve fund is the establishment of the accommodation school in the McGee district. This was necessary because of the Twin Buttes-McGee road dispute."

Burton's policies appear to have provided the necessary push to address the need for the proper allocation of funds because, on June 6, 1939, the *Arizona Daily Star* reported that, "On the recommendation of Mrs. P. H. Ross, county superintendent, the board set up a new school district in the Twin Buttes area now served by the McGee accommodation school. The district, numbered 56 in the county system, will bear the costs of its own one-room school. The present school is financed out of the reserve fund." They announced, on September 1, that Mrs. Isabel M. Schmiedendorf (Mary Isabel Morgan Schmiedendorf) had been hired to teach in the new district.

The Sierrita District was officially reestablished as District No. 56 and opened for students to attend in September of 1939. Cousins Dianne and Lillian McGee, who did not actually turn five until 1940, were given

Norman and Dianne McGee get their photo taken on the first day of the 1940–41 school year. Courtesy of Margaret McGee Elam.

permission to attend. Adding these two students to the roles met the requirements necessary to qualify for county funding. Dianne McGee recalls that Mrs. Schmiedendorf was "sure Lillian and I were too young to be there so we had to take naps and we got to do a lot of playing or whatever we wanted." She also made Dianne and Lillian drink a daily teaspoon of cod liver oil and take naps because they were so small and, in her opinion, malnourished. She doesn't remember much more than that the cod liver oil "was stinky, smelled awful, and I didn't like it. I am sure she thought it would be good for us."

When she started school, Dianne recalls, "We had just moved from the old homestead to our new blue house and the school was right where it is now. I loved school—period. My favorite memories were when we had singing time or playing time outside. It was a new world for me. We had a real turnover of teachers through the years. The living quarters were

Mary Isabel Morgan Schmiedendorf, Dianne's first teacher. Courtesy of Margaret McGee Elam.

just a little room on the back of the main room. There were eight grades of very country kids. It was hard for the teachers to come clear up to this school to face a room full of country cousins who sometimes weren't very nice—to say the least. We were not an easy bunch to handle."

The 1940 census shows Henry Rodee and Mary Isabel Morgan Schmiedendorf on McGee Road, living next door to the Chad and Thelma McGee family, which included five-year-old Lillian. Mary Isabel, listed as the schoolteacher, stayed at the Sierrita School through the 1941–42 school year, and in May of 1942, her three graduates were Betty Jean Heaston, Margaret Norton McGee, and Eldon Bert Heaston.

Sierrita School District No. 56 was on the published list of funded schools for the 1942–43 school year. In the *Arizona Educational Directory*, Margaret Fern Lee is listed as the teacher of record, but on May 24, 1943, the *Star* reported that, "The

A group of "ranch kids" pose for a photo. Boys grouped on the left are Keith and Earl McGee; Gale Bell; Larry Nolen; Jerry and Norman McGee; and Gordon Bell. Girls on right are Betty Heaston; Margaret, JoAnn, and Dianne McGee; and Vera Lou Harris. Courtesy of Lynn Harris.

danger of teaching vacancies in several Pima County one-room schools induced by the reduction of standards in the city schools and the war industry drain on teachers looms large for the next year, Mrs. P. H. Ross, county school superintendent, said today. Already the Sierrita School, 35 miles from Tucson, is without a teacher for next year . . . The Sierrita teacher receives $135 a month on a nine-month basis." Because the September 1943 issue of the *Arizona Daily Star* reports that Mrs. Margaret Fern Lee was a "previously retained teacher" in the Flowing Wells District, it seems that Mrs. Lee may not have been the teacher for the entire 1942–43 school year.

During 1942, the Sierrita Mining and Ranching Company (SM&R) was formed, and in 1943 it became a legal partnership, expanding opportunities for contracting outside jobs. A small adobe building, close to where the school had once been located, became "The Ranch Store." The small community was developing and becoming more self-sufficient, providing a livelihood for more families to settle and build homes.

Family members take a break while making adobe bricks. Courtesy of Margaret McGee Elam.

On January 16, 1943, Matt Ono McGee died after a long battle with liver disease. His widow, Mattie Othello Fox McGee, did not want to remain at the ranch, so Matt's brother, Empy, bought their home and property. Matt and Mattie had built a small adobe home, with a living room, bedroom, and bathroom near where Empy and Mamie were living in the "old blue house." Empy immediately began renovations to make room for Mamie and their children and added a hallway with two bedrooms as well as a cellar.

Dianne remembers the family making their own adobe bricks for construction. Down near the corrals, there was a place with the "right kind of clay." The men dug a pit and mixed the clay with straw and water. When the mixture got really "mushy," they would put it into frames and have the kids "dance on it" to pack it down. When it was partially dry, they would remove the frames and let the bricks finish drying. The bricks were then hauled to the home and stacked. It was quite a long process.

Janet Harris Kidoo taking care of piglets.
Courtesy of Margaret McGee Elam.

The development of the community was good news for the school numbers and on September 10, 1943, the *Arizona Daily Star* reported, "If it is decided to reopen the Sierrita School, Mrs. Cecille Leishman will be [the] teacher." On September 30, the *Star* reported that the Sierrita school opened with nineteen students that year, compared to fourteen the previous year. Former student Dianne McGee was eight years old at the time and she recalls that Mrs. Leishman "had two children who came to school and one was about my age. Lillian and I were not very nice to her because she was smart and had lots of toys. She was also scared to death of the outhouses that were a part of our everyday lives."

On December 19, 1943, the *Arizona Daily Star* reported that, "Formation of a new 4-H club, the Sierrita Cousins, was announced yesterday by Mrs. Cecille H. Leishman, club advisor. It is composed of 12 cousins, who make up the student body of the fourth through eighth grades of the Sierrita School, she said. Boys are doing camp club work and girls are sewing, according to Mrs. Leishman. Members had also helped the school arrange a Christmas program, have written letters to servicemen, and have utilized spare time by picking beans. Meetings are held at the school Fridays after the last class."

The *Star* again mentioned the "Sierrita Cousins 4-H Club" on February 27, 1944. "Almost all of the girls are ready to machine-stitch their tea towels which they are making. Mrs. L. L. McGee is helping the girls in their sewing. The boys are finishing their pot-holders. Friday the School Committee served refreshments after the club meeting was adjourned . . . The pupils of the Sierrita School went to the Sahuarita School Tuesday to see a movie. They all had a very nice time." Cecille Grace Holden Leishman was teaching in Continental for the 1944–45 school year so she stayed with the Sierrita School for only that one year, and Donald Riley McGee was the only graduate from her eighth-grade class.

Newly widowed, fifty-five-year-old Eleanor M. O'Callaghan Bogle moved to Tucson from Inspiration, Arizona. She was hired to teach in the Sierrita School for the 1944–45 school year. After her time in Sierrita she taught in Tucson District No. 1, All Saints, and Saint Ambrose. Eleanor passed away in Tucson on December 21, 1967.

Mattie and Matt McGee in the snow-covered Sierritas. Courtesy of Margaret McGee Elam.

Patriotism was deeply ingrained in the McGee Ranch community. Several family members served in World War II. PFC James Alfred "Jim" Bell enlisted on August 18, 1942, as a member of the U.S. Army's 101st Airborne Division parachute infantry. He was captured in Germany on July 12, 1945, and was held prisoner in Stalag 13B in Weiden, Bavaria. Levi Harris enrolled on November 9, 1943. Gale Stanley Bell was ordered to report for U.S. Army Air Corps basic training on December 28, 1943, at Shepherd Field, and eventually went to Kingman, Arizona, to aerial gunnery school. Gordon Bell enlisted in the navy. Luther McGee Harris enrolled on December 18, 1943. Roy Harris enlisted on April 21, 1945. Gerald June "Jerry" McGee enlisted on January 24, 1946.

At the end of World War II, the first local automotive shop was built, creating a place for repairing personal vehicles and other items used in SM&R's business ventures. As with most things built in the small community, lumber, tin, and other supplies were harvested from former projects and repurposed to build the "new" shop.

Jim Bell and Elmer McVey took out a VA loan to start their own business venture—hog farming. They purchased thirty pigs and brought them home to the ranch, where they penned them up in an area north of the main settlement. All family members collected food scraps for the booming pig business, which at one point had a population upwards of three hundred swine.

On September 12, 1945, the *Arizona Daily Star* reported that, "Hubert D. Orr, Phoenix, has received a temporary appointment at Sierrita, which opened yesterday." On November 25, 1945, they reported, "Hubert C. Orr has resigned as teacher of the Sierrita School, leaving a vacancy there. . . . This is a one-room school located approximately 40 miles south of Tucson."

Mr. Orr's resignation, partway through the 1945–46 school year, resulted in one of the best things that ever happened to the children of McGee Ranch.

In Eulalia Bourne's book, *Ranch School Teacher*, referencing late-1945, she writes:

Lee Harris and Bud McGee working the pig roundup. Courtesy of Lynn Harris.

Hard pressed financially, I told the county office I would do substitute teaching for a week or more at a time in rural areas where I would be accepted in my boots and Levi's. Thereupon one of the luckiest happenings of my life befell me. I was needed. My friend Orpha Mason, the assistant superintendent, told me that nobody else could do it—just me. Resist that? I tried. The job sounded impossible.

The problem school, Orpha said, was Sierrita. The children had been behind in their grades for some time. They had not found the teacher they needed. They had run off the elderly man sent out to them after a woman teacher quit early in the year. The county office tried combining the Sierrita with Twin Buttes, eight miles down the road toward Tucson. It didn't work. Twin Buttes had an all Mexican enrollment. The gringos, when they arrived, were resented as outsiders. Challenged and out-numbered, they fought a race war that was short and furious. Sierrita went back to the mountains. The county office could not find a teacher to take the job.

The Sierrita district, worried about their unschooled children, advertised in a Tucson newspaper. They then hired a young woman who had been employed at a guest ranch on the east side of the Santa Rita Mountains to do tutoring until the ranch ran out of tutorees. The Sierrita board had to pay their new teacher out of their own pockets because county funds could not be used to pay a teacher who did not have an Arizona certificate.

The school was in a long-established settlement on the eastern slope of the Sierrita Mountains. . . . It was forty miles from Tucson, much of the road dirt, or at times, mud. There was no teacherage and little money for teacher hire, as the district had to pay tuition to the city for their high school students.

Eulalia Bourne rings her bell in a portrait drawn by her student, Lucille Fox. Courtesy of Arizona Historical Society.

Orpha called me one morning as I walked past her door on my way to find the cattle

Family members gather at the Ed and Flora Harris homestead in 1933. Back row: Empy McGee, Edward Harris, Raymond Kiddoo, Chad McGee, Florence Lyon McGee Harris, Charles Harris holding Frank McGee, Faye McGee, Janet Kiddoo, Mirma Lively holding Johnny Kent, Arthur Lively, Joan Harris, and Keith McGee beside Gordina Bell. Sitting: Leander Harris, Vera Kiddoo, Luther Harris, and Margaret, Robert, Norman, and Mamie McGee with Cyril McGee Bell and Mickey McGee on the right. Courtesy of Lynn Harris.

inspector.

"You are the one," she declared. "Those children need you."

"But they are not Mexicans," I demurred.

"No, but they're poor children who haven't had the right chance. You have magic with children. You can save this little school."

"They are fighting hill people," I objected. "I've read about them in the newspapers. I don't want to be mixed up in any feuds."

Orpha wasn't sure, but she thought the Sierrita people were in the right in the battle that was described in the newspapers. A stubborn land-owner of a small ranch had closed a gate they had used for years on the way to town. Both sides went armed, but nobody got shot. The court gave the Sierrita people access to their road.

"That's over," she said. "The problem now is the children. You could get them interested. Teach them to read and dance and sing and make things and enjoy school. Shame on you for wasting your energies with a bunch of cows!"

I agreed to go look at the school. I am a softy. I cannot visit a humane society refuge without longing to take the outcast animals home with me. The sight of this attractive little white schoolhouse sitting up on a ridge, crammed to bursting with young ones closed off in isolation from their native country, was like tinkling brass to an old bell mare.

Their people were poor but proud. Years before, they had built this beautiful little frame schoolhouse that needed only a steeple to make it look like a miniature church; in later years, they had moved it up on a windy hill near the center of their restricted settlement. They furnished wood and took turns delivering a barrel of water as needed. Wood became scarce, so they installed a fuel-oil heater . . .

The children were all attractive, some really pretty. They were clean and adequately clothed. But the school atmosphere was not good. They were not involved. They were clock-watchers, without even a clock to watch.

"Sister Bourne" accepted the job immediately and, from the very first time she drove up the dirt driveway of the remote Sierrita schoolhouse, with wary students watching the progress of her little blue car, lives were changed. A more perfect fit between a teacher and her students had never been made. The rough and tumble group of children suddenly had not only a teacher, but an ally, who quickly built up a relationship of trust with her students and their families. With respect as a mutual ingredient, suddenly these students became focused on learning and favorability responded to the challenges offered them.

The students took on a new sense of pride in their school as was evidenced in the *Tucson Citizen* on Monday, February 13, 1950. LaVerne McGee said, "Thank you for putting my name in the *Tucson Daily Citizen* when I won second prize in the Better Breakfast slogan contest last Tuesday, but you put me in the wrong school. I do not go to Sahuarita school, which is 18 miles away. I go to Sierrita school up in the Sierrita mountains. We are a one-room school. Mrs. Bourne is our teacher and Richard and I are in the sixth grade. O please!! I don't want to be in the Sahuarita school. I like Sierrita school."

Eulalia Bourne remained in the Sierrita School for eight consecutive school years—from the fall of 1945 through the spring of 1953—before she was forced to retire a second time to take care of her ranch. At the end of the 1952–53 school year, she said goodbye to her treasured Sierrita School students: Freddy McGee (1st), Betty Jean McGee (2nd), Shelly Fox (2nd), Kelly Fox (2nd), Judy Fox (3rd), Lana Harris (3rd), John Harris (4th), Cynthia McGee (4th), Gary Fox (5th), Eiler Harris (5th), Larry Nolen (6th), Roger Harris (7th), Shirley McGee (7th), Gail Abell (8th), Doris Jane McGee (8th), Lynn Harris (8th), David McGee (8th).

Sierrita School students pose on the steps of the school. Girls: Mary Benson, Shirley McGee, Sandra Harris, Eleanor McGee, Natalie McGee, Gail Abell, and Doris Jane, LaVerne, Lillian, and Dianne McGee. In the middle is Lynn Harris. Boys: David McGee; John C., Rodger, and David Harris; Gary Fox; Bobby and Richard McGee; Eiler Harris; Paul McGee; and Larry and Denny Nolen. Courtesy of Gary Fox.

That same summer, on July 1, 1953, "It was moved by Mr. Lamb, seconded by Mr. Jay, and carried that the recommendation of Mrs. Florence Reece, County School Superintendent, that the boundaries of the Sahuarita School District No. 30 be enlarged to include the Sierrita school District No. 56." When the consolidation vote was approved, it may have closed the book on the story of the little rural school district, but the old one-room building stayed standing tall, watching over the families of the McGee Ranch community, and serving as a memorial to the generations whose lives were shaped within its rough wooden walls.

~ Contributed by Monica Lee Elam Christiansen

NOTES

Arizona Daily Star, Tucson, Arizona
Arizona Educational Directory
Bell, Gale Stanley. Personal history.
Bourne, Eulalia. *Ranch School Teacher*. Tucson, AZ: The University of Arizona Press, 1974.
Elam, Margaret Norton McGee—life story
Fox, Gary. Personal knowledge.
Harris, Lynn. Personal knowledge.
McGee, Mildred Hopwood Norton "Mamie." Personal memoirs.
School Marshal's 1914 Census Report
Trowbridge, Dianne McGee. Personal knowledge.
Tucson Citizen, Tucson, Arizona
Tombstone Weekly Epitaph, Tombstone, Arizona

Portrait of James N. Pemberton, teacher at Sopori School from 1899– 1900. Courtesy of Sandra Jake.

Sopori School

In 1897, Sopori School District No. 32 was established in a facility provided by rancher Juan Elias on his Sopori Ranch property. Sopori School District was renumbered in 1903 as No. 49 after Santa Cruz County was established. Little information is known about the teachers or number of students in this early period at the ranch.

In 1927, a building of two rooms was constructed of adobes for Sopori School on the Bustamante Ranch in Pima County, fronting the Arivaca Road at milepost fifteen. Tomas Bustamante donated the land and adobes. Teachers lived in an attached teacherage. There were indoor restrooms and showers for the students. The district extended from Kinsley's Ranch at Arivaca Junction to the Las Guijas valley. Bus service was established for Las Guijas valley students from the west and Kinsley's Ranch from the east.

Pemberton's bell, still treasured by family, came with him from California. Courtesy of Sandra Jake.

The first two teachers for the fifty-six students were the Romo sisters, Virginia and Genevieve, educated in New York, who taught at Sopori from 1928–40. (They came to the Sopori School reunion in 1994!) During the 1930s some of the older students, who were involved in 4-H, wrote articles for the *Arizona Daily Star* under the headline, "Sopori Willing Workers." Many of the students came from ranches, so roundups and rodeos were covered. In one column, the details of a car accident involving four local men was reported, along with what the children were planning for their Armistice Day float. The Mexican War was to be represented with John Angulo as General Santa Anna, Billy Michael as General Zachary Taylor, and Francisco Santa Maria as General Winfield Scott.

Sopori students and teachers pose for a photo in 1928. Courtesy of University of Arizona Special Collections.

Following the Romo sisters was Eulalia "Sister" Bourne (1941–42), who taught in several rural schools in the Altar Valley and later published several books on her experiences. In 1941, Sopori School had twenty-seven students. She had the children publish The Little Cowpuncher, a newspaper that chronicled life in the area with articles and drawings. Miss Bourne had money collected for a piece of playground equipment, a "Giant Stride" that the students helped to install. (In 1954, Mr. Bradt had it removed because it was all too easy to kick someone's teeth out while swinging around.)

Teaching at Sopori from 1954–60 were George and Mary Alice "Sis" Bradt, recommended by Superintendent Florence Reece and hired by school board member Richard Merchant on a handshake. In an autobiographical memoir, they remembered: "Our six years at Sopori were among our best. We were in our early forties, had a little school with well-behaved rural children with appreciative parents and lived surrounded by miles of desert grassland with its varied plants, birds, mammals, reptiles, and insects." These made up the subjects explored by the students through projects on local history, archeology, science, and natural history.

In this way, the Bradts' educational methodology inspired a large percentage of their students to pursue higher education, including several future teachers, a geologist, a librarian, a biologist, and even a university professor of education. It was named "one of the best school(s) in North America" by Martin Mayer in his book, *The Schools*. (Harpers, 1961) There was a school museum where all kinds of artifacts were neatly labeled and displayed. Mr.

Students demonstrate exercises for health at Sopori School in connection with the Nutrition and Keep Growing Project in 1929. Courtesy of University of Arizona Special Collections.

For the 1937 Christmas program, sponsored by 4-H, Sopori clowns perform in the segment about health. Courtesy of University of Arizona Special Collections.

Bradt was an exceptional photographer of animals and birds, so children learned to take and develop photographs.

One year, the students acted out the story of Henry A. Crabb and his filibustering expedition into Sonora in 1857 (four years after the Gadsden Purchase). An American, Crabb thought he and his one hundred men could take additional territory in Sonora with no problem, but the citizens of Caborca had other ideas. In their play, Sopori students painted a basketball with Crabb's face and put it in a trash can, simulating what happened to Crabb's head after he and his men were shot at the wall of the Catholic church in Caborca (bullet holes are still visible and the story not forgotten). After Sopori, the Bradts taught at Sahuarita School from 1961 to 1963 and went on to teach for many years in Elgin.

Pima County residents had to find their own way to high school. Tucson High and later Pueblo High School were their designated schools. At least one student drove daily from Arivaca to Tucson High on a dirt road. Others boarded in town. The houses at the Marley Ranch are just over the line in Santa Cruz County, but students attended Sopori; however, they were expected to attend high school in Nogales. This continued until annexation to the Sahuarita District in 1967.

In 1963, there were only seventeen students in the whole school. The building was getting old. Annexation to a larger district with a (new) high school was on the horizon. In 1967, Sopori District 49 was annexed to the Sahuarita School district. Two portables were added but the school property had only two acres of land. In 1970, a bond issue included $397,400 for a new Sopori School building to be built next to Lakewood Estates in Arivaca Junction. In 1980, two classrooms and a library were added. In 1984, the board voted to sell the old Sopori School property. Students from Arivaca were (and still are) bused

Girls singing "Marketing for Christmas" snap their fingers and sway while keeping time to the music. Courtesy of University of Arizona Special Collections.

twenty-three miles to the new school and forty-five miles to
Sahuarita Middle School and High School. Interestingly
enough, the Sahuarita School District board allowed a
kindergarten class to be taught in a private home in Arivaca
in 1984, after which it was held in the newly constructed
Arivaca Community Center.

~ Contributed by Mary N. Kasulaitis

*Sopori School students and teachers
welcome visitors for achievement day
in May of 1929. Courtesy of University
of Arizona Special Collections.*

*Children, teachers, and friends gather for the
Christmas program. A boy in the front row
impersonates Santa. Courtesy of University of
Arizona Special Collections.*

NOTES

http://cowpuncher.library.arizona.edu. See Coyote
    School News, published by Joan Sandin in 2003
    for a Sopori-inspired children's book set in the
    mid 1930s.
Mayer, Martin. *The Schools*. Harpers, 1961.

History of the Twin Buttes School and Community

As early as the late 1870s, prospectors roamed the foothills of the
Sierrita Mountains searching for riches. Few families lived in the
lonely uninhabited desert lands, as they were wild places with harsh
seasons and sparse accommodations.

The official name, Twin Buttes, refers to "a pair of ornery
looking, thorny, buff-colored hills, in the country of the gigantic
cactus called saguaro."[1] The first mines in the Twin Buttes region are
accredited to three prospectors known as "the three nations"—John
G. Baxter, an American from Wisconsin, Michael Irish of Ireland,
and John Ellis of Scotland. The trio worked together to build a
company that quickly began to prosper and on June 25, 1898, the
Arizona Daily Star reported that the Twin Buttes boarding house was
already home to ninety men.

At approximately this same time, Baxter, Ellis, and Irish
attempted to sell their property, and apparently felt so confident of
said sale that they started "enjoying the proceeds of the sale by
visiting their old homes. They have already received $20,000 of the
purchase price of $60,000. Michael Irish has gone to Ireland to visit
the scenes of his boyhood days. John Ellis accompanies him across
the Atlantic to visit his old home in Scotland. The other partner, John

VOTE FOR

DAVID S. ROSE

FOR MAYOR.

*Milwaukee election poster for
David S. Rose. Courtesy of
Milwaukee Public Library.*

G. Baxter, has gone to his old home in Wisconsin," reported the July 20, 1899, edition of the *Star*.

In spite of these celebratory homeland visits made by "the three nations," the original $100,000 Twin Buttes sale did not go through and, by June of 1900, the *Arizona Daily Star* reported that Larkin Rockwell of West Pullman, near Chicago, had taken the bond on the properties as a part of the Rockefeller Copper Syndicate. In June of 1901 the *Star* reported that the group of nineteen mines was reportedly sold to a Denver group for $130,000, but all said and done, the mines were on the market for over four years and every sale fell through—with several attempted deals actually ending up in litigation. Throughout those tumultuous years, the mines remained the property of Baxter, Irish, and Ellis. They were active and profitable, employing a large number of miners and shipping out an impressive quantity of ore.

Edward R. Harris, Charles Harris, and water boy Matt McGee work grading the route for the Twin Buttes Railroad in 1904. Courtesy of Lynn Harris.

Finally, on August 21, 1903, the *Star* quoted Mr. Frederic Felker as saying, "The Twin Buttes property will, on or about September first, pass into the hands of a corporation to be known as 'The Twin Buttes Mining and Smelting Company.'" Articles of incorporation were filed on September 10, 1903. The incorporators were John C. Baxter, John Ellis, and Michael Irish with $1,000,000 in capital stock being divided into 1,000,000 shares. "Directors during the first year are listed as William H. Earles; David S. Rose, of Milwaukee, Wisconsin; J. C. Baxter; John Ellis; and M. Irish of Tucson." Baxter, Ellis, and Irish ultimately decided to forego a cash sale of their mines, and instead became shareholders, retaining an active part in the daily operations, something that made them far more money in the long run. They were set for life.

Foy and Duffy family members show off piles of lumber imported for use in railroad construction. Courtesy of James Murphy.

On September 23, 1903, the *Arizona Daily Star* quoted D. S. Rose as saying, "Regarding our properties, I can say we are perfectly satisfied with the outlook, and are pushing the development work as rapidly as money and men can accomplish it. From now on we will have fifty miners laboring, which will make a fair sized camp. We have erected bunk rooms, wagon sheds, a tool house, and other structures, and expect no hindrance in our operations. Almost daily, the arrival of another hoist, an electric plant, and compressed air drills is expected and with these modern additional appliances a great deal can be accomplished. . . . We have a gang of men now at work running a telephone line from the mines to the residence in Tucson of J. H. Blakeley, the general manager, (and step-son of D. S. Rose) who will permanently reside here. The line will be of great assistance to us in ordering goods and transacting the immense amount of business which will be necessary in connection with the enterprise."

With the influx of funds and strategic planning by the wealthy Wisconsin investors, the new Twin Buttes Mining and Smelting Company immediately began the expansion of the camp that was supporting their mining operations. Construction began on a mining office, assay office, and other buildings needed for the company headquarters. The company lumberyard imported large batches of wood from Rancho de

Simplified route of the Twin Buttes Railroad, starting in Tucson. Courtesy of James Murphy.

la Canoa (which was comprised of 17,000 acres of the Old Spanish Land Grant also owned by the Milwaukee investors) which, in addition to being used for mining operations, were offered at reasonable prices to encourage mine workers to build family homes in the Twin Buttes community. Barracks housed single mine workers and company executives. A hotel was built which also provided meals. According to Twin Buttes Hotel advertisements, placed in Tucson newspapers, "Good meals and comfortable rooms" cost three dollars per day. A mess hall provided meals for workers and the Twin Buttes Store sold general merchandise, groceries, hardware, and even jewelry to miners and their families. An advertisement in the *Twin Buttes Times* indicated that a town meat market carried "Fresh Meats received daily from Brown's Ranch" in Sahuarita.

On May, 8, 1904, the *Arizona Republic* reported that, "Mayor David S. Rose, who went out to the Twin Buttes mine this week, is contemplating the building of a railroad from Tucson to this property, a distance of twenty-eight miles."

Rose attempted to convince Southern Pacific to build the railroad, but the most they would agree to do was sell him the supplies.[2] Rose decided to make a go of it without them, so, on September 20, 1904, the *Arizona Daily Star* reported that articles of incorporation had been filed with the Pima County Recorder for the Twin Buttes Railroad Company.

On December 6, 1904, Mayor Rose, along with chief engineer Nic Engel, arrived in Tucson for a six-week stay. The trip's purpose was to plot a path for the pending track and get grading work started within ten days. Rose had purchased an engine from Milwaukee and expected delivery within two weeks. The work was fraught with delays—foreshadowing what was to come. Survey work was not completed until Christmas Eve and graders' tents were not placed until December 26.[3]

On the 29th of December, Rose told the *Star* that forty men were at work in the mines with new equipment and planned to install a new hundred-ton water jacket in February. He reported on the thirty-mile railroad in progress and assured readers that, "There will be ten miles of road constructed by February."

In that same issue, Rose said, "Forty men were set to work in making the dirt fly on Wednesday as a beginning on the grade. There are sixteen teams of horses employed . . . They began operations at 7 o'clock yesterday morning, J.C. McDonald being in charge of the forces, the number of which will be augmented as required. William C. Goetz is the supervising engineer in charge of all the grading and building operations of the railway company. We expect to grade a mile a day, but will not use our locomotive for several days on the line. This engine is not a large one, but it is capable of handling a dozen loaded flat cars with due regularity and speed. A competent locomotive engineer will be in charge of the iron horse when it is on duty. . . . These mines and the railroad combined will be only one of many good things that Tucson will get as New Year's [1905] presents."

More lumber for railroad construction. Courtesy of James Murphy.

In the *Tucson Citizen* for February 27, 1905, Mayor Rose reported that he would be visiting Twin Buttes to "make arrangements for the erection of offices, cottages, ore bunkers, and a company store in anticipation of the business which we shall do as soon as the railroad is completed to the property. The improvements will approximate $50,000 and there will be a town site laid out, also a mechanical plant for the Copper King claim, including a modern house and engine." That visit was delayed by several weeks because, when Mayor Rose attempted to mount his horse, it stepped sideways and rolled on him, injuring his ankle.

Even with Southern Pacific providing the railroad supplies, the project seemed to get further and further behind. The desired date for a July 4, 1905, grand opening was all too soon a thing of the past. Grading, followed by bridge and culvert work, was slow and by the end of May, 1905, only twelve miles of roadbed had been formed. It was not until the end of November that the graders finally reached Twin Buttes.[4]

Finally, with the January 27, 1906, edition of the *Star* came a report of the actual track being laid. "Work began in earnest on the Twin Buttes railroad yesterday. Superintendent Thompson set a gang of fifty men to work on the road, the opening spike having been driven informally, on account of the departure for Milwaukee of Mayor Rose. Grading has been going on for some time, but the actual building was delayed for lack of material,

Men from McGee Ranch work to build railroad bridges. Courtesy of Lynn Harris.

which was held up in the hauling on the main line. It is estimated that thirty-five miles between here and Twin Buttes will soon be covered as it is the intention for the company to push the construction with the utmost speed."

In the February 11 edition of the *Star*, it said, "At the Twin Buttes about 70 men are engaged on the railroad, mines, and buildings. Wednesday being payday, some lively times were seen. There are already three saloons there, with the full quota of the lowest class of men and women. A record equal to that of Imperial Camp in its palmiest days may be expected."

On February 22: "Chief Engineer Thomson of the Twin Buttes railroad tells the *Tucson Citizen* that word had just been received from the freight department of the Southern Pacific that a large quantity of building material for the bridge and track-laying gangs has just arrived. The bridge gang has completed it

The Santa Cruz River flows south near corrals on J. K. Brown's ranch. Courtesy of Susan Strong-Dowd.

for about a distance of three miles out of the city. The gang has been handicapped by a shortage of bridge building equipment and material, but will now be able to go ahead more rapidly with its work. There is now on hand enough ties for about twenty miles of the line. The track-laying gang has been held back owing to the delay of rails in reaching here. At the mines, grading has been commenced for the branches which will run to the various groups."

By the fifth of May, the *Arizona Daily Star* reported that, "The grading of the 27-

mile stretch of the Twin Buttes Railway was completed recently after a second run to bring it up to a perfect state. The camps broke up yesterday. The track laying will be resumed Monday, as bridge timbers have been delayed in arrival from Oregon. There is now sufficient [lumber] in the yards to begin work and other supplies will arrive in time to keep the bridge builders busy to finish at or near the camp. The force will number 125 working after resumption Monday. The road will be completed by July first."

Passengers congregate next to the Twin Buttes Depot. Courtesy of Arizona Historical Society.

The *Bisbee Daily Review*, on May 24, 1906, quoted Mayor Rose as saying, "We will begin shipping 100 tons of ore per day on July 10. . . . Work is progressing rapidly on the railroad" with track being "completed eight miles out of the city." In one day, the railroad crew was said to have laid 3,100 feet of track, with materials being hauled to the workers over the tracks as quickly as it was completed.

"Mayor Rose stated that preparations are already underway for the formal celebration of the completion of the road and the formal observance of the Fourth of July at Twin Buttes. These celebrations will occur on the same day and it is hoped by the Twin Buttes people to have Tucson depopulated for that day and the entire 15,000 inhabitants taken to Twin Buttes to help set off the red fire, the fireworks, and take part in the general celebration."

On the ninth of June, track was laid across the Santa Cruz River at Brown's Ranch, leaving only six miles to reach the Twin Buttes Mining Camp—but on June 20, near Hart's Ranch, a segment of the track was damaged. "The accident was caused by the spreading of rails that had been improperly fastened and three cars laden with construction materials were ditched." The accident delayed work for several days.

Anticipation was building and the end was in sight. In the July edition of the *Twin Buttes Times*, it said, "We Will Celebrate! Upon the completion of the railroad the event will be celebrated in a manner becoming its importance. For it will be an important culmination not only to the officers and stockholders but to the city of Tucson and to the world at large. Important to our officers because it will mark the end of a long struggle, a triumph over discouragements; important to our stockholders because it marks the beginning of an era of material and financial success; important to the city of Tucson because it opens up another avenue to commercialism and makes possible the opening of new mines for which the city will be the basis of supplies; important to the world because the transportation facilities afforded by the road bring new resources to add their products to the sum total of the world's wealth. Indeed, we will celebrate and in right royal fashion."

This same issue also told of immediate plans to open a post office, claiming that the application had already been submitted, but was on hold pending the completion of the rail lines. Establishing a school to benefit the miners' children was "one of the first things to be done by the Twin Buttes people." The county commissioners had given assurance that they would "gladly co-operate to accomplish this." Hopes were expressed that, because of the discontinuation of the school near the Sahuarito Ranch, the "children from the families residing in the Santa Cruz Valley who formerly attended that school could be accommodated at Twin Buttes."

The June 22 completion date was delayed, but on June

(I. C. C. No.1)						

TWIN BUTTES RAILROAD

LOCAL PASSENGER TARIFF No. 1

BETWEEN TWIN BUTTES, ARIZONA, AND TUCSON, ARIZONA AND INTERMEDIATE STATIONS

EFFECTIVE OCTOBER 1st, 1906.

FROM TWIN BUTTES TO	Miles	Rate per Mile	Amount of Fare	BETWEEN	Miles	Rate per Mile	Amount of Fare
SAHUARITO	9	6c	$ .50	Twin Buttes — Sahuarito	9	6c	$ .50
PRECIADO	15	6c	.90	Sahuarito — Preciado	6	6c	.35
TUCSON	27	6c	1.60	Preciado — Tucson	12	6c	.70

This Company does not make or charge rates, fares or charges for transportation between points on its own route and points on the route of any other carrier by railroad or otherwise, and there has not been established between this Company and any other carrier any through route or joint rate whatsoever.

Organized excursions, of not less than 50 adult passengers, from Tucson to Twin Buttes and return, fare for round trip $1.60 each. This rate to be open to all societies, organizations and associations.

DAVID S. ROSE, *President.*

Tucson, Arizona. September 20, 1906.

Tariff posters for Twin Buttes passengers were posted at the depots as well as published in local newspapers. Courtesy of David Myrick.

30, 1906, the track finally reached the Twin Buttes camp. Preparations for the Independence Day celebration moved forward, and the proposed celebration was truly an Independence Day to remember. The following appeared in the July 6, 1906, edition of the *Arizona Daily Star*:

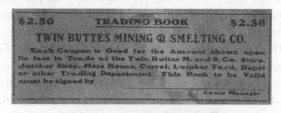

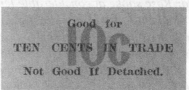

Trading book and torn out coupon from the Twin Buttes Mining and Smelting Company Store. Courtesy of the Revello family.

Twin Buttes-Tucson Now United! Two of the proudest and happiest men in Arizona welcomed the first passenger train to enter the [Twin Buttes] mining camp as they stood on the platform Fourth of July morning. They both looked like mining men, one a pioneer in that line, the other a man who invested capital in making the camp a possible future bonanza." These men were David S. Rose and John G. Baxter.

At 7:30 o'clock Wednesday morning five observation cars and a Pullman of the caboose class formed the makeup of the train that was decorated in view of the day being one that all loyal Americans celebrate. This train pulled out for Twin Buttes followed by another at 1 p.m. The runs were made in one hour and 10 minutes running time. These trains were manned by Engineer A. McGovern, Conductor B. K. Elgin, and Brakemen Wiggett and Sanford, all men who came here from Eastern roads. The paste boards were issued by John Reef, who was for 18 years private secretary to ex-Mayor Rose of Milwaukee and at present, secretary of the Twin Buttes Mining Company.

The Twin Buttes camp was alive to the situation, there being evidence of patriotism, the Old Glory being displayed at every point. The watchword was, 'good fellowship.' The visitors from the city were soon made aware of this, and the watchword stood until the last whistle blew at 11:00 p.m. when the homeward trip was made.

Fourth of July was a most appropriate time to celebrate the day and the linking of Tucson with Twin Buttes, a connection that makes the relationship much closer than ever. Misters Rose and Baxter were loyal entertainers. They left no stone unturned. It was their day. The ex-mayor aided by his lieutenants, Henry Webber, Joe Smith, Captain Bogan, and son Earl B. Rose took care of those who stayed in the camp proper, and John Baxter looked after friends at his bunk house at the Senator Morgan Mine, down which a number descended, among others, several ladies.

Duffy family and friends enjoy an excursion aboard a Twin Buttes train. Courtesy of James Murphy.

The most important event in amusements was the baseball game which resulted in a score of 14 to 9 in favor of the Southern Pacific team.... Following the ball game were foot races, Mayor Rose, et al., engaged. There were other races which filled the time, all interesting and some amusing. The evening program was of a special interest. Captain Baxter was the chairman. A quintet ... sang choice selections and were encored; Tom Kay Richie read the Declaration of Independence . . .; Judge Charles Blenman was patriotic in his utterances . . . Captain Baxter told of his coming to Arizona 22 years ago and what followed up to date, not forgetting his partners John Ellis and Mike Irish who were with him in the Olive and Twin Buttes Camps. . . . Enrique Anaya made . . . his address in Spanish. . . . Steve McKenna sang a selection in Spanish. Charles H Balis, president of the Tucson Chamber of Commerce . . . presented ex-mayor Rose with a handsome silver loving cup. Music was produced by the Montijo-Roldan orchestra.

Mayor Rose spoke at considerable length. It is unnecessary to quote the ex-mayor as all know he is an eloquent talker. He made it clear that he was in Arizona, and had been for three years. Incidentally he referred to Tucson as a suburb of Twin Buttes and the audience smiled audibly. The audience enthusiastically cheered for Mr. Rose just as they did the speakers who preceded him. There was opportunity for dancing on the improvised platform, but owing to the scarcity of ladies, this pleasure was availed of by only a few. Those who did not go out Wednesday have much to be sorry for. Day delightful, scenery fine night and day, and Helvetia smelter in sight after dark.

On July 7, 1906, the *Arizona Daily Star* reported that there were 250 men on the Twin Buttes Company's payroll. The August 16, 1906, edition of the *Bisbee Daily Review* said, "The camp looks not unlike a small fort. The site is ideal for a town. It is 1,200 feet higher than Tucson. It is always cool there at night. A breeze comes up at sundown and stirs until sunup. There is a depot at the camp. The town lies back 100 yards. There is a store, a modern meat market with large refrigerators, apartment houses, which could be called "flats" in a city, a large boarding house and a great many tents."

Duffy family and friends pose for a photo next to a Twin Buttes rail car. Courtesy of James Murphy.

With the anticipation of the long-awaited railroad finally put to bed, and the grand celebration a thing of the past, residents began looking forward with plans to settle into life with the new railroad in their town. The Twin Buttes school district was officially organized on the fifth of October in 1906. Miss Myrtle Hogan was the contracted teacher.

Earl B. Rose became the first U.S. postmaster assigned to the Twin Buttes post office on December 29, 1906. His commission arrived in March of 1907. That made it possible for daily pouch pickup and delivery, and the camp received a cancellation stamp bearing the "Twin Buttes" name. U.S.P.S. ledgers show that, over the next twenty-four years, Rose was succeeded by Perry Wildman, Albert S. Wordell, John G. Baxter, and Otto Hoffbauer.

On Valentine's Day, 1907, the *Tucson Citizen* gave Twin Buttes a glowing report. "Twin Buttes is fast getting and deserving the name of the prettiest mining camp in Arizona. It is situated much the same as is Tombstone—on the slope of a range of foothills looking across a valley. . . . Quite a cluster of buildings now surround the rectangle of which the depot and roundhouse form part of one side. The cabin of John Baxter, which three years ago was the only house in the camp, now forms part of a continuous row of buildings, in which are the mess house, butcher shop, company store, and bunk house. The pretty residence of Earl B. Rose faces the depot from across a wide plaza and the tented city of the mine workers, the schoolhouse, and corrals make the fourth side of the hollow square. A new bunk house is in the course of construction. The little red schoolhouse, presided over by Miss Hogan, has enrolled thirty-six aspirants for education. The County School Superintendent Cullin inspected the school Tuesday and found everything in shipshape."

By March 4, 1907, District No. 21 was without a teacher. Myrtle Hogan had married local miner Peter McFadden on February 25 of that year and resigned from her position. The county ran advertisements to try to fill her position, but there was no indication of a replacement being found. With so many students in a rural area, it must have been a difficult search. There are no records of a teacher for the 1907–08 school year, either.

In the fall of 1908, however, a new teacher filled the open position, but the man hired was less than an upstanding citizen. Mr. Dan M. Whetstone was accused of embezzlement and a warrant was issued for his arrest in November of 1908. The *Tucson Citizen* reported on the November 28 that, "his whereabouts are said to be a mystery." Whetstone had resigned from his teaching position the previous week, claiming a principalship in Yuma. Upon collecting his pay from the county, he was "reported around town spending money like water." He did not return to town after this, leaving behind a long string of residents who claimed to be owed money— including a twenty-five dollar debt to the boarding house and five dollar debt to the boardinghouse keeper. All said and done, it was estimated that he owed the people of Twin Buttes over $110.

Duffy family and friends admire a local donkey in front of the Twin Buttes Mining and Smelting Company Store in 1913. Courtesy of James Murphy.

Miss Clara Thompson Ball was the teacher appointed to fill the 1908–09 school year vacancy left by Mr. Whetstone. It appears that she completed the school year, but did not remain in the small town for long.

In 1910, Southern Pacific purchased a large chunk of the Twin Buttes rail line. The segment from Tucson to Sahuarita was used to complete a line that ran from Tucson to the Mexico border. From then on, the short spur from Sahuarita to Twin Buttes became used mostly for transporting materials to and from the mines.

In April of that same year, Miss Alice L. de Forrest settled in Twin Buttes and began teaching at the rural school there. Alice had been born in Pennsylvania in about 1883. After coming to Arizona, she attended the university in Phoenix and sat for the teachers certification exam in September of 1900. She spent a few years in the Phoenix area before moving south to teach at Twin Buttes for three consecutive school years. She took a year off for the 1912–13 school year during which Amy Irene Hansen was the teacher. Alice then returned for one last school year before moving on to teach in Cochise County. She was seriously injured in a car accident in May of 1933 and never completely recovered from the traumatic injuries to her ribs and back. She died on September 18, 1937, in a Tucson Hospital.

Harriet Duffy visits with Ed and Catherine Duffy Foy. Courtesy of the Revello family.

During Alice's time in Twin Buttes, the mines had stayed busy, but the community itself could have been considered pretty "rough around the edges." By 1913, the smelter in El Paso was receiving over 1,500 tons of copper, silver, and lead shipped out of the Twin Buttes mines each month. A mining group that included John Baxter, Ed Bush, Charles F. Pfister, and eventually

William F. Foy, took ownership of the mines. The highly productive little town had its rowdy side and became known far and wide as "Campo Borracho," or drunk camp. Tradition tells that the Twin Buttes postmaster once received a letter for a Mexican miner, originating in Old Mexico, addressed simply to: "Camp Borracho, Arizona, U.S.A." Even the United States Post Office Department knew of the Twin Buttes nickname.

In the fall of 1914, Miss Sarah T. French came to Twin Buttes as the new teacher. She stayed through the 1918–19 school year. From the fall of 1916 through the spring of 1919, she was listed as the school principal, and by this time, there were enough students to make it necessary to hire additional teachers.

Catherine Duffy joined Sarah for two years. She was the daughter of Martin and Brigid Egan Duffy and one of "the Duffy sisters" (Mary, Harriet, Alice, Ida and Catherine) after which Duffy Elementary School had been named. After the 1917–18 school year, Catherine Gertrude Duffy stopped teaching in Twin Buttes and on June 4, 1919, she married Edward Nicholas Foy, brother of William G. Foy.

Looking back, this period of time surrounding World War I was to have been the heyday of Twin Buttes. The demand for copper, especially during wartime, had mines running nonstop. The Twin Buttes camp was growing at an astronomical rate and records indicate that, during this time, William and Edward Foy started eleven new mine shafts, connected by underground tunnels. The quality of ore coming from these mines was phenomenal—some were said to contain thirty to forty percent copper.

Full advantage was taken of the Twin Buttes rail lines, and miles of new track were added to connect to each of the mine shafts for easy transportation. New workers were continuously hired and families came with them. In the fall of 1917, Catherine Duffy's second year at Twin Buttes, there were sixty students enrolled and the county hired a third teacher, Bertha E. Pond, to help keep class numbers at a manageable level.

Bertha stayed just one year; she and Catherine Duffy both submitted their resignations in the spring of 1918. Two new teachers, Fosta Ilene Welch and Eleanor Wood, a twenty-one-year-old Kansas native, joined Principal French for the 1918–19 school year. There were seventy-three students enrolled.

Miss Fosta Welch, born in Nebraska in 1894, came to Arizona from California after attending the California State Normal School. She was highly motivated and worked hard to earn scholarship funds to enable her to take musical classes as part of her post-graduate work. She taught at the Twin Buttes School for only one year before marrying Charles Madison Sisson on February 7, 1920, and moving back to El Monte, California, where she continued teaching for many years.

For the 1919–20 school year, there were only two teachers—Eleanor Wood and Grace Wright—but enrollment numbers still reflected seventy-three students combined between their classrooms. Grace Winford Wright was thirty-two years old when she moved to Twin Buttes. Born in South Dakota to Canadian parents, Grace had spent many years in Missouri. Her father died quite young, but she stayed close to care for her mother. With her mother's death in 1912, Grace left Missouri to head west. She was in El Paso, Texas, briefly, where she married Samuel Ebb, in January of 1917, but soon she was on the road to Arizona, having reverted to her maiden name of Wright.

Twin Buttes School teachers and students pose for photos in front of the schoolhouse in 1928. Courtesy of University of Arizona Special Collections.

The fall of 1920 brought Miss Amy Irene Hansen back to Twin Buttes as a replacement for Eleanor Wood, who had married Joseph John Smith in March of 1920. Grace Wright maintained her position as principal of the school, but enrollment numbers had decreased to thirty-nine students, foreshadowing a downward trend in the town population.

Grace and Amy started the 1921–22 school year in July with thirty-seven students, but by November, there were only twenty-five. The November 2, 1921, edition of the *Star* reported that the Twin Buttes school had been recognized for one hundred percent attendance. Sadly, only a few days later, on November 9, 1921, Principal Wright died in a Tucson hospital. She had been battling Bright's disease for years, but took a severe turn for the worse, leaving twenty-eight-year-old Amy Hansen alone for the duration of the school year.

1927–28 Twin Buttes District school marshal's report—Catherine Foy, teacher.
Courtesy of Arizona State Archives.

By the time plans were made for the 1922–23 school year, Amy Hansen was the lone teacher in a classroom with an anticipated enrollment of seventeen students. Born in California, Amy had come to Arizona in 1912 where she graduated from the Tempe Normal School, now known as ASU. Her very first teaching job was at Twin Buttes during the 1912–13 school year. After that, she went back north to teach in Chandler. She never lost her commitment to her lifelong calling to teach. When she died on the fourth of July in 1981, at the age of eighty-eight, she was still an active member of the National Retired Teachers Association.

Being the only teacher in the school did not seem to slow Miss Hansen down. In February of 1922, she organized a young people's Americanization class after school hours from 2 p.m. until 4 p.m. each day. Students were very enthusiastic and excited to attend. Amy worked tirelessly to care for her students in Twin Buttes through the spring of 1924 when she moved to San Bernardino, California, to accept a job there.

Catherine Duffy, now Catherine Foy, returned to the small school and remained there from the fall of 1924 until she retired in the spring of 1946. Enrollment numbers through those years fluctuated in sync with the constantly changing demands of the mining industry. There were periods of time when a second, and even, third additional teacher had to be hired. Emma Johnson, Mrs. J. W. McMahon, Mary Maroney, Lucille Titus, Vera Foster, and Delia Finnerty all came through the doors of the rugged building, but none stayed for more than a year. The consistent face of the Twin Buttes School, over the next twenty-two years, was the beloved face of Mrs. Catherine Duffy Foy.

Irene Foy on the left and Catherine Foy on the right pose with guests in front of the Twin Buttes School. Courtesy of the Foy family.

The population of Twin Buttes continued to dwindle. In 1928, William Foy bought out his partners to become the owner of the Twin Buttes Mining Company and the rail spur that accompanied it. He was seeking to consolidate ownership of all mines in the vicinity, but the crash of the stock market in 1929 took Foy's dreams with it. It seems that the town disappeared overnight.

At the close of the 1929–30 school year, Catherine Foy was the only teacher who remained. On July 22, 1930, it was announced that, effective August 15, 1930, the Twin Buttes post office would close and mail would be routed to Tucson.

A short burst of life came back to the Twin Buttes School when the Sierrita School closed due to a lack of attendance in the fall of 1932. The newly added children were transported to school and back each day, but in April of 1936, a heated dispute over the road and property lines made it impossible for the children to travel down the mountain for school. After over a year with no access to school, the students went back to their own small school for the fall of 1937.

The May 8, 1935, edition of the *Arizona Daily Star* reported:

> The ghost of Twin Buttes is there for everyone to see, with screens hanging on rusty hinges, mill equipment sagging from disuse, butcher shop hooks meatless, company club rooms abandoned, offices without noise except for the scratching of mice and rats, and the railroad being torn up from its bed to be sold for junk. The other day the most active thing in Twin Buttes was the American flag whipping in the breeze over the schoolhouse, from which came the drone of young Mexican voices, led by their teacher, Mrs. Ed Foy. Eight or nine Mexican families live in the camp and couldn't be pried away with the best Apache dynamite; and their children, with those from the ranches back in the Sierrita Mountains, attend the school.
>
> The Twin Buttes claims are now held by William and Ed Foy, the latter living in the ghost town and the former in Tucson. They managed the mine for the Milwaukee company during their best paying days, and when they took them over, expected to return as much to themselves as they had seen go to the Milwaukee stockholders, but copper took a dive shortly after they took hold, and the bottom dropped out of their investment. But there is always that lure of the claims coming back in silver or gold, or the price of copper going up to where production may be resumed. But whether they expect to resume operations or not, they will not say. So three bachelors live in the ghost camp's company houses, with eight or nine Mexican families for neighbors. The Foy home is nearby, and back in the Sierritas are the McGee and Harris families on dry farms and cattle ranches. The quiet life is the good life, and this is the land of tomorrow, so they fret?

By the end of 1935, William Foy gave up on his dreams and scrapped the last of the Twin Buttes railroad.

In July of 1939, the *Star* reported that ". . . Mrs. Catherine Foy [was] recently honored by the classroom teachers' department of the National Education Association, who teaches 21 Mexican children at Twin Buttes, on the windswept slopes of the Sierrita Mountains, 17 miles south of here [Tucson]. Except for five years in the Tucson schools, Mrs. Foy has been teaching since 1916 at Twin Buttes, a copper mining camp of many ups and downs. Pupils from a neighboring community once were transported down to her school but 'feudin' broke up the consolidation. Mrs. Foy's classroom houses pupils ranging in age from six to sixteen, in classification from the first to the eighth grades. At present all are Mexican ranch children. All enroll the first year without a speaking knowledge of English. Her system is to achieve a 'family atmosphere' by keeping all the pupils working on a common project, each according to his abilities. 'When the babies come to school,' she said, 'I try to see there is not so great a change from family life to school.'"

The May 25, 1941, edition of the *Arizona Republic* announced that, "For the first time in a dozen years, the Twin Buttes camp is showing signs of activity." J. J. Williams from California was reconditioning machinery to start exploring the Minnie and Copper Butte claims. He was working out arrangements with William Foy, the current owner representative, to take over those claims. Foy had been working several other sites in the area and Charles M. Taylor had leased the old Morgan Mine for exploration. This may have been a step to reopen the mines, but it was not an attempt to revive the Twin Buttes camp.

On May 23, 1944, a petition was filed to annex the Zinc School to the Twin Buttes district. It wasn't until May of 1945 that the proposed combination occurred. The Twin Buttes school, deep in the middle of the empty town, was made ready and three teachers were once again in the building. When the 1945–46 school year started, Catherine D. Foy, head teacher and teacher of grades one through three shared space with Mrs. Ann Freeman, who taught grades four through eight.

Ann Freeman and Catherine Duffy Foy sit on the steps in front of the school in 1946. Courtesy of the Revello family.

The freshly painted rooms did not stay filled for long. By July 21, 1946, the *Star* reported that the Twin Buttes school was once again reduced to one room, but, unlike years before, the teacher to submit her resignation was Mrs. Catherine Duffy Foy. With her departure, it would not be long until the school doors closed permanently. Mrs. Ann Freeman taught through the fall of 1947 and Ruth Barker, along with Dorothy Irvin, closed out the final year in the tired abandoned town. The annexation petition was cleared and Sahuarita would now welcome the children from Twin Buttes. In the fall of 1948, for the first time in over forty years, the school doors did not open on the first day of school.

Teachers, District No. 21

1906–07	Myrtle Hogan
1908	Dan M. Whetstone (disappeared in November)
1908–09	Clara Thompson Ball
1910–12	Alice L. de Forrest
1912–13	Amy Irene Hansen
1913–14	Alice L. de Forrest

1914–16   Sarah T. French
1916–17   Sarah T. French (principal); Catherine Duffy
1917–18   Sarah T. French (principal); Bertha E. Pond; Catherine G. Duffy
1918–19   Sarah T. French (principal); Fosta Ilene Welch; Eleanor Wood
1919–20   Eleanor Wood; Grace Winford Wright
1920–21   Grace Winford Wright (principal); Amy Hansen
1921–22   Grace Wright (principal); Amy Hansen
1922–24   Amy I. Hansen
1924–25   Catherine D. Foy (principal; lower grades); Emma Johnson (upper grades)
1925–26   Catherine D. Foy (principal; grades 1–3); Mrs. J. W. McMahon (grades 4–7)
1926–27   Catherine Foy (principal); Mary Maroney (grades 1–3); Lucille Titus (grades 4–8)

Teachers, District No. 31

1927–28   Catherine D. Foy (grades 1–8)
1928–29   Catherine D. Foy (grades 1–8); Vera Foster

Teachers, District No. 21

1929–30   Catherine D. Foy (principal; grades 1–3); Delia Finnerty
1930–31   Catherine D. Foy (grades 1–6)
1931–33   Catherine D. Foy (grades 1–7)
1933–45   Catherine D. Foy (grades 1–8)
1945–46   Catherine D. Foy (head teacher; grades 1–3); Ann Freeman (grades 4–8)
1946–47   Ann Freeman (grades 1–8)
1947–48   Ruth Barker (grades 1–4); Dorothy Irvin (grades 5–8)
1948–49   School is annexed to Sahuarita

~ Contributed by Monica Lee Elam Christiansen

NOTES

1. Kalt, William D., Jr. *Awake the Copper Ghosts! The History of Banner Mining Company and The Treasure of Twin Buttes.* Tucson, AZ: Banner Mining Company, 1968.
2. Myrick, David F. *Railroads of Arizona: the Southern Roads.* Berkeley, CA: Howell-North Books, 1975. 1:394.
3. Ibid., 1:394.
4. Ibid., 1:306.

Zinc School District and the History of San Xavier, Olive Camp, and Surrounding Ranches

Like many of the early Pima County Schools, students in Zinc School District No. 32 were from extremely diverse backgrounds. The district boundaries encompassed Helmet Peak, a tall, ruggedly steep landmark, that could be used as an easy point of reference in pinpointing the general location of the Zinc School District. Land in the local area was rich in minerals, bringing an endless parade of mining companies into the area. Individual families came to work their small mining claims, with dreams of "striking it rich." Others came to take advantage of the opportunities to file for "free land" through the Homestead Act, while the sloped landscape was wide open and perfect for raising cattle.

The view looking southwest from San Xavier Mine shows the road to Olive Camp which is near the two small mountains on the left. Courtesy of U.S. Geological Survey.

As early as March of 1859, the *Weekly Arizonian* briefly made mention of the "San Xavier Mining Company located approximately 15 miles from Tucson, near the San Xavier Mission." This was one of the area's earliest mine sites responsible for bringing an increased number of people into the area.

In the mid-1880s, the Emperor Copper Company opened mines at a site known as Mineral Hill, and by the end of that decade the Azurite Copper and Gold Mining Company operated a thirty-ton smelting jacket, with the active Azurite Mining Camp built near the smelter. The camp was primarily home to men working at the Mineral Hill and Azurite mines. Families were not commonplace because the camp consisted mostly of tents. "Azurite increased to a population of 125 by March of 1899, and reported the need for appointment of a peace officer, since liquor conveniently smuggled into camp . . . was causing the working schedules to be disrupted."[1] Within the next few years, silver prices peaked and receded resulting in the Azurite Mine's closing, and ultimately, the demise of the Azurite Camp.

Panoramic view of Olive Camp illustrating how large the area was. Courtesy of Susan Strong-Dowd.

Olive Camp, another active site in the shadows of Helmet Peak, was the result of successful operations of the Olivette Mine. Olive was one of the longer-lived camps in the area. On September 17, 1886, the *Arizona Daily Star* reported that, "A representative of the *Star* visited Olive Camp on Wednesday last, taking the new stage line of Mr. Geo. L. Johnson, who made the trip in 2:30 hours. The camp presents a very lively appearance, with two boarding houses, an assay office and a saloon. There are over one hundred men at work in this district and there is room for a good many more. There is a movement on foot to establish a post office [which eventually opened on March 4, 1887]. The name will be Olive, and they have recommended Mr. Owen J. Doyle to be the postmaster of that camp. Mr. George L. Johnson will take the contract of carrying the mail, under the present arguments. They have a pouch, with a key at the post office in Tucson and one kept by Mr. J. K. Brown who receives and [sorts] mail for

Olive Camp view of homes and company buildings. Courtesy of Susan Strong-Dowd.

the camp free of charge . . ."

Olive Camp was "named in honor of Olive Stephenson Brown. Olive was an active silver camp during the 1880s and 1890s. Serving such mines as the Olivette, San Xavier, Wedge, Michigan Maid, and Richmond, the camp was unique in that there was no mill, smelter, or machinery. Ore was merely extracted and sent elsewhere to be processed, and the miners received their returns by check. Olive Brown, whose husband James Kilroy Brown was one of the owners of the Olive Mine, gave more to the camp than just her name. While living there, Mrs. Brown formed the habit of treating the employees of the Olive Mine to a free chicken dinner every Sunday. Soon Sunday became a day of feasting and fun, and was eagerly anticipated by the men."[2]

With silver prices declining in the late 1890s, mines in the Pima District began to focus on copper production. Some of the smaller mines, including the Olivette, were closed. The Olive post office closed on May 23, 1892, and the Brown family sold its interest in the Olivette Mine to move into Tucson. With the focus shifted to copper, the San Xavier Mines remained open as the industry moved into the 1900s, and the area once again became known as San Xavier.

As is normal with the cyclical nature of metal markets and the mining industry, the Mineral Hill Consolidated Company soon came into the area and bought out nearby mines to seek its fortunes in the search for copper. The company opened the Pittsburg Camp to house workers at the site of the old Azurite Camp. The June 21, 1905, edition of the *Arizona Daily Star* reported that, "Three loads of merchandise will leave for the Pittsburg camp store this morning. The Mineral Hill Consolidated Company [is the owner] of the store in camp, which is doing a good business." The company built structures to house the company headquarters on-site and arranged for stage service three days a week.

In November of 1912, the Empire Zinc Company purchased the San Xavier Mine, in addition to six other mines in the vicinity. This purchase once again brought life to the area mines, setting the stage for another population boom as the camps were quickly resurrected.

In 1928, students at the Zinc School squeeze together for a mountainside photo. Courtesy of University of Arizona Special Collections.

On October 11, 1913, the *Star* announced that, "Three New Schools Will Start Monday." Included in this list was the Zinc School in the San Xavier Mining District. "The Zinc school will be taught by Miss Annie Moran. It will be held in a frame building erected and used formerly by the San Xavier Mining Company and will be attended by children of employees of that company." The 1913–14 school records show sixty-five children on the rolls for that first year.

It was around this same time that some of the larger ranches began to form, adding additional students to the new school district. On June 30, 1913, Antonio Navarro had filed paperwork to homestead 160 acres of ranchland near the mines, creating what would be known as "Navarro Ranch."

On January 6, 1919, Florencio Gallego filed for 159 acres and, over the next four years, the Gallego family added to their holdings, creating the original La Sierra (later renamed El Ocotillo) Ranch—an operation covering over 639 acres. According to Salina Barajas, a Gallego descendant:

The ranch was known as a place of herding, roping, and branding cattle but also a place for family, roundups, and fiestas. According to my Tia Lydia (deceased), both Florencio and Mercedes loved to dance "rancheras" and "chotis." In 1935, during the Great Depression era, they moved to South Tucson and had a business selling wood and would go back and forth to the ranch until they sold it in 1959. My great grandparents had a total of (12) TWELVE children (6 boys and 6 girls): Lupe, Cruz, Florencio, Antonia, Francisco (my grandfather), Lydia, Lolita, Casimiro, Delia, Jesus, Mike, and Armando.

The older Gallego siblings attended school by the mines. It was called Zinc School and only had 2 classrooms. The capacity of the school was twenty students and nine of those children were Gallego children! I heard stories that they were often late because the horse that pulled their wagon was too slow. The children named their horse "Franque."

The Gallego children pose in their wagon near the Zinc School while Franque waits patiently. Courtesy of the Gallego family.

Between October of 1923 and July of 1924, Rafael Peyron homesteaded over 800 acres and Ventura Maldonado claimed another 600 acres in January of 1936. While small in comparison to huge cattle ranches elsewhere, these "small spreads" took up a lot of the property near the existing mines. They brought ranch owners, foremen, and *vaqueros* (cowboys) with large families to areas once dominated by the mining camps and small single-family properties.

The Zinc School was the first rural school in the area with a vocational program that started in the fall of 1927. Otto L. and Roxy Dustman, the teachers hired for the 1927–28 school year, inaugurated the vocational work and the program was so successful that Annie E. Daniels, county school superintendent, hired another teacher for the regular classrooms so Mr. Eastman would be able pursue this branch of instruction full time.

According to the November 13, 1927, edition of the *Tucson Citizen*, "While not repairing decrepit articles of furniture for the neighborhood, as a means of practice, the boys have found the time aside from their academic studies to improve the school building and remodel their workshop. They have also been taught to fashion their own work desks and have excited interest to a point where every boy of school age is now in daily attendance at Zinc and older boys, who had left school, are returning for vocational instruction, and even the fathers of some of the pupils have enrolled. To instruct the older boys and men, a night class is to begin at the school on Monday. Carts are being made for the hauling of water, and as a means of branching out from woodwork, tools for repairing harnesses were purchased yesterday."

The December 20, 1927, edition of the *Tucson Citizen* further reported that:

Ramona Pemberton takes aim near Las Palmias in December of 1949. Courtesy of Sandra Jake.

The entire course of study at this school is based upon the fact that most of the foreign-born pupils leave school at the age of 16 to become wage earners. The course is attracting the interest of men who have been out of school for years, but who have joined the shop work class.

The course taught in farm mechanics includes wood work, mechanical drawing, rope work, sheet metal work, farm blacksmithing, plumbing, and concrete construction. The projects involved include making and repairing home, farm and shop appliances.

The boys, before the opening of school in the fall, remodeled part of the school house, tearing out old windows and building in a panel of five new windows on one side, building new cupboards and installing new blackboards. They remodeled an old house into a shop, making it six feet longer and putting in new windows and doors. Each boy has an individual bench.

Ramona posing in front of a Rome café in her W.A.C. uniform. Courtesy of Sandra Jake.

In January of 1928, the rapidly growing Zinc School needed additional property to make room for all of the children in the district. Mrs. Annie Daniels, county school superintendent, resorted to creative expansion methods. She filed a mining claim on government property to secure the needed land.

Throughout the 1930s and '40s, classes at the Zinc School were taught by Marguerite Schneider and/or one of the Pemberton sisters. Marguerite Schneider was the daughter of Frank Edmond and Kathleen M. Correll Schneider. She graduated from the University of Arizona in June of 1928. In the fall of 1930, she started at Zinc School and, aside from one year, worked there until the spring of 1937. She moved to San Francisco soon after that to be close to her sister, Kathleen M. Schneider Baker. The Gallego family remembers that the girls from her class stayed in touch with Miss Schneider after she moved to California.

Ramona Hopwood Pemberton, born February 25, 1906, and Maria Tempe Hopwood Pemberton, born September 1, 1910, were daughters of James Nicholas and Ramona Araiza Pemberton, of Tucson. On January 30, 1933, Ramona Pemberton homesteaded 640 acres west of Mineral Hill, on what today is known as Wrangler Ranch. On October 7, 1937, James N. Pemberton filed for an additional 640 acres of adjacent property. Beth Pemberton, widow of James Pemberton, Jr., filed for 639 acres of adjacent property on January 8, 1940—giving the family a total of 1,919 acres in the Zinc School District.

Ramona graduated from the University of Arizona in 1928 in the same class with Marguerite Schneider. She was very involved in hiking, tennis, and the Girls "A" Club. Her sister, Tempe Pemberton, also attended the University of Arizona and graduated in May of 1936. She was on the women's hockey team and in the varsity villagers club.

The February 20, 1930, edition of the *Tucson Citizen* includes a brief article about the Zinc School. It states, "The Zinc school is located 21 miles from Tucson on the road to Twin Buttes, also known as the South Nogales Road. The camp was formerly called Olive Camp and hasn't been operated for over 10 years. Members of the school board are Mr. Place and his daughter, Mrs. Altfillisch. There are 34 pupils in the school. The upper grades are taught by Miss Marguerite Schneider, and the primary grades by Miss Ramona Pemberton, head teacher. Teachers, with the help of

Tempe Pemberton in her backyard in Tucson. Courtesy of Sandra Jake.

the board, have completely repainted the inside and outside of the schoolhouse this year. Although there are no grades above the fifth, manual training and sewing are being taught. The girls are organizing a 4-H club. Special stress has been placed on health work. At the beginning of the school year a tooth-brush drill was initiated. It has proved very successful and the children now brush their teeth twice a day. The children are greatly interested in outdoor sports. Baseball games have been played between Twin Buttes and this school. Soccer ball will be on the schedule later on in the season. At the present time the children are greatly interested in preparing exhibits for the County Fair."

Tempe Pemberton posing for a photo. Courtesy of Sandra Jake.

The May 8, 1935, edition of the *Arizona Daily Star* tells readers that, "Only 2 white women remain in the San Xavier Ghost Camp—Mrs. George H. Place (Sally Louisa Oliver Place), caretaker for Empire Zinc Company and Miss Marguerite Schneider, teacher in the little school." The mining families were no longer a source of students for the Zinc School population. The focus had shifted to the local farmers and ranchers.

In the "Zinc Zippers" segment of the *Arizona Daily Star* on October 14, 1935, student reporter Concha Coronado tells that the Zinc Zippers held their first meeting on October third and elected officers. The group of girls, including those with the family names of Maldonado, Coronado, Barredaz, and Vindiola, had planned to meet every other Monday with Miss Schneider as their club leader. They were working on making dish towels by learning to hem and miter fabric corners. The school was small that year, with only sixteen total students.

On May 22, 1936, the *Arizona Daily Star* reported, "The little gray schoolhouse at Zinc, one-room unit of the Pima county rural school system, rose to the educational heights of glory Wednesday night when Ernesto Coronado and Frank Gallego graduated. . . . This is the first graduating class of two earnest students, who in all the years of the school's existence have been the first ones to stay long enough to complete all eight grades of work, brought out the entire population of the countryside to celebrate. There was a 'hot time in the old town' that night. The fathers of the two boys, in well justified pride, provided a big barbeque and just as the sun set and the afterglow lighted the hills around the tiny mining camp not far from Twin Buttes, the barbecue pit was opened, the proud *señoras* bustled around a savory kitchen, dogs barked excitedly, the seniors came galloping into camp on horseback and the party was on. Paper plates piled high with food were handed out with typical western hospitality. There was handshaking and congratulations."

In May of 1940, a petition was circulated to consolidate the Twin Buttes and Zinc School Districts—an area of about sixty-three square miles. This was not passed because on December 15, 1944, the *Arizona Daily Star* reported that, "Zinc, smallest school in the county, will have a Christmas play, program, and tree at 8:00 p.m. next Thursday under the direction of Mrs. Margaret McNeill, teacher. There are 10 pupils in the school. Since there is no electricity, the program will be held under lantern light."

The 1944–45 school marshal census listed students as

The Zinc schoolhouse at Mineral Hill on Twin Buttes Road stands proud with new windows on May 13, 1937. Courtesy of University of Arizona Special Collections.

Andrea Granillo (1), Robert Buelna (2), Leslie Pittman (2), Frank Hernandez (2), Billy Kraft (3), Joe Pittman (3), Rudy Ortiz (3), David Garcia (3), Gabriel Garcia (3), Virginia Buelna (4), Gilbert Coronado (4), Nieves Ortiz (5), Dorothy Pepper (5), Albert Buelna (7), Frank Coronado (7), and Robert Coronado (7). All of the students were from six local mining families.

On May 30, 1945, the *Arizona Daily Star* reported that, "School electors of the Zinc school district have petitioned for annexation of that district to the Twin Buttes district, it was announced yesterday by

May 13, 1937, finds students and teachers building a soil conservation dam on the Zinc School grounds. Courtesy of University of Arizona Special Collections.

Mrs. P. H. Ross, Pima county superintendent of schools." In this process, the electors of the Zinc district petitioned the board of trustees of the Twin Buttes district for annexation. After Twin Buttes approved the proposal, it was submitted to the county school superintendent. It was expected to be approved because the Zinc school building was located on the Eagle-Picher Mining Company property where a new shaft was planned to be sunk. With the small number of students and only five miles between the schools, it was much easier to combine than to find a new site and rebuild the Zinc school. Plans were under way to arrange a transportation schedule. The Twin Buttes building was going to be repainted and repaired to accommodate two additional classrooms and teachers.

This simple vote, logically processed sometime during the summer of 1945, forever changed the dynamics of the small community. The schoolhouse and outlying buildings—a source of much pride to hard-working vocational students—were torn down and replaced by the gaping mouth of a hungry new mine shaft. Mrs. McNeill packed and moved away, seeking a new classroom full of children to teach. Helmet Peak remains, standing tall against the skyline, forever without the laughter of lively students at recess and the echoing tones of the Zinc School's bell.

Zinc School Teachers

1912–13	J. F. McCall
1913–14	No teacher listed
1914–15	Louise K. Ball
1915–16	Mabel R. Kerrigan
1916–17	Mabel R. Kerrigan (principal); Gladys Reidel; M. Hellert
1917–18	Mabel R. Kerrigan (principal); Olive J. Bashford; M. Hellert
1918–19	Olive J. Bashford (principal); Ruth E. Zeigler
1919–20	Olive J. Bashford; Vannette Barrett
1920–21	J. B. Robinson
1921–22	Alma Faulkner; J. F. McDole
1922–23	J. F. McDole
1923–24	J. F. McDole (grades 1–6)
1924–25	J. F. McDole
1925–26	Helen Worth

1926–27   Helen Worth (grades 1–7)
1927–28   Rony P. Dustman (K–8)
1928–29   Helen E. Worth (principal; grades 2–8); Ramona Pemberton (primary); A. G. Hansen
1929–30   Ramona H. Pemberton (1-5)
1930–31   Marguerite Schneider (grades 2–6); Ramona H. Pemberton (1)
1931–32   Ramona H. Pemberton (grades 1–3); Marguerite Schneider (grades 4–7)
1932–33   Ramona H. Pemberton (grades 1–7)
1933–34   Marguerite Schneider (grades 1–7)
1934–37   Marguerite Schneider (grades 1–8)
1937–44   Tempe Pemberton (grades 1–8)
1944–45   Margaret McNeill (grades 1–8)
1945   Annex petition (May 30)

~ Contributed by Monica Lee Elam Christiansen

NOTES

References

1. Sherman, James E. and Barbara H. *The Camp Ghost Towns of Arizona*. Norman, OK: University of Oklahoma Press, 1969. 100.
2. Ibid., 110.

Additional resources

Arizona Daily Star, Tucson, Arizona
Barajas, Selina. *Gallego Family—Tucson's Original Vaqueros*. Retrieved January 28, 2022, from https://mireinaboutique. wordpress.com/tag/gallego-family
    Gallego family Facebook page.

PART III: SAHUARITA

An Overview of the History of Sahuarita from 1821 to the 1970s

This is the story of how the town of Sahuarita began, the significance of its location, and what has kept it going economically over all the years.

Sahuarita name origin

In 1854, after the signing of the Gadsden Purchase that brought Southern Arizona into the United States, a few hardy Americans began to move into the Santa Cruz Valley following in the footsteps of the Spanish (later Mexican) missionaries, military, miners, and settlers. In the beginning, it was only miners. Pete Kitchen, one of the earliest American settlers, said in that year the area was depopulated due to the Apache depredations. Despite this, the Canoa Ranch land grant was still claimed for cattle grazing by the Ortiz brothers, Tomás and Ignacio, even though they were often forced to live in the more protected communities of Tubac or Tucson. When the Canoa grant was surveyed in 1821 by Tubac Commander Ignacio Elias Gonzales, he located the northern boundary on a rocky hill near a place by the Santa Cruz River called "El Saguarito," Spanish for "small saguaro" cactus. (Willey, 156) To be named, it must have had some prominence. This is the elevation at which the prime saguaro habitat begins and continues downhill toward Tucson. Saguarito, as a place name, has thus been acknowledged at least as early as 1821. Later, the name was given as Saguarita on a map drawn in 1861. (Biertu)

1861 map made by F. Biertu, mining engineer, showing the early spelling of Saguarita. Courtesy of Henry Huntington Library.

According to the Encyclopedia Brittanica, "saguaro, (*Carnegiea gigantea*), also spelled sahuaro, is a large cactus species (family Cactaceae), native to Mexico, Arizona and California." The base of the word (saguaro) is thought to originate in the Uto-Aztecan language family spoken by several tribes of Native American peoples of southern Arizona and northern Mexico. Since a hard "g" sound is not pronounced, some preferred to spell Sahuarita with an "h," which is silent in Spanish. In Spanish, saguaro and its diminutive saguarito are always spelled with a final "o." Even though *saguarito* is grammatically correct, perhaps some people just liked the sound of *saguarita* better. According to old Tucson newspapers, in both articles and ads, Sahuarita and Sahuarito were used interchangeably from the 1870s until about the 1940s. A fixed spelling had never seemed to be important, although the name of the school has always been spelled Sahuarita. (Sah-wah-REE-tah) The "h" was almost always used, not "g." There also continued to be a difference of opinion about the spelling of saguaro (h or g?) for years in the Arizona State Legislature and in the school districts, as reported in a letter to the editor of the *Star* from local rancher and Spanish speaker Fred C. Noon. He believed that the "sahuaro" spelling reflected the pronunciation of a Native American name, which was later modified by speakers of Spanish. He went on to describe the 1901 naming of the flower of the Territory of Arizona as a *sahuaro* blossom, which was then approved by the State Legislature in 1931, but in 1933 it changed the spelling to *saguaro*. The stronger political will predominated (*Star,* Oct 19, 1966) but preferences remained: now there is a Sahuaro High School in Tucson and a Saguaro High School in Scottsdale.

Earliest settlement

The Canoa grant was centered on a place halfway between Tucson and Tubac, where there was relatively easy access to underground water. Digging a few feet down would reward the thirsty man and animal with safe water to drink. (Bolton, Vol III, 3) But because the distance from Tucson to Tubac is forty miles, early day travelers needed multiple resting places where water could be found. Some, like Captain Anza and Father Kino, went directly from Canoa to San Xavier on the west side of the river. El Sahuarito's location was about halfway between Tucson and the Canoa watering place, twenty miles, or about the distance someone could travel in a day. El Sahuarito's water supply was not, perhaps, as productive as that of Canoa, but better than nothing. Fairly shallow wells could be dug, but apparently there was no spring. Some nice large washes run out of the Santa Rita mountains just upstream of where the current town is located. They would have provided a jolt to the water table at that point.

Later on, homesteaders would take advantage of the water and good soil in that area. Mexican settlers had probably lived in the area when not under immediate threat by Apaches, whose raids limited settlement from the 1700s to the early 1870s. The first occupants could be called squatters, because American land ownership laws took a while to develop. Exactly where people lived is difficult to determine now, because in the interim there have been many other settlers. When the Gadsden Purchase brought this area into the United States in 1854, Mexicans were allowed to become U.S. citizens if they chose. When the Tucson Presidio's soldiers were finally transferred south to Sonora in March of 1856, some Mexican settlers went with them and some stayed.

Beginning in 1855, more American miners and mining companies began to move into the area, including the Sonora Exploring and Mining Company, headed up by Charles Poston, Samuel Peter Heintzelman, and mapmaker Herman Ehrenberg. (North, 20) They usually arrived in Tucson and then traveled south along the Santa Cruz River to Tubac, a distance of forty miles. They would make a stop if lodging was available.

The first known American map that shows *Saguarita* (with an "a" at the end) is *Silver Mines of Arizona* by H. C. Grosvenor, published in 1861. Another map was drawn in 1861 by mining engineer F. Biertu. He also spelled it *Saguarita*. The first known non-Mexican to live nearby was Allen Cullumber (sometimes spelled Collumber), who was born in Ohio in 1815 and came west, via Texas, to do some farming and mining. He settled near Sahuarita and provided food and lodging to travelers, besides farming. He had three sons. He appeared on an Arizona census in 1860, farming in the San Pedro Valley; probably from there he went to Sahuarita. It is likely that he spent only a short time in Sahuarita due to the Apache threat, leaving by 1861. In 1874 he was living in Yavapai County.

One of those mining companies, the Sopori Land and Mining Co., incorporated in Rhode Island, was represented by Richmond Jones, who arrived in Tucson in February of 1860. On his way south, he stayed overnight at Cullumber's, noting in his diary that between San Xavier and Cullumber's place was the heaviest growth of mesquite he had seen. A couple of months later he was surveying north of Canoa and located Cullumber's place on a map, where apparently there was sufficient water to be shared. Cullumber had either dug a well or improved on one already there. By the late 1860s there is no mention of Cullumber, so he must have left by then. However, Jones does mention Sahuarito on March 4, 1861, where there was still a place to stay. (Judkins and Bingham, 30, 40–41; Robinson, 21)

During 1861, Apache attacks increased and the Butterfield Overland Mail was halted. Then the War Between the States began to affect Arizona by the withdrawal of troops from Fort Buchanan. With the loss of troops, Apache attacks continued to increase and most settlers and miners left the valley. Richmond Jones and H. C. Grosvenor were among those killed by Apaches. (North, 201) The surviving owner of the Canoa Ranch, Tomás Ortiz, lived in Tucson. His brother, Ignacio, had been killed west of Tucson by Native Americans on his way back from California in 1857. Survivor of an Apache attack, Larcena Page's family members were not as lucky as she, including her husband, brother, and father. Bandits also were active, killing John Poston and two German miners at Cerro Colorado in 1861. (North, 174)

Right and left, vacant ranches would have met the eye for some time. The Confederacy took possession of Arizona for a brief time. When Carleton's Column arrived from California in April 1862 and successfully opposed the Confederate soldiers, the Union flag was raised in Tucson. In the meantime, politics was working its way through Congress in the interest of making Arizona a separate territory from New Mexico. Heintzelman Mine silver was waved around by Charles Poston and those supporting the Sonora Exploring and Mining Company. On February 24, 1863, the Territory was established. The law came, too: Joseph Pratt Allyn was appointed associate judge and he came west, writing letters everywhere. He did not mention Sahuarita so it was probably still deserted. In 1862, Major David Fergusson, stationed with the California Column in Tucson, reported that the Sahuarito Ranch was abandoned and the well had caved in. (*Star*, May 5, 1910; also Major Fergusson's report)

Established settlement

The late 1860s were still tenuous, but one Cyrus S. Rice came back through the Territory with the California Column and decided to settle on the Sahuarito Ranch. At that time, in 1867, there was a lone saguaro cactus that served as a landmark. Rice built a house, or perhaps repaired one that was already there, but did not stay long. (*Arizona Daily Star*, Feb 9, 2016; Ancestry.com) In 1868 he sold the Sahuarito Ranch to Albert C. Benedict, who was raised in Michigan. The latter had gone to the gold fields in California and joined the California Column before doing some prospecting near Prescott. Leaving there, he arrived in Southern Arizona in about 1864. Albert married Gregoria Alvarez (born in 1844 in Santa Ana, Sonora) in 1865, and they had four children—three boys and a girl. (Their daughter Mary became a professional woman and eventually made a place for herself in Arizona history by marrying Colonel W. C. Greene of the Cananea Cattle Company.) (Sonnichsen, 82–88) At this point the name of the ranch changed

Horses and Mules Ranched
By A. C. BENEDICT,
—on—
SAHUARITO RANCH
—in—
SANTA CRUZ VALLEY,
—at—
$2.50 per Month for Each Animal.
Careful Herders Always with the Stock.

This ranch has ample water and the BEST of GRASS in unlimited quantity.
When ordered by the owner, stock will be fed grain at an additional price to be agreed upon.
Stock for this ranch, left at R. N. Leatherwood's corral in Tucson, with instructions as to feed, time, return, etc., will have prompt attention.
As the care of stock will be made a specialty on this ranch, owners can rely upon their animals sent to it, receiving the best of care.
January 31, 1874.   17-6m

Arizona Weekly Citizen,
February 14, 1874

from Sahuarita to Sahuarito, possibly at the behest of the Spanish-speaking Gregoria. They began supplying food to travelers and their stock. Albert knew by then to keep one hand on a gun, since Apaches were still a serious threat. In July of 1872, while planting beans, he and two farm hands, Jose Padilla and Tomas Tapia, were attacked by a group of fifteen Apaches. Ever wary and ready, Benedict and the others began firing and succeeded in running them off. However, Benedict took a bullet in the ankle which did serious damage and caused him trouble the rest of his life. (*Arizona Weekly Citizen*, July 27, 1872) This did not stop him from politics however, and he began serving as treasurer of Pima County within a few months, and later as territorial auditor. Soon he began to attempt the sale of the Sahuarito Ranch, moving his family south to his Huababi (Guevavi) Ranch near Pete Kitchen's place. It was not until 1877 that he found a buyer.

James K. Brown acquires the Sahuarito Ranch

James K. Brown and longtime miner Tom Roddick bought the Benedict ranch. (By then the threat had abated as the Apaches were being put on reservations.) In 1879, Tom Roddick took sick and passed away. His death was accompanied by an infamous court case between two doctors, J. C. Handy and C. V. P. Watson, over the cause of death; the latter being the one who had been caring for him. Dr Handy accused Watson of incompetence. Violence ensued in the courtroom, but eventually, after an independent autopsy, it was determined that the death was due to multiple factors, and Watson was exonerated. A. C. Benedict died in 1880 and Gregoria in 1884, leaving their children as orphans. (*Star*, Mar 28, 1880) Mary was adopted by another pioneer rancher, Frank Proctor, and his wife Mary Dowdle Proctor, and ended up in Cananea where Frank was working for Col. Greene as his ranch manager. She married Col. Greene in 1901. (Sonnichsen, 82–88)

Charles and Jesusita Proctor. Courtesy of the Proctor family.

Out of a large family, there were three Proctor brothers—Charles, Frank and Henry—who established themselves in Southern Arizona in the late 1870s. Charles A. Proctor ran several large ranches in the Sahuarita area, including the Canoa under Maish and Driscoll, the Tesota, and the Vail, and also had mines at Helvetia and property at Box Canyon and Madera Canyon. His homestead, however, was in Graham County. He had friends and business associates in the Sahuarita area, including J. K. Brown. Charles Proctor married Jesusita Salazar, whose adopted father had had the Tesota Ranch, and they had four boys and two girls. He was a Sahuarita school trustee. In 1910, Proctor obtained property and built a house next door to the Elías family's Sopori Ranch, where he died in 1913. (*The Oasis*, Dec 16, 1911; *Citizen*, May 17, 1913).

In 1879, J. K. Brown had become the sole owner of the Sahuarito Ranch and decided to return to his birth home in Ohio to claim the bride who was hopefully waiting for him. He married Olive L. Stephenson and brought her back to the ranch. Olive remembered the house as having eight rooms with thick adobe walls—two rooms with wood floors and the rest were dirt. The dining room table could seat twenty to twenty-five people, and so portions of the house were used as a restaurant and hotel. Subsequently the couple had five children: Clara (Clarissa), Marguerite, Harriet, James K. Jr. (Roy) and John S. Brown. Olive homeschooled the children until they reached high school age. J. K. operated a post office from 1882–86, where he was designated postmaster with Olive as assistant (she said she did the work). (Olive Stephenson Brown memoirs) The Sahuarito Ranch was never called Sahuarita during Brown's tenure, but he did rename the location Brown's Station, because of its status as a stage stop. Over the years, stage operators such as Pedro Aguirre and Mariano Samaniego (Samaniego Peak) ran a stage line from Tucson through Sahuarita to Arivaca and the Oro Blanco mines. Wagons continued to operate until the auto became prevalent in about 1914. (*Arizona Weekly Citizen*, Nov 23, 1878; *Star*, Oct 5, 1879; *Star*, Aug 20, 1910; *Citizen*, Sept 30, 1914)

Between 1890 and 1908, Brown acquired a homestead and three

Arizona Weekly Star,
April 4, 1878

other properties that increased his acreage. Much of this was good farmland, but he used it primarily as a cattle ranch. (Bureau of Land Management) He also developed mines, including the Olive Mine west of Sahuarita in the Pima Mining District in the Sierrita Mountains. The San Xavier Mine, Mineral Hill, Zinc Mine, and several others were developed in this area. Further south was the Twin Buttes Mine. While working as postmaster, Brown separated out the Olive Camp mail and hauled it and a load of water to the camp every day. Brown had also been involved with several mines in the Helvetia district from the beginning, including the Narragansett Copper Mine, and so became a prominent citizen with many business interests. (James Kilroy Brown) Many of these early miners were mining gold and silver, but in 1893 the silver market collapsed. Luckily for miners in the area, the copper industry had been developing in response to the needs of the electric industry. With copper having been found in the Sierritas west of Sahuarita, the development of this mineral and others associated with it would prove to be of great benefit to the area. (*Star*, Feb 26, 1922)

Seward Brown, brother of James Kilroy Brown. Courtesy of Susan Strong-Dowd.

In the spring of 1886, Geronimo and several of his men got off the Apache Reservation where they had been forced to live since the early 1870s, and went on a rampage for a few weeks down the Santa Cruz Valley, causing fear among the settlers. The Brown family took refuge at Olive Camp and were not disturbed, but they did lose some horses and cattle from a corral near the ranch house. (Olive Brown) Other homes in the area were burned, but no one in the Sahuarita area was killed. However, Mrs. Peck and her baby who lived in Peck Canyon near Nogales were killed, as well as Phil Shanahan and his horse, who were at Yank Bartlett's place in Sycamore Canyon. (*Arizona Weekly Citizen*, May 8, 1886; *Star*, May 2, 1886; Willson, 259)

Seward Brown, younger brother of James K. Brown, arrived in Southern Arizona in 1881 at the age of seventeen (he was fourteen years younger than J. K. B.) and settled first in Tucson, where he worked at making enough money to go back to Ohio and retrieve his bride, Elizabeth Blackmore. They had five children. Moving to Sahuarita, he obtained a homestead in 1899 and by 1905 had a ranch and stage stop (separate from his brother's) and was selling beef to the Twin Buttes Mining Company, located due west of his property. (*Star*, Feb 24, 1905 and Mar 4, 1910). His ranch was located a few miles south of Sahuarita, southwest of his brother's

Si quiere vd. comprar muy buena carne de ganado excelente, y que prontamente se le lleve á su casa la carne, ocurra á la carnicería de

ALFREDO DURAZO

Que se ha cambiado al magnífico edificio de Altos del Sr. Andres Rebeil en la calle de Meyer. Allí encontrará toda clase de carnes.

El Fronterizo, *June 1, 1895.*

property, and on a stage line. (U.S. Army Corps of Engineers) In 1913, he sold out and moved back to Tucson where he lived until he died in 1934. (Seward Brown Obituary, *Star*, Jul 29, 1934)

Alfredo Durazo, a well-known butcher with a shop on Meyer Street in Tucson, had a ranch adjoining J. K. Brown's from the 1880s, which he used for raising the meat he provided. Durazo proved up on his homestead in 1892. Durazo was crotchety, but was well known and ran in the Hispanic circles of Tucson where his wife, Eloisa, could be part of society (*The Oasis*, Jun 3, 1905). On the 1926 U.S. Army Corps of Engineers topographical map referenced previously, Alfredo's Ranch was well marked, no surname needed.

In the early 1890s, William A. Hartt began developing a farm adjoining J. K. Brown's, and made improvements such as irrigation wells and windmills. The two of them had partnered on at least one property. He had installed a Portuguese pump at Sahuarita where he could get 2,500 gallons per minute and fill an irrigation ditch that would water fifty acres per day. He was also involved in politics and specialized in water rights legislation, although he did not run for office. He invited the Populist candidate for President, Gen. James Weaver, to come see the verdant Santa Cruz Valley. Weaver was duly impressed, saying, "Hartt's ranch is a magnificent place, full of wonderful possibilities." (*Star*, Jan 26, 1893) Hartt married Blanche Smith in Chicago in 1895 and it was widely advertised that she would not promise to "obey." (*AZ Republic*, Aug 24, 1897) Hartt was an innovative inventor who held several patents. He had great hopes for his farmland but also for his "El Oro" mining property in the Oro Blanco District south of Arivaca. (*Weekly Star*, Dec 13,

Olive and James Brown pose with their children John, Roy, Clara, and Billie in the fields of the Sahuarito Ranch circa 1887. Courtesy of Arizona State Historical Society.

1894) But it was not to be. He passed away of pneumonia at the age of 43 in 1899. (*Star*, Dec 23, 1899) In a few short years, visitors lamented that his Sahuarita property was going to the dogs. (*Star*, Mar 22, 1902) In 1911, it was sold to George M. Holmes who, in turn, sold it in 1913 to the Tucson Farms Company. (*Star*, Aug 25, 1911; *Citizen*, Apr 12, 1913)

J. K. Brown ran for sheriff in 1890 and won, despite the efforts of Allan Bernard of Arivaca to overturn his election. (*Star*, Nov 29, 1890) He held that office for only two years, during which time the family lived in Tucson. At first they lived in the Sanford House. (*Weekly Citizen*, Aug 30, 1890) For a time, they lived in the Silver Lake Hotel, which they renovated and offered room and board. In 1893, J. K. was having financial troubles and his properties, including the Narrangansett mine, went up for sale. (*Weekly Citizen*, Nov 23, 1895) He probably leased it out to relieve a debt.

The Browns moved back to Sahuarita in 1894, and with their five children and apparently around fifteen other children living in the Sahuarita area, the Browns decided to support the building of a school. Sahuarita School District No. 29 was established, with Brown building the school himself and furnishing it with purchased desks. (*Weekly Citizen*, Dec 29, 1894) Olive Brown was obliged to assume the duties of teacher herself, at no pay, until enough money had been accumulated in the Pima County coffers to hire another teacher. By 1897, Olive's sister Bertha, was teaching about 18 students in Sahuarita. (*Citizen*, Oct 1, 1897) In 1899 the apportionment for Arivaca, Sahuarita, and other schools of their

Front and back of an April 4, 1900, Sahuarito district supply receipt. Courtesy of Arizona State Archives.

size was $48.50. Exactly where this school was located isn't known but it was probably near the J. K. Brown ranch. It would be typical for a rancher to provide a school building separate (at least a short distance) from the house, as this happened all over Southern Arizona.

By 1900, the Browns had moved to Tucson but retained ownership of their Sahuarito Ranch property and mines. (*Star*, Nov 23, 1900) One reason for the move was to take advantage of the Tucson school system and the University of Arizona; it was very common for ranchers to have houses in Tucson if they could afford them. Clarissa was of age to attend St. Joseph's Academy in 1897, and she went on to the University of Arizona. At some point the Browns purchased the Fitch House in Tucson. (LoVecchio, 3–4) J. K. Brown passed away in Los Angeles in 1922. (*Star*, Mar 5, 1922) Olive died in 1953 in Tucson. (*Star*, May 6, 1953) Some of the children continued to have an interest in holding property in Sahuarita, including son John Stephenson Brown, who had his own homestead and ran cattle. John also had a store in Sahuarita, on the Old Nogales Highway at Sahuarita Road. He was the census taker in 1920 for the whole area. In his autobiography, Phil Clarke referred to him as Brownito, which might be a reference to his height or his status as son of J. K. Brown. John moved away from Sahuarita to California and then to Ajo where he passed away in 1962. (Carolyn Honnas interview)

Commercial mining and farming begin

After 1900, a period of serious mining and commercial farming development began in the area around Sahuarita, with infrastructure to support those industries provided by both private enterprise and the government. The post office was reestablished in 1915, with T. G. Dumont as postmaster. (*Copper Era*, Oct 29, 1915) Railroads were being developed. The automobile was replacing the wagon. Mining equipment was being improved. Deep wells were now possible. The

From the Twin Buttes Copper Glance Mine looking northwest toward the Copper Queen Mine and the settlement of Twin Buttes. Courtesy of U.S. Geological Survey.

reasonably priced Model T automobile began to be produced in 1908, with the Model T truck becoming available in the early '20s. All this attracted entrepreneurs, workers, and new businesses to the Sahuarita area.

In 1877, the whole mineralized area on the eastern slopes of the Sierrita Mountains was established as the Pima Mining District. (*Weekly Citizen*, Mar 31, 1877) From then until 1900, small mining operations at Mineral Hill, San Xavier Mine, Zinc Mine, Helmet Peak, Olive Camp, Esperanza, and Twin Buttes showed the promise for copper, lead, and zinc that was later developed into the enormous businesses we see today. David Rose of Milwaukee incorporated the Twin Buttes Mining and Smelting Co. in 1903. (*Citizen*, Aug 19, 1903; Keith, 36) The American Smelting and Refining Company (ASARCO), established in 1899, leased the Twin Buttes mines from 1915–16. (*Star*, Aug 14, 1915) After that, William Foy with two others began to operate the Copper Glance mine in Twin Buttes and soon found high-grade ore, raising hopes for future development. As yet, mining had been on a fairly small scale. A necessary smelter had been completed in 1912 by the Pioneer Smelting Company, about one-and-a-half miles west of Sahuarita, but it was short-lived. The industry was always dependent upon the price of metals and the ability of developers to interest investors. Foy and partners continued working mines in Twin Buttes between 1916 and 1928. When the Depression hit, things went downhill. Foy got control but couldn't maintain it. He had the railroad scrapped. (Kalt, 29; *Star*, Oct 13, 1963) Some mining continued but it did not take off until after World War II. During the war, the Eagle-Picher Mining and Smelting Company, formerly based in Ruby, Arizona, moved its headquarters to Sahuarita and built a mill on the Pioneer smelter site, which operated until 1960 when Anaconda bought it and dismantled the buildings. (Arizona Department of Mines and Mineral Resources, Sahuarita Mill; *Citizen*, Nov 6, 1944) Eagle-Picher also operated the San Xavier Mine, an underground lead and zinc mine, as was the one at Ruby. In about 1960, Banner bought the San Xavier Mine. (Arizona Department of Mines and Mineral Resources, San Xavier Mine)

It was not until the 1950s and '60s that the mining operations really began to be developed. (Keith, 36, 133–139; Heinrichs) This was in part due to the new ability of geophysicists to create and use devices that could locate the gigantic bodies of low-grade copper ore that could subsequently be mined with open pits. In 1950, Banner Mining Co. acquired Twin Buttes and Mineral Hill and reopened operations, acquiring claims by purchase or lease to create a large block of ownership and opportunity for open-pit mining. Extensive drilling pinpointed the best ore bodies. (Kalt, 39) Anaconda Mining Co. acquired the Banner operation in 1963 (which had also had an underground operation and small mill), and began the open pit, removing "overburden" and exposing the low-grade ore, the first ingot being produced in 1969. (Ascarza, Sept 14, 2020) By 1965, Duval, ASARCO, and Pima Copper Co. had also begun operating. (*Star*, Jun 27, 1965) In 1973, Anaconda partnered with Amax Mining Company to create the Anamax Mining Company and subsequently developed an enormous open pit. In 1985, the Cyprus Minerals Company purchased Twin Buttes from Anamax Company and the Esperanza-Sierrita complex from Duval.

Duval had bought the Esperanza mine, located at the south end of the ore body, and acquired mineral rights near there. Rancher neighbors began to realize the difference between their surface property rights and subsurface mineral rights; some to their dismay. Meantime, the science behind milling and processing was improved and became highly sophisticated. Specialized heavy equipment was developed.

The mining industry continued to be influenced by wars, other world events, and the U.S. economy, which created an up-and-down tendency in the local operations, always affecting the employees who had come to depend on the mines, not just for jobs but also careers. (*Star*, Apr 29, 2012; Kalt, 39) Over the years, mining companies came and went, split and merged. ASARCO formed a partnership with Anamax Mining Company to mine the Eisenhower property between Mission pit and South San Xavier pit in 1976. Then, in 1985, ASARCO acquired the Pima Mine. In 1999, Phelps Dodge merged with Cyprus Climax metals and attempted to get ASARCO, but Grupo Mexico, a Mexican conglomerate, won the bidding war and purchased controlling shares of ASARCO for $2.2 billion, retaining ASARCO as a wholly-owned U.S. operating subsidiary. (www.asarco.com; *Citizen*, Oct 6, 1999) ASARCO now owns the Mission Mine Complex.

Phelps Dodge was sold to Freeport McMoRan Copper and Gold Co. for $25.9 billion dollars. (*Star*, Nov 20, 2006) In 2010, Freeport bought the Twin Buttes Mine and so, with large overseas operations as well as domestic, this made Freeport the world's largest copper company. Freeport owns the Duval-Sierrita Mine and Twin Buttes.

Water rights emerged as a big issue, with the mining companies competing for water (used in milling) with their Green Valley and Sahuarita neighbors and Farmers Investment Co.'s big pecan farm. Anaconda purchased Bull Farms in 1969 for its water rights. (*Citizen*, May 24, 1969; *Citizen*, Jan 2, 1970) Into the picture came the Gila River Indian Community's suit against all water pumpers upstream of their reservation. This was not settled until 2004 when President George W. Bush signed the Arizona Water Settlement Act.

Water from the Central Arizona Project (completed in 1993) arrived in Tucson in 2000, greatly increasing the available water for Tucson residents and relieving the pressure for all. In 2020, Farmers Investment Co. (FICO) completed a pipeline and is now able to use CAP water for some of its pecan trees between Sahuarita Road and Pima Mine Road. (*Star*, May 9, 2021) As the Santa Cruz Valley population grows, water issues continue to affect development as do environmental problems. (*Star*, Mar 21, 2021) According to Georgia Spivey Martin, residents in the area around the mines west of Sahuarita and in the

foothills of the Sierritas know that you can't easily get water just by drilling a well. That area never had water. Most residents have to haul water, still, to this day, limiting the amount of animals they can raise or yard or garden they can support. It's hard to imagine how different this world is from Rancho Sahuarita, only a few miles away down in the valley. Many of the long-time residents still tend to have negative feelings about the mines and their enormous dumps, but the Arizona economy depends on mining.

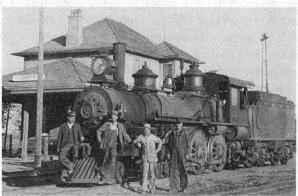

The Twin Buttes train stops at the Preciado Station. Standing on the tracks are Mr. Stevenson, Mr. Johnson, Charles Ashburn, and James R. Ashburn. The faint lettering on the station sign reads "Sahuarita." Image courtesy of Arizona Historical Society. Image details courtesy of the Revello family.

Railroads

The Southern Pacific Railroad arrived in Tucson in 1880 and spurred great development in that city and the mining camps and ranches in the vicinity. In particular, copper was needed in the newly developing industries that used electricity. Surviving the vicissitudes of the copper industry was a challenge. When the Twin Buttes mines showed promise, the Twin Buttes Mining & Smelting Company was incorporated in 1903 for one million dollars by David Rose, mayor of Milwaukee, Wisconsin. It acquired sixty mining claims. (*Star*, Jan 6, 1907) In need of ore processing and transportation, it branched out into the construction of a smelter and railroad to serve the company. (*Star*, Sept 9, 1905) Construction material like railroad rails and ties as well as a locomotive were purchased from Southern Pacific. (Myrick, 306)

The Twin Buttes Railroad line ran from Tucson to the south on the east side of the Santa Cruz River to Sahuarita, and then angled west to the mines all the way past Twin Buttes to the Senator Morgan mine. Completion was celebrated on July 4, 1906. (Myrick, 307) A lovely station building was constructed at Sahuarita. In 1910, the Tucson-to-Sahuarita section was taken over by Southern Pacific and a railroad from Sahuarita to Nogales was then constructed by a subsidiary of Southern Pacific, the Tucson and Nogales Railroad Company. (Myrick, 313) Plans were made for a

spur to Mineral Hill and another to Helvetia, but those did not happen because, as usual, copper prices dropped and work slowed. After the mining boom faded, the railway to Twin Buttes was used sporadically and was scrapped in 1934 as mining had slowed during the Depression. (Myrick, 303–312) The Sahuarita Railway Station House burned down in 1939. A fire in the attic consumed the building, which then was being used for housing two or three families. All got out safely but there was no fire department to assist the neighbors in putting out the flames. (*Star*, Jun 21, 1939) In the 1960s a new rail line was constructed because by then mining had picked up again.

After a fire destroyed the station, converted passenger and box cars became a replacement station. Courtesy of Don Bufkin via David Myrick.

Roads

In the early years, the main road from Tucson to the Twin Buttes mines was what is now called Mission Road, several miles west of the Santa Cruz River. (*Citizen*, Oct 14, 1916) But times were changing. By 1915, the automobile industry had prevailed over the wagon and the need for good roads, professionally maintained, was imperative. A large number of roads were needed and Pima County began planning big. After much controversy as to a new location (west or east side of the river) a bond issue succeeded on October 26, 1915, to support the construction of the Nogales Road from South 6th Avenue in Tucson to Sahuarita on the east side of the Santa Cruz River. This included a bridge crossing. The estimate was $300 per mile for a properly graded and drained road, not paved. (*Citizen*, Aug 12, 1916; *Star*, Apr 12, 1917) This road would provide access to the mines on the east side of the valley and on the west via the Twin Buttes Road, as well as the farms in the middle. The population was greater on the east side.

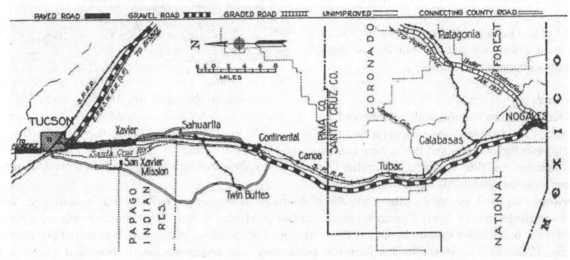

The Tucson–Nogales route in October of 1925. Courtesy of Arizona Highways.

In 1915, Santa Cruz County started building a road north toward Tucson, and they were proud to say that once finished, all the bad road on this highway would be in Pima County! (*Citizen*, Jul 3, 1914) Citizen Auto Stage began to run from Tucson to Nogales. Any stage, horse or auto, that ran to Nogales stopped at Sahuarita. (Both J. K. and Seward Brown operated stage stops and had done so for years.) In 1920, more bonds were issued for $1,500,000 to fix all of the roads in Pima County that had been either petitioned for or determined to be necessary, and this time paving was included for some. Funding came from both bonds and the federal government, because even in those days the federal government was supporting local highway construction. (*Citizen*, Oct 8, 1919) All of this infrastructure would be necessary for the development of the Sahuarita area mines and farms, and to attract willing developers.

Stores

The western corners of Sahuarita Road and the (old) Nogales Highway became used for businesses and the post office. There was Epp's Store in 1920. (*Star*, May 23, 1920) John S. Brown also had a store there for a while. Then T. H. Irwin had a store, serving lunches and soft drinks, until it burned in 1925 along with a house and garage. Two rocking chairs that usually sat on the porch were the only things salvaged. (*Star*, Jun 23, 1925) By 1930, there were two markets across the street from each other at the junction. In both the 1930 and 1940 censuses, one was owned or run by Harry Manelos and one was owned by Roy Brown. The two stores existed until recently, when that portion of the Nogales Highway was rerouted to the west and they were demolished. (Oscar Gomez notes; Lynn Harris notes)

By 1930, Greek immigrant Harry Manelos had opened the Sahuarita Bar and Grill on the north side of Sahuarita Road. He also sold beer and wine. Manelos's daughter Maria took over management at a certain point and expanded the bar area of their store. Hours for the bar included a night shift when miners returned to town. Later, part of the building became a dance hall.

In June of 1930, J. K. Brown, Jr. (Roy) opened a store on the south side of the intersection, and according to the *Star*, "had a formal opening attended by all the people in the community. It was in the nature of an old-fashioned housewarming, and a dance culminated the evening." He suffered some robberies during the Depression 1930s. (*Star*, Jun 13, 1930) Roy died in 1942. (Roy Brown obituary, *Star*, May 15, 1942) His store on the south side of the intersection was purchased by the Oro Verde Farm. Manager J. P. Corcoran renamed it Oro Verde Store and also got a beer license. (*Citizen*, Dec 3, 1948) During the war years they cooked lunches for farm workers. This store also held the post office. When Corcoran sold the Oro Verde Farm, Harry Foster took over management of the store. It went through a couple of hands and then Mildred and Harold Ellis obtained it. They held onto it for over twenty years. (*Star*, Nov 30, 1954; Mar 29, 1963) The post office remained there until it was moved in 1960. In about 1977 it became known as One Stop Market.

School beginnings

By 1915, the Sahuarita area was growing rapidly, with mining and farming, so that a larger school was needed. Bonds were approved in 1915 and a school was built east of the river and railroad tracks. (*Star*, Aug 20, 1915) The farm developers hired locally but also began importing workers such as cotton pickers, who brought their families. Migrants from Mexico were fleeing the Revolution and looking for jobs. The U.S. census of the greater Sahuarita/Continental area showed about 650 residents in 1920. A majority were Hispanic (57%) and most had jobs in mines or on farms. There were twenty-eight students in the school, at least for part of the school year. (*Star*, May 23,

Teachers pose in front of the redbrick Sahuarita School building. Courtesy of Arizona State Library, Archives and Public Records, History and Archives Division.

1920) As late as 1925, the school district approved the feeding of horses that children had ridden to school, because some students had no other transportation and frequently the children could not even provide for their horses at home. Without this supplement, attendance would have dropped. (*Citizen*, Jan 9, 1925)

As time went on, there was the need for another bond election in 1926, which led to an addition to the school, designed by well-known Tucson architect Henry O. Jaastad who had designed 45 other schools as well. (McCrosky, 1990: *Star*, Oct 3, 1926) In this same year, the consolidation of Sahuarita with Continental school districts was voted down and to this day has not happened. (*Citizen*, Apr 25, 1926) The increase in Mexican immigrant workers also brought about the opening of a night school for adults with classes in reading, writing, arithmetic, and citizenship, taught by Mrs. Ethel Taylor, similar to one offered at Continental School. (*Star*, Jan 25, 1926) During the 1930s, 4-H Clubs for children were established by the Cooperative Extension service at each rural school: members of Sahuarita Blue Jays learned many useful skills including sewing and woodworking, which was reported along with local news in articles in the *Arizona Daily Star* newspaper. (*Star*, Apr 1, 1934) Homemakers clubs were also established for the women of the area. Besides providing a social network, they were taught home-economics-type skills including nutrition, home budgeting, balancing a checkbook, gardening, landscaping, and other life skills. (*Star,* Aug 7, 1938; Arnold, 5–7) The school was used for many civic activities in the Sahuarita area for years.

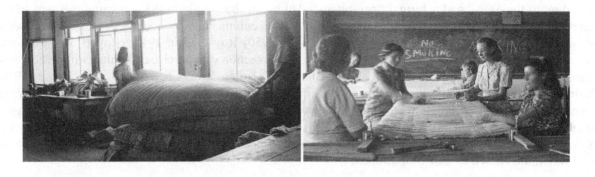

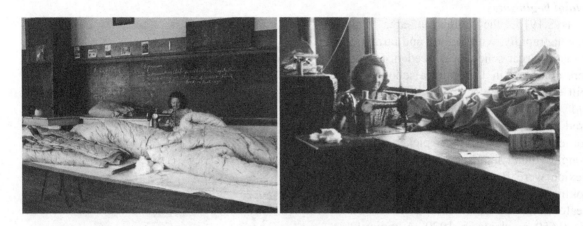

Above and below: Sahuarita School was used as a mattress and quilt making center in June of 1941. Courtesy of University of Arizona Special Collections.

Commercial farming and water issues

Commercial farmland, other than just homesteads, was starting to be developed in the 1890s. Farm real estate was being publicized widely in the U.S. In 1911, the *Arizona Daily Star* reported the sale of the J. K. Brown and neighboring Hartt ranches to New York developer George M. Holmes for $60,000. This was 4,000 acres of bottom land in the Santa Cruz Valley and was valuable for farming, although Holmes reportedly had planned to subdivide it into home lots. (*Star*, Aug 15, 1911) The next year the Tucson Farms Company was incorporated by Chicago businessmen and brothers C. C., G. J., and Paul Magenheimer with Howard Morris. (*Star*, Feb 3, 1912) Thus began the largest farm investment in the Santa Cruz Valley. In 1913, Tucson Farms purchased the 4,000 acres from Holmes for $110,000, making a total of 13,000 acres in possession of the company. The Sahuarita tract was called Unit 3. (*Citizen*, Sep 30, 1913) TFC's other tracts were at Midvale Farms,

Cotton pickers' camp near the gin in Sahuarita. Courtesy of Mercy Angulo Teso.

Flowing Wells, Jaynes Station, and Marana. At first, barley and alfalfa were being planted, but many other crops were being suggested. Initially, thirty German farmers were brought in by the company to plant cotton on their Jaynes Station parcel. (*Citizen*, Dec 7, 1913) Egyptian long-staple cotton was first planted in 1918, by then already known as Pima cotton. Soon it became a staple crop. By 1920, 12,000 acres area-wide were under cultivation, with 4,000 at Sahuarita. (*Star*, Sep 19, 1920) A sales campaign with large newspaper ads promised much profit at a reasonable investment. (*Citizen*, May 30, 1920) A competitor, Edwin R. Post, had established farms north of Tucson, which became the Pima Farms Company. (*Star*, Jan 1, 1922) Dairies and poultry farms were being established in the Flowing Wells area. The *Star* reported in 1920 that 600 acres of cotton and 400 acres of alfalfa had been planted there. The Santa Cruz Valley was becoming an agricultural centerpiece. (*Star*, May 23, 1920)

In the Sahuarita unit, Tucson Farms reportedly constructed twenty-four irrigation wells and eighteen miles worth of canals. By 1914, it had organized the Sahuarita Water Company with irrigation water rights. (*Citizen*, Jun 12, 1914) Tucson Gas, Electric Light and Power Company subsequently began constructing a suitable power line to serve the Sahuarita farms (but not families), to be completed by 1916. (*Star*, Oct 4, 1914) In 1915, Douglas Smith of Chicago bought out the Magenheimers but Paul remained in control of Midvale Farms. (*Citizen*, Aug 22, 1916)

The rubber plantation in Continental, located about thirty miles south of Tucson. Courtesy of Arizona Historical Society.

Initially, farm acreage was sold to individuals who were interested in either large or small farms. Tucson Farms used nationwide newspaper advertising in its promotions. Improvements included clearing the land, cutting wood (mesquite bosques), maintaining irrigation wells and canals, and plowing and harvesting, which provided many jobs for laborers. A Mennonite colony was even established at Sahuarita for a couple of years just as the state called up the National Guard to protect the border. (*Star*, Apr 12, 1917) Mexican workers had been arriving, escaping the civil unrest in Mexico during the 1910–20 Revolution. By 1920, the population of Mexican workers in the area was large. Given that a number of workers were not citizens, an interesting legal opinion came through in 1915. An

Arizona "Alien Law" stated that at least 80% of the workers on one payroll must be American citizens. This law was declared illegal and unconstitutional by a federal judge because it conflicted with the fourteenth amendment to the Constitution, which gives equal protection of the law to all. By 1920, Sahuarita was established as an important cotton-producing area and began to be commonly known as "Sahuarita Farms." (*Star*, May 23, 1920)

In 1916, the Agricultural Products Corporation, a subsidiary of the International

A young boy and his father work the potato fields in Continental, Arizona, on May 23, 1922. Courtesy of University of Arizona Special Collections.

Rubber Company, planted 4,500 acres of Mexican guayule at Continental Ranch, the name they gave to their new holdings. They had bought 9,200 acres from L. H. Manning on the north end of the Canoa ranch. (*Citizen*, Jul 18, 1916) After some serious study of the guayule plant, they determined that this drought-resistant plant produced a rubber that, it was hoped, could be used for automobile tires. Four years after the purchase, most of the local people counted in the 1920 U.S. census were working at the rubber farm. After several years, however, the price of rubber went so low that the company went out of

Constructing irrigation systems on Bull Farms; Jeanne and John Klingenberg look on. Courtesy of the Bull/Klingenberg family.

business; it was revived in 1929 and began planting alfalfa, cotton, and forage crops, so the town of Continental stayed. (*Star*, Nov 22, 1929) In 1920, a Sunday motor trip on the new Nogales Highway was featured in the *Arizona Daily Star*. It described Sahuarita as "a garden spot in the desert. Little homes are springing up everywhere and the valley is fast coming into its own." (*Star*, May 23, 1920) Besides Continental, some of these little communities, including La Villita and Valle Verde neighborhoods, inhabited by the descendants of the early families, still exist near the river in Green Valley and Sahuarita.

Pima County provided an agriculture extension service for farmers, with Agent C. E. Brown dispensing advice, information, and statistics as needed. A long newspaper article by Agent Brown reported on the history of agriculture in the Santa Cruz valley up to 1927. (*Star*, May 31, 1927) In that year, over $7.5 million dollars' worth of agricultural products, not including cattle, was produced. He promoted other crops such as sweet potatoes, which were considered suitable for the climate. In 1925, Lee Moor, a West Texas cotton grower, was one of the out-of-towners who saw opportunity in the area and purchased 160 acres on which to plant cotton. (*Citizen*, Mar 28, 1925) His operation would last until the 1960s. (*El Paso Times*, Dec 16, 1968)

J. B. Bull began another farm in 1930 with 160 acres, but by the time it was sold in 1969 it had been increased to over 6,000 acres. (*Citizen*, May 24, 1969) He began with cotton but expanded to peanuts, sorghum, and corn. He also raised steers. It was on his property that a German POW camp was constructed during World War II. The inmates were put to work on the local farms. (Rookhuyzen, *Green Valley News*, May 29, 2016) A road trip down State Route 89 through Sahuarita by the writers of the Works Progress Administration state book project indicated that in the 1930s, the country was irrigated and cotton was the main crop being farmed. (Arizona WPA Guide, 299) By 1930, Sahuarita showed a population of 271 with twenty farms operating. (*Star*, May 17, 1930)

Tucson wanted water. In the mid-1920s the City of Tucson, realizing its exponential growth, began looking for sources of water to supply the population for the foreseeable future. (At that time the city wells were located near Midvale Farms at Irvington Road and the Santa Cruz River). This provided much controversy, from those who said new sources were necessary to those who said Tucson already had all the water they needed for years to come. In 1928 the Rillito River Development Company began offering water rights to the City, unleashing the issues of need, cost, capacity, and parcel size. Storage and piping needs were raised. City water department officials and a consulting engineer created reports that evaluated the potential sources, including the Santa Cruz River valley south of the City, the Rillito River, and Flowing Wells locations. (*Star*, Feb 22, 1929) The mayor was in favor of moving ahead and approved sales without a council vote. Jack Ryland sold the City eighty acres of farmland in 1929, near the existing wells. (*Star*, Jun 18, 1929) The Flowing Wells District presented a proposal to the City in 1930, in which a thirty-nine-inch main would bring water from its wells. (*Star*, Aug 19, 1930) The City was seemingly inundated with water offers.

Ferd Itzweire observes water pumping on his property. Courtesy of Sutah Thomas Harris.

In the Sahuarita area, cotton farmer M. B. Watson of Coolidge was expanding his business. Watson had moved into the area in the mid-1920s, first buying a cotton gin at Rillito. Then he purchased the Sahuarita Farms, some of which he flipped. The Western Ginning Company, under R. E. Butler of the Tucson Cotton Oil Co, planted 200 acres of cotton and erected a ginning mill on land purchased from M. B. Watson in 1928. (*Star*, Nov 8, 1929) Apparently, Watson was primarily looking to resell his Sahuarita parcel to the City of Tucson for a water source. Once again, without council approval, Mayor Julian purchased Watson's Sahuarita farm eighteen miles south of the City for $141,000, (*Citizen*, Nov 10, 1930) but he had jumped the gun. The opponents of the Mayor took legal action and Judge Fred Fickett quickly ruled that the purchase was not legal. (*Star*, Dec 7, 1930) Arguments went back and forth. Watson filed a counter suit. Finally Watson gave in and moved on, taking a position as superintendent of the Tucson City Farm in July of that year, while continuing to farm cotton in Sahuarita. (*Star*, Jul 31, 1931) In 1936, he moved back to the Phoenix area where he continued farming. (Watson obituary, *Arizona Republic*, Oct 21, 1956)

The first field of flax ever grown in Pima County was on Wiley Lane's Sahuarita Ranch in 1936. Courtesy of University of Arizona Special Collections.

Watson and some partners sold six sections of his Sahuarita Farm to the W. H. Lane family of Coolidge in 1935. Cotton, not water, was back on the table. At Sahuarita Farms, there were eighteen wells for irrigation and four tenant residences of six rooms each. (*Star*, Nov 17, 1935; Dec 8, 1935) In a 1941 article in the *Star*, Lane said he had to restore the farm but was doing well, planting cotton, alfalfa, lettuce, and potatoes, with twenty steady workers and up to 300 at peak employment. By then Lane was considered the largest agricultural operator in the county.

In 1942, probably due to wartime issues such as lack of workers and market, Lane sold the farm to Helena and John J. Raskob, Sr. who called it the Green Gold Ranchos, which was later changed to Oro

Verde Ranchos. (*Citizen*, Mar 6, 1942) Under the operation of J. P. Corcoran, they opened the Oro Verde Store. (*Citizen*, Dec 3, 1948) John J. Raskob was a financier, involved with General Motors and the du

Loading leaf-worm spray into the airplane for dusting cotton at Lane's Farm in 1937. Courtesy of University of Arizona Special Collections.

Ponts, part owner of the Empire State Building, and involved in Democratic politics, but he stayed in New York. Wife Helena was the farmer, an asthma sufferer, who had come to Arizona for her health, bringing with her John Corcoran. (*Star*, Mar 7, 1942) Corcoran had been manager of the family's large farm in Maryland before they moved to Arizona; thus the interest in Sahuarita Farms. Corcoran's name appears on the incorporation papers for Oro Verde Ranchos. He also bought the store and renamed it Oro Verde, getting a beer license for it. He raised exotic grasses that could be adapted to the climate.

John J. Raskob passed away in 1950. J. P. Corcoran married Helena Raskob in 1952. Like his mother, John Raskob, Jr. was active in farm interests until he moved away in 1958. Among other donations, the Raskobs were generous benefactors of Salpointe and Brophy High Schools as well as St. Mary's and St. Joseph's hospitals, and donated their model dairy farm on River Road to the University of Arizona College of Agriculture. In 1950, Kemper Marley, owner of United Liquor, became the next owner of Sahuarita Farms. (*Star*, May 10, 1950) Marley was a Phoenix cotton farmer and cattle rancher. In 1955, Marley went on to sell the 5,000-acre Sahuarita Farm to Producers Cotton Oil Co., which flipped it to Jack Harris, a Chandler rancher and farmer. (*Star*, Aug 1, 1955.)

Ranching

A large ranch was being developed in the 1920s to the southwest of Sahuarita. La Canoa Ranch owner Levi H. Manning, with his son Howell Sr., had decided that they would take advantage of the opportunities for accumulating state land leases and homesteads. In 1915, the Arizona State Land department was created and land that had not been homesteaded began to be allocated in leases to suitable ranchers, a section at a time. In addition, the teens had been good years for homesteaders.

But many soon found that 160 acres was not enough for a real ranch, water was scarce, and a horrible drought in 1920–22 was discouraging. So Manning picked up these ranches and the accumulated leases. Among the properties

Las Tinajas Ranch was one of many purchased by Manning. Courtesy of Lynn Harris.

were those of Robert Catlett, Jesus Proctor Elias, Jesus Zepeda, George Edwards, J. C. Kinney, and Las Tinajas ranch. Others, like those of Paul Bell and Julia Ahumada, came later. Most of these were located between Arivaca Road and the Sierrita Mountains. Eventually the Manning ranch extended all the way from the Santa Cruz River to the Altar Valley, north of the Cerro Colorados and south of the Sierritas, and it was all known as La Canoa. (*Citizen*, Feb 11, 1926; Nov 11, 1926; Mar 27, 1927; Mar 5, 1930) The Mannings expended much time and energy on improving their rangeland and raising prime cattle and horses for over twenty-five years. (*Star,* Feb 19, 1926; Dec 31, 2000) Levi Manning passed away in 1935 (*Star*, Aug 3, 1935), but Howell's son, Howell, Jr. became the most avid rancher in the family.

In 1951, Howell Manning, Jr., was killed in a car accident. (*Star*, Dec 23, 1951) His father was devastated. Howell Manning, Sr., lost interest in the enormous ranch he had developed with his son. Kemper Marley realized the opportunity he had to buy the Manning Ranch, so in 1953 Marley bought most of the Canoa Ranch, but not the south end with its headquarters nor the Navarro Ranch to the west of Sahuarita. Marley's portion was made up of 20,000 acres of deeded land and 100,000 acres of leased land, some 200 sections, as well as the cattle. Howell Manning, Sr., lived on the Canoa Ranch until his death in 1966. (*Star*, Oct 11, 1966; Nov 24, 1968) Marley had come along at an opportune time. (*Star*, Nov 15, 1953) He went on to purchase more land to the west of the Nogales highway, all the way to Kinsley's Ranch. Some of this was purchased from Mrs. Arminal Patterson of Tucson. Using property acquired from Basilio Caranzano, Marley's headquarters home was located on a hill between Amado and

the Halfway Station, (*Citizen,* Oct 3, 1957) but his ranch headquarters was (and is) on Arivaca Road at about milepost eighteen on the former Proctor property. Although some Marley parcels have been sold in the vicinity of Green Valley, Marley Ranch is still one of the largest ranches in Southern Arizona and is still owned by Kemper's descendants. (Pima County flyer)

Keith Walden and the Green Valley Pecan Company

Perhaps no individual had the impact that Keith Walden of Farmers Investment Co. has had on the Sahuarita area. From Southern California, he came to Arizona in 1949 and bought the 10,000-acre Continental Farm, which at the time was planted in cotton. (*Star,* Sep 7, 2008) In 1958, he bought Jack Harris' Sahuarita Farm, which

Wheat fields are harvested while young pecan trees thrive around the field edges. Courtesy of the Walden family.

included about 4,000 irrigated acres planted with cotton. (*Star*, Sep 17, 1958) Walden opened a feedlot which at one time held 16,500 head. (*Star*, May 29, 1976) As time went on, he expanded his land holdings and closed the feedlot. Pecan trees replaced cotton in the Sahuarita area. Green Valley Pecan Company is now known worldwide and the Walden story continues to this day.

~ Contributed by Mary N. Kasulaitis

NOTES

References

Allyn, Joseph Pratt. *The Arizona of Joseph Pratt Allyn, Letters From a Pioneer Judge: Observations and Travels, 1863–1866.* John Nicolson, ed. Tucson, AZ: The University of Arizona Press, 1974.

Altschuler, Constance Wynn, ed. *Latest from Arizona! The Hesperian Letters, 1859–1861.* Tucson: Arizona: Pioneers' Historical Society, 1969.

American Smelting and Refining Company (ASARCO). www.asarco.com.

Arizona Department of Mines and Mineral Resources. Field Engineers Report: *Sahuarita Mill.* June 2, 1966.

Arizona Department of Mines and Mineral Resources. *San Xavier Mine*. As reported in *Mining World*, May 1960: 87.

Arizona, the Grand Canyon State, a state guide compiled by workers of the Writers' Program of the Work Projects Administration in the State of Arizona. Revised by Joseph Miller. Henry G. Alsberg, ed. New York: Hastings House Publishers, 1940, rev 1956.

Arnold, Eleanor, ed. *Voices of American Homemakers: An oral history project of the National Extension Homemakers Council*, 1986.

Ascarza, William. *Southeastern Arizona Mining Towns*. Charleston, SC: Arcadia Publishing, 2011.

Biertu, F. Journal, HM 4367. Hand-drawn map of Santa Cruz Valley, 1861. San Marino, CA: Henry Huntington Library.

Bolton, Herbert Eugene, Trans. *Anza's California Expeditions*, Vol III. Berkeley, CA: University of California Press, 1930. Retrieved January 31, 2022, from https://openlibrary.org/books/-OL24993640M/Anzas_California_expeditions_Vol._3

Brown, James Kilroy. Brown Papers, 1876–1914, MS 0210. Arizona Historical Society Library & Archives.

Brown, Olive Stephenson. Brown Papers. MS 0210. Arizona Historical Society Library & Archives.

Clarke, Philip. Autobiography of Phil M. Clarke, July 1938. Typewritten manuscript; original in Arizona Historical Society Library & Archives.

Cullumber, Allen. www.ancestry.com.

Eagle Picher. Report. Arizona Department of Mines and Mineral Resources.

Fergusson, Maj. David. Letter of the secretary of war, communicating, in answer to a resolution of the Senate, a copy of the report of Major D. Fergusson on the country, its resources, and the route between Tucson and Lobos Bay. United States Army, Department of New Mexico, 1863.

Gomez, Oscar. Interviewed by Mary N. Kasulaitis. March 2, 2021.

Grosvenor, H. C. *The Silver Mines of Arizona*, map. Santa Rita Mining Company (affiliated with the Sonora Exploring and Mining Company).

Groundwater Awareness League. "History of Mining in Green Valley Area." *Augusta Resource/Rosemont Copper Project*. 2009–2011. Retrieved January 31, 2022 from http://www.-savethesantacruzaquifer.info/History in GV.htm

Harris, Lynn. Interviewed by Mary N. Kasulaitis. August 25, 2021.

Heinrichs, Walter E., Jr. *The Pima Mine Story*. Marana, AZ: Western Economic History Center, 2000.

Honnas, Carolyn Pine. Interviewed by Mary N. Kasulaitis. January 27, 2021.

Judkins, Daniel G., and Mary Bingham. *Whose Turn Next? The Diary of Richmond Jones, Jr.: Life in the Santa Cruz River Valley, 1860–1861*. Unpublished manuscript. (Special thanks to Ellen Kurtz)

Kalt, William D., Jr. *Awake the Copper Ghosts! The History of Banner Mining Company and The Treasure of Twin Buttes*. Tucson, AZ: Banner Mining Company, 1968.

Keith, Stanton B. *Index of Mining Properties in Pima County, Arizona*. Bulletin 189. Tucson, AZ: Arizona Bureau of Geology and Mineral Technology, University of Arizona, 1974.

LoVecchio, Janolyn G. "A Tale of Two Cities: Preserving History in Yuma and Tombstone," *The Smoke Signal*, Tucson Corral of the Westerners, No. 107, December 2020, 3–4.

Martin, Georgia Spivey. Interviewed by Mary N. Kasulaitis. August 27, 2021.

McCrosky, Mona Lange. "Henry O. Jaastad: Architect of Tucson's Future and the Governor's House-Boy and the Mexican Ambassador." *The Smoke Signal,* Tucson Corral of the Westerners, No. 53, Spring 1990.

Murphy, James M. "The Twin Buttes Railroad," *Arizoniana*. Vol. V, No. 1, Spring 1964.

Myrick, David F. "Twin Buttes Railroad Company" and "Tucson and Nogales Railroad Company." *Railroads of Arizona: the Southern Roads*. Vol 1. Berkeley, CA: Howell-North Books, 1975.

North, Diane M. T. *Samuel Peter Heintzelman and the Sonora Exploring and Mining Company*. Tucson,

AZ: The University of Arizona Press, 1980.

Pima County flyer.

Proctor Pioneer: The American West Generations. Family history, proctorpioneer.com, n.d.

Ransome, F. L. "Ore Deposits of the Sierrita Mountains, Pima County, Arizona." *Contributions to Economic Geology*. Bulletin 725, Part 1, 1921.

Robinson, Samuel. "Arizona in 1861: A Contemporary Account." *The Journal of Arizona History*. Spring 1984, 21.

San Xavier Mine. Report. Arizona Department of Mines and Mineral Resources.

Sonnichsen, C. L. *Colonel Greene and the Copper Skyrocket*. Tucson, AZ: The University of Arizona Press, 1974.

Spicer, Edward H. *Cycles of Conquest: The Impact of Spain, Mexico, and the United States on the Indians of the Southwest, 1533–1960*. Tucson, AZ: The University of Arizona Press, 1962.

"Twin Buttes Mining and Smelting Company." Stock Certificate issued in 1903, David S. Rose, President. The James Garbani Arizona mining stock and document collection, Fred Holabird Americana Auction #12, March 23, 2002, catalog page 168.

U.S. Army Corps of Engineers. Tactical map, Arizona Helvetia quad. T18S, R13E, USGS, 1926.

U.S. Department of the Interior. "Arizona Water Settlement Act of 2004." *Reclamation: Lower Colorado Region*. Retrieved January 31, 2022 from https://www.usbr.gov/lc/phoenix/AZ100/2000/az_water-_settlement_2004.html

U.S. Department of the Interior, Bureau of Land Management. Land patents.

Walenga, Karen. *The Santa Cruz Valley: a Centennial Celebration*. Sahuarita, AZ: Green Valley News and Sun, 2011.

Willey, Richard R. "La Canoa: A Spanish Land Grant Lost and Found." *The Smoke Signal*, Tucson Corral of the Westerners, No. 38, Fall 1979.

Willson, Roscoe G. *No Place for Angels: Roscoe G. Willson's Stories of Arizona Days*. Tucson, AZ: Arizona Silhouettes, 1958.

Walls, Deborah Spivey. Interviewed by Mary N. Kasulaitis. June 14, 2021.

Walls, Jack. Interviewed by Mary N. Kasulaitis. June 14, 2021.

Additional resources

Arizona Daily Star (Tucson, AZ) (abbrev. Star)
Arizona Weekly Citizen (Tucson, AZ) (abbrev. Weekly Citizen)
Arizona Weekly Star (Tucson, AZ) (abbrev. Weekly Star)
Arizona Republic, (Phoenix, Arizona)
Border Vidette (Nogales, AZ)
El Paso Times (El Paso, TX)
Green Valley News (Green Valley, AZ)
Tucson Citizen (Tucson, AZ) (abbrev. Citizen)
The Copper Era and Morenci Leader (Clifton, AZ)

Sahuarita History 1930–80

To understand what Sahuarita was like in the 1930s, we need to remember what the world was like back then. The stock market had crashed in 1929, creating the Great Depression and a time of immense suffering and job scarcity. In Sahuarita, there were mines to work, vegetable farms to help harvest, and cattle ranches to man. Hard-rock mining had begun in Arizona in the 1850s, yielding copper, zinc, silver,

A train leaves the Eagle-Picher Mill, bound for Sahuarita. Courtesy of David Myrick.

and gold. In 1912, there were 445 active mines in the state.

The Twin Buttes Mine in the Sierrita Mountains west of Sahuarita had just closed down in 1930. The San Xavier Mine operated until 1918 and was bought and reopened from 1943 to 1952 by the Eagle-Picher Mining and Smelting Company. They also operated a mill behind what is now the Sahuarita town center at La Villita and El Toro roads. The tailing mounds are still visible. The Pioneer smelter was built along the railroad to Twin Buttes in 1912 and smelted ore from the Twin Buttes Mine to the west. During World War II, the Eagle-Picher Company built a custom mill and replaced the old railroad up to the mill on what is now Twin Buttes Road in Sahuarita. It also serviced other mines in Arizona including about 1,000 tons per month from the San Xavier Mine to the northwest of Sahuarita.[1] The zinc was shipped off, but the lead concentrates were stockpiled on-site and capped there for over fifty years. The mine is doing a remedial reclamation of the site now to make it safe for recreational use in the future. It was later bought by Anaconda and dismantled in 1966.

The newspaper was the best form of communication of news around the country, so that is where ads were placed back east to attract people to the state. The Great Plains Dust Bowl had crushed the dreams of many farmers in the Midwest in 1934, and people from Oklahoma and Arkansas were eager to answer the ads in the newspapers and come out west looking for a fresh start and to make new lives for themselves. Living conditions in rural Sahuarita were difficult, but when compared to what they left behind, these families found a sense of renewed hope. One family member would usually move out west first and others would come and live with them for a while until they had enough money to get their own place.[2]

Students and teachers gather for a photo in front of Continental School in 1930. Courtesy of University of Arizona Special Collections.

It was standard to live in a tent when people first came to work on the farms, and then make their way up to a one-room house. It took people years of hard work and saving to be able to build a house and acquire land. The neighborhood of Santo Tomas was started in the late 1950s, and Green Valley's first neighborhood started in 1963. Before that, houses were few and far between. The "Camp" east of Nogales Highway and Sahuarita Road was built for migrant workers.

In 1915, three financiers, Bernard Baruch, Joseph Kennedy, and J. P. Morgan started Continental Farm to produce guayule (pronounced why-YOU-lee) that would be made into rubber if and when the war cut off other rubber imports.[3] In 1918, World War I ended and there was no longer a need for the rubber products. The operation later became the Intercontinental Rubber Company, and Queen Wilhelmina of the Netherlands bought a controlling interest in it. The land was later leased out to locals and cotton was grown on it. In 1948, Farmers Investment Co. (FICO) bought the farm from Queen Wilhelmina. There was a school, housing for management staff, barracks for the workers, and a railroad station in Continental.

James B. Bull answered an ad in the paper for a bookkeeper and came to Continental, as it was called, in 1926. He found 3,000 acres of cotton being grown there with a population of 200. There was no gas or electricity in the homes, only kerosene lamps and wood burning stoves. He was lucky enough to have indoor plumbing because not everyone did. In 1931, Bull bought 160 acres of foreclosed land north of Continental, near what is now Quail Creek. He had dreams of being a farmer like his father had been in Arkansas. He lived his dream for thirty-six years and created Bull Farms which grew cotton, corn, maize, sorghum, alfalfa, and, later, peanuts. He found workers first in the "hobo jungle" in Tucson where unemployed men waited to find odd jobs but ended up liking the Native Americans best because they were dependable. They would be picked up and driven to the farm. Some later used the barracks left behind after the POW camp closed as living quarters, and eventually adobe buildings were built. The migrant workers who came from Mexico were given tents and wood-burning stoves.[4]

During World War II, Arizona had over twenty-one German POW camps.[5] The one near Quail Creek Crossing Boulevard and west of Nogales Highway was opened in 1944 and was called Camp Continental. The inmates worked in the cotton fields on Bull Farms, as well as on other vegetable farms in the area, cleaning irrigation canals, hoeing fields, and helping with the harvest. They were given eighty cents a day in script that they could exchange for goods at a small post set up at the camp.[6] Some were hard workers, but others were Hitler fanatics that would break out in fights and be unruly.

Gladys Klingenberg described the camp as having a high barbed-wire fence with four twenty-foot-high guard towers. She remembers there being about 250 prisoners and forty guards.[7] The government said it was cheaper to ship prisoners to America than to ship supplies overseas. Most states had some prisoner camps.[8]

A Bull Farms worker poses with her son for a photo. Courtesy of the Bull/Klingenberg family.

Barbara Brown Bennett tells of her deep Sahuarita roots beginning in 1935, when her father, Orval "Red" Brown, moved to the area from Ada, Oklahoma. He first worked on the Oro Verde Farm harvesting vegetables. He later went back to Oklahoma and married his sixteen-year-old sweetheart, returning with her in 1941. When his new wife, Richadeen, saw the Santa Cruz River, she made the same comment as everyone who was not born locally: "There's no water!" Back then, there were also no telephones, only a few roads, and no doctors or churches in Sahuarita. Richadeen delivered her first son in Tucson at the "Stork's Nest." It was a ten- to fourteen-day stay for the mother and baby, and rooms were rented for twenty-five to thirty dollars. All of the caregiving, meals, and doctor fees were included in this price.[9]

Mothers of that time sewed clothes, made meals from scratch, and washed and hung clothes by hand for their families. Richadeen once had a friend with a battery operated radio and would sometimes go over to visit and stay to listen to a radio show for entertainment. They lived in a tent with a wooden floor and had a portable table and chairs. Their dishes were stored in a wooden apple box. The toilet was outdoors. Richadeen washed the baby's diapers in the irrigation ditch on a rubboard, but later had a washing machine that required the use of a stick to grab the clothes and put them into the wringer. She remembers visiting Orval's family, who also lived in Sahuarita, and their having a long table with a bench on one side for kids, and one chair at each end for the parents. Orval was the oldest of twelve children, and many of his siblings had to eat while standing.

Orval was drafted into the navy in 1943, and his wife and young son went back to Oklahoma to live with family while he served. In 1947, the family moved back to Arizona. After trying to make a living with a hauling truck, and then running a service station with his brother in Phoenix, he found himself back in Sahuarita working in the fields harvesting vegetables. Richadeen had four children by then and worked in the fields as well. The family lived in a small house with a kitchen, living room/bedroom, and a small bedroom added onto the back.

Barbara remembers being in the cotton fields with her parents, who wore big canvas bags on their backs. They pulled the bag down the row, filling it with cotton bolls—the unrefined lint with the seed still intact. They worked as quickly as they could, being paid by the pound, not the hour. Her mother wore gloves with the fingertips cut off and put glycerin on her fingers so the sharp shells would not harm her, and the cotton would stick better to her hands. The children would gather the hard-to-get cotton because it took longer. There were a lot of people in the field at once during the harvest and it was hot. Barbara says, "There ain't no shade in a cotton field." She thinks it genius that her mother found a way to get out of picking and make more money by selling a hot lunch of beans and cornbread that she kept warm on a Coleman stove to the other workers. The work crews consisted of local and migrant workers. Richadeen says trucks went to Texas and brought back seasonal workers for the harvest. Barbara says the classes at school swelled during the harvest time with the migrant families in town, and they all played together at recess not knowing anything about segregation until they watched TV.

The family of Orval and Richadeen Brown pose for a photo on their 25th wedding anniversary in 1966. In the back row stand Orval "Red" Brown, Edward Brown, Charles Brown, and Fred Brown. Richadeen Brown and Barbara Brown Bennett are seated in the front. Courtesy of Barbara Brown Bennett.

Orval's father, Finis Brown, came down twice from Phoenix and built two cotton gins, one of which is defunct but still standing across from the FICO building east of Nogales Highway on Sahuarita Road. His wife said she wasn't moving again the second time and they made Sahuarita their home. Orval had moved up from driving a tractor to running the pumps on the farm and began making thirty-five cents an hour enabling them to move into the small house. One of Barbara's classmates at school later told her she thought Barbara was rich because she lived in a house rather than in the migrant camp, which was a row of white block buildings on the farm. Orval's brother and wife lived with them in the small house, so the farm paid for an addition to be built on the back for the kids to sleep in. They had purchased a used car for $200 and drove across the border to Nogales once a week to buy extra things like shoes and sugar because the government rationed things with coupons in the U.S. They drove to Safeway in Tucson every other week to buy groceries. They stopped at a butcher shop for meat, but also hunted javelina and deer. They were allowed to eat as many vegetables as they wanted year-round from the fields as long as they didn't sell it to anyone. The government would put dye on the surplus potatoes so they couldn't be eaten or sold to keep the prices up for farmers some years, R. A. Davis recalls.

They could buy lunch meat, bread, and milk to tide them over until the next Tucson trip at "Greek's," or Sahuarita Bar and Grill as it was later called. Located on the north side of Sahuarita Road and Old Nogales Highway, it was the only place between Tucson and Amado that was open at night.[10] They had hamburgers, pool tables, and live music on the weekends. The owner, Harry Manelos, allowed everyone to buy goods on credit by signing a piece of paper, and then they would cash their checks there and square away their accounts each pay period. The Oro Verde Store, later the One Stop Market, was south across Sahuarita Road from the Sahuarita Bar and Grill. Barbara was sent over to get bread with her brother as a child—Old Nogales Highway wasn't very busy in the '50s! It was the only road with a real name; all of the other roads were just roads leading to farms. She once signed off on a big bag of candy and when she got home she was told by her uncle that she'd better not do that again. The Oro Verde Store had the post office inside where boxes with combination locks were on the wall. Josephine Jungen sold stamps and worked at a little window. Later, Rachel Davis replaced her. R. A. Davis mentioned that Rachel didn't want the title

Finis Brown, Jr. Courtesy of Barbara Brown Bennett.

or responsibility, so she was never postmaster; just an employee for fifteen years. The intersection of Old Nogales Highway and Sahuarita Road was at the center of town[11] and was the meeting place for adults to get the talk of the town, or " jaw" with each other, as Barbara put it. It was the hub of the town and everyone enjoyed visiting the only local stores around. Teens would also hang out and buy candy, chips, and ice cream.

When the farm was sold, Orval went to work for Pima Mine and stayed there for twenty years. Barbara enjoyed her mother's good cooking, and being from Oklahoma, she cooked southern style. They

Richadeen York Brown. Courtesy of Barbara Brown Bennett.

had potatoes—mashed, fried, or baked—at every meal and meat, roasted or fried, a vegetable, and a salad. They drank iced tea and baked desserts on the weekend to last the week. Shamrock Dairy delivered milk products in Sahuarita. The family would leave a key for the milkman to put the milk in the refrigerator.

The Browns, like many local families, came from humble beginnings and worked their way up in the world. They knew how to fix things up over and over again instead of buying something new every time things went wrong. When her children were grown, Richadeen became a licensed nurse and eventually retired in Green Valley with all of those years of hard work finally paying off.

~ Contributed by Amy Millet and Barbara Brown Bennett

NOTES

References

1. "Eagle-Pitcher [*sic*] Mill Tailings." *Arizona Department of Mines and Mineral Resources Mining Collection*. Phoenix, AZ. September 4, 2012: 8. PDF available from http://docs.azgs.az.gov/OnlineAccessMineFiles/C-F/EaglepitchermilltailingsPima573.pdf
2. Davis, R. A. Interviewed by Barbara Brown Bennett. 1994.
3. "Guayule Grew Town Near Tucson." *Arizona Daily Star*. May 21, 2013. Retrieved January 31, 2022, from https://tucson.com/guayule-grew-town-near-tucson/article_f6745018-c249-11e2-8cb0-0019bb2963f4.html
4. Klingenberg, Gladys, and Jeanne Birdsong. *My Life Story*. 2010, 2012.
5. Ellis, Tim. "Sahuarita Once Had a POW Camp." *Arizona Daily Star*, May 25, 2006: 10.

6. Rookhuyzen, David. "The Home Front: German POW Camp in Sahuarita Gone, but the Memories Aren't." *Sahuarita Sun*, May 29, 2016. Retrieved January 31, 2022, from https://www.gvnews.com/sahuarita/news/the-homefront-german-pow-camp-in-sahuarita-gone-but-the-memories-arent/article_5019acff-d1c2-5656-8295-2b0b5f7f3b5e.html

7. Klingenberg, Gladys, and Jeanne Birdsong. *My Life Story*. 2010, 2012.

8. "Auxiliary POW Camp Is Being Planned Now." *Tucson Daily Star*, October 31, 1944: 2.

9. "The Stork's Nest," *Historical Marker Project.* October 14, 2014. Retrieved January 31, 2022 from https://historicalmarkerproject.com/markers/view.php?marker_id=HMKVK

10. Franchine, Phillip. "Historic One-Stop Market, Nearby Bar Come Down in Sahuarita," *Green Valley News*, August 25, 2013. Retrieved January 31, 2022 from https://www.gvnews.com/news/local/historic-one-stop-market-nearby-bar-come-down-in-sahuarita/article_c6c22cca-0c48-11e3-af13-0019bb2963f4.html

11. Goorian, Philip. *Images of America: Green Valley Arizona*. San Francisco: Arcadia Publishing, 2002: 64–65.

Additional resources

"Mining in Arizona. Arizona Mining, Minerals, & Copper: A Primer." *The University of Arizona Geological Survey*, n.d. Retrieved January 31, 2022, from https://azgs.arizona.edu/minerals/mining-arizona

Brown, Richadeen York. Interviewed by Barbara Brown Bennett and Gael Mufasta. June 20, 1998.

Bennett, Barbara Brown. Interviewed by Amy Millet. August 31, 2020.

Sahuarito? Sahuarita? What Does It Mean and Where Is It?

Sixth Avenue is a major north-south corridor in Tucson, Arizona. Traveling south will take you out of the city and quickly into the desert. This transition becomes the Nogales Highway, continuing to Nogales, Arizona, and Nogales, Mexico.

Leaving Tucson, copper mines with enormous mounds of dirt and rock can be seen on the west side. These mounds are the overburden from the open-pit process used to find and remove ores from the dirt. Although many ores are found in Arizona, copper is the most desired. The overburden removed from the pit remains on the surface as permanent residue. The open-pit mines came to the Tucson area in the late 1950s. Prior to that, mining for various ores was done with underground tunnels and small railcars. Open-pit "tailings" extend for many miles.

As one heads south on the Old Nogales Highway, there are also miles of pecan tree orchards. The orchards were started as a crop in the late 1960s and began producing significant quantities of nuts in the 1970s and beyond. The pecan trees make up a large farming area of many acres. Both the orchards and the ore production use groundwater. New techniques such as recharging the water table are being implemented to preserve water in the desert.

There is also a railroad track parallel to the Nogales Highway. The tracks cross the highway at a point where roads converge. The road going to the east brings one to a small community of farmhouses, equipment, and a redbrick school. This is the traditional Sahuarita!

In the past, this was the Oro Verde Farm, producing mostly cotton and beef livestock. The cotton was grown in many fields, "picked" by hand and later by machine. A cotton gin processed the cotton into large "bundles" to be shipped out on the railroad. There were two cotton gins, both built by Finis Brown at two separate times. Mr. Brown was the elder of a large family. Many of his sons also worked on the farm—the oldest son, Orval Brown, was the irrigation foreman and a welder. He built a small welding shop on the farm.

Turning north at the first road after crossing over the railroad tracks, there are farmhouses on both sides of the road. One of the houses on the left is an adobe structure with a high wooden porch on the front. On this elevated porch sat a large blue metal box for outgoing mail. As a young girl, I remember my mom sending me up to the mailbox to send letters out. I don't remember getting incoming mail or buying postage stamps. Continuing north on the dirt farm road we could see white buildings and cotton fields. Children were playing; clean clothes were hung on wire lines. Those without regular clotheslines used other wire or wooden structures to dry their laundry. If available, wooden clothespins were used to secure the laundry. Because Arizona has low humidity, it took only a short time for items to dry. The dust from the dirt road was more of a concern. The dirt around the cotton field was soft and made a "fog" when several cars or trucks passed by.

The area of the white buildings was used by mostly transient workers who came to Sahuarita during seasons when workers "chopped weeds" in the field and during harvest times when white puffy handfuls of cotton were picked. Local workers were also hired in order to increase production. The small house on the corner was the residence of Mr. Orval Brown and family, home to four adults and four children. Across the road was "the camp."

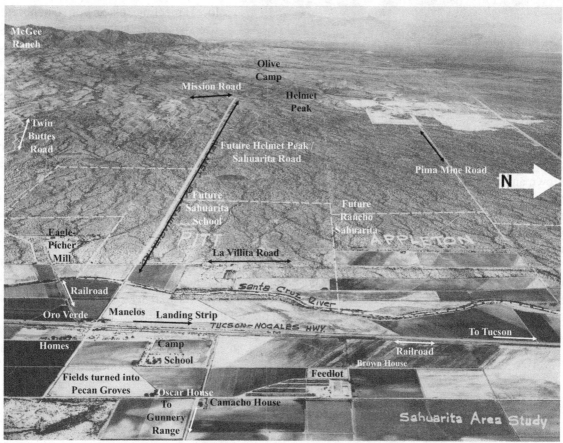

Sahuarita aerial photo showing locations pertinent to the Barbara Brown Bennett story. Courtesy of Barbara Brown Bennett with edits by Monica Lee Elam Christiansen.

Turning around, we travel south back to the railroad tracks and Nogales Highway. Continuing west across the Nogales Highway are two buildings on either side of the east-west farm road, named Sahuarita

Road in 2022. On the north side was the Sahuarita Bar and grocery store where they also sold gasoline. It was unfortunately demolished to make way for a safer road design. The store and the bar were owned and operated by Mr. Manelos and family. There was an airplane landing strip just north of the building and parallel to the Nogales Highway. Across Sahuarita Road there was a second grocery store where the post office was located in the back of a large room. Mailboxes were numbered and they each had a brass door with separate combinations to open each box to retrieve the mail. People could also get mail by "general delivery" at the post office service window. This store was called Oro Verde Store in its early days. The store had a cement floor in the front and a wooden floor in back that was built using wood from the original train depot that had burned down. Very few residents had telephones, but there was one public phone outside the store. This store was later called One Stop and was operated by Harold Ellis and later by Richard and Bernice Jensen. The gasoline part of the business was run by "Red" Tyra.

Workers are ready to begin hoeing weeds in the cotton fields at Bull Farms. Courtesy of the Bull/Klingenberg family.

As Sahuarita grew, a large post office was needed, so a redbrick building was built just south of the store. The postmistress was Mrs. Jo Jungen. This new building also had small brass boxes but many more. The post office was a local meeting place for neighbors and friends. There was no home delivery, so residents came to the post office building. When Sahuarita grew even more, rural delivery began. The community incorporated in 1994 and became an official town. Another post office was built on Sahuarita Road where it stands today as part of a government complex of new buildings to support the operations of the town and includes courts, the police department, mayor and council member offices, and a large room for town meetings. Our trip has taken us west from the Nogales Highway and across a bridge over the Santa Cruz River. Back then the bridge was one-way only, so we had to wait our turn to cross. In earlier days we drove through the dry, sandy river bottom. I remember how we had to "gun" the accelerator so as not to get stuck in the sand. When it rained a lot there was no access.

After crossing to the west side of the river, we see that the road goes north and south. North is where many Mexican-American families live. Most are employed in mining or farming. Going south takes us to the original James Kilroy Brown Ranch. The actual location is verified by Barbara Brown Bennett's husband, Gaylen Bennett, as told by Finis Brown who played there as a child.

~ Contributed by Barbara Brown Bennett; transcribed and written by Amy Millet

The Story of Sahuarita's Schools

This entry was first written in December of 1970 by Paul S. Frick, Superintendent of Pima County School District No. 30, and was originally titled "The Sahuarita Story." It was revised in July of 1973.

How can a better job be done of helping each student enrolled in the Sahuarita Schools achieve the maximum development of his [or her] innate abilities? This is the central question which challenged the educators and parents of the Sahuarita area during the middle and late 1960s. The responses to this question have resulted in the creation of an individualized curriculum designed specifically to meet the needs of Sahuarita's youth.

The historical sketch that follows is presented as a background and guide to Sahuarita's educators and parents as they face the challenge of fully implementing an individualized curriculum during the 1970s.

Sahuarita School District No. 30 approximately doubled its size to 108 square miles on July 1, 1948, when it annexed Twin Buttes School District No. 21. This newly acquired area was located immediately west of Sahuarita and included the communities of Twin Buttes and San Xavier.

The Sahuarita School District was just beginning its period of expansion. During the winter of 1950, school patrons contacted Mrs. P. H. Ross, the Pima County school superintendent, about the procedure for annexing the unorganized territory in the Helvetia area to School District No. 30. Mrs. Ross spoke to the Sahuarita School Board, the members of which were receptive to the annexation of the area east of Sahuarita, and signed a letter of acceptance. A petition to be signed by a majority of the qualified voters of the Sahuarita District was circulated and returned to Mrs. Ross. As no one objected to the annexation during the subsequent fifteen days, Mrs. Ross recommended to the Pima County Board of Supervisors that the Helvetia area be annexed to Sahuarita School District No. 30. Her recommendation was approved, and the annexation became effective July 1, 1950. The District had now grown to 187 square miles in size.

Paul S. Frick photo from the 1968 Sahuarita High School yearbook.

During the spring of 1953, Pima County School Superintendent Florence Reece was actively encouraging the merger of the small, rural elementary districts and the annexation by these districts of the unorganized territory in their areas. As a result, Sierrita School District No. 56, on April 20, 1953, annexed thirty-seven sections of unorganized land located immediately east and south of the present-day Duval Esperanza Mine.

Several weeks later, in May of 1953, the Board of Trustees and citizens of Sierrita School District No. 56 petitioned the Sahuarita School Board for annexation. The procedure described previously for the Helvetia area annexation was again followed and on July 1, 1953, Sierrita School District No. 56, seventy-five sections in size, was officially annexed to Sahuarita District No. 30, thereby increasing the area of the District to 262 square miles.

At the same time that Mrs. Reece was urging the Sierrita School Board to annex the unorganized territory east and south of the present-day Duval Esperanza Mine, she was suggesting to the Sahuarita Board that they annex a strip of land one mile wide and fifteen miles long that separated the Sahuarita School District from the southern border of the San Xavier Reservation, as well as

Sahuarita Elementary School opens to students in 1959. Courtesy of Arizona Daily Star.

nine sections near the present-day location of the Wrangler Ranch subdivision. These twenty-four sections of land were annexed to the Sahuarita School District on April 20, 1953. The size of the district now stood at 286 square miles. It is interesting to note that American Smelting and Refining Company's open-pit copper mine and mill complex and a portion of Pima Mining Company's open pit and mills are today located in the mile-wide strip mentioned previously.

On November 18, 1958, the voters of the Sahuarita School District approved by a vote of thirty to zero the formation of a high school district, although there were no plans at that time to build a high

Principal William E. Gregory and student Jerry Mitchell stand under the covered walkway of Sahuarita Elementary School in 1959. Courtesy of Arizona Daily Star.

school or offer a high school program. The boundaries of the high school district would be the same as those of the elementary school district. The first high school budget was adopted for the 1959–60 school year.

Sahuarita District No. 30 again increased in size when the Board of Trustees successfully initiated action to annex seventy-five sections comprising approximately the southern two-thirds of the San Xavier Reservation. This annexation was effective on July 1, 1959, and it increased the area of the District to 361 square miles.

Sahuarita residents were erroneously led to believe, through a mistake on the petition describing the area to be annexed, that Pima Mining Company and American Smelting and Refining Company's land was annexed in 1959, and that these two companies had existed on unorganized territory during the several years of their local existence. This is not the case, as the minutes of the Pima County Board of Supervisors show that the land on which these two mining companies are located had been annexed to the Sahuarita School District on April 20, 1953.

Following the annexation of the Twin Buttes and Sierrita School Districts, the students were transported to Sahuarita Elementary School, which was located just east of the Sahuarita cotton camp. The overall inadequacy of these facilities was recognized by the educators and citizens of the district. During the 1956–57 school year, the school board began to investigate ways to solve this problem. The solution arrived at, through the discussions among interested citizens, teachers, and the board members, was the construction of a new school at a new location.

The new location became the forty acres upon which the present Sahuarita Elementary School is located. It was purchased from Mr. Francis H. Appleton on August 19, 1957.

The Tucson architectural firm of Blanton and Cole worked with the school board and faculty to

Ethel Black at the piano teaching students in 1959. Courtesy of Arizona Daily Star.

design a nine-classroom elementary school with space for shop classes, home economics, a kitchen, a multi-purpose room, and an office area. Bids were opened on March 4, 1958, but the awarding of the contract was delayed. The reason was that a prospector had located a mining claim on the School District's forty-acre site and it necessitated special action by the U.S. Congress to withdraw the mineral rights from this land. The contract to build the school was awarded to the Craven-Hague Construction Company for $349,516.00 on June 2, 1958.

The new Sahuarita Elementary School was ready for occupancy in March of 1959; but rather than wait until the fall, students, teachers, and bus drivers pitched in and moved the teaching supplies, furniture, and equipment that was not being discarded to the new facilities along Helmet Peak-Sahuarita Road. On March 17, 1959, classes were conducted for the first time in the new school.

Even though Helmet Peak-Sahuarita Road was officially dedicated on April 2, 1934, no work took place on that portion of the right-of-way near the new school property until the construction of the elementary school began. At that time, a relatively primitive roadway was bladed in the right-of-way from the school district's property to the existing Sahuarita-Twin Buttes Road about three quarters of a mile to the east. On November 11, 1958, the Board of Supervisors widened the right-of-way from sixty to 150 feet, and by the time the new school was occupied in March 1959, the County highway department had bladed Helmet Peak-Sahuarita Road west from the school to connect with a portion of the road that extended east about three miles from Mission-Twin Buttes Road.

Sahuarita High School, which opened in 1967.
Courtesy of Arizona Daily Star.

During the 1940s and 1950s, Sahuarita's high-school-age students were bused first to Tucson High School and then to Pueblo High School when it opened on April 1, 1956. In spite of the excellent education provided by these two schools and the free bus transportation, many of Sahuarita's eighth-grade graduates dropped out of school. The reasons vary: the change in going from a small rural school to a large, city high school; the long bus rides and long days; the expense of purchasing books, supplies, etc.; and the difficulty in participating in athletics and other extra-curricular activities because of late-afternoon transportation problems.

The problem became acute in the early 1960s when Pueblo was forced by increasing enrollment to adopt a double session. Sahuarita's students attended split sessions, with part of their classes in the mornings and part in the afternoons. This meant boarding the school bus at a very early hour to arrive at Pueblo by 8:00 a.m. Their class load was also limited to five subjects.

The school board discussed these problems at length and after consulting with the Pima County School Office and the State Department of Public Instruction, voted unanimously on March 11, 1964, to build a high school. On April 21, 1964, the qualified electors of the district voted forty to two in favor of

Sahuarita High School resource center, opened to students in 1967. Courtesy of Arizona Daily Star.

purchasing forty acres of land adjacent to and to the east of the existing school district property on which to construct the high school.

Because of the increase in the responsibilities of the board members created by the decision to build a high school, the Board asked the voters to approve enlarging the Board of Trustees from three to five members. The qualified electors approved the request by a vote of thirty-eight to zero on September 15, 1964.

During the November 10, 1964, Board meeting, Superintendent Paul Frick's recommendation "that the goal of both our grade and high school should be to individualize the instruction to fit as much as possible each child's needs and permit each child to progress at his [or her] own rate of speed" was approved. The Board reaffirmed its support of the school's individualized instruction in a resolution during a meeting on March 17, 1965.

Strolling on the sidewalk of Sahuarita High School in 1967. The gymnasium is on the right while the football field and track are straight ahead. Courtesy of Arizona Daily Star.

Mr. Carl L. John, Tucson architect, was employed to design the high school and the Educational Planning Service of Colorado State College, Greeley, was hired to assist the District in developing an individualized educational program to meet the specific needs of the Sahuarita area. A $995,000 bond issue was approved by the voters by a margin of thirty-one to nine on August 3, 1965. Construction of the campus-style facility began in October of 1965 and was completed in December of 1966. The 250-pupil capacity school opened its doors to 142 students on August 31, 1966.

On June 8, 1966, the school district was notified by the National Education Association (NEA) that Sahuarita Elementary School had been selected to receive the 1966 Pacemaker Award for the State of Arizona. The award was made in recognition of the school's program of individualized instruction and its new resource center. The award was co-sponsored by the NEA and Parade magazine.

When the Helvetia area was annexed to the Sahuarita School District in 1950, one family lived just inside the District at the extreme south end of Wilmot Road. This family had access to the Sahuarita area by means of a road that crossed the Sahuarita Bombing and Gunnery Range—which meant that during the early 1960s, a school-age child would have to cross the Range to meet a Sahuarita school bus. It became obvious to the school board that when the air force had padlocked the road across the Bombing and Gunnery Range, it became impossible for the District to provide educational services for this family. The Board circulated a petition proposing that the area on the east side of the Range be de-annexed so that this family could look to the Vail or Sunnyside School Districts for

Sahuarita High School as pictured in the 1967 yearbook.

the education of their children. Sufficient signatures were obtained on the petition, Mrs. Reece approved the request as did the Board of Supervisors, and on July 1, 1966, these eighteen sections were removed from the District. Sahuarita School District was then 343 square miles in size.

The dust created by automobile and truck traffic on Helmet Peak-Sahuarita Road adjacent to the eighty-five-acre Sahuarita campus rapidly became a major health and safety hazard with the opening of the high school in the fall of 1966. Discussions with the Pima County highway department engineer's office resulted in the paving of the road in the early winter of 1966, from the entrance to Sahuarita Elementary School to the cattle guard a short distance east of the high school baseball field.

The importance of Interstate 19 to the residential, commercial, and industrial development of the Sahuarita area and the influence of this development on the increasing enrollment of the schools, the need for additional rooms and schools, and the convenience to school district employees, many of whom lived in Tucson, cannot be overestimated. Knowledge of the approximate future location of I-19 was known to area residents in the early 1960s. The Helmet Peak-Sahuarita Road overpass bridge was completed and opened to traffic on November 6, 1969. The three-mile section of the divided highway between Pima Mine Road and Helmet Peak-Sahuarita Road was opened for use on approximately November 1, 1970.

Sopori School as it appeared in 1954. Courtesy of Mary Kasulaitis.

During the mid-1960s, the trustees of Sopori School District No. 49, which bordered the Sahuarita District on the south, employed the Bureau of Educational Research and the services of the University of Arizona's College of Education to conduct a study of the educational and financial needs of the District. Among the Bureau's recommendations was a strongly worded suggestion that they ask the Sahuarita District to annex Sopori. This action was urged because the Bureau felt that it was difficult if not impossible for the Sopori School Board to provide a first-rate education for the district's children when the assessed valuation in 1965–66, for example, was only $670,717. New facilities were desperately needed, but the District's bonding capacity was only $67,071. To complicate matters, the enrollment of Sopori School was increasing, mainly due to the families moving into Lakewood Estates, many of whose breadwinners were employed by the mines located in the Sahuarita District.

The Sopori School Board formally requested the Sahuarita Board to annex the Sopori School District and presented a petition signed by a majority of the Sopori District's landowners favoring the annexation. On May 15, 1967, the Sahuarita School Board approved the annexation of the 283-square-mile Sopori School District, thus increasing the size of District No. 30 to 626 square miles.

Census Data							
Date of Census	April 1965	May 1966	August 1967	August 1968	August 1969	June 1971	July 1973
Sahuarita Area	787	844	1062	1248	1554	1885	2325
Sopori Area				342	377	504	669
Total	787	844	1062	1590	1931	2389	2994

Table 2. Sahuarita and Sopori Census Data

Although the annexation was approved by Pima County School Superintendent Florence Reece and the Board of Supervisors during the spring of 1967, the two districts were not merged until July 1, 1968, by the mutual agreement of the two school boards. The reason for the delay was the heavy workload on the Board and administrators resulting from the opening of the high school. It was agreed that the assimilation of Sopori would be much smoother with a year's delay.

The population of the Sahuarita area remained relatively constant during the 1950s and the first half of the 1960s, with one exception. Before and during the 1950s, the yearly influx of migrant farm laborer families in the summer and autumn months swelled the fall school enrollments by fifty to seventy-five students. These families would move on to the Phoenix area and then to California between November and January as the cotton harvest in the Santa Cruz Valley came to a close. The advent of highly mechanized cotton cultivation and harvesting plus a steady decrease in cotton acreage in the 1960s brought an end to this seasonal population influx.

Sahuarita Student Enrollment Data										
Date	High School	(9-12) **	Junior High School	SJHS Grades	Elementary School	SES Grades	Sopori	Sopori Grades	**Totals**
Sept 1963		51			210	1-8			**210**
Sept 1964		52			230	K-8			**230**
Sept 1965		38			281	K-9			**281**
Sept 1966	142	6			260	K-8			**402**
Sept 1967	201				315	K-8			**516**
Sept 1968	240				389	K-8	84	K-8	**713**
Sept 1969	286				492	K-8	73	K-6	**851**
Sept 1970	325				532	K-8	86	K-6	**943**
Sept 1971	394		143	7-8	436	K-6	83	K-6	**1056**
Sept 1972	456		166	7-8	433	K-6	94	K-6	**1149**

** Students residing in the Sahuarita School District attending high schools in Tucson

Table 3. Sahuarita Student Enrollment Data

The increase in mining activity in the Sahuarita area during the 1950s and 1960s stimulated slow but steady population growth until the mid-1960s. Two housing developments came into existence at this time—Santo Tomas in the Sahuarita area, and Lakewood Estates at Arivaca Junction. Student enrollments have increased rapidly, especially at Sahuarita, as population and enrollment figures indicate. (See tables 2 and 3.)

The school board took action on December 2, 1969, to de-annex the "Mexico corridor" portion of the school district located south of Arivaca because of its remoteness [actually in Santa Cruz County]. This boundary change, which took place July 1, 1970, reduced the district's size by approximately nineteen sections to its present 607 square miles.

The evaluation also made an extensive study of future building needs and recommended the construction of a Sahuarita Junior High School, a Santo Tomas Primary School, and a new Sopori Elementary School. The Santo Tomas school was tabled later when it became apparent that the housing boom in that area had ended.

Planning for the new junior high and Sopori elementary schools took place during the spring of 1969 under the leadership of Tucson architect James L. Merry. The real property taxpayers, however, turned down the $1,180,000 bond issue on July 8, 1969, by a one-vote margin: sixty-one to sixty-two. The ten-cent levy election, to acquire the sites for the new Sopori and Santo Tomas schools, was also turned down sixty-one to sixty-four.

As it turned out, the election was invalid because of a U.S. Supreme Court ruling in June of 1969 that raised the possibility that limiting bond elections only to property owners was unconstitutional.

During the spring of 1970, the Arizona Supreme Court ruled that school districts could legally hold dual bond elections with one set of ballots for use by property owners and the other set of ballots for all qualified voters. If both ballots passed, the bond had passed.

Another bond and ten-cent levy election [was] scheduled for June 23, 1970. The bond election this time was for $1,220,000. Both the property

Aerial view of the Sahuarita Junior High School from the 1971 graduation program. Courtesy of Charles Oldham.

owners and qualified electors approved the ballots by approximately a four to one majority. Ironically, the U.S. Supreme Court ruled the day of the election that all qualified electors may vote from that day on in all school bond elections.

At the December 22, 1970, board meeting, a contract in the amount of $721,430 was signed with Defco Construction Company to build the Sahuarita Junior High School and a contract for $359,210 was awarded to Ruck Construction Company to construct the new Sopori Elementary School.

Sopori Elementary School, located in Lakewood Estates, opened its doors to students on September 7, 1971. The school has eight classrooms, a library, a multi-use room, and an administration building, and has a capacity of 200 students.

The two, relocatable, prefab classrooms that had comprised half of the "old" Sopori School were moved to the Sahuarita campus and remodeled as the school district's administration building. The business and superintendent's offices were moved on October 4, 1971, from the high school to their new home along the north edge of the high school visitor parking lot.

On November 1, 1971, the students and faculty held school for the first time in Sahuarita Junior High School. The circular facility is situated along the west side of the high school entrance road. The junior high has a capacity of 350 students and consists of eight classrooms surrounding a learning resources center, boys' and girls' locker and shower rooms, general shop and drafting rooms, a science lab and classroom, home economics classrooms for cooking and sewing, and an art and crafts room.

Visitors to the Sahuarita area invariably comment on the fact that the school district is composed of numerous small inhabitations scattered widely over 607 square miles. Some of these villages, such as Arivaca, San Xavier Mine, Arivaca Junction, Sahuarita, Sahuarita Village, and McGee Ranch, have been in existence for many years. The area boasts two ghost towns—Helvetia and Twin Buttes. Other inhabitations, including Lakewood Estates, Curley Horn Ranch, Wrangler Ranch, and Santo Tomas are of more recent vintage. Sahuarita Heights and Los Arboles Trailer Court are relatively new and have grown rapidly during the past several years.

The rise in the School District's assessed valuation during the late 1950s, 1960s, and early 1970s has been phenomenal. Prior to the start of the development of the area's mineral deposits in the mid-1950s, cotton farming, cattle ranching, the Southern Pacific Railroad, and [Tucson Gas, Electric Light and Power Co.] provided the bulk of the school district's modest tax base. Since then, Farmers Investment Co. has greatly reduced its cotton acreage and replaced it with pecan orchards; [Tucson Electric Power] and Trico Electric Cooperative have greatly expanded their lines to meet the rapidly growing industrial, commercial, and residential needs; the railroad and cattle industries have remained relatively unchanged and the continually expanding operations of the four major mining companies—Pima Mining Company, American Smelting & Refining Company, The Duval Corporation, and the Anaconda Company—have made the Twin Buttes and Mineral Hill mining districts one of the largest and most active copper mining areas in the world.

School Year	Assessed Valuation	School Tax Rate
1950–51	1,235,598	1.46
1951–52	1,907,167	2.89
1952–53	1,490,464	3.2926
1953–54	1,466,066	5.343
1954–55	1,313,486	6.02
1955–56	1,801,667	3.00
1956–57	3,406,984	2.05
1967–58	5,002,847	2.0746
1958–59	5,634,621	2.4582
1959–60	13,473,336	1 .3270
1960–61	16,737,523	1 .3882
1961–62	22,583,324	0.9164
1962–63	44,081,419	0.5706
1963–64	45,951,149	0.5386
1964–65	45,729,246	0.7626
1965–66	48,738,500	0.8662
1966–67	55,423,792	1.3914
1967–68	66,895,271	1.2976
1968–69	69,322,632	1.4280
1969–70	77,987,691	1.4895
1970–71	113,554,755	1.3356
1971–72	152,188,877	1.5320
1972–73	189,824,919	1.5458

Table 4. District Assessed Valuations and Tax Rates

The growth in the school district's assessed valuation and the effect on the school tax rate are indicated in Table 4.

During the 1971–72 school year, it became increasingly apparent that the central kitchen located at Sahuarita Elementary School would soon be inadequate in size to prepare noon meals for a steadily increasing student enrollment. As space for the expansion of this facility was limited, the concept of building a combined central kitchen and cafeteria, located midway among the elementary, junior, and senior high schools was conceived. The voters approved the construction of this facility by a four to one margin in the November 7, 1972, general election.

On March 12, 1973, a contract in the amount of $550,979.00 was awarded to the W. F. Connelly Construction Co. of Tucson by the school board to construct the central kitchen-cafeteria. Mascarella/-Merry and Associates, architects from Tucson, designed the facility.

Superintendent: Paul S. Frick

Principal: Earl J. Kelly

Science: Robert Hesser & Robert Lane

Business Education: Susan Shoemaker, Roger Gerdenics & Barbara Larremore

Math: Gordon Becker, James Madeheim, Dewayne Kurtenbach & Burton Tingle

Industrial Arts, Welding & Carpentry: Donald Graf, Barry Callaway & David Wear

Fine Arts: Janice French

Band: Wayne Webb

Spanish: Carol Gebauer

English: Teresa Bissen, Sam Fadala, Katherine Weaver & Charles Jaquette

Auto: Archie Romney

Library: Shirley Brantley

Counselor: Thomas Beattie

History: Pam Sparks, Mrs. Hoffman, Wes Gentner & Michael Singman

Home Economics: Wanda Miller & Judith Forster

Physical Education: Richard Dombroski, Nancy Williams, Marilyn Schnur, Don Udell & Dave Green

Teachers and administrators as featured in 1967–70 Sahuarita High School yeabooks.

PART IV: STUDENT MEMORIES

Thousands of Southern Arizona students have fond memories of their school days that were created within the boundaries of what is today known as the Sahuarita Unified School District No. 30. The small rural districts of Arivaca, Cerro Colorado, Helvetia, Liberty Mine, Sahuarita, Sierrita, Sopori, Twin Buttes, and Zinc provided a foundation for the current-day boundaries that are comprised of nine schools on multiple campus locations.

In addition to bringing families, communities, and businesses together, schools created memorable moments for many students. Reading and writing were taught, but some of the real lessons the students learned sprang from the cultural and linguistic diversity of the student bodies and the individual care shown by the teachers who had bravely ventured into these rural communities.

School Memories of Barbara Brown Bennett

All of our crayons, pencils, erasers, and paper were supplied by the school. The Sahuarita School District was a wealthy one because of money from the mines. Later, the state equalized the money given to each district. The school was the hub of the community where everyone met together. With only newspapers and radio for communication, there could be a flyer sent out to the community to inform them of events through the students. Prominent ranchers and farmers were on the school board.

My first-grade teacher was Mrs. Black. She also taught music at the school. I thought she was very nice to everyone. My second-grade teacher was Mrs. Stock. Her husband was the administrator for a Native American medical clinic. We went to her house for an Easter egg hunt one year. We were taught cursive and didn't use print very often.

For third grade, my teacher was Mrs. Dorothy Irvin. She was tall and kind. She really taught me how to read well. Her son went to the school also and my older brother Edward was his friend.

My fourth-grade teacher was Mrs. Iola Dudgeon. We didn't get along very well. She snapped her fingers to get our attention and I didn't like that very much. This was the year they closed the school at McGee Ranch and all of the children from there started to come here with us.

In fifth grade my teacher was Mrs. Greenberg. She didn't stay very long. First through fifth grades were held in the red brick building. Sixth grade was held in the old military barracks. There was a gunnery range to the east of the school and one day a balloon from the gunnery range fell into our school yard causing much excitement but hurting no one.

My sixth-grade teacher was Mr. Porter Wilson. He was a World War II vet, having served in Burma. He would get a piece of chalk and start at the left side of the board and make a timeline. He never got past World War II—he just started telling stories then. He thought there was too much roughhousing happening on the playground during recess, so some of us older students started acting as security. We had plastic belts around our waist or over our shoulders and wrote tickets to other students who broke the playground rules by throwing things, turning on the hose, or standing behind someone when they were on the swing. Mr. Wilson was also the advisor; he was more involved and interactive with students than most of the other teachers. He drove us to Tucson in the summertime to certify us in swimming lessons. He told me I was the only student ever who learned how to swim with their eyes closed. My eyes were very sensitive to the chlorine. My friend Sutah Thomas saved my life twice, once jumping into the deep end when I went stiff. After some questionable comic books got on campus, Mr. Wilson went to the board and got a sex education class approved.

The first student council elections for Sahuarita School were held in 1958. Campaigning and elected on the Sputnick ticket were Barbara Brown for vice president (center, in white dress); and Jesus Felix, Jr., for president (second from left). Courtesy of Barbara Brown Bennett.

My seventh-grade teacher was Mr. Gregory. He was the principal and class was held in his house on the property because we had outgrown the school. Anita Maloy was the eighth-grade teacher. She was a little strict, but a good teacher and she liked me. Our class started the student council. The first president was Junior Felix and I was the first vice president. We gave speeches and got to vote for each other. For the eighth-grade graduation, a stage was built on the side of the building. There were plants on the stage and folding chairs for the audience. There was a program to hand out that Mrs. Maloy had made. It was printed on white paper with blue mimeograph ink. There was a prayer, a salutatorian speech, the announcement of citizenship awards, and another prayer at the end of the ceremony. We walked across the stage and Mr. Gregory gave us our advancement diplomas. The girls all had on nice party dresses and wore high heels. There was music playing from a vinyl record.

Mr. Philip Espino lived on the school grounds with his wife and children; he was the custodian.

At recess we played on the merry-go-round or swung on the wooden swings. I saw Junior Felix go so high that he went around the top of the swing set. Girls couldn't use the monkey bars because we all wore dresses. My mother made my dresses and used the same pattern year after year. It had a bib around the collar and three tiers of ruffles—one at the waist, one in the middle, and one on the bottom. I wore a matching ribbon in my hair. At that time, girls wore crinolines—net slips around their waists to make our skirts puff out more. Mother would have to wash and starch them each week. I wore oxford shoes, called saddle shoes. I had to polish them every weekend to keep them nice looking. In our home, we only got one pair of shoes a year so I took them off after school to reduce wear. In seventh and eighth grade I was embarrassed because some of my friends had purchased their clothes from a store and I was still wearing homemade dresses.

We all brought lunches from home and ate outside at a picnic table. Most people had paper bags; it was a big deal if you had a metal lunchbox with characters on the side. I folded my paper bag carefully and used it over and over again. The Mexican children brought bean burritos. My mother made little hamburgers out of

Sharon Davis was elected student council secretary in the 1958 run-off. Courtesy of Barbara Brown Bennett.

processed deer meat that my dad had hunted. They were mixed with sausage or suet for flavor. I had fruit each day and bought a small carton of milk at school. On special occasions, we lined up to get free apples and cheese.

There was a big carnival every year to raise money for the school that the whole community came to. Mr. Espino helped make the booths that the students decorated with crepe paper. Activities included the fishpond, throwing a ring on a bottle, throwing darts at balloons, or doing a cakewalk that everyone had to bring a cake for. That was the most popular booth! Another hit with the kids was to "Dunk the Dummy." Mr. Wilson was a good sport and volunteered to be the teacher getting dunked many times. There was a dance afterwards sometimes.

I only got in trouble one time. I had to write something on the chalkboard a hundred times. I enjoyed my experiences in grade school and loved my teachers.

The Catholic nuns came down from Tucson to a migrant ministry and taught catechism classes. The Sisters of the Mission Servants of the Most Holy Eucharist came by train and used the Farm Bureau building just off campus for those who wanted to attend.

We were bused to Pueblo High School in Tucson for ninth through twelfth grades because

The merry-go-round was popular during recess in 1958. Members of this group include Judy Fox, Sharon Davis, Sutah Thomas, Leandra Harris, Patricia Hartley, Ruth Gilliam, and Mary Traslaviña. Courtesy of Barbara Brown Bennett.

there was only an elementary school in Sahuarita. In high school we were branded as the "Sahuarita bunch." It was a new experience being in the city with crosswalks and paved roads. The seniors initiated the freshman by making them dust their shoes. It was fun watching our friends have to do it and we felt more like we belonged afterwards. I never went to any dances or basketball games because I didn't have

Students perform during the Sahuarita School District eighth-grade graduation ceremony in the spring of 1958. Courtesy of Barbara Brown Bennett.

transportation, but on occasion, I would go with a friend to Johnny's Hamburger Stand. My dad was very strict and didn't want us to get in trouble. I did go to one prom with my brother and the brother of his date in my dad's car. The theme was kept secret until the night of the prom, and I felt perfect in my blue dress when the underwater theme was announced. It was exciting to be in high school with so many different classes and teachers.

The freshman had to walk a half mile to the Old Indian School for homeroom because of overcrowding. We had to buy a uniform for gym class and dress in a locker room with gang showers. We played hockey with a stick and ball out on the field and were expected to take a full shower afterwards. We had to take math and English all four years, but some of the electives were Spanish, Latin, general business, typing, camping, and home economics. I learned so much and still use my education. Latin class helps me define words I see and the business class taught me how to balance a checkbook. I learned how to cook and sew in my home economics class. I learned how to cook on cast iron by making a lemon cake in my camping class. I made a belt out of cedar squares by burning a picture on each one, drilling holes and tying it all together with leather laces. Because I was in an advanced English class, I was selected to represent Pueblo High School at the University of Arizona on a discussion panel that was broadcast on TV. I was very nervous about how I looked.

There was a cafeteria where we all met together and socialized, laughing and carrying on with friends. They served food like meatloaf, mashed potatoes with gravy, green beans, and fruit cocktail. There were sectional trays with stainless steel utensils and we scraped our food off into a garbage can when we were done. There were activities held in the cafeteria. At the sock hops we had to take off our shoes so we wouldn't scratch the basketball court floor. Our socks were pulled up and folded down at the ankle. The shoes we wore were saddle shoes or canvas shoes and later flats.

I had a unique learning experience going to school here and in Tucson. I was a good student and had my friends from Sahuarita to help me feel comfortable and like I fit in. I enjoyed learning and went to the University of Arizona after high school, earning my master's degree and working in the field of education.

~ Contributed by Barbara Brown Bennett;
transcribed and written by Amy Millet

Home: Steve Brown's Personal Reflections on Continental and Sahuarita, 1946–66

My grandfathers were immigrants from Scotland. My parents were born in Illinois and my father was one of five children; my mother one of six. They met in 1936, were married the following June, and had three children in rapid succession: my siblings Julia, Katie, and Keith, Jr. (known by his middle name, Spalding) Brown.

This young family lived in a small town outside Chicago, and my father worked in that city. My ancestors' lives, like so many, changed dramatically on December 7, 1941. My father and uncles went off to war; their wives stayed home in Illinois, and two became war widows. When the war ended in 1945, as men came home all over America, many of them found themselves to be simultaneously exhausted and restless, uninspired by the jobs they had left to fight for their country.

My father had been in the ordnance department and had learned lots about vehicles and munitions, but came home only to fall sick with pneumonia. In early 1946 he was still sick, so he and my mother, Kay Brown, fled the Chicago winter of 1945–46 for a vacation at a dude ranch in Sonoita, accompanied by my siblings, who were in primary school. My parents had a wonderful respite, and the day before they were scheduled to take the train back to Chicago, they made a decision that changed everyone's life in my family.

That day, they were shown the Santa Rita Ranch on Box Canyon Road, and my mother told the story many times for the next forty years of her first sight of the ranch: "We drove up the driveway, and when the car passed between the two live oak trees at the cattle guard, I knew I was home."

They went back east just long enough to pack up their household and hire a moving van to bring everything west—which is a whole other story. My grandfather and grandmother Brown were thrilled with my parents' decision; the rest of their families, not so much. My grandfather knew the Sonoran Desert, having jumped ship in San Diego in 1893, fled into Mexico, and worked a great variety of jobs; then he went off to the Alaskan Gold Rush and to the Philippines during the Spanish–American War. He was adventurous! A decade later, at the age of twenty-seven, he met and married my grandmother, and they left San Diego for the Midwest.

My mother's family, entrenched for generations in the Chicago suburbs, thought my parents were crazy to take up ranching at the old ages of twenty-nine and thirty-three. My maternal grandmother, widowed by then, predicted they would last six months before coming to their senses and returning to the Midwest. She lived on for more than thirty years, and my recollection is that she visited the ranch once a year or so, and may eventually have come to appreciate the desert for short periods of time.

For my parents and my siblings, Santa Rita Ranch became home. I was born in 1949, and lived there until 1969, when I married and moved to New England. I still feel most at home in the Sonoran Desert. What "home" meant to this one child and adolescent is the subject of this reflection. I touch on three themes: safety, friends, and truth.

Safety: I never remember feeling in any sort of danger anywhere in the desert. Naturally, from the time I learned to walk, I was taught about rattlesnakes, scorpions, and black widow spiders, but I also learned how to avoid them: "Never put your hand where your eye can't see" was my mother's mantra. The Arizona Sonora Desert Museum educated me about all the other creatures (it was called the Desert Trailside Museum in those days). Hal Wooden, the museum director, drove a battered old Studebaker to the Continental School, accompanied by a mountain lion named George, that we children learned to love.

Steve Brown poses with his 4-H steer in 1963.
Courtesy of Steve Brown.

As the youngest of four, I was given plenty of slack. I spent untold hours exploring the Santa Rita Experimental Range and the Coronado National Forest, where we ran cattle. I had a horse and a dog and later, a Jeep. What else could a kid ask for?

Friends: I might have been termed a "lonely child," but I had no sense of loss, no words to describe that sensation. In some ways, I felt much more at home with the ranch animals than with people. I went off to Continental School, eleven miles downhill on a dirt road, when I was six, and the children I went to school with for the next eight years were my friends. This was before the mines, before Green Valley, before the pecan groves. Continental and Sahuarita were Farmers Investment Co. (FICO) company towns, and cotton was king. Continental was known for the feed yard, where cottonseed meal fattened the calves from the surrounding ranches; Sahuarita was known for the cotton gin.

Agriculture connected all my friends' families. The schools were what today we could call diverse, equitable, and inclusive. The good teachers were loving to all the children; the mean teachers were mean to all. Discipline was swift and harsh. My brother was paddled often. I learned to avoid trouble. Like everyone, I played sports, studied my lessons, and counted the days until vacation. Once in a while I'd go to a birthday party, or for a sleepover, but I was always homesick for the ranch. It was only when I grew to adolescence, and was sent away to boarding school, that I came to have any understanding of racial, social, or economic class issues. Then I grew to understand some of the deeper meanings of "safety" and "friends."

I was one of two white children in my graduating class. Continental School educated between forty and sixty children per year in the 1950s and 1960s. The student population was predominantly Mexican American, and others were from various backgrounds, including about a dozen Black students, and maybe a dozen Anglos. I remember a Black girl calling our teacher a racist when I was in eighth grade (this would have been 1963). I remember she was slapped and had her hair viciously yanked for using that word.

As I grew into adolescence, I realized my classmate had spoken a truth that was not to be uttered aloud, especially by children. Racism and classism must have defined my childhood world, but like fish sharing an ocean, we children didn't know what water was, and together we formed a community that kept us all safe.

This community of students was, in the deepest sense of the word, true. The only time I got paddled at Continental School was for telling a lie in third grade. I had been sent in from the playground for not paying attention to the baseball coach/school bus driver/custodian, who had asked me if I knew how many outs there were. I didn't. When I got inside, I told my teacher I had felt sick. She found out the truth from the custodian at lunch, and I got paddled. I learned my lesson. My parents reinforced it, reading the note I took home, and approved the paddling.

Truth: When I became a teacher, truth stayed with me, and I hope my experience influenced my students over many years. Truth matters. Whatever judgments today's world might make about the composition of small Southern Arizona agricultural towns like Continental and Sahuarita in the 1950s and early 1960s, these towns rang true. What happened there, good and bad, just or unjust, really happened, and everyone witnessed it together. As far as I can remember, everyone who talked to anyone about anything told the truth. I never recall any adult accusing any other adult of lying. Our families certainly didn't all get along, and they undoubtedly had their faults, but as far as I can ascertain, adults habitually told the truth and taught their children to do likewise. The things they could not share openly and truthfully, they simply internalized without comment, or denied. Our parents were products of the Great Depression and two world wars.

They represented a wide range of cultures, and over the last sixty years the children I shared Continental School with have populated the world with their stories and cultures, and that's a good thing. I can honestly say I had a wonderful childhood, and a wonderful life. I was safe; I had whatever friends I needed to feel safe; we were, and are, truthful. As I age, I am filled every day with gratitude for my life.

~ Contributed by Steve Brown, July 21, 2021

Robert Bruce Elam's Memories of Sahuarita

I was born in September of 1952 in Pecos, Texas. My dad worked very hard as a farmer while my mom stayed home and took care of our family. I was the third of what would eventually be ten children. Every day was a struggle to keep food on the table and work wasn't always easy to find. We moved quite often and always seemed to be

Tom, Bruce, and Terry Elam go for a ride on a patient Texas donkey in 1954. Courtesy of Robert Bruce Elam.

starting over in a new school or a new town. We were definitely a wild bunch, but learned early to take care of each other.

My sister, Terry, was the second child, sandwiched by four brothers. She was not only the "big sister," but was a force to be reckoned with. For much of our early childhood, we were the only "white kids" in the area. Every time we moved, it seemed like a new pecking order had to be established, and Terry was definitely the person you wanted on your side when things got rough. We learned to stick together and weren't afraid to fight for one another.

I remember once when Terry got in a fight in Barstow. There were three of us—Terry, me, and Andy. We walked to the community building where there was grass and a tennis court. We hung out and there was no one around but Mexicans. It seemed like we were fighting all the time. This time, we got over there and the Mexican guy was going to fight Andy. In those days, OK, you would fight. It wasn't going well and Andy finally said, "I have had enough! I quit." The Mexican kid said, "No, you're going to get more." Terry said, "He said it's over." The guy turned and said, "You

The Elam children hold still for quick snapshot in 1959, when Marley was a baby. From the left are Suzi, Jay, Andy, Bruce, Terry, Tom, and Marley. Courtesy of Margaret McGee Elam.

want . . .," and she jumped on him. She bit his eye. She was hitting and scratching. She tore him a new one. She tore him up. She was very interesting. This guy was kind of a bully. She sent him away. That was about 1961.

In 1965, when I was in the seventh grade, my family moved to the Sahuarita area to be near my grandparents, Empy and Mamie McGee. My dad got a job with the Banner Mine and we moved into a very small building at the McGee Ranch. Life at the ranch was a new adventure for us. Instead of having flat dirt fields and ditches, we had free run of the mountains with cattle and horses to get acquainted with. We suddenly had cousins everywhere.

I started school in spring of my seventh-grade year. At that time the only Sahuarita School buildings were those now (in 2022) occupied by the Sahuarita Primary School, minus all of the portable buildings.

Robert Lee and Margaret Elam family stop for a photo in 1963. From left are Tom, Bruce, Terry, Suzi, Bob, Camie, Marley, Margaret, and Jay. Perhaps Andy is taking the photo or hiding behind the car. Rest assured, he hasn't gone far. Courtesy of Margaret McGee Elam.

The basketball gym also served as an auditorium and cafeteria and was used for special events. Food for the cafeteria was prepared in a connected building on the north side of the gym toward the home economics room. It was served through a roll-up door. The multipurpose shop was north of the home economics room. The library was completed around 1966.

Mr. Hahn was my base classroom teacher in seventh grade. Porter Wilson was my teacher for health, physical education, and shop classes. I remember when I first got to Sahuarita and we were playing volleyball. I started jumping up and hanging on the net. Mr. Wilson showed me really fast that this was not acceptable. Mr. Wilson taught swimming over the summers and was the lifeguard and bus driver.

We spent an hour or so every day in the

plastics lab or wood shop with Porter Wilson. It was just a little bit north of the home economics building. We made salt and pepper shakers and I still have mine. We hand cut clear plastic into two-by-two squares of the same thickness. We used different colors of glue on each piece and stuck them together. We put them in the vice and let them sit. We drilled a big hole through the middle to hold the salt or pepper and then glued it to the base plate. We drilled small holes in the top and a hole in the bottom where a screw would work as a plug.

Paul Frick was the principal. Our classroom was the first one down the hall on the right. The home economics room was south of the shop where we built stuff. The school was south of the bus barn where the primary school is today and held kindergarten through eighth grade. The gym and cafeteria were in the same room (which is, in 2021, the gym), and the stage was where they held programs and graduations. That's where I graduated from the eighth grade. When I started, there was no library. They built that and another wing during my eighth grade year. Mrs. Brantley was the librarian.

Salt-and-pepper shakers made in the plastics lab under Porter Wilson's supervision. Courtesy of Robert Bruce Elam.

In eighth grade, we were planning the new high school—what the mascot would be; what the colors would be. I remember that Kathy Duncan wanted the mascot to be a roadrunner. Another guy wanted it to be "the gladiators." We ended up choosing the name "Mustangs" and our colors were blue and gold. A lot of the older guys were really involved with that.

My sister, Terry, graduated from eighth grade a year before me, in May of 1966. Those kids stayed at Sahuarita Elementary School and their freshman year was spent there instead of going to Pueblo or Sunnyside High Schools in Tucson. The tenth-, eleventh-, and twelfth-grade students went to other school districts.

Dave Harris was our bus driver. He lived at the top of McGee Ranch, so it was convenient for him, after doing the sports run, to park the bus overnight at his house and pick up the kids on the way to school in the morning. Because Dave Harris lived at the ranch and knew all of our parents, we knew that if we misbehaved he would go straight to them, and if that didn't work, he would go to the school. We knew we would be kicked off—not permitted to ride the bus, and that would not make things good at home. If you got kicked off the bus and your parents would not take you to school, you were given numerous chores to keep you working all day at home, and that made your stay at home nothing but misery.

We rode an old Bluebird or Crown bus. In the morning, on the way to school, the bus was full coming off the ranch. We picked up everybody at the ranch and went down Twin Buttes Road. We crossed the first railroad track and kept going past the mountain in front of where Kerley Chemical had an operation. Denny Brown lived just east of the mountain where the dirt turned to pavement. (Denny and I used to hang out a lot.) There was a road that went into some houses near him. There were also houses on the north side of Twin Buttes and kids had to walk out to the bus. Sometimes we stopped to pick up Debby Craven on the corner before we crossed La Canada. Santo Tomas was just barely growing; another

Bruce's gold 1955 Chevy parked in front of the home of Bob and Margaret Elam. Courtesy of Robert Bruce Elam.

bus picked up those kids.

We would stay on Twin Buttes Road (before they built the freeway) and pick up the kids from the various houses and trailers. Some kids were picked up at the old mine building near an old wooden mining head frame. We picked up Lupe Lerma near some large eucalyptus trees. Lupe was a young girl who was our age, but she had to take care of four or five younger kids. I remember her bringing them with her on the bus and trying to finish getting them ready for school. The Gonzalez family was on the other side of the road at that same location. After the freeway was built, Twin Buttes didn't go through any more. After that, we would go down La Canada to get to the school.

The regular after-school bus went the same route home. All of the schools started and ended at the same time so there were all ages mixed together on the bus. It seems like they were always trying different bus routes, but we never went on Mission Road to Duval Mine Road—only Twin Buttes Road.

On the way home from after-school sports, the bus route was interesting. We would get out of the school and go toward the town of Sahuarita. When we got down to the intersection before the Santa Cruz River, where you now go into Rancho Sahuarita (La Villita Road), the bus would turn north on this bouncy dirt road and we would drop off Jesse Grenhough. Then we would get onto Pima Mine Road heading west all the way up past Mission Road. We would drop off two or three sports players in the Wrangler Ranch area, then we would come back, get on Mission Road, and follow it south all the way to McGee Ranch Road and drop everybody off there. Kids were also dropped off at Ocotillo Ranch as we headed down Mission Road. I was always very glad when there was no one to drop off at Ocotillo or Wrangler because it shortened the ride and we got home about a half hour sooner.

Initially, we were able to go west on Pima Mine Road, all the way to the Ocotillo and Wrangler Ranches, but that changed. The mine said they had to have Pima

Sahuarita High School cheerleaders Rose Courtney, Debby Tate, Terry Elam, Chris Tate, and Molly Davis pose for a photo for the 1968 Sahuarita High School yearbook.

Mine Road closed. I remember their saying, "Oh, it's not going to make it that much longer. We're going to fix up Helmet Peak Road for you." The Helmet Peak-Sahuarita Road was a dirt road and the mine made it a really good road, but we then had to go up Sahuarita Road and turn north on Mission to drop off all of the Ocotillo and Wrangler kids before driving clear back south to get to Twin Buttes and McGee Ranch. It made it a lot farther.

When the freeway wasn't there, to go to Tucson we had to use Mission Road or Nogales Highway. I remember right after I was legal to drive, a girl named Debbie and I went to Tucson. I decided I could take the freeway home. They had barriers and signs that said it wasn't completed. I was in my old gold '55 Chevy. It was very smooth and I was going down past Papago Road. There was nobody else on it because it was closed. I got right there, almost to the paved main road and there was a policeman. He stopped me and said, "What are you doing?" I said, "Going home." He said, "You can't drive on this." I said, "But it's a good road, boss. What are you doing up here?" He was going to make me go all the way back, but he let me off. He said I could go ahead and get off, but that I couldn't drive that way anymore. I got busted on that one and had to use Nogales Highway or Mission Road instead. The police officer had been using the freeway for his own personal transportation back to Tucson, rather than taking Nogales Highway or Mission Road.

The 1970 Sahuarita High School varsity football team pausing for a photo in the bleachers. Courtesy of Robert Bruce Elam.

After that, we were the first freshman class in the new Sahuarita High School (1966–67) and the first senior class to graduate after all four years at SHS (spring of 1970). The high school gym was where the Sahuarita Middle School gym is today. There was a big swimming pool, built in 1967, that is gone now. The administration office was southwest of the pool. The automotive shop was to the north and right; next to that was the science building.

During my high school years, Paul S. Frick was the principal my freshman year, but Earl J. Kelly took over in May of 1967 and Mr. Frick was the superintendent. The science teachers were Doc Hesser and Mr. Lane. Mr. Becker, and Mr. Madeheim; Mr. Kurtenbach taught math. Mr. Calloway and Mr. Wear were in the welding and carpentry shop and Archie Romney was in automotive. Mr. Gerdenics and Miss Larremore were the business teachers and Mrs. Miller was followed by Miss Forster, teaching home economics. Miss Gebauer taught Spanish. Wayne Webb, from McGee Ranch, was the band director. I took baritone with him my freshman year and he was one heck of a musician. In the English department there were Mr. Fadala, Mrs. Weaver, and Mr. Jaquette. Mrs. French taught fine arts. Mrs. Hoffman, Mrs. Sparks, and Mr. Gentner taught history, and Mrs. Brantley took care of the library. Mrs. Williams, Mrs. Schnur, Mr. Udell, and Mr. Green taught physical education in the gym that was built in 1967.

While I was in high school, they started an early morning seminary program for church scripture study. Mr. Merrick, the maintenance guy at the schools, lived in a trailer right next to the bus barn and that's where we had seminary. His wife, Mary Merrick, was our teacher. She had arthritis so bad that she really couldn't do anything. She couldn't go anywhere so we went to her house. There were about six of us, Terry, me, Randy McGee, the two Merrick girls, and Debbie and Chris Tate.

Alex Romero and Robert Bruce Elam pose for individual photos for the 1970 Sahuarita High School yearbook.

Our first year at the high school, we played in Class C with six-man football and did pretty well, but starting with the 1967–68 school year, we moved up to Class B so we could play eleven-man football. The football field was in the same place that it is today; they just added bleachers. We played Benson, Tombstone, Thatcher, Florence, Marana, and several others. When I first started, I remember playing against Sells in the dirt on their rodeo arena.

In the fall of 1967, Mr. Udell was hired as head basketball and baseball coach, and was the athletic director. In 1967–68, DeWayne Kurtenbach was the head football coach and Barry Callaway was the junior varsity coach. In the fall of 1969, Barry Callaway became the head coach and Dave Wear was the assistant. On the 1969–70 varsity team there were Lee Taylor, Vincent Fuentes, Ed Depper, Mike Stout, Alvin Wright, Paul Murrieta, Ernie Alvarez, Wade Clark, John Black, Robert Espino, Ramon Delgado, Merrill Bell, Carlos Torres, Andy Monzingo, Alex Romero, Fred Depper, Armando Salcido, Peter Olivas,

Denny Brown, Frank Gonzalez, and me.

Frankie Gonzalez was our football quarterback my senior year. We had been running and practicing all summer. Coach Calloway said, "This coming Thursday, we are going full contact. Don't hold back!" Well, Frankie was on the other team and I was the monster lineman/tackle. I blitzed, grabbed him by his butt and his front pad and drove him into the ground. It broke his collarbone and put him out for the senior year. I remember the coach yelling, "No, Elam! Not that hard!" Frankie was a little guy. There went our top quarter-

Sahuarita High School varsity basketball team with Coach Green posed for the 1970 Sahuarita High School yearbook.

back just before the season started. We never got to see how good he was. Coach didn't tell me to "not hold back" during practice again. My junior year I received a trophy for "outstanding lineman."

Sugar Bear (Alex Romero) lived in Tubac next to the Chili Factory. He went to Eastern Arizona College with us and we were good friends. He retired from the Pima County Maintenance Department. We went through automotive together. Alex was an awesome baseball player. He was left-handed like Babe Ruth. He was kind of heavyset and really strong. He would just, "whack!" and could knock the ball over the fence almost every time. He never even had to run—he just trotted around the bases.

I also played basketball. During my senior year, Coach Green was the varsity coach. Our team consisted of Mike Stout, Bruce Stephenson, John Black, Fred Depper, Randy McGee, Andy Monzingo, Ed Depper, Charlie Alegria, Ronnie Serr, Leonard Quihuis, and me. Archie Romney was the junior varsity coach and Wes Gentner coached the freshman team. I received a trophy for "most valuable

Sahuarita High School basketball game in 1970 with Robert Bruce Elam, number 34, shooting a free throw. Courtesy of Robert Bruce Elam.

player" my senior year. Fred and Eddie Depper also received trophies. At awards ceremonies, comments were made that, for both football and basketball, "the ranch boys took all the awards."

In high school, I learned the basics of what an engine is and how it works, as well as front end, rear end, brakes—everything. I learned just about everything that needed to be done with a car in the automotive classes at Sahuarita High School. When they implemented the automotive program, Archie Romney was there. I think I took all four years of automotive with him. Archie came to the school from working in a dealership and was able to get a lot of money for the programs. The mines

put the money in. He had a deal with the mines. They would give him the latest motors—the latest everything—and thousands of dollars of testing equipment. They donated all the Snap-on toolboxes and tools and they told Archie, "On your word, anyone who graduates and is a good mechanic will have an automotive job at the mines." All they had to do was mention Archie. The mine contacted him for a reference and if he said they were good, boom, they had a job—a good paying job. That's why they gave him all the equipment and all their engines and everything. He was training their mechanics. They came out freshly trained on all the latest technology.

We had a $3,000 machine to test injectors. Volkswagen donated a $1,000 engine training kit. Plymouth gave Archie brand new cars to work on. Twin Buttes and Anaconda donated a $6,500 diesel Caterpillar engine. It was delivered on a mine truck. Anything Archie wanted, they would give him.

Auto Club members Fred Depper, John Plemons, Randy McGee, Armando Salcido, Al Wear, Robert Bruce Elam, Archie Romney, Mike Bodine, Donald Johnson, Paul Murietta, Herbert Chapman, and Alex Romero in the 1970 Sahuarita High School yearbook.

Sahuarita's program had the best.

We called ourselves the "auto club." We got started taking cars apart, fixing everyone's cars, and charging a little money that went to the "club." It gave us the funds to compete.

Archie loved competition. He entered us in about every competition there was. One of the biggest was the Plymouth Trouble Shooting competition that was nationwide. Another one was Vocational Industrial Clubs of America Inc. (VICA), which involved competition in many other areas in addition to automotive. Archie would get a team of troubleshooters. He would teach them how to find problems within a car. He would have other kids put special bugs or problems or broken parts in the car and then the next hour the team that was going to be in a national competition would come and try to find the problem in a few minutes. My job was putting in the bugs and trying to stump the diagnosis team. I would throw bugs in the car and Fred Depper and Alex Romero were the ones who found the bugs. The ones who were going to be the competitors would try to find the bugs I put in there, using testing techniques they had learned from Archie. I competed in VICA, but not Plymouth TroubleShooting. That was the big one. They got big money for that—also tools and scholarships. My senior year, Alex Romero and Fred Depper got to go to Indianapolis to compete.

We all knew what needed to be done to make an engine work—what was needed to make it fire and where each spark came from. I loved putting a piece of paper underneath the points so there was no ground. I would cut a part out of the distributor cap to make the cap no good or cut the center part out of the resistor wire so there was no power getting in. We would bug it and they would unbug it. My senior

Robert Bruce Elam and Kerry Lynn Johnson celebrating their wedding in June 1973. Courtesy of Robert Bruce Elam.

year, there were eleven of us in the auto club—John Plemons, Armando Salcido, Al Wear, Mike Bodine, Paul Murrieta, Herbert Chapman, Fred Depper, Randy McGee, Donald Johnson, Alex Romero, and me.

One year we went to a VICA competition in Tucson. They showed us the car we were supposed to diagnose. We had all of our own personal testing equipment. We had a certain amount of time to find as many bugs as possible. The official said "Go" and started the stopwatch. He observed us as we popped the hood, doors, trunk, every moving thing on the car. Windshield wipers, headlights, everything. We found broken parts, accessories not working, windows that wouldn't roll up, broken parts in the engine, flat tires—anything possible could be wrong. We were supposed to record each problem we found and turn it in on our master sheet for grading. To make a long story short, it never got recorded. We thought our recorder was recording everything, and he thought we were each recording the problems we found, so nothing got recorded. The officiator said we hollered out about every bug on the car, but he couldn't give us credit because we didn't mark anything down on the grade sheet. So we didn't do well at all.

After I graduated from Sahuarita High School in May of 1970, I decided to go over to Eastern Arizona College in Thatcher, Arizona, to get an automotive degree. Several people I knew from Sahuarita also went, so I had friends there. When I got over to college, I was able to challenge a couple of courses for credit because of everything I learned from Archie Romney.

In June of 1973, I married Kerry Johnson and we moved back to the Sahuarita area. My grandfather, Empy, owned a house near my parents. He asked the current renters to find somewhere else to live so we could move in while we built a home on property about a mile north of my parents. My parents had lived in the same old house we lived in while they built our new home soon after we came back from Texas. It had originally been owned by the Ramon Sandez/Sanders family.

I became a firefighter for the Tucson Fire Department on July 23, 1973. In April of 1982, I was promoted to engineer and in June of 1986, I became a captain. On May 21, 2010, I retired after thirty-seven years of service.

We have four children and fourteen grandchildren. All four of our children and four of our grandchildren have graduated from Sahuarita High School. There are eight more of our grandchildren attending school in Sahuarita and are likely to graduate from SHS. Three generations of my family have walked the same halls, played on the same fields and in the same gyms, and, in a few cases, even had the same teachers that I had.

~ Contributed by Robert Bruce Elam; edited by Kerry Lynn Elam
and Monica Lee Elam Christiansen

Student Memories of Gary Fox

I spent my childhood at McGee Ranch and started school in the fall of 1948. On my first day, I had to walk up the road from my parents' house near the bottom of the ranch to the schoolhouse near the top—a distance of about two-thirds of a mile. My cousin Eiler Harris lived very close to us and we started school together, so we walked with Eiler's older brothers Lynn and Roger.

The Sierrita school was a small two-room building sitting on a little rise. There were eight grades taught by one teacher, Eulalia Bourne. Parents called her Sister Bourne and she lived in a little room attached to the back of the schoolhouse.

I do not remember very much about the first years of school, so my story is a mixture of memories from the first through fifth grades.

Rodger Harris, Dave McGee, John C. Harris, Lynn Harris, Denny Nolen, Bobby McGee, Dave Harris, Paul McGee, and Richard McGee, with Larry Nolen, Eiler Harris, and Gary Fox in front, pose in front of the Sierrita School. Courtesy of Gary Fox.

I was not very good at keeping a neat row of numbers on the big blackboard hung on the wall of the schoolhouse. To me, the blackboard seemed to be very large, but was likely only about two feet by three feet. I struggled to figure out where all of the answers were located in the jumble of numbers and math

The Fox children—Shelly, Kelly, Judy, Scotty, and Gary—stand in front of their McGee Ranch home. Courtesy of Gary Fox.

calculations scattered all over the board.

In 1953, Trico Electric Cooperative brought electric power to the ranch. This project made it hard for the teacher to keep our attention because we could see the linemen working near the school. We watched them as they dug the holes for some of the power poles, set the poles, and put the electric lines in place. It was much more interesting to me than what was going on inside the schoolhouse.

Just to the west of the schoolhouse was a clear area big enough for the kids to play softball. The space didn't need to be very big because the oldest kids in school were in the eighth grade. The ball did not get hit very far. The outfield was on the ridge above the infield. We had one ball and it was used until there was no cover on the ball—just a tight roll of string. We kept using it until there was not enough tight string to hold it together. Try hitting a loose ball of string and see how far it will go.

One day while we were playing ball, I was the catcher. A girl was at bat. She swung at the

Sahuarita gunnery range. Courtesy of University of Arizona Special Collections.

ball, missed, and let loose of the bat as it went over her shoulder. The bat hit me in the mouth and I ended up with a ball in my hands (we did not have any baseball gloves) and a bat in my mouth. It broke my front teeth below the gum line. Over time my teeth grew back and I still have them.

A man named Lee Harris (not related to us) was in the air force and knew some of the guys on the ranch. I remember him flying an early fighter jet near the school, doing what I called barrel rolls—turning the jet over and over as he flew down from the mountains. That also made it difficult for Sister Bourne to keep us focused on school.

Sahuarita gunnery range. Courtesy of University of Arizona Special Collections.

Gayle Abell was one of the older kids in the school. She helped the teacher with the younger students and I remember her spending time working with me on some of my math problems. As I have gotten older, I realize the teacher was able to watch the older kids teach the younger ones and by doing that, she could see if the older kids understood what she had taught them.

Sister Bourne really liked baseball and during the World Series, she would listen to the games on the radio during lunch while we played outside.

We played several different games during our recess time. One I remember was called Annie Over. We would divide our group, with one half on one side of the school building and the other half on the opposite side. We used a small ball, about the size of a tennis ball, to throw back and forth over the steep roof of the schoolhouse. If the ball was caught by one of the kids, they would try to sneak around the side of the building so they could throw the ball and hit someone on the other side. If they were successful, the person who was hit had to go back with them.

I have many fond memories of my years at Sierrita School, but our small school district was annexed into the Sahuarita School District in 1954. I started the sixth grade in the old Sahuarita School building located about a quarter of a mile east of the current-day Pecan Factory.

I really liked my teacher, Mr. Porter Wilson. He taught me about the game of football, which I had never played before. We also learned how to march in formation—Porter was famous for having the kids march around. It helped keep the kids under control during physical education classes.

On duty at the Sahuarita gunnery range. Courtesy of University of Arizona Special Collections.

I believe 1954 was Mr. Wilson's fourth year of teaching.

During that time, the air force had a gunnery range near the school where they had a fifty-caliber gun mounted on a platform. The air force had drones that they flew inside the area. I do not know how large an area it was, but we could hear the guns from our classroom when they were training at the range.

Mr. Wilson took the eighth-grade kids over to the gunnery range to shoot the fifty-caliber guns at the drones. It was discontinued when I was in the seventh grade so I never got to shoot the guns, but we could go to see the equipment used to follow the drones and shoot the guns. There was a device that looked similar to a pair of binoculars that they used to look through to guide the gun and a handle with a knob trigger to fire the gun.

When a drone was hit, it would lose power. A parachute would come out and it would bring the drone slowly down to the ground so the air force could pick it up to rebuild it for another flight. From the school, we could see the drones go down, and once in a while, it was close enough that we could see the air force guys pick up the downed drone.

Gary sitting in the beginnings of his "Fox" hole. Courtesy of Gary Fox.

I do not remember much about eighth-grade graduation. I sort of remember getting a white shirt and a tie to put on, but little else. That would have been in the spring of 1956.

In the fall I started high school in Tucson at Pueblo High, located on South 12th Avenue near Ajo. Today you can see the field lights from the freeway between Ajo and I-10. The Sahuarita School District transported the high school kids to school every day, and the bus I rode picked up the kids on the west side of the district. The homes were very spread out so the bus ride was very long. For my freshman year, the kids on the ranch caught the

Gary posing for a photo in Vietnam. Courtesy of Gary Fox.

school bus just after 5:30 in the morning and arrived home around five o'clock in the evening.

By the time it was my senior year, we were on the bus a shorter time—about an hour each way. I did not play sports through my high school years because of the long rides on the bus, but I was a manager for the gymnastics team that Eiler was on. There were only a few meets each year so he and I could use a car to go to Tucson. That was the extent of my high school sports experience.

I received my diploma on my birthday in June of 1960. After the ceremony, I went home with my parents, so not much of a celebration. Dad wanted to take mother and I out to eat, but I just didn't feel like going out.

I immediately started working with Sierrita Mining and Ranching and stayed there until January 1, 1966, when I entered boot camp. I volunteered for the Seabees instead of being drafted into the army.

~ Contributed by Gary Fox

John R. Gayler's School Memories

Rudy Cubillas, John Gayler, Maria Gallardo, and Jose Gallardo stand beside Mission Road waiting for the Sahuarita School bus. Courtesy of the Gayler family.

John R. Gayler went to school at Sahuarita through the eighth grade. He started out in the old, redbrick Sahuarita school in the pecan fields. He thinks there were four rooms, with two classrooms added on. The first grade was in another building.

When John started first grade in 1955–56, His friends Marie, Jose, and Rudolfo Gallardo started with him. They were all in Mrs. Burrell's class. Cecelia Stock taught John and Rudolfo for second grade, but Marie and Jose were in Mrs. Ethel Black's class. Dorothy Irvin taught third grade in 1957–58. John called his fourth-grade teacher Mrs. Dungeon (Iola Dudgeon), but is sure that wasn't her real name.

He remembers cotton fields surrounding the school—not pecan trees like there are today. Old biplanes were used to dust the fields. The planes flew all around the school so when they crop-dusted the cotton, the kids got dusted, too.

When he was in fifth grade, the students moved into the new elementary school where he went until he graduated from eighth grade in 1963. His fifth-grade teacher was Mrs. Winifred Templeton. His teacher in sixth grade was new to the school and he does not remember the name [G. L. Miller]. Porter Wilson taught him in seventh grade and Mr. William H. Hannum was his eighth-grade teacher.

Mr. Wilson invented a flag football system, but didn't get the credit he deserved for it. John has many memories of Porter Wilson and of playing flag football with his friends.

Crop-dusting planes prepare for takeoff. Courtesy of the Walden family.

There was a prominent farm family in Sahuarita whose son drowned in one of the irrigation ditches. Every summer they paid Porter Wilson to give swimming lessons so the local children could learn to swim. Porter drove the children to Tucson in an old bus. They would have their swimming lessons and then about an hour of free swim time before boarding the hot bus to go back home. A lot of the Spanish-speaking kids didn't know much more than how to wade in water, so it was important for them. The pool charged twenty-five cents per person to swim, but if the kids couldn't afford it, Porter would just cover it for them. The pool was on South 12th somewhere at a local church.

John spent his freshman year at Pueblo High School and then, after his family left the Ruby Star Ranch, he went to

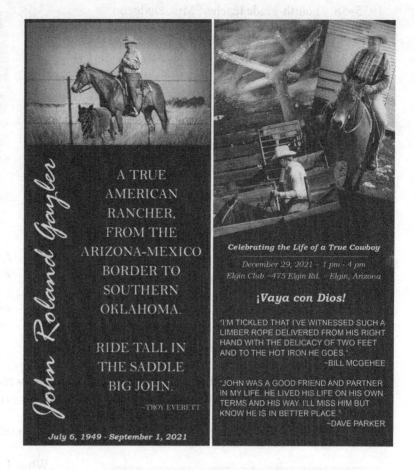

John Roland Gayler

A TRUE AMERICAN RANCHER, FROM THE ARIZONA-MEXICO BORDER TO SOUTHERN OKLAHOMA.

RIDE TALL IN THE SADDLE BIG JOHN.

~TROY EVERETT

July 6, 1949 · September 1, 2021

Celebrating the Life of a True Cowboy

December 29, 2021 ~ 1 pm - 4 pm
Elgin Club ~475 Elgin Rd. ~ Elgin, Arizona

¡Vaya con Dios!

"I'M TICKLED THAT I'VE WITNESSED SUCH A LIMBER ROPE DELIVERED FROM HIS RIGHT HAND WITH THE DELICACY OF TWO FEET AND TO THE HOT IRON HE GOES."
~BILL MCGEHEE

"JOHN WAS A GOOD FRIEND AND PARTNER IN MY LIFE. HE LIVED HIS LIFE ON HIS OWN TERMS AND HIS WAY. I'LL MISS HIM BUT KNOW HE IS IN BETTER PLACE."
~DAVE PARKER

Nogales High School for his sophomore, junior, and senior years. He graduated in 1967.

His older sister, Frances, was six years older than he was—the same age as Jack Murietta. She went to Sopori while they were in Canoa and then moved to Sahuarita when the family purchased the Ruby Star.

~ Interviewed and compiled by Monica Lee Elam Christiansen

Oscar Gomez: Memories of Sahuarita School in the 1950s

1950	Sahuarita Elementary School consisted of six buildings located in the Farmers Investment Co. housing area. The principal lived in a house that was also used for seventh grade. Another house was occupied by the school bus driver, who also worked as a custodian, mechanic, and groundskeeper. Students were not allowed to speak Spanish, making things difficult for those whose primary language was Spanish. Migrant students attended school September through January.
1951–52	First-grade teacher: Mrs. Burrell
1952–53	First-grade 1A and school music teacher: Mrs. Black
1953–54	Second-grade teacher: Mrs. Stock
1954–55	Third-grade teacher: Mrs. Irvin

1955–56   Fourth-grade teacher: Mrs. Dudgeon

1956–57   Fifth-grade teacher: Mrs. Templeton, who was also the school librarian. Students were introduced to encyclopedias and an abundance of books.

1957–58   Sixth-grade teacher: Porter Wilson, who taught and told stories about World War II, flag football, and swimming. He introduced us to University of Arizona football and Dairy Queen.

1958-59   Seventh-grade: Moved into the new elementary school in March of 1959. The new school provided a cafeteria, gym, locker room, library, indoor plumbing, and air conditioning. Mr. Wilson started a swimming program and once a month drove us to different pools, which allowed us to learn to swim. For many years, Mr. Wilson dedicated his summers to giving swimming lessons. Mr. Wilson piqued my interest in geography and for two summers I received a subscription to Weekly Reader, which included a booklet that focused on a different country each week.

Moses Torrez, David Ybarra, Jaime Estrada, and James Tolliver stand behind Raul Lopez, Rocky Lopez, Eddie Ybarra, Jose Castaneda, and Kenny Hammond after a baseball game in the field near Nogales Highway. Courtesy of Oscar Gomez.

1959–60   Eighth-grade teacher: Mrs. Maloy. Academics were emphasized, concentrating on reading, writing, and math. It was a great learning experience.

1960–64   Attended Pueblo High School in Tucson.

1972   Returned to Sahuarita to teach at the new junior high school.

The 1959–60 eighth-grade class, standing in front of the school, included Ingrid, Lupe Olivas, Carmen Olivas, Helen Tyra, Olga Estrada, Frances Vavage, John Thomas, Ysidro Martinez, Oscar Gomez, and Charlie Ybarra. Courtesy of Oscar Gomez.

When I attended Sahuarita School District in the early 1950s, the district consisted of six buildings—a house where the principal lived that was also the seventh-grade classroom; a small white building that housed the first grade; a long building in the back for 1A, sixth and eighth grades; a house where the bus-driver-mechanic-custodian-grounds man lived; and a big red building in the middle for second, third, fourth, and fifth grades. There was also a garage next to the house where the bus driver lived. All of the buildings are still standing. The playgrounds are now pecan orchards; the entire complex is owned by Farmers Investment Co. (FICO).

After moving to the Sahuarita area in 1950, we lived on Lee Moor Ranch No. 2, a cotton farm that is north of what is now Pima Mine Road. From the first grade until the middle of third grade I rode a bus to school. In 1954, after Christmas our family moved into a house a bit closer to Sahuarita. I walked to school until the new elementary school was completed. The school district did not have a cafeteria. Students who lived close by in the labor camp or houses walked home for lunch. During the primary grades, seventh- and eighth-grade boys would often come into the classes with boxes of fruit to distribute to all of us. I was most impressed when pears were passed out because they came with a wrapper.

Mrs. Burrell, the first-grade teacher, was the only teacher that I remember who spoke Spanish. Very little Spanish was heard throughout the school. We were not allowed to use Spanish on the school grounds. It was difficult for me as my knowledge of the English language was very limited. The small classroom impressed me because it had indoor plumbing and separate bathrooms for boys and girls. Up to this point the farmhouses I lived in did not have bathtubs or

Ysidro Martinez, Charles Ybarra, Luis Dominguez, Tony "Bobby" Gonzales, and Leon Gonzalez pause for a photo during their field trip to the Tucson airport with Porter Wilson. Courtesy of Oscar Gomez.

indoor toilets. In September, migrant families would arrive at the start of cotton-picking season. The classroom was filled with desks and had very little room to maneuver. By January when the picking season was over, the migrant families left the area. The permanent residents were very happy to have a bit more space in the small room.

After first grade, I had to attend a 1A class taught by Mrs. Black. I could not advance to second grade because it was believed that my command of the English language was not sufficient to be promoted. Mrs. Black was also the music teacher for the entire school. She had a keen interest in patriotic songs. We

Wally Hammond shows Jaime Estrada some fancy footwork with Lorraine Hammond, Bobby Gonzales, Yolanda Galvan, and Maria Estrada in the background. Courtesy of Oscar Gomez.

sang quite a few John Philip Sousa songs! In eighth grade when my voice was changing, she asked me to just mouth the words. My second-grade teacher, Mrs. Stock, became involved in making sure students attended catechism classes. She drove students to classes and helped them make their first Holy Communion. Mrs. Stock also took students to her home for an Easter egg hunt. Mrs. Stock's husband was a doctor at the Indian Bureau hospital close to the school district.

During third grade, I was taught by Mrs. Irvin. I remember her as being very tall and very strict. Fourth grade introduced me to Mrs. Dudgeon. She was very fond of hands-on activities. Once a week we listened to classical music provided by the Standard Oil Company. I discovered that a caterpillar could turn into a butterfly. I also discovered that I loved history, the Swamp Fox (the nickname of a military officer who had served in the American Revolutionary War), hominy, grits, and all the [details of the] Revolutionary War!

Mrs. Templeton taught me in fifth grade. She was also the librarian. Her classroom was filled with books. She would not allow comic books to be read during library time. Students could come in for lunch and read them. I discovered encyclopedias. I

Oscar Gomez entertains at the eighth-grade graduation ceremony while Charlie Ybarra, Ysidro Martinez, Mrs. Maloy, and John Thomas look on. Courtesy of Oscar Gomez.

found an overwhelming amount of information and facts.

Sixth and seventh grades are a blur! I spent two years with Porter Wilson. The class was small. The thirteen students had been together since the second grade. We learned about World War II, flag football, storytelling, Tom Sawyer and Huck Finn, University of Arizona football games, swimming, and Dairy Queen. During seventh grade the elementary school was completed. In the spring we were told to collect our books and move to the new school.

I recall that there were times during these years when we would hear guns/cannons shooting off in the distance east of the school. I was told it was a gunnery range where the soldiers practiced shooting drones. The range was part of Davis Monthan Air Force Base.

The drones, flown electronically, were occasionally misdirected and, after being shot down, landed on the school grounds. I remember one landing on the baseball field, but another got far too close to the school building. It came down with the parachute draped over the merry-go-round. Fire alarms went off and classrooms were emptied out. While we congregated outside waiting to see what was going on, we could hear sirens coming our way. We watched curiously as vehicles from the gunnery range came to retrieve the drone. By the following year, all drone activity had ceased at the gunnery range.

Before the range was completely shut down, Porter Wilson was able to take his students to observe the operation. A few of Mr. Wilson's students even got to shoot some of the guns. This was my first and only visit to the gunnery range. While there, the gunnery range personnel treated all of us to a traditional Thanksgiving meal. This was my first experience with this kind of holiday meal, and it wasn't until later that I realized the significance of it.

The area of the gunnery range is now where Walden Grove High School was constructed. Close by, cement slabs can be found there along with small pieces of debris from a bygone era.

The new school offered a cafeteria, gym, locker room, new desks, and air conditioning. It seemed like another one of Porter Wilson's stories. Mr. Wilson started a swimming program. At least once a month he drove a bus to different sites allowing us to have the opportunity to swim. He dedicated his summers to giving swim lessons. Mr. Wilson also piqued my interest in geography. For two summers I

Yolanda Galvan, Cliff Hammond, Janice Hammond and Maria Estrada rest from dancing while at the Hammond home in about 1965. Courtesy of Oscar Gomez.

received a subscription to the Scholastic Weekly Reader. Along with the readers came a weekly booklet focused on a different country. I loved to read about all of the countries in the world.

In eighth grade, Mrs. Maloy really emphasized academics! We read, wrote, and did a tremendous amount of math. It was an immense learning experience for me.

When we moved to the new elementary school in the spring of 1959, a new road had to be blazed through the desert to get to the school. I recall asking Mr. Wilson, "Why is the school facing west instead of east where we can see the valley below us and the Santa Rita Mountains?" He informed me that a new freeway was going to be built in a few years from Tucson to Nogales and it would allow travelers to see the front from the highway. When I left the district in 1993, the entrance to the elementary was still on the west side of the complex. Much to my surprise the new entrance to the elementary school is now facing to the east which I believe makes more sense.

In September of 1972, I returned to Sahuarita school district as a teacher. Two of my former teachers retired just before I was hired; however, Mr. Wilson was still teaching.

Yolanda Galvan dances with Ramon Estrada while Olga Estrada and Oscar Gomez also take a turn on the floor. Courtesy of Oscar Gomez.

~ Contributed by Oscar Gomez

Oscar Gomez's third-grade teacher, Dorothy Irvin, posing in the desert. Courtesy of Oscar Gomez.

The next three pages show the results of the 1951–52 Sahuarita School census, courtesy of Arizona State Archives. Oscar Gomez is listed as a member of the first-grade class.

1st Grade—Chonita Burrell

Bejarano Ernest	1
Brown Chas, DeWayne	1
Camacho Eddie	1
Durham Robert	1
Gastelum Nacho Junior	1
Gonzalez Leo	1
" Procopio	1
Martinez Raymond	1
Parker Sidney	1
Partida, Frank	1
Carabello, Junior	1
Johnson Garland	1
Garcia Sam	1
Gomez, Oscar Alberto	1
Miller Edward Ray	1
Calhoun Robert Ray	1
Questas, George	1
Canady, McAuther	1
Walker, Charles	1
Tanori, Leonard	1
Harvey, Clarence	1
DeMoss, Robert	1
Corella, Armando	1
Delores, Elila	1
Baptista, Lorena	1
Chilson Barbara Mary	1
Estrada Olga	1
Hernandez Petra	1
Johnston, Barbara	1
Olivas, Lupe	1
Ortega, Erminia	1
Vanages, Rachel	1
Vejar, Beatrice	1
Moreno, Marcella Maria	1
Olivas, Marie Elena	1
Clements, Lucille	1
Eaton, Ella Faye	1
Guardado, Janie	1
Martinez, Isabel	1
Carmen Saldate	1
Chilcoat, Joann	1
Kelly, Deanne	1
Larson, Lola	1
Ledezma, Julia	1

1st & 2nd Grade—Ethel Black

Austin Alice Fae	1B
Body, Carol	1B
Contreras, Elvia	1B
Felix Angie	1b
Felix Celia	1B
Gainous, Easter Mae	1B
Gonzalez Angelina	1B
Hernandez, Carmen	1B
Narcho Cecilia	1B
Ruelas Ofelia	1B
Sanders Margaret	1B
Tanori Ramelia	1B
Vasquez Patricia	1B
Olivas Mary Helen	1B
Brent, Addie	1B
Cachora Gwendolyn	1B
Blanton Obie	1
Garcia Joe	1
Mims John H	1
Sherman, Harold	1
Dews Fred	1
Miller, Floyd	1c
Thomas Fernando	1c
Cantley Bernice	2
Estrada Maria	2
Neal Lucy	2
Dews, Annie Mae	2
Cotton, Albert	2
Ervin, James Earl	2B
McFarland Jess	2
Nays Melvin	2
Walker, Larry Lee	2
Gonzalez Alfred	2
Carr Chester Lee	2
Tillman Lorenzo	2
Brent Le Varn	2

2nd Grade—Cecelia Stock

Baptista Daniel	2
Brown Barbara	2
Brown Billie	2
Carrasco Yvonne	2
Carrillo Josephine	2
Cantley, Bertha Lee	2
Dickard Jan T3	2
Felix Janie (Jesus)	2
Grashon Dale	2
Gildon Edward	2
Moreno Fernando	2
Musgrove Susie	2
Neal Robert	2
Ramirez Gloria	2
Saunders Faustina	2
Tanori Frank	2
Thomas Sutab	2
Johnson Bobby Wayne	2
Traslavina Mary	2
Alvarez Edilia	2
Huss Edna Mae	2
Haggy Dale	2
Eaton Raymond Joe	2
Vasquez Josephine	2
Vasquez Charles	2
Kelley Deanna	2
Oneal Richard	2
Walker Barbara Jan	2
Hill Buddy	2
Hill Gene	2
Teyechea Rodolfo (Rudy)	2
Hansen Lynn	2
Brent Ruby	2
Castillo Gilbert	2
De Moss Robert	2
Cachora Ronald T3	2
Brown Patsy	2
Corella Pedro	2
Denton Barbara Kaye	2
Cartwright Julie Ann	2

3rd Grade—Dorothy Irvin

Name	Grade
Angulo, Mercy	3
Burrell, Charlie	3
Burrell, George	3
Chilson, Richard	3
Cuestas, Linda	3
Felix, Manuel	3
Gonzales, Andreas	3
Gonzales, Florentina	3
Gonzalez, Leonard	3
Harris, Loramay	3
Hernandez, Carlos	3
Johnson, Sandra	3
Johnston, Kathryn	3
Moreno, Elsie	3
Moreno, Peter	3
Moreno, Steve	3
Nunez, Robert	3
Quiroz, Ruth	3
Ramirez, Lillian	3
Ribera, Mary	3
Ruelas, Josephine	3
Sanders, Ramon	3
Sherman, George	3
Smith, Ardell	3
Tanori, Rogelio	3
Tapia, Frank	3
Vejar, Charles	3
Watkins, Joey	3
Anderson, Ira	3
Caraveo, Mario	3
Kelley, Wilbur	3
Nays, Melvin	3
Walker, Wilbert	3
Dews, Annie May	3
Saldate, Mary Frances	3
Canada, Bethel Ruth	3
Walker, Woodrow	3
Botts, Reuben	3
Yates, Shanna Rae	3
Slaut, Vivian	3
Rowley, Hugh Charles	3
Brent, LaVerne	3
DeMoss, Eva Lee	3
Ledezma, Jesus	3

4th Grade—Iola Dudgeon

Name	Grade
Austin, Willie	4
Blanton, Jodie	4
Brown, Edward	4
Carr, Chester	4
Cotton, Eddie	4
Dickard, Joe	4
Felix, Frank	4
Gallego, Richard	4
Garcia, Pablo	4
Gonzalez, Geronimo	4
Johnson, Billy	4
Linker, Donnie	4
Matlock, Ray	4
Moreno, Ablardo	4
Narcho, Fred	4
Narcho, Raymond	4
Nays, Sylvester	4
Ortega, Juan	4
Ruiz, Jerry	4
Tapia, John	4
Baldwin, Philip	4
Waters, Frank	4
Alveaz, Richard	4
Miller, Joe	4
Brent, Barney	4
Tillman, Lorenzo	4
Corella, Juan	4
Anderson, Norma	4
Angulo, Clara	4
Blanton, Doris	4
Clark, Natalie	4
Gonzales, Olga	4
Harvey, Katherine	4
Jungen, Jean Ane	4
Matlock, Martha	4
Mims, Barbara	4
Moreno, Frances	4
Musgrove, Luetta	4
Quiroz, Elizabeth	4
Tanori, Ophelia	4
Waters, Joline	4
Stout, Dixie	4
Hill, Agrieree	4
Hill, Dorothy	4

5th Grade—James Soder

Name	Grade
Camacho, Ernest	5
Campbell, Jessie	5
Caraveo, Manuel	5
Carranza, Danny	5
Corella, Felipe	5
Cotton, John D.	5
Cotton, Travis C.	5
Johnson, Eddie	5
Gainers, Loyd	5
Gasho, John	5
Gonzales, Guadalupe	5
Martinez, Louis	5
Moreno, Frank	5
Larsen, Leslie William	5
Murray, John	5
Oneal, Mike	5
Rowley, Robert Allen	5
Saldate, Nick	5
Saldate, Mack	5
Turner, James Edward	5
Austin, Ira Jewel	5
DeMoss, Doris R. TH	5
Reiarana, Alma	5
Felton, Bobbie Jean	5
Cana, Guellermina	5
Canada, Bettie Joyce	5
Cuestas, Virginia	5
Dews, Frances	5
Felix, Maria	5
Hill, Docie	5
Harris, Sandra Ellen	5
Huff, Earma Gean	5
Johnston, Louise	5
Harris, Tiny	5
Lucas, Elisa	5
Mims, Dorothy Mae	5
Miranda, Georgina	5
Miranda, Maria Elena	5
Ramirez, Norma	5
Sanders, Mary Rose	5
Smith, Linda Fae	5
Smith, Marjorie	5
Soto, Cruz	5
Spivey, Emma Lee	5
Stuart, Gladys Astorleta	5
Tanori, Edelia	5
Vaughn, Margaret	5

6rd Grade—William Gregory

Name	Grade
Brent, Dorothy	
Camacho, Sarah	6
Canada, Mary Lois	6
Cantley, Zelven	6
Castillo, Carmen	6
Cuestas, Martha	6
Estrada, Frank	6
Gallega, Fred	6
Gomez, Arturo	6
Gonzalez, Margarita	6
Huff, Waddy	6
Johnston, Earline	6
Johnson, Ida Mae	6
Moreno, Alice	6
Miller, Ruby Jewel	
Morgan, Leon	6
Nielson, Billy	6
Musgrove, Billie	6
Olivas, Eugene	6
O'Neal, Robert Patrick	6
Ortega, Gregorio	6
Ortega, Maria	6
Ruelas, Jess	6
Salazar, Cruz	6
Smith, James Leon	6
Traslavina, Nancy	6
Vega, Raymond	6
Walker, James Elwood	
Walker, Lorle D.	
Hales, Billy	6
Luera, Elisa	

7th & 8th Grade—Lester Olsen

Name	Grade
Austin, Johnny Lee	7
Kelly, Floyd	7
Cant, Raymond	7
Clark, Shirley Ann	7
Cuestas, Mary Helen	7
Eastman, Keith Edward	7
Gurken, Georgia	7
Gastelum, Arnold	7
Eaton, Norma Jean	7
Luera, Mary Ellie	7
Kelley, Norma Lee	7
McFarland, Ronnie	7
Miranda, Ramon	7
	7
	7
	7
Smith, Christine	7
Naash, Bennie	7
Rivera, Albert	7
Ruelas, Joe	7
Ortega, Patkin	7
	7
Nielson, Albert	7
Stout, Emma	7
Luera, Glennie	7
Castillo, Gregorio	7
Gasho, Marvin	

Name	Grade
LeCamp, Peggy	8
Lumber, Lorletta	8
Luther, Jean	8
Morgan, Pete	8
Miller, Joann	8
Olivas, Dolores	8
Walker, Shirley Ann	8
Vega, William	8
Livingston, C.	8
Toledo, Christina	8
Brown, Wilson	8

James Eiler Harris's Fond Memories of a
One-Room Schoolhouse: Sierrita School

From time to time, they show up. Sometimes, when I least expect it, there they are again. Precious and fond memories of a day and era that are no more. Of a time so different than what we are experiencing these days in which I now live. The year was 1948; the American president was Harry Truman.

The Korean War had yet to start. The New York Yankees were, that year, once again, favored to win the baseball World Series, as they were fortunate to have on their team stars such as Mickey Mantle and Whitey Ford.

In 1948, the nearest paved road was the Old Nogales Highway. In that year, as you began traveling south from Tucson toward Nogales, the view of the beautiful Santa Cruz River Valley took in not huge copper mines, nor mining waste dumps, nor large groves of pecan trees as you drove through the tiny towns of Sahuarita and Continental. Your view was of cotton fields, cotton gins, and cattle feedlots. Your view of the landscape just up from the farmland was that of cattle ranches and grazing land. On the east side of the Sierrita Mountains, approximately fifteen miles west of Sahuarita, a small one-room schoolhouse sat on a ridge not too far from the road at McGee Ranch. There are still several people living at McGee Ranch who vividly remember attending Sierrita School in the 1940s and early 1950s.

Yes, and memories of a proud and excited little six-year-old finally in the first grade! And of walking up the trail and road with my little lunch box in hand, walking side by side with my cousin, Gary, who was also starting first grade. After walking a little more than half a mile, we reached the one-room elementary schoolhouse, which sat alone on a little hill. At the Sierrita School, there was no bus to transport the pupils.

When almost there, I have memories of looking up at that flagpole in the school yard and seeing that 1948 American flag gently waving in the morning breeze. Also of noticing the homemade merry-go-round in the northeast corner of the school yard, at the edge of the hill where the terrain drops off sharply.

As we climbed the hill, we could see the little Radio Flyer wagon next to the building, kept there for

Rodger and Lynn Harris stand in the yard with their lunch boxes. Courtesy of Lynn Harris.

the smaller kids, like ourselves. At times during recess or the one-hour lunch break we would hop in it and coast down that steep, hard-packed little road on the east side of the school yard, quite often flipping over when reaching the softer sand and flatter portion of the road near the bottom. Lots of fun!

I also remember noticing the two outhouses out back on the south side, one for the girls and one for the boys, and the cleared area on the west side, which came in handy for red rover, slow-pitch softball, and Pick-Up Stix games during lunch hour and recess.

We walked up the big porch steps and into the schoolroom and stood there, inside the door, looking around. In the big schoolroom were four rows of the old-style desks, of the same style used even back in the 1800s. The smaller ones on the left side were for the younger kids. The larger ones on the right side

*The Sierrita School building standing tall on the
hill. Courtesy of Margaret McGee Elam.*

were for those in the upper grades.

Large blackboards covered the south and east sides of the room. At the top of one blackboard in large letters was:

SIERRITA SCHOOL DISTRICT NO. 56

Current day, month and year

On the different blackboards the day's assignments for all eight grades were printed out. Then, looking straight ahead, we noticed the big coal-oil stove that was our only source of heat.

McGee Ranch did not have plumbing for water or pipes for gas and would not have electricity for another four years. Tall windows that took up most of the north side along with a couple of smaller windows on the south side let in sufficient light for the classes to function.

Looking straight ahead at the far west end of the room, the door was closed which led to the teacher's private weekday residence and sleeping quarters. It was a small room containing, among other things, a bed, a little table with a coal-oil lamp on it for light, and a wood-burning cooking stove with a small stack of wood near it.

Our attention was then diverted to the large teacher's desk not far from the door with books and papers spread out and a second coal-oil lamp sitting on it. Next to the desk were cups and a fifty-gallon drinking-water barrel with a spigot at the bottom.

There she was, Sister Eulalia Bourne, whom after all these years I am able to picture perfectly in my mind, sitting there at her desk and when realizing her two first graders, Gary and I had entered the room, she turned and gave us that friendly smile and greeted us saying, "Good morning."

We then walked to the desks in the left row, the smaller ones designated for the first and second graders, noticing that a few of the older kids were already at their desks. Before long, she got up and reached for the brass bell and went out onto the front porch, ringing the bell and saying, "Come on in, it's time to start."

After the pupils of all eight grades were in their seats, approximately twenty of them, Sister Bourne stood in front of the room and gently tapped the big stove to quiet everyone and get their attention. This remarkable and unforgettable lady, now in her fifties, was always appropriately dressed as a "ranch school teacher" in Western clothes—her attire being Levi's jeans, ladies' boots, and a Western-style blouse. And I cannot forget that familiar ladies' cowboy hat that she always wore when going outside. In the schoolroom it was always lying on her desk. She wore reading glasses, which were usually tucked up in her hair. Often when preparing to read something or contemplating what to say next she would pull them down off her head and chew on one of the ear pieces, which would always leave a bit of red lipstick on the end of the earpiece.

This was in a time when, in many rural schools, one teacher would be assigned to teach all eight grades. Her only help was the older students who would help the younger. When needed, a substitute teacher would take over for a day or two. Every now and then the county superintendent would show up to evaluate how things were going. At the time it was Mrs. Florence Reece.

Sister Eulalia Bourne chose to teach the last eight years of her long and successful career in Southern Arizona at Sierrita School. She was willing to sacrifice much of her time and energy and even at times personal finances to give us a well-rounded, excellent primary school education. On weekends she was usually working on her ranch near Mammoth, Arizona. She would leave there very early on Monday morning to get to our school in time for the start of another school week.

There were school plays, parties at Christmas and the end of the year, along with field trips, with Sister Bourne teaching us dances such as the Highland fling and the Mexican hat dance. She also taught us to appreciate good classic books, such as Mark Twain's "Tom Sawyer" and "Huckleberry Finn," as well as Ernest Hemingways's "The Old Man and the Sea." She took time to read something to us for a half hour each day, and helped us to learn and appreciate classic poems such as Edgar Allen Poe's "Under the Spreading Chestnut Tree." She also insisted that we become reasonably good with penmanship and spelling.

One of her ways of improving the grades of her students was giving verbal praise and congratulations to those who turned in good papers and excelled in the schoolwork they were assigned, as well as putting blue, silver, or gold stars beside a student's name when they did well.

It still amazes me, when I think back to that room of kids with their ages ranging from six to fourteen years old, that Sister Bourne was able to single-handedly keep control of that many grade levels and assignments at the same time and was able to somehow keep the focus and attention of each young pupil of each class on their respective assignments for the day.

Just as amazing, this teacher always demanded that we continue to be a disciplined and polite group of schoolkids, showing respect toward her and one another. She was ready to use discipline, if necessary, yet very seldom actually had to use it in order to accomplish that goal. For the most part, just a serious and stern look in the direction of the student who was out of line was all that was needed.

For those of us who were fortunate enough to be called "her kids," it didn't take long at all for us

A group of students poses on the homemade merry-go-round at the Sierrita School, circa 1950. John C. Harris holds hands with Gary Fox while sitting on the shoulders of David McGee. Barry Webb stands in front of the group with Richard McGee looking over his shoulders while Larry Nolen clings to David Harris. Laverne is holding hands with John T. Harris and Sandra Harris while Deanna Webb and Eiler Harris balance bravely behind. Courtesy of Arizona Historical Society.

to see and realize what a patriotic person Sister was. She had a love for this country and affection and respect for the principles and ideals of our founding fathers—the principles of freedom, liberty, and justice for all.

She felt it was one of her most important duties as a teacher to do her best to instill within her students this same respect and appreciation for America, insisting we learn and even memorize portions of the Declaration of Independence, the Bill of Rights, the American Creed, and the Preamble to the Constitution. Also, she taught us how to respect and properly raise and lower the American flag.

It wasn't until much later in my life that I began to fully realize how fortunate and blessed I had been to have had this remarkable person as my teacher for the first five years of my schooling. She was always going beyond in many ways to make those first few years of my education enjoyable and fulfilling.

~ Contributed by James Eiler Harris

McGee Ranch Experiences of Lynn Harris

In 1911, most of the settlers of McGee Ranch moved to the Canoa Ranch. They had an option to buy the Canoa Land Grant. The grant was nine miles long and three miles wide along the Santa Cruz River. It began at Duval Road and ended at Elephant Head Road. My great-grandfather, James Riley McGee, hired a teacher for the children in the group because there were no schools in the area. The teacher taught the children during the day and the adults, who had never been to school, at night.

During the fall of 1913, the group left the Canoa Ranch and moved back to McGee Ranch, teacher and all. A small one-room school was built, and again, the teacher lived at least five days a week on the ranch. My dad, Leander Harris, started school on the ranch in 1915. My grandmother, Mirma McGee Harris, graduated from the eighth grade in 1914. She was a grown woman who was married with three children at the time of her graduation.

James Riley McGee, Luther Harris, Mirma McGee, Leander Harris, Empy McGee, and Matt McGee stand near the barn at the Canoa Ranch. Courtesy of Gary Fox.

Making a living was very difficult, so most of the families moved away in about 1918 and the school closed. Better jobs were to be found in Tucson, Nogales, Douglas, and elsewhere. Some of the families moved all the way to California.

The Desert Homestead Act was enacted in 1916, which allowed a family to take up 640 acres. This attracted more people to homestead and secure land.

Matt and Mirma McGee stand in front of the bean barn. Courtesy of Lynn Harris.

Around 1930, there were enough children to bus them to the three-room Twin Buttes school. My great-uncle Robert McGee was the first bus driver, with his Model A Ford station wagon. He made a loop down by Tinaja and picked up children along the way. Their parents worked in the mines and on ranches in the area, and Robert delivered the children to Twin Buttes mining town.

During the thirties, four of the students rode a horse to school every day, a little more than two miles over the hills.

In time, there were enough students at the ranch to have Pima County furnish a teacher. I think the number of students needed was twelve. This included children from neighboring ranches as well. A new school was built and the families resumed their schooling back on the ranch—Rero Ranch School District Number 6. It was difficult to find teachers to live on the ranch five days a week. Sometimes the teachers had families back in Tucson.

When I started first grade in 1945, we did not have a teacher so we were bused to Twin Buttes School for half of the year. The buses consisted of two family cars. The

County school superintendent found a teacher who would teach only at small country schools: Eulalia Bourne, or Sister Bourne, as we called her. She retired from teaching when I was promoted from the eighth grade. Sierrita School District merged with the Sahuarita School District at the time, which was 1953. The elementary students were then bused to Sahuarita. The kids in ninth grade and above were bused to schools in Tucson. They went to Roskruge Junior High, then Tucson High, and finally Pueblo High School. My final year was Pueblo's first class to graduate, which was in 1957.

Ruth, Betty, Jerry, Margaret McGee, Gordon Bell, JoAnn McGee ride tandem on their decked-out donkeys. Courtesy of Lynn McGee.

Smiling photo of Lynn Harris. Courtesy of Lynn Harris.

When I was attending the school at the ranch, we all walked to school and brought our lunches with us. My brothers and sister and I walked a half mile each way, lunch intact. All students participated in sports: softball, Annie-Annie Over, and other games. Our teacher taught us to dance many different dances: early American, Scottish, and Spanish. We put on plays for the folks, sometimes three-act plays. And always, there were spelling bees.

In school, the seventh- and eighth-grade classes had to help the younger classes with their studies. The teacher stayed in the one-room teacherage connected to the back of the school during the week. The older students, if the teacher was lucky, cleaned the school every day and chopped wood for the kitchen stove every week. The students were paid five dollars per week by the school district. Oh yes, and the two outhouses were about 200 feet from school, with the doors facing the mountains. The teacher had a view of both outhouses at all times.

Our school always entered paintings, poetry, and pottery in the Pima County Fair, which was held in the Quonset buildings at the Tucson Rodeo Grounds.

~ Contributed by Lynn Harris

Mary Kasulaitis's Memories of Sopori School

I attended the old Sopori Elementary School from 1953 to 1961, all eight years. My fellow students and I rode a small bus from Arivaca to Sopori, located at milepost fifteen on the Arivaca Road. A couple of the mesquite trees are still there. You can still see the bus pull-out in front of an empty lot on which

Arivaca first-grade students wait for the bus to Sopori in 1954. Courtesy of Mary Kasulaitis.

once stood the adobe two-room school built in 1927. A bus coming from Kinsley's Ranch (Arivaca Junction) brought the students that lived in that area. The bus drivers that I remember best were Irene Bell and Ernest Grimm. No one messed with either of them.

My first-grade year was blessed with Mrs. Ann Boice as teacher of the primary grades. In the other room was Mrs. Fournier, who taught the upper grades. I am still friends with Ann Boice, after whom I named my daughter. It happens that when I started first grade I could already read at the third-grade level because my parents highly valued education. I lived on an isolated cattle ranch with nothing much for me to do except read. My nanny for the preschool years was Jennie Smith, who had taught at Ruby School until it closed and then lived with us for three years. She brought with her many of the Ruby School books and that's how I learned to read. I still have them. I think those 1930s textbooks were much more interesting than most of the readers they provide today. After she moved away, Miss Smith continued to send me books and folders of famous artwork that made an impression on my little mind.

My second-grade year was blessed with Mary Alice "Sis" Bradt. She taught grades one through three and her husband George had the upper grades. They lived in the teacherage attached to the school. I don't remember much about second grade except that I had run a big sticker into the bottom of my foot while playing on some piled up lumber after school in Arivaca. After it was extracted, a few days after the event, Mrs. Bradt put it on a poster and pinned it up on the wall. I learned about festering but fortunately did not have to learn about infections.

I moved in my third-grade year, along with Judith Casey, to Mr. Bradt's classroom with the big kids. His method of teaching was to use a several-weeks-long project on a featured topic and include all the subjects like social studies, science, math, and reading. For example, we studied our school district, No. 49. It had an interesting boundary line, so all of us were involved in surveying it, making a scale model, writing reports, identifying the plants and animals that lived there and learning the history of it. Then it was displayed in a museum room in the school. We had our own library of reference books. If you had to do something and didn't know how, you might ask one of the older kids for help. Helen Oros taught me to divide; later on she became a teacher.

Most of the history we learned was local history, so we learned that in 1857 a man named Crabb collected one

Sopori School in 1957. Courtesy of Mary Kasulaitis.

hundred Californians who thought Sonora needed to cede more of its land to the U.S. and came down to Caborca where they soon learned that folks didn't appreciate this expedition and lined them up in front of the church and shot them all, except one. (1854 had been the year that Mexico lost the Gadsden Purchase to the U.S.) The Caborcans then took Crabb's head and pickled it and carried it around Sonora to show that they weren't going to put up with any more filibustering Americanos. The one young man who had not been shot was allowed to escape up Tres Bellotas Road through Arivaca and over to the Santa Cruz

Valley where he reported what had happened. We, the students, acted this out in a play. Crabb's face was drawn on a basketball and put into a trash can. I remember this well (but not what part I played) and now I have the book on which the play was based: Crabb's Filibustering Expedition into Sonora, 1857, by Robert H. Forbes, published in 1952. Later in life I saw the bullet holes still existent in the church wall to help Caborcans remember what can happen if you aren't watchful and what it might take to save yourselves. It didn't hurt that we had a schoolmate from Caborca and we knew it was only about sixty miles away. This kind of school

George and Sister Bradt pose with Sopori students in front of the school. Courtesy of Mary Kasulaitis.

activity made me into the local historian that I am today. It also made researchers of us, so that in later years you could find teachers, professors, a librarian (me), geologists, and others in academic life who graduated from the School of Sis and George.

My class of six had George Bradt for six out of the eight years of elementary school. They loved our school. I know this because in their older years they made a book about all the schools where they taught. My eighth grade year, 1960–61, George and Sis moved on to Aspen, Colorado, where they stayed one year (too cold). They also taught at Sahuarita for a year or two in the 1960s before they finally found Elgin School and stayed there for years. Those of us left behind had to find our own way to high school: drive, ride the bus, board in town, or go to boarding school. Everyone found a way. I boarded with four different families. I wouldn't recommend it. But you do what you have to do to get an education. Our little group of students has reunions every once in a while so that we can keep up with each other.

~ Contributed by Mary N. Kasulaitis

The 1928 road to McGee Ranch. Sierrita School stands off to the right side in the distance. Courtesy of University of Arizona Special Collections.

School Memories of Margaret McGee Elam

I was born at the Stork's Nest in Tucson, Arizona, on January 21, 1927, and came home to the McGee Ranch, where I spent most of my childhood.

JoAnn, Empy, Jerry, and Mamie McGee in the Canoa House circa 1925. Courtesy of Margaret McGee Elam.

My older brother, Jerry (Gerald June McGee, born in June of 1924) started kindergarten at the Sierrita School in 1929 when he was five years old. My sister, JoAnn, born in 1925, also went to the Sierrita School. She was a year ahead of me and one year behind Jerry in school.

I started kindergarten in the small one-room schoolhouse at McGee Ranch in the fall of 1931. I was only four years and eight months old. They needed ten students in order for Pima County to keep our school open, so I was allowed to start early. The tiny one-room schoolhouse was on the small slope where the community building and store are today. Water for the school was brought by wagon in fifty-gallon barrels from the ranch well. This was the same way my father, Empy McGee, hauled water to our place at the homestead. A small two-room teacherage was behind the school that had a kitchen and small living area. The teacher had to use the same water that was hauled in for the school and she shared the school outhouse.

I remember my teacher, Mrs. Jones, wanting me to write so many pages and I just couldn't do that. I traded my peanut-butter sandwiches to the two Lopez girls so they would write papers for me. I am sure the teacher had to have known that we did that.

In September of 1932, the Sierrita School was closed due to lack of attendance. I attended first through fifth grades (fall of 1932 to spring of 1938) at the Twin Buttes School. Catherine Foy was my teacher. The school building was much larger than Sierrita and there were three wings. Mrs. Foy taught all eight grades in the first wing. The second was used for storage and the third was where we had to go when we got sick at school. If we were not feeling well during the school day, there was no way to take us

JoAnn and Margaret McGee stand in front of their grandma's chicken coop. Courtesy of Margaret McGee Elam.

home so we had to go to the third wing and lie on the floor on one of eight mats until the bus came to take us home. It was kind of scary being back in that third room alone. I remember my sister JoAnn getting appendicitis at school and having to lie there all day.

My uncle, Robert McGee, drove the kids from McGee Ranch to the school in Twin Buttes. We rode in an enclosed old panel truck with boards across the bed for benches and a door in the back. They would also stop along the route to pick up the Lopez kids who lived at Tinaja. The road down was a two-wheel track that everyone used to get to town, very close to

The student body of the Twin Buttes School pauses to show off a part of their school ground conservation project on March 19, 1937. Courtesy of University of Arizona Special Collections.

where the paved road is today.

Going down to Tinaja, we would come to the Cowboy Arroyo, a little way down from where the Cowboy Dam is. It was quite a deep arroyo. When I was in second or third grade, Empy told Robert that he could let us off at the arroyo so we could walk home and he would not have to drive clear back into the homestead. Robert would let us off and I still can't believe Empy let us walk that far because it was a long way. One time, the weather was bad. Robert still let us off and it rained on us. Jerry was older. He always took off in a hurry because JoAnn and I were too slow. On this day, we were pretty wet and miserable by the time we got home. Empy blew a fuse. He said, "I don't care if you let them off when it's good weather, but you shouldn't have let them off when it was bad." We didn't have to walk anymore after that. Empy said, "You just bring them home."

Swinging at the Twin Buttes School. Courtesy of the Foy family.

There was a big mailbox down at Twin Buttes where the store was. I don't remember how many people were living up at the ranch at that time, but it would be quite a bundle of mail in the box. Whoever went down to Twin Buttes would pick it up. It only came two or three times a week. It was always fun to go get the mail.

The school was just like the one in *Little House on the Prairie*. They had the blackboards, desks, and on the wall the ABCs were hung so we could learn to write. I can still see it in my mind.

Mrs. Foy was the only teacher. She would say, "All right. It's spelling time. Everyone get out your spellers. We are going to have spelling." Then, she would go through all eight of the grades, giving them their assigned words, and then start back at the beginning. She would repeat that until every grade had finished. Then we would hand them in.

At the Twin Buttes School, JoAnn and Margaret McGee are in the middle of the back row wearing matching dresses. Norman McGee is sitting fourth from the right. Courtesy of Margaret McGee Elam.

For geography, she had a little circle of four to five chairs. We would sit there around her. She would say, "All right, third grade, come up for geography and the rest of you guys get your geography books and study the lesson." The third grade would finish and another group would go up with her. There weren't that many of us, but we didn't dare make any noise.

We always had reading first and then spelling, followed by a recess. We came in from recess for geography, history, and math in the afternoon. We even had art—papers she would pass out for us to color on.

Mrs. Foy was quite strict, especially about holding your pencil

Margaret Elam standing in the yard at the Drachman house after eighth-grade graduation. Courtesy of Margaret McGee Elam.

correctly. We had writing tablets. We had to do very precise ABCs and your hand had to hold the pencil "just so" or you would get your hand smacked. I think about that when I see kids holding their pencils wrong.

JoAnn on Soppy, Betty on Chapo, and Margaret on Chubby. Courtesy of Margaret McGee Elam.

We played out in the school yard for recess. I remember once when the kids were getting some wasps out of the wall. They set a piece of paper on fire and put it in this knothole to kill the wasps. There was big excitement about the school catching on fire. It didn't go anywhere, but I sure remember that.

Near the school was Revello's little store. It was kind of like the stores in Mexico along the roads into town. We could go there during lunch to get candy or trinkets if we had the money.

I also remember an old woman who lived in Twin Buttes. She would always come into town with a bunch of dogs following her.

In the fall of 1937, the county reopened the school at the ranch. Before school could begin, the old schoolhouse was moved down the ranch road to a small ridge of land that was donated by my father, Empy McGee. I remember their moving that school building. It was quite a big deal. The big metal wheels they used are still by the road. They put the school on wood to support an axle and pulled it down the hill to where it is still located today. We all went out to watch.

Mrs. Squire was our teacher that first year back at the ranch (1937–38). There was still only one classroom with a small two-room teacherage at the back. Empy McGee, my father, took us to school that first year from the homestead. After that, we rode Little Bay over the mountains.

Miss Mullins was the teacher for the 1938–39 school year. My teacher was Mrs. Schmiedendorf in 1939–40. There were ten to fifteen kids attending school by then. I was the only one in eighth grade. We were taught reading, writing, math, spelling, geography, and history, with an occasional art lesson.

I remember that one of the teachers always brought her daughter with her. To the daughter, of course, she was not the teacher—she was just "Mom." At recess, the daughter would come out with some soda crackers and we were always so jealous. Something like soda crackers was a real treat. She would eat those in front of us. If we ever had oranges, they were such a treat that we would even eat the orange peels.

When I was in eighth grade—my last year of school at the ranch—they had the Pima County Fair in Tucson. The schools all put on skits. Mrs. Schmiedendorf arranged for Don McGee and I to dance a Russian dance. We had to do this Russian step where you squat and you jump, put your foot out, put your foot out. I remember having to do that. It was really hard. The entire group did things, but it was just Don and I doing that dance.

They also had spelling bees. I remember I lined up and I spelled my word right. I got on the other aisle. They tapped on my shoulder and said, "You're disqualified." I said, "Why?" They said, "You didn't pronounce it first." You were supposed to pronounce the word and then spell it." It didn't hurt my feelings too badly because I didn't want to go out because I couldn't spell a

Margaret Elam posing in her nursing uniform in 1945. Courtesy of Margaret McGee Elam.

word—only because I didn't pronounce it.

Mrs. Schmiedendorf also liked to diagram sentences and I really learned to do that.

The County provided schools only through the eighth grade so when I graduated, I went to live in Tucson. During the 1940–41 school year, I attended Mansfield Middle School for ninth grade. Then, from the fall of 1941 to the spring of 1944, I attended Tucson High School.

After graduating from Tucson High School, I decided to enroll in a nursing school. It started in September of 1945 and was a government-sponsored program through St. Mary's Hospital, training nurses to help during World War II.

While I was preparing for that training program, there was a severe drought and my parents moved their cows down to a pasture in Continental. They stayed down there in a company house. My father, Empy, got acquainted with O'Dell Massey, the manager at Lee Moor Ranch No. 2. He invited the Massey family to a dance at the Continental School.

My future husband, Robert "Bob" Lee Elam, was staying with the Massey family and working at Lee Moor No. 2. He grew up in Fabens, Texas, on the Elam family farm. He became good friends with William and Bill Massey at school. Bob had lost his father when he was only seven and Mr. Massey was a surrogate father to him. Bob came to the dance with the Masseys and that is where we first met. My father told

Margaret and Bob dance at a Halloween party. Courtesy of Margaret McGee Elam.

them they could come to visit any time and they took him up on that offer.

It was very common for them to load the piano belonging to my parents, Mamie and Empy McGee, in the back of a truck and take it to different locations for dances each weekend. They planned a dance at Kinsley's. Bob asked me if I would go to the dance with him. Since neither of us had a car, my family took my sister and me to the dance and Bob went with the Masseys. We had a great date at the dance and then went home with our families.

We got better acquainted through letters and brief visits. Bob injured his right hand badly in a poison machine (a spray rig used to distribute a light layer of poison on the cotton plants to kill insects) and couldn't work. He boarded at our house while he healed. Eventually, my father hired him to work at the ranch. I was very happy and Bob loved working as a cowboy. Eventually, we were married on December 24, 1947.

After our marriage, we lived in Tucson. I worked at the police department and Bob worked with the Masseys again at Lee Moor No. 2. When a house opened up, we moved to a small house on the farm with no running water, no kitchen, and no bathroom. I had to cook on a small kerosene stove and Mr. Massey

The Elam family, minus Tom, stands for a photo in July of 1963. Bob is in the back beside Margaret, who is holding Cammie; Terry, Bruce, and Andy are in the middle row; Jay, Suzi, and Marley are in the front. Courtesy of Margaret McGee Elam.

*William Massey, Bob Elam, O'Dell Massey, Billy
Fred Massey, and Milton Massey stand in front of
the Massey home at Lee Moor Ranch No. 2.
Courtesy of Margaret McGee Elam.*

helped us buy an electric refrigerator. We
bought a #3 washtub to wash in and of course,
we had the outhouse. What more could we ask
for?

In May of 1948 we left Lee Moor and
moved to Texas to help Bob's mother with
their farm. His brother, Henry, was sick and
she could not manage without help. We
packed up my father's truck and headed to
Fabens, Texas. I had sad, sad feelings leaving
my family and home.

Bob had various jobs in several different
Texas towns over the next fifteen years, but in
September of 1964, he finally returned to the
McGee Ranch. Unlike when we left, our
family of two was now a family of eleven. At
the time, the closest school was in Sahuarita. It
was a nice big school with a fleet of buses to
gather up all the kids.

Our oldest son, Tom, was a sophomore (1964–65) when he came from Texas with my father, Empy.
There were no buses so they had to take him to football practice every morning, stay in town until his
practice was over, and then bring him home. This was for the practice session before school started. That
was quite a chore. I believe that went on for two weeks. Because there was no high school offered at that
time, the school paid his tuition and helped provide transportation. We would get him down to Sahuarita
and then he would catch a Citizen bus from there to Tucson. He would catch it home in the evening and
my husband, Bob, picked him up after work. He did that for his sophomore and junior years (1964–65,
1965–66).

Tom would be a senior for the 1966–67 school year when
the new Sahuarita High School opened. He had been going to
Pueblo High School and was involved in sports with many
friends there. With Sahuarita School ready to teach all grades,
we had a problem. Tom wanted to go to Pueblo to finish up there
with his friends. He was very involved in the sports program. If
he continued to go to Pueblo, Sahuarita District would not help
us. He would have to pay tuition and all the transportation. My
father helped pay for him to stay in Tucson through graduation
in the spring of 1967.

Our daughter, Terry, born 1951, was in the eighth grade our
first year back in Arizona. The Sahuarita School offered just
eight grades. There were plans to build a high school, but it
wasn't ready for her grade when she finished elementary school,
so a plan was devised to keep the students in the elementary
school for an extra year. The improvised plan allowed the
freshman class of (1965–66) to avoid having to pay tuition and
transportation costs to Tucson for the year. By the time they
were sophomores (1966–67), the new school was open. Terry
graduated from Sahuarita High School in 1969 (1968–69).

Bruce, born in 1952, graduated from Sahuarita High School

*Bob takes a ride on his horse, Billy.
Courtesy of Margaret McGee Elam.*

in the spring of 1970. He was a member of the football and basketball teams, and he excelled in the automotive program run by Archie Romney. Their class went to nationals to compete. The kids were really good. Bruce was in the first graduating class to go completely through (freshman to senior) at Sahuarita High School.

All of our other children also went to Sahuarita. They caught a bus on the road by our home at McGee Ranch. It all seemed so nice. There was a program offered at the school that was a head start for four-year-olds. Our son, Marlin, born in 1959, was old enough to go to that.

We have ten children and nine of them attended Sahuarita High School.

~ Contributed by Margaret Norton McGee Elam and Monica Lee Elam Christiansen

Sutah Thomas Harris: My Sahuarita School Memories 1950–58

1950–51   First-grade teachers: Mrs. Chonita Burrell (bilingual) and Mrs. Ethel Black (also taught music for the entire school)
1951–52   Second-grade teacher: Mrs. Cecilia Stock
1952–53   Third-grade teacher: Mrs. Dorothy Irvin
1953–54   Fourth-grade teacher: Mrs. Iola Dudgeon
1954–55   Fifth-grade teacher: Mrs. Harriet Greenberg (taught just one year)
1955–56   Sixth-grade teacher: Mr. Porter Wilson
1956–57   Seventh-grade teacher: Mr. William Gregory (also the principal)
1957–58   Eighth-grade teacher: Mrs. Anita Maloy

When I started at Sahuarita School in 1950, the school was located on the east side of the railroad tracks. It consisted of a large red brick building with barracks on the south and northeast sides. The first grade was in the south building. The second, third, fourth, and fifth grades were in the brick building, and the sixth and eighth grades were in the northeast building. The seventh grade was in a building on the north side of the house of the principal, Mr. Gregory. There were probably fifteen to twenty students on average in each class. That could vary

A 1956 aerial view of the school shows the placement of all the buildings. Courtesy of Sutah Harris.

depending on the laborers working the crops. Integration was not a problem. We were about a third each—white, Hispanic, and Black. I don't remember any kind of prejudice. We all studied, ate, and played together.

I lived on a cotton farm about three miles south of the Oro Verde Store. The name was later changed to the One Stop Market. Most of the kids were from farm and ranch families or from the labor camps just west of the school. We were a small community that was very spread out.

My first school bus driver was Philipe Espino. I was picked up right at my house as it was at the south end of the district and the bus turned around in our yard. Phil and Pila Espino lived on the school grounds where they had a home and a mechanic shop behind it for maintaining the buses. I believe Phil also did other maintenance and janitorial work at the school. His wife Pila was an amazing seamstress and cook.

Playing on the Sahuarita School playground during recess. Courtesy of Sutah Harris.

Jay Pelton, Red Tyra, and William Spivey were also drivers.

All through my years at Sahuarita, the classes would meet first thing every morning by the flagpole and we would say the pledge of allegiance before school started.

I started at Sahuarita School in 1950. My first-grade teacher was Mrs. Chonita Burrell. She spoke Spanish as well as English so was able to help the children who did not speak much English. Mrs. Ethel Black also taught first grade and was the music teacher for the entire school. She taught a lot of patriotic and Stephen Foster songs, among others.

The first-grade classroom was in a barracks building south of the redbrick building. It also had separate restrooms for that class. There was a desk for each student and a large blackboard across the front of the room. She would let different students take turns writing on it and using the eraser to clean it.

There was a playground outside which consisted of several swings, a slide, and a tether ball. On the north side of the brick building was a merry-go-round which was a novelty and used a lot. All eight grades used the same playground. There were also a few ball fields on the north side of the buildings. Their boundaries were marked off with chalk depending on the games to be played. There was also a basketball hoop.

There was no cafeteria or lunchroom. We all took sack lunches. There were a few picnic tables outdoors or we could eat under the trees or on the steps to the brick building. When the weather was bad we would eat inside at our desks. It was fun to see what we could trade with each other at lunchtime.

In the second grade, 1951–52, my teacher was Mrs. Cecilia Stock. She and her husband lived on the grounds of the Indian Hospital just south of Tucson and there were nice green lawns there. Every Easter she would take us to her place for an Easter egg hunt. The school bus transported us and I believe several of the other classes also went with us. In addition to her regular teaching I remember she liked to have us put on plays. That was a lot of fun.

In the third grade, 1952–53, my teacher was Dorothy Irvin. She lived just south of Tucson on the Nogales Highway. Her classroom was on the west end of the brick building. In addition to her regular teaching she also taught sewing to the older girls who were interested. There were only about four machines, so everyone had to take turns on them. I remember making a skirt and it seemed like it took most of the year to finish it because we all

Mr. Wilson's sixth grade class poses under the tree. Front row: Leandra Harris, Yvonne Carrasco, Barbara Denton, Sharon Davis, Judith Fox, Celia Felix, Barbara Brown, Sutah Thomas, JoAnn Smith, Mary Traslaviña, Mary Estrada, and Frances Lopez. Standing in back: Melvin Hill, Duane Havins, Spencer Anderson, Kenneth Hopkins, Mr. Wilson, Lavern Brent, David Soto, Frank Soto, and Danny Vavages. Courtesy of Sutah Harris.

Spinning on the merry-go-round with the flagpole in the background. Courtesy of Sutah Harris.

had to wait and take turns on the machines.

My fourth-grade teacher was Mrs. Iola Dudgeon in 1953–54. She was a very prim and proper lady. I remember we had to complete a lot of mimeographed sheets with multiple choice questions. There were music and educational programs on the radio that she would tune in to and we would listen to those. All through my Sahuarita School years the radio was used quite a bit in the various classes for different programs.

Mrs. Harriet Greenberg was the teacher in 1954–55. She was very young and pretty. She taught at Sahuarita only that one year and I have always been so thankful to have had her. I think this might have been her first year as a teacher. I kept in touch with her for many years after she left. She was very strong on penmanship and her goal was that each of her students would end up with, at the very least, legible handwriting—and she accomplished that. She always had a smile on her face and seemed to love her job. I think this might have been my favorite year. After she left, Mrs. Templeton (who had been a teacher at Continental School) took over the fifth grade.

In the sixth grade, 1955–56, my teacher was Porter C. Wilson. He also helped out with any sports that were played at the school. Porter Wilson had invented flags for football. We spent many hours assembling them for him. Sahuarita boys got first use of them and flag football was played often. He had been in the military in Burma and liked to tell war stories. He also liked to teach the boys to march. My husband, James Harris, remembers that one day Mr. Wilson took a group of boys and marched them all the way to the gunnery range east of the school.

We had "duck and cover" drills in case of a bomb or nuclear threat. We hid under our desks (as though that would do any good). The Sahuarita gunnery range was to the east of the school and we could hear noise from shells coming from there. One day one of the shells landed in the school yard and the military had to come and get it.

When Porter Wilson first came to the Sahuarita area, he, his wife Betty, and their daughter Kathleen, lived at the Thomas farm in the long house. Mr. Wilson started teaching children in the area to swim. At first we went to the Kinsley ranch in Amado where there was a large pool fed by freshwater from a well. I remember it being very cold. Some school parties and picnics were also held there. Later he used the House of Neighborly Service pool in south Tucson. The school bus transported us there during the summer. This was a huge success

The eighth-grade graduating class of 1958 poses for a photo. Back row: Mrs. Maloy, Danny Stewart, Judy Fox, Harrietta Hartley, Armando Wilson, Pat Hartley, Ruben Federico, Barbara Denton, Sharon Davis, and Junior Felix. Front row: Barbara Brown, Sutah Thomas, Yvonne Carrasco, Leandra Harris, Mary Estrada, Celia Felix, and Frank Soto. Courtesy of Sutah Harris.

A special-request photo of "The Gang" that always enjoyed school days together. The boys are Jack Collins Jr., David Ellis, Dennis Fairless, and John Harris. Girls are Barbara Denton, Sharon Davis, Mary Traslaviña, Sutah Thomas, Barbara Brown, Leandra Harris, and Yvonne Carrasco. Courtesy of Sutah Harris.

and we all loved it.

We were able to take quite a few field trips during our school years. I remember one especially, when Mr. Wilson took us to the Tucson Airport. We were able to go up into the control tower. He had a small plane arranged for several of us at a time to take a ride from Tucson and fly over the school at Sahuarita. It was the first time I had ever been in a plane. I have a picture of the school grounds that I took from the plane that day. Unfortunately it is a little blurry due to an amateur photographer and a fast plane!

In 1956–57, the principal of the school was Mr. William Gregory. He was also the seventh grade teacher for the time I was at Sahuarita. He and his wife Frances lived on the school grounds and the seventh-grade class and school office were on the north side of their house. When Mr. Gregory had to be out of our class for other school business, he would give us our assignments and open the door to the office so that the school secretary (who was also my mother, Katie Thomas) could keep an eye on the class and make sure we behaved. According to an article I wrote for the *Pima County Farmer*, the enrollment was 184 students for the school that year.

Anita D. Maloy was our teacher in 1957–58. I believe this was her first year in the district. She moved on to the new school when it was built on the west side of the Santa Cruz River. Her goal was to prepare us for high school as best she could. We would be going from a very small school to a much larger high school in Tucson and she knew it would be a challenge for us country children. I remember a lot of math and English being taught. At that time, each month I wrote an article for the *Pima County Farmer* paper about Sahuarita school news. I graduated from Sahuarita and was class salutatorian at the end of the year.

Mrs. Florence Reese was the county school superintendent at the time. She was frequently at the school and always wore the prettiest Western [broomstick] skirts. It created a fad and quite a few of the girls had similar ones made which we wore to the square dances after the new school was built with a gym where we could hold events.

There was also another barracks building outside of the school grounds to the south and east a bit. The local Farm Bureau

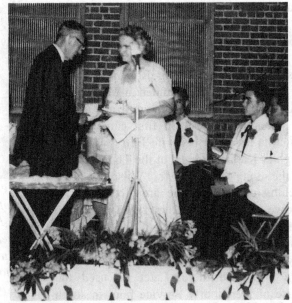

William Gregory and Anita Maloy at the 1958 eighth-grade graduation ceremony. Courtesy of Sutah Harris.

meetings and socials were held in that building for many years. Many farmers and ranchers in the area were very active in that. That was one way so many people in the areas around Sahuarita stayed connected and got to know one another.

When I started school in 1950, most of the kids were from farm and ranching families or from the labor camps just west of the school. There was the Oro Verde Store with a post office and a butcher shop and a bar across the street. At that time Harold and Mildred Ellis owned the Oro Verde Store. They would extend credit month to month to some of the residents. Their son, David, attended Sahuarita School and was a grade ahead of me.

Producers Cotton Oil had a gin on the east side of the railroad tracks and south of Sahuarita Road. (Harry Timmons and Jack Collins were the gin managers.) Farmers Investment Co. had a gin on the north side of Sahuarita across the road from Producers. There was a third cotton gin, Cotton Producers Association, several miles south of Sahuarita on the west side of the Nogales Highway. Joe Ingram was the gin manager and I believe John Klingenberg also worked there. We were a small

Red Tyra and Gary Fox carry out a can of ice for the bus picnic. Courtesy of Sutah Harris.

community that was very spread out. The main crops in the area at that time were cotton and some alfalfa, and to the south some fields were planted in peanuts. This information was given to me by my brother, John Thomas, who was a cotton gin manager in Marana for many years.

The pecan orchards came about later. Dad brought in about six pecan trees from Del Cerro in Las Cruces, Mexico, and planted them in our yard. He monitored their production for years and decided that they could be a productive crop in the Sahuarita area. He was not well enough to put in orchards, but Keith Walden and Warren Culbertson were also watching the trees and Farmers Investment Co. decided to go ahead and plant trees. That was how the pecan orchards began.

Most of us were bused to school. My first bus driver was Philipe Espino. He and his wife Pila lived in a house on the south side of the school grounds. He was also the custodian and did some mechanic work on the buses. Jay Pelton was another bus driver and also Red Tyra and William Spivey. Red Tyra was the driver who took us into Tucson to Pueblo High School.

There was a very active PTA in our school and carnivals were held every year to raise money for the school. We would all work together to make the booths with the help of the custodians, and the community would supply the prizes. These were big social gatherings for the community. Food was served and the women of the area were excellent cooks. I remember my mother and Pila Espino, among others, making tamales for days to serve at these events.

We did not have a school nurse. Mrs. Gregory and Mrs. Espino took care of minor problems and took ill children home if needed. There were very few telephones in the community so calling the parents was not an option.

I remember that there was a pay phone outside of the Oro Verde Store, one at the school, and one at each of the cotton gin offices, but most households did not yet have telephones.

I graduated from eighth grade in 1958. We were then bused to Tucson to attend Pueblo High School, as Sahuarita did not yet have a high school. It was an hour to an hour-and-a-half ride twice a day. Whenever possible, some of us would try and get some of our homework done on the bus.

After graduating from Pueblo High School in 1962, I married James Eiler Harris from McGee Ranch and have lived there ever since.

~ Contributed by Sutah (Thomas) Harris

PART V: TEACHER AND EMPLOYEE MEMORIES

Some of the gracious people who taught in the schools of Sahuarita were homegrown; others landed by kismet in one isolated small town or another. Whatever the case, the memories of these teachers and school employees stretch across circumstances and generations. What follows is a compilation of assorted student memories spanning a time period of over ninety years.

Scott Boyter: Bleed Blue and Live Gold

The best part about growing up was attending Sahuarita High School (SHS) athletic events. Friday night football or basketball games always gave me something to look forward to. The atmosphere for home basketball games was one of a kind—[watching the players] running onto the court with the band playing the Lone Ranger theme and watching the spotlight player introductions would give you goose bumps every time. Being able to sit on the bench, ride the team bus, or hang out in the locker rooms before and after games are some of my best memories. The players on my dad's team always treated me like I was part of the team; it led to my being very motivated to attend SHS and play sports.

In the fall of 1986, I became a student at SHS. Finally, after all the years of being a fan I got to be the one to create excitement for the fans in the stands and hear the cheers. I enjoyed my high school experience to the fullest and got to live out my dream of playing for the Mustangs like so many of the great players I had grown up admiring. I also got the privilege of being a student to the many wonderful teachers who helped create the culture I so longed to be a part of. Mr. Rieman, Mr. McQuown, Ms. Brantley, Mr. Cleveland, Mr. Elias, Mr. Harrington, Mr. Price, Mr. Miranda, Mr. Flannery, Mr. Gentner, Mrs. Vorhees, Mr. Wear, Mr. Encinas and many more taught me so much about responsibility, integrity, and most importantly how to be a good person. I am sure I am missing some others who served long and productive years at SHS, helping me and so many others along the way. To all I would like to simply say, "Thank you," for being great at what you did!

I have come full circle and have been teaching and coaching at SHS since 2005.

Sahuarita High School basketball team photo with Coach Ron Boyter. Courtesy of Scott Boyter.

Each year I have more admiration for those listed herein because they gave so much to SHS for so many years. Longevity is not something that you find in the education field, or especially at staying with one school in this day and age. Each day that I come to school I remind myself to treat the students with respect and try to put a smile on their faces—that's what those teachers did for me. I am grateful that my father, Ron Boyter, chose to take a job at SHS in 1977 where he became a great role model for all his players, students, and fellow co-workers for the next thirty-plus years. I cannot stress enough how the influence of this place has given me so many fond memories and opportunities to be happy and content with my life choices. I wouldn't change a thing!

~ Contributed by Scott Boyter, Sahuarita High School, Class of 1990

Barry Callaway's Memories of Sahuarita 1967–95

The brand new, $1.1-million Sahuarita High School opened its doors in September of 1966 with a student population of 131 students. The football team played eight-man football the first year with Dewayne Kurtenbach as coach. During the summer of 1967, after teaching for two years at the Arizona State Industrial School for Boys, I was hired as an industrial arts teacher and athletic coach. Within that one-year space of time between the opening in September of 1966 and when I started teaching in September of 1977, the student population increased to 201 students, so we had to move up a league and play eleven-man football. We were the smallest school in the league for the next few years, and for the first few seasons, there were no lights on the football field, so playing day games in the heat definitely took its toll on the players. When lights were finally installed, making night games possible, it made our games much more pleasant.

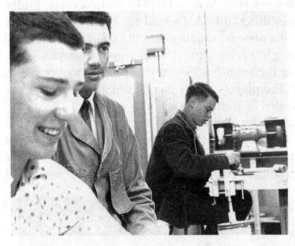

Barry Callaway supervises Eddie Depper and Ronnie Serr in an early 1970s crafts class. Courtesy of Barry Callaway.

The I-19 freeway to Nogales was still being built, so the Old Nogales Highway was the route to work from Tucson, where most of the teachers lived. Occasionally, the Santa Cruz River would flood from the Sahuarita Store intersection to Valle Verde Village Road. We would have to take Valencia Road to the upper mine road (now Mission Road), and go down Helmet Peak-Sahuarita Road to avoid the flooding. Later, when the freeway was finished, it was never a problem getting to work.

I taught in the industrial arts program from 1967 to 1974. For the first two years, 1967 to 1969, I taught woodworking, welding, crafts, and mechanical drawing classes all at the same time, in four adjoining rooms. Needless to say this was not only challenging but sometimes overwhelming. The third year, 1969 to 1970, Dave Wear was hired to teach crafts and mechanical drawing, so I could focus on teaching woodworking and welding, both of which were in the same shop. When Bill Furnas was hired in 1973 to teach welding, we were able to split some welding classes. Our programs were not only focused on developing skills in the industrial arts, but also in [peaking students'] interest in home repair, whether that meant pursuing careers in the building trades or being a hobby. The "Golden Hammer" award, a mounted Stanley bronze claw hammer, was given annually to the best industrial arts student. One student who I remember received the award was Rick Karasch, who went on to graduate from the University of Arizona and became a successful remodeling contractor in the Green Valley and Tucson area.

I was the junior varsity football coach from 1967 to 1970, and then the head football coach from 1971 to 1973. During baseball season, under head coach Wes Gentner, I was the junior varsity baseball coach from 1967 to 1978.

One of the biggest thrills I experienced at Sahuarita High, aside from my two children graduating, was in 1974 when Sahuarita High won the Arizona State Class B Baseball championship in extra innings at Arizona State University stadium. Coach Gentner and I were thrilled to take the Mustang team to Sahuarita High School's first state championship game. In 1984, the Mustang team, still led by Coach Gentner, went on to win a second state baseball championship in Class A.

The state championship game was against Benson and definitely had some odd twists. Benson, at a game played on their home field, was the only team to beat Sahuarita during the regular season. Sahuarita beat Benson when they played in Sahuarita. Ironically, these same two teams were the ones to meet for the State B championship. The game went into the sixth inning and Sahuarita was forced to pull their starting pitcher, Curtis Serr. Per the rules, a pitcher could pitch only for a total of twelve innings in a thirty-six-hour period. Serr had pitched the entire seven-inning semifinal game the day before, leaving him with only five innings in the championship game.

Sahuarita's shortstop, Ramon Orozco, came in and pitched the next four innings. In the bottom of the ninth inning, the score was tied two to two. Sahuarita was at bat and David Stout had made it to second base. Melvin Johnson was the next batter. I was standing at third base where I could see which pitch had been called in to the Benson pitcher. Melvin had been instructed that if I called out his first name, it was a fastball, and if I called out his last name, it was a curveball. It was a curveball and Melvin drove it into right field between the outfielder and the second baseman. David Stout raced home from second base and, under the errant throw of the Benson outfielder, the score was Sahuarita three to Benson's two—game over! This was Sahuarita High School's first championship win for any sport.

Five members of the championship team made the B East All-Star Team. They were catcher Ray Granillo, second base Javier Blanco, short-stop Ramon Roozca, outfielder David Stout, and pitcher Curtis Serr. Throughout the 1970s and '80s, under the coaching of Wes Gentner, Sahuarita High School was a dominant force in Southern Arizona high school baseball. They were always in the state playoffs, bringing home state titles in 1974 and 1984.

Over the years, I had the opportunity to coach many highly skilled athletes with great potential. Some who went on to college athletics were Fred Depper, who played football at Mesa Community College; Eddie Depper, who joined the Glendale Community College football team; and Curtis Serr, who continued his baseball career at Pima Community College. Others I didn't coach but remember are Marc Livingston, who went to the Naval Academy for wrestling; Michelle Williams took her track skills to West Point; and Chris Fanning was All Conference and Academic All American at New Mexico State playing baseball.

Athletic travel from the late '60s to late '90s was often to distant opponents requiring long bus rides. Over the years, Sahuarita teams traveled to Benson, Willcox, Tombstone, Safford, Thatcher, Eloy, Clifton, Coolidge, Florence, Morenci, Marana, Hayden, Ray, San Manuel, Apache Junction, Gilbert, Sells, and Ajo. At times, when we would arrive back at school after a late travel game, the bus lights illuminated the baseball fields to reveal javelinas and/or jackrabbits feeding on the grass. Thankfully, we never had a problem with javelinas, as they always ran away. One of our favorite things to do on night bus rides home from Ajo was to count the number of coyotes that ran across the road in front of the bus. Quite a few!

There were several times when we went to the baseball practice field and found a rattlesnake coiled on one of the bases. Careful removal of the snake became the order of the day. A big rock usually took care of them, but one time a baseball player, who will forever remain nameless, came flying out of the locker room door chasing another player with one of the dead snakes. We quickly put a halt to that activity, advising him that what he was doing "wasn't very smart" because rattlesnake post-mortem nerve contractions, on occasion, have been known to result in a venomous bite.

The much needed Sahuarita baseball team dugouts were built in the early '70s in a cooperative effort among Coaches Barry Callaway, Wes Gentner, and Dave Wear. It was a summer project financed by the school district.

In October of 1970, Sahuarita played an intense and memorable football game against Benson. In an unusual late-season rainstorm the day before, the Sahuarita field had been soaked. Neck and neck throughout the entire muddy game, Sahuarita's much smaller team scored a touchdown in the third quarter and missed the extra point. Benson scored a touchdown and a two-point conversion. Field goals were a rarity in Class B football in those days, so when sophomore Steve Alvarez lined up for a fourth-quarter, twenty-nine-yard field goal attempt, the Benson line hesitated, allowing the kick to sail through. Final score Sahuarita nine, Benson eight. It was the only game Benson lost in the conference that year and Coach Mike of Benson accused us of watering down the field so his players had a disadvantage. I told him it works the same way for both teams. Mike was a friend of mine, and while we rarely beat him in football, we always kicked his rear in the junior varsity baseball games. His only junior varsity baseball win was in Benson due to a terrible umpire call that ended up costing us the game. Mike never let me forget that game, just like he never forgot that field goal.

The 1987 Sahuarita Stingray swim team poses with their coaches Barry Callaway, Ron Gerhart, and Heidi Lukow. Courtesy of Barry Callaway.

In April of 1972, during an after-school junior varsity baseball game, I happened to turn back toward the high school buildings and saw flames and smoke coming from a modular science classroom. I immediately called a time out to the umpire and ran back to the administration building to call the Green Valley Fire Department. There were no cell phones in those days and the modular unit was burned to the ground by the time the fire department arrived.

Another incident that sticks in my mind was during a practice when players were running a drill to learn how to slide into third base. There were large cardboard pieces on the ground in front of the base to prevent road rash. One student tried to slide into the base, but tucked his leg and foot incorrectly. I heard a loud "pop," just like breaking a carrot in two and unfortunately, the sound had come from his leg. I carried him "fireman-style" up to the nurse's office and called an ambulance. His season was over, but thankfully he had a full recovery and was able to play the next season.

A few years after I quit coaching football, I was at a home Sahuarita football game. Sahuarita had a fourth-down situation and was forced to punt the ball. The punter for Sahuarita was a student named Jay Elam. Jay received the snap and punted the ball thirty-five yards—straight up! There was a gasp from the crowd as the ball came down and the other team recovered. Immediately, Jay's dad, who was in the stands, stood up and yelled "Whose boy is that anyway?" Needless to say, the entire crowd roared with laughter.

In the early 1970s, I worked for two summers as a school recreation director at Sahuarita Elementary School. During that same time period, I taught an adult evening woodworking class for Pima Community College at the Sahuarita High School woodshop. These classes were composed of nine female students who had been unable to take woodworking classes in high school and were anxious to get experience. After demonstrations and safety checks on the woodworking machines, they each chose a project to build.

Some chose fairly complicated items to build, giving me concern that they might struggle with completion, but to my surprise, they did quite well cutting, sanding, building, and finishing their projects. It was a treat to have students who really wanted to learn and who never needed my promptings to get to work.

Having previously completed my master's degree in counseling and guidance, in 1974, when our student population increased enough to require a second counselor, I was hired to work with the freshmen and sophomores. During this time, I was able to lead the effort in establishing a Future Farmers of America Vocational Agriculture program. The FFA Vocational program of the 1970s and 1980s was primarily a horticulture-oriented program. Darrell Brinkerhoff headed up the program for three years before he resigned and started his own business. The next agriculture teacher was Gary Campbell, who brought in a more animal, crop, and farm-mechanic oriented program. The students would compete in Agriculture Field Days against other FFA chapters judging livestock, crops, soils, bugs, and farm mechanics. Students also participated in prepared speech and parliamentary procedure competitions. Each year, the Sahuarita High School FFA invited the elementary students to "animal day," which was another event that was very successful. Some of the students in FFA were also 4-H members, but focused on other areas of interest. Sadly, the program was discontinued in the late 1980s due to budget cuts. I was disappointed when it was scuttled because the FFA program was my favorite subject and it was instrumental in keeping me in school.

I was hired as assistant swim-team coach in 1977. This was a summer program that I coached for eleven seasons, the final three of which I was head coach. I believe the Sahuarita Stingray Swimming program started in 1974 and was funded by the Sahuarita School District as a summer program. The team belonged to the Southern Arizona Aquatic Association, Santa Cruz league, and swam against teams in Tucson. In the late 1970s or early 1980s, the program broke away from the school district and became a

Sahuarita High School Mustangs, 1984-85. Courtesy of Barry Callaway.

community-funded program, paid for by parents and the community. A fee was charged per season, but no child was turned away as we had scholarships available from donations. The Stingrays never won a league championship, but the team was a consistent runner-up as reserve champion. All workouts and home meets were held at Sahuarita High School pool in the early summer mornings. The program was based on age-group swimmers: six to eight years old; nine to twelve years old; thirteen to fourteen years old; and sixteen to eighteen years old.

In 1990, after sixteen years as the freshman-sophomore counselor, I was appointed junior-senior counselor. Serving as head counselor, one of my duties was to meet with parents of eighth graders in our tuition districts of Continental, Calabasas, and Vail. I would hold evening meetings, with discussion sessions for incoming freshmen students, along with a video presentation of the programs and opportunities offered at Sahuarita High School. It was vital to our budget that we secure as many out-of-district tuition students as possible.

I spent a great deal of time with students. I remember one time when an upperclassman came into my counseling office and closed the door. His name was Cliff Honnas and he said his ambition was to become a veterinarian. Unfortunately, his advisor had told him she didn't think he was capable because of his grades and the classes he was taking. I advised him that, if he really wanted to do this, he should pursue it, no matter what roadblocks he might encounter. He was a ranch kid and, having been raised working with animals and doing things that gave him experience that most other veterinary applicants would not have, he actually had a head start. To make a long story short, this former Sahuarita student and his Sahuarita-graduate wife, Lorie, now own and operate the Texas Equine Hospital in Bryan, Texas, with seven veterinarians on staff besides Cliff. He also is a former professor of equine surgery at Texas A&M.

Robbie Carr, Flint Callaway, Jim DeVere, and Justin Rosson face John Knuer during a performance at the 1987 Sahuarita High School talent show. Courtesy of Barry Callaway.

As senior counselor, our scholarship program was also under my direction. Our goal was to provide financial assistance to graduating seniors who planned to go on to post-secondary education. Some of the contributing scholarship sponsors from the Green Valley area were Green Valley Community Church, Rotary Club, Optimist Club, Kiwanis Club, Lions Club, Lutheran Church, Valle Verde Catholic Church, Daughters of the American Revolution, the Women's Club, White Elephant resale store, and others, including the State of Arizona universities and colleges. Many of these sponsors gave multiple, renewable scholarships each year. I always tried to maintain a good working relationship with the sponsors by distributing and collecting applications on time, making sure each student wrote a thank-you letter, and staying in contact with the organizations as needed. Sponsors were invited to our annual scholarship presentation ceremony during which each was able to personally present a scholarship to the chosen winner. Our students were very fortunate to have that resource available to them. When I took early retirement in 1995, the scholarship program exceeded $100,000 available for our students, with the community of Green Valley being the major source of awards.

Between 1967 and 1995, Sahuarita High School had five students who were nominated and chosen to attend various United States military academies: Marc Livingston (Naval Academy), Michelle Williams (Army-West Point), Strom Brost (Air Force Academy), Mike Stout (West Point Prep), and Wayne Brown (Coast Guard Academy). Truco Fuhst, a Sahuarita High graduate, became a career air force officer, having matriculated through the University of Arizona ROTC program at the top of his class and moving on to the air force flight school where he again graduated at the top of his class. Tara Thacker received a scholarship to Dartmouth, where she studied pre-med.

I was honored to be able to conduct twenty-one graduation ceremonies in my tenure at Sahuarita High, with many second-generation Sahuarita High students graduating on my watch. Over the years, when second-generation students were attending Sahuarita High, I would occasionally have a conversation with a parent I had taught or had counseled in the early years of my career. More than one was known to say, "Please don't tell my kid what kind of student I was!" My standard reply was always, "Your secret is safe with me!"

My wife, Laurie Callaway, was employed as a paraprofessional at Sahuarita Elementary School for a number of years before she transferred to Sahuarita High School to assume the job of production clerk in the curriculum print shop. Many of her elementary students were now high school students, including her own two children. Needless to say, with both mom and dad working at the high school, our two children could get away with nothing. The only perk was that we were a close source of funds when needed.

In 1987, the *Tucson Citizen* newspaper chose our son, Flint Callaway, to receive the Tucson Citizen Award as the most outstanding high school senior in the Tucson area. The award was based on academic excellence and citizenship. Flint was the first student in Sahuarita High School history ever to receive this award. We were so proud of him.

During my twenty-eight years at Sahuarita High there were five different superintendents, three high school principals, and four counselors, including me. The student ratio of ethnic population was sixty percent white and forty percent Hispanic for many of those years. When I retired in 1995, the enrollment at Sahuarita High was 740 students.

Many of my teaching colleagues at Sahuarita High are deceased, with the majority of deaths due to cancer. We moved to Sahuarita in 1968 and lived in the community until 1995 when I opted for an early Arizona retirement. After thirty years of service, my wife and I moved to Colorado where I worked in the Cortez and Dolores School Districts for five years. From there, in 2000 we moved to Ellensburg, Washington, where I worked at Easton School in Easton, Washington, until 2003 when I fully retired from counseling and teaching.

~ Contributed by Barry Callaway

One-room Rural School in Twin Buttes

The following entry was written by Catherine Duffy Foy in 1939.

This past summer our little one-room rural school of Twin Buttes was honored because of the fact that its teacher was chosen by the Department of Classroom Teachers of the National Education Association to be its guest at the convention held in San Francisco this past July. I feel that the boys and

girls should share equally in this distinct honor, for they too contribute to the success of our school. Here, I may truthfully say, we live together as one large, happy, family.

And so I have been asked by Mr. Nolan D. Pulliam, executive secretary of our association, to prepare an article which deals with some phases of the one-room school.

Before I do this, I feel that I should state my philosophy with regard to my work. I am deeply interested in helping my children build happy and significant lives. I have a personal interest in every child in my room and at all times I prefer to stress the cooperative rather than the competitive. When I say that, as all teachers, I place health first, I wish it to be understood that under that main objective, I include mental as well as physical well-being. My playground, too, is a community center and here personality is developed from the first grade on.

Children from the Twin Buttes School pose for a photo during the 1942–43 school year. Most of the children are from the Laborin, Sanders (Sandez), and Vidal families. Courtesy of the Revello family.

This one-room school, which I represent, is located in Southern Arizona, twenty-six miles south of Tucson. A few years ago, Twin Buttes was a flourishing copper mining camp which paid its owners handsome profits. Today it is awaiting the time when it may again operate profitably. Since 1931 there has been a one-teacher school here.

In this community I have taught from 1923 to the present time. I have a feeling that my problems are not much different from those found in many such rural schools in Arizona. My enrollment includes Mexican children from first to eighth grades.

In making out my program for the past year, I included in it a unit of work which I think was enjoyed very much by my first and second grades and one I shall review briefly.

These children were very anxious to make and furnish a dollhouse. For this they selected an orange box and of course this led to planning for doors, windows, a roof, and even to painting. Now before its completion, my entire group, of its own accord, wished to work on some phase of this activity. The smaller children made simple furniture, clay dishes, curtains, and doll dresses; the girls of the older group made little bedspreads, tablecloths, and various articles of crocheted work. Some of the older boys, upon their own initiative, made some of the furniture. Now each day, as the work progressed, we had the opportunity for much oral English, too; we enriched our vocabulary by learning names of familiar articles in the home. Each day we made a reading lesson of four simple sentences which told of our work for that day. I placed the sentences on the board and each day I typed our written lesson—a separate page for each lesson. By the time our unit was completed, we had made our own reader; its contents were actually built upon the children's experiences. From many different sources I gathered magazines which contained pictures of rooms and homes. But this is only one part of my program.

Students at the Twin Buttes School show off a dollhouse they made. Courtesy of the Revello family.

My geography in the upper grades also centers around a unit of work. Here too, I must gather appropriate reading material to carry on successfully. The homes in the district do not have much reading material for children.

I believe in the three Rs! Children must know how to write and must master the fundamentals in arithmetic. And here, I want to say that I know children are persons— each one is different from the other. Perhaps some do not master all, but I feel it is my duty to discover any such cases that arise. I want my children to know how to read so that their reading will be of real value to them whether they read for recreation or information. And here, may I say that I spend part of my time on Saturdays gathering suitable books and magazines for my reading table. I want the small children to read a great deal of very simple supplementary reading matter.

Another activity which we carried out was our school lunch. This gave opportunity for an emphasis on cleanliness, not only of the dishes and the cooking equipment, but the personal as well. These children learned to serve a simple meal correctly and here entered the subtle teaching of table manners. Unfortunately, this project did not continue throughout the year owing to the expense entailed. (I was paying for the food.)

We have what I like to term meaningful programs in Twin Buttes. In our little plays, children acquaint themselves with stories of good citizenship, sportsmanship, loyalty, honesty, and fair dealings. Perhaps they dramatize a reading lesson and to these affairs our parents are invited. I make a special effort to have every child responsible for some part of the program.

At the present time there seems to be a desire to consolidate all one-room rural schools into a larger unit. The question which clamors for answers is, "Should the one- and two-room rural schools be consolidated?"

To that question I would answer most emphatically, "nothing"—especially in a sparsely settled district where there are children not too far removed from the school. We do have an excellent system of paved and graded highways of which Arizona can rightfully boast, but the fact remains that many of the outlying school districts do not have adequate roads for transportation. This fact, coupled with the great distance a school bus must travel, increases the transportation cost to a marked degree.

Another question which often arises is, "To what extent may a rural teacher influence the school and the community?" In answer, I would say that a teacher's sympathy, influence, and understanding can be potent. Especially if she is one of long tenure, she knows the parents intimately and is aware of the children's home environment, and in many cases of their hereditary influences. If I may refer to my personal experience in the Twin Buttes School where I have taught for many years, I know it to be a fact that the children whom I have taught still come to me for advice and guidance in regard to their problems which may be anything from marital to looking for a job.

I think the one-room rural teacher has a wonderful opportunity for her creating a real home-like situation with a group of children ranging from six to fifteen years of age. The older ones become interested in the problems of the younger ones and vice versa. The whole group can work together toward a common end. The rural child is entitled to inspirational leadership, which only a real teacher can give.

Before closing, I would like to point out a few of the things which, if brought about, will make for better rural schools.

First, there should be new standards for buildings and the equipment necessary for instruction.

Second, if supervision, and I mean the supervisor, not in the capacity of a critic but rather a helping teacher, is good for a city school, why is it not valuable in a rural district?

Third, there should be help given to teachers in directing them to the acquisition of desirable materials in connection with their work.

Fourth, there must be a better salary for the rural teacher than we have at present.

I feel that the rural school is one of our most difficult educational situations, and if our American system of public education considers all the children of the United States, it must continue to improve the rural school.

~ Catherine Duffy Foy, 1939

Ron Gerhart's Career in Sahuarita

1. Tucson Unified School District (TUSD): 1967–70
2. Sahuarita Elementary School: 1970–78
3. Sahuarita Junior High School: 1978–92
4. Sahuarita High School: 1992–2000

I started my career as a fifth-grade teacher at Mary Lynn Elementary School in TUSD after graduating from the University of Arizona in 1967.

After completing my first teaching position in 1970, I was contacted by a friend who worked at

Kiki Ochart and Ron Gerhart stand on the stairs of the Sahuarita Junior High School with the boys' basketball team. Courtesy of Oscar Gomez.

Sahuarita Elementary. She was leaving to raise her family, so I went to an interview with John Zuchowski and accepted a fifth-grade position at Sahuarita Elementary.

In 1978, I was being considered for a move to Sahuarita Junior High School. After being accepted, I was offered a position to team teach a sixth-grade class with Mrs. Brewster to prepare them for middle school in the same room. It was definitely a unique experience!

When I moved to Sahuarita Junior High School, I began teaching sixth-grade math. Not only did I teach math, but I became involved in coaching. I was able to help coach boys' basketball with Kiki Ochart, girls' volleyball with Gayle Hobrock, and boys' and girls' track with, I believe, Dave Green. During the summer, I would teach summer school as needed and coach the Sahuarita Stingrays swim team with Heidi Lukow.

I remember late-afternoon away games at places like Tombstone, Benson, Safford, and Nogales, returning back to campus around midnight in some cases. Cell phones were not prevalent in those days, so we had to do our best to meet the projected hour of return. Most parents were very patient, but there was an occasional parent for whom we had to wait. Amazingly, the students always made it to school the next day.

Those were the most amazing and satisfactory years of my career. Not only did I make lasting friendships, but each day was filled with the typical drama, sadness, and happiness of middle school students. I honestly looked forward to arriving at school each day and hoping I was able to make a difference in some way!

In 1992, I accepted the position of assistant principal at Sahuarita High School. Other than the usual responsibilities of an assistant principal, I was very pleased to become involved with the grad-night experience. The committee was incredible in organizing activities, food, music, and prizes for the evening. The biggest prize would be a car to give away to some lucky senior. Each of these evenings were magical in their own way and, I'm sure, have been remembered by many students who graduated from Sahuarita High School.

After my daughter graduated from Sahuarita High School in 1999, I remained one more year and left in 2000 to accept a counseling position at Amphitheater High School until my retirement in 2016.

~ Contributed by Ronald Gerhart

Recollections of Oscar Gomez, Teacher

I attended the Sahuarita Junior High School dedication ceremony in the spring of 1971. I was fascinated by the circular layout with eight classrooms opening to a central library. In August of 1972, I began teaching eighth-grade social studies and Spanish at Sahuarita Junior High School. A few years later, I requested to teach seventh-grade geography. My teaching schedule became two classes of social studies for eighth graders, two classes of geography for seventh graders, and two classes of Spanish. In the beginning, the school accommodated only seventh and eighth grades. The total student population consisted of one hundred and fifty students. Frequently, the physical-education teacher would ask if he could combine two classes so he could conduct large group activities. The junior high school shared the playground with the elementary school.

The teaching staff consisted of twelve to fourteen teachers. All of the core subjects were taught in classrooms around the library. Approximately three years later, the school added sixth-grade students. The classrooms did not have rectangular walls. An elementary school teacher once came into my room and asked, "Where is the front of the classroom?"

Oscar Gomez teaching in his classroom at Sahuarita Junior High School. Courtesy of Oscar Gomez.

In 1974, I contacted the YMCA-Knothole University of Arizona football coordinator about taking students to the University of Arizona football games. The gentleman encouraged me to do so. The coordinator explained to me that many years earlier, a teacher from Sahuarita had taken students to football games. I explained to him that the individual was Mr. Porter Wilson, and I was one of the many students who participated in the trips. I expressed to the YMCA coordinator that Porter Wilson had been my sixth and seventh grade teacher.

Volunteer chaperones and bus drivers were never an issue for the next sixteen years. On every trip, forty to sixty students would sign up to attend. I met the students at the middle school on game nights. I had a list and gave instructions to all of the students as to what to expect and any circumstances that might occur. The most important rule was they were not to become separated as we were leaving the stadium. If they became separated, they were to return to the stadium and stand by a huge eucalyptus tree on the southwest end of the stadium. On one occasion, I discovered that a student was missing. I went to the tree and, much to my delight, there he was, waiting for me. He was the only one who ever became separated. Many years later, we crossed paths. He was wearing a Pima County sheriff's uniform! I shall not mention his name, but I could not resist asking, "Aren't you the one who waited for me by the tree?"

One night as students were debarking from a very full bus, a parent commented to me, "Oscar, you should get a medal for bravery or stupidity! There is no way I would take fifty students to a University of Arizona game." A fellow teacher met a

Oscar Gomez leading students out of the gym on his first day teaching at the Sahuarita Elementary School. Courtesy of Oscar Gomez.

former student from the 1970s. He was at a University of Arizona game with his young son. The teacher asked about driving all the way from Phoenix just to watch a University of Arizona football game. The ex-student responded, "I am a University of Arizona graduate and I got hooked when Mr. Gomez brought us to football games!" These trips were terminated in the 1980s when the district had to cut many activities due to budget constraints. I simply could not ask students to bear the expense of the field trips.

An exciting day at the Sahuarita Junior High School in the classroom of Oscar Gomez. The entrance to the library is directly behind Oscar. Courtesy of Oscar Gomez.

In later years, many younger brothers and sisters would inquire about attending football games. They wanted to go because they had heard about how much fun the students had experienced.

In 1977, I mentioned to the principal my interest in being the student council adviser. The following year Mr. Charles Oldham offered me the extra-curricular activity. It became a large part of my workday. Student council officers attended the Arizona Association of Junior High Student Council Leadership camp every summer. I volunteered as a camp counselor and, later on, I served on the board as the southern region representative. The middle school held regional student council workshops. High school students helped tremendously by presenting small workshops on various student council activities. Every year a student council convention was held and schools throughout the state shared successful activities. One year the convention was held in the district auditorium.

Student council activities were well attended because the district had activity buses to run students home at 5:00 p.m. It meant we could plan two-hour activities. Every student had a ride home!

Some of the most popular student council activities included:

Dances—School dances were held in the science room the first few years. When the cafeteria was built, we were allowed to use that facility. The student council members brought records and used a record player. Quickly, we progressed to hiring a DJ. The students' favorite was Windy City DJ. As the students moved on to high school, they took their preferences with them. Soon thereafter, Windy City DJ was also playing at high school activities.

Carnivals—Carnivals were held often. Some were scheduled during the school day but most were after school. Teachers made them a success by their willingness to stay after school to sponsor games and activities. Opportunities to buy food were provided at just about all after-school activities. It was almost a requirement because some middle school students did not get home until very late. The students who lived in Arivaca did not get home until after 6:00 p.m. Students loved the dunking machine. The line was long, especially when Mr. Charles Oldham volunteered to get up on the tank.

Birthday parties—This activity was presented three times a year. All students were allowed to participate during their birthday sessions. A large birthday cake was provided. Games were held that definitely appealed to students. One

Students giving Mr. Gomez a soaking at the Sahuarita Junior High School. Courtesy of Oscar Gomez.

favorite was to find a pack of gum in a bowl full of whipped cream. Biting an apple on a string, a water balloon toss, a peanut race, a ping-pong ball march, and an egg toss were always included. The boys complained to me about the water balloon toss being unfair because the balloons were always on the girls' side of the line. If the boys wanted to have an opportunity to throw a balloon, they first had to catch one thrown by the girls.

Movies—After school, movies were shown in the auditorium about three times a year. Students were unhappy not because of the movies selected, but because we were not allowed to sell food on the premises.

Later, we moved this activity to the middle school building. It worked out well because of the VHS system in the library. Students were never charged to attend. Money was generated from selling hot dogs, nachos, chips, candy, sodas, and popcorn. Our only limitation was that the movies had to be less than two hours long. Students had to be out before the activity buses left.

Oscar joins the Sahuarita Junior High School cheer-leaders at a school party in the library. Courtesy of Oscar Gomez.

Student council was able to sponsor some activities during the school day. Annually a Halloween costume contest and a bulletin board holiday contest were included. Lunchtime activities were common. For quite a while, break dancing was fun to watch. The radio system played music. Students were always volunteering to handle the chores.

Raggedy Andy celebrates Halloween with the Sahuarita Junior High students. Courtesy of Oscar Gomez.

The biggest fundraiser for the student council was a magazine sale. This activity raised enough money to pay for the officers' leadership camp expenses, fund the yearbook, and buy toys for the Christmas toy drive. The local Walmart always helped with a large discount. Monies spent had to be accounted for to the district office. Regular student council meetings were held and minutes were written up to show the authorization for monies spent.

Food drives were held every Thanksgiving. Originally, the donated food was given to the Community Food Bank in Green Valley. Later we determined that the high school student council was sponsoring turkey boxes at Christmas time, but they had difficulty coming up with nonperishable items. Soon we started taking the middle school food donation items to the high school.

The student council made visits to a nursing home in Green Valley, but they were not just limited to student council members. Mr. Oldham agreed to let us go there twice a month—once during the school day, and then once after school. The district supported us by providing transportation. It was encouraging to me to watch the response from students interacting with senior citizens. Later on, some students told me that they had started going there on their own time.

Soon student council members thought of having "doughnut days" before school and "pizza days" at lunch. The details were worked out and presented to Mr. Oldham. The idea was approved and put into motion. Once a month, treats from Dunkin' Donuts were brought to school. Peter Piper Pizza was sold every other

Sahuarita Junior High School student council float, being pulled by Oscar Gomez in the White Elephant Parade. Courtesy of Oscar Gomez

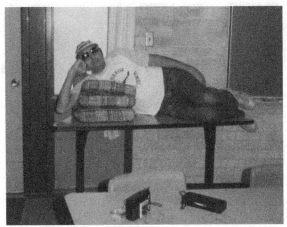

Oscar chilling after a long day of work at Sahuarita Junior High School. Courtesy of Oscar Gomez.

month. Everything went well until, a few years later, when the idea was taken to the high school. It so happened that both schools had pizzas at lunch on the same day! Very few students ate in the cafeteria. The manager was not forewarned and prepared lunches as usual. He blew up! That was the last time pizzas were brought to both schools on the same day.

In the early 1980s, I was asked to apply for a position as assistant principal in Chandler. During a Sahuarita High School graduation, sitting next to a dear and longtime friend, I explained to her about the opportunity that had been offered to me. Very seriously, she turned around, stared straight at me, and with a stern tone said, "You can't leave, you haven't taught my daughter yet!"

My twenty-one years at Sahuarita Junior High School were memorable. I left Sahuarita Junior High School in June 1993 to become a school administrator in another school district. I was close to retirement and had to consider my future. I departed with many regrets but wherever I went, Sahuarita followed me. I encountered new teachers who also knew Sahuarita families and friends. The children of students I taught continue to approach me and remind me that I was their parents' teacher.

I always felt honored and privileged to work at Sahuarita Junior High School because of the opportunities, trust, and support given to me by my fellow teachers and the school administration. I consider my time at the middle school a joy because I grew up in the area and had the honor of teaching the children of family friends. Thankfully, my family supported my endeavors.

~ Contributed by Oscar A. Gomez

Bob and Nita Ham

Bob and Nita Ham posing for their annual school photos. Courtesy of Garrett and Kris Ham.

Bob and Nita Ham were exceptional educators, champions of children, and well respected in the community. As a team, they had a huge effect on Sahuarita.

Bob was born in Chambersburg, Illinois, which is a very small town in the southern part of that state. He had a younger brother, Larry. The family moved to the Chicago suburb of Des Plaines when Bob was six. With the exception of two years during World War II, when his parents went to Portland, Oregon, to work in the shipyards, Des Plaines was home.

In Des Plaines, Bob's mother worked as a bookkeeper. His father worked as a carpenter and later as the superintendent of the local water plant.

Bob was a dedicated student at Main High School. He especially enjoyed English and appreciated a challenging teacher. He was a dutiful son, often holding down the home front for his busy parents.

After receiving his bachelor's degree from Cornell College, Bob joined the army. While in the service, Bob worked as a postman. After his service in the army, Bob received his master's in education from the University of Illinois.

Nita was born in Tucson, Arizona, at St. Mary's Hospital. Her parents lived in Marana at the time. When she was four, her family moved to a farm north of Coolidge where the house they lived in had been a stagecoach stop. Her parents remodeled it into a home for their five children. Her father farmed cotton and was a cattle rancher.

Nita used to try her hand at picking cotton with the migrant workers and Native Americans who worked on the farm. She also loved to run her own backyard school with the children of these families.

While Nita loved to ride horses, tag along with her dad to the corrals and fields, and help with the branding chores, her dad would have preferred she stay in the house helping her mom with the household chores!

Bob Ham working on art projects with children. Courtesy of Garrett and Kris Ham.

Early years were filled with church, choir, and Girl Scouts. Later, drama, friends, journalism, swimming, and Rainbow for Girls kept her busy. After high school Nita received her bachelor's in education degree from Arizona State University.

Bob and Nita met as first-year teachers in Pomona, California, in 1958. Bob started out in sixth grade and Nita in fourth. They ran around with a group of crazy young people who liked to water ski and snow ski. Nita kept trying to fix Bob up with her roommate.

After teaching in Pomona for two years, Bob accepted a job teaching at the Department of Defense Dependents' School in Ingrandes, France. As Bob was leaving Pomona, he and Nita took a closer look at their own relationship. Bob invited Nita to spend some time in Des Plaines and meet his family. Nita was working on her master's at Arizona State University that summer but found time for a visit. They decided to marry in France in December if Nita could be released from her teaching contract.

Nita flew to France and Bob and Nita were married twice, once in a local courthouse in French and later in the base chapel in English. They honeymooned in Majorca, Spain.

Nita soon got a job teaching second grade at the Dependents' School where Bob taught fifth grade. They spent their weekends traveling to Paris, Italy, Germany, Holland, and Switzerland.

Nita Ham working on art projects with children. Courtesy of Garrett and Kris Ham.

They decided to return to the United States, as their first child was well on his way by the end of the school year. They traveled to England and Scotland before returning to Illinois for a homecoming and wedding shower where Nita, seven months pregnant, was introduced as Bob's bride!

Upon their return to the United States, Bob returned to teaching at the previous school in Pomona. Nita stayed home and completed her master's in education from Arizona State University one week before their first child arrived.

They stayed in Pomona for ten years. Bob was a district "helping teacher" for two years and even spent one year teaching kindergarten. Nita started doing day care in their home, which provided extra income, satisfied her yearning to teach, and allowed her to stay home with their three children while they were young.

Having grown tired of the smog and congestion in southern California, they started looking for a better environment in which to live and raise their family. Nita's brother was friends with a Sahuarita School District Board member who mentioned that Sahuarita was looking for first-grade teachers. So, in 1971, the family moved to Sahuarita and Bob and Nita started their twenty-year teaching careers at Sahuarita Elementary School. At first, Bob was told that husbands and wives couldn't teach in the same school, so Nita volunteered and subbed until a permanent sub was needed. Rules changed and Nita got a permanent teaching job the next year. It was a real family affair at Sahuarita Elementary with Bob and Nita teaching and their older children in the third and fourth grades and their youngest starting kindergarten at Sahuarita. Not exactly ideal for three children to endure growing up right under their parent's eyes! But they turned out to be super kids, so it didn't hurt.

Bob and Nita Ham standing on their back patio. Courtesy of Garrett and Kris Ham.

These years were busy with scouts, swim team, 4-H, FFA, Optimist Club, and many educational and recreational activities. Bob and Nita taught at Sahuarita Elementary for over twenty years, retiring in 1994.

During his career at Sahuarita, Bob was a first- and second-grade teacher because he thought that was when many children had their "aha" moments and he could have the biggest impact. Nita taught fourth grade and was renowned for the program she developed to teach kids about Arizona history and Native Indian culture that involved an annual overnight adventure camp at the Tumacacori Mission. It was a huge job and took great dedication and stamina to see it through from beginning to end. It was a family commitment, with Bob as her right hand and with help from their kids and friends.

In retirement, Bob and Nita enjoyed dancing, traveling, playing canasta, and watching their grandchildren grow up. While Bob enjoyed working in his yard, working on pinecone and seed-pod wreaths and crosses was Nita's passion. She had her family and friends trained to always be on the lookout for material for her crafts. Money from the sale of her wreaths and crosses went to the Sahuarita Elementary School for children in need.

Nita passed away in 2014 and Bob in 2018. A scholarship fund has been established in their honor with the Sahuarita Educational Enrichment Foundation.

~ Contributed by Garrett and Kris Ham

Donald Honnas Memorial Page, Representing Arivaca and Sopori

Arivaca cattle rancher Donald Honnas was a member of the school board of Sopori School District in the transition period between self-governance and the merger into the Sahuarita School District. Don was elected to the school board of Sopori District No. 49 in 1961, seven years after the Arivaca District had merged with Sopori. He served from 1961 until he was elected to the Sahuarita District School Board in 1969. He retired from Sahuarita District in 1972.

Don was raised in the Sonoita area where his family had lived since the late 1880s. His parents, Cecil and Lottie Honnas, had a cattle ranch there and did whatever it took to make a go of things. His mother was a schoolteacher and instilled the importance of education in her boys.

Don married Carolyn Pine, who had lived most of her life in Sonoita. But she had a connection to Sahuarita—her step great-grandfather John K. Brown built the Sahuarita School, which had been founded by his wife. Carolyn's step-grandfather, John S. Brown, raised cattle in Sahuarita. Her father, Kenneth Pine, was from the Box Canyon area.

In 1961, Don's parents bought the Jarillas Ranch south of Arivaca and Don and his brother Ray brought their families to live there. Soon Ray had sold out, but Don built a house just west of Arivaca on a hill facing Baboquivari Peak. Don was always a community minded person and would help anyone who needed it, dropping whatever he was doing to help them deliver a calf or drive a sick person to the hospital. He donated the land for First Baptist Church. Right away he began serving on the Sopori School board with fellow rancher Fred Boice.

At that time, Sopori School had two rooms and children were bused fifteen miles over a dirt road from Arivaca. Other children were bused from Arivaca Junction, also known as Kinsley's ranch, seven miles to Sopori School. There were only

Don Honnas smiling for the camera. Courtesy of Mary Kasulaitis.

a few other children who lived on nearby ranches. Don and Carolyn had three children: Debra, Jacqueline, and Cliff, who attended the Sopori and Sahuarita schools. Sopori School had been built in 1927 by rancher Tomás Bustamante who donated the land. It had a minimal footprint of land (two acres) with barely enough playground area for the twenty to thirty children who usually attended it. Attached was a teacherage with a kitchen, bedroom, and large living room, suitable for a couple or one teacher.

Don Honnas signing his book at the Arivaca Library. Courtesy of Mary Kasulaitis.

Sometimes teachers lived elsewhere. The school board had to worry about the students, parents, and the school facility as well as the teachers (and substitutes), teacherage, buses, and bus drivers. In this rural area, having a minimum number of students was always an issue, for that was what had closed the Arivaca school. According to former Sopori teacher Ann Boice, there is an optimum number that will benefit the students' social and educational development. Attendance varied annually, and at one point in the 1960s a separate portable building was added. Sopori School closed in 1970 and, as Debra Honnas Wehrman remembers, she went to Sahuarita Junior High school in the eighth grade. She and her sister and brother went on to graduate from Sahuarita High School, riding the bus from Arivaca to Sahuarita every day, some forty-five miles one way. By 1973, Arivaca Road was finally paved.

Don was not separated by bureaucracy from budgets, textbooks, buses that didn't run, teachers who were sick, parents with demands, or heating systems that went down. The school board was on the front line, and both Don and Fred knew what it was like to have children at Sopori, and for children to ride the bus thirty miles a day, or more, on a dirt road. Then when it was time for them to go to high school, a family decision had to be made: would they drive or ride a public bus to Tucson? Which high school would they attend, Pueblo or Sunnyside? Would they board with a family (related or not) in Tucson, or in another town that had a high school? Could they afford boarding school? Until Sahuarita High School was built, these were always issues. Even then, the Arivaca children were and are still to this day bused the forty-five miles to Sahuarita.

Don Honnas at the book-signing event. Courtesy of Mary Kasulaitis.

When the opportunity came, in the late 1960s, to consider merging Sopori School District with Sahuarita, it was a move that could not be passed up. At the time, Sahuarita was growing in population and there was planning in the works to build a school at the south end of the district at Arivaca Junction, soon to be known as Lakewood Estates. The school district authorities could not ignore the merits of having lower taxes due to the increase in Sahuarita's tax base from the large farms and mines that had been established in the Santa Cruz Valley. But Sopori District could bring into Sahuarita District a number of students, which it would need. The Green Valley area was not yet very developed. The person who initiated this merger was Pima County Superintendent of Schools, Florence Reece, a hands-on official who would visit all the little districts at least annually. She knew Don and Fred, the teachers, and even many of the parents. Having taught in country schools for many years, she realized the benefits of consolidation for the children. But in the first bond issue in March 1967, the Sahuarita improvements were voted down and the merger with Sopori not approved. So they tried again, and later that year the Sopori district was annexed, adding 375 square miles to the Sahuarita district. In 1970, a bond issue was finally approved, enabling the construction of the new Sopori School at Amado as well as the Sahuarita Junior High School.

In 1969, Don Honnas ran for the Sahuarita School Board and won over two other candidates in the largest voter turnout ever. In the three years he served, he saw the new Sopori School constructed and the old one removed from service. He resigned in 1972 when he found that driving home at night after a meeting was too much and the curves on the Arivaca road too dangerous. That did not stop him from his church and community efforts; it just kept them closer to home.

In 2001, after forty years of ranching, Don and his wife Carolyn sold their Pocahonnas Ranch in Arivaca and retired to Sahuarita, where Carolyn still lives. In 2008, Don Honnas published a book of stories about his life in Sonoita and Arivaca, including the memorable events that took place in that town from the 1960s on. Some of those stories exist nowhere else in publication except in newspaper articles, but Don always kept notes of anything interesting. Many stories are about the beloved animals on his ranch: cattle, horses, dogs, and cats. Don passed away on August 12, 2020, at the age of 86.

~ Contributed by Mary N. Kasulaitis

NOTES

Arizona Daily Star and *Tucson Citizen* newspapers
Honnas, Don. *Happenings on the Pocahonnas: a Southern Arizona Cattle Ranch*. 2008.
Interviews with Carolyn Honnas, Debra Honnas Wehrman, Ann Boice, Fred Boice, and Charles Oldham

Madeheim Memories of Sahuarita High School: May 1965–May 1984

In May of 1965, I graduated from the University of Arizona with a Bachelor of Arts degree in education with an emphasis in Spanish and secondary education. Now I was ready for my first job teaching high school Spanish!

Surprisingly, I received a call from Sahuarita two weeks later. Paul Frick, the district superintendent, wanted to talk with me about a teaching position . . . in the elementary school! Huh?

Mr. Frick explained that a new high school was being built to the east of the existing K–8 elementary school. The students in grade nine were going to remain at Sahuarita for the coming school year and then move into the new high school the following year along with students in grades ten through twelve, who were currently attending Pueblo and Sunnyside High Schools.

I guess Mr. Frick really wanted me to stay and so I was hired to teach Spanish to grades one through nine at the elementary school until the high school was completed. But I had a secondary teaching certificate! This was a challenge! Maybe this was not on the "up and up" as far as Arizona teaching certification regulations were concerned, but if Sahuarita wanted me, I was in. I had to develop lessons for nine grade levels and then plan schedules for each class. I also needed lessons for both the non-Spanish-speaking and native Spanish-speaking kids! *Ay de mí!* As I had no experience teaching elementary kids, I spent the summer asking little kids "How old are you?" and "What kind of games do you like?" I got some strange looks from parents, but they would eventually decide that I was harmless.

So, OK, I was young, naive, and yes, pretty darned motivated and so I tackled the assignment. My office was in the elementary school library and I shared space with Lavone Baker, the librarian. My desk faced a large window with a view into the adjoining AV room. Mr. Lockett was the AV coordinator. Thanks to him I learned all about Wollensak tape recorders, filmstrips, film, and overhead projectors, as well as ditto machines (copiers that produced alcohol-scented copies that the students loved to smell!), "Language Masters," and more—all now considered "vintage."

Each school day I trucked materials from one room to another—games, bouncing balls, and Velcro story boards for the younger kids and Spanish literature and grammar books for the older kids (some games, too).

I remember that the first-grade teacher was very young, cute, and had a red Mustang (convertible, I think). I was impressed! I'll probably remember her name tomorrow—or next month! Mrs. Higgins was the second-grade teacher; Mrs. Iola Dudgeon was the third-grade teacher (little Todd used to hide under her desk); Chuck Gatterer taught fifth grade; Mrs. Nastre (sp?) was the sixth-grade teacher; and Porter Wilson, seventh grade. I don't remember who the fourth- or eighth-grade teachers were. They were memorable I'm sure, but just aren't in my senior citizen memory bank.

The elementary faculty referred to the new high school under construction as "the great Taj Mahal to the east." Just a bit of jealousy for funneling district funds? Because of taxes from the mines, the Sahuarita District was one of the richest districts in Arizona with the highest-paying salaries. Those were the days!

Teachers were required within five years of receiving their bachelor's degrees to either complete an additional thirty units of college credit beyond the bachelor's or to earn master's degrees. Since thirty units was basically the equivalent of a master's degree, most of us opted for the master's degree. Chuck Gatterer and I carpooled to the University of Arizona for several summers to complete our master's degrees in education. I enjoyed his dry humor and sharp wit. He had coined the sobriquet "the great Taj Mahal to the east" for the high school and I was considered a bit of a traitor for moving over there to teach. I was living with my parents in one of the original apartments facing the highway in Green Valley. And that was pretty much all that was there—apartments, Safeway, a gas station (still there), and a bank.

I kept a horse named Two Bits at the Green Valley Stables to the west of the Nogales Highway on

Continental Road. One afternoon after working Two Bits, I went shopping at Safeway, still in my riding gear—chaps, boots, and hat. A first grader was in the store with her mother. She stopped when she saw me and said, "Look, mom. I think that's my Spanish teacher. Do teachers do grocery shopping?" and "She looks like a cowboy." I gained some type of reputation, I guess.

Carol Madeheim in 1978.
Courtesy of Carol Madeheim.

I also taught evening Spanish classes for adults. Misters Elam, McGee, and Harris were particularly memorable. I was the newbie just out of college. They had all the Spanish regional and local idioms down pat and enjoyed quizzing me on their meanings "What's a *papalote*? A kite? No! Around here it's a windmill!" *Ja, ja.* So as I taught, I learned too.

Pima cotton fields (replaced by pecans) grew to the east and south of Sahuarita. The bar and grill and One Stop Market were on the corner of Sahuarita Road and the Nogales Highway. Kids used to hang out there before and after school. The railroad tracks were just south of there and were the site of several accidents before railroad crossing lights were finally installed. (I understand that accidents still occur anyway.)

Several families lived in the housing provided for migrants (the "cotton camp") and worked picking the cotton. Kids from there also attended Sahuarita Elementary School. It was a challenge to help these kids keep up with their education when their families continually moved following the harvesting of seasonal crops.

Each morning, elementary school faculty met informally to review some individual student's progress—or lack of it. We tried to share ideas on ways to assist struggling students or to encourage those who were doing well. We really enjoyed this. The meeting was informal rather than "required" but was borne of our real desire to help.

Teaching the seventh and eighth graders was a challenge too. Those middle school years are unique. Porter Wilson (seventh grade) always encouraged me to hang in there and did a good job of settling his kids before I came in for the Spanish lesson. Some of the other teachers saw Spanish time as their time-out—a few even using it as time out of their rooms!

Being the oldest kids in the elementary school, the eighth graders thought they were pretty tough. One afternoon, a big kid, Alex, mouthed off and left the room. I followed him into the boys' restroom. "Miss, you can't come in here!" "Well, I just did!" I grabbed his arm, pulled it up behind his back and marched him back into class. What a rep I got then. I was the "teacher who grabbed Alex in the boys' restroom" and "she knows karate so watch out." He was very sweet ever afterwards. No way could a teacher touch a kid nowadays or even follow them into the opposite-sex restroom.

I survived that first year of teaching and thought that I had really paid my debt to society. Little did I know that I would spend the next eighteen-plus years teaching in the high school.

The following year I continued teaching Spanish to the seventh and eighth grades in the elementary school and to grades nine through twelve in the new high school. For Spanish levels one through four, there was different curricula for the non-Spanish speaking and native Spanish speaking kids. It was a definite challenge to develop continuity from one Spanish level to the next across different grade levels. I don't think I ever did this successfully. Perhaps it just couldn't be done.

The first day of high school Spanish classes, I geared up to welcome the "kids." Gee, they were big kids and some were even my contemporaries. José C. greeted me with "Mi abuelo colgó los tenis y tengo sueño y voy a planchar la oreja." Huh? What? "My grandfather hung up his tennis shoes and I'm tired and I'm going to press my ear"? This wasn't the Spanish I had learned. (Translation: "My grandfather died and I'm tired and I'm going to lie down.")

I learned a lot from the kids. Part of the individualized curriculum for the Spanish-speaking kids was the development of a dictionary of local idioms. It was fun and educational for both me and the students and gave validity to their local idioms and in some cases even archaic Spanish. One of many examples is saying "pos" instead of modern Spanish "pues," the former of which is fifteenth-century Spanish!

High school kids traveled from Arivaca and at times missed school due to floods (and sometimes for other questionable reasons). "But Miss, we couldn't get to the bus. The water was too deep!" Yeah. Sure. And the dog ate my homework.

The Halfway Station—located halfway between Tucson and Nogales—was a favorite for its tasty tacos and carne asada. On weekends students regularly attended dances and quinceañeras (fifteen-year-old girls' coming out celebrations) and on Mondays they would recount the exciting times there (fights frequently broke out!).

We had a Spanish club and practiced Mexican dances and songs at club meetings. The kids performed several times for school Christmas celebrations. They were proud of their achievements performing Mexican regional dances and songs and dressing up in traditional charro and china poblana outfits.

Each year the club made a trip to Tumacacori for the Christmas season's "Fiesta de Tumacacori." We set up a booth to raise money for the club. Nancy Williams (art teacher) and I loaded up a big white van to haul all the materials for the Art and Spanish Clubs' booths. The smell of the mesquite fires and the club girls dressed in their finest were always part of the festive atmosphere.

It was usually pretty cool in December at Tumacacori—and so, one year, we decided to sell hot chocolate at our booth. Oh yeah! This would be a good money maker! Of course, the best laid plans . . . It turned out to be eighty degrees that day! Boy, did the kids work hard to sell that hot chocolate.

Jim Madeheim smiling for his photo in 1978. Courtesy of Carol Madeheim.

During my first year as the Spanish club sponsor, we sold tamales for Christmas. The Hispanic girls all pitched in to make them. We used Wanda Miller's home economics room. The girls were very experienced at preparing Mexican food and really took over the whole project. Thank goodness they did, because I had never prepared even one tamal (loved eating them, though!). They proceeded to put a whole green olive, pit included, in each tamal. I questioned the wisdom of doing this (broken teeth!) but they knew their traditions— "Oh, Miss. We always put olives in the tamales!" Families who knew this had no problem with the olives and pits and, in fact, expected them; others not so knowledgeable complained about the hard pits and olives. However, no broken teeth were reported. But those tamales were authentic!

Individualized instruction was "in" during the '60s and the high school faculty was involved in developing instructional packets that could be used for individuals and groups of students. "Learning contracts" were a part of this; goals and objectives were developed to be met for each student and each level. For several summers, teachers were paid to develop high school curriculum with individualized goals and objectives. For classes in history, English, etc., this was a relatively attainable goal, but you can imagine the difficulty in developing individualized lessons for four levels of Spanish, plus one track for the non-Spanish speaking kids and another for the Spanish-speaking kids? Then we added an English as a Second Language (ESL) class and more levels within that. I spent my time orchestrating and monitoring learning centers and moved from one to another as the kids listened to audio tapes, watched filmstrips, and used the Language Master. It used recordable cards with two tracks—one with my pronunciation of words and phrases and the second for the students to record theirs.

When the junior high was added, Oscar Gomez taught Spanish. Once again we tackled the challenge of providing credit for junior-high Spanish as the students moved into ninth grade. This necessitated providing another intermediate level of Spanish, again for both non-Spanish speaking and native Spanish-speaking students. We really needed another Spanish teacher or two!

I was still teaching Spanish classes two nights a week for the adults in the community. I also taught a guitar class for Pima Community College one night a week using the high school classroom. The school was compensated by Pima for the use of the classroom.

My favorite part of the week was "Project Day." This was one way I discovered that I could individualize lessons. On Fridays, individual students or small groups of students worked on projects of interest to them related to the Spanish language and culture. Kids really enjoyed this, and I had time to work with them one-on-one. We had some really "cool" projects, from making piñatas, to learning the history of Padre Kino and the Spanish missions, exploring the Anza Trail, making models of missions, and painting Spanish-themed murals on the classroom walls. (We had to get permission from the principal for the latter.) I think the murals were painted over after I left and the classroom use changed. Taking photos wasn't done as easily or commonly as it is now, so, sadly, there are no records of the students' budding talents.

Thinking of the walls reminds me of the building's ceilings. They were coated in asbestos for sound control. The teachers joked about brushing off the desks each morning before the kids arrived. The asbestos fell each night like snow (or dandruff) onto the desks. After several years, the District decided that the asbestos should be removed. A hazmat team fully attired in protective gear came to do the removal. Bemused teachers were asked to stay outside their rooms when the teams were working; then, when the hazmat teams were finished, we could come back to work.

Mine tailings from the Anaconda (later renamed Anamax) copper mines regularly blew over the school on windy days. One day it was particularly bad and the students were sent home. The teachers had to stay and continue working. Amazing that between breathing the tailings dust and asbestos we still had working lungs!

Students taking Spanish who had averages of As and Bs were rewarded by taking a school bus field trip to Nogales, Mexico, for shopping and lunch, which they had to order in Spanish. They were divided into groups of five with a parent in charge of each group. One year, as we were crossing back into the U.S., the border patrol stopped the bus and boarded carrying buckets. Oh my! Having lots of experience with high school kids, they were ready to confiscate contraband fireworks. One of the girls called me back to where she was sitting and told me that one of the boys (José C.) had asked her to put his fireworks in her purse. She asked if I thought she should turn in the fireworks. I told her it would probably be a good idea. Other kids were muttering to each other and wouldn't you know, the border patrol guys came away with two large buckets filled with fireworks. Sneaky kids! I sure hoped Mr. Kelly (the principal) wouldn't hear of their exploits. Apparently, the parent chaperones hadn't been too observant. No one said a word about this when we returned to school.

Nancy Williams and I had horses and were really into all things horse related. We were frequently seen in the hallway next to the Resource Center (not the "library") discussing the latest in bits, saddles, training, vet care, and more. The principal, Earl J. Kelly, used to kid me about my needing to gesture with my hands while talking. As he passed us one morning before classes, he grabbed my hands and said, "Now talk!" I couldn't say a word! He was one of my favorite people—a kind, compassionate, people-person who was respected by the faculty, staff, and students. He always "told it like it was," had a dry sense of humor, brooked no nonsense, and always got good results.

One morning, as I walked into my Spanish class, one of the students, knife in hand and raised overhead, had another kid backed up against the wall. I came up behind him, pulled the knife-wielding hand back over his head, pinched his upper arm, and escorted him to the office. Here we went again with,

"Miss. You can't do this. I was only kidding." Today the knife wouldn't even have made it onto the school grounds, or I'd probably have been fired and sued by the family. This same kid was later arrested after trying to pull a heist in Green Valley. He was caught when his motorcycle got stuck in the Santa Cruz riverbed sand.

Years later, when working for the Arizona-Sonoran Desert Museum, I helped bring desert animals to the juvenile detention center on Wilmot Road. Guess who was there? My knife-wielding student himself. One of the young men came up after the program and said there was a guy who wanted to say, "Hi," but was embarrassed. He finally came over and we reminisced about "fun times at SHS." I hope he straightened out and found a better path in life.

The high school classrooms in the main building were located around the Resource Center, which in other less technologically oriented schools was called the library. Movable classroom walls could be folded back so the classrooms could open to the Resource Center. The original concept was that classes would be integrated into a general learning area. In reality, the walls were closed most of the time because most classes needed their own space and relative quiet for studies—mine, especially, for language learning.

Shirley Brantley was the librarian. Mr. Lockett (elementary school) helped the high school with audio-visual (AV) materials and equipment. John Flannery later took that position and worked specifically in the high school. All the AV equipment was stored in a room next to Shirley's. At the beginning of each year, teachers hurried to requisition (and sometimes carry off) the equipment needed for their classrooms. It was a good idea to be on friendly terms with Lockett and Flannery.

Shirley was definitely the librarian; not the Resource Center manager. "I am NOT a babysitter! Your kids must have specific projects to be researching in the library. And they must have a library pass (which was usually written on pink paper)." Kids without passes or just hanging out were frequently sent back to their class, to the chagrin of the teacher.

Around 1969, Jim Madeheim came on board as a computer and math teacher. He developed and set up the first Apple Macintosh computer lab. I didn't know anything about computers but was curious about them. Jim showed me how to play Pac-Man and not only was I hooked on the cute Apple Mac computers, but in time I also became hooked on Jim. My interest in computers and lessons learned from Jim have helped me over the years as I developed learning packages for SHS and later designed teachers' brochures and activity packets for the Desert Museum, as well as newsletters brochures and for several dog training clubs.

Jim's room became a gathering center for kids before and after school and during lunch. Budding computer geeks—and some not so geeky—were drawn to Jim's easy-going personality and neat computer stuff. Jim never needed that lunch break that most of the rest of us looked forward to (and needed!). He genuinely enjoyed sharing time with the kids; some were not even in his classes. He was known as the "cool" teacher with his imposing size, beard, mustache, cane, sandals, and laid-back teaching style.

I thought he was pretty neat, too, and I became Mrs. Madeheim during Christmas break in 1974.

Jim was the girls' volleyball coach and I became his assistant. Another learning opportunity! I coached the junior varsity girls and Jim had the varsity team. As with math and computers, Jim's enthusiasm was catching and the kids loved him. One of his favorite sayings was, "Ain't it great?" When he passed away in 1994 (after only two years of retirement), we established the "Big Jim Ain't It Great" award. The plaque reads: "Presented to the player who really loves volleyball as Jim Madeheim did. SHS Volleyball Coach 1970–1980. Teacher and friend 1969–1992." Lynette Thompson was the 1994 recipient.

Then came the Great Flood of October 1983. It was the largest flood of record in the Tucson area. Between six-and-a-half to seven-and-a-half inches of rain fell across the Tucson area in five days. Whenever a tropical storm made its way into Southern Arizona, the Santa Cruz River overflowed its banks. Houses along the Rillito in Tucson fell into the river as the banks crumbled. Bridges and underpasses were flooded. The Elephant Head crossing was washed out and residents on the opposite side of the river were stranded. The San Xavier mission bridge off I-10 was badly damaged (read impassible!) and the river cut a new "canyon" as it swept around and under I-10 at the San Xavier exit.

Students living along the Santa Cruz River told harrowing tales of rescues off their roofs by helicopters and those involved became local heroes and celebrities. The Santa Cruz Valley and Tucson became worthy of national news.

Teachers always hope that perhaps through encouragement, a kind word, or some action even unknown to them, "their kids" will be helped along the road of life—that they will have the opportunity to achieve their very own best and to become lifelong learners. Most of the time, we don't really know how we may have touched their lives; sometimes we do.

Amazingly, they really do grow up, mature, and become good parents and community members. They become the entrepreneurs, the professionals, the educators. Gee—I know a few who became school principals, teachers, and even Spanish teachers! Who would have guessed?

On another note, I still cringe when I hear Sahuarita pronounced "Serita" as in "Rancho Serita" or "Swa Rita" (argh!) instead of Sah-wah-ree-tah (with a trilled "r"). Originally the name was Sahuarito (correct for the diminutive—"little sahuaro" the "h" being the original, and some insist the correct, spelling of the name of the cactus. According to some local historians, the name was misspelled (the final "o" being changed to an "a") due to a post-office glitch and thus it became today's frequently mispronounced "Sahuarita."

Sorry—once a teacher, always a teacher! Go Mustangs!

~ Contributed by Carol Madeheim (née Gebauer)

Hands Across the Border: William McNarie

William McNarie posing for a quick portrait. Courtesy of William McNarie.

In 1992, Sahuarita High School became part of the Hands Across the Border Student Exchange Program with a high school in Hermosillo, Sonora, Mexico. The school was called COBACH Villa de Seris, "Home of the Seris," after the Seri Indians. In October of each year, we would take twenty to twenty-five students to Hermosillo in our school bus on a Thursday. After a welcome at the school, our students would be paired with students from that school and go to their homes. Staff would also be paired up with local staff members. On Friday, students would attend classes and on Saturday we would have a beach party and picnic at Kino Bay. Sunday morning would be a farewell brunch and the trip home. In April, the students from Hermosillo would come to Sahuarita. Since they had no buses, they came to Nogales by commercial carrier, walked across the border, and we would meet them at the local McDonald's.

The program was basically the same—classes on Friday and an activity on Saturday. In Sahuarita, it was usually the Pima County Fair or the Arizona-Sonora Desert Museum, with a farewell brunch on Sunday. Some of the farewells were tearful because the students had really bonded.

Our students found it interesting that the students in Hermosillo were assigned to a classroom and the teachers moved from room to room. They were also surprised to learn that on Saturdays, the students would take turns cleaning their classrooms. The exchange program was dropped in 1996 because no faculty sponsor could be found.

When I arrived at Sahuarita High School as principal in the fall of 1984, the enrollment was approximately seven hundred students. About 150 of these students were from districts other than Sahuarita. There were students from the Continental District, Rio Rico, and a few from Vail and Tucson.

Just prior to Rio Rico opening its own high school, they were bringing ninety-eight students (two busloads) to Sahuarita High from Santa Cruz County. Vail was transporting between twenty to twenty-five students daily, and Continental thirty-five to forty students.

~ Contributed by William McNarie

Charles Oldham

Charles Oldham's first encounter with Sahuarita Unified School District No. 30 was in 1957, the same year that he moved from Oklahoma to Arizona. "My dad had a glass-cleaning business and we had the contract to clean Sahuarita Elementary School (SES) and get it ready for occupancy," Oldham remembers. "We spent three days camped out in our travel trailer by the school getting it ready for children to occupy."

At the time, Oldham was in high school and lived in Tucson where he attended Catalina High School. After graduating and marrying his high school sweetheart Marcia in 1959, they started their life together. "It seemed preordained that we would end up in Sahuarita at some point—we kept returning there. In college I worked for Tucson Gas, Electric Light and Power Company and we surveyed all the water wells in Pima County. I remember coming to Sahuarita and running into Elizabeth Hazen in Santo Tomas, and the mine tailings weren't there! When we permanently returned to Sahuarita, I was never oriented because it was a different landscape altogether, with no visible tailings by her home."

Oldham spent a stint teaching in Las Vegas in 1969 and the whole family—he, Marcia, and their son, Charles Richard—discovered it was not for them. During spring break, they ran into some friends at a McDonald's in Chandler, Arizona. "Barry [Calloway] mentioned they needed an industrial arts teacher at SES for the coming school year, so as soon as I got to my parents' house, I called SUSD and asked for an interview," says Oldham. "John M. Zuchowski interviewed me and before I left that day, he offered me a contract. He was the principal of SES. Dr. Paul Frick was the superintendent. We were elated to be able to return so close to our families and we knew in our hearts, we were home."

"I worked as an industrial arts teacher for two years at the elementary school and at the beginning of my employment there was no bridge across Santa Cruz River, which has a dry bed, but there was a road. The bridge came quickly afterwards, because workers had to service Farmers Investment Company, with its pecan groves. In my second year, we moved into the new Sahuarita Junior High School (SJHS). On moving day all the kids grabbed a chair and we moved along the elementary school playground and into the new building. Dr. Kenneth Gose was our principal at that time and five years later he became the superintendent and I became principal of SJHS."

Before the high school was built, students had to go to Pueblo High School in Tucson by bus. It was quite a relief for

Charles Oldham's portrait in the 1972–73 Sahuarita Junior High School yearbook.

people in that age group to have their own high school. "I coached junior high school football. We had tackle football for a number of years which at the junior high school level is exciting and worrisome. You'd go to play someplace like Eloy and invariably they'd have some 250-pound eighth grader. You'd breathe a sigh of relief when you got back on the bus without any injuries. I coached football and wrestling."

"When I was principal of SJHS, you're always trying to figure out a way to make school life enjoyable for the students. We would have our dances in the afternoon at the end of a school day so the kids could take the activity bus home. Sports were a big draw for our kids and we were always looking for ways to keep kids involved in the school and in the community. Before the state equalization, the physical education classes would be about the same size as a regular class, so you could do things like gymnastics and archery and broaden the scope of things that students could be involved in. After the equalization, those things began to disappear, and I think the kids lost a great deal of positive activities that helped them grow." The effects of equalization in 1983 will be discussed in greater detail later in this story.

"We had, in the early years, a summer program with transportation to bring children in for reading and math programs at the elementary level; then the school district, in connection with the county, would have the recreation program. I ran that recreation program. The kids would go to the classroom during the morning and then in the afternoon they'd take swimming lessons or play recreational games on the campus.

"There was a relationship between the Sahuarita Stingrays Swim Team and the district. The district provided the pool, and I don't think they charged for the use of that pool. I'm deaf in one ear because I was the starter for the swim team for a long time, and it never entered my mind to use an ear plug. The Stingrays were a great summer activity. You took your kid to swim practice at six in the morning and then they'd get tired and spend the rest of the day in their rooms sleeping.

"The school district, at the beginning of 1969, had about 850 students spread over the district's 626 square miles,"[1] Oldham said. "It was a challenge because I felt responsible for those kids until they got home. If they missed the bus, someone had to come get them. If someone couldn't come get them, I had to take them wherever they lived. I took students home to Arivaca. If there was a storm and you couldn't get down Arivaca Road because buses would hit high ground going through those washes, I had to make sure Sopori School was open and there were supplies for the students on hand—although I never had a student spend the entire night at Sopori, because their parents would know where they were and come and get them with a four-wheel-drive vehicle."

During the '83 floods, Elephant Head got marooned. People couldn't get out of Elephant Head without going across the desert to Green Valley. The mothers ended up homeschooling their children for about three weeks. They were glad Sopori was waiting for them when the bridge was rebuilt.

"Within the school buildings, people were pretty close with each other, but I don't remember a camaraderie between the buildings. We celebrated Ruth Moyer, who was a reading specialist in SJHS; she recently celebrated her seventieth birthday. She and her husband live in Birmingham, Alabama, now, but when she comes to town the great bulk of the junior high staff gets together to see her: Len Miller; Oscar Gomez; Helen Brewster. Sadly, we've lost Dick Bennett and Wes Hesser.

"One of the most interesting adventures I had was in the early part of the district—there was no way to know who was going to show up on the first day of school, so the district would hire a census taker to take a census throughout the district—so designated census takers would visit every house. Sometimes we weren't totally welcome. You would knock on every door in the school district in the heat of June to record the ages of every child in that household. That was the only way Dr. Paul Frick knew how to staff the schools. Chuck Gatterer and Oscar Gomez served as census takers for a number of years and I took the census for a couple of years, too. Most of the census takers were warmly received. It would take about forty-five working days. People didn't realize how important those figures were.

"In 1983, I became interim superintendent for six months while a search committee was formed to hire a new superintendent. The district was suffering under a re-evaluation process that required us to give reduction-in-force letters to about forty teachers. It was really very traumatic. We had to develop a policy of seniority and how you go about displacing people in the classroom by bumping some of them. As a result, not everyone who came back returned to their original position. The state's equalization project allocated monies previously given solely to SUSD No. 30 from the mines to other local school districts. The SUSD No. 30 school board authorized an override vote that allowed us to bring back all but twenty-three of those teachers. The people in the Sahuarita Unified School District are supportive of their schools and always have been.

Charles Oldham portrait from 2001. Courtesy of Charles Oldham.

"Everyone who came back was happy, but overall morale was really down. We recovered quickly in the coming year and a new superintendent, Steve Lebrecht, was hired. I moved back to junior high as principal and continued there until 1993. When I was offered the opportunity to move to Sopori Elementary School as the principal, I jumped at it. Sopori is a little piece of heaven. When you go from four hundred kids to 130, the workload is significantly different. Junior high kids can be very trying. You can't help but love them, but you need the patience of Job. The biggest challenge at Sopori was how to appropriately let little kids hug you. They all wanted to come up and wish you a good morning.

"I think the district made every effort to be innovative in providing a quality education for children. Individualized Educational Plans or IEPs—the district was at the forefront of that movement. I've seen four generations go through this school district and I marvel at how well they have done. It is quite gratifying to have adults come up and say, 'I want you to meet my grandson.' For the most part I would say they've been the most successful group of children that I have seen. I also marvel and feel honored that the teaching staff was outstanding: Burton Tingle, Archie Romney, Chuck Gatterer, and many others.

"In my opinion, we've been blessed with some very good superintendents. They've helped the district to manage the growth quite well. They've kept our mission on track. I have spent thirty-six years with SUSD No. 30 from the time we moved here to the present. I've spent fifty-two years within the community. I've been able to serve that community as a town council member and as a mayor. Those have been exciting—to be at the forefront of the sudden growth. It's not the same place as 1969. Sahuarita was quiet; it really was a bedroom community for the mining industry and Hughes Aircraft. Sahuarita Road didn't go beyond FICO's farm; it stopped at Santa Rita Road. People had to go through the bombing range if they wanted to access Vail.

"I thought it might be time for my family to move when they built the Circle K on the corner of La Canada and Duval Mine Road. I talked to Marcia about how maybe it was too crowded. When the town of Sahuarita was incorporated in 1994, there were about 1,900[2] people who lived in the boundaries. Now we're pushing over 30,000.[3] We've got Subway sandwiches and Eegee's is here. It used to be that you had to go to Tucson to go to those places."

"The school district began to interact with the mines mostly at the high school level. Job-ready programs have always been a plus for the school district and the business community. Archie Romney's auto diesel program was one example. Jim Smith went through Archie Romney's auto diesel program and he later became executive vice president of Empire Cat Southwest. Adrianne, my daughter, is another example. She learned to take apart small engines under Archie Romney. When she was in her graduate program, they were impressed she could take apart the vacuum pumps and fix them without the maintenance men.

"I think the mines didn't necessarily depend upon the graduates, but were happy to see kids come out of there with skills applicable to their industry. Bill Furnace and the welding program provided a good welding vocation. I don't think the connection was overt, but it happened."

~ Interviewed and Written by Barbara Tingle and Emily Tingle Soto;
edited by Mary A. "Mac" Chernoski

NOTES

1. Frick, Paul S. *The Sahuarita Story*. December 1970; revised 1973.
2. Walenga, Karen. *The Santa Cruz Valley: a Centennial Celebration*. Sahuarita, AZ: Green Valley News and Sun, 2011.
3. United States Census. Retrieved January 21, 2022 from https://www.census.gov

Joe Prince

Joe Prince has always struck a formidable figure at Sahuarita High School (SHS): tall, with the straight-backed bearing of a younger athlete, and with a wide personal space around him. Prince's bearing is not in any way a tell of his life, which is a chronicle of obstacles, setbacks, and accomplishments.

Joe Prince racing during his college and high school career. Courtesy of Joe Prince.

Prince, a former special-education teacher, is still, in 2022, the track and field coach at SHS. His chances at Olympic glory were sidelined—first by cancer and second by an international crisis. He is a career educator, but one who learned to read in fifth grade. Diagnosed as mildly autistic, Prince daily held court, for thirty-three years, with a classroom of special-education teenagers, and he continues to inspire excellence on the track as well as admiration from his athletes. And yet, his early life reads like preparation for the life of a gang member.

Raised by his illiterate grandparents in East Palo Alto, California, his part of the city was crime-strewn, and he saw corpses on his way to school. The classroom, where many students find safety and encouragement, failed him for years. His first day in kindergarten, he was placed in a closet for fear he might 'agitate' other children."[1] Eventually, he transferred to the Black Panther Liberation School in Oakland, where he finally learned to read. By high school, he was wearing hearing aids.

At Ravenswood High School in East Palo Alto, a new coach encouraged him to run track—that coach was Olympic Gold Medalist Tommie Smith. Although Prince, a freshman, was only 5'5" and 103 pounds, Smith noted his speed and nicknamed him "Joey Jets."[2] During his senior year, though, Prince had a back injury which prevented him from running.[3]

Prince signed up for a crop science associate degree program at San Luis Obispo. The associate-degree dorms were separate from those for four-year-degree students. His obvious talent led his coach to find him a scholarship to pay for a bachelor's degree and get him into his teammates' dorm.[4] Prince won the 1974 California Conference Championship in the 220-yard sprint. In 1975, attending Fresno Pacific University, Prince was clocked for the second-fastest time in the country in the 100-yard dash. He appeared destined for the 1976 Olympics when, at age twenty, he was diagnosed with testicular cancer.

Two years of treatment followed, including radiation, before Prince was pronounced in full remission. He underwent additional surgeries after the first bout, as the cancer was found to have spread to lymph nodes in his abdomen. A third surgery removed a benign tumor.

He graduated in 1977 and was selected later to run for Athletes in Action, a program developing teams for the Olympic trials.[5] This was his second chance to shine, but the Soviet Union chose to invade Afghanistan, bringing worldwide condemnation and the withdrawal of the United States from the 1980 Olympics in protest.

Joe Prince sits in the bleachers at Sahuarita High School. Courtesy of Green Valley News.

Prince first moved to Arizona to join the Arizona Wranglers' football team, but he could not pass the physical.[6] At that point he went back to school, switched his major to education, and earned degrees in both special education and physical education. He taught at Eloy Junior High School and was named acting principal there for his final year, recognized for his commitment to students and his work ethic. Prince also coached track and field at Santa Cruz Valley Union High School in Eloy, and it was during a competition that he began to be wooed to Sahuarita—initially, by an SHS runner.[7] Sahuarita's coach, who was retiring, joined in pressuring Prince to change schools. He began teaching at SHS in 1996, becoming the first Black certified staff member in the entire district.[8]

Joe Prince coaching at the Sahuarita High School track. Courtesy of Green Valley News.

One of his best-known traits is his patience, which matters greatly in working with teenagers. Still, the SHS auto shop kept Prince's beautiful convertible until he forgot he owned it. The car, a 1993 emerald-green Cadillac Eldorado with a tan phaeton top, had pack-rat damage to its wiring, and so Prince brought it to the school's auto shop. Over a decade later, after great pressure from then Principal Mark Neish, the entire school assembled on the commons to see the car driven on the green, wiring now intact, and delivered to a very surprised Prince. Two security guards fell in love with the Caddy, and Prince sold it to Liz and Hector Romero.

Prince is adept at one-on-one teaching and at calmly disciplining students with dignity. He would have conversations just outside the door with a single student, listening and giving choices with consequences. Prince was also a supportive colleague, offering to help supervise myriad student activities and staying the positive force for everyone. He earned admiration for so many of his qualities, not the least being that his kindness and generosity were unsurpassed. His selflessness inspired everyone, from the front-desk staff to the entire school, to "have his back" and be there for him. When he adopted his niece, Diamond Prince, she entered SHS knowing her adoptive father was one of the best men on campus at any given time.

Prince retired in 2020, after thirty-three years of teaching. Known for working with students one-to-one and coaxing their best behavior and efforts, he drew the line at continuing online teaching. His own health had become a priority because, as so often happens, the cure for his cancer in the past brought new concerns: a failing kidney. His autobiography, *Liberation Saturday*, was published in 2003 and a short film documenting his life became available in 2008. A major commercial film has been in the works for years and is still being developed as of this writing.

What began as a possible tragedy took chapter turns—obstacle, triumph, obstacle, triumph—and ends with the image of a man who, despite disability and disease and international invasion, is so much more than an Olympic runner. He is the teacher who understood disability and methods of learning that led many special-ed students to graduation and beyond; the coach who for years inspired high school runners to be their best on and off the track; the colleague whose generosity with his time and support knew no boundaries; and the adoptive father who taught and reinforced avenues of success and ethics to see a young woman blossom. A hero.

~ Contributed by Lori Punske

NOTES

References

1. Verwys, Jamie. "A life well-lived: Longtime SHS coach Joe Prince retires from teaching." *Green Valley News.* July 7, 2020.
2. Boan, Christopher. "The long run: Sahuarita coach's life is story of overcoming." *Sahuarita Sun.* July 15, 2016.
3. Ibid.
4. Ibid.
5. Verwys, Jamie, "A life wee-liver."
6. Ibid.
7. Ibid.
8. Ibid.

Additional resources

Prince, Joe. Interviewed by Lori Punske. July 28, 2021.
Prince, Joseph E. *Liberation Saturday: An Inspirational Tale of Going the Distance.* Dustan Everman, 2003.

Memories of Kay Richardson

Timeline

October 1968	Moved to Sahuarita
Aug 1975–Feb 1983	Employed as an instructional aide to seventh- and eighth-grade social studies teachers as well as to reading specialist and special education teachers at Sahuarita Junior High School.
Feb 1983–Jun 30, 2002	Secretary to the superintendent of Sahuarita Unified School District. Retired

	June 30, 2002. Served under the following:
	Charles Oldham as interim superintendent February 1983 to June 1983 when the superintendent left mid-year
	Dr. Stephen Lebrecht from July 1983 to June 1993
	Dr. Thomas Neel as interim superintendent from July 1993 to June 1994
	Dr. Donald Wright as superintendent July 1994 to December 1998
	Dr. Jay St. John from January 1999 to June 2002
January 2003	Returned to the superintendent's office at the request of Dr. St. John because my replacement left the district. I stayed until a replacement was found in April 2003.
Apr 2003–Jun 30, 2003	Trained new secretary to the superintendent until the end of June.
Jul 1, 2003–Dec 30, 2003	Moved to the HR office to assist when the HR clerk resigned and until a replacement could be found. I stayed until that position was filled and a new position of HR director was created.
Jan 2004–Jun 30, 2007	Served as part-time secretary in the newly created construction office. Served there until Anza Trail Elementary School was completed. Re-retired.

Stories

The first story that comes to mind is the RIF (reduction in force) initiative that took place in March and April of 1983. It was a horrible situation brought about by the determination by the legislature to equalize funding for all school districts.

Sahuarita was considered one of the "rich" school districts and thus had to cut its budget over a three-year period and return monies to the state to be distributed elsewhere.

We had to send letters to certain teachers to notify them that they were not being rehired for the coming school year. They then had the opportunity to "bump" another teacher if they had the proper certification to do so. It was a long, horrible process. Charles [Oldham] and I left the office each day sick in spirit.

The district went for its first (I believe) override that May and it passed. We were able to offer re-employment to the staff and also a raise in salary. Some staff returned and others had already found employment elsewhere.

One thing that always stands out to me is that the school district was community based. The surrounding communities and the school district always seemed to

Kay Richardson snapshot taken in 2022. Courtesy of Kay Richardson.

work as one. There wasn't much around in the area but the school district buildings and the surrounding communities—Santo Tomas, Wrangler Ranch, McGee Ranch, Curly Horn Ranch, FICO, the One Stop Market, the Sahuarita Bar, and the post office. The district opened its swimming pool in the summer to the local swim team and the entire community. It was that way for many years. With the advent of Rancho Sahuarita, it doesn't seem quite the same. It's not necessarily a bad thing, just different. It's called progress, I guess you'd have to say.

All in all, not a bad place to live and raise your children. Our children were born here and went through school here. We still love it after fifty-three years.

~ Contributed by Kay Richardson; revised July 30, 2018

Archie Romney, Industrial Arts Teacher at Sahuarita High School

Sahuarita High School opened in 1967, and three years later Archie Romney's students began winning the state and national championships in auto and diesel troubleshooting contests; they kept on

In the 1968 yearbook, Sahuarita High School Auto Club members Harry Brown, Jim Weining, Fred Sanchez, John Kane, Joe Angulo, Greg Gonzales, Craig Wayne, and Archie Romney show off the engine they are repairing.

winning for nearly thirty years. From 1970 to 1997, the year Romney retired and left Sahuarita, he had taught thirty-eight national champions. They had competed in auto mechanics, diesel mechanics, prepared speech, extemporaneous speech, job interviews, engine mechanics, and a troubleshooting contest (diagnosing and fixing a car within ninety minutes). In actuality, if they couldn't finish in eighteen to twenty-two minutes, they wouldn't win. The Vocational Industrial Clubs of America (VICA) competitions were sponsored by General Motors Corp. and Chrysler/AAA. One hundred and twenty-five schools from Arizona participated. Romney was awarded Arizona Automotive Teacher of the Year by Valvoline Oil Co. in 1990, a title that he would go on to receive seven more times. (Roderick)

He was also awarded by the state Board of Education as "Arizona Teacher of the Year." State Superintendent for Public Instruction Carolyn Warner said, "He is a teacher among teachers, an outstanding example in all that is right with public schools." (State) The motto engraved on his plaque was, "Students don't care how much you know, until they first know how much you care." He is also honored on a plaque in front of the Sahuarita District auditorium. (Romney)

Romney helped hundreds of students excel and become either state or national champions. Some went on to have careers in auto mechanics. Many local dealerships and employers knew the reputation of Romney's program and liked to hire his students right after high school. They knew he taught life skills

like responsibility, values, and attitudes as well as mechanics. (Roderick) Along with auto mechanics, he taught his students how to be good citizens; to be honest and work hard. He helped them excel, and when they honored him at his farewell party, his students said they had learned more about how to be a good father and a good citizen with pride for their community than anything else. About thirty of his students have worked for Caterpillar either at the proving grounds or at the retail Caterpillar shop. One student ascended to vice president of Caterpillar in Phoenix, Arizona. Several state champions went on to the Air Force Academy.

The new Sahuarita High School shop, offering all the best equipment to facilitate student learning. Courtesy of Arizona Daily Star.

Romney helped design the auto shop for the brand-new high school building with state-of-the-art equipment. It included a 10,000-square-foot classroom with computer training programs, auto bays, and a big diesel bay as well. (Sorenson) The mines in the Sahuarita School District have given it the wealthiest tax base in Pima County, and the affluence shows in the equipment. (Cornelius; Kimmey)

He was very invested in the program and thought the most important thing was the students. (Mendoza) He would volunteer an hour before school, an hour at lunchtime, and two hours after school in training every day. He was totally dedicated and the students could see it and they knew it. That's why they would excel. He also had the students set goals as to which award they wanted to win and work toward that. (Cornelius) "Auto mechanics gives the students immediate rewards. I'm teaching them to take something apart and to put it back together. Accomplishing that makes the students feel capable and able," said Romney. (Lefcourt) He also

Archie Romney, Craig Tate, and Ralph Nowak displaying the trophy won during competition. Courtesy of Monica Lee Elam Christiansen.

helped students get scholarships and jobs after high school. He was a role model, inspiration, and friend.

For Romney, volunteering was routine; however, the superintendent's wife worked to ensure that he eventually had a coaching salary offered to him. He had earned an associate of applied science degree from Eastern Arizona College, a bachelor of science and a master of science and arts degree from Northern Arizona University, and a master of education degree in educational administration from the University of Arizona. (State) By 1990, he left the classroom to become assistant principal, but his replacement quit and he went back to the classroom that he loved, now performing dual roles. (Roderick)

Romney's influences were community-wide. Every Christmas, his VICA club would fix up a car and donate it to a needy family. The students themselves would then pick the family that would receive the car from a list Romney had gathered from pastors or word of mouth and deliver it to that family. (Romney)

The 1970 Sahuarita High School junior varsity basketball team—Manny Oros, Dick Drow, Charlie Scott, Andy Elam, Jim Herde, Ernie Alvarez, Mark Wyland, Archie Romney, Bob Eck, Del Rickgauer, Chris Wootan, Robert Valdez, Scotty Fox, Gilbert Delgado, and Nick Olvera— line up for a photo for the yearbook.

Another thing Romney was instrumental in starting was Grad Night Lockdown—a way to keep students from being killed on graduation night after it had happened once. Students had been going out partying, getting drunk, doing drugs, etc. There were cars donated to the school or to Romney from Jim Click Ford or a used car dealership that had been enlisted for the project. The students would repair the cars and polish them up first, then have a raffle on graduation night and give them away. Every student would be in lockdown at the gym and would

Archie grins while repairing the family sand buggy.
Courtesy of Kerry Elam.

have to stay from when graduation was over until 7:00 a.m. At that time, a name was randomly chosen and that student won the car. To get the excitement going, the car would be sitting out the week before graduation. Romney helped start a tradition that is being carried on today at both Sahuarita and Walden Grove High Schools.

Romney's legacy will be remembered always in the hearts and minds of the students he taught. He believed he could take any student and make them into a winner. It was very motivational to them that someone could believe in their potential so much. (Sorensen) Romney loved teaching and he loved the students and that made a difference in the confidence they gained for life.

His contributions to Joint Technical Education District (JTED) teaching, his generosity to the community, and his lessons in citizenship, pride in community and ethics live on.

~ Contributed by Amy Millet

NOTES

Cornelius, Terry. "Sahuarita Turns Out Automotive Champions." *Tucson Citizen*, May 21, 1981: 45.

Kimmey, Bill. "New Sahuarita High Will be Small, but With Ambitious Program." *Tucson Citizen*, July 15, 1965: 13.

Lefcourt, Marc. "Sahuarita Instructor Gets an A+ As State's Top Teacher." *Arizona Daily Star*, December 8, 1983: 25.

Mendoza, Monica. "Award-Winning Automotive Teacher Retiring." *Arizona Daily Star*, July 31, 1997: 15.

Roderick, Gary. "These Auto Mechanics Instructors Teach Work Ethics, Too." *Arizona Daily Star*, September 27, 1992: 73.

Romney, Archie. Interviewed by Amy Millet. January 10, 2021.

Sorenson, Dan. "Fixing Cars a Snap for His Students: Sahuarita High Teacher's Pupils Win Pile of Trophies." *Tucson Citizen*, May 27, 1988: 69.

"State Board Picks 'Teacher of the Year.'" *Arizona Republic*, November 29, 1983: B18.

Dr. Jay St. John

Dr. Jay St. John came to Sahuarita in July of 1994 as the curriculum director of Sahuarita Unified School District No. 30. Hired by Dr. Donald Wright, the superintendent at the time, St. John had worked in Illinois for sixteen years before completing an eight-year stint in Douglas, Arizona. During his early time as curriculum director, St. John worked on several crucial projects, including the design of what was to be the new Sahuarita High School campus and the establishment of advanced placement (AP) classes.

At the time, Sahuarita High School had no AP classes, and St. John was asked by Dr. Wright to implement an AP program. St. John quickly set up eight classes and sent eight teachers to training over the summer. These classes were up and running when school began in the fall of 1995 and are still an important part of the Sahuarita curriculum.

In May of 1996, with financial concerns brewing in the district, Wright asked St. John to move to the position of business manager. The loss of students from the Tubac and Rio Rico areas, as their respective schools had been built, had caused a significant cut in funding. St. John had a degree in school business management and gladly accepted the challenge of the new position—one of many instances in which he pivoted his efforts to whatever the district needed at the time. This title and responsibility change meant that St. John was working on some of the same projects as those he had tackled during his time as curriculum director, but with a different focus. As curriculum director, St. John had met with each of the subject teachers at the high school to discuss what they needed in a classroom and how the district could support their instruction with the design of the new high school. As business manager, he was still focused on the construction of the new campus, but with an eye to the financial aspects of the project. "I had never been involved with anything like that in Illinois or Douglas, and I enjoyed that quite a bit," remembers St. John.

Just over a year later, in the summer of 1997, the governing board elevated St. John to the position of assistant superintendent of schools. Sadly, in the summer of 1998, Dr. Wright was diagnosed with non-Hodgkin's lymphoma. Wright retired and the governing board asked Dr. St. John to assume his duties as superintendent. "On his way out the door he reminded me that the district needed to ask the voters to renew its maintenance and operations override," says St. John.

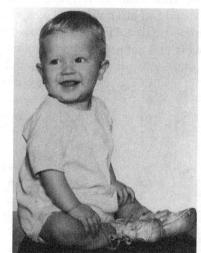

Renewing the override proved to be a challenge, and when the renewal failed to pass, the district lost 3.33% of its override funding. St. John led the district through navigating this reduction in funding, but in March of 1999 a second renewal attempt failed, resulting in a loss of 6.66% of its override funding. This caused financial problems for the district, compounded by the fact that the Vail voters had approved a move to become a unified district, which meant even fewer students and less funding for SUSD.

Finally, in March of 2000, a maintenance and operations override was passed, allowing the district to again have the benefit of a ten percent override. Shortly thereafter, the district began to receive an influx of

Baby Jay St. John shares a heart-melting smile. Courtesy of Jay St. John.

students from Rancho Sahuarita. Ground was broken on the development in 2000, and the thousands of homes planned for the area would mean unprecedented growth for SUSD. "In one summer, we registered 700 new kids," remembers St. John.

As the district handled the expansion of its student population, St. John was contending with a new challenge as well as the ever-present financial matters. The families that were moving into Sahuarita to take advantage of the new development and amenities sometimes found themselves at odds with the long-time residents of the town. Sahuarita was undergoing massive growth in population, and growing pains arose as some tenured citizens found discomfort with the changes being made to their home.

Dr. St. John approached the conflict through a strategy that had served him well: communication. "My doctoral dissertation was on communication and how important it was. You communicate and listen to people so they know who you are and you know who they are. It was a lot of work. It was important to make personal connections with all the parts of the district, especially those parts that had been neglected. It builds trust. I wanted the community to trust our staff, employees, administrators, and the Board of Education; that trust leads to great results for the children," he says.

When priorities differed between the newcomers and longtime residents, St. John focused on building an understanding that working together was the only way to accomplish anything meaningful. "We deliberately got folks from the old guard and the new guard and got them to know each other. [We got them to] work toward doing what needed to be done, even if it was hard. The community now realizes that they've got to work together, both the newbies and the old folks," he says.

The district grew exponentially during St. John's tenure, bringing new and different challenges. St. John approached each new hurdle with a pragmatic mindset. While his role as superintendent required big picture thinking, he also saw the value in taking on problems one step at a time. "I never thought this stuff up," he says. "I just dealt with whatever the problem was next. It wasn't because I had any great plan to unify the district, it was just dealing with the next problem. You don't get to pick what you deal with. You just don't."

That pragmatic approach to problem solving was on display one summer, several days before the school year was to start. "I will never forget that mom that came into the central office right before school started. She asked about enrolling her children. Our office was short of help (as it always was) and I was manning the receptionist position so the regular receptionist could have lunch. I asked (in my own way as always), 'How many do you have and how big are they?' She looked a little bedraggled. She told me that her husband had just transferred jobs to the Tucson area and she had driven a rental truck from the state of Washington. She told me she had five children and they came with her. We got together the necessary paperwork and got her children enrolled. "We didn't send the parent to all five schools, that doesn't make any sense. So, I just got the papers and we did it right there. She turned out to be a great parent in our

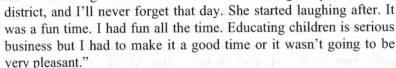

district, and I'll never forget that day. She started laughing after. It was a fun time. I had fun all the time. Educating children is serious business but I had to make it a good time or it wasn't going to be very pleasant."

St. John continued to lead with his pragmatic, communication-based approach as the district continued to change and grow. After an initial rejection, the Arizona School Facilities Board approved a donation of land from Rancho Sahuarita where the Anza Trail School was built. Shortly thereafter the district received a donation of property for Walden Grove High School from Farmers Investment Co., and after another battle received approval from the School Facilities Board, which paved the way for construction of the new school.

Dr. Jay St. John retired on June 30, 2010, handing the mantle of superintendent to Dr. Manuel O. Valenzuela. After over fifteen years of leadership in the district, St. John remembers his time at SUSD fondly. "I got lucky when I came here," he says. "It was a great experience for myself and my family. It was great."

Dr. Jay St. John poses in front of a collection of books. Courtesy of Jay St. John.

~ Interviewed and written by Barb Tingle and Emily Tingle Soto

Burton Tingle

I started my teaching career in 1966 at Buckeye Union High School, where I taught for five years. In the spring of 1971, a former colleague, David Green, informed me of an opening at Sahuarita High School (SHS), where Green was an assistant principal. My job in Buckeye was secure, but school financing was different at the time and I decided to see what a job in Sahuarita would look like.

During the spring of 1971, I had a formal interview for the position at SHS before I went to Colorado State University to finish my master's degree. I knew where Sahuarita Road was but I-19 wasn't finished, so I had to come through Tucson by the rodeo grounds and turn off at Sahuarita Road. As I started up toward the high school, there was only a one-lane bridge across the Santa Cruz River. Right before I got to the bridge, a vehicle that had gone too fast had tried to stop and was turned sideways. I asked at the One Stop Market how to get to the high school. I had to drive all the way around to Duval Mine Road, and then come to La Canada and drive up that road to get to the interview. I was told by Principal Earl J. Kelly, "I can't allow you to come here unless you're going to have discipline in your classroom." A firm hand was needed because at the time, Sahuarita had a lot

A studious Burton Tingle looks up from reading during his early years as a teacher. Courtesy of Barbara Tingle.

of hippies living in the community. The position required a person with a reputation for classroom discipline and setting high standards. David Green knew that I was that kind of person. I would make sure that students remained on task, which was quintessentially important as this was the era of "the dawning of the age of Aquarius," according to the song by The 5th Dimension.

I signed my contract with Sahuarita Unified School District and resigned from Buckeye Unified School District before leaving for Fort Collins, where I finished my master's degree. My wife, Gilda Joy Baxter, and I bought a trailer and we moved it to Sahuarita, into Los Arboles Trailer Park. In the spring of 1972, we bought the property in Sahuarita Heights where I currently reside.

When I came to Sahuarita in 1971, I had a five-figure salary. It was approximately $3,000 less than what both my wife and I would have been making if we had remained in Buckeye. The tax revenues that were being generated by the local mines resulted in a generous salary for those times and that was part of the reason I moved to Sahuarita.

During my first year at SHS, I was a roving teacher. I didn't have a personal classroom—I taught in classrooms during other teachers' planning periods. That first year I taught Algebra I for three of my classes, and one class each in general math and geometry. My first AP class that I taught was calculus. Later on I taught statistics.

Burton Tingle hard at work in his classroom in 1985 and again in 1990. Courtesy of Green Valley News.

Most Organized

Burton Tingle

Burton Tingle cheering his football team forward in 1989. Courtesy of Adrianne Oldham.

At Buckeye I had coached basketball, cross country, tennis, and baseball, and it was my intention to be a basketball coach at Sahuarita. I wanted to get involved in sports right away, but during my first year all the positions were already taken, so I did some supervision of athletic events. Head football coach Barry Calloway knew that 1971 was going to be his last year, and Jack Leonard took over as head coach for the 1972 season. Leonard was a physical education teacher who had started at SHS the same year that I did, and he asked me to be a coach because he also knew about the way that I conducted business in the classroom. This was my first football job. It had a pretty big stipend, which I appreciated as my family was growing. I started as an assistant coach in the fall of 1972, so in the fall of 2022 it will be my fiftieth consecutive year of football at SHS, including some time as the head coach of the junior varsity team.

At SHS, I have coached track, football, basketball, and cross-country running. I grew to love football the most. It wasn't my favorite at first because I didn't understand the game; I hadn't coached it before and I wasn't a huge fan of high school football. It slowly grew on me because it takes good thought and strategy to make sure that you get the job done. What I liked the most was the exchange among the various high schools. Who knew when I began that of all the sports, football would be my passion?

When I moved to the new high school, the landscape had dramatically changed. Where SHS is now was totally desert. When the surveyors started to take the measurements for the new high school, they dug up some of the cacti and took them to the University of Arizona to make sure they weren't endangered species. When the high school was completed, I chose the second floor of the building on the east. The buildings had windows all along its eastern side. And I liked that because I liked the early morning sunshine. Teachers and staff on the eastern side of the building were able to park near their classrooms. I could see my car from my classroom window and I enjoyed walking up the stairs to my classroom. Today the population here has risen dramatically. If I had that same classroom, I wouldn't like it very much because my eastern sunshine would be blocked by the two-story buildings right across the street. But that's progress. You gotta adjust to change and do what you gotta do. If things could have stayed the same as they were, I would have liked it better, but you just have to adapt to change. You just do.

Today there are probably ten to twelve math teachers at SHS. There used to be fewer, but they have always been good, good people. When I started there were two math teachers: me and Jim Madeheim. A couple of years later, Andy Longton joined. Bob McQuown and Gary Switzer were hired, and later Myrna Hunt. They were a good group of colleagues, and I really enjoyed my

A little bit of drama goes a long way when it comes to getting the team excited in 1990. Courtesy of Green Valley News.

exchanges with them—especially the humorous ones. I would call them Bob (or Harvey or Ralph) and they'd call me something else and we'd continue the banter throughout the day! In the social studies department, I fondly remember Weston Gentner—I'd actually gone to high school with him in Willcox, where I grew up. I was close with Tom Dorgan.

He was a man of principle, a good history teacher, and a good wrestling coach. I was also good friends with Coach Joe Prince. For a while, he had a room right next to mine. Our doors were adjacent to each other, so when we stood out between classes to supervise the halls we would talk. I enjoyed Coach Prince a lot. I also enjoyed coaching track with him. When I wasn't coaching, I helped at home track meets.

I undoubtedly appreciated my colleagues, but it was a love of the kids that kept me teaching for so long. Near the end of my career at SHS, there were two girls who came by my room every day. They were always cordial and we had a good relationship, even though they had both failed my math class the year before. There wasn't any animosity, because they knew that I wanted the best for them. The bottom line is the kids knew that I cared about them and I tried so very hard to help them to succeed. I did not want any student of mine to drop out of school. That's one of the biggest reasons that I

Burton Tingle pausing for a quiet moment of prayer and encouragement with one of his football players in 2019. Courtesy of Bobby Joe Smith.

stayed with it so long. I never dreaded doing it—I never wished I was somewhere else. It's always what I wanted to do, go up there and teach mathematics to the kids. I taught math at SHS longer than anyone else. It was my pleasure to do so.

David Rodriguez, Burton Tingle, and Joe Prince show off the scoreboard on Burton Tingle Field. Courtesy of Sahuarita Sun.

Two of my fondest memories involved a student observation and a request. One morning in the early '90s, before class started, there were two girls who came in early for extra help. It was sometime between Thanksgiving and Christmas, and one of the girls said, "Hey, do you know what my aunt did the other day? She made a pumpkin pie with a real pumpkin." The other student replied, incredulously, "No, she did not."

I said, "My family makes a pie like that every year. Would you all like to come over to my house sometime and do that? We'll provide everything, but you'll have to make a pumpkin pie with a real pumpkin." That simple observation began a household tradition with my senior-level math class. It was interesting when the kids came over because they hadn't done much kitchen work. My wife, Barbara Ann Vesterdal, and I had the pumpkin cooked when they got there and provided plenty of guidance, but it was up to the kids to make the pie. Most of the students initially didn't know how to use a mixer, but they learned and we had fun. It was really a heartwarming exchange because many of the girls and boys who came over had never made pie crust or seen cooked pumpkin, and it was special to introduce them to something new.

A Burton Tingle portrait shared by the photographer, his wife, Barbara Tingle.

Another endearing memory that I have started with a student request for a mud pit at my house. One year, the AP class came over to make pies in the fall, and one of the boys said, "What are we going to do in the spring?" I told him that we only did something in the fall, but I asked what he would like to do. Another one of the boys who was a wrestler said, "We want to mud wrestle." It was just a joke, but that day I came home and I dug a mud pit in my backyard and I asked them over. Ever since then there's been a mud pit behind my house.

In 2008–09, I had a beautiful and humbling experience when the SHS football field was named after me. It is one of the things that I brag about—not about the field itself, but the way that it was done. One day five boys walked up to me and said, "Would you mind if we named the field after you?" I actually had coached three of their fathers; at this time I was coaching kids whose fathers and grandfathers I had coached. The kids went to the school board and asked, "Can we name the football field after Coach Tingle?" The board told them that the field could only be named after someone once the honoree had died, but at the next board meeting the students came back with a petition with sixteen hundred signatures on it, and they were successful. I really liked that—that's the right way to do things. It was a tremendous honor. That was one of the greatest things that was ever done for me.

I'm also so proud of the careers of the students that I have taught. There are at least twenty medical doctors whom I taught in high school, at least five veterinarians, and three dentists that I know for a fact. One former student has a PhD in math! Several of them are high school math teachers. To say that I taught those kids has meaning to me; it also has meaning to me that I have four daughters and all of them have college degrees and two have master's degrees. Education is important, and I'm proud that I was a part of so many students' educations.

I retired from teaching in the spring of 2014, and have continued to coach football. Throughout my career, I looked for fun things to do: pep rallies, skits, talent shows, etc. I just enjoyed the high school kids. I sang at a talent show one night with Gary Switzer. We sang a made-up ballad, "What You Gonna Wear to the Wedding?" I sang and played my guitar in more than one show—it was usually humorous or whatever I was asked to do. I said "yes" a lot. I never wanted to move into administration because I just enjoyed teaching math in the classroom. As the kids say today, I just wanted to "be with my kids every day." They brought me joy. What else could you ask of a lifelong profession? Joy.

~ Interviewed by Barbara Tingle and Emily Tingle Soto;
edited by Mary A. "Mac" Chernoski

The David Wear Family Sahuarita Legacy

In the spring of 1969, Dave returned home from his middle school teaching job in TUSD, with a big smile on his face. I knew he must have good news of some kind, because he had been hoping to secure a position teaching and coaching at the high school level, as he had enjoyed at Grand Canyon High School before we moved to Tucson in 1967. We both were longing to get back to life in a small community once again. He happily announced that he had been offered a job at a new high school in the town of Sahuarita, south of Tucson. He would be teaching industrial arts and would be the head track coach and assistant football coach. Being from northern Arizona, we hadn't heard of this little town, but were overjoyed nonetheless, and to top it off, he would be receiving a substantial raise in pay.

Varsity football assistant coach David Wear and head coach Barry Callaway kneel on the fifty-yard line of the Sahuarita High School field. Courtesy of 1970 Sahuarita High School yearbook.

We immediately began hunting for a place to live in our new community, and we were able to purchase one of the few houses available in Santo Tomas. It seemed to us our dreams were continuing to come true. So, in June of 1969, David and Rachel Wear and their four children moved into their new Sahuarita home. Dave soon reported to his new job at Sahuarita High and we registered three of our kids at Sahuarita Elementary School. It turned out to be the beginning of the rest of our lives in this community and school district that we came to love and call home.

Through the years we watched Sahuarita Unified School District gradually grow and change together with the community. In 1969, there were approximately 260 students at SHS, with students being bused from as far away as Sasabe, Arivaca, Amado, and what is now the Rio Rico area. Others attended, and still do, from McGee Ranch, Sahuarita Heights, and surrounding ranches. The town itself, often referred to as "a wide spot in the road" on the Nogales Highway, consisted of a U.S. post office, the One Stop Market, and a bar. Turning west onto Sahuarita Road from the highway, drivers would come to a one-way bridge over the Santa Cruz River and have to wait for their turn to cross. Continuing on, the traveler would soon come to the new state-of-the-art high school, followed by the elementary school for grades kindergarten through eight. In the 1970s, the sixth, seventh, and eighth grades were moved to the new, modern Sahuarita Junior High School, and a large district auditorium was constructed. In advance, a heated debate took place regarding the need for such an elaborate auditorium in comparison to the size of our district. The building of the auditorium was approved in the end, with the stipulation that it could also be used by various organizations throughout the community.

As the years went by, we eventually sold our home in Santo Tomas and had a new home built on a small acreage just west of La Canada Drive, where we have resided since 1974. We were blessed with a fifth little Wear child in 1977. All five of our children attended Sahuarita schools and graduated from SHS. Any one of them, if asked, would acknowledge how glad they are to have grown up in a small town and attended small schools. In the words of our eldest son, who now helps children as a pediatrician, "I am being truthful when I say that each time I look back on growing up where I did, I smile to myself knowing that I did so in a small desert town that afforded me opportunities and memories and incredible friendships I'm quite certain I'd never have experienced in a larger city. The schools were relatively small, so the wonderful teachers who mentored and instructed me could spend more time with each student. My dad eventually coached nearly every sport SHS had to offer, and as a young boy I got to watch him do so up close. I admired the way he built up his student athletes, encouraged them, helped them succeed in team sports, but also helped them be good students and better people. My siblings and I got to participate in many organized school athletics, and be integral parts of many different teams, and excel as individual student athletes. [The influence of these teachers] still guides me every day because of the time they were able to give to their students and athletes."

Dave often remarked about how satisfying it was to be able to reach students on an individual basis in order to better understand their problems and special needs, and that it would have been more difficult in a large school setting. Throughout his tenure at Sahuarita High, as an industrial arts instructor, he

A treasured portrait of a smiling Dave Wear. Courtesy of Rachel Wear.

guided his students in the building of houses for Habitat for Humanity and was awarded one of the first Special Education Vocational Industrial Arts Certificates given in Arizona. He demonstrated his individual teaching methods while coaching a variety of sports for many years, including track, swimming, football, baseball, and girls' and boys' basketball. After retirement, he served as SHS athletic director and coached golf. He loved to laugh and spend time with friends and his family, which always was the most important thing in his life, until he bid us farewell in July 2019. He always told his children and students, "It's okay to make mistakes, just take time to learn from them."

In the late '80s, Rachel had decided to take a job at Continental School. She really enjoyed working with the students and began wondering whether it was too late to jump in and work to earn a degree and get certified as an elementary teacher. With an abundance of encouragement from an exceptional teacher she admired very much, she enrolled at Pima College and got started. After two years she transferred to the University of Arizona, graduating with a BA in elementary education in 1987, at the age of 48. She taught second, third, and fourth grades at Sahuarita Elementary in Nogales, Arizona, and at Great Expectations Academy for several years. Her teaching career may have been shorter than some, but she cherished each year, and she always urges others not to be afraid to step up and strive for anything they want to achieve, no matter when in the course of life the opportunity comes along.

This has been the story of a young couple that came to Sahuarita many years ago, with their little children, and stayed for the remainder of their lives because it was a wonderful place to raise a family, to teach school, have great experiences, and enjoy wonderful people. They watched as so many changes took place—changes they thought would never happen—but the heart and soul of this very special community will always remain steadfast.

~ Contributed by Rachel Wear

Nancy Williams's Sahuarita Memories

I completed my four years of college in three years, so I was twenty years old when I went to interview for the girl's physical education position at Sahuarita High School. Because at that time there were over 250 applicants for every teaching position in Tucson, I ventured to schools farther from town and applied for a job in my minor, physical education, instead of sticking to my major, which was art education.

As we began our interview, Principal Earl Kelly told me was that he thought I should know that his personal policy was to never hire a teacher with fewer than two years of experience. I still had to finish some courses in summer school, just to get my degree and a teaching certificate. After thanking him for that information, we continued with our interview. To say the least, I was ecstatic and shocked when he offered me that teaching position. My gratitude for his trust in me and willingness to give me a chance has never faded in the fifty-two years since that day.

The next surprise in my life was when I found out that I was pregnant with our first child during that summer. I met with Superintendent Paul Frick, as Mr. Kelly was on vacation. I explained my situation to Mr. Frick and told him I did not know if the school district had any policy about pregnancy. He studied me carefully and explained that the district had a policy that the teacher must resign at the end of the first trimester of pregnancy. I told him, "I wanted this job when I took it and I still do." Then he said, "We wanted you when we hired you and we still do." We worked out the situation for me to start teaching and left the rest "to be determined." Later I learned that during that same

Nancy Williams demonstrating illustration techniques of the art room's resident skeleton. This full-sized skeleton was shared with the science department and spent many days and nights posing in the art room waiting to startle an unsuspecting night custodian who came in to clean. Courtesy of Nancy Williams.

summer, two female educators had taken that same policy held by most public school districts to the U.S. Supreme Court, and the policies were determined discriminatory and unconstitutional. I had no idea that I was ahead of history.

My job was to teach driver's education and the girls' physical education classes, as well as to sponsor the GAA (Girls Athletic Association) which included coaching all of the girls' sports in addition to cheerleaders and pom-pom girls. I would say I really had my work cut out for me. I coached freshman, junior varsity, and varsity basketball all at the same time with no assistant coach or budget. That was in addition to all of my other duties such as chaperoning dances and doing cafeteria and bathroom duty. I was young, healthy, and energetic and it never occurred to me that I could not handle it, so I did.

My career at Sahuarita High School began in the fall of 1969. It was the third year of existence for SHS. The community was very different back then. The crossroads of Nogales Highway and Helmet Peak-Sahuarita Road was next to the railroad track near the FICO headquarters. There were Mary's Bar, the Sahuarita U.S. Post Office,

Art club students posing with the resident art-room skeleton as Carrie Browning shares a "stage kiss." Courtesy of Nancy Williams.

Early photo of an exhausting McGee Ranch roundup. Courtesy of Lynn Harris.

and Yoder's convenience store with gas pumps. That intersection no longer exists.

The pecan orchards which are now next to that intersection were cotton fields. The cotton fields gradually transitioned to strips of barley. There then appeared rows of sticks (pecan saplings) between the bands of barley. Within a few years, it had been entirely transitioned to pecan orchards.

Our students were almost entirely rural residents who lived on ranches, in FICO housing, or in other rural communities. The only major employment that was not agricultural was the copper mines surrounding the schools. The original part of Santo Tomas was the only sizable housing development. Our district took in students from an area of about 640 square miles. Many students rode buses for hours a day. For some it was a school bus and for others it was a Greyhound bus. There was one high school (Sahuarita), one middle school (Sahuarita), and two elementary schools (Sahuarita and Sopori).

As Sahuarita High School was the only high school in the Santa Cruz Valley, we had both district and tuition students from the entire valley including Rio Rico (just north of Nogales), Carmen, Tubac, Tumacacori, Arivaca, Amado, Madera Canyon, Continental, McGee Ranch, Wrangler Ranch, Curley Horn, and so on. We had 152 students when I started teaching. The beauty of it was that everyone seemed to belong and got along well. This was a beautiful area filled with beautiful, unique people and it was a joy to work with these students.

Finishing roundup. Courtesy of Lynn Harris.

In the early years of teaching, I discovered lots of common interests with the students. Lori McGee had an incredible love of horses and my life revolved around horses. Before long, she invited me to come on the round-up at McGee Ranch with her. I looked forward to it for days. Round-up consisted of collecting the cattle with their calves from the range, then working the cattle to brand, vaccinate, and castrate the male calves and doctor anything that needed attention. After work comes a great meal. It was at the meal that I encountered my first greenhorn test.

The families were all there and the dads were in charge of the work and the moms were in charge of the meal. I met the McGees, Elams, Foxes, and Harrises and likely more that I can't identify. I was out

Bob Elam and Empy McGee immunize a young calf. Courtesy of Margaret McGee Elam.

there with cattle and horses and life was amazing. The dads saw to it that my plate was continuously filled with "mountain oysters." "Do you want some more of these mountain oysters?" Sure I replied as I gobbled them down. Then they started asking me, "Do you know what these are?" I answered in the affirmative. "No, you don't know what they are, do you." "Yes I know what they are . . . they are OYSTERS!" The test continued for some time. After they seemed certain that I had no idea what I was eating, I grew weary of the game. "All right, all right! They are testicles from the calves you just castrated." The dads were shocked. They thought I was a city girl and that they were pulling one over on me. The fact is that I was born and raised on a dairy farm with both dairy and beef cattle and, yes, I like mountain oysters.

In 1971, I began the transition from teaching physical education to teaching art and taught both in the 1971–72 school year. Shortly after I began teaching art full time, we started the SHS Art Club. For many years we made *ojo de dios* (God's eye) and many other arts and crafts projects; we also recycled paper to earn money for our club. In the spring of each year we used those funds to take a trip. Usually, we went for three days and visited art galleries such as the Phoenix Museum of Art; as well as the Phoenix Zoo; shops and galleries in Sedona, Cottonwood, and Jerome; as well as hiking trails, natural sites, and Native American sites. Two of those trips were backpacking trips. One trip was to Havasu Canyon, which is a side canyon of the Grand Canyon, and one to Sycamore Canyon in Southern Arizona near the border with Mexico. Our world was very different then and we traveled with no worry or fear of danger or problems. The students and I relied on each other and worked together to take successful and exciting journeys.

Jerry, Margaret, and Empy McGee take a short break. Courtesy of Margaret McGee Elam.

Later I was teaching art, arts and crafts, and a personal growth class called Life Enrichment. In addition to my teaching responsibilities, I drove the "handicapped bus" for the students needing specialized transportation. I drove that bus for several years and during the year after the flood of 1983, I drove it seven miles through a cow pasture to get the students back and forth to school.

By 1981, our family had moved from Tucson near the airport into the Sahuarita School District in the country near Amado. In the years before and after I drove the "handicapped bus," I often rode the regular school bus with our neighborhood students. It was great to have extra time with these students and neighbors. Often the return trip was on the "late bus" which took students home after sports and school activities.

In the late '90s (probably 1996 or 1997), Sahuarita High School offered a challenge to all homeroom classes. Each homeroom class was asked to do a project with the theme "make a difference." The plan

At the Art Club booth for the first annual Tumacacori Fiesta, students sell crafts to raise money. Courtesy of Nancy Williams.

was that each class would do a project that would make a positive difference in our school or community. My homeroom class was Life Enrichment, which was a personal growth and personal skills class. This was a beautiful fit for such a project. For several days the students tried to decide what they would do for our project. Nothing seemed to be the right idea. Then I suggested to the students that maybe our approach was wrong for us. Instead of trying to think of a project, we should identify the problems that needed to be addressed. Bingo!

Immediately one of the girls said, "There is nothing in the community for us to do. The retirees don't want us around. There are no places for our age group to hang out or entertain ourselves, so we end up out at 'doughnut land' doing things we shouldn't be doing." Well, that certainly identified a problem. The next person said, "There is that big empty Kmart building just sitting there. Why couldn't that be a skating rink?" That began our project, with investigation and lots of work. We spent the entire semester on this passionate project.

Art club students recycled tons of paper as an environmental project and fund-raiser. Courtesy of Nancy Williams.

My first effort was to contact the local commercial real estate agent who had the Kmart property contract. He was also a former student of mine and immediately offered to come speak to our class. He informed us that the building could not be a skating rink because the building was not a clear span and had large pillars that held up the roof. That would make it a liability risk. He also informed us of the annual lease cost which would require more skaters on a daily basis than the population of our community if they all skated regularly. He did, however, bring us a copy of a survey that had been done with the retirement community that asked what type of amenities the residents would like to see in their community. He suggested we might like to use that survey or do one of our own. Our project took off immediately. After securing approval from our principal, Dave Holmer, we were committed to "making a difference."

The students set to work writing a survey that would ask the students what amenities they would like to have in our community. This was no small task, but the students were on fire. After reworking the survey over and over to be sure we left out our bias and got the information we were seeking, we gave the survey to a small test group of the student body. Then we went back to work correcting and rewriting our survey to make it more accurate. Next we gave the survey to all classes in Sahuarita High School and Sahuarita Middle School. Now we had to tabulate the results, which was another huge task because these were no "yes" or "no" answers. Once the counting had been accomplished, we had to categorize and interpret the results. One student who was quite adept at the computer (it was early in the individual computing era) put our results into graph formats. The next portion of the project was to write an interpretation and explanation of what these results meant and how they could be used.

Art club students are ready to head out on a backpacking trip into Sycamore Canyon. Courtesy of Nancy Williams.

Our real estate friend had also introduced us to a local person with commercial property who had been trying to convince Burger King to put a franchise in the community even though Green Valley had a policy of not allowing fast-food businesses to come into the area. All of this was happening just as Sahuarita had become an incorporated town. We had a new town council to address and convince of our ideas.

We slaved over corrections until we had corrected every typo, margin error, etc. Once we were armed with our survey results and they had been printed and bound for public consumption, we had to sell it to "the powers that be." The next part of the lesson was to learn public speaking, which was also entirely new to these students. Our first presentation was to the high school faculty, who then gave us both encouragement and feedback to help us improve our skills. Next we presented this to the Sahuarita School Board. At that presentation I asked the students to share what they felt they had learned from this project. There were many positive answers to that question, but the one that remains in my mind verbatim is, "I learned that one person really can make a difference."

The Art Club visiting the Phoenix Museum of Art—one of many ways fund-raising proceeds were used to benefit students. Courtesy of Nancy Williams.

The big test was to present our survey, results, and conclusions to the Sahuarita Town Council. To say the least, these students did an incredible job and were extremely well received. Our work and project paid off in a big way.

The survey results of both the retirement community and the students showed that the number one entertainment desired was a movie theater. The students wanted restaurants as much as did retirees. The students' first choice was Olive Garden and their second choice was Burger King. The Burger King was built a short time after our project was completed. The movie theater took a little longer but did get built in the Kmart complex. It was very rewarding to go to Burger King and see both students and retirees sharing the amenity together in lovely harmony. These students were willing to work hard to accomplish what they believed in and truly made a difference in their community.

Sue Simpson was, at the time, a local wildlife rehabilitator who approached some of the Sahuarita High School staff members about starting a club to teach about raptors. Val Faulkner, an English teacher on staff, and I decided to take it on with Sue taking the lead to teach all of us about raptors. We chose to call this new club "Wild Wings," and it was great to share learning with our students while building our knowledge of these magnificent birds. The students soon were becoming educated and Sue decided to step it up a notch.

She had an adult female Harris's hawk that had been injured and could not be released back to the wild. Although the hawk's injuries had healed, she was unable to survive on her own with a permanently damaged wing. Sue contacted the appropriate authorities and arranged licensing for us to use this hawk as an educational ambassador, which allowed the students to handle her.

Next came the lessons on how to correctly handle the hawk on the glove and jesses. This was quite an experience for all of us, and Mr. Faulkner and I were no better students than any of our other members. The students learned well and eventually our

Art club students pause for a photo in adobe ruins on an after-school field trip to the Helvetia ghost town in the Santa Rita Mountains. Courtesy of Nancy Williams.

hawk (we named her Herra) was more comfortable with us. I believe she just became tolerant of our efforts, which led to the next step in our education.

We now started learning about public speaking and answering questions about Herra and raptors in general. We prepared an educational program that we could take to the public and teach others what we were learning. This was our transition into taking our hawk ambassador to visit other groups and schools. It was both challenging and fun for all of us. It was so exciting to share what we had learned and everyone was fascinated by this beautiful bird. Our members became good teachers and speakers. It was a wonderful experience to take Herra to visit the students at Carpenter Middle School in Nogales, Arizona. We arrived on a Friday afternoon for an assembly just before dismissal for the week.

Students working on quilts that were donated to local hospitals to be given to babies born to drug-addicted mothers. Courtesy of Nancy Williams.

The students arrived at the school cafeteria with excitement and middle-school energy. Herra decided she did not like the looks of this situation and wanted out of there. We went to the microphone and advised the students of how anxious Herra was becoming from the noise and large group and that she was still a wild bird. Her instinct was to escape but she was tethered with the jesses and was feeling trapped.

That whole student body quickly checked their energy and enthusiasm and became very quiet and orderly. They listened with great intensity to the presentation and asked wonderful and meaningful questions. Herra became calm and the whole experience was a great success. It was wonderful for all of us to share learning about raptors, Herra, and each other.

Sue was not done yet, though. She felt the Wild Wings members had done a great job and arranged a very special treat for all of us. She was friends with a glider pilot and arranged for our whole club to go to Marana where each of us was given a ride in a glider so we could experience riding on the thermals and soaring like the raptors we had been learning about. It was an amazing way to complete our experience with Wild Wings and Herra.

Please note that Sue Simpson went on to complete her degree in education and became a middle-school teacher for Sahuarita Unified School District, where she continued to inspire students with her enthusiasm for learning and teaching.

Truly, one of the greatest privileges in my life was teaching at Sahuarita High School. The students were for the most part from wonderful families and many had lived in the area for decades to generations.

It was a joy to get to know many of them on a personal level and even to be included as a friend or adopted family member.

These are the kind of people who lived by their values and stood for what is right and good. You learned to trust them and knew that these are people of character who would do the right thing because "it was the right thing to do," even when doing the wrong thing or nothing at all would be easier.

Although it is true that not everyone was perfect all of the time, I understood a basic goodness in these people. Yes, sometimes students did things they shouldn't and I made

Nancy Williams and Sue Simpson study with the Wild Wings Club members in 1992. Courtesy of Billy Lichtenwalter.

mistakes as well. Nevertheless, I celebrate the honesty, integrity, and work ethics that I observed in them. The result was that my husband and I moved our family into this community to raise our children among my students and their precious families.

I certainly would not name family names in fear of forgetting so many. I leave no one out in my heart because I understood that we were all doing the best we knew at the time. Surely, we learn more throughout our lives and hopefully we continue to grow to become our best selves. That is the benefit of starting with a great family or creating one if there isn't one to start from.

Thank you to these wonderful people and students for helping me become my better self, day by day. It was a joy and privilege to learn and grow with you.

~ Contributed by Nancy Williams

Art students gather for a photo with Nancy Williams after painting holiday designs on the windows of a Green Valley bank. Courtesy of Nancy Williams.

Porter Wilson

Athlete, inventor, teacher, lifesaver, decorated veteran: Porter Wilson was all of these and more. An exemplary Sahuarita School District employee for over thirty-two years, Wilson touched generations of students and adults. He received a Purple Heart for injuries suffered during World War II in the China-Burma-India [Theater], according to his obituary. He received his bachelor's degree from Phillips University in Enid, Oklahoma, and his master's degree from the University of Arizona. Certified in Red Cross lifesaving and as an emergency medical technician,[1] Wilson was skilled in many areas, incredibly personable, and committed to helping children.

A young Porter Wilson posing for a School Days portrait. Courtesy of Oscar Gomez.

An athlete of imposing size (6'4"), Wilson was initially hired to teach physical education in 1951 and, according to him, "The real reason they hired me was they were having some real racial problems . . . fights all the time."[2]

According to Oscar Gomez, a student who later became a fellow teacher and friend of Wilson's, Wilson incorporated military drills and science into his classes. He would line students up on the playing field and have them raise their hands when they heard his gun fire; the farthest student heard it last. As the football and basketball coach, Wilson not only drove a bus to out-of-town games but also to Dairy Queen afterward and paid for anyone without money.[3] Wilson and colleague Barbara Lewis were instrumental in Sahuarita's designation as a 1978–79 demonstration site for the President's Council on Physical Fitness in Sports. A "Porter Wilson Presidential Fitness Award" was initiated in 1982 to honor deserving fifth-grade boys and girls.

Wilson wrote an opinion/rebuttal in an *Arizona Daily Star* "Voice of the People" column in 1958[4] in which he argued that the state of Arizona

FLAG FOOTBALL BELTS
Vacuum/Sonic
Ball & Socket

ADJUSTS TO SIZE

• Conversions • Game Books • Storage Rings
Program Kits • Cones • Glo Spots • Throw-Down Bases

FLAG-A-TAG, INC.
– Porter and Madeline Wilson –
5630 N. Via Latigo • Tucson, Arizona 85704
(800) 747-3402 • (602) 690-1660

Flag-A-Tag business card. Courtesy of John Gayler.

had been instrumental in the development of "pre-high school football," disputing another opinion writer's laser focus on Pennsylvania. Wilson had every right to disagree—according to Ray Penzarella and Tom Faust, Wilson and fellow teacher Norman Adams were working on a flag football belt that would allow the game to be played consistently and would be far safer than touch or tackle football. After ten years of effort, their company, *Flag-A-Tag*, turned flag football into a nationwide and perhaps worldwide sport for both genders. Tucson Unified School District purchased the belts in 1962[5] and, by 1963, according to Faust, "orders had been received from 32 states" and "the Armed Forces were using the game both in the States and abroad." Both genders developed leagues. In Tucson, city and county schools plus the University of Arizona and Davis-Monthan Air Force Base played Wilson and Adams' version. More than 40,000 adjustable belts, the only necessary equipment for players, were sold per year; Wilson donated 300 of the belts to an *Arizona Daily Star* children's camp.[6] Flag-A-Tag modernized and stabilized a game that otherwise often resulted in injury. The belts were adjustable and held vinyl-coated nylon flags so tough that Wilson offered to pay anyone who could rip one.[7] Wilson then co-authored an official rule book on the game with Augie Acuna, then program director of the Pima County Recreation Department; more than 25,000 copies were sold quickly.[8]

When an abandoned gravel pit filled with water and a young student fell in and drowned, it became suddenly obvious that many, many Sahuarita students did not know how to swim. The PTA initially ran a swimming program with the schools themselves providing student transportation, but eventually swimming became a school district—and a Mr. Wilson—project. He focused on nine basic strokes and saved countless student lives.[9] Wilson drove sixth-, seventh-, and eighth-grade students to Tucson and used the YWCA pools to teach and practice.[10] More than 15,000 children learned to swim in the program.[11] Eventually Wilson pushed for a district pool, according to Charles Oldham, then principal of Sopori.[12] He taught students lifesaving and artificial respiration techniques, which led to another Wilson invention: a mechanical respirator or, in his words, "exchange lung." Working with Dr. Maxwell Palmer,

an anesthesiologist, Wilson spent two years developing a workable air exchange tube with a slide valve that allowed nearly one hundred percent air exchange and allowed the rescuer to feel the victim getting air.[13]

Gomez, whom Wilson taught for two years, remembers him as a man adept at "influencing the young, mostly migrant, farm children" and as a storyteller who loved the novel, *Tom Sawyer*. Wilson tried retirement for one school year, 1984–85, and then returned on a half-day contract, eventually volunteering his time the

A Sahuarita Junior High School flag football game with Porter Wilson acting as referee. Students playing are John Gayler, Jamie Estrada, Joe Gallardo, Robert Estrada, and Rudy Cubillas. Courtesy of John Gayler.

remaining half day. His second retirement in 1989 inspired the district to name its pool after him. Wilson was named to the U.S. Flag Tag League Hall of Fame in 1999.

Wilson died of cancer on September 17, 2000, leaving behind a legacy of intellectual curiosity, creativity, and selflessness. Having touched so many lives in so many ways, his name still conjures up remarkable memories, praise, and love in the town where he gave his all to all students.

~ Contributed by Lori Punske

NOTES

References

1. Penzarella, Ray. "Inventor Hopes to Score with Flag." *Arizona Daily Star.* June 14, 1984.
2. Ibid.
3. Gomez, Oscar. Interviewed by Amy Millet.
4. Wilson, Porter. Voice of the People column: "Arizona Football." *Arizona Daily Star.* December 11, 1958.
5. Penzarella, Ray. "Inventor Hopes."
6. Chanin, Abe. "Young Campers to be Given Free Belts." *Arizona Daily Star.* December 18, 1968.
7. Faust, Tom. "Tucsonans build 'Flag' into nation-wide sport." *Arizona Daily Star.* May 5, 1963.
8. Penzarella, Ray. "Inventor Hopes."
9. Kimmey, Bill. "Witness to tragedy acted to prevent future ones." *Tucson Citizen.* August 11, 1965.
10. Gomez, Oscar. Interviewed by Amy Millet.
11. Penzarella, Ray. "Inventor Hopes."
12. Ricker, Dave. "Sahuarita Residents Fondly Remember Porter Wilson." *Green Valley News & Sun.* September 27, 2000.
13. Hodge, Carle. "Mechanical Resuscitator Perfected." *Arizona Daily Star.* October 8, 1963.

A smiling Porter Wilson shares his story. Courtesy of Barbara Brown Bennett.

Additional resources

"'Coach' Porter C. Wilson." Obituary. *Arizona Daily Star.* September 24, 2000.

PART VI: FAMILIES AND COMMUNITIES

The diverse experiences of certain families contributed to the formation of the Sahuarita community's spirit and grit. Their stories are told in the following pages.

John Austin Family

John D. "Johnnie" Austin was born on November 28, 1910, in Yancy, Arkansas, to Norman and Maggie White Austin. Cora Lee Smith was born on September 15, 1913, in Saratoga, Arkansas, to Willie and Hannah Hopkins Smith. John and Cora met in the small country town of Cora's birth, where they were married on December 24, 1931. Because of the times in which he lived, John's formal education was limited and he attended school for only a short time. Cora attended school longer than John, but only by a few years.

Alice and Willie, two of the eight children born to John and Cora Austin, have many fond memories of their childhood. All of the children (Roy, Cornell, Fern, Johnny, Jewell, Willie, Alice, and Ruby), were born in Arkansas. They were raised in a home where religion and respect were taught and expected of everyone in their family.

John was a sharecropper and the main source of the family's income came from growing cotton, or, as Willie likes to call it, "white lilies." The family farm had a big house. Willie's recollection of Tollette, Arkansas, was that "everything was green." He remembers big trees and a small pond with fish very close to the house. Tollette was the closest town to their rural farm in Blackland Township.

Hunting and fishing were easy. On rainy days, the pond would overflow. After the rains stopped, Willie remembers going out and picking up fish off the ground. The family had its own garden and there was work for every child on the farm.

"White lilies" ready for harvest. Courtesy of the Bull/Klingenberg family.

John owned two mules, Dan and Kate, that he used to work the land and cotton fields. He also used the mules to pull the cotton wagon to the co-op cotton gin. All members of the family worked together to pick the heaping stack of "white lilies" that filled the wagon bed.

On Sundays, John would hook the mules up to a different wagon that was used to drive the entire family into Tollette for church. John and Cora's religious faith was an influential force in their lives. Even before they married, each was raised with a strong belief in God. After their marriage, their dedication to family and church was a driving force that has carried forward for generations. Before leaving for Arizona, John became a deacon in his church. This choice would bless not only the lives of his family, but also the lives of many people he would come to know in Arizona.

While in town one day, John had heard that Willie Brown was back from Arizona and was looking for more workers to relocate to Southern Arizona. There was said to be a great need for farm workers, and Roy Lee and Cornell, the oldest Austin boys, had been out west looking for work on previous trips. With

Early Arizona cotton fields. Courtesy of the Bull/Klingenberg family.

their input and after much prayerful consideration, John and Cora decided this would be a good move for their family. They sold what they could, packed up their meager belongings, and loaded them, along with all eight of their children, into the back of Willie Brown's old truck. There were several other families that joined them, including widow Ethel Bishop Smith and her younger children (Nora Lee, Willie B., Shirley M., James L., Pleas Ardell, George W., and Linda). The children settled into the truck bed and the adults took their places on the hard wooden benches anchored to the truck bed. With only a huge canvas tarp for protection from the wind and sun, the family left Arkansas behind them and set off toward Arizona.

Prior to leaving, the families had been prepared beforehand for what they would encounter on the three-day trek. Each family had to bring enough food to last the whole trip, as not all places along the route would accommodate them. In some locations, when the truck stopped to refuel, the travelers were not even permitted to get off the truck. Willie Brown and another man took turns driving and for little Willie and Alice Austin, the almost nonstop trip to Arizona was very bumpy and crowded.

Willie had been born June 9, 1942, and Alice on January 25, 1945. Though young at the time, they vividly recall the trip from Tollette, Arkansas, to Sahuarita, Arizona, in that early summer of 1951. Every one of those three days of traveling was hot and dusty. As they came into Tucson on Highway 89, they drove past rows and rows of airplanes at Davis Monthan Air Force Base. Willie remembers saying, "Just look at them all!"

Upon arrival in Sahuarita, the very first thing the children noticed was that, "It was not very green and there were no large trees or ponds." Green vegetation was limited to the fields, and the air was extremely dry. As she got off the truck, five-year-old Alice took one long look at the place and asked her mother, "Is THIS IT?" She was sure they had "been had."

Booker Musgrove, born in October of 1909 in Lexington, Texas, another African-American living on the farm, was a labor contractor for Harris Ranch. Part of his job was to provide new workers with a place to live and assist them in

Hanging scale for weighing bags of cotton on Bull Farms and a worker to log each bag. Courtesy of the Bull/Klingenberg family.

locating essentials for living and working. There were many other families on the Sahuarita farm who had arrived under circumstances similar to what the Austin family experienced. The Austins quickly came to know other families who had come from Texas, Arkansas, Oklahoma, New Mexico, and Louisiana.

The block homes provided in the camp were very bare. There was no indoor plumbing, no insulation on the walls, and most of the rooms had only a bare lightbulb hanging from the ceiling. The conditions of their home didn't matter so much because John and Cora raised their family with complete love and affection.

Mr. Musgrove also supervised the cotton-chopping and cotton-picking crews, so the Austin family was quickly put to work. Pay for chopping cotton was six dollars a day, and in the fall they received three cents a pound for picking cotton. Willie recalls that johnsongrass was a terrible weed that would sprout up between the cotton plants. It was very difficult to control. He laughs as he tells the story of a farm up on the Nogales Highway that tried to use geese to control the wild-growing grass. "If humans with a hoe could not kill it, what's a goose going to accomplish?"

John was taught by Red Brown, who was a foreman for Harris Ranch, how to drive a tractor and operate other farm equipment. Red Brown and John became good friends. Both being from Arkansas must have helped them develop a bond. Over the years, the children of both men remained friends and gathered frequently to share memories of growing up in Sahuarita together.

John worked at the cotton gin on the farm during the cotton harvest for a few years before the gin was dismantled and moved to Gila Bend. John worked to take the gin apart and then assisted in reassembling it at its new location.

After recording the weights of the bags of cotton, workers climb the ladder to dump the cotton into the trailer. Courtesy of the Bull/Klingenberg family.

John and Cora never neglected their dedication to religion and the Lord. Their efforts motivated other African-American families wherever they lived. For quite a while, they took turns holding church services in the homes of different families. Eventually, John convinced the main supervisor, Mr. Stout, that families needed a permanent place to worship. Immediate work began on a small block building that was constructed very close to the railroad tracks between two rows of houses on the farm.

Early on, everyone was expected to work seven days a week. John asked and was allowed to work half days on Sundays so he could attend church and conduct services. The church building was constructed in the early 1950s while John was working for Dick Walden, and John believed that small space in the pecan orchard was truly holy ground. He believed that God uses people in your life to accomplish what needs to be done and, as the owner of Farmers Investment Corporation, Dick Walden was one of those people. The small brick building is still an active church today (2021). Many houses have been removed, but the small church still stands, with the name, "Sahuarita Church of God in Christ," proudly displayed as a reminder for those who knew and will always remember John Austin.

Sahuarita's Church of God in Christ standing in 2022 as a monument to the strength and faith of early Sahuarita families. Courtesy of Monica Lee Elam Christiansen.

John worked for Farmers Investment Co. until he left the farm. His last years were spent on the Continental feedlot. Willie remembers receiving a call from Margaret Gonzales one day telling him, "Mr. Austin was in an accident. He is all

Continental feedlot. Courtesy of University of Arizona Special Collections.

right, but is on his way to St. Mary's Hospital." John had been working on the silo when his jacket got caught, pulling his arm into the auger. He always said, "If I hadn't been a strong man, I would have died." The other workers heard him, shut the machine off, and got him to the hospital. His arm was never the same, but he survived. He still had his church and that kept him going.

John always had fond memories of his years working for Dick and the friendship that grew between the two men. Willie smiled as he thought back and said, "Dad always said Dick gave him a job and a place to worship. My dad was a happy man—ooh-eee, he was a happy man."

Upon request to Dick, improvements were made to John's home. Indoor plumbing, a restroom, bathing facilities, and other repairs made it more accommodating. The opportunity to own a home was made available to farm employees in the late 1960s. John was offered a home site in the Valle Verde area, close to where the Sahuarita Walmart now stands. He declined the opportunity because it would require him to move too far away from his church.

The Austin family is very appreciative of Dick Walden and his respect for their dad. One time, John requested time off to visit his ailing mother in Arkansas. Upon learning why John was requesting leave, Dick told him he had a trip scheduled to visit Oklahoma City on business. He offered John a ride on his airplane as far as Oklahoma City if John could then proceed on his own to his mother's hometown.

John had never in his life flown in an airplane. At first he was extremely reluctant and Willie thought he might back out of going, but John trusted Dick completely, and found that he thoroughly enjoyed flying. Much to John's surprise, upon arrival in Oklahoma City, he found that Dick had arranged a private ride for the rest of his journey to Tollette.

Late in their lives, John and Cora moved to Tucson and lived in a house near Main and Speedway. John loved Sahuarita and hated to leave, but their daughter, Alice, worked for Mr. Maxwell, who owned land in Tucson. He told Alice he would help her get a house for her parents. They built it from the ground up and had a nice, clean home in Tucson where they lived out their lives. They could have all of the kids and grandkids over to visit; Cora never tired of spending time with everyone.

Rounding up livestock at the Continental feedlot. Courtesy of University of Arizona Special Collections.

John remained a deacon at the church for the rest of his life. Even after he and Cora had moved to Tucson, he would still insist on driving the twenty miles to the small church in Sahuarita. Willie remembers that it got to a point where John was really too old to be driving. Whenever possible, Willie would take him and sometimes other members with a van would pick him up because many of the others who attended church also drove out from Tucson. On the days when nobody could offer him a ride, he would climb in his blue 1953 Dodge to make his own way to Sahuarita. He had no business being on the road, and may have been on the wrong side, but he made it. John and Cora faithfully went to church every Sunday and were both active members at the time of their deaths.

Willie laughingly remembered that his older brother used to come over to visit John and Cora. He finally took the distributor cap off so John's car wouldn't start. The next thing he knew, John would be out driving again. It turns out that he had gone across the street and asked the neighbor, who happened to be a mechanic, to fix it. They finally had to ask the man to please leave it broken for the safety of everyone.

Willie remembers that work was hard on the farm. When he turned fourteen, his days of playing on the farm ended and he quickly learned what real work was. Toiling all day long in the heat was not easy. Willie says, "There is no substitute for youth and what you can endure." He remembers that his dad set a good example and was always a hard worker, doing what he needed to do to support his family and give them the things they needed. Willie remembers being there working with his father when they started replacing the cotton fields with pecan trees in 1969.

Willie and his older siblings attended segregated schools in Arkansas. Willie recalls riding the school bus and passing the schools where only white kids attended. Their school was completely separate and located several miles up the road. It was a complete shock to him when he walked into Mrs. Durbin's third-grade classroom for the first time at Sahuarita Elementary School. Unlike what he had experienced in Arkansas, there was only one school for the whole community, and every student was welcome.

School was fun and Willie thoroughly enjoyed sports the most. Mr. Porter Wilson was Willie's sixth-grade teacher, and he coached all the boys' sports at the school. Willie excelled at football, basketball, and baseball. He always looked forward to competing with the schools in Tucson. Willie and his friends were in awe the first time the other team showed up in sports uniforms. Kids in Sahuarita had no uniforms to wear. From then on, Mr. Wilson made attempts to have some sort of uniform for his team, but somehow they always looked more like those of the military rather than a school.

Willie speaks with fondness and enthusiasm as he recalls Porter Wilson. He has always been

Operations of the Continental feedlot. Courtesy of University of Arizona Special Collections.

grateful for the support Mr. Wilson gave to all of his students. Once, Mr. Wilson had arranged for a weekend match and Willie was expected to participate. Willie did not show up because his father said he had to work. Upon finding out, Mr. Wilson drove the whole team over to find John Austin. Willie remembers him privately pleading his case saying, "Mister Austin, we got to have Willie. Without him there, it's no use in going." John relented and Mr. Wilson quickly drove out to the field where Willie was working. All of the team members got off the bus, went into the cotton field, and said, "Come on, man. Your dad said we could take you." They drove Willie home to quickly wash up and change for the game.

They rushed off to Safford Junior High School, where they found the other team waiting. Boy, did they have a game! Willie remembers yelling, "Come on! Let's fight! We're not gonna let those city kids win!" Willie also recalls the other team's comments about the "dusty-legged girls down in Sahuarita." To this day, Willie still laughs when he remembers someone saying, "Skyrocket's down there pickin' white lilies." He told them, "But at least I got some green money in my pocket from pickin' those white lilies." That shut them up really fast. Their team may have, in the end, lost that hard-fought game, but they still had a team picture in the newspaper in which they referred to Willie as "Skyrocket." This experience was something he will never forget.

In 1955, while in eighth grade, Willie made a record five-foot eleven-inch high jump at a track meet being held at Sunnyside. Prior to the meet, Willie recalls "The old coach from Wakefield was braggin', 'Ain't none of you guys gonna do what Valentine [Wakefield's best athlete] can do.'" Every once in a while, he would see Mr. Wilson who would tell him, "Willie, your record still stands."

Willie also remembers Mr. Mecham, who always wanted the kids to work arithmetic problems on the board. He liked to call on the kids he thought wouldn't know the answer because he thought embarrassing them would encourage them to learn. Willie walked into class the day after the basketball game and Mr. Meacham said, "All right, Skyrocket, you go up to the board there this morning." Willie said Mr. Mecham gave him a hard question, but he eventually got the answer. As he was going back to his seat, he said, "Mr. Mecham, you could have gone easy on me since I'm the star."

Cora Austin, left, sharing the stories of her life. Courtesy of Barbara Brown Bennett.

He also remembers some very intense after-school boxing matches—"Texas against Arkansas." Groups of the older farm kids got pretty skilled. Willie was especially fast and good with his hands. Some of the kids compared him to Muhammad Ali. Most of the time, the teams were pretty evenly matched.

Sahuarita School went up only to eighth grade, so after graduation the Austin children went to Pueblo High School in Tucson. Red Tyra drove the bus that picked the kids up to go to Pueblo. Mr. Tyra was a country boy and they had to listen to country music all the way there. They asked him if they could listen to some rock and roll. Mr. Tyra said, "Not on this bus, you won't." Mr. Gregory, the principal, finally told him to mix it up a little, so they were very happy.

John Austin worked hard all of his life to care for his family, something Willie and Alice will never forget. Willie remembers fondly his school years and the great memories he made with schoolmates: Juan Ortega, Clara Angulo, Richard Gallego, Cuate Velasquez, Luetta Musgrove, Barney Brent, Juan Tapia, Sue Lyons, Bob Jones, Abelardo Moreno, Frances Moreno, Olga Gonzalez, Edward Brown, and Billy Johnson.

Willie says, "Life was hard, but there is a God who loves us all. We just hung in there and by the grace of the Lord Jesus Christ, we survived." Willie left the hard work on the farms when he had an opportunity to get a job in the operations department for the City of Tucson. He laughed as he said, "I liked Sahuarita—liked to get out of there. I left Sahuarita so fast there were dust clouds behind me." He was tired of the long, exhausting

Willie Austin with Alice Austin Bailey and her husband posing for a photo. Courtesy of Barbara Brown Bennett.

days on the farm and was fortunate enough to have the option to explore something new. He started out at the bottom and worked his way up to a supervisory position. His dad was so proud of him. He told Dick Walden, "That's my son—a big-time supervisor for the City of Tucson."

Willie attributes his ability to have a successful career to his dad, John. "Dad was a good Christian who believed there was a God. He would never give up hope. He endured a lot. Dad did not have an education, but he laid the foundation for the next generation to have more choices and opportunities." Willie has a son who was city all-state in Pueblo basketball. He had many scholarship offers and spent two years at Arizona Western followed by two years at Cal State, Bakersfield. Willie credits his father's dedication to hard work for some of his grandson's success.

John passed away on December 7, 1998 and Cora followed on April 6, 2005. They were treasured parents, grandparents, friends, and neighbors who are missed to this day.

As one listens to Willie's thoughts and memories of his father and family, there is an overwhelming feeling of admiration and respect. Says Oscar Gomez, "Those of us 'young ones' who lived on the Sahuarita farm never called Willie's father by his first name. He was, and always will be, 'Mr. Austin.'"

~ Written by Oscar Gomez and Monica Lee Elam Christiansen,
as told by Willie and Alice Austin

Ollie and Jim in Sahuarito, Arizona Territory

James Kilroy Brown, also known as "J. K." or "Jim," was born on the family farm in Marion Township, Ohio, on December 9, 1849. Hyman Brown, Jim's father, had been born in Virginia on March 21, 1800, but spent a majority of his life in Marion Township. His mother, Harriet Wakefield, was born in Saint Clairsville, Ohio, on December 22, 1822. Their Ohio farm was a beautiful place where their nine children grew to adulthood.

On May 3, 1863, the oldest son, George C. Brown, was killed in the Battle of Milliken's Bend during the Civil War. The loss of this twenty-year-old son must have been difficult for the family. At the time, Seward Ellsworth "S. E." Brown, the youngest child, was only six months old.

While Hyman Brown was content to spend his life farming in Ohio, his sons were born with the desire to seek adventure. Nathaniel Wakefield Brown, born in 1848, Robert Samuel Brown, born in 1856, and Seward Ellsworth Brown, born in 1863, all eventually headed west, as did Jim.

According to the writings of Eleanor Winsor Davis, Jim's first travel adventure occurred in 1869 when he set sail from New York, destined for San Francisco by way of Panama. It is said that he "fell in love with California," but a shipboard illness quickly

James Kilroy and Olive Stephenson Brown sit for a photo soon after their marriage. Courtesy of the Brown-Strong family.

used up his savings and, with empty pockets, Jim returned to the farm where he worked for a number of years to finance his next adventure.

In 1872, while working in Chauncey as a clerk at the Ohio Coal & Co. store, he met Olive Letitia "Ollie" Stephenson who was attending the Weethees School for Girls. A friendship turned into an engagement on Olive's sixteenth birthday, but a wedding was not planned for the near future as Olive's parents, John A. and Clarissa S. Burge Stephenson, insisted that she first finish her education.

In 1874, Jim began to dream serious dreams of living happily ever after with Ollie as soon as she completed the education her folks had insisted upon and he made his fortune in the west. In the fall of 1875, Jim left his folks, his young sweetheart, Olive Stephenson, and his home in Summerfield, Ohio, traveling by train to California. Before he left, he said, "Ollie, I'll not bind you by a promise, but if you'll be as true to me as I will be to you, I want to claim you for my own on my return."

While studying a California newspaper, Jim read, "Modesto City, County Seat of Stanislaus County Central California, on the Tuolumne River and southeast of Stockton, in the San Joaquin Valley; founded in 1870." Modesto was located in an agricultural area, and good reports were being circulated about the mining that flourished there. The train went as far as Modesto, so that city was his first stop.

There he farmed with a couple of other young men. They did well, but not well enough to satisfy Jim. His mind was on Ollie, and his fortune wasn't growing as fast as he desired. He was a faithful correspondent with Ollie, and in a letter—one of hundreds over the years—dated July 9, 1876, Jim declared his undying love:

> *Dearest Darling Ollie,*
>
> *I have received from you two of the dearest best letters that ever were received by man. I know they are the dearest and best ever received by me. Dearest charming love, do you have the least fear of me forgetting you? If so, please remove that idea and let your mind be at rest. Dearest, if you will just prove as true to me as I have done and intend to do with you, we need not doubt each other for one moment. I am sure I have the utmost confidence in you and hope that you can say the same of me. There is not an hour in the day but my mind is resting on you—your noble heartedness, your kind ways, your beautiful form all appear to me in my mind's eye. I sometimes get so homesick to see you that I almost think of going back. Were it not for the name of so short a stay, I spoke at one time of not staying two years, I don't think now that I can ever stay that long from your dear darling presence. As for you calling me yours, if you are not safe in doing so, it is a fault of your own for I am sure it is my intention to be yours and yours alone if you will only be so kind as to partake of my offer. There was quite a big time in Modesto on the fourth, but I did not go. We worked. There was rain here on the sixth—wet the ground about two inches, something I never knew here before in the summer. Darling Dearest, a good night kiss. Please write soon and give all the news.*
>
> *~ Jas. K. Brown*

The urge to go to Tucson, within the Territory of Arizona, kept growing in Jim's mind month by month. So, in the spring of 1877, Jim and his farming companions left Modesto with their teams of horses and wagons and headed for Tucson. While on their journey southward Jim wrote to Ollie:

> *Ollie my darling, you may think my chances for returning to Ohio are scarce as I am now in such a wild country, but if I have any kind of luck at all, it shouldn't be long I assure you. My precious dear, if luck is against me, I will return anyhow and give up this wild life. I do not really like it. Rough life I mean, but will stand it for a short time hoping to be benefited by so doing.*

There is a grand rush to Arizona this spring from all directions. Some are after land; some are going into the mines; and some are seeking stock range. Of course, every man has his own object in view. If I can locate a good ranch, I will do so and if not, I will go into the mines and try my luck. This country has a beautiful climate. We are now on Latitude 34 and still going south. We had a splendid rain yesterday. The weather is very pleasant and warm today and sunny. Our party is now composed of seven men. When we started there were three of us, but while at San Bernardino, before starting across the desert, we fell in with a second party of four men from San Francisco. They are going to the gold district to the mines and perhaps we will go with them. Little did I think a year ago while in Chauncey, Ohio, that I would ever be here in this wild country. . . . Why is it that a man will stray off from civilization, from those that are so near and dear to one's heart? Excuse my poor writing and mistakes. I cannot write to do any good on account of the boys bothering me and talking to me all the time. Ollie dear, I will write again soon.

> *A hundred kisses,*
> *James K. Brown*

Somehow, Jim and his companions crossed the desert from San Bernardino and ferried across the Colorado River at Yuma. They made the journey in about a month, arriving in Tucson safe though slightly bedraggled.

They followed the road on the west bank of the Santa Cruz River, passing by the foot of Sentinel Peak on Mission Road, which led directly to a Native American reservation. They camped near the San Xavier Mission.

Jim poked around the little pueblo of Tucson, which then consisted of three dusty, dirty streets, each three or four blocks long. Main Street, the principal one, was lined with adobe dwellings built close to the street, with Mexican-style courtyards behind them. There were also several business establishments, livery stables, and a couple of hotels. The town, by this time, was much better than the Tucson described by J. Ross Browne, a visitor in the early 1860s when there were no hotels and travelers slept under the stars with the pigs that roamed the streets.

Jim wasn't a drinking man, but since the town consisted largely of saloons, he frequently wandered into one and hobnobbed with the various town characters. His dignified, quiet, but friendly manner won him many friends.

One of them was Tom Roddick, who had been in the territory for quite some time, having come from the goldfields of California in 1865. He was an indefatigable prospector and miner, having

Freight wagons pause near Tucson. Courtesy of Susan Strong-Dowd.

staked out several claims in the Santa Rita Mountains that had panned out quite well for him in the dozen or so years before Jim Brown came seeking his fortune. Tom was about twenty years older than Jim and quite a boozer, but he was an agreeable sort and an experienced miner. He and Jim hit it off well and made a little money working several of the mines together.

Jim, however, had his heart set on getting into the cattle business and was earnestly looking for a ranch so that he could offer his beloved Ollie a home. It so happened that Albert Case Benedict, a pioneer of pre-Civil War days, had abandoned the Sahuarito Ranch on the Santa Cruz River (the oldest ranch on the Santa Cruz), originally purchased from C. S. Rice in 1868, and converted it into a place for boarding horses and mules. Benedict had given up the Sahuarito Ranch and returned to his Huababi Ranch several miles south of Sahuarito to farm and raise stock. It may be noted here that Benedict died in 1880 at the home of Pete Kitchen in Tucson, leaving four children. The youngest, Mary, was adopted several years later by Mary and Frank Proctor. Benedict's wife, Gregoria Alvarez, died in 1884.

Early in November 1877, Thomas Roddick and Jim Brown acquired the Sahuarito Ranch. A notice in the *Arizona Weekly Star* dated November 8, 1877, advertised their new venture in the following language:

Entry to the Sahuarito Ranch with the windmill in the background. Courtesy of Arizona Historical Society.

Messrs. Roddick & Brown have purchased the Sahuarito Ranch, located twenty-two miles from Tucson, on the Tubac road, and intend opening it for the benefit of the traveling public. Meals will be served at all hours of the day or night. They will also keep on hand hay and grain for stock. Mr. Roddick is well known in Arizona, and his partner, an old Californian . . . will be on hand to attend to the wants of the public. Give the boys a call.

By the end of December, Tom and Jim, with the help of Jim's brother Nathaniel, began to receive high praise for the quality of food being served at their Sahuarito Ranch station. The *Arizona Weekly Star*, dated December 20, 1877, gave them a plug by publishing a portion of a letter from a traveler making a trip from Tucson to the Oro Blanco mining district.

Arriving at Roddick and Brown's Ranch, quail on toast was a good feature among the various condiments [sic] that greeted our astonished gaze and to which we set to [sic] with the very best of intentions. We wish Roddick & Brown had a ranch a trifle closer to town, say on the Plaza here in Tucson.

The mines kept Tom and Jim busy, and the stage station was prospering. Nathaniel was hard pressed for help in the kitchen, so Roddick moved in a woman friend from Tucson, named Guadalupe, to keep house for them, wait on tables, and do the laundry.

Jim heard less and less often from his Ohio sweetheart, Ollie. Day after day Jim watched for the mail stage to arrive bearing a letter from Ollie. He was bitterly disappointed as a single day stretched into months without a word from his sweetheart. Also, he was becoming increasingly anxious about the situation at the Sahuarito Ranch Stage Station.

Although marriage was uppermost in his mind, he could not propose a marriage date because his business partner had brought a woman to live with him in the only home he could offer Ollie at the time. Jim pondered his personal problems for a good period of months. He and Roddick had located the Excelsior Mine in 1878, a year after Jim had arrived in Tucson. There was money to be made, but it was slow in coming.

While the area of the Santa Rita Mountains looked promising for mining in the 1860s, there had been little activity at that time because of the uncertainties of the war between the North and South, and the hostilities with the Native Americans. Some claims had been staked, but not recorded. However, in the late 1870s, several prospectors discovered limestone on the northwestern slope of the Santa Ritas and organized a mining camp which they named Helvetia. About the same time, another group of men formed a camp on the eastern slope, which they called Rosemont Camp.

Jim browsed around in this area and in 1879 located a copper mine on the saddle between Helvetia and Rosemont. He named it the Narragansett. He hoped that this mine would make him rich. Meanwhile, he was making a little money from holdings in the Tyndall mining district, which included the Hidalgo and Tubac mines, jointly owned by Messrs. Brown, Phillips, Ammet, and Brottam. In that same district, the Leticia Mine, referred to in the August 25, 1877, edition of the *Arizona Daily Star* as the "joy of its owners with four or five tons on the dump," and a vein that was "three feet through," was "owned by the Khedive Company, Roddick, Buck, Britton, and Brown." Unfortunately, Jim's income from ownership in the mines was not netting enough to buy out Roddick.

Roddick, meanwhile, had accumulated $6,000 in the bank and was contemplating a trip to Texas to buy range cattle for the ranch, in which Jim would share, but he became seriously ill around June 1, 1879. On June 4, he went to see Dr. J. C. Handy, whom he had seen on previous occasions. Dr. Handy was not available on this occasion so Tom was attended to by Dr. C. V. P. Watson. On Saturday morning, June 7, Tom died.

After the initial shock of his partner's death, Jim realized that he was free to plan for his future. However, Guadalupe, the Sahuarito Stage Station housekeeper and the late Roddick's companion, filed a petition July 16, 1879, in the probate court of Pima County, Arizona Territory, claiming she was Roddick's widow. She asked for the house, twenty acres of land, two cows, five swine, and a six-month supply of feed for the animals. She also wanted furniture, utensils, wearing apparel, and household goods. Finally, she demanded $75 per month for maintenance of the place during settlement of the estate.

J. S. Wood, Probate Judge, denied the petition, and on August 6, Guadalupe appealed to the Supreme Court. Attorneys for Roddick's absent heirs (his mother and a sister) filed objections to the petition, which was again denied.

When the court proceedings were final, on August 21, 1879, the ranch

James Kilroy and Olive Stephenson Brown had portraits taken while visiting Tucson. Courtesy of the Brown-Strong family.

was sold to J. K. Brown for $1,000, and Roddick's personal property for $659.

While the probate court proceedings were taking place, Jim got a letter from Ollie in which she broke off their engagement and announced her plans to marry an old beau, George Smith. George had just graduated from Harvard and gone to work in his father's haberdashery shop in Chauncey.

Jim was a gallant suitor, not easily discouraged, so he left his business with his brother, Nathaniel Brown, sold the horse he had ridden into Tucson, boarded the stage, went to California, and took the train for Ohio.

Jim went to see Olive. She told him at once that she was going to marry George Smith. Jim's response was in the form of a question. "Ollie, do you care more for him than you do for me?"

She told him he had no right to ask a question of that sort and went on to say that she was fond of George and respected him deeply.

Stagecoach racing on its way. Courtesy of Susan Strong-Dowd.

Before long, Ollie's mother saw that Ollie was unhappy, and asked her if she really cared more for Jim than for George. Ollie admitted that she did. Her mother advised her to marry Jim and "go to the ends of the earth with him."

Jim and Ollie were married in her mother's little parlor at nine o'clock in the morning on November 6, 1879, and all too soon they started on the long journey to a new home in the Territory of Arizona. Jim had expected work on the Southern Pacific Railroad to be further along by the time he returned to Tucson from Ohio, and thought he and Ollie could go right into Tucson on the train. The summer heat and scarcity of water had delayed the work on the Tucson terminus, though, and Casa Grande was the end of the line.

A stagecoach met the train at Casa Grande, but Jim had neglected to wire ahead for reservations on the stage, and there was room for only one more passenger. Jim wanted Ollie to go ahead. He'd follow on the next coach and meet her at the hotel in Tucson. Ollie refused to leave Jim, so Jim wired his brother Nathaniel to bring horses and a buggy to take them to Tucson.

Ollie, Jim, and Nathaniel drove into Tucson the evening of December 26, 1879, stopping at the Cosmopolitan Hotel on Main Street. The next day they set out for Sahuarito by way of Mission Road along the Santa Cruz River. Late in the afternoon of December 27, Ollie laid eyes for the first time on the big adobe building situated on the west bank of the Santa Cruz that was to be her home.

The Sahuarito Stage Station, Ollie's new 7,608-acre home, lay in a broad, picturesque valley, shadowed on the south and east by the lofty Santa Rita Mountains, rugged and beautiful. Looking west through the open valley, heavily forested by mesquite trees, she saw the box-shaped Baboquivari Peak some fifty miles away, towering over this great desert country, its silhouette cut shapely in the big sky.

Ollie loved the big, rambling, eight-room adobe building, with extra thick walls and high ceilings. The two front, or living rooms, were floored, while the other rooms had hard-packed dirt floors. A porch, twelve feet wide, extended around three sides of the building, and was topped by an awning. A high, thick adobe wall surrounded the entire structure. She loved the fireplaces in several of the rooms which were constantly kept bright with burning mesquite logs.

Her first report home said, "The stage station has a big room with long benches at the dining table which is a crude affair made to accommodate twenty or thirty people." She further wrote, "More often than not there are

Tucson's Palace Hotel around 1880. Edited digital image courtesy of the Getty Open Content Program.

nights when we have a full house of nice courteous men. I expected to see men who use their forks and daggers to pick their teeth—not doctors and lawyers and refined people."

On New Year's Day, 1880, Jim drove Ollie to Canoa Ranch to introduce her to and visit his friends, Mary and Frank Proctor. Mary and Frank lived in a hacienda on a large cattle ranch on the Santa Cruz River about fifteen miles south of Sahuarito.

Ollie soon became a favorite with the Mexican ranch hands, cowboys, and miners. She made good friends in Tucson, where she and Jim enjoyed little vacations for several days at a time. They would stay at the Palace Hotel, eat good meals, dance, sleep in pleasant surroundings, and go shopping.

Ollie was wild with excitement when she learned of the big celebration scheduled to take place in Tucson when the first Southern Pacific train was to roll in on March 20, 1880. Of course she and Jim had to participate. It would be just three months since they had gotten off the train in Casa Grande.

View from the Palace Hotel rooftop around 1880. Edited digital image courtesy of the Getty Open Content Program.

The great day finally came. They stayed at the Palace Hotel. Ollie wrote her Ma and Pa describing the band and the speeches, the booming cannons, and the 38-gun salute of the sixth cavalry, but the party at Levin's Park was the best part. The nice people she met, and the dancing, were highlights. Ollie loved to dance. "Ma," she wrote, "I waltzed and waltzed and it was lovely. I looked nice in my blue taffeta that I had made at Middlefield, and Jim was so handsome. I am proud of my precious husband. Do you remember how you approved of my dancing everything but the waltz? Well, Ma, I waltzed on the sly then, and I'm waltzing now."

In the month of April, 1880, Ollie and Jim headed out through the sage brush, across the vast sandy desert, thick with mesquite trees, saguaros, and the many other species of cacti that cover the southwest desert.

Through big sandy washes and over rough, rocky, bumpy roads, Jim Brown took his lovely young bride of a few months in his horse-drawn buggy to Arivaca and to Baboquivari.

Ollie wrote in a letter to her mother, "Jim had to make a trip to Baboquivari on mining business and I went with him. We packed a lunch for the first day and in the late afternoon got to the little hotel at Arivaca, about thirty miles from home, where Camile Roseilles [*sic*], a Frenchman, was a fine host. We spent the night there and the next morning started out bright and early to finish our trip of twenty-five miles. Camile fixed us a splendid lunch and the trip was ideal. The travel was good and the weather was all that could be desired.

Pete Kitchen posing for a formal portrait. Courtesy of Marshall Trimble.

"I have never seen any place so carpeted with flowers, mostly snow lilies. It was enchanting. We did not get to our destination until almost evening, but then we were beautifully entertained by the Rainey boys in their camp. They are doing some prospecting in the Baboquivari area."

In the late spring of 1880, Jack Rockfellow and Bill Hart came from Devil's Cache mine in the Santa Ritas (up in White House Canyon—later known as Madera Canyon) to Sahuarito Ranch. Pete Kitchen and young Rockfellow had become great friends, and Pete had told him of the "good little woman" of Jim

James K. Brown's family and friends gather in front of Sahuarito Ranch circa 1896. Clara is the second from left, Olive is fifth from left, and James Kilroy is on the far right leaning against the fence. Courtesy of Arizona Historical Society.

Brown who had come from back east, as Jack and Bill had.

They had a pleasant visit that day and Ollie was entertained with a recital of harrowing experiences they had endured in 1877 while en route from California to Arizona loaded down with their prospecting gear. Bill Hart was the owner of a misfit burro that he had named Balsam. The burro was long legged, short bodied, red eared, and cussedly stubborn. On occasions when Hart was riding him, the burro gave an exhibition of her stubbornness by suddenly stopping and apparently becoming anchored. Hart [dismounted] and gathered a fistful of dry grass and remounted. Striking a match, he lit the grass and shoved it under the burro's tail. The burro left the spot in a hurry and the future striking of a match was enough to cause the animal to forget her stubbornness. Although the remedy was effective, it cost Hart the loss of much dry grass and several stacks of hay one time when he accidentally lit a large grass fire.

Another time, they were up on a mountain trail with a deep canyon on one side and a high mountain on the other. All at once, Balsam brayed in her loudest voice, broke into a run with pots and pans making a fearful chorus, with her mouth wide open. Terrified into bravery by the sight of a huge bear, she was going right for him. The bear, equally terrified at such an unusual encounter, folded himself up into a ball and rolled down the canyon wall.

Of Kitchen, the story is told that on one occasion, contrary to the admonitions and advice of friends, he went into Sonora, Mexico, to buy sheep. He returned to the Santa Cruz Valley without any sheep, and broke, which caused the Mexican people in the neighborhood to say that, *"El fui por lana y salió trasquilado,"* or "He went for wool and returned shorn."

Ollie was impressed with the modest manliness of Jack Rockfellow, a refined young man—a gentleman, and as she put it, a "good Christian." He was well educated and interesting. She sized up his partner, Bill Hart, as a man hewn of rougher stuff, but being the kind of person she was, she saw the good in both men and enjoyed their company many times after that.

One story they told that really impressed her was about a young man named George Atkinson, who had contracted to burn brick for the beautiful hotel being built by Colonel Sykes at Calabasas on a spectacular site overlooking the junction of the Sonoita Creek and the Santa Cruz River. Atkinson had stumbled into the rain-soaked camp of a crew that had been on a truck from Tucson to Sonora, and of which Jack and Bill were members.

They were just about to eat dinner around the campfire when suddenly a disheveled young man burst out of the thicket of mesquite, sans most of his clothing and even his boots. He had been robbed by a gang of bandits of his horse, saddle, gun, and the new attire he had just purchased in Tucson. One of the bad men had put on George's fancy new boots and then kicked him in the rump and told him to scram.

"He was really mad when he came upon us," Jack said. "We shared our beans and bacon and coffee and he was truly grateful." He was hired back on his job at Calabasas and stayed around and became a good friend to Jack and Bill. Olive got acquainted with George Atkinson sometime later and heard the story firsthand, as well as some others, equally bad if not worse, about a gang of cutthroats known as the Celia outlaws.

At this time, in 1880, not only was Ollie getting acquainted with the many frontier people who stopped at the stage station and little store, but she was also preparing for a baby.

Mary "Mamie" Bernard Aguirre, sister of Noni Bernard from Arivaca, had stopped one time at the Sahuarito station to visit Ollie. They were charmed with each other and, woman-like, talked about their families. Mamie was considerably older than Ollie, but she was still a pretty, gracious lady. She was the mother of three sons, Pedro the eldest, eleven, and his two younger brothers, Bernard and Stephen, who were in Westport, Missouri, attending school and staying with an uncle, William R. Bernard. In the course of the visit Mamie Aguirre told Ollie of the brutal slaying of her young husband, Epifanio Aguirre, a freighter, by Apaches in January of 1870 near Sasabe, Arizona. Her story did little to allay Ollie's fear of Native Americans.

Epifanio Aguirre was sixteen when his family moved from Chihuahua, Mexico, to Las Cruces, New Mexico, in 1850, where he engaged in freighting by mule and ox trains between New Mexico and Missouri. During his trips over the Santa Fe Trail every few months, he met sixteen-year-old Mamie Bernard. Though neither spoke the other's language, they fell in love and were married in 1862. An interpreter and a neighbor friend in Westport, Missouri, Steven B. Elkins, aided and abetted them in this romance and even accompanied them on the wagon train trip when Epifanio brought Mamie and their three-month-old son, Pedro, to his home in New Mexico in 1863. Six years later, Epifanio moved his family to Southern Arizona where his other two sons were born. A year later in January 1870, Mamie became a widow when Epifanio was killed.

General George Crook was sent to Arizona in 1871 to quell Apache hostilities. Some of the Apaches were trying to work and live peacefully with the white settlers, but in about 1872, it became obvious that attacks were continuing in Arizona.

In 1882, Olive Stephenson Brown poses for a formal portrait. Courtesy of Arizona Historical Society.

One of Crook's prime considerations was a first-class pack train, and he thought the mule was about the most important part of his military deployment. A couple of young men who had been teamsters (bushwhackers) on the west coast, known in their firm as Hank and Yank, were chosen by the general to follow him over dangerous mountain trails. He chose them because of their honesty, dependability, and congeniality, and for the scrupulously good treatment they gave their mules.

Hank and Yank followed General Crook from one end of Arizona territory to the other. They became known as "the inseparables" because of their close partnership.

When General Crook left Arizona, Hank and Yank left the government service. They invested their savings in mines and land in Oro Blanco, several miles southwest of Sahuarito and close to the Mexican border. It was a mining town, and Yank operated a general store there and carried on his business as a teamster. Hank and Yank also located ranches in Bear Valley, a few miles east of Oro Blanco. While riding his wagon from Oro Blanco to Tucson, Yank became a regular patron of the Sahuarito stage station, beginning when it was operated by Tom Roddick and Jim Brown in 1879.

One winter day in 1880 Hank and Yank rode up to the Sahuarito Ranch, tethered their horses, and entered the stage station. They had come to meet their friend Jim's young wife. Ollie thought Mr. Henry Hewitt (Hank) and Mr. John Bartlett (Yank) to be pretty "crude at first meeting, but interesting." Hank, busy at his Bear Valley Ranch, wasn't often seen at the Sahuarito stage station, but Yank continued to stop his wagon at the ranch and rest his team.

The Brown's had a Mexican maid named Chona Ruiz, who was employed by the family. She was very intelligent and gave excellent service. A visitor, commenting on the maids' apparent efficiency, asked her about her education and how many languages she spoke. Chona promptly replied, "Three—Spanish, English, and Mrs. Brown's Spanish."

In the latter part of August, 1880, Ollie and Jim went to Tucson and rented a house on McCormick Street. Their baby was due to be born soon. It was as convenient a place as could be found. They ate their meals at a small boarding house close by, managed by a man named Sue Donny. Jim tried to make everything as comfortable for Ollie as possible. She was trying to be brave but Jim knew she was nervous and frightened.

Mrs. Coughlin, an Irish woman, was hired to be Ollie's nurse, and Dr. John Handy was a big and brusque man in some ways, but also kind and comforting. Just before the stroke of midnight, September 3, 1880, the doctor delivered a sweet, fat baby girl. Dr. Handy stayed, giving directions to Mrs. Collins, until he was satisfied that mother, father, and baby were doing just fine.

The baby was named Clara Beatrice, but Yank Bartlett teasingly dubbed the new baby Keno. Ollie didn't care much for that nickname, but it wasn't long before she, too, began using the pet name.

Salero mining camp, in the foothills of the Santa Rita mountains, was a pretty place where a number of Ollie's and Jim's friends worked and lived. The two highest peaks in the range, Mount Wrightson and Mount Hopkins, were named for two men who were part of the Salero Mining Company, which had worked the mine since 1857. Both had been killed by Apaches, but the Salero mine working continued. One winter day in December 1880, John and Alice Campbell, with their two children, came from Salero camp to visit Ollie and Jim. These friends frequently visited and stayed the night.

Christmas of 1880 fell on a Saturday. Jim went to Tucson during the week for supplies, anticipating that many travelers would stop by for something to eat. William, their splendid Chinese cook, would set a good table with plenty of meat, potatoes, vegetables, and pies. Of that Jim was certain. Jim was more concerned about Ollie's Christmas in Arizona so far away from her family. Jim got her a small pine tree from the Santa Rita mountains. Following the custom of her folks, she decorated the Christmas tree with whatever she had at hand—cards, paper chains, bows of calico, ribbons, and lace. Her mother had tucked in her trunk some of her Pynchon candleholders when she left home the year before, and Jim brought some tiny candles from town, as well as a few trinkets for his brothers Nathanial and Seward, the latter of whom had come to Sahuarito in June. They would all celebrate the baby's first Christmas together.

James Brown, having arrived in Tucson, a town of about 4,000, in June 1877, had escaped the Indian atrocities that had befallen some of the earlier settlers. Even after that date, people along the Santa Cruz River and in the vicinity of the Santa Rita mountains lived in fear of marauding Apache bands, who kept slipping in despite the Indian reserves that had been selected by the Indians themselves. Geronimo, the famous Apache chieftain, refused to be transferred to the San Carlos reservation, and fled to New Mexico. He was finally captured and sent to San Carlos in June of 1877, the same time Jim Brown had come to

Tucson.

Under the pseudonym "Spider," Ollie had been the vivacious social reporter of the *Echo*, a local newspaper in the village of Chauncey, Ohio, from whence she had so recently come to the southwest.

Being a natural born [writer] she entertained herself not only by writing constantly to her folks, but also by frequent contributions to the hometown newspaper under her pseudonym.

Sahuarito Ranch, A. T., April 27, 1881

Editor, Echo

Thinking that a small space would be accorded me in your valuable paper, and believing that a few items from far away Arizona would be interesting to the many readers of the Echo, I send the following:

We are situated on the Santa Cruz, a subterranean river about 20 miles from the honorable and ancient Pueblo, Tucson, a city of about 10,000 inhabitants, principally the natives of the territory and the "noble" Redman. The Santa Cruz Valley is 200 miles in length and about 40 miles in its widest part, and one of the finest and richest valleys in the territory, and for stock the grazing cannot be excelled. Arizona will probably never be an agricultural country on account of the scarcity of water. Artesian wells have thus far never been a success and all the water is raised by windmills and by "whims" for irrigating.

We are hemmed in by mountains on all sides. To the north is the Santa Catalinas, whose rock capped peaks look like they are covered with snow all the year round, and hidden treasures consisting of gold, silver, and copper mines are being brought to light day after day by fortunate prospectors. To the west of the Sierrita Mountains, rich in silver and copper, and to the east and south are the Santa Rita Mountains, the largest and highest range in the territory, of which "old Baldy" peak is the highest point. The mineral wealth of the Santa Rita mountains is most fabulous. Reduction works for milling the ore are going up and the camps are the scenes of excitement in life. Among the richest mines of the Santa Ritas are the Copper World, Scorpion, Narragansett, Kolkata, Excelsior, and many others too numerous to mention. The Narragansett has an open cut 40 feet and a tunnel 60 feet. It has a good foot wall with 14 feet solid ore, or carbonate, and red and black oxide. Mining experts claim this mine to be a "second Copper Queen." Miners' wages are $3.50 to four dollars a day. The celebrated Copper Queen mine sold at Bisbee a few days ago for $1,250,000. At present writing the weather is warm and delightful. I haven't known winter since leaving dear old Ohio. In conclusion I will say to those who have romantic ideas founded on rumors of [life out west], if you don't wish them dispelled like mist before the morning sun, don't come to Arizona.

Ollie summed up her first year at Sahuarito stage station as "nondescript, full of love, pain, and curiosity." She wrote her Ma and Pa that she had met charming people, queer people, people seeking adventure, people seeking fortunes, and that was exciting. Yet she could not overcome her nervousness and fears. The newspaper accounts of atrocities involving conflicts with Native Americans were beginning to distress her.

As if that weren't enough, Mexican bandits were robbing and murdering people in the vicinity of the Santa Cruz Valley. To add to all this nervousness, the frequent roundups of cattle by *vaqueros* (cowboys) caused great amounts of dust and confusion, and a steady flow of people arriving by stage had to be fed and oftentimes bedded down for the night.

When Ollie realized that she was pregnant again, she told Jim that she couldn't go through the ordeal of having another baby on the ranch, and even suggested that he give up Western life and move back east. They finally decided that she should spend her prenatal months in Chauncey, Ohio, with her folks until Jim could decide what he could afford to do. Ollie wrote her Ma and Pa that she was coming home.

In the latter part of June, 1881, Ollie, Jim, and baby Clara slept two nights on the roof of the Palace Hotel. It was unbearably hot to sleep indoors, but there was hardly a breath of air stirring outside, either. Many people the length and breadth of Meyer Street were sleeping outside on cots or blanket pallets spread on the ground.

Mary and Frank Proctor drove them from the Palace Hotel to the Southern Pacific depot a few blocks away. Then Ollie and Clara caught the eastbound train for Ohio, with Jim and the Proctors seeing them off.

After she was gone, Jim wrote Ollie that he had attended to business in town the rest of the day and left Tucson for the ranch in the evening. He

A cactus garden thrives out front of the Sahuarito Ranch. Courtesy of Susan Strong-Dowd.

said he was nearly home at about 10:00 p.m. when the powder house north of town blew up. The explosion was tremendous; nearly all of the glass windows in Tucson were broken, and the noise was so loud he heard it as far away as Sahuarito. Some professed to have heard it as far away as Arivaca and others believed that Halley's comet had struck the earth. It panicked many Tucson people, but actually very little damage was done.

The balance of the year 1881 was one of uncertainties and grueling work for Jim. Besides maintaining the stage station, he was raising hay for the cattle herd he was building up. Jim patiently carried on at the ranch, hoping he could salvage enough from his mining enterprises to make it possible for him to go back to Ohio and make Ollie happy if that should be where she preferred to live. She seemed torn by indecision and asked him to tell her what to do. He responded, "Please, Darling, do not ask me what you should do; ask yourself what is best for you and your health and the health of our sweet little darling baby."

On July 5, 1881, part of Jim's letter said "I wrote to you last Tuesday, Thursday, and Saturday. In fact I have written every day there was a stage. Also, I sent you the paper containing the account of the explosion. The cook is about the same as when you left and old sleepy George is alive yet looks as though he might not get through the summer. We have had two or three good rains since you left. Frank Proctor went in on Saturday's stage and has not heard anything from J. H. Campbell and Mary Proctor since you went away. When we went back to the hotel, I gave Mary her comb and brush and did not see her anymore. I have not been in town since you left. I presume the world has had its Fourth of July, but I did not see any celebration as I was home all day and there was no trouble to amount to anything. I am very anxious to hear from you since your arrival home. I am very lonely."

Roy and Clara Brown photographed circa 1886 in Nelsonville, Ohio. Courtesy of Arizona Historical Society.

A few days after Ollie had left for Ohio, an assassination attempt was made on the life of President James Garfield on July 2, 1881, by a disgruntled office seeker. After lingering a few weeks, Garfield died on

September 19, 1881. Following the script of his Republican father's politics, Jim deplored the violent death of the new president. Generally, however, he followed the national political scene with only half-hearted interest. His thoughts were mainly on Ollie, baby, and work, though he did keep abreast of local politics through the *Arizona Daily Star* and the *Arizona Weekly*.

On July 7, Jim went to Tucson on business to make out a deed for the Williams brothers. He wrote: "I will get $2,000 if all goes right, which I think it will, although I never count on mining money until I get it in my fingers. Now that you've gotten home please don't strain yourself in any way. Get everything you need or want and when you want any money please let me know and I will send you whatever you need."

Sandwiched in between his many other chores from July until the time Ollie came back from Ohio about fifteen months after her departure, Jim kept her posted about the Narragansett mine. He never lost faith that the mine was going to net him a sizable amount of money. He also wrote all the accounts of a number of smaller mines he was selling or hoped to sell. It was from the smaller workings that he actually made his sales, but it was obviously slow going and he frequently remarked that, "You can't rush a mine sale."

When Jim's brother Nathaniel had followed Jim to Tucson in 1879, he had left his wife Kate and two children in Ohio, hoping to strike it rich in mining and make a home for them in a new land. Kate, in order to be closer to her husband, moved to Santa Cruz, California, and stayed with relatives until such time as he could join her in California or she could join him in Arizona. The summer of 1881 was unusually stormy. Kate wrote to Jim inquiring why her husband had not written and Jim answered that Nathaniel was still up in the mountains and could not get home now even if he wanted to because the river banks were full. Nathaniel had gone up into the mountains to work for the Williams Brothers where he was paid four dollars a day.

Lord and Williams had been one of the well-liked general merchandising establishments in Tucson since 1870 and they had branched out into the banking business. Over the course of several months, Jim kept Ollie apprised of how he and some of their neighbors had put money into the Lord and Williams depository with confidence. Suddenly, without warning, the great Lord and Williams enterprise collapsed and became a total failure. Many, including the Browns, lost money when the company fell apart.

John and Tootsie Brown had their portrait taken at the same time as their siblings. Courtesy of Arizona Historical Society.

About fifteen or twenty miles from Sahuarito Ranch, on the road leading to South Tubac, Tumacacori, Calabasas, and Pete Kitchen's Potrero Ranch, to name a few locations along the way, was another road that turned west at almost a 90° angle. It led to Arivaca. This formed a junction. Within the junction, a store and corral were built to accommodate travelers going north, south, or west. It became known as "junction corner" and years later was to be called Kinsley's corner.

A number of Jim's friends at Calabasas had stocked and opened the store unsuccessfully. Jim did not think it looked like a very lucrative business for Ed Wood, who had lost everything in the Lord and Williams' failure.

Jim continued to manage his business dealings in Arizona. Ollie remained in Ohio and gave birth to a baby boy on March 9, 1882. Jim wrote to her, "Mama wanted me to send a name for our little man. I think he is big enough to name himself." They named the baby James Kilroy Brown, Jr., after his father, and nicknamed him Roy.

Plans were being made for Ollie to return to Arizona in May, but that did not work out. Nathaniel and Kate came to stay with Jim. While there, their children became ill. Jim's letter, dated April 1, said, "I will try to tell you something about the sadness of our brother and sister and losing their two sweet little darlings. They came out here to the ranch on Tuesday evening of the 21st (March) and when they came Aubrey was broken out some and Kate thought it was heat from getting too warm in the cars. The next morning he was quite sick. Little Minnie was playing around the yard until nine or ten o'clock when she came in and told her mama that she felt sick at her stomach and was taken very severely ill so the next day which was Thursday she was delirious and stayed so until death which came ten minutes after two o'clock on Monday, March 27. Poor little Aubrey died the following evening fifteen minutes before six. Just about the time I was laying poor little Minnie down to sleep, the sleep that knows no waking, little patient Aubrey was dying. It rained very hard. Neither of the parents could go to the funeral of little Minnie, as they could not leave the other dying child. Kate stands the loss splendidly. I think she has more nerve than any little lady I ever met. Darling, I mentioned your staying at home until fall which I think best for you as the hot summer will be here. Now because of this disease it might be best for our babies to stay home. We will consider the matter when you get well and then can decide what to do."

In another letter to Ollie on April 3, Jim identified the illness as scarlet fever. Kate and Nathaniel went back to Ohio. They later moved to Oregon, where Kate had two more babies. They remained there the rest of their lives.

Jim did not go to Ohio in the fall to bring Ollie back to Sahuarito. Ollie had lingered in Ohio because Jim was fearful that if she came too soon after the deaths of Minnie and Aubrey the babies might be exposed to scarlet fever, despite the fact that he had carefully scrubbed and whitewashed everything.

An image of a picnicking Brown family shows Olive in the wagon and Harriett sitting on the ground near their poor dejected Bobby horse. Courtesy of Arizona Historical Society.

It was running late into summer and Jim's fear that Ollie would suffer such discomfort from the heat that it might affect her health made it easier for her parents to put pressure on her to stay with them. And so, month after month passed, until the hottest part of the summer was over.

Ollie finally got her dander up and said she was going home to Jim which she did, in September of 1882.

The American philosopher Irwin Edman is often quoted as having said: "The gift of gaiety may itself be the greatest good fortune, and the most serious step toward maturity." This—the gift of gaiety—is the gift that was given to 21-year-old Olive Stephenson Brown.

Her husband Jim was an excited man that warm September day in 1882 when he went to Tucson and met the train that was carrying his beloved Ollie. When the porter gently put his little girl, two-year-old Keno, on the ground, Jim lunged for her and gathered her up in his arms so feverishly that she whimpered as she turned her head anxiously to look for her Mama, who was coming down the steps with fat, six-month-old Roy in her arms. Jim soon had all three encircled in his embrace —all three crying—Ollie for joy, the infants from fright.

It was a happy couple that took the long buggy ride back to Sahuarito Ranch. The babies were soon fast asleep. Jim had made arrangements to go in with the wagon the following day and pick up the trunk.

When they entered the house after Ollie's fifteen-months absence in Ohio with her folks, she immediately saw why Jim had so persistently, in his many letters, urged her to take music lessons and practice as much as she could so that she would be a good performer when she got back. A lovely square

Steinway piano was standing proudly in one corner of the "long" room (the dining room for travelers), a homecoming gift from Jim. Tears were always as close to the surface as laughter with sentimental Ollie. She cried.

A frequent visitor to the Sahuarito Ranch was Ollie's devoted friend, Mary Proctor. Mary and Ollie were mighty glad to see each other after Ollie got home from Ohio and they visited often. They had grand visits. Mary enjoyed the children and confided to Ollie her longings to have a family but that, as time passed, her hopes waned.

It was a joyous Christmas in 1882 at the Sahuarito stage station ranch, with Jim's family safely back from Ohio. Ollie had her piano; Mary Proctor had brought Ollie's canaries, Rosa and Dick—gifts from George Hand—back after caring for them while Ollie had been in Ohio; and the station was again filled with merriment and song. When Ollie was not singing the popular songs of the day to Jim and visitors, she was singing to her babies all the songs her grandpa had taught her as they rode around the Ohio farm on horseback when she was a small girl. With both arms around her grandpa's waist, she had clung for dear life. She sat behind him bouncing around on the horse's fat rump while Grandpa Stephenson warbled away. Those were happy, carefree days, before her Pa enlisted in the 63rd Volunteer Infantry during the Civil War.

Bertha Stephenson and her niece, Clara Brown sit at the family piano at Sahuarito Ranch in January of 1901. Courtesy of Arizona Historical Society.

Ollie also reminisced about her sweet Ma who, like Pa, sang a lot. Her thoughts were often with her folks in Ohio, but Ollie had decided that her home was now in Arizona with Jim in the land he loved, and it was her desire to make him happy. She said Jim made up for her defects with his nobleness; he was so modest and so thoroughly good and true.

Ollie made so many friends with her singing and hospitable ways that a custom was born that lasted many Christmases while they were at the ranch. Along with their friends on the Santa Cruz they staged a "baile" (a dance gathering) at Christmas time. All the neighboring *vaqueros* and their families were invited. The babies and small children were bundled up in blankets and tucked in every nook and cranny while the older children and their families enjoyed refreshments, and sang and danced to the guitar music of some of the local Mexican musicians.

Jim brought Ollie to Tucson on or about July 12, 1884. He rented a house at 215 Camp Street, next to the Prince Brothers carpenter shop, in anticipation of their third child who was soon to be born.

On July 15, Jim and his friend, Sheriff Bob Paul, went to Sahuarito Ranch to tend to some business, expecting to return in the evening. A fearful storm came up. Trees were uprooted; telegraph polls leveled. Ollie was so terrified that she became sick. Her joy knew no bounds when Jim and the sheriff came back safely late in the evening. The next morning, July 16, the baby was born. Mrs. Coughlin, the same Irish nurse, attended Ollie during Harriet Estelle's arrival. Good Dr. Handy officiated at the delivery, as he had done at her first child's birth. Jim immediately called the beautiful new miss his little "Tootsie," as he relished pet names.

While Ollie was in bed, a fire broke out next door in the Prince carpenter shop. Ollie was still weak.

Jim had brought an unopened bottle of Three Star brandy in case it was needed. Alcohol was considered good medicine on some occasions, but this bottle had never been opened. The fire seemed to be gaining headway and folks were commencing to move out. Mr. Fries, who was visiting his wife in a house nearby, and another man carried Ollie and her baby across the street to the home of Mrs. White, a Tucson schoolteacher.

Mrs. Collins was loaded up with satchels and other items when she spied a . . . [foreigner] with the bottle of brandy. She dropped everything, collared . . . [him], and proceeded to treat every person—and herself—to the contents of the bottle. She said, "The dev'l of a [foreigner] was thrying to gid away wid the brandy." (Personal notes, Olive Stephenson Brown)

The fire out, Ollie returned to her bed with her brand new treasure beside her. The food Jim brought her from the Russ House was unappealing so Jim located William, the Chinese cook who had worked for the Browns in 1880. William had opened a restaurant in Tucson and he began bringing food to Ollie. She wrote to her Ma and Pa: "Jim found William and he is bringing me the grandest things to eat I have ever seen—whole ducks and all good and dainty things. Today Jim said, 'William, you are bringing too much, you must not do it.' William replied, 'Oh that's all lite, what I lose on Missie Blown I make up on lail-load men.' William continued to bring Ollie her meals until Jim took her back to the ranch."

There was a wave of sentiment against the Chinese people about this time in Tucson. Ollie stoutly defended them, for she liked the Chinese people.

On September 4, 1884, the first post office was established in Sahuarito with Jim the first postmaster. Ollie was in charge of the office, as his assistant. She once commented, "Jim had the honor and I had the work."

After Ollie's Tootsie was about six months old, Mary and Ollie decided to go to town arrayed in their most modish attire to have their pictures taken. Although they were now country girls, they had not lost their desire to look stylish and pretty. Spruced up in their hats and elegant pinched-waist dresses, corseted of course, they made their way to Buehman's studio and had their pictures taken with baby Tootsie, in her fashionable long white dress, sitting on her mama's lap.

Mary Proctor and Olive Brown, holding baby Harriet, dress in their best to pose for a portrait with a Tucson photographer in January of 1885. Courtesy of Arizona Historical Society.

That was their last fashion spree for some time. The following year on January 26, 1885, the adoption and guardianship of Mary Benedict was granted to the Proctors, and on December 20, 1885, Ollie had another baby, John A. Brown.

Many years later when Ollie was living in Tucson alone, both Tootsie and Jim having died, Ollie wrote her friend Mary, who then lived in California, and sent her the following poem:

To Mary Proctor
How little we knew then of care
How fair the days of youth

As o'er the glistening sands we sped
The river forceful the willows gray
The golden sunshine overhead.
And in each heart a prayer was born
Hand clasped in hand
Two happy girls
With not a thought of aught but joy
To still the tripping happy feet
Sweet pure content without alloy.
But Mary through the changing years
We both have supped the bitter cup
Within our hearts we've each a grave
And fancy brings the phantom up
But changing years have brought to us
The cup from which we all must drink
A grave stands through the mist of tears
Which we never cease to think.
So while I sit alone tonight
And dream my dreams of long ago fled
When we were girls on the Santa Cruz
And listened to its ripples flow
I'll weed within my dream dear Mary
Prayer that God may bring you joy
Upon the coming Happy New Year's Day
And peace be yours always.
And when I lay me down to sleep
May dreams of dear old days be mine
When I first met you New Year's day
In eighteen hundred and seventy nine.

~ Olive Stephenson Brown ~

Jim Brown was the original locator of the Olive Mine, named in honor of his wife, which was the beginning of the Olive Camp, famous during the '80s as a producer of silver. More than two hundred miners worked in that camp, and shipments exceeded $1 million from the shallow workings. Colonel Sykes had predicted, before he left on extended business in the east, that Olive Camp would be the "bonanza camp of the territory." When he returned after a few years, his prediction had been realized.

Owen Doyle, a promising young miner, was interested in mining in the Sierrita Mountains and became acquainted with Jim while he was working his Olive Mine in the early '80s. After Geronimo had been subdued, Jim and Owen did some more mining in the Sierritas and got out very good ore.

The sons of Jim's friend George Allison, Warren and Frank, also became interested in the San Xavier Mining District after their father's death in 1886. They worked the Olive Mine with Jim Brown and Owen Doyle with considerable success. The Olive Mine was eventually sold at a profit for all of them.

In an 1886 newspaper account, it was reported that very few people in Tucson, outside of those directly interested, knew or realized what was going on in the suburbs of the city. "Out at the old Olive Camp, 20 Miles south, a section that has a very interesting record as an ore producer in the 1880s; a camp that has produced more local business for Tucson than any other, has in the last few months taken on new life and promises to be in the very near future one of the great mining Districts of Arizona."

James Kilroy Brown gathers wood at Olive Camp. Courtesy of Susan Strong-Dowd.

A much later *Arizona Daily Star* account dated Tuesday, March 3, 1891, reported that "O. J. Doyle of the Olive Camp was in yesterday, buying supplies and making a mining 'dicker' with someone. He reports that chloriding is going as usual, and that all the ore is shipped principally to El Paso. The Westinghouse Co. is at work with as much rigor as ever, and shipping ore right along. Mr. Doyle owns the Annie mine in company with Mr. Covel, who is now east, and is paying good wages every day. Olive is a lively camp just now, and for its size holds its own equal to the largest mining camp of the territory." Olive Camp came to be known as the "Leadville of Arizona."

In the year 1886, Olive Mine, San Xavier, and many other mines were running full blast, but many people still feared attacks by rogue bands of Native Americans. General Nelson A. Miles, who succeeded General Crook, arrived at Fort Bowie on April 1, 1886, hoping to put an end to the skirmishes, but Geronimo had escaped. He and his band gathered together, eluding soldiers and ambushing and murdering people.

Ollie wrote her Ma and Pa about her sadness at the killing of their young friend Charlie Owens by Geronimo's gang. "The Apaches continue to harass the ranchers and miners, killing and stealing livestock along the Santa Cruz River as far south as the Mexican border. People are being killed on every hand, and the survivors are extremely nervous.

"All of our horses have been stolen from the pasture a mile and a half north of our house. Because of the nerve-racking events taking place all around us, we have moved to Olive Camp for protection. We have banded together with several families and are helping each other."

Following Geronimo's raid, the family returned to find that all the horses and a large portion of their herds had been run off by the [Native Americans], but luckily their home was intact—although the homes of some nearby farmers had been burned to the ground.

Interest in schools in Tucson began as early as 1864. In 1867, when R. D. McCormick was governor of the territory, a school was organized and run for a short while, but had to close for lack of money. An act was passed in the legislative assembly of 1867 that required the supervisors, on petition, to organize a school district. The Tucson district was formed.

After Anson P. K. Safford was appointed governor of the territory in 1871, he was untiring in his efforts to put three public schools on a sound

Brown family members pose in the doorway of the family home at Olive Camp. Courtesy of Susan Strong-Dowd.

financial basis. "Free education for all" was his theme. On March 4, 1872, a school building on the northwest corner of South Meyer and McCormick streets was opened to about seventy boys, with John Spring as their teacher. Although Governor Safford left Arizona in the early '80s and took up residence in Florida, he never lost interest in educational matters. Because of his unceasing interest in education of the Mexican and American children in Arizona, he is called by many "the father of our public schools in Arizona."

Ollie wrote home about the day and night the Saffords spent with them at Sahuarito Ranch in 1887. The governor had approached Ollie, asking her to consider teaching school again.

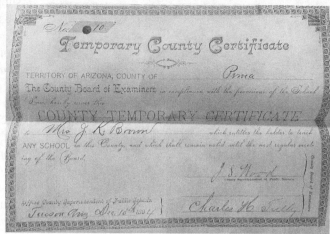

Olive Brown's temporary teaching certificate, issued on December 15, 1894. Courtesy of Arizona State Archives.

She consented to study for an examination so that Keno and Roy could go to school, along with the other children living in their area who needed an education. She got out her old McGuffey reading and spelling books and studied. Jim drove her to Tucson where she took an examination. Mrs. Satterwhite and Judge Woods were the examiners. Ollie was awarded a four-year certificate. She was pleased, for she feared she had failed. It was not too long afterward that she got her children started. Keno was already eight years old, but all along Ollie had been teaching them their numbers and the basics of reading and writing.

Ollie wrote that she passed her examination with "flying colors, applied for the Sahuarito School, got it, taught it for quite a while and had a very good attendance of pupils. Seward Brown and I rode miles on horseback rounding up the pupils and my roll numbered twenty-eight, I believe. 'Them was the days,' and with but few exceptions I'd love to have them over again."

John, Clara, Roy, Harriett, and Marguerite Brown, children of J. K. and Olive Brown, stand in a photo with their young cousins, Harriett Ann and Ruth Olive Brown. Ann Lewis and Samuel Blackmore, seated, are parents of Elizabeth Ann Blackmore Brown and are visiting their daughter and her husband, Seward Ellsworth Brown, at the Sahuarito Ranch circa 1896. Courtesy of the Brown-Strong family.

Although she was to be the teacher, Ollie felt that Jim was the real benefactor and promoter of the school. Jim's youngest brother, Seward, helped Jim build the schoolhouse, a rather nondescript structure made of odds and ends of lumber, boxes, and galvanized iron. From the outside it was a nondescript looking building, but within, it was well equipped and comfortable. Ollie liked it, and called it a nice little school. A well was dug to

Olive, James, and Clara Brown pose for a photo at the Sahuarito Ranch when James was elected sheriff of Pima County in 1892. Courtesy of Arizona Historical Society.

supply water for school uses. The first attendance was fifteen pupils.

Seward, in compliance with the terms of the Homestead Act, had erected a one-room adobe house in which he lived during the years he was digging a well, building a corral, and developing his own cattle business. He didn't know, being a bachelor at the time, but while they were erecting the schoolhouse and Ollie was ordering desks from a catalog, they were creating a schoolhouse that would be for some of his own children. Many years later, Ethel Brown Tolley, third daughter of Seward Brown, wrote her story, *A Family History*. She said, "The year I began school at Sahuarito, the accommodating of a teacher was a problem so we all moved over a little in our four-room ranch house and took in the teacher—a young man named Mr. Poorman. I often wondered about Mr. Poorman. He had no privacy. I guess he just lived as part of the family."

Ollie and Jim's fifth child was born in Tucson on August 14, 1888. Ollie was happy that another little girl had made her advent safely onto the stage of life. She was named Marguerite Bernice. Of course she had to have a nickname and it was Billie.

On the hot August evening when Ollie returned from Tucson and carried her brown-eyed baby into the Sahuarito Ranch house, she felt weak and weary. Although a nursemaid, Maggie Nannia, the nannie Ollie had brought out from Ohio on her last trip home, had taken good care of Ollie and the baby while they were at the McNeil house, Ollie's strength seemed to have played out. When John Weigle, a long time friend, saw her looking so thin and wan after they got home from the twenty-mile buggy ride that hot August evening he said to Ollie, "Mrs. Brown if you have any more children it will kill you." Jim was listening. There were no more.

About this same time, Jim was building a dam to conserve water. Some Yaqui Indians were hired to help with the construction. They were good and dependable workers. The chief, Crecensio, had a stately and beautiful wife who lived up to her name, Cleopatra. She ruled her husband and the children, Jose and Chema, with an iron hand. They all camped in the corral and said chants while sitting by their campfires. Ollie thought them picturesque and interesting.

While Ollie was teaching one day, Chema walked into the school without a single stitch of clothing on his body. Ollie said, "Jose, Jose, take him out and get some clothes on him." Chema looked up at her and asked, *"Que te importa?"* meaning, "What's it

Bertha Stephenson and Clara Brown pose inside Sahuarito Ranch surrounded by an abundance of collectibles and priceless artifacts. Courtesy of Arizona Historical Society.

to you?" Ollie laughed, but she was mighty glad when Crecensio and Cleopatra returned to the ranch to finish their work and take care of their children.

Jim ran for sheriff of Pima County in the general election of 1890. His opponent was Democrat Allen C. Bernard of Arivaca. In a very close election, Jim became sheriff by a margin of two votes. Jim hired his brother Seward to take charge of the Sahuarito Ranch and moved his family to the Silver Lake Hotel at the beginning of the 1891 school year. After he had served for two years, during which time he faithfully performed the duties that fell to his lot, guarding the interest of the people he served fearlessly and conscientiously, Jim did not run for reelection in 1892. It was assumed that he did not run because the duties of the office interfered with his tranquil domestic life, and his cattle business required too much of his attention.

By the early summer of 1892 there was very little water and practically no grass on the range, and ranchers lost as much as 75% of their cattle. During that time, Jim, too, struggled trying to save his cattle. Ollie related, "It was a sad thing to see beautiful young cows come into the corrals with young calves and drink and drink, and finally drop down and die. Jim moved his cattle three times in order to have a good supply of feed and water for them."

At the end of 1892 Ollie's younger sister Bertha, age eighteen and a graduate of the high school in Nelsonville, Ohio, came to Sahuarito. She had agreed to teach in Ollie's little school for four years. Bertha Stephenson, only a couple of years older than Ollie's daughter Keno, was well liked and enjoyed the experience of being a schoolmarm at Sahuarito Ranch. With a youthful spirit of fun in her heart, Bertha tackled her job with enthusiasm. The one-room schoolhouse, close to the ranch but not built on Brown property, accommodated a small group of children ranging from six years upward. Bertha taught her pupils to read, write, sing, draw, use numbers, and speak English. Other than the Brown children, most of the school's population was Mexican. Bertha said, "I learned to dearly love those little brown-skinned children."

As they sit together on the front porch, James Jr. is being held by James Sr. Olive is holding John, Clara is holding Marguerite, and Harriett is in the center. Courtesy of the Brown-Strong family.

Jim loved his Sahuarito Ranch and hated to leave it, but he felt that it was necessary to get the children into schools of higher learning. They had spent many happy years on the ranch. Ollie said, "We had good years and bad years, for Jim was a cattle man and had hard grueling work sowing alfalfa seed; watering, cutting, and baling hay."

Jim moved his family to Silver Lake for the second time in the latter part of 1899, where a few years previously they had enjoyed good times dancing, swimming, and boating when it was first opened as a resort.

Jim and Ollie continue to live at Silver Lake. Ollie busied herself with her Tucson friends. She made scrapbooks, wrote letters and poetry, and looked after her family while Jim divided his time between the ranch and mine and casting around in Tucson for a business in which to invest.

Jim and Ollie and their family stayed in Tucson. In 1910 Jim gave the Twin Buttes and Nogales railroad permission to cross the southern end of his ranch and was instrumental in having the Southern Pacific Railroad establish a freight and passenger station at Sahuarito. The following year, 1911, he sold most of his Sahuarito Ranch holdings, stock and barrel, to George Holmes, for $68,000. However, he retained several parcels of the many acres he had acquired, bordering on the Sahuarito Ranch, which he gave to his children. Holmes was a friend of Pancho Villa and had many dealings with the Mexican leader. Later, he was shot and killed while smuggling merchandise from Mexico to the United States.

Jim's health began to fail in 1918 and he died in 1922 of pernicious anemia. At the time of his death, Ollie stated, "It was the end of all my lovely life with the best man I [ever] knew."

Ollie lived in her home at 422 South 5th Avenue for thirty-one years after the death of her husband. She died May 5, 1953, at the age of 94. Throughout her long life she maintained a closeness with her children and grandchildren and the ranch-day friends, several of whom lived within a block of her home.

"We felt sorry for the children because we were out in the country, but after it all, they have never regretted the ranch days and I can see them yet, gathering baskets of flowers, riding horses, and playing as hard as ever children could play. We had little plays, too, and with plenty of lumber at their command, the children built stages in the long room where they tried their histrionic abilities and did pretty well. Such happy evenings we used to have at the old ranch. Reading aloud to the children, who were breathless with delight and would beg for just one more chapter. Our picnics were a happy part of existence. We had many charming and many strange people who came to the ranch. Our lives were varied by many strange things. I learned a lot about life that I'd never dreamed of while I lived at Sahuarito. Time stops for no one and my lovely babies became men and women. These were the happiest days of my life, and I look back to them with a heart full of longing for my precious young husband and our lovely little babes," wrote Ollie.

~ From the stories of Eleanor Winsor Davis and Olive Letitia Stephenson Brown; condensed by Kerry Lynn Elam and Monica Lee Elam Christiansen

Bull Farms—1926 to 1969

Jeanne, John, and Dan pose with their mother, Gladys at her ninetieth birthday celebration. Courtesy of the Bull/Klingenberg family.

June 12, 2021

Dear Readers:

I am Jeanne Lee Klingenberg Herrman, the youngest grandchild of James B. Bull and Lee Ethel Bull. Mr. Bull moved to Continental, Arizona, in 1926 as a bookkeeper for a group of El Paso cotton farmers. Soon after, Mrs. Bull and their daughters, Gladys and Margaret, followed.

James Bull bought his first parcel of land in 1930 at a tax sale and continued to acquire land until 1969 when he had more than six thousand acres of crop and grazing land, which is now within Sahuarita and the Sahuarita Unified School District but had been entirely within the Continental School District from 1926 to 1969.

When I began working on this project, I was struck by the number of other participants with whom I grew up or shared close family ties. It has been an unexpected pleasure talking and connecting with old friends and making new ones—all through the wonders of twenty-first century technology and despite being hundreds or thousands of miles apart. Our forebears would have been pleased at the strength of the bonds through the history of the generations that followed them.

In 1950, when my father became the manager of Bull Farms, my parents (Gladys and Paul), my brothers (John and Dan) and I moved to Bull Farms from Tucson. We lived in a new house just west of the Santa Cruz River, near old Highway 89.

Newcomers to the valley will continue to make changes to the land, as my family did from 1926 to 1969. I hope the story of Bull Farms will contribute from a very personal perspective to the history of the valley and its development. I will always miss Bull Farms and cherish the memories that were made there.

A big thank you, Granddaddy and Grandmother Bull, for your years of hard work and perseverance, migrating to Continental, Arizona, from Fort Smith, Arkansas, and El Paso, Texas, to establish Bull Farms. Thank you to Paul Klingenberg, Gladys Klingenberg, John Klingenberg, Dan Klingenberg, Mary Jean Harper Klingenberg, Rena Allen Klingenberg, Bishop Harp, and Edward Epps for your written histories, as well as to Janie Bowden Harris, Lynn Harris, Steve Brown, Sutah Thomas Harris, Angelita (Angie) Espino, Mark Culbertson, and Dick Walden—your contributions to this effort brought back many happy memories.

For history buffs, a timeline of the events that shaped Bull Farms and to a large extent the Santa Cruz Valley from 1887 to 2021 is shown at the end of this section.

Pictures of Bull Farms were taken by Bishop Harp and Paul Klingenberg unless otherwise credited.

Now, I invite you to enjoy the story of Bull Farms as told by the family members of James Burton Bull and Lee Ethel Bull:

> Gladys O. Bull Klingenberg, eldest daughter
> Paul John Klingenberg, son-in-law
> John Burton Klingenberg, eldest grandson
> Mary Jean Harper Klingenberg, John's wife
> Dan Allen Klingenberg, second grandson
> Jeanne Lee Klingenberg Herrman, granddaughter
> W. Edward Epps, grandson
> Bishop Harp, great nephew

Life on Bull Farms

Sometime in 1950, my memories begin at a brick house on Bull Farms, located three-quarters of a mile from Highway 89 on the west side of the Santa Cruz River. My family moved into our newly built house on

In February of 1950, Paul Klingenberg moved his family into their new home on Bull Farms. Courtesy of the Bull/Klingenberg family.

the farm in February of that year, and my father became associated with grandfather Bull's farming operation shortly thereafter. A house design was selected by my parents from a magazine. The magazine concept was adapted by Paul Klingenberg and an architect friend. This was the beginning of my life on Bull Farms, experiencing the unique joy, solitude, and sadness of rural living. I was almost two years old.

The brick house, where I had a room of my own, looked out to a large grassy yard and to the fields beyond. The yard was watered by flooding. My brother Dan kept it mowed, often getting reprimands for speeding from our mother, Gladys. The mower was a birthday gift to *her* one year (not totally appreciated!)—a gas-powered mower, I think. I ran around the yard, sometimes hopping over a snake, a rattler perhaps, but I would not waste time identifying the species and instead would rush inside the house. The snake appeared again when my brother, Dan, went out the back door one night and shrieked at

The Klingenberg family home 1950–58 stands to the left of the old stage stop—home to the Lewis family during that same time period. Courtesy of the Bull/Klingenberg family.

the realization that he had almost stepped on a rattlesnake on the doormat. Forever after, when I visited my parents in Green Valley, I stepped outside cautiously if the light was dim for fear of meeting the snake again.

The desert land and the fields surrounding the house were filled with endless hours of fun and make-believe. I would play in the sandy wash beds with my Native American friends, Jimmy, Arlene, and Laura Ann Lewis. Other days we would swim in the irrigation ditches, sliding on the algae that grew on the concrete walls. When the planted fields around the house were producing their crops of cotton or sorghum, we would find reasons to play hide-and-seek in the planted rows. At harvest time we would try to participate in the picking of cotton. I had only a pillowcase, whereas the men and women toted long bags over their shoulders, dragging them on the ground behind them. The task, overwhelming for me, would be replaced with jumping in the trailers full of fluffy cotton. A lot more fun, by far! Toward lunch or dinner, mother would often call, "Jeanne, time to come in," and I would be so involved in our games that Laura Ann and Arlene would have to tell me, "Your mother is calling. You'd better go home, now!" Mother never could understand why I took so long in reporting home after her call.

A small distance to the east of the house was a fascinating adobe building.

Laura Ann, Arlene, and Jimmy Lewis waiting for the yellow Continental School bus. Courtesy of the Bull/Klingenberg family.

After locating water by witching near the old stage stop, a drilling rig was brought in to complete the well. Courtesy of the Bull/Klingenberg family.

This was home to Jimmy, Arlene, and Laura Ann and their family. The floors were well-swept dirt. Smells of homemade tortillas made on a mesquite wood-burning stove would fill the air in the evenings. Later I learned that this had been a stagecoach station on a route from Tucson to Sasabe.

My friends' mother and aunt sat for hours making woven baskets from yucca and devil's claw. Occasionally, for a change of pace, they would switch to wire with the same fine craftsmanship, forming baskets that were just as intricate. Still cherished are my special woven gift baskets of amazing quality and technique that are rare today. I guess out of respect for their heritage and not wanting to intrude, I never learned their craft or their language, instead quietly marveling at their work.

Talk of their homes far away in Sells, Arizona, inspired me to climb aboard my red tricycle and pedal to the "reservation." Shortly thereafter, in a pea-green pickup, my father and brother John came down the dirt road through the fields near the Santa Cruz River to pick up me and my tricycle. I was safely returned home and never asked to go to the reservation again, at least not without a chaperone and motorized transportation.

Our brick house was a short distance from the corrals and a big shed. I still happily remember a black-and-white goat brought home by my brother John from a livestock auction. The goat was my closest playmate, letting me dress, push, and pull him while riding my bike. But one of my first memories of death happened when he got into the fertilizer in the shed and died a few days later.

The shed also housed tools, including those for removing the training wheels from my Schwinn bike. Daddy came home early one hot afternoon and I hurried to the shed so he could remove my training wheels. I jumped on the bike and pedaled, maneuvering down a dip into a small wash only to tip the bike and my lightly clothed body fully into the arms of a cholla cactus, followed by days of baths, mother using tweezers, and my sitting on pillows at mealtime with the family.

Jeanne's treasured collection of beautiful Native American baskets. Courtesy of the Bull/Klingenberg family.

Jeanne on her little red tricycle peddling to the reservation. Courtesy of the Bull/Klingenberg family.

We had a hand-crank phone with a ringing system to identify the intended recipient of the call. Ours was one long ring and two short rings. My bedroom became a hideaway due to my many medical conditions (allergies, measles, and valley fever). I have fond memories of opening exciting "get well" gift boxes sent by my first-grade teacher, Mrs. Hughes. The boxes were filled with one gift per day and letters from my classmates. The letters were on wide-lined writing paper with near perfect penmanship, decorated with colorful crayon drawings.

The back laundry room was where my mother washed clothes in a Maytag wringer washer. Rinsing the clothes required two large laundry tubs and moving the Maytag with wringer from tub to tub to thoroughly rinse and wring the water from the clothes. This took hours; drying was done by hanging the clothes outside on the clothesline with clothespins. It was an all-day chore and heavy work, considering the quantity of Levi's and T-shirts the three men of the house would dirty. Mother would be wet all over. The next day was spent ironing.

I would have dearly loved to ride the horses in the corrals, but I could not master that skill. One fall in particular is still vivid in my mind, as well as the scary fall Dan took between a car and the back

Gladys hanging clothes on the line. Courtesy of the Bull/Klingenberg family.

patio wall that resulted in a broken nose. Because riding a horse was not for me, I turned to reading books of horse fantasy and the mysterious "hidden valley."

John and Dan raised 4-H calves at the corral. Dan also raised rabbits. The Hereford calves impressed me with their beautiful bright white and red fur and the longest eyelashes. I learned a lot about life when one of John's calves ate poor feed and bloated. John, Dan, and father walked and walked the animal attempting to save her, but she died. Her remains were left in the riverbed.

Life was good at the new house. Father built a great swing down by the water tank that stood high in the air. He built the frame out of pipe with long chains and a wooden seat. The wooden seat was wide enough that two of us could swing together.

Jeanne sits on a wicker bench with her babysitter. Courtesy of the Bull/Klingenberg family.

Sometime around age five my cousin, Elaine, moved to the farm, across the river, near my grandparents. It was a short memory. She was playing one day with my brother Dan and his friend, Janie Bowden, at a new well site past my grandparents' house. It was safe, but she was small and thin. She slipped through the narrowly spaced railroad ties that covered the well and plunged a couple of hundred feet below. The phone rang (one long, two short rings) at our house and my mother and I rushed to the well. My dad had lowered himself down the well shaft on a rope and pulled her out. An ambulance from Tucson was at her house when we arrived but they could not save her. She died on the couch in her new home. I lost my new best friend and experienced the funeral of a little girl in a white casket. Her mother, Ina, fainted and had to be revived with smelling salts. The family gathered at grandmother and grandfather Bull's house to console Elaine's family.

Jojo and Jeanne stand outside the 1947 Bull house. Courtesy of the Bull/Klingenberg family.

Soon it was off to first grade. We rode in a yellow bus—me with my metal lunch box and thermos, and my friends Jimmy, Arlene, and Laura Ann. Mother usually drove us through the fields, down through the Santa Cruz riverbed, to the Bull Farms' mailbox on the Old Nogales Highway to wait for the bus. The bus seemed big (seating probably twelve kids) and the ride seemed long through the big dip by the FICO feedlot and past the Continental Store over the railroad tracks to the three-room Continental country schoolhouse.

The school had wonderful sights and sounds—blackboards that covered a full wall in each room; erasers with chalk dust that we each used to take turns at cleaning; clocks with pendulums. The call to class was made with a handbell, usually rung by Mrs. O'Brien. Three lines of students formed outside, facing the porch and front doors by the assigned classroom. Each morning at 8:45 a.m., a different student stepped out from the line formation to state, "Ready," and the rest of us followed with "I pledge allegiance . . ." I had friends of all colors with lots to learn and to share; friends who spoke different native languages, who were strongly punished for not speaking English on the school grounds, and friends who could not stay the entire school year because their fathers followed the harvests or the availability of work on ranches in Southern Arizona.

At the end of the school day, we would ride the bus back to the mailboxes and walk three-quarters of a mile to my grandparents' house to watch TV (we did not have one) until mother came and picked us up. Grandmother would leave snacks, often warm pot roast on Rainbo white bread with room-temperature mayonnaise, a flavor I still remember but have never duplicated. Granddaddy always kept Juicy Fruit and Doublemint gum in the secret drawer of his giant rolltop desk in the office space at their house.

Jojo Henry stands with Janie Bowden beside his sister, Melissa Henry, and Shirley Jones. Courtesy of the Bull/Klingenberg family.

On special nights of the week our family would visit the grandparents to watch TV (specifically: *The Twilight Zone, Alfred Hitchcock, The Ed Sullivan Show, Lawrence Welk, Gunsmoke,* and *Maverick).* On Sundays, grandmother often fixed fried chicken, pressure-cooked fresh snapped green beans with salt pork, homemade biscuits, and fresh peach pie. The peaches came from the trees behind their house, another taste I cannot find today. At special times, she prepared homemade ice cream which we cranked and cranked. I loved the mystery of the salt and ice chemistry turning a liquid into ice cream. During those years, I became closer to my grandparents, Lee Ethel and James B. My grandmother possessed, in addition to her cooking skills, the art of sewing and crocheting. Granddaddy, although a very stern and demanding person most of the time, could be fun and mischievous. When we watched TV, if someone performed an athletic feat, he would pinch my elbow and say, "Jeanne girl, bet you can't do that!" I remember grandfather would often swirl together honey and butter on his plate to put on grandmother's biscuits.

When I was ten, the folks decided to move. That was scary because they were looking at houses in Tucson. I did not want to leave my house, my school, and my friends. Finally, father decided to build on

Lunchtime at Continental School. Courtesy of University of Arizona Special Collections.

the hill just above the Bulls' house. His nights were spent designing the house himself, using the current brick-house layout as a model. It was great fun watching him create the plans and then to see his ideas turn into a new house. In 1959, we moved. Stake-bed trucks full of our possessions made many trips back and forth to the new house. The view from the hill was wonderful. We looked out over our grandparents' house and across to the Sierrita Mountains, Twin Buttes, and just barely visible was the Magee Ranch. I was away from my friends, who lived in the stagecoach house across the river, but more friends were near my grandparents' house—Melissa, Jojo, Pauline, Yvonne, Vickey, Brenda, and many others.

Two rows of adobe apartments were just beyond my grandparents' house. Native American women often cooked outside on large mesquite fires when the weather was good. The women patiently formed flour tortillas from small balls of dough. The tortillas were cooked on oil-drum lids placed carefully on the burning mesquite logs. At Christmas, they cooked special tamales. The adobe apartments had wooden screen doors and shutters covering deeply set windows. These have always remained as an architectural implant in my brain.

I had new areas to explore and new adventures to experience. The hills were covered with broken, painted pottery pieces from Native American tribes of centuries past. A grave protected by a wrought-iron fence sat silent just north of my grandparents' house east of the dirt old-Old Nogales Road. It was the grave of a former owner of the land. At another corral, I would watch cowhands brand calves. I had continual memories of Elaine, as the corral had been built near the well—mostly happy memories, though.

I went through the years adapting to life on the farm—going to and from Continental School; participating in school plays; raising 4-H lambs and a calf, sewing and cooking for ribbons at the Pima County Fair; waiting for out-of-state visits from my cousin Ed; and playing with my cat Mimi and dog Penny and numerous other cats and dogs including the white kitten, Frosty, given to me by Steve Brown after Mimi died.

Mimi watching for jack rabbits. Courtesy of the Bull/Klingenberg family.

Before long, the yellow school bus changed to a Citizen's Stage Line bus, which took me and my other classmates to Tucson, either to Pueblo High or Sunnyside High. The time on the bus was long, with the bus stopping whenever the pull cord directed it to. We, the schoolkids, enjoyed our time to socialize in the back of the bus. The paying passengers were diverse, and interesting events sometimes unfolded. At high school we met the "rich" kids from the district of Sahuarita arriving in their yellow bus and merged with the city kids. I went to Pueblo High School with 1,800 students, which involved rotating classes of seventy-minutes' duration. Our interests and circles of friends began to change.

Adobe apartments for farm workers with deep-set windows and doors. Courtesy of the Bull/Klingenberg family.

In 1968, my grandmother passed away, setting in motion the decision by my grandfather to sell the farm to Anaconda Mining. At the age of twenty, my life on Bull Farms was concluded. We could see the farm from the new house in Green Valley. My father designed this house, too, with a small apartment for my grandfather, basing it on the floor plan of the second house. This time the house was located near Continental Road and Interstate 19 (the highway I had first seen on the blueprints my grandfather showed me).

My grandfather spent six years in the apartment at the new house with my parents, always having lunch at 1:06 p.m. after listening to the CBS radio news. My visits were spent with him reminiscing about many special times on the farm. He often would direct tours of the old farm and the Green Valley area when family came to visit. He would sit in the passenger seat and point silently in the direction he expected the driver to take at a moment's notice!

Today I live in northern California with my husband, Tom. Visits to Green Valley to see my parents were always reminders of the past and I was astonished by the growth of the area. I take great pride in knowing I am a descendent of Mr. and Mrs. James B. Bull and Mr. and Mrs.

Early motorized equipment used for the planting of crops. Courtesy of the Bull/Klingenberg family.

Transportation for field workers and families by Mr. Bull, Bishop, or Paul from other parts of Arizona, to Bull Farms 1940s–1960s. Courtesy of the Bull/Klingenberg family.

Paul Klingenberg, who had the vision and fortitude to cultivate the potential of the land in this gorgeous and historic valley.

~ Contributed by Jeanne Lee Klingenberg Herrman

Bull Farms operations—1937–40s

Bishop:

When we first went to Continental, the irrigation system used to be two ditches side by side. The main ditch moved the water into a ditch that had rubber hoses within the walls of the bank that let the water flow onto the cotton rows. These rubber hoses were discarded air hoses from railcars. To keep the water flowing, we had sticks that we used to clear mud and debris from the hoses. As we became better irrigators, we found that a single ditch with flexible hoses could siphon a more efficient flow of water to the cotton.

The source of water we used was a 1,500-foot well that was pure, sweet, and cold. Our main pipes connected through a standpipe to the ditches that carried water and took off from the well in three different directions. The southwesterly supply moved through an underground concrete pipe to the big ditch. The outlet area was covered in Bermuda grass and was six to eight feet deep. Our irrigation crews worked around the clock to keep the water moving.

The machinery on the farm consisted of a John Deere Model G tractor, a two-row cultivator, a disc, a harrow, a three-bottom turning plow, and a two-row cotton planter (converted from horse-drawn). During cotton-planting season the school authorities were very generous about letting me miss school so I could ride the cotton planter pulled by the tractor. The cotton planter was really designed to be a corn planter but with the proper insert could be used to plant cotton seeds.

We had chickens, cows, pigs, and steers for our food sources. We also had a garden and were able to supply the needs of the Bull and Harp families. We grew a great many of our own vegetables. We had rows of potatoes, corn, tomatoes, green beans, etc.

When we first started farming in 1937, the cotton was picked by migrant workers who wandered through following the harvests. They were mostly families that were supplied with tents and wood-burning stoves to cook and heat with. Most of the migrants had their own lanterns and the stores in Sahuarita and Continental stocked kerosene for them.

Uncle Jim and dad also made frequent trips to the "hobo jungle" in Tucson to hire migrant cotton pickers. The workers

A "rent-a-cowboy" on Bull Farms. Courtesy of the Bull/Klingenberg family.

would work all week and after they were paid on Saturday at noon, they would take their bedrolls and disappear. On Sunday afternoons dad would take the truck back to the "hobo jungle" and pick up a new crew for Monday. A great many of those who had left on Saturday afternoon were already broke, hungover, and ready to come back to work another week. Uncle Jim had an arrangement with the Sahuarita store to give the workers enough food to live on but not over what they would earn.

Field hands at Bull Farms. Courtesy of the Bull/Klingenberg family.

The unstable work force caused Uncle Jim to go to the Native American reservation and get several families and transport them to the farm. We built a migrant workers' building of corrugated metal and provided a water supply as well as wood for the cookstoves. The children would travel to Continental School on the school bus—a Ford farm pickup with a wood frame, covered by canvas with wood benches.

We would drive the farm truck as a flatbed to the reservation and transport people, bedrolls, groceries, pets, and belongings, and bring them to the farm. We had another corrugated building that during harvest time was turned into a store. We had all types of non-perishable foodstuffs—flour, lard, beans, vegetables, cornmeal, salt pork, canned tomatoes, and such. The workers would sign IOUs that were deducted from their wages on Saturday. Uncle Jim would drive down from Tucson on Saturday morning at about 11:30 to figure the payroll and make the deductions. Then, sitting at a table with a muffin tin as a cash drawer for silver and stacks of twenties, tens, fives, and ones in front of him, he would start to pay the workers. The Native American men would have on their Levi's, colorful shirts, neckerchiefs, and big black hats. They would stand patiently in line

Clearing the land on Jack Rabbit Hill. Courtesy of the Bull/Klingenberg family.

waiting their turn. When it was a worker's turn to be paid, his wife would hold out her hand to Uncle Jim to accept her husband's pay, then give her husband ten or twenty dollars, keep a few dollars for herself, and put the balance back in Uncle Jim's hand to be on deposit with him until the cotton-picking season was over and they returned to the reservation.

~ Contributed by Bishop Harp

Bull Farms operations—1950 to 1968

Paul:

The farming operation in the early days primarily produced cotton as well as corn and other grains. Later, peanuts and a specialty crop of various love grasses were added. Sorghum grain such as milo maize was sold to the nearby feedlot for silage. We always knew when the silage was "ripe" because we lived downwind from the feedlot. Any cattle ranching activity would take place whenever the range feed was adequate. Usually a hundred yearlings would be bought, and a cowboy would be "rented" to look after the herd. When the cattle had gained enough weight, they would be sold at the Tucson auction and the cowboy would move on.

Labor was hired primarily from the Native American reservation. In the early days the cotton harvest was done by hand; at that time the labor camp could have as many as a hundred people in residence.

Anchor chains used for clearing brush on Jack Rabbit Hill. Courtesy of the Bull/Klingenberg family.

To recruit these people, it was frequently necessary to provide transportation from their homes on the reservation. Many came on their own, but I found myself available most of the time as the "gofer" or go-to person. It certainly was an opportunity to get acquainted with a good many villages on the reservation. There were some Native Americans who lived on the farm most of the year for irrigating, weeding, carrying sprinklers, driving tractors, etc. In later years harvest was mainly done by machine, but "scrapping" still had to be done by hand.

When you have many folks on the farm, medical issues will develop such as sickness or births, so it was my job to transport pregnant mothers to Tucson Medical Center in the middle of the night or to the Native American hospital at San Xavier Village. Perhaps I felt a kinship as I had been born on a Native American reservation in North Dakota myself.

There were other people living year-round on the farm who had specific duties peculiar to the farming operation. As for myself, I never had a title for the duties I performed unless I could be satisfied with the "Mr. Bull's son-in-law" handle. Maybe "gofer" would have been appropriate after all.

Milo maize was harvested with a conventional self-operating combine. The stalks were generally not put into a bale but plowed back into the soil. Occasionally, yearling cattle were put out to graze on the desert range when the feed justified doing it. We also planted love grass with seeds from Africa. Two of the varieties were Weeping LG and Boer LG. Weeping was the predominant crop on the farm. Most of the grass was on a field near Sahuarita.

John:

Grass-growing was really dad's project. He probably had to convince granddaddy to allow it. It was the one crop that he had complete control over, without Mr. Bull interfering with the operation. The grass seed was sold for erosion control and for reseeding forest and rangelands after fires. The seed was generally planted by airplane ahead of the monsoon rains, to get the grass established in

Thresher bagging peanuts on Jack Rabbit Hill. Courtesy of the Bull/Klingenberg family.

Peanuts being bagged after picking.
Courtesy of the Bull/Klingenberg family.

the early fall. The grass was harvested with an Allis Chalmers combine that was pulled by a tractor—I did that one summer. The seed was combined when it was green and placed in large cotton bags to be transported to Ryan Airfield, near Three Points. The seed was then taken to a large abandoned hanger to be spread on a concrete floor, to be scattered by hand. This was to allow the green/wet seed to cure. If this is not done in a timely manner, the seed loses its potential to germinate. I was also given that task to do. As for the hay, it was usually formed into small bales by a custom operation. The hay was probably fed to cattle and horses.

~ Contributed by Paul and John Klingenberg

Bull Farms: Growing peanuts on Jack Rabbit Hill

John:

Mr. Bull's farming operation introduced peanut production to Arizona. Jack Rabbit Hill, where the peanut crops were grown, can still be seen from Interstate 19, several miles west on the mesa. Today it is called Quail Creek.

I do not remember a lot about the clearing of the farm ground on Jack Rabbit Hill; this is the name we gave that part of the farm because of the antelope jackrabbits that wreaked havoc on the cotton or peanut seedlings. They would come off the experimental range, east of Jack Rabbit Hill toward Helvetia. We would go out at night in trucks with spotlights and shoot some of them. They could eat an acre of peanut or cotton seedlings in a night.

I do remember that dad was greatly involved in the project. In order to clear the land of brush, cholla cactus, mesquite, and catclaw trees, they used two Caterpillar dozers to push the bigger trees down. They also used large ship-anchor chains hooked to each machine that formed a semicircle. Each Cat would pull in the same direction to let the chain drag a large group of plant growth at once to form a pile of brush to burn later. I might add that in the clearing project, dad took great care to assure that saguaros were not damaged. Dad also did the surveying to mark the elevation level to form the fields for irrigation. I helped dad with the survey work by holding the

Peanuts bagged and drying in the fields. Courtesy of the Bull/Klingenberg family.

survey rod at each place where lath stakes had been placed. While clearing the land, I believe that two wells were drilled along with small concrete ditches placed around the farm.

Bull Farms started growing peanuts probably in the early '50s and continued into the 1960s. They were usually planted in the spring and harvested in the fall. They were planted in furrows and cultivated by tractor until the vines were too heavy or long for the equipment to get through without damaging the vines. The plants were watered by sprinklers for about twelve hours per day. Then the pipes for the sprinklers had to be moved to another part of the field for the next twelve-hour water cycle. This was all done by hand and was very labor intensive. It probably took eight to nine men to do this, mostly in the mornings. The crew was made up primarily of Native American men.

Aerial photo of the main section of Bull Farms, 1964.
Courtesy of the Bull/Klingenberg family and Monica Lee Elam Christiansen.

Key: 1) House of Mr. and Mrs. Bull in 1947; 2) Front lawn and front door; 3) Main office entrance for Mr. Bull and Paul Klingenberg for meetings with farm workers and salespersons; 4) Maid's quarters with separate porch; 5) Old-Old Nogales Road; 6) Campbell Avenue North (2021); 7) Road to 1959 Klingenberg house and Jack Rabbit Hill (now to Quail Creek and Stone House developments via Quail Creek Parkway); 8) Fields under cultivation were part of the 1938 purchase; 9) Location of Bull Farms Quonset hut where harvested peanuts were stored; 10) Current Quail Creek Air Gun Club; 11) Fields currently under cultivation that were part of the 1938 purchase; 12) House and garage, often home to family members working on the farm; 13) Adobe housing units for field workers and families; 14) Arroyo, mostly dry—rain and flash floods required use of a tractor to cross; 15) Mr. and Mrs. Bull's first house on the farm 1940–47 and later home to many farm managers and families; 16) Railroad tracks; 17) Old Nogales Highway/Continental Road; 18) Entrance to Bull Farms, location of mailboxes, bus stop for younger Continental School kids, and Greyhound bus stop for picking up high school students

Jeanne:

I learned that Bull Farms was the largest producer of peanuts in Arizona. Peanut harvest was as much fun as the cotton season. First, I learned that peanuts are the only nut that grows underground. Mr. Bull grew only Spanish peanuts, the smaller type of peanut. The peanut plant grows low to the ground, unlike cotton plants. With time, the plant expands and blooms with beautiful pink and white blossoms. When time came, a potato digger, a type of machinery, was started up and the peanut plants were gently pulled up by the machine and left on top of the ground to allow the peanuts in their shells and the roots to dry further. After the peanuts were dry enough, a pull-type thresher came in and processed the peanuts off the vine and loaded them into burlap sacks, machine-tying the sacks with string, and dropping the full bags to the ground. Often families on the farm and other special guests would go out and collect the peanuts that either fell off the machine or did not get picked up.

Later the filled sacks were loaded onto a flatbed truck and transported a short distance down the hill to a Quonset hut built specially for the storage of the bagged peanuts. The bags were stacked perhaps ten to fifteen bags high. After inspectors graded the peanuts, the harvest was usually sold to peanut brokers for conversion to cooking oil.

Peanut bags are placed in the Quonset hut to be graded, stored, and eventually shipped. (The Quonset hut still stands near the Quail Creek Air Gun Club in 2021). Courtesy of the Bull/Klingenberg family.

The coyotes really liked this time of year. Lying in my bed at night I could hear them chatter as they ate the peanuts in the fields and ran back and forth in the desert. The javelinas loved my dachshund, Suzie, and they all loved peanuts. When the javelinas roamed the desert at dusk, Suzie would chase them until the javelinas ganged up on her and chased her back to the house. When mother baked the nuts in their shells and someone started to crack open the shells, Suzie would come running to eat the nuts. She was very particular, though—the outer red skin had to be peeled off or she would spit the nut out onto the floor!

~ Contributed by John Klingenberg and Jeanne Klingenberg Herrman

Continental, Arizona, before Bull Farms

Gladys:

During World War I, rubber was in great demand because rubber imports from the Malay states had been cut off by Germany. President Woodrow Wilson authorized the establishment of the Intercontinental Rubber Company to produce and process guayule as a rubber substitute.

The Intercontinental Rubber Company guayule farm and processing facility were located in

Bags of peanuts are loaded into trucks. Courtesy of the Bull/Klingenberg family.

Continental, Arizona, and the company established the town in 1916. The Intercontinental Rubber Company land was the northern half of the 9,700-acre San Ignacio de la Canoa Land Grant that had previously been acquired by the Manning family in 1908. In addition to the guayule processing buildings—which consisted of a chemical laboratory, an extractor-compressor facility, and a power plant to fuel the lights and machinery—the company built Continental School, ten houses, and workers' quarters. The Intercontinental Rubber Company also drilled irrigation wells for the guayule production.

When World War I ended, however, the demand for rubber decreased and the guayule was no longer needed, so the Intercontinental Rubber Company abandoned the acres of guayule production and the facilities that had been built for processing it. In 1926, the entire land was leased by Ivey-Dale-Owens Co. of El Paso, Texas; three thousand acres of cotton were planted and harvested for only a few years. The old guayule chemical plant building was later used for additional classrooms for Continental School until it collapsed in the early 1950s.

In 1948, the Continental farm was purchased by Keith Walden with one-half interest owned by Henry Zellerbach of Crown-Zellerbach. Their corporation was named FICO (Farmers Investment Co.), and their farm on the old Intercontinental Rubber Company land first produced cotton, then cereal grains, followed by vegetables, fruit, and wine grapes, and finally pecans. The first young trees began to be planted in the early 1960s.

Making of The Westerner *on Bull Farms. Courtesy of the Bull/Klingenberg family.*

Filming the burning of Mr. Bull's cornfields. Courtesy of the Bull/Klingenberg family.

~ Contributed by Gladys Bull Klingenberg

Hollywood comes to Bull Farms

Gladys:

In 1939, while the Klingenberg family was living in New Mexico for Paul's job, back home in Arizona the movie, *The Westerner*, an Academy Award-winning film starring Gary Cooper and other well-known actors, was filmed in Southern Arizona. The film production company was headquartered at Canoa Ranch, south of Continental, and the scenes and action were shot in other locations. The spectacular scene of the burning cornfields was shot on Bull Farms between the Santa Cruz River and west of the Old Nogales Highway and Continental Road, near the present (2021) Quail Creek entrance.

The movie was released in theaters in October 1940 and became available on videotape in 1987. In the October 7, 1940, issue of *Life*, then an extremely popular weekly magazine, *The Westerner* was featured in a prominent story with pictures of some of the scenes, including the spectacular fire filmed on the farm.

The farm employees enjoyed the filmmaking. Daddy particularly liked getting to know Gary Cooper and the director, William Wyler.

Bishop:

The making of *The Westerner* was a financial boon for all of us. I was hired as security to keep people from entering the

Lunch being served to the cast and crew. Courtesy of the Bull/Klingenberg family.

farm during filming, and dad was hired as a technical advisor. I made $3.50 per day and dad made $5.00, I think. The movie company also fed us lunch, and if filming took place late in the afternoon there was also a meal or snack for us.

Gary Cooper and Doris Davenport between scenes on Bull Farms. Courtesy of the Bull/Klingenberg family.

As a technical advisor, dad's main function was to record the use of crops or property that were to be paid for, and he kept a daily diary of what was used or misused.

Settlement day came when the movie was completed. Uncle Jim, dad, and I had our bills ready. We had stopped at a little cafe to have a glass of iced tea, and dad and Uncle Jim went over the list and priced the items that the movie company was to pay for. Later, after the producer paid dad and me in cash, he asked Uncle Jim if he had his statement ready. Uncle Jim gave his statement to the producer, but after studying the list, the producer asked, "Are you trying to make me the laughingstock of Hollywood?" Uncle Jim was taken aback and told the man he had tried to be realistic but if it were too much, he would refigure the statement. The producer told Uncle Jim that it was not enough and that he should refigure the statement at ten times what he had submitted. The producer added, "Refigure it and bring it back." After another glass of iced tea, Uncle Jim had refigured it and presented his bill; the producer said, "That's more like it." He gave Uncle Jim a check which we took across the street to Valley National Bank, and Uncle Jim paid off his mortgage.

Jeanne:

Until approximately 2021, I remember seeing reruns of *The Westerner* on TV and telling friends and family to be sure and watch it or at least until the cornfields burned. Today in 2022, the movie is hard to come by in a format suitable for use with today's technology—except, of course, on the internet: https://en.wikipedia.org/wiki/-The_Westerner (1940s film).

> ~ Contributed by Gladys Bull
> Klingenberg, Bishop Hart, and
> Jeanne Klingenberg Herrman

Bull Farms' WWII POW Camp—"The Continental Camp"

John:

Granddaddy was engaged in a contract with the U.S. government to have a prisoner of war camp constructed right on the farm. This camp was to be used as a German prisoner of war facility. The camp was under construction on the day we left for Oklahoma so my dad could report for duty.

Prisoner-of-war farm labor camp in Continental, Arizona. German prisoners of war from this camp picked 1,860,863 pounds of cotton from September 17, 1945, to February 10, 1946. Besides cotton picking, this camp furnished field workers for cleaning irrigation canals, hoeing and thinning lettuce and cotton, and harvesting vegetables. Photo by John Craft. Courtesy of University of Arizona Special Collections.

We stayed in Oklahoma until after the war ended in August 1945. When we returned to Tucson, the POW camp was still in full swing, so I got to see some real Germans. These prisoners were used as farm labor, mostly for weeding and picking cotton. I heard that a couple of Germans had actually escaped but were caught. Looking back, it must have been strange for my dad to come home and find German prisoners on the farm after he had just come back from the war with them.

The workers' quarters built on Bull Farms after WWII housed many families over the years. Courtesy of the Bull/Klingenberg family.

Gladys:

The camp for about fifty German prisoners of war was located on the Bulls' land, on the west side of Continental Madera Canyon Road, three miles north of the Continental School. The camp consisted of barracks to house the prisoners and four twenty-foot-tall guard towers, one at each corner, surrounded by a ten-foot-high barbed-wire fence. It was run by army personnel and served as a labor cooperative, with the prisoners of war repairing roads as well as weeding and picking cotton on the surrounding farms in the Sahuarita/Continental area. The cotton produced with their labor was used in the war efforts of the United States.

Paul:

During the 1950s, the old POW camp buildings were used to house farm laborers. Jim employed a number of Native Americans on his farm, and their families lived in the old barracks, cooking their meals over wood fires outside the buildings. The Native American children attended Continental School. Eventually, in the late 1950s, buildings in the camp caught fire and burned down.

~ Contributed by John Klingenberg, Gladys Bull Klingenberg, and Paul Klingenberg

Lee Ethel and James B. Bull, fiftieth anniversary, 1962. Courtesy of the Bull/Klingenberg family.

Our memories of living and working on Bull Farms

Gladys:

Mr. Bull was living in El Paso, Texas, in 1926 with his wife, Lee Ethel, and their two daughters, Gladys and Margaret. He worked as a bookkeeper for several prominent business firms after his arrival there in 1916.

In September of 1926, Mr. Bull accepted a bookkeeping job with a group of Rio Grande Valley farmers, namely Messrs. Ivy, Dale, and Owens. The group had leased the holdings owned by the Intercontinental Rubber Company in Continental, Arizona. During the first years, three thousand acres of cotton were planted and harvested on lands which

Home of J. B. and Lee Ethel Bull on the farm, 1940. Courtesy of the Bull/Klingenberg family.

have now been developed into a retirement community in Green Valley, Arizona, or planted with pecan trees. Both ventures began in the early 1960s. The entire holdings of the Intercontinental Company were sold to a group of investors in 1949 and are now known as Farmers Investment Co. (FICO).

In 1931, Mr. Bull had succeeded in acquiring his first parcel of land of approximately one hundred acres located two miles north of Continental, lying west of State Highway 89 and to the east of the banks of the Santa Cruz River. In 1933, he began his farming in a primitive way with the help of a few people. The year 1937 brought more farming production and continued activity.

In the fall of 1940, Mr. and Mrs. Bull moved to the farm and continued to live there until their holdings were bought in 1969 by the Anaconda Mining Co. Through the years Mr. and Mrs. Bull continued to acquire additional adjacent lands. They owned 2,200 acres of patented land located on both sides of old Highway 89. In addition, several sections of state and federal land leases were held. (This part of the highway is now designated a Pima County Road called Continental/Madera Canyon Road.) In 1989, a retirement community was reestablished and the development is known as Quail Creek and includes the Stone House residential area added many years later.

Bull Run vegetable label from Sahuarita.
Courtesy of the Bull/Klingenberg family.

Shortly after Mr. and Mrs. Bull moved to their farm, he became the full-time manager and bookkeeper for his growing farm operation. In the World War II years, the production and demand for cotton were tremendous.

Beginning in the mid-1940s and continuing for the remainder of the farming years, diversified crops were rotated. In addition to cotton, both short- and long-staple, other crops included vegetables, various grains, peanuts, and grasses for seed production.

Harvesting and packaging Bull Run vegetables in the fields. Courtesy of the Bull/Klingenberg family.

Back in the early years of the Great Depression, financial help for small farms was almost nonexistent. When Mr. Walter Bimson of Gila Valley Bank acquired the old Consolidated Bank in Tucson, he saw a definite need to finance agriculture in Pima County. Subsequently, the banks were renamed Valley National Bank of Arizona. An agricultural department was established, and Mr. George Pond of that department handled the financial needs of Bull Farms for many years.

In 1955, Mr. Bimson and the Valley National Bank recognized Mr. Bull, together with other Arizona farmers, in a ceremony in Phoenix as outstanding agriculturalists in the state.

Through recommendations of the Valley National Bank, Mr. Bull was sought as an active independent farmer by the Cotton Producers Association in Georgia. From 1954 through 1967, Mr. Bull served as a director on the association's board, representing the interests of Pima County. The Tucson Kiwanis Club presented Mr. Bull with an award for the outstanding Farmer of the Year in 1962.

The Pima County Soil Conservation District was established in 1949. Mr. Bull served as a supervisor for the district from 1949 through 1962.

Loading Bull Run vegetables on trucks. Courtesy of the Bull/Klingenberg family.

Locally, Mr. Bull was active in the Farm Bureau of Pima County. Also, for many years he served on the Continental School District No. 39 board as a trustee.

Early in his farming venture, Mr. Bull was receiving information first through the Pima County Extension office and then the agriculture agent, Mr. C. B. Brown. For the most part, Mr. Bull had had no contact nor interest in higher educational institutions. At one point, however, he befriended a young University of Arizona professor in the plant breeding department, William (Bill) Thomas, whose family had moved into the local farming community. Mr. Bull became more interested in engaging his contacts in the College of Agriculture from whom he received a great deal of information that benefited his farming.

Three of Mr. and Mrs. Bull's grandchildren and two great-grandsons have received degrees from the University of Arizona: John Klingenberg, eldest grandson; Dan Klingenberg, second grandson; Jeanne (Klingenberg) Herrman, granddaughter; and Jeffrey Klingenberg, eldest great-grandson. All received bachelor of science degrees from the College of Agriculture; Douglas Klingenberg, second great-grandson, received a bachelor of arts degree from the Liberal Arts College.

Due to health problems related to severe allergies, Mr. Bull was eventually forced to give up his job and the pleasant lifestyle with his family in Continental. He truly regretted having to leave the area. However, he and his family settled in Tucson, Arizona, where Mr. Bull continued his bookkeeping career with several prominent businesses. Through the ensuing years Mr. Bull longed to be able to return to the Continental area and to farm on his own. Farming was his boyhood family's background and livelihood in Sebastian County, Arkansas. As a young man, after only a seventh-grade level of formal education, he had enrolled and excelled in a business school in Fort Smith, Arkansas.

Loading Bull Run vegetables onto a Southern Pacific Railroad car in Sahuarita. Courtesy of the Bull/Klingenberg family.

Paul:

On February 15, 1950, we moved to our new house on the farm, a beautiful setting, and I began commuting to my job in Tucson. The catch was that Mr. Bull would stop me on the way out to the highway to request that I do an errand for him in town. That would have been fine except that my job took me all over Pima County with little chance to run errands. I guess he got the picture, so he decided to invite me to join him full time on the farm.

The Klingenberg family on moving day in 1958. Courtesy of the Bull/Klingenberg family.

This proposition took some soul-searching, as I was well situated with the Soil Conservation Service. After Gladys and I talked it over, and considering all family factors, we decided to accept the offer. We spent the next twenty years as a family: Gladys, Paul, John, Dan, and Jeanne along with Mr. and Mrs. Bull on the farm.

In 1958, after eight years living in our new home, which was located on the west side of the river, it was decided that our home was now on the wrong side of the river due to a land deal which isolated us from the main body of our farm. There were mixed emotions for everyone because it had really become home for us. We built another house.

Second house designed by Paul and ready for the Klingenberg family, 1958. Courtesy of the Bull/Klingenberg family.

We chose a site on high ground not far from the Bulls' house. It was a place where a stack of baled love-grass straw was located and provided ample level area for a house. This location was administratively best because it was located between the valley farmland and the Jack Rabbit Hill fields on the mesa. This land had been cleared and put under cultivation since we moved to the farm in 1950.

This new house was to be built out of homemade adobe instead of concrete brick. By using adobe, we could employ Native Americans, who were experienced in making adobes. In due course the home was completed, and we moved in. Never again would I have to cross country on high ground, where Green Valley is now located, in order to get to the Continental Bridge and across the Santa Cruz River at flood time, a round trip of twenty-five miles. Another reason that this location was important was because the workload had been increasing due to the fact that, in addition to Jack Rabbit Hill, two hundred acres of rental farmland had been acquired at Sahuarita. Initially this property was used to establish the Lehman love-grass crop. Now, to make the rounds of the entire operation, I would travel twenty-five

Paul Klingenberg teaching "tractor" to Perez, an exchange farmer from Israel. Courtesy of the Bull/Klingenberg family.

miles. Being in a central location was a big help. A bonus with the move was the view of the mountains and the valley. We were given a view of the first Green Valley lights as they came on.

The farm crop program that had developed up to this time (1958) would continue pretty much the same for the next ten years when the property would be sold. During this period Mrs. Bull passed away (1968), leaving Mr. Bull alone in his big house. Gladys and I became more involved in his personal needs; however, he was able to function very well as far as the farm was concerned.

As for the Klingenberg family, moving to the farm was good from the standpoint of providing a stable environment for growing children, with all of them completing their educations. In fact, all three graduated from the University of Arizona College of Agriculture with bachelor of science degrees.

~ Contributed by Gladys Bull Klingenberg and
Paul Klingenberg

Memories of growing up on Bull Farms

John (Johnny):

Cotton bolls are vacuumed up into the gin from a wagon at the Santa Cruz Valley Cooperative cotton gin in Sahuarita, 1961. Courtesy of Arizona Daily Star.

Granddaddy and grandmother, James B. and Lee, lived in a small frame house just east of the Old Nogales Highway and the railroad tracks. A cow barn and corrals were nearby. When agricultural activity increased in the Santa Cruz River Valley around 1950, granddaddy started asking my dad to come to work on the farm. My parents decided to move down to the farm and to build a new house. I was very much in favor of this move, as I had always dreamed of living on a farm or ranch. I was in the seventh grade when we moved, and Dan and I enrolled at the Continental School. The two years that I attended, through the eighth grade, were a good experience. We then had to go to Tucson to attend high school, which was a bus trip of about thirty miles each way.

Clean, dry bolls tumble through the gin. Courtesy of Arizona Daily Star.

My earliest memories of my grandparents, Lee Ethel and James Burton Bull, are probably from when I was three or four years old. This would be about 1939 or 1940. I recall seeing photographs showing both of my grandparents with me in various activities and places. However, because my granddaddy was developing his farm operation south of Tucson in the late 1930s, I became acutely aware of some of the farm activities early in my life. I even got a job helping build the cotton gin on Highway 89 across from where Walmart is now.

My grandfather was the president of the Santa Cruz Valley Cotton Gin Cooperative. The gin was used in Alabama and was shipped to Arizona to be reinstalled.

At the onset of World War II in 1942, my father, Paul J. Klingenberg, was sent overseas to be a part of the North African Campaign. He was gone from our family for over two years. At that time my mother, Gladys (Bull) Klingenberg, took up residence in Tucson at 1236 North 4th Avenue with my brother Dan and me.

During the next two or more years, I saw quite a lot of my grandparents. They lived "down at the farm," as it was described for many years.

Grandmother and granddaddy would come to Tucson to attend the First Baptist Church most every Sunday, after which we either went out to Sunday dinner somewhere in Tucson or to our house on 4th Avenue, where mother would have a dinner prepared.

I know that I would look forward to trips down to the farm before I was five years old.

Cotton is baled at the Santa Cruz Cooperative gin in Sahuarita in 1961. During its peak, the plant processed 160 bales. Courtesy of Arizona Daily Star.

Granddaddy and grandmother lived in a small frame house just east of the Old Nogales Highway and the railroad tracks. Their house was near a small cow barn and corrals. I suppose I started getting my farm and ranch interest about this time.

I remember grandmother milking a Guernsey cow by the name of Bossy. She also had chickens for eggs and meat. It always fascinated Dan and me when she would kill a chicken by cutting off its head, and sometimes the bird would jump away and flop all around the yard without its head. Very intriguing to small boys.

Another memory of the house site was an old mule that was kept in the corral. Granddaddy would saddle that mule for me to ride, and as I was only four or five (I think), they would let me ride this mule around the house in the yard. I would ride around and around so many times that grandmother would come out of the house and say she was tired of watching me go around in the same direction. She would then turn the mule around to go in the opposite direction. The farm was primarily a cotton farm, but granddaddy also fed cattle in a small lot. At that time, he was putting up silage in a pit for some of the feed. I can still smell the odor of the silage pit.

It was not uncommon for me to ride

A giant pile of cotton seeds is the byproduct of bolls processed at the Santa Cruz Cooperative cotton gin in Sahuarita. Courtesy of Arizona Daily Star.

around the farm with my granddaddy, so I had lots of time to visit with him as a small boy. During the war years, granddaddy drove a pickup truck, but later he began to drive a sedan car. I liked the pickup best. I remember one time when he had Danny and me with him in the car and for some reason, he needed

to cut across a field that was furrowed up. The car was jumping up and down so hard that Dan and I could hardly sit in our seats. We had a great time that day.

When I was five years old, we visited the farm for a few days. Granddaddy had come back from Tucson with a load of plumbing pipe tied to the side of the pickup. He had parked out on the road, south of the house. I climbed on the truck and promptly fell off and broke my right elbow. My mother and granddaddy had to rush me to Tucson to have me attended to, along with a police escort down 6th Avenue to the Thomas-Davis Clinic. I had a bad time with that arm for several years.

I started first grade in 1944. Dad came home from overseas duty in the Army Air Corps in the early fall of that year. Mother had gone to get him from somewhere, and Dan and I stayed with grandmother and granddaddy during that time. I remember seeing my dad for the first time in

John playing in the cotton trailer. Courtesy of the Bull/Klingenberg family.

grandmother and granddaddy's house on the farm. It was a strange feeling to see him after not having seen him for so long. He came into the house in uniform. Dad was a lieutenant colonel, and I was immensely proud of him. I guess the old farmhouse created some special memories of my early childhood.

In that same time period of the fall of 1944, dad was transferred to Tinker Field Air Base at Midwest City, Oklahoma. On the morning we left to travel from Tucson to Oklahoma, we went down to the farm to say goodbye to my grandparents. At that time granddaddy was engaged in a contract with the U.S. government to have a prisoner of war camp constructed right on the farm. This

John wandering through the tall cotton plants. Courtesy of the Bull/Klingenberg family.

camp was to be used as a German prisoner of war facility. The camp was under construction on the day we left for Oklahoma.

Later we again lived at the 4th Avenue house in Tucson, and Dan and I went to University Heights Elementary School. I finished through the sixth grade. Dad had gone to work for the Soil Conservation Service during the late 1940s. Jeanne was born in 1948. Dan and I then had a cute baby sister to look after.

In 1950, granddaddy had been asking my dad to come to work on the farm. My parents decided to move down to the farm and to build a new house. I was very much in favor of this move, as I always dreamed of living on a farm or ranch. I was in the seventh grade when we moved, and Dan and I enrolled at the Continental School. Our granddaddy was a member of the school board at that time. The school was basically a three-room school, with three teachers. The two years I attended, through the eighth grade, were a good experience. We then had to go to Tucson to attend high school, which was a bus trip of about thirty miles.

John waiting for Paul's return from the War. Courtesy of the Bull/Klingenberg family.

During the years I actually lived on the farm and before college, I think Dan and I gained a good rural upbringing. Life was probably harder on dad

Dan and John hanging around Bull Farms with friends. Courtesy of the Bull/Klingenberg family.

and mother than us kids as far as keeping a good balance between farm operation demands and family life. However, I believe it all turned out very well in the long run. Our grandparents bought a television set in the late 1950s. We kids were allowed to go to their house to watch *The Ed Sullivan Show* and a comedy called *Private Secretary* with Ann Sothern. We looked forward to that time all week.

Granddaddy always had time to chat with his grandchildren. One of his favorite questions to any of us was whether we "thought we would amount to something." While this was somewhat of a negative comment, it did make one think about the future a little more strongly.

Grandmother was always near the house. She did not drive a car herself. She said that she tried to learn but felt dizzy while steering the car. It could be that she came from such a different time that acceptance of a contraption like a car was difficult.

Sunday dinners at my grandmother's house on the farm were always a treat. Grandmother could really cook and was able to present a table such that you could not go away hungry. Her pies and fried chicken were especially wonderful.

As we grandchildren got older, I can remember becoming more aware of how granddaddy vocalized the economics of farming. He seemed to be constantly wanting to remind the family members of how tough it was to farm and keep the finances together. As for me, in the farming business now, I can readily see what his problems were. Sometimes, when he would indicate to me how tough times were in the farming business, he would ask me if I wanted to "buy a farm." I, being very naive about what he was talking about, would say that I would not mind owning a farm. Again, sometimes granddaddy's remarks were negative, but at the same time I believe he felt that we should be forewarned of difficulties one might encounter in business.

After I had completed college and started my own career in agriculture in the Yuma, Arizona, area, Bull Farms was sold. I was sad to see the farm operation cease, but sometimes good things must end, and new endeavors begin. At this time granddaddy was about eighty years old. Each trip to Green Valley was an education for us, as granddaddy wanted to get us aside and explain everything he was doing to build the income from the growing farm sale payments. I know that I have always been grateful for the knowledge that we received and have tried to put it to use, and I believe he would have approved.

In conclusion, I have to say that I am grateful and proud to have had grandparents who struggled to do something positive with their lives and to have given me a good heritage to pass on to my

Lee Ethel and James B. Bull standing by their first house near the railroad tracks circa 1942. Courtesy of the Bull/Klingenberg family.

own family in the American tradition.

~ Contributed by John Burton Klingenberg

Memories of visiting Bull Farms

Mary Jean:

During John's and my courting years at college, I have many fond memories of interesting lunches after church with Grandmother Lee Ethel and Granddaddy James B. Bull. Granddaddy would fill me in on the Bull family and what they were all doing; he had a good gift of storytelling and a sense of humor. He seemed dominant in the family. Grandmother was always the sweet, gracious, obedient wife.

Granddaddy gave me fair warning about marrying into such a large family one day when we visited the farm.

I can remember grandmother's kitchen with her big chiming clock, and the good smells that came out of there. One day when she was making her notably good lemon pie, I followed her around the kitchen to discover her

Mr. and Mrs. Bull inspecting cotton in the mid-1950s with a motorized cotton picker in the background. Courtesy of the Bull/Klingenberg family.

secret. I watched her add twice the recommended amount of butter to the recipe and that was what made the creamy difference!

For their golden wedding anniversary, I was given the honor of doing the drawings for their special history book.

Also, early on the day of the party, I had the privilege of combing out her soft curls. It was just beautiful.

John and I both loved them dearly and miss them.

~ Contributed by Mary Jean Harper (passed away in the winter of 2020)

Life on the farm

Dan (Danny):

I doubt I was really born to be a farm kid. An army brat, maybe. But when I was ten years old, my folks gathered up my brother, sister, and me and we moved to my grandparents' farm in 1950. I took to it like a duck takes to water. There was plenty of space. Picking cotton was a kick, and attending an eight-grade, two-room schoolhouse was an experience to treasure. I learned to hunt, and the folks put on

John and Mary Jean helping Gladys celebrate another birthday. Courtesy of the Bull/Klingenberg family.

great hayride parties for their church friends.

Why we moved to the west side of the Santa Cruz River and closer to the Old Nogales Highway, I am not quite sure. This meant quite a walk or drive through dusty roads to catch the school bus (a pickup truck until 1954), to go to town (Tucson), or to visit the grandparents who had a TV. In August, there was also the problem of getting trapped when the river flooded.

A redeeming feature of being on the "west side" was the magnificent view of the Santa Rita Mountains, a memory I have always carried with me and return often to enjoy. I guess the "west side" was also a good place to conduct my 4-H Club projects (mostly raising beef calves), and I have a fond memory of a marshmallow roast with my friends from town when our house was being built. I am not sure I liked very much having to mow our huge Bermuda-grass lawn with a push mower. Was this a form of character building?

Santa Rita 4-H Club at Ruby Star Ranch, circa 1955, is ready for the Pima County Fair. Dan Klingenberg is on the left with his heifer and John is on the right. Those standing in the background include Mr. Hibbetts, the Gaynon boys, the Raye family, and Gladys and Jeanne Klingenberg. Courtesy of the Bull/Klingenberg family.

Needless to say, I was glad when we moved to the "east side" in the foothills just behind my grandparents' house. Dad built our house with the same floor plan as the other one; but this house faced west, and the view of the Santa Rita Mountains was not as good. Still, we were closer to the school bus and to grandmother's Arkansas-style family dinners, which always seemed to include fried chicken, fresh vegetables, and homemade ice cream. I remember the ice cream especially because I got to turn the crank and add the ice and salt.

I knew that as a farm family we were making progress when an electric ice maker was purchased, and

Jim and Ethel Bull stand in the backyard of their home in 1947. Courtesy of the Bull/Klingenberg family.

my folks bought a TV for our very own. Even so, we still enjoyed getting together at the grandparents' to watch *I Love Lucy* and *The Ed Sullivan Show*. Progress was also shown in that the grandparents no longer raised the chickens and milked the cows as they did in the early days before we moved to the farm. As long as I lived on the farm, however, the cotton was sprayed by low-flying aircraft. Never knowing or even thinking of this as a harmful practice, the buzz of the airplane and the smell of the insecticide in the early morning hours is a vivid memory.

By now, supermarkets were coming to Green Valley, which curiously was being developed on the "west side." And who would ever have thought that they would put a super-highway over there? I guess stranger things have happened. After all, the Continental School board (my grandfather was a member) voted to add a third classroom and to replace the pickup truck with a real school bus with flashing lights and all. Imagine my surprise when they built a brand-new school to the east on the mesa. It was sad to see the old school close.

Life on the farm had its ups and downs, however. The folks

insisted that if we were going to buy a horse, it would best be procured at the livestock auction in town. The price was right, although I doubt they realized the wild nature of an auction horse. Larkey, for example, seemed to be the perfect horse for a kid; but get him out in the open plowed field and there was no question of who was in control. All I could do was hold on for dear life. And why he always decided to buck me off in the middle of the labor camp right in front of everybody, I will never know.

My worst memory on the farm took place when I was fifteen years old. Some of us kids had decided to shuck dried ears of corn that were stored in a shed just behind my grandparents' house. My six-year-old cousin, Elaine, and I chose to do this while sitting on the edge of the old well that was nearby. That is when tragedy struck. For a fleeting moment, I turned only to see Elaine slip without a sound between the railroad ties that held the newly installed pump apparatus. She fell sixty feet; and we knew, when dad retrieved her with a carefully and quickly made rope cradle, that she never had a chance. Farm accidents occur all the time, but I still find it hard to believe it could happen to us.

Dan A. Klingenberg. Courtesy of the Bull/Klingenberg family.

My grandfather had a part to play in my career in banking, which at this writing spans more than twenty-seven years. I do not think he ever wanted me to drive a tractor. "To be a success, Danny boy," he used to say, "you have to take bookkeeping, and I'll give you a job in the office so you can get some experience." And that is what happened. I enrolled in bookkeeping at Tucson High School and worked part-time recording time and payroll records for the farm. This all seemed like a good idea because that is how he got his start. I got paid "something" and the office was cool. I vowed, however, that I would never start work as he did, at three o'clock in the morning.

Well, so much for life on the farm. They say, "You can take the boy out of the country, but you can't take the country out of the boy." And that is the way it has been, as virtually all my career has been related to agriculture: county extension agent in Yuma; Peace Corps in Venezuela; cattle feeding in Montana and Arizona; and agricultural banking for Chase Manhattan Bank and Farm Credit Services of Southern California. And, yes, I still mow my own lawn as that is good for character, and I tell any kid who will listen to me to be sure and take bookkeeping, as it is the secret of success.

~ Contributed by Dan A. Klingenberg (passed away in the fall of 2020)

Eddy Epps smiles for a photo. Courtesy of the Bull/Klingenberg family.

Memories of my grandparents

Ed (Eddy):

There is a flood of memories that fills my head concerning my grandparents and their effect on my life, and they are all positive. My grandparents, James B. and Lee Ethel Bull, represented stability and success for me. I admire the saga of leaving Arkansas before World War I in 1916 and heading west for a new life. They had humble beginnings and worked hard to make a new life for their family. Apart from a few business trips, they did not seem to know how to enjoy their wealth according to today's standards. I was proud of the awards that grandfather won in his field. Knowing them in those days, my formative years, gave me an appreciation for all the hard work that small farmers across America do.

Grandfather cared for all of us and showed his love in many ways, but he was not affectionate, as were not many men of that era. I was always glad to be with him. We shared a bedroom when I visited. Sometimes he would scratch my back at night and pretend to be planting and caring for cotton. He always had to be "working."

My grandmother made up for any faults that grandfather may have had. She was very affectionate with me and always seemed to have a sweet spirit. The meals we had on the ranch were legendary. Great cook! I can also remember her having headaches and having to go to bed.

Driving around with grandfather as a boy and later as his chauffeur is an important memory. He talked; I listened. Cruising the ranch, checking on the irrigation and the farm hands, was fun for me. I can remember him signaling me to turn the car with the slightest flick of his finger. The car was followed by billows of dust no matter how slowly we drove, and the tires somehow always got covered with mud. This provided a job for me when we returned to the house—I spent many hours washing his car.

Bishop Hart, family photographer and great-nephew of J. B. Bull. Courtesy of the Bull/Klingenberg family.

On these drives, grandfather would always get around to discussing what I would be when I grew up. At that time, I was living from day to day and could barely think about what I would be doing during the next summer. So, to forestall the big question and to put him off, I would say that I wanted to park cars for a living. I do not know if he thought it was a joke or not, but I meant it that way. He cared for me and was concerned that I would make a good living as an adult. I always got the feeling that it would be great if I were a bookkeeper like he was, something for which I had no aptitude whatsoever.

He did help me out financially with my college education and eventually with the purchase of our first house. A lot of what I remember about my grandparents centers around their ranch, although I got to see them doing the "California scene" once a year during hay-fever season, which was in August. And I have inherited something besides their wealth—I have inherited my grandfather's genes, which leave me susceptible to allergies. My sons, too, have the same problem. And so it goes down the generations.

In California they would always rent a place at the beach, and we would be invited to be with them there. It was great fun. Grandfather rented our first TV during one of those times. This was my exposure to technology in the 1950s. I suppose if he were alive today, we would be hopping on the information highway together.

Back to the ranch . . . Holidays were always special for our extended family in those days. Grandmother was a great cook and enjoyed seeing all of us eat up. Her pies and biscuits were outstanding. Being part of a large family felt like I belonged to someone besides my parents. The things we did, and the old house, seemed to have almost a magical quality. I am very thankful for that experience.

The house was a real shelter from the summer storms that blew across the desert. The sky would turn black. Lightning would strike the earth, knocking out the electricity, and the wind and rain would rage on the land. The smell of kerosene heaters and lamps takes me back to that era. I felt safe inside the thick adobe walls. Occasionally the arroyos would flood, cutting off the ranch from the rest of the world. Exciting! In the summer, the house was a shelter from the killing heat. The drone of the air conditioner meant all was well and cool inside. After the ranch was sold, I returned with my wife to show her the house and it seemed so small and frail, hardly the place that I had remembered. I have learned since growing up that a child's view of things is always different from what really happened.

In summary, my grandparents did what they could to make the best of life at that time and they did an outstanding job. The unique circumstances they had to deal with did not stop them from getting what they thought was best for them. They provided a stable relationship and family in spite of the challenges of that day. I know they would be proud of their grandchildren for what we have accomplished, as well as their great-grandchildren. They certainly did their best to help us all get a good start in our various lives.

~ Contributed by W. Ed (Eddy) Epps

The J. B. Bull I knew

Bishop:

Mr. Bull with his foal. Courtesy of the Bull/Klingenberg family.

My family went to Uncle Jim's farm in 1937. My father, A. A. Harp, was a nephew of J. B. Bull. During the Depression years, dad was laid off from the Southern Pacific Railroad and needed work. So Uncle Jim gave him an opportunity to farm for him.

Dad had been a farmer in Mansfield, Arkansas, before he went to El Paso, Texas. Dad, Uncle Jim, and I would walk the ditch banks making sure that the water was within the ditch banks and was being moved onto the fields.

Around 1939, Uncle Jim's prized possessions were two big, dapple-gray Percheron mares. Both were with foals when he bought them. I cannot remember their names, but we used them to pull stumps as we cleared additional acres and to pull the forty-foot float we used to level the fields so that water would flow properly. During the summer months, Uncle Jim would come down on Sunday afternoon and we would give the mares a swim in the irrigation ditch outlet. Then Uncle Jim would brush their manes and tails, clean their hooves, and take care of their teeth.

One of the mares had a beautiful foal, black with a white blaze on his forehead. Uncle Jim halter-broke him and was training him. When I was working the team in the fields the colt would cavort around for a while, then walk alongside his mother; then I would stop the team so he could nurse. The other mare's foal was stillborn. It was a sad day on the farm. It took a great deal of coaxing to get the mare away from her foal's body.

J. B. Bull in 1971 working in his Green Valley garden. To his left is the former Bull Farms across the Santa Cruz Valley. Courtesy of the Bull/Klingenberg family.

The introduction of Pima cotton to the Bull place was exciting. Our short-staple cotton was about forty-eight to fifty inches high, but the Pima cotton (extra-long staple) grew to well over six feet tall.

Uncle Jim walked the fields of his farm, but he also wore out many cars in his career. The closest way to any destination for Uncle Jim was right across the fields.

The corn grew to great heights, sometimes as high as fourteen feet. The green corn was made into silage that was put into a pit silo, and the Percheron mares would pull a four-wheel steering wagon down into and out of the pit for long periods of time. The feedlot was lit with electric lights and the cattle were fed twenty-four hours a day. The fermented smell was intoxicating to a boy. The four-wheel steering wagon was made by putting together two Model A front ends that were fixed to steer in a very tight circle.

~ Contributed by Bishop Hart (passed away in the winter of 2009)

Timeline of Bull Farms in the Santa Cruz Valley

1887, November	James Burton Bull is born, the seventh of fifteen children in rural Sebastian County, Arkansas, south of Little Rock.
1888, February	Lee Ethel McConnell is born in Arkansas, the fifth of five children.
1897	Mr. Bull finishes seventh grade and goes to work as a farmhand.
1905	Jim goes to Fort Smith, Arkansas, to attend bookkeeping school. He stays in Fort Smith working as a bookkeeper.
1908	The Manning family purchases the 9,700-acre San Ignacio de la Canoa Land Grant. Their holdings in the Santa Cruz Valley eventually exceed 500,000 acres.
1912, February	Arizona becomes the forty-eighth state.
1912, June	Jim's last job in Arkansas is in Mansfield at a mercantile store. There he meets a salesperson, Lee Ethel McConnell. They start dating and are married in Fort Smith, Arkansas.
1913	Mr. Nelson Sawyer purchases 320 acres of the Manning holdings. President Woodrow Wilson signs the deed on August 28, 1913.
1914	Germany stops shipments of rubber from Asia from going to the U.S.
1915	Both Jim's brother and sister-in-law contract tuberculosis (TB) and die, leaving Jim as the only brother to nine sisters.
1916	Mr. and Mrs. Bull move to El Paso, Texas, in hopes of improving his health—Jim was afraid of TB. Due to the rubber shortage, President Woodrow Wilson directs the Intercontinental Rubber Company to start growing guayule, a plant that could be converted to a rubber-like product. The company was owned by Thomas Fortune Ryan, Nelson W. Aldrich, Bernard M. Baruch, and Daniel and Solomon R. Guggenheim. The Continental Farm is established from the northern part of Manning's 1908 purchase. Approximately seven thousand acres are planted with guayule, and a plan to convert guayule into rubber is created. The farm is located seven miles from the newly formed Town of Continental. Intercontinental Rubber also builds the Continental School, workers' quarters, and ten homes. The project winds down when World War I ends.
1917	Post office in Continental is built. Lee Ethel Bull is to be postmistress from 1926 to 1927.
1922–49	Queen Wilhelmina of the Netherlands buys the Continental Farm with Henry Zellerbach forming Crown Zellerbach and rents it to cotton growers.
1926, early fall	Mr. Bull takes a bookkeeping job in Continental, Arizona, with a group of El Paso farmers who are harvesting their first three thousand acres of cotton from leased land on the Continental Farm.
1926, late fall	Lee Ethel Bull with daughters Gladys and Margaret moves to Continental, Arizona, from El Paso. Gladys is enrolled in eighth grade and Margaret in fourth grade at Continental School.

1927, late summer	Mr. Bull develops severe allergies and moves his family to Tucson to avoid local weeds and pollen.
1927–29	Mr. Bull keeps an eye on affordable farmland in Continental, Sahuarita, and the Santa Cruz Valley. Despite his allergies, he wants to farm there.
1928–41	Mr. Bull works in accounting jobs at several well-known businesses in Tucson.
1928	The Bulls open a grocery store in Tucson. Lee Ethel runs the store. Gladys is the primary employee until 1934.
1929–31	The Tucson grocery store is closed and moves to Emery Park, south of Tucson.
1931	The Bulls open "Bull's Grocery" in Tucson, at Tucson Boulevard and 6th Street, and sell the Emery Park store.
1935–37	Mrs. Bull also operates "Bull's Grocery Store" at 4th Avenue and 5th Street. Margaret helps her mother in this store.

Nelson and Florence Sawyer burial site in 2022. Courtesy of James A. Christiansen.

1931	Bull Farms is established with a mortgage on the first parcel of land, 126 acres, purchased at a tax sale. The land is west of the Santa Cruz River, two miles north of the Continental Farm, and adjacent to the Itzweire Ranch.
1932	Mr. Bull works part-time on Bull Farms while working in Tucson. He hires local and transient farm laborers and a supervisor.
1933	Paul Klingenberg and Gladys Bull meet at the First Baptist Church in Tucson. They began dating and are married in 1934.
1935	Paul starts work for the Soil Conservation Service (SCS) as an entomologist covering territories in New Mexico, southern Colorado, and the Navajo reservations in Arizona.
1937	Mr. Bull hires his nephew, A. A. Harp, his wife, Audry, and great nephews Bishop and Jess Harp, to run the farm and manage local laborers until 1938.
1938	Mr. Bull purchases his second parcel of land to add to Bull Farms. The land, 311.85 acres, lies east of the Santa Cruz River, on both sides of the Southern Pacific Railroad tracks.

Deed: Patented Land of Nelson Sawyer purchased
by James B. Bull on 3/03/1938
E1/2 Sec. 1, R13E, T18S
Source: Option, 03/03/1938, Approximately 311.85 Acres
Excluding a 12 x 12 foot parcel for Mr. Sawyer's Grave Site

Mr. Sawyer specifies that upon his death, he will be buried on the hillside just above the Old-Old Nogales Road. He dies sometime before 1938. Mrs. Sawyer keeps the land until she remarries. When the 311 acres are sold, she keeps the small portion of land where Mr. Sawyer had been buried in a concrete vault within an iron fence, per stories passed on to Paul and Gladys. Mrs. Sawyer-Gorman and family often come to clean the burial plot. After Mrs. Florence

Sawyer Gorman's death, her ashes are spread over her first husband's grave, just north of Mr. and Mrs. Bull's house on the Old-Old Nogales Road and just northeast of the Klingenberg home. Their granddaughter, Jeanne, often visits the site until the sale of Bull Farms in 1968. It should still be a separately deeded plot of land designated as a burial site.

1940, September	Jim and Ethel move permanently to Bull Farms.
1941	Mr. Bull signs a contract to build a Prisoner of War camp, later to become known as Camp Continental.
1941–42	Mr. Bull leases the Continental Rubber Company's entire holdings for one year—seven thousand acres. He cultivates the land suitable for crops, and subleases the remaining land for cattle grazing to a rancher from the McGee Ranch, west of Continental.
1941	Norman Bowden, Janie Bowden Harris's father, works for Mr. Bull on Bull Farms.
1945–46	Although cotton has been a major crop for Bull Farms during World War II, years of producing it depleted the soil so Mr. Bull grows vegetables, alfalfa, and grains in place of cotton under the Bull Farms brand.
1945	Mr. Bull is elected to Continental School Board.
1946	The Bulls have a home designed and built just east of their first house on the Old-Old Nogales Road, which runs north along the west side of the foothills of the Santa Cruz Mountains.
1947	Norman Bowden returns to work on Bull Farms with his wife, Cora. Their children, Jimmy and Janie, go to Continental School and then on to Sunnyside middle schools and Tucson and Pueblo high schools.
1947	Mr. Keith Brown and family from Chicago buy the Santa Rita Ranch at the northern end of the Madera Canyon Road. Soon, Mr. Brown is also elected to the Continental School Board.
1947	Jim and Lee Ethel Bull move into their newly built home. This is to be the final home until Mrs. Bull dies in 1968 and Jim sells Bull Farms in 1969. Norman Bowden remains as a permanent employee through 1969, along with Cora. Jimmy returns in the late '50s or early '60s with his family (Virginia, Vicky, and Brenda) for three years.
1948	Mr. Keith Walden acquires the Continental Rubber Company's farm, named Continental Farm, before it becomes Farmers' Investment Co. He and his wife Barbara Culbertson Walden and two sons, Dick, and Tom, move into a home that was the boarding house where Mr. Bull and his family lived in 1926–27. Soon Mr. Walden is also elected to the Continental School Board with Mr. Bull and Mr. Brown.
1949	Mr. Bull purchases and leases land in three separate transactions: *1. State Lease Agriculture and Grazing Bill of Sale, 220 acres* *2. State Grazing Lease Purchase, 2,080 acres* *3. Bureau of Land Management Grazing Lease, 1,835.20 acres* *Total leased or purchased in 1949 = 4,135.20 acres* *Total land previously purchased = 437.85* Total Bull Farms acreage in 1949 = 4,573.05 acres
1948–50	After Mr. Bull offers house sites on Bull Farms to Paul and Gladys, Paul selects a house site and designs the first Klingenberg home just west of the Santa Cruz River, east of Nogales Highway 89, adjoining the Itzweire Ranch. The site also

borders the William Thomas family homes and farm. Jeanne, Sutah, and Sutah's brother, John Thomas, become friends.

1950, February 15   Paul, Gladys, John, Dan, and Jeanne move into their new home.

1951   Paul Klingenberg joins the Bull Farms operation full time until it is sold.

1952   Mr. Bull adds two more parcels of land to Bull Farms.
Amado purchase, 632.72 acres; Morrison purchase, Jan 1952, 1,152.00 acres = 1,784.72 acres

1952, December   Total Bull Farms acreage (agriculture and grazing): 6,357.77 acres

Late 1950s   WWII POW camp, Continental, buildings burn down except for the superintendent's house.

1958   Paul designs a second home, east of the Santa Cruz River, in the foothills above the railroad tracks, the corrals, and the Bulls' house.

1959   Paul, Gladys, John, Dan, and Jeanne move into their second home on Bull Farms. Their view is now to the west, looking over the Santa Cruz River, their first house, the Sierrita Mountains, and McGee Ranch. The sunsets could be spectacular. But little did we know that the mines would soon start piling tailings to heights that would obscure the view of the Sierrita Mountains.

1960   On Jeanne's twelfth birthday, Mr. Bull shows her the blueprints of a retirement development named Green Valley. The blueprints are borrowed from Keith Walden. In addition to the retirement town and shopping center, there are to be tennis courts and a community pool. Highway 89 eventually becomes Interstate 19, a four-lane highway straight into Tucson.

1962   Jeanne graduates from eighth grade, the largest class ever at Continental School with nine students.

1968, February   Lee Ethel Bull passes away, leaving Mr. Bull alone in his house.

1968   Paul begins to site and design a third house, this time in Green Valley.

1969   Bull Farms is bought by the Anaconda Mining Co., primarily for the water rights.

1969   Paul, Gladys, and Mr. Bull move into their final, new home. This time their view faces east to the Santa Rita Mountains.

1970, January   Bull Farms ceases operation, and the name is retired.

1976, September   Mr. James B. Bull passes away in Green Valley after a long battle with cancer.

1970–2009   The land referred to in the Santa Cruz Valley as Bull Farms remains dormant. Except for the land acquired by Green Valley and Quail Creek, most of the Bull Farms buildings, equipment, and Quonset hut are left as they were in 1970. Over the next several years, the 1947 Bull home and the second Klingenberg home are occupied by Joe Martin and his family members. Joe becomes a security person for Anaconda Mining Company and runs some cattle for himself.

1981   The first Klingenberg house built in 1950 west of the Santa Cruz river and the former adobe building used as a stagecoach stop and later as a residence by Bull Farms field workers and their families are torn down by Anaconda per a handwritten note by Gladys Bull Klingenberg found by her daughter in 2021.

1989   Quail Creek, a retirement community, is established in Green Valley, Arizona.

1999, Summer   Ed Robson purchases the existing 2,500-acre Quail Creek community in Green Valley, with sold homes or sites (minimum one hundred sales), establishing Robson Ranch Quail Creek, LLC, a Robson Company.

2000   The City of Sahuarita annexes Quail Creek Community. The former footprint of Bull Farms within the Continental School District for thirty-nine years is now entirely within the border of the City of Sahuarita.

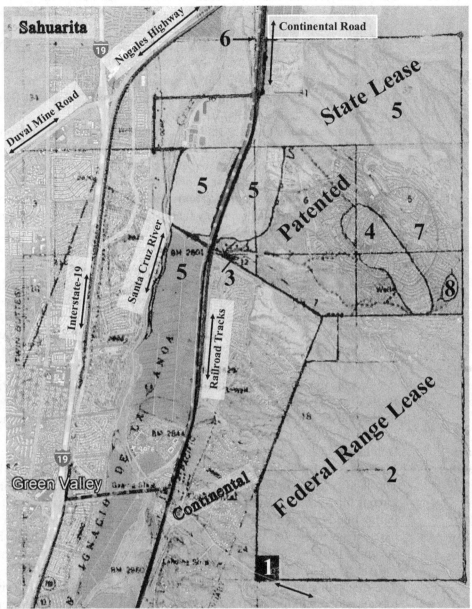

Map of total 1969 Bull Farms acreage and property outline, per Paul Klingenberg in 1987, superimposed over a 2021 Google Earth map. Courtesy of the Bull/Klingenberg family and James A. Christiansen.

Key: 1) White House Canyon Road beside the 2021 Continental School site; 2) Federal range lease land used to graze cattle; 3) Main section of Bull Farms houses, corrals, equipment sheds, and Quonset huts; 4) Jack Rabbit Hill cultivated land; 5) Cultivated land sections on both sides of the railroad tracks—patented and state lease; 6) State lease land ending near Thomas family homes; 7) 2021 Quail Creek on Jack Rabbit Hill; 8) 2021 Stone House on southern and eastern end of Jack Rabbit Hill

2002, February	Paul Klingenberg passes away at La Posada Health Care in Green Valley, just a mile away from the third home he designed.
2009, January	Martin Bishop Harp, age 83, passes away on January 1, 2009, at the Homestead Hospice House in Owatonna, Minnesota. He is buried in Fort Snelling National Cemetery.
2010, November	Gladys Bull Klingenberg passes away after three years in La Posada Assisted Living.
2013	An archeological dig at Quail Creek is reported in the *Green Valley News*, proving that others had walked and lived many centuries earlier in the Santa Cruz Valley area that briefly was known as Bull Farms.
2021	The 1950 Klingenberg house and the adobe building once stood roughly where the entrance to the Llano Grande Trailhead parking area is today. The section of land east of the Santa Cruz River and west of Old Nogales highway or Continental Road is now mostly barren, but includes the GV water treatment plant and the Quail Creek Veterans Municipal Park and Playground. Any remaining vestige of Bull Farms is completely gone except for a lone Quonset hut next to the present Quail Creek Air Gun Club. The potato digger used to cultivate peanuts on Jack Rabbit Hill (now Quail Creek) sits just across north Campbell Avenue near the intersection of Quail Creek Parkway. The gravesite for Mr. Nelson Sawyer and Mrs. Sawyer-Gorman is roughly a short city block or two north of the potato digger just east into the slight elevation of the land and vegetation.

The Carrasco Family of Sahuarita

I appreciate the opportunity to contribute my family's story to this history of Sahuarita schools. It incorporates input from siblings, cousins, and historic records, and was written in the summer of 2021.

My parents, Joseph J. Carrasco and Mary L. Soto, were married at Holy Family Catholic Church in Tucson on September 4, 1940.

In November of 1943, I was born at the Storks Nest, a birthing center in downtown Tucson. At that time my dad Joe worked at Davis-Monthan Air Force Base as a sheet-metal worker. In the mid 1940s, Joe and Mary Carrasco of Tucson purchased a farm on the Old Nogales Highway between Sahuarita and Continental with plans to establish roots and farm cotton. It had been my dad's dream to be a farmer, especially a cotton farmer. Our mother was supportive and willing to move to this quiet, desolate, and dusty farming community, which included a bar, post office, cotton gin, and general store.

Joe and Mary Carrasco posing after their wedding in 1940. Courtesy of Yvonne Carrasco Clay.

Joe and Mary with baby Yvonne in 1943.
Courtesy of Yvonne Carrasco Clay.

Ancestry

Joe Carrasco was born in 1918 in Mammoth, Arizona, to Manuel Carrasco (born in San Diego, California) and Carmen Araiza (born in Sonora, Mexico). Joe's grandfather was Rafael Carrasco, Jr. (born in San Gabriel, California), and his grandmother was Filomena Quijada (born in Los Angeles, California). After having moved to Tucson with his family, Joe attended and graduated from Tucson High School in 1935, and then attended the University of Arizona for two years. It is unfortunate that we don't have more information on Joe's ancestry.

We are fortunate to have much more information on Mary's family history thanks to cousin Martha DeSoto Green, a genealogist for forty-plus years.

Mary Louise Soto was born in 1919 in Tucson, Arizona, to Rudolph Carrillo Soto and Clara Otero Castro Coenen. Rudolph's parents were Ramon Comaduran Soto and Maria Carrillo Soto. Maria's uncle was Leopoldo Carrillo, who built the Carrillo home on Main Street. He had purchased the land from the Sosa family. The house was built in 1880 and today it is on the National Registry of Historic Places and is the home of the Mexican-American Heritage and History Museum.

Maria Carrillo's father, Don Francisco Carrillo (Rudolph's grandfather), was a rancher and the founder of La Sierrita Ranch, southwest of Tucson in the Sierrita Mountains. The Soto Ranch is now owned and operated by the Sierrita Mining and Ranching Company of Sahuarita.

In 1928 our mother, Mary, was almost ten years old. She lived at La Sierrita Ranch with her parents, Rudolph and Clara Soto and siblings, Hortencia and Rudolph. Families requested a school in 1928 and in 1929, Pima County approved an accommodation school for the Soto Ranch so she and her sister attended

The Soto Brothers posing on horseback in
1947—Pancho, Dad, Robert, Buck and Ronaldo.
Courtesy of Martha DeSoto Greene.

school in the main headquarters of the ranch. They had a school room for the fifteen children that lived on the ranch property. With the large number of children wanting to attend school in the ranch house, the County soon decided to send the students to Three Points. Clara Cohen Soto became the bus driver to take the children back and forth to school.

The ranch was eventually divided between Rudolph and his three siblings. Rudolph and his family homesteaded in El Toscalito where they raised and sold cattle. They supplemented their income by cutting and selling firewood. Mary's lineage also includes Jose Maria Sosa and Captain Antonio Comaduran, who were among the first soldiers at the Presidio San Agustín del Tucson and the Presidio San Ignacio de Tubac.

The ancestral Otero family from Tubac

originated in Spain with Don Torivio de Otero, who received a land grant from the king of Spain in 1789. The terms of the grant required that a home be built on the land and a school be founded; this school became the Old Tubac Schoolhouse. Fruit trees were planted—pomegranate, fig, and quince. Eventually the descendants, Sabino and Teofilo Otero, built Otero Hall, which today still stands on the grounds of the Tubac Presidio State Historic Park, and financially supported St. Ann's Catholic Church of Tubac. Sabino was considered the "cattle king" of Southern Arizona and had other entrepreneurial businesses. He also built two homes for the Coenen and Otero families in Tucson on Main Street near the Carrillo home. The Otero porch from the home on Main Street in Tucson is currently in the courtyard of the Arizona History Museum on 2nd Street. The Otero and Coenen homes were demolished during the urban renewal of the late 1960s.

La Sierrita Ranch tucked away in the Sierrita Mountains. Courtesy of Martha DeSoto Greene.

Mary's mother, Clara, was the daughter of Anthony Coenen (born in 1847), who with his brother Eugene immigrated from Lier, Belgium, when he was twenty-nine years old. They lived in Kentucky before venturing out west to Arizona and settling in Tucson. Brigida Castro Otero (born in Tubac in 1866) married Anthony in 1883 in Tucson at the Cathedral of St. Augustine and her cousin, Ana Maria, married Eugene.

The grounds of the Otero Ranch are now the Tubac Golf Resort. The original ranch house still remains; it has been renovated and is used as guest quarters. On the grounds are the silos and the stables (now the Stables Restaurant), as well as the pasture that still has cattle grazing. Visitors at the restaurant can view and enjoy watching the cattle from the restaurant patio. The conference rooms have photos of the Otero family and the original ranch on display.

As for Joe's and Mary's family life, after having purchased their Sahuarita farm in the 1940s, Joe needed income to purchase equipment to cultivate the land before planting and raising cotton and other crops. To accumulate the funds, he took a position with the United States Department of Agriculture helping Mexico with the vaccination of cattle during the outbreak of hoof and mouth disease in 1947–50.

My mother, Mary, and I accompanied Joe on the journey to Mexico. During this time our family lived in Mexico City, Pueblo, and Cholula.

I loved Cholula because there were a lot of dogs. Many dogs also lived in our household! My memories of that time include anticipating a package from my grandmother in Tucson, with bubble gum as a special gift. I never received the package—it was stolen en route. Can you believe that to this day the memory is still so vivid? It's so

In 1928, one room of the old ranch house was being used for a school room at the Soto Ranch because the Spanish-American ranchers were so anxious to have a school for a dozen children. Courtesy of University of Arizona Special Collections.

significant at a young age to wait and wait for a package that never arrives.

On a side note, in 2008 I traveled to Cuernavaca, Mexico, with teacher friends Clara and Liane to attend a Spanish language and cultural immersion program at the Universidad Internacional. Lo and behold, we went to all three places where I had lived while a five-to-seven year old. No surprise that Cholula still has a lot of dogs! Such a wonderful experience to return for a visit.

Clara Martinez de Otero, center, poses with her daughters Manuela Otero Quesse and Sister Mary Clara. Sister Clara Otero, with the order of Sisters of Carondalet, was inducted into the Arizona Women's Hall of Fame. Courtesy of Martha De Soto Green.

The family returned to Sahuarita in 1950 and began the journey of setting up their household, working the land (which was just dirt and tumbleweeds), and preparing to farm the first crop. We had to start by planning where to put the first irrigation ditch and how to get the water routed to start the hoses. I got good at siphoning the water from the hoses. Farming was hard work and required a lot of perseverance and money. Joe worked in the lab at Anaconda Mine by night and farmed by day. An amazing feat is that Joe built his own tractor out of parts from other tractors. Oh, to have a photo of that tractor!

It was springtime when we returned to Sahuarita. I started first grade in the original Sahuarita School of grades one through eight, which included four buildings. I graduated the eighth grade in 1958. The teachers I remember from that time period include Mrs. Black (she taught us to play the piano on cardboard keyboards); Mrs. Dudgeon, Mrs. Greenberg, Mrs. Maloy, Mrs. Stock, and Mrs. Irvin (the latter taught us to sew). I also remember Mr. Wilson and Mr. Gregory, the latter of whom served as principal in addition to teaching seventh grade.

When I was twelve, my sister Bridget was born and a year later brother Joey was born. With the addition of farm animals including Voltaire, the Charolais bull, the family was complete. We always had dogs with their offspring that we loved and enjoyed. I named one dog Pink Pajamas. It was a silly name that just came out of nowhere! She was a beautiful, loyal mutt and a wonderful mom to her litter of pups.

One of my fond memories was to pass the time away in the summer by making adobe bricks. I guess there were future plans to build a house. Another fond memory is of "playing school" on the farm. All the animals were my students, especially the dogs. The idea of being a teacher was planted long before attending college.

It was very special when my dad had to go into Tucson for business and mom and I would go with him. We spent quality time reading books at the Carnegie Library (which today is the Children's Museum). I checked out books to bring back to the farm. I also remember when the scheduled bookmobile came to Sahuarita and it would park by the post office. Also, there was a toy store in a basement on Congress Street next to the Fox Theatre. I remember getting a box of sixty-four Crayola crayons! We went to

Sabino Otero
Born, Tubac, 1844. Died, Tucson, 1914.

Sabino was heir to the first Spanish land grant in Arizona. It had been issued to his grandfather, Toribio, in 1789 and passed on to his father, Manuel. It became the region's largest cattle ranch. Sabino lived in Tucson for 50 years until his death where the Tucson Community Center now stands.

Sabino Otero tribute at the Tubac Presidio. Courtesy of Yvonne Carrasco Clay.

that toy store when in Tucson and boy, was that special.

My friends consisted of Sutah from the farm next door; other school buddies included Sharon Davis, Barbara Brown, Barbara Denton, Judy Fox, Mary Traslaviña, and John and Lana Harris.

I remember going to Kinsley's Ranch in Amado for end-of-the-year swim parties sponsored by the Sahuarita School. Oh! And to the Easter egg hunts in the grass fields by the Santa Cruz River. We walked the distance from the school to the river to hunt eggs. It was an enjoyable time to goof off! We looked forward to these small and far-between outings.

High school, for myself as well as for my classmates (1958–62), consisted of traveling by the Sahuarita school bus to Pueblo High School in Tucson. I started the day at the bus stop at 6:15 a.m. and returned home at 5:15 p.m. My years in high school were highlighted by joining activities, which included cheerleading as well as being a class officer and I was a member of the National Honor Society and Future Teachers of America. I was also president of the Pueblo chapter and Arizona state officer for Distributive Education Clubs of America, (DECA). During my senior year I spent weekends working at the Southgate Shopping Center through the DECA program. One very fond memory is of my geometry teacher, Mr. Gene Troutner, who is now ninety-five years old and lives in Cascabel, Arizona, with his wife Maria. Gene and I have remained friends all these years and visit with each other and talk about our years at Pueblo High School.

In 1962, I graduated from Pueblo High School and enrolled at the University of Arizona, where I chose education as a major. I traveled from the farm to the university in a 1956 Chevrolet with a transistor radio sitting on the dashboard and, later, in a VW bug. Eventually I lived in a dormitory on campus, within walking distance to everything! What a treat.

Yvonne holding her baby sister, Bridget Carrasco, on the family property. Courtesy of Yvonne Carrasco Clay.

I graduated from the University of Arizona in 1967 with a bachelor's degree in education. That fall I started my first teaching job, teaching first grade in Marana School District. The next year I went back to the University of Arizona to study for a master's in bilingual-bicultural education through a fellowship awarded by the Department of Education of the federal government. I then returned to teaching, this time in the Tucson Unified School District (TUSD), teaching kindergarten through third grade.

In 1977, I applied for and received a sabbatical leave from TUSD to study for a master's degree in school counseling. I graduated in May of 1978. I taught one more year and then started my career in school counseling in elementary, middle, and high school.

I retired from TUSD after thirty-four years. At that time I had the opportunity to be an adjunct instructor at the University of Arizona, working with graduate students studying school counseling. My career in education spanned forty years. I feel privileged to have had these wonderful opportunities.

Pink Pajamas soaking up the sunshine with her pups. Courtesy of Yvonne Carrasco Clay.

In retirement, giving back to the Tucson community was important. I am currently serving on three boards involving Southern Arizona history. The first is the Arizona History Museum of the Arizona

Yvonne, second from the left, with her friends Judy Fox, Mary Traslaviña, and Lana Harris. Courtesy of Yvonne Carrasco Clay.

Historical Society; also the Friends of Arizona History and Southern Chapter Board. I spearheaded the restoration of the Otero porch in the courtyard of the museum, which included an engraved brick fundraiser to support the restoration.

I am on the board at the Presidio San Agustín del Tucson Museum to preserve Tucson's history. There I work on several projects, one of them being the online auction fundraiser and another being the yearly celebration of Tucson's birthday (1775) on August 20. The Presidio is just a few yards from the Stork's Nest where I was born. The third board is for Los Descendientes del Presidio de Tucson. I also serve as a docent at the historic Sosa Carrillo House, which is host to the Mexican-American Heritage and History Museum.

My son, Matthew, was born in 1978 and lives in Tucson. He graduated from the University of Arizona with a BA in philosophy (specializing in ethics) and an MA in counseling rehabilitation. He works at Pima Community College on the west campus in the access and disability department, assisting students with their accommodations to find success in academics.

I live on Tucson's northwest side, enjoying dogs as always. Traveling and studying history are two great passions of mine that are very rewarding, in addition to enjoying the desert, volunteering, and the company of friends.

My siblings Bridget and Joey attended Sahuarita School from the 1960s into the mid-'70s and had a much different experience from mine. Everything was new, including the location of the schools. Grades one through twelve (now with kindergarten) were in new facilities with the latest equipment in the classrooms. The home economics wing and shop classes had the latest technology. By the time Bridget and Joey were in high school they enjoyed the addition of a state-of-the-art swimming pool.

Yvonne with her lunch packed and ready for school. Courtesy of Yvonne Carrasco Clay.

Yvonne and Sutah Thomas sitting with puppies. Courtesy of Yvonne Carrasco Clay.

Their high school years were 1970–74. Bridget was involved in Future Homemakers of America, Government Club, and Student Council. In 1972, the Government Club raised enough money for a bus trip to Washington D.C. That was the highlight of the year for the students!

Another highlight for Bridget was being a teacher's assistant for home economics teacher Mrs. Miller. In her senior year, Bridget received the award for "Most Outstanding Home Economics Student."

Bridget remembers that during high school the Spanish teacher, Ms. Gebauer, married math teacher Mr. Madeheim. Other teachers included Mrs. Burrell, with whom she had first grade, and

Mr. Gatterer as her sixth-grade teacher. She also has fond memories of the bus drivers, Bart Quihuis and Fred Espino. Student Mary Esparaza was a good friend. She came from Continental to attend high school in Sahuarita. Mary went on to become a librarian at the Pima County Library in Green Valley. Another fond memory includes the Tanori family, good friends of our parents'.

During high school, the school secretary was Mary Ann Clark, who was in the job for twenty years (deceased 2017). Bridget and Joey grew up as neighbors and friends to Mary Ann, her husband Jack, and children Wade (deceased), Diane, Doris, Donna, and Walter. The two families had many adventures—among them were pulling taffy, cooking, contriving family pranks, playing baseball on the farm, and in the later teenage years participating in drama skits and helping each other with homework.

Yvonne graduating from the University of Arizona. Courtesy of Yvonne Carrasco Clay.

Bridget and Joey's school friends included Wade McGee, Jay Elam (deceased), Javier Blanco, Theresa Estrada, Oscar Ahumada, Ricky Fielden, Frances Gonzales, Mark and Phil Davis, Arnold Burrell, Vanita Toliver, GoGo (deceased), and the Lerma family that lived next to the old school.

Bridget remembers that, during the time of the Bay of Pigs in 1961, there were bomb threats and the drills included having the students hide under their desks at school. Another event was an incident with the coyotes seen regularly on the school grounds—after all, it was their territory before students arrived. During seventh grade there was a bear in Sahuarita. It apparently came down from the Madera Canyon area and caused a lot of excitement. It was seen on the school grounds, at the farming camp, and by the grocery store.

During the growing-up years on the family farm, Bridget and Joey became very passionate about agriculture and still are to this day. They were involved in the Sahuarita 4-H club as well as the Pima County Rabbit Breeders Club. Joe, their dad, was the beef and sheep 4-H leader and my mom, Mary, was the cooking and sewing leader.

Bridget and Joey participated in showing sheep, goats, rabbits, and poultry, as well as steers and heifers. Bridget excelled in cooking, sewing, public speaking, and livestock judging and also exhibited at the old Pima County Fairgrounds. I remember taking my first-grade class to see the livestock at the fair in support of Bridget and Joey's accomplishments.

Bridget's first market lamb was named Sam. She became very attached to him and he ended up staying on the farm as a pet. We had a dog named Duke that was a Rhodesian Ridgeback, and that was feisty and unafraid! We also had a milk cow named Sugar and our mom made cheese and sold it at the general store. Bridget remembers several cows from throughout the years on the farm. Two in particular were Lucinda and Barbie, a couple of Herefords. Even today, Joey raises miniature Herefords.

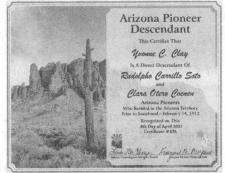

Arizona Pioneer Certificate. Courtesy of Yvonne Carrasco Clay.

Raising steers for 4-H included giving them names like PeeWee and Jumbo and we had a Hereford named Duke, just like the dog! The family coped with the inevitable grief of selling their prized animals for meat.

As Bridget and Joey got older, they began to exhibit livestock at the Arizona State Fair and the Arizona National Livestock Show in Phoenix, Arizona. Their dedication to the 4-H programs led to winning many distinguished awards in Pima County, the State of Arizona, and also at the national level. They won scholarships in addition to trips to Washington D.C. and New York State.

The farm produced lots of corn and barley in addition to cotton. Summers were spent irrigating, hoeing, and cultivating the corn. Once the corn was ready for harvest, we would sell to people who would drive from Tucson to purchase fresh corn for roasting. The corn was also popular for making green-corn tamales. Bridget and Joey would pick the corn and fill a pickup bed with it to sell to produce stands and restaurants in Tucson. They had fun and enjoyed their independence in farm life.

Joey and Bridget pose with Yvonne in her Pueblo High School cheerleading outfit. Courtesy of Yvonne Carrasco Clay.

Sahuarita did not have a Catholic church, so to attend mass the family went to Tucson. Going to Tucson was enjoyable because we would get the opportunity to visit grandparents and cousins. Bridget and I became founding members of a church that Bridget named "San Martin de Porres." For a long time, masses were held at the old school and a traveling priest would say the masses. The Sahuarita community can be proud of this early established church. I taught catechism for several years.

Bridget and Joey remember the flood of 1968 because the students were kept at the school until the parents could cross the Santa Cruz River to pick them up. They also remember the flood of 1977 in which the families had to evacuate because the river overflowed and a gas line exploded! The animals had to be encouraged to flee to higher ground. Rabbits and goats had to be loaded into Bridget's car and taken to safety.

Bridget and Joey graduated high school in 1974 in a class of ninety-six students. Both attended college. Joey later graduated from the University of Arizona with a BA in agricultural economics in 1980. Shortly after that their dad, Joe, died from lung cancer and the farm was sold to Granite Construction. Joey went on to farm in Stanfield, Yuma, Coolidge, and Chandler. Joey currently owns and operates (along with Bridget's son, Joseph) a five-hundred-acre vineyard in Paso Robles, California.

The Carrasco children pose for photos in the fields. Courtesy of Yvonne Carrasco

Bridget received an associate of arts degree in social work from Pima Community College. She then received a BA in special education and rehabilitation from the University of Arizona. She retired from the State of Arizona after several years of working as a vocational rehabilitation counselor and rehabilitation teacher for the visually impaired.

Bridget moved to Paso Robles, California, after retiring and works at a small elementary school. She participates in farmers' markets, selling the best apple pies in the valley as well as "Last Chance Salsa."

Her son Joseph, in addition to managing the farm, owns a trucking company and hauls grapes. Joseph is married to Brianna, whom he met when both were active in livestock shows. They have a son, Joey, who is one year old and is growing up to be an eighth-generation farmer and rancher. Bridget and son Joseph are both 4-H leaders in San Miguel, California. Bridget gardens and raises goats. Joseph raises Hampshire hogs just like his grandparents, Mary and Joe, did back in Sahuarita.

Joe, my dad, passed away in 1976 and Mary, my mom, in 2007.

~ Contributed by Yvonne Carrasco Clay

Yvonne and Joey posing behind Joe, Mary, and Bridget. Courtesy of Yvonne Carrasco Clay.

The Chilson Family Story

Growing up I didn't realize I was part of history—or would be. Mom gave me my name so I would have the same initials as my father, D. G. Chilson. Unfortunately, the feminine form of my father's name (Dan), i.e. Danielle, wasn't a name she was familiar with, so instead she named me Donna Gail. I wasn't called Donna very much until I went to high school. Dad nicknamed me Chici and that was pretty much how I was known among all our friends. I rebelled against my mother in so many ways, and one of them was to finally drop the name Donna, altogether, around 1978. I started going by Gail, spelling it Gale, then finally Gael in 1988, even though I never changed it officially. But I use the initials D. G. to this day, being proud of my heritage.

"Chici" and Dan Chilson. Courtesy of D. G. Chilson.

I remember being carted off as a child to numerous mine sites or claims that were being prospected. I remember my dad carrying the apparatus around that was known as the Chilson Pipe Detector—also known as the Chilson Ore Locator. It consisted of two boxes of finely coiled copper wire at either end of a frame that had straps for hanging over the shoulders and a meter in the box in front that a person could read.

Dad always referred to his experience being a telegraph operator on a ship sailing between Seattle and Juneau as the beginning of his fascination with using radio waves to find metal under the ground. He first started using his invention in Los Angeles to discover underground pipes. After perfecting his invention, he brought it out to the field and used it all around the Southwest. There are many of my father's maps and materials in the archives here at my home at San Xavier Extension that have never been cataloged. The remains of the actual apparatus can be found in the old shed.

It was said that dad was more interested in the actual discovery of ore bodies than in patenting the ore detector, which was the reason that another man/company got the patent first.

Dan and Marian take turns posing with "Chici" at the mines. Courtesy of D. G. Chilson.

As foretold by my distant cousin, Carl Chilson, in his story about Chilsons in the 1926 Mining Journal,[1] I tried to carry on in the family tradition in the early 1980s. My partner at the time and I invested in creating a corporation and hired my nephew, Bill Yarter (my half-sister's son), who had graduated from the University of Arizona Mines Division with a master's degree in disseminated gold, to locate a bunch of claims in the Harquahala Mountains near Salome, Arizona, as well as some others near Douglass, Arizona. We imagined his finding a lot of disseminated gold. Mom died in February 1983, and I put the money she left me into the project. What had been earned by my dad from finding the ore body that became the first pit mine in the region when it was sold to Pima Mining Company around 1955 or '56 by dad and his partners "Chilson, Wilson, and Todd" was invested back into the ground and the family member most interested in mining. This all came to naught and caused a lot of ill will among family members in the end, especially after Bill died of a brain aneurysm on December 24, 1987.

Later, another partner of mine tried to do something with the claims before giving up in the early 1990s. The claims near Douglass, although very promising, lost their appeal to mining companies when a portion of land that included the only possible route to develop a road out of the projected ore deposit was purchased by Nature Conservancy to protect the native species of fish in the creek it would have crossed.

It seems that the development of mines in this day and age runs counter to any consideration of protecting the environment for the generations to come. In my dad's era, he was a hero for expanding the knowledge of what lay beneath the ground that could be exploited to increase expansion, development, and the enrichment of people. Now we realize that this exploitation has its consequences in ways that those early pioneers had no way of foreseeing. Trucks became massive haul-packs, carrying more tonnage than my dad could have imagined as he gazed upon the pit

Dan Chilson at Goldendale, Washington in April 1909 when he was the sole radio-telephone operator on the west coast. Courtesy of D. G. Chilson.

mines in Montana and places around the Southwest. Did he imagine how vast would be the mountains of overburden that would forever testify to the capacity of man to move dirt around, visible all around this property and down the road? More earth was moved out of one pit mine near us by the mid-1980s than was moved to build the Panama Canal. We have three of these massive pit mines in the area now.

I practice forgiveness of myself and my father every day by trying my best to support the wildlife in its habitat, giving water to the critters and trying to preserve a small piece of the area for them as I turn this family property into a trust called San Xavier Peak Sanctuary.

Water

When I was young, the water table in the shaft in the front yard—San Xavier Extension—was around the 150-foot level. We pumped some of it up to a tank on the hill and gravity fed it to the house for a while. There was also a time when dad arranged to have the water from the mine across the street that was pumped up to the water tanks on the hill across from us (which is still there today, rusted and full of holes) and gravity-fed to the whole mining camp that surrounded Eagle-Picher Mine piped over to us so that we had plenty of water for a while. Those iron pipes could be found even when I returned home in 1985 although they had long since stopped carrying water.

Dan Chilson displaying his Chilson Pipe Detector. Courtesy of D. G. Chilson.

Dad loved growing plants. He grew the most beautiful red rosebush in front of the porch. I remember it grew as high as the roof. He planted honeysuckle in the back and nurtured the morning glories and the tobacco trees. He created a tub out of an old bladder tank. We used to enjoy taking a dip in it when it got hot. He also strung a hose along the roof of the porch that was punctured intermittently so that it would spray water down and cool off anyone sitting on the porch in the summer. We had a hammock hung there that we kids took turns on.

Art Burns helped my mom put a pump down the shaft in the front yard sometime in the '60s so she could have water. That pump burned out when the water gave out later in the '70s as the pit mine across the street got deeper and deeper and drought struck the region. Mom's second husband, Fernando Orozco, devised a system of barrels and started hauling water from the pumping station on Twin Buttes Road called Las Quintas Serenas.

Dan Chilson exploring Arizona in 1928. Courtesy of D. G. Chilson.

After I returned home in 1985, I hired a company to see about putting another pump down the shaft but the casing only went down to the 400-foot level and Fernando wouldn't hear of placing the pump below the casing.

There was a time in the late '80s that I would fill a barrel of water in my car and drive it around back and above the house to gravity feed it to another barrel on the roof, leaving Fernando to his own supply.

After Fernando died in 1997, I hired a water hauler and bought a large tank to hold water and a friendly plumber to install a pipe from the water tank to the pump in the back of the house.

In 2003, I hired a company to put a pump down the shaft again. The water was measured at being around the 480-foot level. They had to drill through the old casing at one point, in order to run

Dan admiring his mariana bush in August of 1946. Courtesy of D. G. Chilson.

a new, smaller four-inch casing down partially inside the old iron pipe but breaking through that and continuing down to 517 feet. They put the pump just above the bottom of the shaft so it wouldn't suck too much mud. I had the water tested and it was better water than what was coming from the wells in Green Valley where arsenic was a problem.

The only issue with the water from our shaft was that it was so hard. I remember as a kid watching a man testing the water when we first had a pump put down the shaft back in the '50s. He stood at the kitchen sink and just kept counting the drops of some chemical that he was measuring into the vial of our water. He got to fifty drops and proclaimed our water the hardest in the country!

When we started pumping that water in 2003, even the plants didn't like it much. But it kept them alive. We went back to hauling water for the house because it tasted good, even though we

Donna Gail Chilson standing by Dan's fragrant red rose bush in 1963. Courtesy of D. G. Chilson.

had the pump down the shaft. The water from the shaft was so alkaline that our carbon water filters didn't improve the taste enough to make it palatable.

We pumped water for about ten years and then the pump stopped working for some reason. We can't get a plumb bob down the shaft because of all the fallen timbers, so we have no way of checking where the water table is now.

The project of pulling the pump to see what state it is in has seemed to be more than we are up to currently, but we do keep in mind getting a truck into the site at some point.

Right now we have a water hauler bringing in 2,000 gallons every week

Pink House on the hill, approaching from the south (left), and from the north (right). Courtesy of D. G. Chilson.

and a half or so, plus hauling by ourselves another 300 to 900 gallons a week for the garden in the hot, dry summer. We also have rain catchment tanks and barrels situated under every gutter downspout. A good summer rain can provide us with garden water for a week.

Going to school in Sahuarita in the 1950s

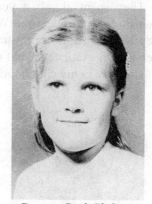

Donna Gail Chilson posing for her third-grade portrait in 1956. Courtesy of D. G. Chilson.

Donna on the last day of school on May 29, 1957. Courtesy of D. G. Chilson.

I was only five and a half when the 1954–55 school year began but I was allowed to attend first grade at the old Sahuarita School in the midst of the cotton fields on the east side of the railroad tracks. The pecan store and processing plant now stand where the old school buildings were.

The first grade was in a small stand-alone classroom and taught by Mrs. Burrell. I was shy and the experience was daunting. I was promoted into third grade taught by Mrs. Irvin, skipping second grade. Then came fourth grade with Mrs. Dudgeon and fifth grade with Mrs. Templeton.

It was during that fifth-grade year that my parents took me out of school to spend several months in Mexico. I continued my schoolwork under my mom's tutelage, making sure I wouldn't fall behind my classmates.

I can remember riding the bus every day, catching it by walking up the road to where other children caught the bus at the mining camp next to Eagle-Picher Mine. The ride home was sometimes very long if the bus driver had to take the McGee children home first.

My favorite teacher was Jeanne Dunn in the eighth grade. She got me started acting—a passion I continued to follow through college. In April of 1961, the students of her class put on *Faust*. I got to dress up as a maid—a fat maid with a pillow cinched around me, and had ever so much fun! Freddie McGee played Faust and that made being involved with the play even more fun and exciting.

My mother, Marian Chilson

Mom definitely has a place in this history. She was born in Massachusetts. Her cousin traced the family line back to Captain John Smith, one of the early colonists in Jamestown, Virginia, who came over from England. My mother graduated from a teacher's college in New England and went back to school after dad died to become a librarian.

Mom decided to come west after living in New York City in her twenties. She first landed a job in Prescott working for the sheriff's

Mrs. Irvin's third-grade class in the spring of 1956. Courtesy of D. G. Chilson.

department. A friend of hers lived in Tucson and urged her to come stay with her. Mom found an ad in the classified section of the newspaper placed by a man seeking a secretary for his mining business. She answered the call and met my dad!

They spent almost a year camping in a mine tunnel before they decided to live at San Xavier Extension. Mom loved the West and the desert. She loved my dad and going on all the trips with him. They bought a little camp trailer in the mid-'50s and took that around the West and into Mexico on a three-month excursion. That was luxurious camping, for sure; a darn sight better than that old army truck we had early in my childhood. Later on that trailer became my bedroom.

Mine shaft in the Chilson front yard that was used for water. Courtesy of D. G. Chilson.

Mom worked as a librarian at the Green Valley Library for some years. She was an avid reader—and newspaper clipper! I remember getting lots of clippings with every letter she wrote and came home after she died to find clippings in lots of books and in those recycled Kleenex boxes that were too pretty to throw away.

Mom was also a staunch member of the Republican Party. That's how she met her second husband, Fernando Orozco, local builder and inventor of building materials. She married him in 1969. The debacle with President Nixon made her decide to put away the pictures and silver plate she had been awarded for her dedication in getting him elected. She died at the same age as my father, only twenty-three years and a few months later.

~ Contributed by Gael (D. G.) Chilson

NOTES

1. Chilson, Sajas Carl W. "Mine Locations of the Chilson Brothers." *Western Mining History*. May 15, 1926. https://westernmininghistory.com/library/37951/page1

Friday, May 1, 1959: Dedication Day for the Sahuarita School (and a long ride on Jennifee)

Mom wrote in her diary:

Chici [Gael] was up at 5 a.m. to ride Jennifee. Decided it was too windy so went back to bed. Up at 6 a.m. again deciding it wasn't too bad; was going over at first to tell Normague 'not going' but Normague was over here and wondering what had happened to Chici so they left here on Jennifee and Fury at 6:30. It was ten to seven before they left Fuell's and about 10:30 when they got to school. They got home at 6 p.m. We went to Sahuarita School dedication at 7:30. McGavocks went with us. Saw Becky and Hircel; the Wilsons, McGees. We missed the Fordhams who came while we were gone and left Chici a dress and another Hobbit book.

I still remember that long ride there and back again. Long and kind of boring. When we finally got to school we tied the burros to the tetherball

"Chici" and Marian Chilson doing laundry with the help of a cat. Courtesy of D. G. Chilson.

poles in the yard in the back of the school and went into class. At break time all the kids ran out to see the burros. It caused quite a stir among the staff. When we left that afternoon, as we passed the front walkway, Mr. Gregory, the principal, came out shaking his finger at us, telling us to never do this again unless we warned them ahead of time and asked permission.

Dan and Marian Chilson's first home in the mine tunnel. Courtesy of D. G. Chilson.

That was okay; once was enough. It was a long day. Burros don't run, at least my burro never ran unless I was trying to catch her and she was running away from me. She plodded slowly along, steady but slow. I loved Jennifee—learned how to cuss, too, because of her, when I wanted her to do something she didn't want to do, both of us being very stubborn.

Dad got Jennifee for me for my seventh birthday. I would lie on her and read books as she munched her way around the yard. We would let her run wild with the other burros in the neighborhood, catching her when we had hay and I wanted to ride her, or when family was visiting or other kids wanted to ride, too.

We used to sometimes keep the burros in a fenced area, down behind San Xavier Mine, where the extra water from the mine first flowed into an old tank we could dunk ourselves in when it was hot, then down the wash, almost turning the area into a swamp. It was a lot of fun to go looking for the burros and play in the swamp.

Dad had a truck full of dirt hauled in from a local ranch yard and I tried my hand at gardening one summer. I had some watermelons coming along and Jennifee chomped on all of them, checking to see which were ripe. I was so mad!

When we had her penned in the yard at home, Jennifee liked to stick her head in the back door of the house if she wanted a treat.

I rode Jennifee in the Rodeo Parade twice, once in 1961 and again in 1963. In 1961, Ann and I created costumes as if we were Seminole Indians (Ann was from

Donna Gail in front of the Sahuarita School on April 25, 1959. Donna Gail and Normague Fuell ride Jennifee and Fury to commemorate the dedication day festivities on May 1, 1959. Courtesy of D. G. Chilson.

Florida). I especially remember the second time, though, when it was so hard to find and catch Jennifee and the other burros that Ann Fordham, I, and one other girl wanted to ride. Mom hired the local rancher finally, after I had run all over the desert, to round them up and trailer them into Tucson. We stopped the whole parade at one point because the burro the other girl was riding had a young colt with it that wanted to nurse right there in the middle of the parade. A guy in the band behind us hit the burro on the rump with his French horn and made it get moving again.

One hot summer day my friend Brenda and I and one other neighbor girl rode three burros way back of San Xavier Peak, around where the Ocotillo Ranches are today. We didn't notice the clouds building

"Chici" and Jennifee. Courtesy of D. G. Chilson.

up until all of a sudden it was pouring. Then it started hailing and the only refuge we had was to huddle under the burros. The younger girl started crying and I freaked out and ran home, braving flooded washes, to try and get mom to drive back there and bring the girl home. Mom basically said that we got ourselves in that fix and we could get ourselves out. By the time I had walked all the way back there again, I found the girls and the burros walking down the road, headed home. The washes had pretty much stopped running and peace had been restored to the desert.

Remembering people from my childhood: Traslaviña, McElvane and Herde

My memories of Olivia Traslaviña are based around the wonderful ceramic pottery and artwork she fired in her backyard kiln. One afternoon, Olivia invited my mother to bring me over to make something with clay that she later fired and gave back to me. I couldn't have been more than ten years old at the time, maybe younger. There may have been other children and mothers there that day—I can only remember feeling special because Olivia made me feel that way. I was a ceramic artist for a day. Wish I knew what happened to that special object.

Fortunately I still have two of Olivia's ceramic art pieces on my living room wall. She painted the lovely desert scenes on them before they were fired—typical of her work.

Dad had a truckload of rich earth full of cow manure brought in from the Traslaviña ranch a few years before he died. I loved growing things in that soil—especially sweet peas and watermelons (as mentioned, my burro loved those melons, too).

My memories of Mrs. McElvane are similarly dim. The first time I remember visiting her was with both of my parents. It was at night and Mrs. McElvane was caring for her husband who was very ill. He must have passed on not long afterwards. The second time was when I was a little older, not sure what age exactly, but Mrs. McElvane had invited a number of ladies to attend a function which, for some reason, she hosted in her large Arizona-style living room in the separate building that also included the bedrooms. She had a grand piano in the part of the living room that was a step higher than the rest, in front of a large fireplace. My mother wanted to show me off by having me play some piece of music that I'm sure I should have practiced a lot more than I did. The piano was daunting, especially because I was used to my small electric organ with two keyboards rather than a single long one. My memories of that day will always be associated with my lackluster performance and shame. But the piano was a lovely instrument in the right hands and I'll bet someone, maybe even Mrs. McElvane, played it well.

Donna Gail and Ann Fordham in the February 1962 Rodeo Parade with Jennifee. Courtesy of D. G. Chilson.

Mrs. McElvane and her husband had built that home in the desert back in the '30s or '40s. It showcased the southwestern style with thick adobe walls, a rounded turret at one end of the large living area to help with keeping the place cool (hot air rises), saguaro-rib ceilings, large beams with bark still on them, rustic fireplaces, and a long way down a winding dirt road coming from the west on Mission Road. Stone edifices guarded a small cattle guard as you drew near the house.

Gael's treasured ceramic decoration painted by Olivia Traslaviña. Courtesy of D. G. Chilson.

In 1960, ASARCO installed a new general manager at the Mission Mine. Roy Herde was transferred to this location from the Silverbell Mine with his wife, Marion, and young son, Jim. By that time a road had been run straight through from Mission Road that met up with Sahuarita Road so that the driveway to the property was very much shortened. This road was named Helmet Peak after the gray limestone hill near its inception at Mission Road.

Roy used to let a friend from Tucson keep his horses on the property. I had a lot of fun riding them and taking girlfriends over to enjoy horseback riding, too.

When Rancho Sahuarita was in the early phases of development, the town decided to have the exit from I-19 renamed Sahuarita Road instead of Helmet Peak and even wanted the whole of the road's name changed to Sahuarita. Herde was against the name change and got a few of the other longtime residents of the area to go along with him, refusing to sign the petition allowing the name change. It was meant to keep things simple for those who didn't want change, but it has caused problems ever since in explaining how the very straight road coming all the way from Route 83 across the valley changes its name for the last few miles. People trying to find their way back to Sahuarita or Green Valley from Mission Road, looking for the Sahuarita Road that they thought they came west on, have ended up going a long way out of their way only to get to either Duval Mine Road or realizing they were headed for Tucson.

Herde home in the spring of 2015. Courtesy of D. G. Chilson.

Roy Herde may also be remembered as serving on the Sahuarita School Board for a period of time in the '60s. He continued to live in that special house long after he retired from ASARCO and his wife died, until he died in early 2015.

Now, thanks to the fact the place has such historical value, ASARCO has turned it into a company meeting place with a fancy new gate that can be seen when driving down Helmet Peak Road.

~ Contributed by Gael (D. G.) Chilson

Marion, Roy, and Jim Herde stand near an agave in the front yard of their home on Helmet Peak Road. Courtesy of D. G. Chilson.

The next five sections were written by Gael's mother, Marian Cole Webb Chilson.

House by the mine shaft: a new note in landscaping and interior decorating

There was the hill, rocky and barren, except for cacti. To call it a cactus-covered hill would be more fitting. Below it was the mine shaft. We had been working around the mine shaft for years, wondering all the time whether to build there or closer to town. One day a discovery was made of a young stripling of a tobacco tree making its way out of the hill. Big green leaves. We tended the tree and watched over it for a year until it acquired the stature of a young giant. This is the place for our home, we agreed. And building our plans around the tobacco tree we set to work. Arrival of the tree made the decision simple. We had been toying so long with the idea of using a mine-shaft headframe for the motif of our house, but while the shaft was in use, house building had to be delayed.

But now with a tree! We set to work planting seeds in line where the porch of our house would end.

On life at the Dimple Camp—August 1947

Above arched the Milky Way and around—all around —was the rim of the world we had left. Black curves of mountains with a dim glow behind them reminded us of the cities of men. But in the vast space encircled by the hills it was only us and the stars.

The night was quiet yet active. A cat bird squawked at intervals below us; coyotes laughed derisively in the distance. A whir of wings passed over our bed. And the millions of stars glowed above us from north to south in a broad band. Dan tried to explain to me how we belong to the Milky Way; the feeling of

The Sahuarita School Board in 1968 consisted of Dennis Nolen, James Bell, James Coile, Roy Herde, and Harry Timmons. 1968 Sahuarita High School yearbook.

association with it was beyond me, though. I listened and wondered how we could be below looking at it and yet still be a part of it. Looking up a few hours later while the world was still dark, I was surprised to see how the stars no longer arched over us; the band's course was east to west. Of course, I smiled happily, because for the first time I had a realization of the earth's rotational movement. We were getting farther away from the vision of the Milky Way as we sped toward the morning sun.

Our days in paradise are perfect. No other human comes to distract or torment or harry us. Time is entirely of our own will. We can breakfast with the mood, or dress as we please, or work when we please. It is day or night as we please for our abode is in an abandoned mine tunnel which we make light or dark with a twist of an electric bulb. The tunnel stretches farther into the hill than we feel like walking and, besides, there are bats.

My garden stretches as far as I can see. My world reaches to the sky and is encircled by a horizon of hills curved and undulating, broad tops and high peaks. Cloud ships rest on them by day, lights of the other world glow behind them at night and make a rim against the starry sky.

The world is round to me—here as it is nowhere else. A band of hills surrounds me, a

Dan standing beside the porch of the Chilson home. Courtesy of D. G. Chilson.

ring for a jewel setting of paradise where I dwell for free—a rocky and thorny jewel, studded with cacti, beautiful with rugged wildness and at night the arc of the Milky Way overhead.

With us life has been reduced to four people. From all the people we have known, from all the things we have done or owned or places we have been there is nothing now but the four of us. We have left conventions if we wished—we have left competition—we have left strident noises and appointments and buying and selling and storing and saving (for how long, though, can we exist today without some forms of buying and selling and storing and saving?)—but not learning or seeing or hearing or dreaming.

Riding the trailer with Candy

Sunday was the appointed day for moving. Dick had arranged for a truck to move the family and belongings. Dan had arranged for a trailer to be hitched to the car to move Candy, the milk cow, so that she would be established in Helvetia and ready for business at the same time the family landed.

Dan arrived at the ranch on schedule with Candy's conveyance. The truck was held up, however, and as later proved, did not show up until the next day. Meantime, Dick and Alice and family waited amid boxes and barrels to get moved out of sight and memory of the ranch.

As the trailer was available for only that one day, Dan went ahead with his program of moving Candy. Candy would arrive ahead, in the vanguard, and would have set up housekeeping in the delightful setting of the "Swiss Mountain Alps" minus family.

There was a slight delay to the program while Dan and Dick tackled the finer points of enticing Candy into the trailer quietly and efficiently. She had resisted first efforts wherein Dick tied her and looped the rope around the trailer and then tried to draw her in from the front. She refused to be enticed by the fresh green hay in the trailer. She put her foot down on the ground and refused to raise it to climb the boards. A cow does not aspire to heights even

Dan and Marian Chilson pausing for a quick photo. Courtesy of D. G. Chilson.

Dickie Chilson at 59 Ranch before the move to Helvetia. Courtesy of D. G. Chilson.

when she is but two feet off the ground. Solid comfortable footing is her motto.

Candy munched on a tree where Dick had tied her while they cogitated all possibilities. From time to time she eyed them, watchful and yet bored at the same time.

Dan and Dick engaged in backing up and moving forward to set the trailer in a favorable spot so that Candy wouldn't be raising herself too much. They wanted Candy to slip in easily before she realized it. They also wanted the trailer to rest straight once she got in, and not tip forward. It meant unhitching the trailer, with nuts and bolts to loosen and tighten again and finally, success. Like a charm, Candy allowed herself to be enticed into the trailer, and we were off.

Candy was anxious to ride in front with us. She made several attempts to climb out of her trailer. Not in an obstreperous way, but more or less venturing. Dan stopped each time and pushed her forelegs back. Candy was becoming accustomed to the idea and was beginning to feel like a lady in coach (who knows?) when we came to a dead halt, stuck in the sandy wash.

It was a long, tedious job. Dan jacked up the left rear of the car trying to keep out of Candy's affectionate way. Candy enjoys licking people within her range. Dan shoveled dirt into a bucket and then dumped it under the car wheels. Many times he did that. Then he piled dirt in the road ahead of the wheels. Then he let down the left side and jacked up the right side, to repeat the process of digging and dumping. Candy watched absentmindedly as if it were no concern of hers. She didn't seem to mind standing under the blazing sun.

"Let's try it!" But the car would not move ahead. Instead it sank deeper into sand. Just then, along came Dick to the rescue. He was on his way downtown with his family to find out what had happened to the trucker. It was a matter of minutes before he had plunged ahead of us, chained our car to his, and pulled us out. Candy viewed from the rear in her trailer, rode majestically up the bank of the wash, unflurried and as a matter of course.

Dick took her from then on so that Dan could get away to town. Alice said that Candy mooed at every cow they passed—we think she wanted to call attention to her grandeur. On arrival at Helvetia, Candy partook of a long drink of water, emptying two tubs, and proceeded to munch on her new landscape.

Taffy followed the trail blazed by her mother two days later. Only one mishap occurred. Taffy, being of a smaller size, rode in a more sedate style. She rode like a lady in the back seat of a Studebaker, chauffeured by Dick. She behaved like a lady, too, even though she broke out one window on the way. She wanted to gaze out the window—she couldn't help it since her head stuck way out anyway—and munch on green grass when

Dick Chilson milking Candy. Courtesy of D. G. Chilson.

she could. Dick had tied her tail down so she wouldn't swish it in his face. Instead, Taffy could wave it out the window every time they passed another cow.

Operation No. 3: an insight to mining, May 1946

You hear the truck coming a mile or more away—at fifty miles per. Up the hill to the Elgin it comes, swings around, and backs under the bin. Immediately the dragline goes into operation. Its huge scoop pushes the pile of waiting ore into the truck. Four to five pushes and the truck is loaded—in three minutes. Away rolls the truck down the hill and along the eighteen-mile stretch to the ramp at Sahuarita. Five loads a day; sometimes six for each truck, with an eight- or ten-ton capacity. At the end of the day, another car is ready to be hauled away to the smelter.

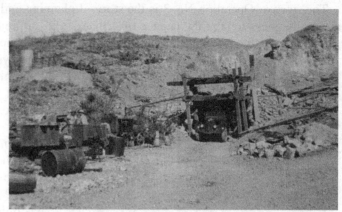

Loading haul trucks at the Elgin Mine. Courtesy of D. G. Chilson.

What goes on at the mine between truckloads? Plenty, and yet the work is so planned that it can be handled efficiently by only two men working a full day steadily—one man to run the dragline and look after machinery; another man to drill.

But before that comes the plan of operation—a prime necessity. The open pit, which is the Elgin Mine, at present, came about by design and location of ore. A hill has been pulled away. The framework of it still stands, like a pair of shoulders and outstretched arms, but the front slope is going fast.

The dragline rests on a foundation to the northwest, its cables stretching across the top of the hill. It is pulling ore from the right side of the cut. The drums of the hoist rumble and turn; the cables quake. Back, dig in, and forward goes the scoop in its lumbering fashion. It soon has a pile of rock ready by the bin for the next truckload.

On the left bank of the pit, there is drilling in preparation for blasting the entire side. Behind the present face is more copper to be exposed in the multitude of fractures in the rock. Up and down, across and sideways the fractures appear, showing rich deposits of copper. In another day or so, this whole side will be blasted away, leaving much for the dragline to clear away, and then the pit will be larger than ever.

Dragline at Elgin Mine stretches across the ground. Courtesy of D. G. Chilson.

There is more ore atop the tunnel opening of yesterday, too, in the center of the pit. Good green copper extending across the entire face. South of the tunnel stands the steam shovel, now idle before the wide opening in the face it scooped out in January.

Dan says there are at least 1,000 more carloads of ore that can be taken out to the smelter—1,000 cars at a car per day, or 1,000 cars at two per day when the strike ends.

It has taken ten months to dig the pit. Before that, in July of 1945, the Elgin Mine was a tunnel opening into a hill with a big stope going into it from above. High-grade copper had been extracted. Lining the sides of the tunnel and over the surface of the hill was copper ore of a lower grade, but mineable and profitable with premiums. Two men had tried to mine there a year before but they had passed over the mineable copper and left it. Not since the previous World War had this mine and the Helvetia District been mined seriously.

The story of Operation No. 3 is the story of planning and vision, an envisioning of the whole process and a willingness to take the chance of setbacks and surmount obstacles; of adjustments and successes; wages paid and food bought; 252 carloads of ore; new trucks; a bulldozer; a loan paid back in full; a geophysics survey instrument and a diamond drill hole; nine months of living—that is what has come out of the tunnel in the hill. It is what the pit represents.

Dan Chilson running the hoist. Courtesy of D. G. Chilson.

Operation No. 3: Elgin Mine at Helvetia—a diary of daily life

Up to June 1946, things looked bleak—in debt $3,450 (loan plus interest) to Dean, six months of gas bills due him as well; nothing in sight to make money. The Bull Docer Mine was finished; San Xavier Extension was finished, unless we could get a $20,000 loan to develop further, which Dan had talked over with Ballam.

On June 9, the light broke. Dick talked with Dan about development on the Blankenship property in Helvetia. Further investigation of the possibilities began when Dan returned from a trip on June 22. That day they found a tunnel prospect (Elgin) and also a dump. Immediate need would be a compressor.

By June 26 they had received first assays from Jacobs, ranging from 1.4 to 2.6—the big dump and iron dump respectively. The first thirty feet of the Elgin tunnel was 2.11; the next ninety feet was 2.5; the average of the overall surface was 2.4; little dump over tunnel was 2.5. Good enough to start work. Plans were to ship dumps first and then go ahead with a tunnel, but the second set of assays convinced them to leave the dumps alone—the dumps assayed at .71 and .95, whereas the tunnel came out as before, 1.4 ranging to 2.6.

On June 27, they were negotiating with Mrs. Blankenship for the lease. Dan and Dick drew up a tentative lease; Mrs. B considered it for several days and worked it over with her lawyer.

All clear ahead—Owens has promised a first month's payment on a compressor to get us going; Richard of AS&R told Dan to go ahead shipping fifty tons a day for at least thirty days or until the smelter hollers.

Sunday, July 1, we picnicked at the Elgin tunnel. Dan and Dick were prospecting and laying plans. At present there is the tunnel extending 200 feet and overburden and dumps. First things to do is build a bin and lay tracks. They plan to shoot from above, filling up chutes into the tunnel and loading cars from there, and then into the bin at the end of the track where the truck road ends.

Monday, July 2—Dan and Dick put up the first cent in the ore bin. Until work got underway, we were still borrowing from Dean.

Thursday, July 5—Looked around for a compressor.

Friday, July 6—We began laying track in the tunnel. It was about finished, also to the bin, by July 11. On a suggestion from G. T., we located and bought a Rix compressor in Patagonia for $1,000. Later Dan was able to negotiate for a final price of $850 in view of the repairs necessary before we could use it. Dick and Alice went to Patagonia after it while Dan collected pipe from Bull Docer hill to lay at Elgin. Owens gave us a deposit for the first payment on the compressor.

Saturday, July 14—Dan overhauled the compressor engine and Dick worked in the tunnel finishing track. More assays: 2.2 (twenty feet in tunnel) and 1.7 (eight feet in crosscut south from big stope over tunnel).

Operating the hoist at Bull Docer Mine. Courtesy of D. G. Chilson.

On the sixteenth, they took up car and track from San Xavier Extension to take over to Elgin. Dan took the engine of the compressor into town, and on the following day put it together. They drilled first holes on the eighteenth—eight holes and each was five feet deep.

July 19—Dick shot the first round. The first carload of ore is in the bin. On July 20, Dick added thirty more cars (mine cars) of ore to the bin. We borrowed another $100 from Dean to run us until returns came in. Total to date borrowed is $2,450.

On July 23, we hired our first worker for the Elgin-Frank Coronado. We did more drilling from the surface through the tunnel roof and finished filling the bin. We would have shipped the first carload of ore on July 24, but Mrs. B's carload was tying up the works. The bin assayed at 2.85, but the first lot from the smelter came out at 2.12.

July 26—We shipped the first carload of ore from the ramp. We would eventually receive returns on August 23 for $523.35 on the first and second cars. To be deducted from this was $188.56 for trucking and labor for one man.

Also on July 26 they hired a new man for Elgin while Frank was working at Bull Docer Mine for Owens. Pay for the new man was $6.00. More assays provided some disappointments: 1.90 was the cut under the bin and 3.15 was from the first raise from eight feet above the tunnel to roof. The face over the raise in the big hole was 2.6.

By July 28, Dan had overworked himself and was too exhausted to go to the mine so he had to take the day off. Dick is considering working for Owens at Bull Docer as manager for $350, while keeping his eye on Elgin. (He begins on August first and continues until the end of year when Bull Docer closes down.)

July 31—Our bank account is zero.

Dan back at Elgin on August first and the fourth carload is on the way. Owens loaned us $100.00 more for two men's wages at Elgin.

Dick is spending most of his time at Bull Docer Mine. Frank is the only worker at Elgin beside Dan; the two Mexicans we were depending on didn't show up. (Just the start of labor difficulties that would continue throughout.) At this point, Frank was working in Chute No. 2 from within. Dick was able to work on it the next day, finishing

Dragline at Bull Docer Mine. Courtesy of D. G. Chilson.

it. We are averaging three carloads a week. Mexicans came in to work again and then were out again. Dan and Frank were the only ones working at Elgin on the tenth. They finished the sixth carload from the mine to the smelter. The new assay numbers are encouraging—2.35 in the face in the big hole over raise; 2.45 in the muck at the bottom of the big hole over the shaft and raise; 3.50 from the south wall of the big cut; 2.45 from the No. 15 car sample; 2.27 from the smelter; and 2.25 in waste ore.

A view of the newly dozed road up to Elgin Mine. Courtesy of D. G. Chilson.

On Sunday, Dick went pirating and got a chunk of track from Esperanza Mine. On Monday, there were three at the Elgin—Dan, Frank, and Gregorio, one of the Mexicans. On August 14, Dan found out at AS&R that our ore has been averaged with Mrs. B.'s, so he sent word to El Paso. They took over more track from Extension and are waiting for the compressor from El Paso. (Dan did too much lifting at the mine and was tasting blood).

Labor problems again! Dick suggests a bonus for workers when they work a whole week continuously. Dan thinks otherwise; that they should be fined for a day's absence if they don't let us know they will be out.

On August 18, we borrowed our last from Dean—$200, bringing the total due him with interest to $3,975. Our first check from the smelter arrived five days later. We are working on a Sunday schedule at the mine with one worker and truck driver. Dick and Alice were tramming together on August 20.

We are running an ad for workers. Dan is still going over to mine during the days. On August 23, Frank had an accident, injured his foot, and was laid up. We now have James Murray working and two new Mexicans from Bull Docer Mine.

On August 26, one month from the first shipment, we began to get ore out of a new raise going into the big pit. The following Sunday the big stope caved in. On August 27, Dan was about ready to turn his hand to something else. He says last week he was in charge of a mine, but now Dick says he can handle both Bull Docer and Elgin himself.

On August 28, Dan went over to see what Dick was doing and there was on hand a crew of one man, and he had only one eye. Charlie the truck driver did not show up, either. Dan is still going to Elgin as usual. On Wednesday, August 29, all hands were on deck. Now we are being held up at the ramp. The Southern Pacific doesn't get full cars moved out fast enough. On Thursday Dan and Dick stayed at Elgin late, working on a switch in the track.

September 1—Dan made the first payment to Dean on our loan.

Labor Day—Gip began work at Elgin, one week after returning from the east. He'll be on the shaft. The next day, he was caved in, but dug out and no harm done. The other three men were on the job. We received a payment for the third, fourth, and fifth cars. The assays were 2.18, 2.37, and 2.27.

On September 5, we began a night shift and had two of the Mexicans tramming. We gave Dean

Dan enjoying the borrowed steam shovel at Elgin Mine. Courtesy of D. G. Chilson.

a second payment on the loan. On September 8, Frank Coronado came back again. Dan and Gip were still planning to go over. On September 14, we enlarged the bin to make more space.

On Saturday, September 15, Dan caved in and will have to take it easy for a while. He has been doing too much. The following Monday, Gip and Pinky worked alone. They shipped out the twenty-first carload, but there will be no ore ready tomorrow. Dan wants to stop shipping from the No. 2 chute on account of the low assay—only 1.6. Dan tried going back to Elgin on September 19, but had too many pains. He is on a light diet. Dan insisted on going the next day, though, because he was anxious to get the hoist moved over from Bull Docer hill.

There seemed to be an interlude of trucks breaking down at this point. We would get a truckload or two in the bin and then have to go to town for parts. If a truck was missing, there could be no cars at the ramp for them to load. It always seems to be one thing or another.

On September 28, Dan did too much again, lifting cables and such while getting drag lines underway at Elgin.

Dick speeds up the work. He was over there on October 2 and trammed ninety cars together with the others. Gip, Frank, and Pinky were working.

Gip is suggesting to Dan that he stay home and let Gip take over. Gip finally persuaded Dan to stay home on October 5. There were days from then on when Gip was doing it alone. Dick would come in each afternoon and tram until dark.

By the middle of October, we were looking for more workers. Owens is getting peeved at Dick for not spending more time at Bull Docer. By the end of October we had shipped fifty carloads of ore and had received over $11,500, from which we had to deduct trucking, labor, and materials. We had also been able to pay back Dean $1,550 on the loan.

By November, we were ready to open up more of Elgin. All of the ore to date has been coming from the big pit. Dan prospected and found a good body at the north end of the Elgin claim on November 4. We would have started work on it, but found out later that it was on the Franklin claim, so will drop it.

The total crew with Gip and night shift on November 7 was eight. Of these, we had an African American, an Indian, and several Mexicans, as well as two white men through the middle of November. Owens was averaging a carload of ore a day in the trucking and we hope to keep it up. We want to speed it up to two cars a day.

November 19—We had no cars, no trucks, and no men.

November 25—Gip began work on radio geophysics so he will not be at the mine hereafter. Leo began work over there that week and the other men came back so things will be in operation again. We shipped twenty-seven carloads in November.

Marian and Dan Chilson at Elgin Mine with their burro. Courtesy of D. G. Chilson.

In December, the weather got unpleasant and the crew wanted to quit. We still have the night shift on tramming. Sunday, December 9, with Dick, Leo, and one other working at the mine, Dick got most of the carload himself. They began bulldozer work at Elgin on December 11, opening up more developments and clearing away waste. They moved the dump and swept away the side hill. We made grade on the upper workings and moved six carloads of ore into a bin from the side of the hill to the east, mostly off the surface. We were also able to put in a new road for trucks with the bulldozer. (Dan and Dick are getting more and more anxious to own a bulldozer.) The total time spent using the bulldozer was thirty-nine hours.

Yes, we like burros! Courtesy of D. G. Chilson.

In the week ending December 23, Owens reports fourteen cars shipped so we are now averaging two a day.

On January 2, 1946, we finished paying Seaman for the compressor. This month we tried using a steam shovel for taking ore out of the cut to the northeast of the tunnel, but it was too low grade. The assays from the smelter came out as low at 1.59. We were using Scott's steamshovel and are still taking ore from the tunnel, but the whole front side of the hill is gone.

Just as we were preparing to ship four carloads a day and had made arrangements to buy a tractor, the smelter went on strike on January 22. We canceled the tractor purchase and will cut down on employees. As of January 23, the strike had been postponed.

On the first of February, we were using a bulldozer again. Dick says it got out enough good ore for twenty carloads. Owens drew up an agreement whereby he would hire a steamshovel for loading waste and loading ore into the bin. Gip was back at the Elgin again; survey work over for present. On February 12, he was the only one there, though, on account of a storm. We're getting a series of low settlements from the smelter, just enough to cover trucking and nothing else.

On February 20, in preparation for the smelter strike going through, we negotiated with Magma for shipments. They will take one per day. This means the end of the Owens steam shovel deal and no extra help will be needed. Dick has worked out a new plan for operation at Elgin using a big dragline and pulling ore from the slope into trucks directly. This makes it into almost a one-man operation, except for Buck who will be doing the drilling.

Collins Family

Jack and Joyce Collins (originally from Texas) and their three children, Jack, Jr., also known as Jackie, age eleven; Kay, age six; and Pam, age two, moved to Sahuarita from Tucson in the summer of 1955. Jack was gin manager for Producers Cotton Oil Company in Sahuarita, and had worked in Southern Arizona's cotton country, including Amado, which also had a Producer's gin. Jack was friends with all of the farmers whether they ginned with him or not.

That fall Jackie and Kay enrolled in the small Sahuarita Elementary School across the railroad tracks from the Oro Verde Store. Jackie was in the seventh grade and Kay was in second grade.

Sahuarita was a fun community to grow up in. Joyce was involved in PTA, as well as Farm Bureau potlucks and square dances which were well attended. Jackie raised a calf for 4-H and cried when auction day came for "Capitan." We took school buses to Tucson in the summers for swimming lessons. Kay was best friends with Judy Davis and spent lots

Joyce and Jack Collins. Courtesy of Sutah Thomas Harris.

of time with the Davis family. Our families were also friends with the Thomas family. When the grown-ups had their canasta games, the kids had their own game nights.

We made lifelong friends in Sahuarita and some of my fondest childhood memories were from that time. For years, Judy Davis and I would spend two weeks every summer at each other's houses and I would again be a part of farm life.

We had lived in Sahuarita for only two years when Producer's moved Jack to their Gilbert, Arizona, gin. We lived in Chandler for the next seven years.

The rest of my family members have passed on now, but I will always remember the small farming community of Sahuarita where we were blessed to have been a part of those two short years.

~ Contributed by Kay Leta Collins

Warren Eldridge Culbertson

Warren Eldridge "Toops" Culbertson was born to James D. and Bertha Culbertson and they had four children: Jimmy, Barbara (Bobbi), Helen Jean, and Warren. His father, J. D., was the manager of the Limoneira, an agricultural company that grew citrus and avocados. That company still produces quality citrus fruit today. Many folks wonder how Warren got the nickname Toops. According to his family,

Mary Alice Harding posing for a portrait. Courtesy of the Culbertson family.

Barbara (Bobbi), who was married to Keith Walden, gave Warren the nickname Toops after a character in the J. K. Gray children's book series, Penny and Tuppence. She would read him this book often when Warren was a child. Keith Walden, Bobbi's husband, was well known in the Santa Paula community for his citrus operations and knew Bobbi's father, J. D. Culbertson and his family, especially little Warren.

As time passed, Warren excelled in school. At Santa Paula High School, he became senior class president and played a variety of sports, including football. It was here that Toops would meet his high school sweetheart, Mary Alice Harding. Unbeknownst to either of them at the time, they had attended kindergarten together. Mary Alice would later attend Pomona College. This is an important nugget to remember as our story unfolds.

In Toops's junior year, he was selected for the navy's V-12 program—a World War II-era program designed to recruit technically savvy students to study foreign languages, medicine, and engineering. Since Toops's father knew he was a brilliant academic scholar, he was left to his own resources to pay for his education. He applied to the Webb Institute and graduated at the top of his class in architectural and mechanical engineering. Upon graduation he procured a job at General Electric (GE). Although he did not relish the job, he remained there for approximately a year and planned to stay on the East Coast when fate took his hand.

Toops had written his high school sweetheart, Mary Alice, a "Dear John" letter while Mary Alice was attending Pomona College. She was certainly disheartened, but like many folks, she moved on with her life. She met someone else and decided to marry him.

Radios control operations by land and air. Warren Culbertson ranges his domain with radio-equipped car and plane. Courtesy of University of Arizona Special Collections.

When J. D. found out about Mary Alice's engagement, he sent his son a very frank and candid letter telling Toops that his high school sweetheart, Mary Alice, was engaged to someone else. J. D. thought he was making a huge mistake that he would regret. Toops took his father's advice, quit his job, hitchhiked across the county, knocked on Mary Alice's door, and proposed. She promptly broke off the engagement with the other gent. Mary Alice's parents, Beatrice and John Harding, were pleased with her decision.

Toops and Mary Alice Harding had five children: Steven, John, Nancy (Scott), Mary Ellen (Hitchiner), and Mark. Mark, John, and Mary Ellen all expressed the sentiment that their parents were well suited or an idyllic couple. Toops was offered a job almost immediately after his marriage to Mary Alice by Keith Walden, and the newlyweds traveled to Continental, Arizona, where he began as a bookkeeper for Farmers Investment Co. (FICO). Later, he became the operational manager, and one of his duties was the development and implementation of efficient irrigation systems.

With the new irrigation system underway, Keith Walden had a conversation with Toops about making the switch from cotton to pecans; Toops oversaw the change and managed the people tasked with the job. FICO, which is a group of corporate investors, had many locations and Toops managed the ranch operations at most of the locations, such as Aguila (near Wickenburg), Sahuarita, and Continental in Arizona as well as Wewahitchka, Florida. The sheer size of the operations meant that Toops had to learn to fly and flew to most of these locations from a company airstrip located near the back of his home.

Toops coordinated all operations among the various FICO sites, including the planting of 4,500 pecan trees which encompassed five to six thousand acres of land in the 1960s. Toops's eldest son, John, worked putting the saplings from Las Cruces, New Mexico, into the soil in Continental, Arizona. It is interesting to note that saplings are now being planted in the Willcox area near San Simon, Arizona, because operations will be moved there in the future.

At this juncture, John, Mark, and Mary Ellen were asked to tell about some of their fondest recollections of their father Toops and their mother Mary Alice. John fondly remembers that in the 1950s, the main street in Continental, Arizona, consisted of "ten houses and a camp"[2] where Mexican and African-American families lived. The main stores in town were the Continental Store and the One Stop. The Continental Store was owned by the Tang family and the Tangs and Culbertson children knew each other well. In the summer John worked in the cotton fields alongside the Mexican workers on their plot of land and this job provided him with some income for about four or five years. John also recalled the freight trains that stopped in Continental with tanks of ammonia to mix with water and enhance the soil for farming.

John spoke with his father only at the breakfast or dinner table or on the weekends. The weekends were family time spent with mom and dad and often the neighborhood children. The Culbertsons loved to entertain, and the in-ground

Warren Culbertson in the pecan groves. Courtesy of University of Arizona Special Collections.

pool, barbecue grill, and basketball hoop meant hours of enjoyment. John especially enjoyed playing basketball and baseball and going bowling. He and his friends often played a basketball game called "horse."

John recalls walking eight miles by foot down to the man-made Canoa Lake to fish. His love of

Warren Culbertson inspecting pecans still on the trees. Courtesy of University of Arizona Special Collections.

fishing was inherited from his dad. Bowling was another activity that John truly enjoyed in Tucson and his mother, who was a women's auxiliary volunteer at Tucson Medical Center, would drive him to the alley. When he played baseball at Sunnyside High School, there was a Greyhound bus that he could take home.

Because Mark was the youngest child, he spent a lot of time with his dad. He worked with his father, Toops, on many of the ranches owned by Keith Walden in Arizona and the one in Florida during his summer breaks from school. Mark noted the difference between the work ethic and the camaraderie in Arizona versus Florida. A cordial spirit of work and play permeated the atmosphere in Arizona, but it was lacking in Florida. Toops was a workaholic and had amazing stamina. Fueled by a twenty-minute power nap after a fourteen-hour work day, he would go play bridge with friends late into the evening.

According to Mark, his parents went on annual two-week family vacations—but these were not typical vacations. They once went on a fishing trip to Idaho via a private plane. The entire family went to the 1964 New

York World's Fair. For six or seven years his father rented a home on Mission Beach in San Diego, California, where he and his neighborhood friends joined the family for some fun in the sun.

Mary Ellen fondly remembers Toops coming home and clapping his hands saying, "Let's go, let's go! We're going to the Halfway Station." The Halfway Station was the only restaurant around unless the

Mary Alice and Warren "Toops" Culbertson sit for photo. Courtesy of Culbertson family.

family traveled to Tucson. While Mary Ellen did not recall the name of the restaurant, after hearing its name her brother, Mark, confirmed that this was their family's favorite dining location. According to Mary Kasulaitis, a collaborator on this book, the restaurant was located halfway between Tucson and Nogales, Arizona. The remnants of the restaurant are located twelve miles south of present-day Green Valley on Old Nogales Highway. "It was a Mexican restaurant run by a husband and wife with five children," stated Mary Ellen. The wife was the cook and her husband was the bartender. When the restaurant owners saw the Culbertson kids coming, they would say, "Uh-oh, here come the hot sauce kids!" Some children are ketchup aficionados, but the Culbertson kids loved hot sauce on everything. Mary Ellen also fondly remembers Toops shopping for presents the day before Christmas and then he would be up for twenty-four hours straight putting bikes and other assembly-required gifts together.

Everyone that the editor of this article spoke with, including Oscar Gomez, a retired educator from Sahuarita and a former employee of FICO, spoke fondly of Toops, whom they truly respected. Toops did not work over them in the fields, he worked with them. He was truly a hard-working and admired member of our community. His beloved wife Mary Alice was his soul mate and John, Mark, and Mary Ellen all agreed that they were a quintessentially matched couple.

~ Interviews by John, Mark, and Mary Ellen Culbertson;
edited by Mary Chernoski and the Culbertsons

NOTES

References

1. Intercontinental Rubber Company. *International Rubber Company records, 1903–1955*. Southern Methodist University, Texas Archival Resources Online. MSS 0146, MSS 0146X DeGolyer Library. http://legacy.lib.utexas.edu/taro/smu/00376/smu-00376.html
2. Walenga, Karen. *The Santa Cruz Valley: a Centennial Celebration*. Sahuarita, AZ: Green Valley News and Sun, 2011.

Additional resources

Green Valley News

Davis Farm

Sahuarita, Arizona: home to copper mines, cotton fields, pecan orchards, homemade tamales, and the R. A. Davis family farm. It is our pleasure to share memories of living in and enjoying our beautiful desert here on the outskirts of Tucson, Arizona.

Robert Alexander Davis, or R. A. as he was known and called, was born in Texas and was one of five siblings. All but one worked and lived in and were part of the settlement of the Sahuarita area. R. A. was married very happily to Rachel Rebecca Graham. They built a house, farmed, and raised four children—two girls and two boys: Sharon Kay, Judy Dianne, Philip Brian, and Mark Craig. R. A. moved from Texas to the Continental-Sahuarita area in the early 1930s. He worked for Mr. Lane, Keith Walden, then for Mr. Bull. He worked at the cotton gin, saved up money, then drove back to Oklahoma and married Rachel. R. A. and Rachel had met in Carnegie, Oklahoma, when she was about sixteen. Her father was a minister at a church there and they met at a young people's meeting. It took R. A. five years to ask for her hand in marriage. Rachel's father married them. They then moved to Continental and R. A. worked with his brother Gibb and Mr. Bull. He

Davis family with Mark, Philip, and Judy standing in the back. Sharon, Rachel, and R. A. sit in the front. Courtesy of Philip Davis.

and Rachel lived in a little adobe house with a white picket fence around it on the Bull Farms and Sharon was born while they lived there. Rachel took on the role of farmer's wife and did some cooking for the German POW camp that was out in Continental at the time.

When Sharon was two years old, in 1946, the family moved to Willcox where they stayed for about five years. Judy was born there.

In the late 1950s, dad got a loan from Mr. Bull and bought some property a half mile east and a half mile south of Sahuarita. The farm was two hundred acres, one-half mile square, and fenced in. Dad had it cleared and built a three-bedroom brick house on it. He dug an irrigation well and planted cotton, peanuts, and maize. He also leased some land at the Lee Moor Ranch No. 2 north of Pima Mine Road and the Bull Farms on the west side of the Santa Cruz River. At one time he had 350 acres planted in peanuts and 620 acres in cotton. Mark remembers riding in the truck after the summer rains to check on the wells to be sure no damage had been done. He also remembers working on the farm hoeing weeds in the summer. It was very hot work and when possible he would go to the ditch at the top of the row and get a drink of water out of the irrigation ditch. The water came right out of the well so it was very clean and refreshing. He also remembers swimming in the ditch on occasion. During the cotton-picking season he was allowed to play in the cotton trailers to help tamp down the cotton. R. A. would take the boys with him while hunting jackrabbits on the farm because the rabbits would destroy the crops. R. A. worked seven days a week, taking off only Sunday mornings for church.

R. A. grew cotton, both long- and short-staple, as well as various grains and peanuts. He grew

Putting peanuts into bags.
Courtesy of Arizona Daily Star.

Spanish peanuts and Virginia peanuts (also known as "cocktail peanuts"). They were put into forty-pound gunny sacks and stacked next to the house before being sent by truck back east to Planters Nut and Chocolate Company for processing. The peanuts sold for six dollars per sack, according to Mark. Peanuts grew well in Arizona and he made money from them. Cotton was the main crop; the short-staple cotton was ginned south of Sahuarita at the Cotton Producers Gin. The long-staple cotton was trailered to a gin in Marana. Farming made us a good living and supported our family of six.

Mark remembers always having dogs when he was growing up. They were not allowed in the house.

Mom and dad were incredibly involved in the Farm Bureau. R. A. was one of the square-dance callers for the Farm Bureau dances and later at the new Sahuarita School gym where dances were held for the community. Dad was on the Sahuarita School Board from 1957 to 1965, involved with building the new Sahuarita Elementary School. The previous school was in the old town of Sahuarita, north and east of the railroad tracks (a little north of where the Pecan Factory is today) and the new school was built about three miles west of the old school. R. A. Davis' name is on the historic plaque that is on the elementary school building to this day.

Sharon started school at the old Sahuarita school when she was in fourth grade and graduated from there in 1958. She was then bused to Pueblo High School where she graduated in 1962. (At the time there was no high school in Sahuarita, so students were bused to Pueblo High School in Tucson.) Sharon then finished her schooling at the University of Arizona. Judy also went to the old school and then on to Pueblo High School in Tucson. Phil was the first class to be in the first grade at the new elementary school. He was also in the first class of freshmen in the new high school. Mark attended the new Sahuarita School and graduated from there also.

Judy remembers that Rachel was PTA president and held many church offices. She was also a 4-H leader and Boy Scout leader at times. She always took meals to people in need and helped her neighbors. She was an excellent cook. R. A. kept two or three rows in the field for Rachel's garden. She raised corn, watermelon, okra, cucumbers, and tomatoes, among other things. Rachel canned what she could. Judy remembers learning to make green corn tamales. She also has a fond memory of riding her bike around the farm to where the workers lived. They had a fire where they made flour tortillas and she loved those. It was a great life!

As the children grew up, Rachel went to work at the Sahuarita post office where she was a clerk for fifteen years until she retired, according to her son Mark. She was well known by all in the community at that time.

Mom retired and dad quit farming. They sold the land

R. A. Davis examining the peanuts on his farm. Courtesy of Arizona Daily Star.

to Pima Mine in 1972, when Mark was a junior in high school, and moved to Show Low in the White Mountains. Pima Mine wanted the water rights. They lived there for years until dad could not take the altitude and they moved back to Tucson. Mom passed first and dad passed ten years later. All of dad's farmer friends and Sahuarita acquaintances, his brothers and sisters, had passed before he did. He was the last man standing.

Sahuarita was formed and shaped and guided with the help and involvement of Robert and Rachel Davis. The children and grandchildren of all the farmers and friends keep in touch to this day. We are immensely proud of the legacy left by our parents.

~ Contributed by Sharon Davis Atwater, Phillip Davis, Mark Davis, and Judy Davis Branson; compiled by Sutah Thomas Harris

Interview: Robert A. Davis, 1994

R. A. Davis grew up on a farm in Texas and later went with his father to Oklahoma. They grew some of the same crops that were grown in Arizona including cotton, corn, alfalfa, and maize. They farmed with mules rather than horses back then. He attended a two-room school that went through high school. He only made it to ninth grade there and then worked on the farm.

The November 15, 1945, Pima County Homemakers Annual Achievement Day at the Tucson Indian Training School was highly successful for Sahuarita homemakers Mrs. M. Evans, Hazel Jones, Mrs. O. W. Dishaw, Mrs. Rachel Davis, Mrs. Nell Davis, and Mrs. Lee Ethel Bull. Courtesy of the Bull/Klingenberg family.

After his sister came home for Christmas in 1934, R. A. followed her back to Arizona where she lived. First he worked for a farmer in Coolidge, and then followed W. H. Lane to Sahuarita when he bought a farm there. R. A. lived with his sister and her husband in a twelve-foot by fourteen-foot tent with an outhouse beyond the yard. It had room for only one bed, so he slept on the porch.

The post office was run out of a Dollie Luken's house next door. There was a store and bar (Sahuarita Bar and Grill) on one side of the street and a service station and store on the other side (Oro Verde Store). There was a packing plant where lettuce was shipped off via train nearby. There was a dance parlor at the

Sharon Davis Atwater and Judy Davis Branson pose with their parents R. A. and Joyce Davis in 1993. Courtesy of Sutah Thomas Harris.

bar run by Harry Manelos, whom the locals called "The Greek." R. A. went dancing on Saturday nights for a dime at Kinsley's Ranch Dance Hall where they had a Mexican orchestra playing. Kinsley's Ranch had a swimming pool there to cool off in as well as a rodeo arena.

He married his wife, Rachel, in 1940. She was also from Oklahoma. Their four children were born at the Stork's Nest in Tucson. Davis bought his first 160-acre farm in Willcox but lived there only for five years. In the 1950s, he had 350 acres of peanuts and 620 acres of cotton growing in Sahuarita.

In 1982, he sold his farm off of Old Helvetia Road to Pima Mine. The mines were buying up all of the land for the water rights. R. A. rented his

Filling field crates with U.S. No. 1 lettuce at the Sahuarita Ranch on November 23, 1941. Courtesy of University of Arizona Special Collections.

house back from the mine and lived there for thirteen more years. He loved what he did for a living. He liked seeing things grow. He loved and got along well with the people he worked with. He was a friend of fellow farmer, Mr. Bull, who had a reputation of being hard to get to know, but R. A. had worked for him twice before. Prominent ranchers and community members were on the school board, on which he served from 1957–65. He had no regrets in life looking back and said he would do it all the same way again.

~ Contributed by Barbara Brown Bennett; transcribed by Amy Millet

Manuela Duarte Lauterio Fuentes

Manuela Duarte was somewhat of a legend in Twin Buttes and the surrounding communities. Nothing is known of Manuela's family, origins, childhood, or even birth date. It is as though she dropped into the world as an adult resident of Twin Buttes, Arizona. The first record relating to Manuela is a 1915 record establishing a simple "justice of the peace" marriage to Juan Lauterio. At the time, Manuela claimed to have been thirty-six years old, and Juan listed his age as forty-one. (It is not known if Duarte was her maiden name or the name of a first husband.)

The quiet start to their marriage gave no indication as to what would lie ahead, and the newly married Lauterios did not stay happy for long. At some point on March 7, 1917, a brawl in their Twin Buttes home resulted in Ricardo Pesqueira and Manuela's nephew, Manuel Lauterio, being charged with violating the state prohibitory liquor law. Manuela was put in jail and charged with assault with a deadly weapon; Juan Lauterio was in the hospital with a gunshot wound to the groin.

The stories about the incident are wild and inconsistent. Some say Juan came home after an evening with another woman to find a very upset Manuela. The sheriff claimed that the four individuals—Manuel, Manuela, Juan, and Ricardo—were all drinking together when Manuela pulled out a .44-caliber revolver and, after shooting her husband in the groin, was felled by her nephew Manuel Lauterio with that same gun. A death-bed confession told of a simple accident.

With Manuela locked away in jail, and Juan in the hospital, everyone looked to the local papers for information. The *Arizona Daily Star* reported on March 22 of that year that Lauterio had taken a turn for the better, but in the March 29 issue, there was a funeral notice telling of Juan's burial on March 28 following his death on the night of March 24. His turn for the better must have rebounded into a sharp turn for the worse, but at some point during those two days, Juan made a deathbed confession stating that the shooting was an accident that occurred while the pair was "wrestling for possession of the revolver." All charges were subsequently dropped and Manuela returned to Twin Buttes to open her home to the town's stray dog population.

The newspapers weren't aware of the promise Manuela had made prior to her court hearing. She made a vow that if she didn't have to go to jail, she would become the caregiver for all stray dogs in the town—a promise she kept until the day she died.

At some point over the next six years, Manuela married again to a man named Refugio Fuentes. Refugio had already had his name in the *Tucson Citizen* for an incident in May of 1923. Feliciano Aleartar had apparently fired a load of birdshot into a group of Mexicans celebrating Cinco de Mayo. Refugio was "nursing a slight wound in his forehead as a result of the shooting." He then, according to the *Arizona Daily Star* on October 26 of that year, added to his notoriety by getting arrested for disturbing the peace at the Twin Buttes Mine on the previous afternoon. It wasn't known if his escapades took place before or after his wedding to Manuela, but he was definitely not a better alternative to life with the dogs.

In 1936, in the December 15 edition of the *Arizona Daily Star*, Refugio made the headlines: "Indian Stages Solo Uprising: Threatens to Kill Off All of Twin Buttes, Goes to Jail Instead." Refugio, identified as a "49-year-old drink-crazed [Native American]," was given six dollars by his wife, Manuela, to spend in Sahuarita on groceries. Instead, he spent the money on liquor and came home intoxicated. Inebriated and angry, he threatened to kill her with his 1861 .45-90 Winchester rifle.

Manuela hid next door at the home of the Revello family. As Refugio searched for her, he "terrorized the whole settlement with threats to kill everyone." By the time law enforcement arrived, everyone in the town was hiding indoors and Refugio had gone off into the hills to search for Manuela. When officers located him, he threatened to kill them, as well as Manuela. He was subdued, handcuffed, and taken to jail in Tucson.

It is assumed that Refugio was eventually released and that Manuela must have let him return home because in September of 1949, Justice Court records indicate that Manuela was discharged after being charged with drunkenness. Refugio was given thirty days in jail for disturbing the peace.

In the *Arizona Daily Star*, on April 5, 1956, an urgent message was published, "Woman, Aged 97, Reported Missing." A search party from the Pima County Sheriff's Office had been called in late the previous night to begin searching for Manuela who had "wandered from her home, accompanied by a small dog about dusk and has not been seen since."

Arrest warrant for Refugio Fuentes dated August 26, 1917. Courtesy of the Revello family.

The next day, the same paper reported that Manuela, a "Slight But Spry [Native American] Wandered All Night After Being Stunned By Blow On Head." According to the story, "A tiny 97-year-old [Native American] woman who was lost for a night in near-freezing weather in the desert 20 miles southwest of Tucson was back home. The night-long search for Mrs. Manuela Fuentes ended shortly after 9 a.m. when a ranch hand sighted her trudging aimlessly in the foothills about four miles north of McGee Road. Sheriff's deputies said the 'spry little woman' wandered directionless for about twelve miles in the rugged mining country in the Twin Buttes area. Cuts above and below her right eye explained her disappearance from her home near the juncture of McGee and Twin Buttes roads. She told officers she was cutting branches off a mesquite tree with an ax when a branch snapped, striking her near the eye. The blow stunned her and she started walking at around 3:00 p.m. Wednesday. She was reported missing about six hours later."

"Dressed in a black coat, she went in a wide circle, twice crossing the Twin Buttes road before wandering onto the Ruby Star Ranch. Her small black dog followed [no mention was made of Refugio].

The Revello sisters crowd in for a photo with Manuela. From left to right is Josefina, Helen, Doña Manuela, Rose, and Yolanda. Courtesy of the Revello family.

An employee of the ranch, Roberto Traslaviña, noticed the woman walking in the rocky terrain. He rode her double on his horse back to a neighbor's home where sheriff's deputies had set up their search headquarters. Deputy Taylor called her 'about the feistiest little woman' he's ever seen. 'She only weighs about 90 pounds.'" Manuela had lived in the area for over forty-five years and had always cut needed wood from mesquite trees. She was treated at the Pima County Hospital for head wounds, exposure, and puncture wounds and bruises on her arms and legs.

The tales of Manuela continued on June 5, 1958, when eighty-seven-year-old Refugio Fuentes hit another car head-on while traveling on Sahuarita Road. Manuela, his passenger, was listed in critical condition, with multiple face and head injuries. Refugio was in poor condition with leg, chest, neck, and head injuries. In addition to his wounds, he was also charged with driving on the wrong side of the road, having no driver's license, and illegally using license plates.

Thankfully, the other driver was unharmed.

Ysabel recalls everyone loving and looking after Manuela. They also never gave up trying to figure out how old she was. Her Aunt Rose once said, "She is so old that she doesn't know how old she is." Uncle Pete guessed that she was around ninety-four, but recalled once when Manuela told him she was a hundred years old. According to Pete, "She's the hardiest person around here. She still goes around carrying wood on her head. And days when I think it's too cold to go get the mail, I'll look out and she'll be walking up the road to meet the mailman."

Ysabel remembers Manuela walking a half mile into town every day. She would come to the store with a gunnysack and purchase three pints of beer. Her ever-present pack of stray dogs would follow her in, and then follow her right back home. At one point, there were at least ten of them.

Sadly, on December 17, 1961, Manuela's name made it into the *Arizona Daily Star* one last time. "Twin Buttes Woman, More Than 100 Years Old, Killed By Fire In Home." Sweet little Manuela, loved by the entire town, was found dead in her tiny home on Ruby Star Route when friends came by to visit. "The dead woman was widely known in the Twin Buttes area and was said to have delivered a great number of babies, most of whom are presently parents and grandparents of their own. She claimed to be 116 years old and to have come to this country before the turn of the century with her first husband . . . She was a tiny, alert woman

Manuela smiling for the camera. Courtesy of the Revello family.

who still chopped mesquite wood every day. It appeared that she was heating her home with a wood fire inside of a gallon can. She apparently brushed too close to the blazing wood and her dress caught fire. She tried to run outside, but couldn't open a door latch which was wrapped with a piece of wire. Her body was found lying at the foot of the door. She was alone except for two pet dogs. . . . Manuela would often play host to many visitors who knew her or had heard of her. She spoke only Spanish. Her memory was described as marvelous for one so advanced in years. She was the godmother of many of the present residents of the ranches near Twin Buttes."

Manuela was buried in the Holy Hope Cemetery on December 20, 1961. Refugio died in the tuberculosis ward of Pima County Hospital on July 23, 1963. He, too, was buried in the Holy Hope Cemetery.

~ Contributed by Monica Lee Elam Christiansen

Estrada Family

Petra Ochoa Acuña was born in Phoenix, Arizona, on June 29, 1884. In April of 1905, in Pomona, California, Petra married Guillermo Armijo and in March of 1911, while living in Paso Robles, Petra gave birth to their daughter, Balbina. Guillermo died in San Luis Obispo on January 4, 1913, leaving Petra a young widow. After moving to El Centro, California, Petra married Diego Gonzales Estrada on June 14, 1915. Diego had been born November 20, 1893, in Fresnillo, Zacatecas, Mexico. Diego appears to have accepted young Balbina as his own, because all future records show her name as Balbina Acuña Estrada.

While living in Brawley, California, Petra and Diego added four more children to their family: Angel (1916), Josefina (1918), Roberto (1922), and Alfredo (1928). Diego's mother, Teresa, and his brother, Angel, both lived in Imperial where they worked on the local farms.

When Diego and Petra separated in the mid 1930s, Petra remained in California and Diego moved to San Agustín, Mexico, just across the Rio Grande from Fabens, Texas. In 1935, Josefina, Roberto, and Alfredo wanted to be close to their dad, so they settled in Fabens to work on Lee Moor Ranch No. 1.

While living on the Fabens Lee Moor Ranch, Josefina married Pedro Llamas and Roberto met his future wife, Alicia. Alicia had been born in April of 1928, in Fabens, Texas, to Gumercindo Gomez and Bersabe Acuña. Bersabe had three daughters from a previous relationship: Julia, Elvira, and Virginia. Alicia's parents had met and married in Antony, New Mexico, and had four children together: Alicia (1928), Alfredo (1929), Felipa (1932), and Arturo (1939).

Until September of 1949, Roberto worked on Lee Moor Ranch No. 1. Then he heard about the need for cotton pickers in Casa Grande, Arizona. The wages for picking cotton were better than in

The Lee Moor Ranch No. 2 cotton harvest in full swing on October 11, 1949. O'Dell Massey, manager of Lee Moor Ranch No. 2, and the agricultural agent pause while recording the weights of harvested cotton bags. A crew of about one hundred pickers was working the fields. Courtesy of University of Arizona Special Collections.

On November 10, 1949, E. E. England, George Durham, G. E. Blackledge, and O'Dell Massey inspect the cotton fields. Courtesy of University of Arizona Special Collections.

Texas. When he left for Arizona, Alicia, three months pregnant, was left in Texas with their four young kids: Maria (1944), Olga (1945), Ramon (1947), and Jaime (1948). Roberto liked Casa Grande and sent money to his wife to join him, so Alicia and her young children made their way to Casa Grande on a Greyhound bus.

Maria does not recall where her father worked in Casa Grande but remembers that accommodations for migrant workers were not very good. The families lived in large army-like tents, including Roberto's family, and everyone slept on army cots. Her mom cooked on a two-burner kerosene stove placed on top of wooden fruit and vegetable crates. Maria vividly recalls large wooly, yellow caterpillars. The company had just sprayed and it looked like it was raining caterpillars. They were everywhere and it was overwhelming to a five-year-old girl. At nighttime the caterpillars would get inside the tent, making their way to the peak of the tent and dropping themselves on the family as they slept.

After the picking season of 1949, Roberto heard about Lee Moor Ranch No. 2, south of Tucson. He had met the supervisor, Mr. O'Dell Massey, on the ranch in Texas and was able to get employment. Maria tells that, as soon as the family arrived on the ranch, the car ended up with four flat tires.

Lee Moor No. 2 was a friendly and warm place to come. There were many longtime Arizona residents and, to their surprise, other families from Texas. There was a mixture of young and old families with large numbers of kids to play with. Some of these families— Ortega, Gonzales, Hernandez, Galvan, Cruz, and many other *braceros*—became longtime friends and even relatives of the Estrada family.

As they drove into Lee Moor, there were three houses where Massey and his supervisors lived. Further north was a little country store, and then the shop and equipment area. Beyond the shop was the area where there were homes on both sides of the road for the families to live in.

When the Estradas arrived, the only place available to live in was a one-room space where the *braceros* stayed during picking season. Maria remembers that her dad was not pleased with the filth and conditions. The family slept in the car their first night there. The next day, her mom washed and scrubbed the floor and walls. Maria asked her mother, "What are those little insects crawling up the wall?" "Lice!" her mom responded.

On October 11, 1949, cotton trailers line up along the field road on Lee Moor Ranch No. 2 waiting to be filled with cotton. Courtesy of University of Arizona Special Collections.

Without furniture of their own, the family made do with items provided at the farm. Wooden crates were used to make tables, chairs, and storage areas. A few days after they arrived, there was a knock on the door in the middle of the night. When Roberto opened the door, an Anglo man was there. The commotion woke Maria. The man explained to Roberto that, as he worked on the Caterpillar during the night shift, he would see a light. He got curious and, one night, with a shovel in hand, he investigated the light. He told Roberto he had discovered a buried chest full of money. The man gave no description of where he found the chest or of what the contents were, but it contained enough money that he was leaving Lee Moor. He offered Roberto everything in his two-room house. His last words to Roberto were "Do not tell anyone about what I have found!"

Maria said all of the kids had lots of fun on the farm. They would come out when all the men were working, but they had to be inside their home by the time their fathers came home. All the kids would run home as soon as they heard the first tractor coming into the shop. On the weekends, most of the men would take off to the bars in Tucson or Nogales. That's when the women would get together to share what was going on in their lives. They sang, laughed, and cried. They all knew each other well. The children would play games like hide-and-seek, freeze tag, and many others. They all felt free for a couple of days until their dads came home.

Roberto worked on the Lee Moor Ranch No. 2 until everyone started moving out two or three years later. During their stay, Armando (1950) was born and later Gerardo (1951). Roberto found employment on the Sahuarita Ranch and moved his family there where they lived from 1952 to 1970. There were happy and sad times. Their first home was a two-room wooden house not far from the Sahuarita Elementary School. It

Roberto Estrada, Cipriano Ramirez, Federico Ramirez, and Juan Lopez in 1961. The Ramirez men were old family friends from Anthony, New Mexico, and Lee Moor Ranch No. 1 in Fabens. The parents of these men knew each other long before these men were born. This photo was taken in Juan's house at Sahuarita Ranch where all the men worked for FICO and Harris. Courtesy of Oscar Gomez.

was here that Esperanza was born in January of 1953 and died forty-two days later of crib death. All of the remaining children were born while they lived at Sahuarita Ranch. In total, Roberto and Alicia had twelve children, including Angel (1954), Alicia (1956), Teresa (1958), Ricardo (1961), and Hector (1964).

In about 1956, Roberto briefly went to Gila Bend to work for Harris Ranch and took his family with him. Maria remembers confrontations with desert critters. Shoes were shaken before putting them on for fear of scorpions. Outside, they were constantly on the lookout for snakes before lifting boards or boxes. None of the family members liked it there, so the family stayed in Gila Bend only for a short time.

At Sahuarita Ranch, Ramon Estrada holds a bucket while Felipa and Rocky Lopez sit by the front door and Delia Lopez hides on the right. Courtesy of Oscar Gomez.

Maria's mom drove the kids to the small school and Maria's classroom had three grades: sixth, seventh, and eighth. They returned to Sahuarita and Maria finished eighth grade there.

The Oro Verde Store, owned by Harold and Mildred Ellis, served the Sahuarita community with groceries, clothing, gas, and mail service. A small corner of the store was dedicated to the post office. The store gave credit to farm employees who were able to charge their purchases as needed, and settle up on payday. Paychecks were delivered to the store on paydays and farm workers would pick them up there. Some did not earn enough to pay off their debt to the store so the balance was carried over to the next pay period.

There were times when this happened to Roberto Estrada. Opportunities to shop in Tucson were few and money was scarce for his family. They, like most other community members, relied heavily on the store. Not until

At Jaime Estrada's wedding in January of 1970, family members gather for a photo. In the back, Arturo, Oscar, and Alfredo Gomez stand. Sitting are Elvira Gomez Galvan, Felipa Gomez Lopez, and Alicia Gomez Estrada holding her son Hector. Courtesy of Oscar Gomez.

Roberto's children started working could the family afford to shop and buy necessities in Tucson without having to rely so heavily on the Oro Verde Store.

Roberto's oldest kids worked weighing barley and milo trucks, chopping cotton, irrigating cotton and barley fields, driving tractors, and picking cotton on weekends, school vacations, and during the summers.

Roberto worked a variety of jobs on the farm. Before FICO and during the years that FICO owned the Sahuarita Ranch, he was a tractor driver, heavy equipment operator, and foreman for FICO. He drove a FICO truck and carried a CB radio to get and give information to other foremen. He also supervised the planting of thousands of pecan trees.

During his life, Roberto also worked in the mines and at the golf course in Green Valley. His health eventually forced him to retire because he was battling Lou Gehrig's disease and prostate cancer. He passed away on January 16, 1995, at the age of seventy-two. While Roberto was still alive, his wife, Alicia worked in the cafeteria at the Sahuarita School District, from which she eventually retired. She was completely dedicated to her husband and stayed home to take care of him until he drew his last breath. She considerably enjoyed time spent with her children, thirty-three grandchildren, and sixty great-grandchildren. The numbers continue to grow.

The family's housing accommodations improved as the years passed, but in 1970, Project PEPP came along with grant money that helped Roberto and other farm families purchase their homes. (PEPP, which stands for "portable, practical education preparation," was founded in 1967 by Dr. John David Arnold "to improve the quality of rural life.") At that time, FICO owned Sahuarita Ranch and provided land for employees to have houses built. Roberto chose to live in the Valle Verde area off Duval Mine Road. As of 2021, some of his boys still live on that property.

Alicia and her sister, Felipa Lopez, were very involved in the Community Catholic Church, where they started the prayer meetings and helped organize all of the special events. Alicia's oldest daughters and other children from the community, with the help of a priest from Tucson, had a chapel started at the old schoolhouse in Sahuarita to

San Martin de Porres Catholic Church stands proudly in the middle of a pecan orchard. Courtesy of Monica Lee Elam Christiansen.

provide catechism for all the children that lived on Sahuarita Ranch and in surrounding areas. The family began attending church when it was held in the old Sahuarita schoolhouse and Alicia was instrumental in establishing the new Catholic church, San Martin de Porres, which currently serves all of the surrounding towns.

Alicia passed away on November 17, 2017. Both Roberto and Alicia are remembered as super parents, grandparents, and great-grandparents; as brothers, sisters, friends, and hard-working individuals.

~ Contributed by Maria Estrada and Oscar Gomez

Felix Family

One of the old families still living in the Sahuarita area is the family of Francisco F. "Pancho" Felix. This family, or at least the Felix name, can be traced back to Jesus Corrales Felix who was born in Pitiquito, Sonora, Mexico (near Caborca), in December of 1864. His wife, Andrea Ariola, born in 1870, stated on immigration records that she was born in Ures, Sonora, Mexico. It is believed that Jesus and Andrea came to the Sahuarita area prior to 1898, and they were the first members of the Felix family to settle along a stretch of the Santa Cruz River.

In the 1900 federal census, the Jesus and Andrea

"On the Wagon" was taken during roundup on the Buck Fletcher Ranch. Standing from left to right are Sally Fletcher, Manuel Quiroz, Tom Welch, Evaristo Angulo, Buck Fletcher, Chico Felix, Manuel Sanchez, Spicer, and Mr. Ballard. Courtesy of the Ray Manley family.

Felix family was enumerated as residing one house over from the James Kilroy Brown family. In 1910, they lived on Nogales Road in the San Xavier Precinct. The family was in the cattle business. During this time, Southern Arizona was open-range country. Jesus had cattle in Arizona stretching from the Nogales area to as far north as the Santa Rita Mountains. The family home was called Rancho de la Providencia.

Jesus and his wife, Andrea, also owned property in Tucson on Meyer Street. Andrea rented out homes in the Tucson area. One of the families that eventually rented from her was that of Catalina Cortez, the mother of Celia Cortez, who became the wife of Francisco F. Felix, Jesus and Andrea's grandson.

The Rancho de la Providencia headquarters and Felix home were where Santo Tomas is today. Manuel Felix remembers that the adobe walls were still standing in the 1950s. The family also had a ranch home in the area close to the current Felix family homes east of the railroad tracks along what was then the road to Nogales.

Felix cattle were herded into Tucson to be sold to buyers from the eastern part of the United States. In the late 1950s, the family of Francisco Felix still pastured cattle in the Tucson area. Manuel, Francisco's great grandson, remembers that cattle were grazed around what is now Ajo Road and the 29th Street/Silverlake area east of Tucson.

Land records show that Ramon Ariola Felix (1894–1939), a son of Jesus and Andrea Felix, and his wife, Amalia Lizarraga Celaya (1899–1957), homesteaded 640 acres of property between Duval Mine Road and Twin Buttes Road. Present-day La Canada Road runs through the middle of that acreage. This property likely included or was adjacent to the original Rancho de la Provencia headquarters. Ramon and Amalia raised a large family with six sons (Ruben, Jesus, Ramon, Manuel, Felivardo, and Gilbert) and five daughters (Lydia, Amalia, Aurelia, Olivia, and Celia). They lost five children as babies: Andrea, Juan, Manuel, Roberto, and Eduardo.

On Wednesday, April 19, 1939, Ramon died from rabies, two months after being bitten on the finger by the family's pet coyote. According to the April 20, 1939, issue of the *Arizona Daily Star*, Ramon had roped and captured a coyote that the family kept as a pet. Two months prior to Ramon's death, the coyote escaped and was recaptured while raiding the family chicken coop. Ramon received a minor bite on his finger during the recapture. When symptoms got severe, he was taken to Tucson to his mother's home and on Monday, April 17, a doctor was summoned. On Tuesday, he was taken to the county hospital, but survived only fifteen minutes after arriving. "(Ramon) Felix was experiencing violent symptoms and several children had to hold their parent to the bed." His passing left Amalia a widow with eleven children between the ages of two and nineteen. It was believed to have been the first Arizona fatality from human rabies in at least twenty-seven years.

Francisco Ariola Felix (1889–1968), also known as Frank A., was the oldest son of Jesus and Andrea. He was born in Tucson on December 31, 1889. He and Carmen "Carmelita" Irigoyen Lizarraga (1890–1984) were married in Carmen's hometown of Pitiquito, Sonora, Mexico, on January 7, 1912. They raised three sons (Jose, Francisco L., and Rafael) and three daughters (Andrea, Carmen, and Elvira) on the Felix family property. Two other children passed away young: Ramon died as an infant, and Carlota died at age one.

The Felix family posing for a portrait. Courtesy of Manuel Felix.

On the 8th of January in 1920, Francisco A. Felix filed to homestead 160 acres. Today, that property runs along the western edge of the Rancho Sahuarita Community. It was another piece of the property on which the Jesus Felix family had already been raising cattle for the previous thirty years.

A second homestead claim made by Francisco A. Felix on October 24, 1938, officially added 640 acres to the family holdings. This acreage surrounds the current-day intersection of Helmet Peak and Mission Roads.

Francisco Lizarraga Felix (1915–2004), the son of Francisco A. and Carmen, also known as Frank L. or Pancho, was born in Tucson, Arizona. Growing up in Southern Arizona in the cattle business was hard and it involved long hours. When the family settled in Sahuarita, Francisco L. was able to attend Sahuarita Elementary School. He and his siblings would have to either ride a horse to school or take a wagon. They would take friends to school with them each day. They attended what is now referred to as "the Old Sahuarita School," which is currently owned by Farmers Investment Co. and surrounded by pecan orchards.

Frank L. married Celia Cortez (1921–2017) on July 29, 1939, in Tucson. Celia was born in El Paso, Texas, to Ezequiel Cortez and Catalina Mora, a native of Mazatlán, Sinaloa, Mexico. Celia's father left his family in Texas so Catalina took her children Celia, Lucia, Cecilia, and Rafael to Mazatlán where her family still lived. Celia had many childhood memories from there.

When Catalina and her children eventually returned to the United States, they rented a home in Tucson from Andrea Felix. Francisco L. rode his horse to Tucson many times to visit his grandparents. It was during one of those trips that he met Celia. Celia's mother encouraged her marriage to Francisco L. Felix in an attempt to provide her daughter with security. La Provencia Ranch was prosperous and the Felix family was quite well-to-do.

Francisco L. and Celia loved to go to dances at the old Mission. She did not dance, but Francisco loved it. He would dance with everyone. He thought he was quite a playboy. They also had races on Saturdays. The families would get together to play baseball; then, they would race quarter horses, complete with lots of betting. The day would end with a dance. Inevitably, someone would get into a disagreement over something—the attention of a woman, a dispute over the horse race, or anything else that came up. No matter what, the participants always ended the night by shaking hands.

From there, Frank L. and Celia went to live in a little farmhouse in the old section of northeast Tucson near the intersection of Orange Grove and Ina Road. The family raised cows, pigs, chickens, and goats. In addition, Frank L. planted corn, chili peppers, and tomatoes while Celia made fresh cheese to sell to local residents in Tucson.

Eugene Olivas and Manuel Felix stand in the yard of their homes after Holy Communion in 1954 or 1955. Courtesy of Manuel Felix.

The family then moved to a ranch house just south of the Hughes Aircraft grounds called El Viejito Ranch de Boten. The owner of the land offered to sell Frank L. and Celia the eighty acres for ten dollars per acre, but they instead moved to Sahuarita.

In 1949, the family pulled together the financing to purchase twenty-five acres along Old Nogales Highway for about a thousand dollars. It was a part of the Jose Soto Ranch that lay along the Santa Cruz River between Sahuarita and Continental. They built a small two-room adobe home and spent the rest of their lives there. The property is still owned by Felix descendants.

Grandma Carmelita surrounded by her grandsons, Jose, Armando, Henry, Frank, and Manuel Felix. Courtesy of Manuel Felix.

On the new property, the family farmed corn, green beans, barley, peppers, squash, and watermelons. They also raised cattle, pigs, and horses. They sold their produce, animals, and the cheese that Celia and her daughters made. Celia also made quesadillas. People would come on Sundays to buy produce and cheese.

Frank L. used to drive into Tucson to go around to restaurants to gather fifty-gallon barrels of scraps to take home to slop the pigs. If there were day-old bags of chips or other items, he brought those home as treats for his family. The children were all taught to work hard. Each time a new son was born, Frank L. was excited to have yet "another ranch hand."

Francisco L. and Celia's child-ren—Maria Elena, Francisco, Manuel, Celia, Martha, Armando, Henry, Andrea, Jose, Juan, and Miguel —all attended the Sahuarita School District. When the Felix children were first attending school in Sahuarita, there was no high school so they attended Pueblo High School in Tucson. It was not until 1969 that Sahuarita High School opened. The first child to attend and graduate from the new high school was Henry Felix.

Frank L. and Celia were foster parents to over 125 children. They often took the most troubled and difficult-to-place foster children—teen boys. The boys would be put to work on the ranch and they played with the multitude of grandchildren on the ranch. When each child came, they were introduced to the family and they very quickly came to love living at the ranch. Sometimes children would stay for an extended amount of time and their departure always left an impression on the family—those such as Jonathan, Freddie, Rob, and Andrew.

Traditionally, every morning, the Felix sons came by the house to have some of Celia's famous *pan de espaura* with bowls of hot, freshly made *frijoles*. Many great memories were made around the family's kitchen table.

Memories of Manuel Felix (son of Frank and Celia)

When I was three years old, I was playing store with Maria Elena and Ponchito, my sister and brother. I went to buy a small wooden boat. Ponchito got mad at me because he wanted more "money"—which was actually little rocks. He pushed a large metal mattress spring on top of me, breaking my hip, leg, knee, and ankle in four places.

For four days I cried all day and night from pain until my grandmother, Catalina, came from downtown Tucson to see what I was crying about. She told my mother that I had broken my right leg. They took me to a doctor in Tucson and he put me in a cast for over a year. Thanks to God that after nine years of limping, the limp went away.

I went to school for eight years at the old Sahuarita school behind the pecan plant. I graduated from the eighth grade, but I could not go to high school. I had to take the cows to the river to eat, come home, cut wood, feed the chickens, and bring in the eggs.

I never had a bike. The only thing I got for Christmas was a yo-yo, a top, and some marbles. My brother, sister, and I played house at night by the back of the house.

There are eleven children in my family—seven boys and four girls. We all live happily, and give thanks to God for his protection all these years in Sahuarita, Arizona.

My first job, at age fifteen, was at a cotton field owned by a man named Mr. Smirhoff. He owned land southwest of the Santa Cruz River. I was hired to give water to the people hoeing the cotton fields. After two days, a one-armed man told me I couldn't work anymore unless I wanted to clear weeds from the cotton plants. After that, I had to pick cotton after taking our cows to the pasture. I was paid sixty cents per hour.

At the age of sixteen I went to work in Tucson with Uncle Gilbert and a man called Mr. Porter, who owned a garden and landscaping company. I was then paid one dollar an hour after a year of working with Mr. Porter. On Christmas morning, Mr. Porter got out of bed and was walking down the hall when he fell down and broke his leg. He called Gilbert, my uncle, and told him that he was not going to work anymore. He told my Uncle Gilbert to take the trailer, all of the equipment, and the jobs he had scheduled.

We were making $1.25 an hour at that point. I thought I would go half and half with Gilbert, but then he said he was going to run the business so I worked for $1.25 an hour for over two-and-a-half years before I quit working with my uncle and went to work for the University of Arizona in the agriculture and animal department. I was there for two years in the animal experimental department.

In 1960, while coming home one Sunday afternoon from bringing the cows to the corrals, I saw a dust storm off to the southwest in the desert area of our farm. I told my brother Panchito we should ride our horses to that area. When we got there, we saw a large Caterpillar bulldozer clearing the desert area. We stopped one of the men working and asked him what the Cat was going to do. He said that they were going to build a town called "Green Valley."

On Saturday nights, my brother Ponchito and I would ride to the dance hall and bar in Sahuarita. We would watch people dancing through the window. One night in 1962, I saw a nice-looking girl dancing. I went home and asked my sister to show me how to dance. The next Saturday we went back to the dance hall. I got off my horse, but it took me an hour and a half to get brave enough to ask her to dance with me.

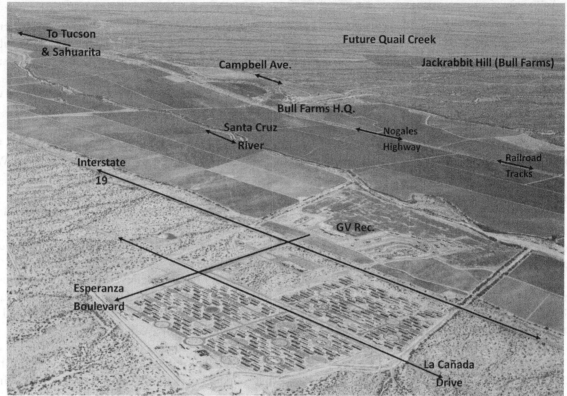

Aerial photo of Green Valley in 1964. Courtesy of Barbara Brown Bennett.
Edited by Monica Lee Elam Christiansen.

We went together for three years. In November of 1964 we got married. Thanks to a great God, we have been married for over fifty-six years.

~Contributed by Mark Felix, Manuel Felix, Oscar Gomez,
and Monica Lee Elam Christiansen

Dudley Harrison and Joan Florence Harris Fox

Dudley Harrison Fox was born on October 16, 1913. His grandparents, John Dudley Fox (born July 12, 1853) and Harriet Othello Bowman (born May 16, 1863), had been born in Flynns Lick, Tennessee, to farming families from Virginia and the Carolinas. The ancestors of these families, some of the earliest Tennessee settlers, lived through the Civil War, with some having been soldiers in the Confederate Army. They went to Texas at the conclusion of the war and settled in Fannin County.

James Hollis, Lucille, Dudley, Mary, and Mattie Fox pose for a photo. Courtesy of Gary Fox.

John Dudley Fox and Harriet Othello Bowman were married on July 17, 1881, in Dodd City, Texas. Over the next sixteen years, at least four children, Florence Othello (1882), Arthur Dudley (1887), Bartlett VanNoy (1892), and Julia Emma (1897), were born to the couple before John Dudley passed away on April 2, 1901. After four years alone, on September 27, 1905, the widowed Harriet Othello Fox married widower John Giles Nichols. To future generations, she was known only as "Granny Nichols."

Dudley's father, Arthur Dudley Fox, was born on November 26, 1887, in Dodd City. On September 26, 1909, in Windom, Texas, he married Mary Etta Glover, born August 25, 1891, in Fanning, Texas. Mary Etta's parents, Harrison Lee and Martha Bertha Clark Glover, were also Tennessee natives who moved to Texas after the Civil War. Arthur and Mary Etta met while he was working either on the Glover family farm or on one of the neighboring farms near the Glover home.

After their marriage, the family farmed near Dodd City where they were blessed with four children: Mattie Othello (1911), Dudley Harrison (1913), Florence Lucille (1916), and James Hollis (1919). The Fox children were all born in a house about three miles south of Dodd City. Dudley remembered being told he was born in the bedroom on the northwest corner of the house.

The members of the Fox family worked as sharecroppers and Dudley believed the property owner's name might have been Baker. He remembered his grandparents, Harrison and Martha Glover, coming to visit the family in 1917 while they were living on the farm. They came in a covered wagon and, as Granny Nichols was living with Harrison and Martha at this time, she came with them in the wagon.

Later in 1917, the family traveled to Tucson, Arizona, on a train. Mattie started school in Tucson and

A fragile Mary Etta Glover Fox shares a photo with her children Dudley, Mattie, Lucille, and James Hollis. Courtesy of Gary Fox.

Arthur Dudley purchased a half-section homestead just outside of Tucson, now bordered by Grant Road to the north and Swan Road on the east. The family home was located near the intersection of Ft. Lowell and Swan.

Their stay in Tucson did not last long, and by 1918 they relocated to Vernon, Texas—about a hundred miles west of Dodd City, where their last child, Mary Elizabeth was born on November 27, 1921.

Arthur Dudley Fox died on April 14, 1923, most likely of congestive heart failure, while working on a farm three to five miles west of Vernon, situated near the Pease River. After Arthur passed away, Mary Etta moved into a house on her Uncle Solon Glover's farm. There she worked in the fields picking cotton until her health began to decline and she was forced to move in with her parents, Mattie and Harry Glover. Soon after that she died on June 19, 1924, in Tolbert. Though her death certificate lists complications of tuberculosis, her son always believed she "worked herself to death." The last photos of Mary Etta seem to support how fragile she must have been near the end of her life. Within the space of fourteen months, the Fox children saw both of their parents laid to rest in the Tolbert Cemetery, in the shadow of an old Baptist church.

Arthur Dudley Fox had joined the Beasley International Order of Odd Fellows (IOOF) Lodge Number 270 on October 16, 1916. Mary Etta, just prior to her death, told her father that after she was gone, she wanted her children to go to the Odd Fellows orphanage. She followed that statement with a promise that, if he did not follow her wishes, she would haunt him forever. Grandpa Glover told her that no one would adopt the children, but her mind was made up. Times were rough in Texas and none of the extended family members were able to take care of the five Fox youngsters so, per Mary Etta's request, the children were placed in the IOOF Widows' and Orphans' Home in Corsicana, Texas, on June 30, 1924.

The facility was situated on a large plot of land where the organization raised crops and ran a dairy. All of the children were expected to help support the orphanage by milking cows, working in the fields, helping out in the laundry room, etc. Dudley remembered working in the dairy where he was able to get cream to eat over his cold cereal from the commissary. It made for a very good breakfast.

Dudley played football, baseball, basketball, and ran track all through his school years in the orphanage. Aside from missing his parents, living there was a wonderful experience and it made it possible for the children to remain together.

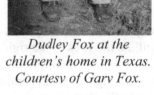

Dudley Fox at the children's home in Texas. Courtesy of Gary Fox.

In 1916, Aunt Florence Othello Fox and Uncle Edgar Potts had moved their family to Tucson, where Edgar was working as a conductor for the Southern Pacific Railroad. When Mattie graduated from high school at the orphanage in 1929, she came to Tucson to stay with them. At that time, Granny Nichols and her husband were also living with Florence and Edgar.

Lee Harris, milk boy at the San Pascual Dairy. Courtesy of Lynn Harris.

In the city of Florence, Arizona, on April 19, 1931, Julia Margurette "Babe" Potts, daughter of Edgar and Florence Potts, married Lanas "Louis" McGee, son of James Riley and Rozinah Diantha Bingham McGee. A little over a year later, in November of 1932, also in Florence, Mattie was married to Edward Aboud in what would become a very short-lived and disastrous marriage.

Dudley had graduated from the IOOF High School on May 26, 1933. He left the orphanage and came to Tucson where his sister, grandmother, aunt, uncle, and cousins were living. He worked in the Coronado Hotel as a dishwasher and enrolled in the University of Arizona where he attended three months of summer school, taking English and Spanish. His three-hundred-dollar inheritance was soon gone and his job could not support him, so he quit school and moved back to Vernon, Texas, where Mattie was living at the time. He returned with her to Arizona in October of 1933.

Dudley and Mattie moved to Yuma, where Edgar and Florence were then living. Dudley immediately started working for Lloyd Marion

Dudley working as a cowboy at McGee Ranch. Courtesy of Gary Fox.

Burkhart at the Double B Garage and Wrecking Yard. After two or three months, he went to work for Stevenson's Service Station. While there, he also worked part-time as a short-order cook. He remembered that, back then, gas was only ten cents a gallon and he made five dollars a week working.

While in Yuma, Dudley bought his first car—a 1921 Model T Ford, with tire size 240 x 21. He paid three dollars for the car and drove it for a little over a month. The roads were very rough in those days. He took a short trip up along the Colorado River where two tires went flat at the same time and the radiator fell apart. After getting it back to Yuma, he sold it to the wrecking yard for fifty cents. Not too long after, he bought a two-door 1929 Model A Ford for fifty dollars. After a five-dollar down payment, he owed five dollars per month until it was paid off.

In 1933, the road through the sand dunes to California was paved. Dudley often took his car out to play in the dunes. In order to drive in the sand, they had to let some of the air out of the tires. Once the pressure was very low, the cars could drive through the sand without getting stuck. When it was time to return to Yuma, they had to pump the tires back up with a hand pump. Fortunately, the tires were small so it didn't take very long to reinflate the tires to the right pressure. In those days, a hand pump was carried in the car at all times. If a flat tire occurred on the road, the driver would pull over, take the tire apart, repair the tube, pump the tire up to the right pressure, and away they would go.

Mattie also got a job in Yuma, and during that same time, she divorced Ed Aboud. In September of 1934, Mattie married a second time to Matt McGee, the half brother of her cousin's husband, Louis. Matt, employed as a fireman for the Southern Pacific Railroad, was still recovering from serious burns received while on duty in the summer of 1928. The couple settled in Tucson for several years.

As each of the younger Fox children graduated from the orphanage high school, they headed west to Arizona to find their older siblings.

In January of 1935, Dudley moved to McGee Ranch to live with Eldon Heaston, husband of Lura McGee. He was hired by Matt and Empy McGee to work cutting wood for three to six months. Soon after that, he moved to the homestead where he lived with Empy and Mamie McGee.

In the early spring of 1936, Dudley was riding in the mountains one day with Bud McGee. They were packing salt and it was snowing and very cold. Bud said he knew of a place to get a cup of coffee and maybe some cold biscuits with honey, so they headed for the West Star cabin. Through the spring, summer, and fall, Joan Harris had been living there with her two brothers, Lee and Luther. She was there when Dudley rode in with Bud. That was the first time they saw each other.

At McGee Ranch, grandmother Martha Thornton Harris stands with Lee, Joan, and Luther Fox. Courtesy of Gary Fox.

Mirma and Charles Harris riding in Mexico. Courtesy of Gary Fox.

Throughout 1936 and 1937, Dudley worked around the ranch and rode the range. Matt and Empy McGee hired Dudley, his brother James Hollace, and Vernon Hanna to build Tascula dam. The boys lived in Tascula canyon in a tent pitched about a half mile below the dam. From time to time, Chad McGee packed sand and helped with the work on the dam. Four burros—Choppo, Brownie, and Soppy, plus an unnamed burro that had been either borrowed or rented—were used for transporting materials. Fifteen-gallon containers, one strapped on each side of the burro, were used to haul water from the well at Bill's Hole to use for drinking and mixing cement. Lumber was hauled up from the main ranch. Cement was delivered to the campsite in vehicles and then carted into the canyon to the dam site. Burros pulled sand up the canyon on a skid built of old sheets of tin.

Dudley's children later rode these same burros when they were young, from the time they could catch them until they were about thirteen or fourteen years old. Joan remembered taking one of the burros to West Star. She wished she could have left him along the trail and walked because he would not lead—he just flat out refused to walk, but she couldn't leave him there with a saddle on him.

During that same time period, Lawrence Saursfield hired Dudley, Bill, Lee, and Luther to survey and do assessment work on some of his claims. They also worked the Boydo Tunnel on Keystone Peak chasing a gold vein.

In 1938, Dudley left the ranch and ended up in Bakersfield, California. He was completely broke and desperately needed work. He learned about a job in Saugus, near Van Nuys, California, but did not have the money to get there. Unsure of what to do, he was walking down the street in Bakersfield and found two five-dollar bills on the street—enough to buy something to eat and pay his way to the town of Saugus where the job was waiting for him.

He immediately started working for the bridge and building department of the Southern Pacific Railroad; but because of the short work hours, he couldn't support himself, so he left to go trapping with Robert McGee in the Sierrita Mountains. Through that winter, they ran the trap lines, slowly moving a little further away from the ranch each week. Eventually they found themselves in Altar Valley, near Silverbell. They made fifty cents for swift foxes and five dollars each for coyotes and badgers.

Lee and Joan help grandmother Florence McGee feed the turkeys. Courtesy of Lynn Harris.

One night, when they went into Redrock for supplies, there was a foot of snow on the ground and two thermometers in at the store both registered negative four degrees. On cold nights, they would build a fire and spread the fire around to heat the ground. After a while they would rake all the coals back into a pile so they could set their bedrolls on the heated ground. Dudley said they could only put part of the bed on the heated ground or the bed would get too hot. Dudley always remembered that winter spent with Robert, learning invaluable skills and sharing wonderful conversations around the campfire.

In September of 1939, the railroad work picked up again and on the fourth of that month, Dudley was recalled to Eugene, Oregon, where he worked the line between Crescent Lake and Eugene. At that point, Dudley and Joan Harris were exchanging letters any time he was away from the ranch.

After about four months, the railroad transferred Dudley back to Tucson from Oregon. On January, 12, 1940, the draft board called Dudley up for service. As he was standing at the railroad station waiting to board the train, he received word that he was no longer required to report. Eventually, he was informed that the railroad had asked for and received a deferment for him. His record of service and reliability kept him at home working on the railroad during World War II.

Joan Florence Fox

Joan Florence Fox was born on November 13, 1913, on the Canoa Ranch, located south of Tucson, Arizona, along the Santa Cruz River. Her parents, Charles Eiler Harris and Mirma McGee Harris were children of the early settlers of McGee Ranch.

At the time of Joan's birth, most of the McGee and Harris family members were living at "the Canoa," farming and establishing a community there in hopes of purchasing the property for a permanent settlement. It was a beautiful place with fertile soil and plenty of water. The Santa Cruz River ran year round, making it possible for minnows to live in the river near the family farms.

Luther, Charles, Lee, Joan, and Mirma Harris all dressed up. Courtesy of Gary Fox.

Some of the older men stayed back at McGee Ranch to take care of the place, with Aunt Hanna Harris there cooking for them. This was fortunate, as the property deal in Canoa fell through and the families were forced to abandon the settlement, returning to McGee Ranch via horse and buggy during a winter snowstorm.

In 1915, several members of the Harris families (Dan, Charlie, Andrew, and possibly Fawnso) moved to Mammoth, Arizona, where they lived in tents and worked for the local mines. Joan remembered wishing for a door to go in and out of because she was tired of camping out.

The boys worked in an underground mine hauling ore to the mill with mules. Sometimes they would get behind with their hauling. Dan, who was known for his strength, would put a piece of timber under the axle of the engine that was sticking out of the mine building. By prying up on the timber, he was able to apply enough leverage to stall the engine to allow them to get caught up.

Andrew, Dan's brother, was not a large person, but was also very strong. One day the foreman of the mine picked a fight with Andrew, and when the dust cleared, the foreman had a black eye. Later, when things had settled down, the foreman told Charlie that his little brother had "cleaned his flues." After the fight, the foreman

Bob King, Joan Harris, Frank King, and Lee Harris pose for a photo on the dairy in California. Courtesy of Lynn Harris.

and the Harris brothers became good friends.

In 1916, the family moved south to Tucson and lived in a place that was called "the drag." It was located on the corner of Oracle and Wetmore.

Not long after that, they moved back to McGee Ranch where Joan started first grade in the small Sierrita School. She was living on the ranch when "Grandpa Jim" (James Riley) McGee passed away in January of 1917. Dr. Snabble, who owned the first car in Tucson, took care of Grandpa Jim during his final illness.

By 1920, the family had moved yet again—this time to El Porvenir, an area near Agua Prieta, Mexico, just across the border from Douglas, where Arthur Lively, Robert McGee, Fawnso Harris, and Charlie Harris were working a farm. Joan stayed there one summer with them. Initially, the guys camped in an adobe shack and it was pretty rough, but Joan remembers that when the women came, they cleaned up the place and served meals.

John Kent Lively toddling around.
Courtesy of Lynn Harris.

Later that same year, Charlie and Mirma moved their children into a small house in Douglas (at 7th and D Avenues) where they lived until the middle of Joan's fifth-grade school year. Luther, Joan's older brother, told the school that his mother, Mirma, was born in Mexico, so they assumed he spoke Spanish and put him in a class with the Mexican kids.

Joan's father, Charlie, worked all around the Douglas area as a carpenter and blacksmith. He used to forge weld with coal to repair broken springs for cars, most of which were for Chandler automobiles that had an elliptical spring that went from front to back.

Lee Harris's baby brother, John Kent Lively. Courtesy of Gary Fox.

In early 1925, Joan's parents separated. Her mother, Mirma, moved to El Paso to live with Eldon and Lura McGee Heaston. After about two months, Joan moved there as well to live with her mother, uncle, aunt, and cousins Virginia and Barbara. Mirma worked in a candy store and in a boarding house helping to serve meals. Joan, only twelve years old at the time, traveled to El Paso on the train by herself. Her Uncle Matt, who was still working on the railroad, was able to watch over her as she traveled.

When the school year ended, Joan moved to Tucson where she stayed with her grandparents, George and Martha Harris. Her Aunt Zinah McGee was living nearby so she was able to spend the summer playing with Adina McGee.

The fall of 1925 found Mirma and her children living in Escondido, California, where they stayed a few weeks with Janet and Raymond Kiddo before moving into a one-room house. Lee, Luther, and Joan attended school there for one year. Mirma was able to get a job working as a practical nurse. Joan remembered traveling to San Diego through the California sand dunes on a road made of boards, with passing spots every couple hundred yards.

Joan was able to visit McGee Ranch in the summer of 1926. Mirma, Luther, and Joan traveled along with George and Martha Harris. They returned to San Diego by train and were picked up by Mirma's mother, Florence, and her stepfather, Ed Harris. Mirma and her children stayed with them on their dairy farm in the San Pasqual Valley where Joan attended the seventh and eighth grades.

Luther and Joan once competed in a track meet at school. Between the two of them, they won all the prizes, which were boxes of candy. Lee was in high school at the time, but he was there to watch and hold all of the candy for them as they continued competing, winning each event they entered.

Joan cares for an orphaned fawn. Courtesy of Gary Fox.

On the dairy farm, Joan had a little goat. Lee used to play with the goat, butting heads with it, until the goat got too big and started hurting Lee. The goat was kept on the farm until he was caught on the roof of the cloth-top car. After that the goat disappeared.

Joan started high school in Escondido, but during the semester break in 1928, they moved to Redwood City, California. Mirma had moved up there and Joan went to stay with her mother. When school ended for the summer, her brother Lee came through town with the King boys. They were on their way to Montana with plans to spend the summer working on the King's sheep ranch.

Mirma and Joan moved back down to Escondido. During the winter of 1928–29, the dairy farm was flooded. The fields were ruined and they could not raise feed for the dairy cows. Mirma and Joan got a place living over a laundry so Mirma could do the ironing for the business. Joan went back and forth from Escondido to the dairy in San Pasqual.

By 1930, Ed and Flora sold the farm and moved back to McGee Ranch. Mirma, Luther, and Joan returned to Arizona with them. They stayed in the Tucson area, living in Binghampton, near Fort Lowell and Dodge. They also lived with Uncle Fawnso and Aunt Vivian Cowen Harris. At that time, Fawnso and Joan's father Charlie were running trap lines and were rarely home. Luther had a motorcycle and worked delivering newspapers. He also had his own apartment and when Mirma married Arthur Lively in 1931, Luther invited Joan to share it with him. She remained there until she graduated from Tucson High School in 1932 and moved to the ranch to live with Ed and grandmother Flora at the place they called the "homestead."

When Arthur and Mirma McGee Harris Lively built a house about a half-mile north of the homestead in 1933, Joan moved in with them. By that time, Mirma had given birth to little John Kent Lively in September of 1932. Joan loved to help take care of him. She remembers having to haul water up to the house in buckets from a little well at the bottom of the canyon, just north of the house.

Uncle Fawnso homesteaded land on the east of the Tinaja Mountain, near where the Caterpillar proving grounds are today. Grandmother Martha Harris' health was declining, so in 1934 Joan moved over to Fawnso's homestead to help care for her. At that time, Uncle Fawnso lived in a tent with his wife, Vivian. Joan's dad Charlie and grandmother Martha lived in a little board house about a hundred feet from Uncle Fawnso's tent. Joan remembers going deer hunting with her dad while living there. He shot a big mule deer and she remembers the meat being very tender.

At some point in 1935, Joan moved to the West Star cabin to stay with her brothers. While there, she found an

Luther with the orphaned fawn. Courtesy of Lynn Harris.

orphaned whitetail fawn that she raised by feeding cow's milk to the tiny baby from a bottle. It was a little male and he was kept in the house most of the time. She remembered that he used to love to chew on the curtains.

One day, her little deer came running from the direction of Red Silver Pass with a coyote in hot pursuit. The little deer ran by the cabin and up the canyon on the bare side of the hill. Joan grabbed a gun and went after them. By the time she caught up, the coyote was standing over the deer, but when it saw her, he left the deer and ran. Joan shot at the coyote, who was about halfway up the bare side of the hill. She probably hit the coyote because he did a flip and ran in the opposite direction. The deer got to its feet and ran up the hill.

Later, the deer ran away, but in a day or two it came back hungry. Joan got a bottle of milk and by holding the bottle just in front of him and backing up one step at a time, she lured the deer back into his pen. The deer stayed a little while longer, but eventually ran away and never came back.

Joan soon went back to Fawnso's to help take care of grandmother Martha. About two weeks after her return, in January of 1936, her grandmother passed away. Dudley was cutting wood with Eldon Heston in the mountains at the time. On the day of the funeral, he was working by himself. As he was coming back to the ranch, he went to the funeral, but he did not know grandmother Martha.

Fawnso sold the homestead to Empy and Matt McGee, so Joan moved back to the West Star cabin with her brothers. Not long after her move, she spotted a rattlesnake in the cabin. She said a little prayer, "Don't let him get me," picked up a poker for the fire, and was able to put it on his head where she ground it down until it killed the snake.

Another day, Mirma was there visiting from Nogales and a rattlesnake was seen lying on a board outside the cabin. Breakfast was about ready and the snake was cold and not moving so they decided to kill the snake after breakfast. When the boys went outside to get ready for work, Mirma said, "Aren't you going to kill the snake?" They looked, but the snake was long gone.

Lee Harris, Janet Ball Harris, Charlie Harris, Luther Harris, Mirma Lively, Arthur Lively, and Joan Harris pose for a photo near homestead. Courtesy of Lynn Harris.

The milk and butter they got from the cow was kept in a bucket and hung down the well close to the water where it stayed nice and cool. When possible, they kept a cow that had just given birth to a calf. The calf was kept in a pen and the cow would stay nearby so it was fairly easy to get her to come in for milking. They would take most of the milk and leave the rest for the calf.

Luther had a German shepherd-type dog named "Cuff." He was trained to get the cow for them twice a day. After milking, the cream from the milk was put into a bottle. When shaken for a while, it would turn to butter. They also made cottage cheese with the milk. Often dessert was wild honey with cottage cheese or biscuits. Also "war cake." There were very few deer in the mountains at that time so they didn't eat much meat.

In 1937, Joan moved in with her dad at the main ranch settlement. They lived in a very small house with a tiny kitchen and a small living room. There was no foundation under the house. Dudley was working over at Tascula, building a concrete dam. One day in the winter, while it was snowing, he and his brother Hollis went over to have dinner with Charlie and Joan. At the time, Dave McGee was just a little guy and he loved to come down to visit Joan, often playing with the dishes and hiding some under her bed. When Dudley and his brother offered to do the dishes after the meal, Joan kept bringing dishes out from under her bed. Dudley and Hollis teased her about that for several years. After dinner and dishes they had to walk back to the camp in Tascula because there were no extra rooms or beds at the ranch.

In 1938, Joan's brother, Lee, married Janet Ball in a little Presbyterian church at North 4th Avenue and University in Tucson. Joan was the bridesmaid and Dudley had come to the ranch in his 1937 Model A Ford to take her to town for the wedding.

Joan continued living with Charlie. She worked helping family members on the ranch, babysat for Lee and Janet, and took care of the house for her father. On Thanksgiving Day in 1940, the little house burned down while Joan and Charlie were down at Luther and Monie's for dinner. They lost everything except the clothes they were wearing. Dudley had just sent her a small watch on a chain to hang around her neck. She had left it in the house, so it was lost in the fire as well.

Gary, Dudley, Joan, Scotty, Judy, Kelly, and Shelly Fox share a photo in their yard. Courtesy of Gary Fox.

After the fire, she moved to 815 East Drachman to live with her Uncle Matt and his wife Mattie. She gathered desert spoons (southwestern plants of the asparagus family) and sold them for money to help her dad build a new house. Dudley would go out to the ranch and bring the desert spoons into town. There was a fairly good market for the arrangements that Joan made to sell.

Joan moved to Nogales with her mother in 1941 and got a job working for the telephone company. On September 1 of that year, Dudley drove to Nogales and asked her to marry him. She finally said "YES!" so on September 17, 1941, they were married in Yuma, Arizona, at the Gretna Green. Matt and Mattie (Fox) McGee and Arthur and Mirma (McGee Harris) Lively came with Joan to Yuma for the wedding. The young couple had been writing to each other for quite a while and they knew their marriage would help ensure that Dudley would be able to stay working for the railroad instead of going off to war.

After about two months in Yuma, they moved back to Tucson to rent the 815 East Drachman house. Four of their five children were born at St. Mary's hospital while they lived in that house: Gary (1942), Judith "Judy" (1944), Marshall "Kelly," and Sheldon "Shelly" (1945). (Their youngest child, Dudley Arthur "Scotty," was born in 1953). They were paying Matt McGee seventeen dollars and fifty cents per month rent on the house in 1942, but when the opportunity arose, they decided to buy the house for $800. (When they sold the house in 1948, they received $4,500.)

In 1946, Dudley was earning about eight hundred dollars per month working for the railroad. The family decided to move back to McGee Ranch so that Dudley could work for the Sierrita Mining and Ranching Company. They packed up their gray 1938 Plymouth and moved in with Joan's father, Charles Harris. Dudley and Joan spent the rest of their lives in that small McGee Ranch home, the same house that Joan had helped pay for with her desert spoon arrangements.

Over the next fifty-six years, Dudley and Joan dedicated their lives to their family and the community. Joan stayed home with their young family and stood by Dudley's side as he served on the TRICO Electric Board of Directors from 1959 to 1989, and was a member of the Arizona Electric Power Cooperative. During his time at TRICO, he was alternately president, vice president, secretary, and treasurer. He was also a member and secretary of the board of directors for the Grand Canyon State Electric Cooperative Association. He was a board member and organizer of the Shiloh Water Association at McGee Ranch, as well as an important contributor to the Sierrita Mining and Ranching Company. Dudley served on the Sahuarita School Board from 1958 to 1966 and, for part of that time, was the board president. Dudley and Joan were devoted to each other and did everything they could to be wonderful parents, grandparents, neighbors, and friends.

On April 1 of 1989, Joan was painting the ceiling of the front porch. As she stepped down off the ladder, her foot missed the bottom rung, causing her to fall backwards. She landed against the wall and cracked her backbone. A chiropractor visit resulted in muscle tears, and from then on she had difficulty even walking. For years, because of terrible pain, she could only walk short distances and was unable to lift anything or clean the house.

A commemorative photo of Joan and Dudley Fox. Courtesy of Gary Fox.

On November 4, 1999, Joan fell and broke her hip. She had been lying on the floor for a couple of hours before Dudley found her and took her to St. Mary's Hospital, where they placed a new ball in the socket of her left hip. Her recovery time was spent at La Posada in Green Valley and she missed Christmas of 1999. Eventually, she came home for a short time, then got sick and had to return to the hospital. After that, Devon Gables became her home for about two weeks until pneumonia set in, requiring another hospital stay. February and March of 2000 were spent at La Posada for recovery and therapy, but surgical complications kept her from healing properly and she never walked again.

Dudley, known for his "quick wit, quiet humor, solid wisdom, sound advice, and stern courage" (TRICO Livewire May/June 1989), died on January 25, 2002. Joan passed away on the morning of Sunday, February 8, 2004. She was buried beside her best friend and husband in the McGee Ranch cemetery.

~ Contributed by Gary Fox

Foy and Duffy Families

Joseph P. and Rose Ann Barga Foy, both born in Ohio to French immigrant parents, were married on October 21, 1879, in Darke County, Ohio. The couple settled in the village of Versailles where Joseph made a living as a carpenter. Six children were born to the family: William Francis (1880), Albert Peter (1881), Edward Nicholas (1886), Mary Ellen (1888), Raymond Lewis (1893), and Emma Helen (1893).

In Indianapolis, on July 10, 1898, a little over a month before his eighteenth birthday, William F. Foy, a carpenter, enlisted in the United States Army as a member of the Seventh Cavalry, Company F. He was discharged on May 12, 1899, in New York City. Although his military enlistment had lasted only ten months, his experiences were retold throughout his lifetime and beyond. It is said that he was in Cuba with Theodore Roosevelt during the final months of the Spanish–American War, as well as in Arizona, prior to being discharged.

In 1899, Henry Foy discovered the well-known Torpedo Mine in Organ, New Mexico. By mid-1900, William had made his way to Organ to work with his Uncle Henry, and appears to have been working

Passengers boarding the train to Cananea,
Mexico. Courtesy of Sandra Jake.

closely with him. The June 18, 1900, edition of the *Albuquerque Citizen* reported that, "Henry Foy and his nephew, of Organ, were here yesterday, leaving last night for San Francisco and Los Angeles." This was one of several trips they took together.

The *Arizona Republic*, on June 30, 1901, reported that William and Henry Foy "were at the Ford Hotel yesterday and left on the southbound train for Tombstone, Bisbee, and other points in Southern Arizona."

By the time Henry married in February of 1902 in El Paso, it appears that William had permanently departed his uncle's home in Organ, New Mexico. As it was well known that William had been exploring mines in Southern Arizona and Northern Sonora, it came as no surprise that he ended up marrying the daughter of James F. and Catharine Lacey Kearney on September 6, 1905, in Phoenix, Arizona. Alice Irene Kearny, the only daughter of the well-known miner, was born on February 9, 1886, in Tombstone, while her father had been working with Ed Schieffelin—but by 1900, the Kearney family was living in Phoenix. Kearney's connections to the mining industry had led his daughter to William Foy.

The Kearneys and Foys were both in Cananea, Sonora, Mexico, with Colonel William C. Greene, "the Croesus of Copper," who had prospected through Southern Arizona and Northern Sonora before making his millions. It is believed that Foy first met Greene when he was in El Paso, Texas, trying to sell stock in the Cobra Grande Mine. From there, Foy and Kearney were both heavily involved in the development of the Cananea Copper Company. According to the *Arizona Republic* on June 17, 1962, "Foy was also there when revolution swept the country and rioting nearly destroyed the mining, milling, and smelting empire which Greene had built. After order of a sort was restored in Mexico, Foy came to Arizona where his father-in-law James F. Kearney was operating the Octave Mine at Congress, Arizona [near Wickenburg]. Kearney, a pioneer in Arizona mining, had operated the Tombstone reduction works at Fairbanks for many years after building the mill for Ed Schieffelin. Foy worked with Kearney, who made the Octave one of the most productive gold mines in Arizona."

William and Irene Foy's daughter, Viviana Beatrice Foy, was born in Los Angeles on August 22, 1906. Her birth certificate indicates that the usual residence of her parents was La Cananea, Mexico, and that her father was employed as a bookkeeper. It is unknown whether William and Irene were in Mexico, or safely in Los Angeles, when the deadly Cananea Copper Strike took place on the first of June, 1906.

The *Arizona Republican* announced on February 23, 1911, that James Kearney and his

Ed Bush and Bill Foy talk business in Twin
Buttes. Courtesy of William Kalt.

wife had returned from Cananea to make their home in Phoenix. Their daughter and granddaughter moved with them. On his November 1, 1911, Certificate of Registration of American Citizen with the U.S. Consulate in Nogales, Foy stated that he left his residence in the United States and arrived in Cananea, Mexico, in 1902 for the purpose of mining. He also certified that his wife and daughter resided in Phoenix.

By 1912, James and Catharine Kearney had moved to Los Angeles and it appears that their daughter and granddaughter resided there as well.

In an interview with the *Tucson Daily Citizen* on February 14, 1962, William Foy

William and Irene Kearney Foy sit for a photo in their home. Courtesy of the Foy family.

explained that, "Mining was considered a major Arizona industry in 1912, but comparatively few mines were in operation. The Ajo mines weren't in production. About the only mines producing in Southern Arizona were at Bisbee, Cortland, and Gleason. Farther north you had the mines at Globe, Ray, Clifton, Morenci, and Jerome."

"'The Twin Buttes area was beginning to develop in 1912,' Foy said. At one time he had options on the Banner Mine there and owned what is now the Pima Mine. He recalled that Twin Buttes was referred to as 'Camp Borracho' because so many drunken miners lived there."

"E. G. Bush, who came to Twin Buttes from Montana in 1912, contributed real impetus to mining development there. According to Foy, 'Bush bought into the old Minnie Mine prospect hole. That was the big push that got the Twin Buttes area going. They sank a 300-foot shaft and got into a beautiful body of ore. Old Man Barnsdall, a big operator, started the Mineral Hill development which is now the Banner Mine.'"

"Foy remembered that the road to Twin Buttes in 1912 consisted of a pair of wheel ruts circling through the mesquite from San Xavier Mission. The government didn't build access roads in those days so eventually Foy built the road where it is now—spent $65,000 on it one year."

"Foy said the hills in Southern Arizona were full of little makeshift mines where mineralization was too low to make a real mining operation profitable. In many areas the land was pockmarked with prospect holes and disgusted cattlemen complained that their range was being perforated with these oversized gopher diggings. Many prospectors, some of them 'burro men,' were still trudging through the desert in search of pay dirt in 1912, and their stories run pretty much to a pattern—the 'big one' was just around the corner."

In 1915, William F. Foy joined up with John Baxter and Ed Bush at Twin Buttes. Within a short time, John Baxter, who had been involved with the Twin Buttes mines for over thirty years,

Catherine Duffy and Ed Foy stand by a building in Twin Buttes. Courtesy of the Revello family.

Lumber operations in Flagstaff, Arizona.
Courtesy of James Murphy.

retired. Foy bought him out and hired his brother, Edward Foy, as mine manager.

Soon war broke out and over the course of World War I, over twenty million pounds of copper were mined in the area, resulting in shipments totaling almost fifty million tons of ore being sent out over the Twin Buttes railroad, which Foy and Bush had purchased. The town was booming and the men profitably operated the Copper Glance Mine.

Catharine Kearney died on August 31, 1917, in Los Angeles. In September of 1918, when William completed his draft registration form, he was living at Twin Buttes and working as a bookkeeper for the Glance Mine, but his permanent residence was listed as Los Angeles. In the 1920 census, Irene and Vivian were still living in Los Angeles with James Kearney.

After 1920, the Twin Buttes properties continued full operations. Thirteen shafts had been dug in the area right around Twin Buttes. William and Ed Foy sank eleven of them between 1916 and 1924, one of which was a 500-foot shaft that was dug and timbered for less than $10,000. They quickly gained a reputation for being the lowest-cost operators in the country. William Foy stated, "We did it, by gosh, in less than ninety days. My brother sure was a dandy!"

In the 1922 Tucson City Directory, William and Irene were living in Tucson at 1500 West Alameda. William was working for the Midland Copper Company with which Ed Bush and John Baxter were affiliated.

The year 1928 found William Foy the sole owner of the Twin Buttes Mining Co. and the railroad spur that connected Twin Buttes to Tucson. He began consolidating and expanding in an effort to purchase almost all of the mines in the Pima, Banner, and Esperanza areas, and part of the Mission mine. Foy began structuring the financing of his plans in September of 1929, but in fewer than thirty days, the stock market crashed and destroyed his dreams. He didn't give up hope, but finding investors was not possible.[1]

In August of 1931, William and Irene's daughter, Vivian Foy, married William Lott in Tucson, and on September 9 of that same year James F. Kearney died in the Pioneer's Home in Prescott. Though the Foys had moved to Tucson and William had clung to his dreams, by the end of 1935 he had given up. He scrapped what was left of the old Twin Buttes railroad and abandoned the engine and cars where they lay.[2]

William F. Foy died in Tucson on February, 25, 1966, and Vivian Irene Foy died on June 18, 1968.

Catherine Foy standing by a mine or well shaft. Courtesy of James Murphy.

Edward N. Foy was born on March 1, 1886, in Versailles, Ohio, and headed to the Southwest when he was about twenty years old. His older brother, William, had arrived there a number of years prior and encouraged Ed to join him. Both men worked in the Cananea Copper Mines and were associated with Edward Bush and John Baxter, founders of the mining community at Twin Buttes.

In August of 1913, Ed was still living in Cananea, but by the time he filled out his draft registration card on September 12, 1918, he was living at Twin Buttes, working as a mine carpenter—a trade learned in Ohio under the tutelage of his father.

In an *Arizona Daily Star* article published on June 4, 1919, it was reported that when Ed had married Catherine Duffy, he was "connected with the local office of Dunbar Brokerage Company of El Paso."

Catherine had been teaching in the Twin Buttes School from September of 1916 until May of 1918.

In the 1922 Tucson City Directory, Edward and Catherine were living near the Duffy family home at 513 South 4th Avenue. At this same time, Patrick Joseph Murphy, husband of Catherine's sister, Agnes Harriet (Hattie), was working as a foreman in Flagstaff for Greenlaw's Lumber Company. In late 1922, Ed and Catherine moved up north where Ed worked with Pat in the small

Ed Foy's pigeons resting in their pens. Courtesy of James Murphy.

town called Cliff's Camp, east of Flagstaff. It was a rough life there and the lumbermen worked hard. They were paid weekly and it is said that Pat had a deal worked out with the Flagstaff sheriff. Every Friday the lumber crew went into town and would invariably get intoxicated or get into fights. At the end of the weekend, Pat would take a wagon into town, bail them out of jail, and bring them all back to work for the new week.

In April 1923, during the time the Foys were living in Flagstaff, Catherine gave birth to a daughter. Complications during delivery resulted in little Mary Catherine Foy's death on the same day she was born.

Undoubtedly, the loss of their infant daughter was heartbreaking for the Foys. They soon left the Flagstaff area and headed south. In the fall of 1924, Catherine accepted a job teaching in the Twin Buttes School and Ed went to work full time with his brother. They settled into the small mining community and made it their home. On April 2, 1931, Ed filed a Stock-Raising Homestead Entry, No. 068315, establishing his intent to lay claim to acreage in the Twin Buttes area.

Catherine was a treasured teacher and Ed also became involved with community families. In the June 6, 1933, edition of the *Arizona Daily Star*, it was reported that Ed Foy had been appointed as the community welfare board representative. He was tasked with taking a survey of families in need of assistance and reporting the results back to the welfare board.

The Foy family cows wander the range. Courtesy of James Murphy.

In late 1936, the "for rent" section of the classified ads in the *Star* offered a slight peek into the Foy home. The September 22 edition says, "Well furnished three-bedroom home, service porch, bath, garage; located on good highway in Twin Buttes, 25 miles south of Tucson. Ideal climate; 1,000 feet higher than Tucson." A second listing on December 13 offers a "Three-bedroom furnished house. Modern conveniences. On good highway; private ranch, riding horse; fresh eggs available. Beautiful view, public school within walking distance."

The *Arizona Daily Star* on February 2, 1938, reported, "A motor trip and hike was [*sic*] held Sunday by the Kum'n Go Club of the YWCA when they were guests of Mr. and Mrs. C. J. Wilkerson at their

Ed Foy and a friend cook dinner at the Foy home in Twin Buttes circa 1913. Courtesy of James Murphy.

homestead, Twin Buttes. The party left Tucson at 9:30 in the morning and returned at 7 o'clock after driving 17 miles south to Sahuarita, and then west to the old smelter site where Mrs. Wilkerson gave the history of the town and smelter deposit. The drive continued over the desert and through the mountains to Twin Buttes and the homestead. It was 2:20 o'clock and time for dinner on an outdoor fireplace when the party finished climbing the mountain and taking pictures. After dinner, the party broke into smaller groups. One group hiked into the desert in search of more cacti plants for the Mexican dish gardens the club will make and another group tried their skill at dart practice. Others rested on the enclosed porch of the homestead."

"At 4:30 o'clock the membership of the club started on the last leg of the trip, hiking from the homestead to the Twin Buttes copper mine, out of operation since 1917. Here they were joined by the host and hostess and taken on an inspection tour of the mine. This privilege was extended to members by Edward Foy, former superintendent. In addition the party visited the home of Mr. and Mrs. Foy and saw their collection of Saguaro cacti articles and freak cacti tumors."

The *Arizona Daily Star* on November 1, 1939, published notice that, "Edward N. Foy, of Twin Buttes, Arizona, who, on April 2, 1931, made Stock-Raising Homestead Entry No. 068315, filed notice of intention to make final three year proof, to establish claim to the land listed on the 5th day of December, 1939."

On November, 18, 1942, Edward N. Foy received stock-raising homestead certificate No. 1115298 for 640 acres in Twin Buttes. This property is now completely covered by the dumps of active area mines.

As the population of Twin Buttes dwindled, the school remained and so did Ed and Catherine. Their Blackacre Ranch supported them. They grazed cattle over their property. Ed trained a beautiful collie mix to assist him in herding. Ed also kept a large pen with homing pigeons. In addition to her duties at the school, Catherine raised chickens and collected eggs to sell.

For the fall semester of 1945, the children from the nearby Zinc School began attending Twin Buttes when their school closed after an annexation petition was passed. The tired Twin Buttes building was given something of a "face-lift" and an additional teacher was hired.

On September 18, 1945, the *Tucson Daily Citizen* announced that, "A four-room, frame

Ed Foy and Catherine Duffy Foy stroll the sidewalks of Tucson in the spring of 1937. Courtesy of James Murphy.

house in the mining settlement of Twin Buttes southwest of Tucson and the property of Ed Foy, was burned to the ground Friday night. The house was vacant and the origin of the fire has not been determined." It is assumed that this was not the primary Foy residence, as Catherine continued teaching until May of 1946 when she retired.

Though Catherine was ready for a break, Ed obviously was not finished with his mining career. That same May, Edward N. Foy and the well-known Colonel Matthew Baird filed articles of incorporation for the Vulcan Copper and Zinc Mining Company. The seven mines making up this group were located northwest of Helmet Peak, along Mission Road, quite a few miles from Twin Buttes.

Sadly, on November 9, 1948, at the age of 62, Edward N. Foy, "pioneer Arizona mining man and cattle rancher in the Twin Buttes area, died here yesterday at the family residence [at the Duffy home at 505 South 4th Street]. Mr. Foy was a member of the Arizona Pioneers Society, the Small Mine Owners Association, and the Holy Name Society of All Saints

Catherine Foy stands on her porch in Twin Buttes. Courtesy of the Revello family.

Church. He was born in Versailles, Ohio, and came to Arizona in 1907. Prior to working in the mining field here, he worked in copper mines in Cananea, Mexico. He was associated with Edward Bush and John Baxter in founding what was once a thriving mining community at Twin Buttes. The Twin Buttes venture continued until 1929 when it declined and most of the community's several hundred people moved elsewhere. Several years ago Mr. Foy entered the cattle business."[3]

Though the usual residence listed on Ed's death certificate indicated "Twin Buttes," it is likely that Catherine did not return there for long. She closed up the ranch and moved to Tucson, where she lived the remainder of her life in the Duffy home at 505 South 4th with her sisters Harriet, Alice, and Myrtle.

The Duffy Family

Martin James Duffy was born in County Sligo, Ireland, to John and Honor Cunnane Duffy. He was said to be somewhat of a "hothead" in Ireland, and a revolutionary. Because of this, in about 1877 or 1878, he was forced to leave the country. He traveled down to Cork and boarded the only ship available, which was headed for Australia. Once there, he worked any job he could find to save enough money to get to San Francisco, California, where he went to work on the Southern Pacific Railroad.

He worked his way south to Los Angeles and followed the railroad west from there toward Tucson where he disembarked, again, taking jobs where he could find them. He had an important purpose for saving money. His Irish sweetheart, Brigid Delia Egan, had made her way to New York from Ireland and was working as a

Martin James and Brigid Delia Egan Duffy in Brooklyn, New York, soon after their arrival in the United States. Courtesy of James Murphy.

servant for the Redmond Keresey family on Long Island. As soon as the couple had the money for her travel, Brigid came to Tucson where they were married in Saint Augustine's Cathedral on July 18, 1887.

Grandson James Murphy reflects, "When my grandparents came over here, they were poor and uneducated. They had nothing. My grandfather went to work on the Southern Pacific. And you can imagine working out on the road in the middle of the summer."

The first child born to Martin and Brigid was Mary Ellen "Mamie" Duffy. The family was living in Rillito and working for the railroad when she arrived on May 8, 1888. Agnes Harriett "Hattie" Duffy joined the family on September 24, 1889, while they were living in Red Rock, north of Tucson. Martin became a naturalized United States citizen on September 29, 1890, so by the time Alice E. was born on

April 18, 1891, the family had settled on the outskirts of Tucson where Martin had gone into the dairy business. Ida Myrtle "Metto" was born on October 26, 1892, followed by Catherine Gertrude "Kaki" on February 26, 1894.

With five beautiful daughters, the Duffy family was thrilled when little Martin James Duffy arrived on October, 14, 1895. Sadly, he died prior to his first birthday and was laid to rest in the Holy Hope Cemetery. Soon after his death, a second son, William Eagan Duffy was born, but did not survive a difficult birth. He was laid to rest beside his brother, William, and thus, Martin and Brigid moved on to raise the five Duffy sisters.

Over the next twenty years, Martin was a very busy man. In 1902, he stopped working his dairy business and moved into Tucson where in 1903 he began building a beautiful high-ceilinged, redbrick home at 505 South 4th Avenue, right on the corner of 15th Street. He worked as a guard in the jail before becoming a member of the city council, but after only about a year, he was asked to join the police force where he served for many years. He was the foreman of a chain gang, and with experience as a section boss, was put in charge of the local stockyards. He also set up his own express wagon service.

The Duffy sisters Harriet, Alice, Catherine, Myrtle, and Mary sit for a portrait. It is said that Myrtle is wearing a gingham dress because her white dress had been partially eaten by their cow, Bonnie Bell. Courtesy of James Murphy.

Martin Duffy is often mentioned in local newspapers, and was a very well-respected man with quite a sense of humor. In the *Star*, on September 1, 1905, he is quoted as saying, "After I go home from nightly rounds, I throw off my coat and take an axe and cut up a cord of wood, and following that milk the cows. Got into the habit when I was in the milk business just outside of town, but which ranch is now in town."

The Duffy girls attended St. Joseph's Academy, which was located only two blocks from their house. When the three older ones finished the eighth grade at St. Joseph's Academy, there were no high schools in Tucson, so they went on to the preparatory school at the University of Arizona where they studied for four years—the equivalent of high school now. Mary received her certificate and was out teaching after a year at the Tempe Normal School. Hattie and Alice went up to the Normal School in Flagstaff for one year and came out certified to teach. Myrtle and Catherine, the youngest of the girls, went to Tucson High School from which they graduated in 1911—the second graduating class. Catherine had been sick and missed school for a while so she went to the university and got a degree. She was the first one in the family with a degree. Myrtle went to Flagstaff Normal and, after being there for two years, was out teaching.[4]

In an interview with the *Arizona Daily Star* on February 18, 1962, the sisters shared memories of their lives in Tucson. "'We remember,' said Mrs. Harriett Murphy, 'wood wagons going by, and huge wagons with watermelons selling for ten or fifteen cents. The dog catcher used to come down the street and pick up all the dogs he saw. How we scrambled to get Carlo in so he wouldn't be picked up! One time we pulled Carlo out of the dog-catcher's wagon. We got into terrible trouble about that. I don't think there was such a thing as a dog license.'

Officer Martin Duffy. Courtesy of James Murphy.

"'Our mother cooked on a wood stove,' said Miss Duffy. 'It must have been terrible in the summer, but we didn't think anything of it. We didn't know anything different. Our house seemed cool—we have thirteen-foot ceilings. In the winter we heated the house with wood stoves in every room.'

"'We went to Saint Joseph's Academy,' said Mrs. Harriet Murphy. 'We walked to school from here and played basketball, too. The automobile has spoiled people.'

"'Social life in Tucson was pleasant and engrossing. There were many parties and everyone knew everyone else. People were very friendly,' said Mrs. Harriet Murphy. Tucson in the Duffy sisters' day was not as tough as the movies show it. 'Things seem to be worse today—all this breaking into homes,' they said. 'There were a lot of saloons, mostly on Congress Street, but saloons didn't enter into the thinking of young women of the times. There was nothing wild about them,' said Mrs. Murphy, 'but of course we didn't go into saloons.'

"'Every year on San Ysidro's Day in the spring, Mexican small ranchers went through the fields in the Santa Cruz Valley singing hymns and praying for a fruitful growing season. Somewhat as in the still-perpetuated Las Posadas, the Christmas processions, the group of singers would stop at every house, where they would be given refreshments.'

"They remember as children the sound of a violin or a guitar as their neighbors in the valley danced outdoors, the dance floor bare ground sprinkled with water to keep down the dust. They went barefoot around home in the summer, but convention dictated long black stockings (held up by round garters in disregard of the circulatory system) and high button shoes, for all other wear."

The Duffy family home in Tucson. Courtesy of James Murphy.

The family was very poor and everyone had to work hard to survive. Teaching was a profession that was very open to women and it was quite easy to get certified to begin working in the classroom. James Murphy, in an interview with Evo DeConcini, stated that the girls, "Got jobs where they could, including in Flagstaff, Jerome, Twin Buttes, Rillito, and Jaynes Railroad Station, but mostly they worked at Safford School in Tucson, where their thorough knowledge of Spanish and English came in handy. In the earlier days, they frequently traveled to their jobs on horseback."[5]

Mary, the eldest, married Thomas Collins, who was born in Ireland and worked as a railroad locomotive engineer. Tom served on the Tucson Board of Supervisors and also as a member of the Arizona legislature. Mamie, as the family called her, was very stern, whereas Tom was much more laid back. His great-grand-nephew, son of James and Alice Murphy, recalls him fondly. After Mamie passed

The Duffy sisters pose for a photo. Courtesy of the Revello family.

away, Tom remained in their home on 9th Avenue, near the University of Arizona. James reflects that Uncle Tom loved to irritate his sisters-in-law. Tom used to drag the garden hose into the kitchen and spray everything down, including the cabinets, when he wanted to clean the kitchen.

Prior to her marriage in 1928, Mary Duffy taught a total of twenty-one years and a few of those were at the Twin Buttes School.

Harriet Duffy met and married logging superintendent Patrick J. Murphy in Flagstaff. Pat had also been born in Ireland. They lived in Flagstaff for many years where he was a logging superintendent, and Hattie taught at the Flagstaff Normal School. Hattie, the last living of the five Duffy sisters, taught in Tucson for many years, but also spent some time in the rural schools, including Baboquivari on King's Ranch.

Alice Duffy married James Sylvester Murphy, who was not related in any way to her brother-in-law Pat. James worked for the railroad as a brakeman and passed away from bronchopneumonia in 1923 when their son, James Martin Murphy, who eventually became an attorney in Tucson, was only five years of age. James was the only grandchild of Martin and Brigid Duffy. In his DeConcini interview, he said about the Duffy sisters, "They went down the street, almost Indian file and kept a pretty close watch over me. Once, when I was about seven, I got away from them, hopped on the side of a streetcar and fell under it. I lost three toes on my left foot, so that made my family watch me every step." After James died, Alice and her young son moved in with Martin, Brigid, and Myrtle. She and Myrtle taught school and cared for their parents until their deaths in 1926 and 1928. Alice eventually became the principal of Elizabeth Borton School.

Ida Myrtle Duffy never married. According to the *Tucson Citizen* on May 17, 1977, "Miss Duffy retired in 1958 after 43 years of teaching in Tucson School District 1, thirty-six of which were at Safford Elementary School." While attending Tucson High School, Myrtle was quite a basketball star, playing forward on the women's team."

Catherine's husband was Edward Foy, who worked for Twin Buttes Mining Company. Catherine's health was fragile for much of her life, but it didn't stop her from working. Her second and third years of teaching were spent at Twin Buttes. This is undoubtedly where she initially met

The Duffy sisters Harriet, Mary, Alice, Catherine, and Ida with flag at the Duffy School dedication in 1954. Courtesy of James Murphy.

Ed Foy, whom she married in June of 1919. When she moved to Tucson to teach for the 1918–19 school year, she was the head teacher for the Mansfield School third grade. In 1939, she was named "Arizona's rural teacher of the year." Catherine Duffy Foy was a source of stability to hundreds of children who passed through the school at Twin Buttes, but she actually made a difference to rural children far beyond that small town. For a number of years, she taught the children from the McGee Ranch Sierrita School. She was also there for the students of the Zinc School when the districts merged. Her legacy lives on in the Sahuarita area.

Ed and Catherine Foy with their animals at Blackacre Ranch.
Courtesy of James Murphy.

In an interview published by the *Arizona Daily Star* on August 24, 1952, reporter John Farh asked the Duffy sisters some candid questions. "Her sisters agreed when Mrs. Collins named as the most important event in the past history of Tucson schools the arrival of the first school nurse about 1910. She was Catherine Kraft, educated in public health in Germany and in the United States, and she faced some terrible flu and smallpox epidemics in Tucson.

"'A great improvement over the years has been in library facilities for school children in Tucson,' the sisters remarked. 'Boys and girls in Tucson schools have been pretty much the same fundamentally during the span of years they have been teaching,' the Duffy sisters believe. 'You must like children to be a success in teaching for many years,' Miss Ida Duffy declared."

In December of 1954, an elementary school at East 5th Street and North Rosemont Avenue was named in their honor—Duffy Elementary. All combined, it is said that the Duffy sisters spent over 140 years serving the children of Southern Arizona schools.

~ Contributed by Monica Lee Elam Christiansen

NOTES

References

1. Parker, John L. "Twin Buttes Story Mostly about Foy." *Arizona Republic*. June 17, 1962.
2. Ibid.
3. *Arizona Daily Star*. "Edward Foy, 62, Claimed by Death." November 10, 1948.
4. Murphy, James M. *Evo DeConcini Oral History Project: Arizona Legal History*. Arizona Historical Society Library & Archives, Tucson. Oral history interview. May 18, 1988, AV 0399: 1–11.
5. Ibid.

Additional resources

Arizona Daily Star. "Dedication, Discipline Was Duffy Technique." May 13, 1976.
Campbell, Barbara. "Five Duffy Sisters Signify Teaching Service to City." *Arizona Daily Star*, February 18, 1962.

Ernenwein, Leslie. "Low Ebb: In 1912, Mining Was Makeshift." *Tucson Daily Citizen*, February 14, 1962.

Farh, John. "Duffy Sisters Represent 140 Years of Teaching." *Arizona Daily Star*, August 24, 1952.

Gallego Family

Casimiro Gallego was born in March of 1854 in Ímuris, Sonora, Mexico. He married Maria Antonio Martinez Lopez, born June 13, 1866, in Ures, Sonora, Mexico, on the November 12, 1888, in Saint Augustine's Church, Tucson, Territory of Arizona. They had seven children: Dolores (1887), Florencio (1892), Rosario (1894), Casimiro (1900), Antonia (1905), Carlota (1908), and Genovia (1911).

In 1900, the family was living in Hartt's Precinct No. 9 near the James Kilroy Brown and Jesus Felix families in Sahuarita. Casimiro was working as a freighter and indicated that he had come to the United States in 1875.

On May 7, 1913, Dolores Gallego married Antonio Bonillas. On January 8, 1914, Florencio married Maria Mercedes Heredia Villa, a nineteen-year-old Magdalena native. Rosario married Maria Jesus Celaya Bustamante on June 20, 1919. Antonia married Pedro Gastelum on June 22, 1925, Manuel Ochoa Burrell on June 21, 1935, and Jose Maria Bernal on March 18, 1944. Genoveva married Manuel Bermudez on July 29, 1931.

In 1920, the Gallego family was living on the east side of the Nogales Highway in Sahuarita. Casimiro was a rancher who was employing all of his sons on the family ranch. Antonio Navarro,

Antonia, Rosario, Casimiro, Florencio, Casimiro Sr., and Dolores Gallego celebrate Lola's (Dolores) First Communion in 1901. Courtesy of the Gallego family.

another well-known area rancher, was living next door and working on Casimiro's Ranch.

Casimiro Gallego named his property the Rancho Casa Blanca and built a large white house for his family to live in. The Gallego family owned an extensive amount of land. According to grandson Federico, their holdings had once stretched from the Mexico Way Station on the south to Pima Mine Road on the north. Property that later became the Lee Moor Ranch No. 2 was once a part of the Gallego family ranch.

Casimiro also owned a section of land around Santo Tomas where the Anamax Park is located today. The land was eventually divided up amongst family members after grandfather Casimiro passed away.

By 1930, seventy-six-year-old Casimiro, along with his wife and daughter, Genovia, were living in Tucson at 578 South Meyer Street.

Casimiro died on December 22, 1934, and was buried in the San Xavier Cemetery on the following day. Antonia died in Tucson on February 17, 1949, and was buried two days later, also in the San Xavier Cemetery.

Florencio Gallego married Maria Mercedes Heredia Villa at El Bajío (Casa Blanca) Ranch. Mercedes was born in Magdalena, Mexico, on

Casimiro, Rosario, and Florencio Gallego in a somber portrait taken circa 1919. Courtesy of the Gallego family.

Gallego family photo with Maria Antonia Martinez Lopez Gallego on the left. Courtesy of the Gallego family.

September 21, 1895. They had thirteen children: Guadalupe (1914), Maria Cruz (1916), Florencio (1917), Trinidad (1917), Antonia (1920), Francisco (1921), Lydia (1923), Lola (1926), Casimiro (1928), Delia (1930), Jesus (1932), Miguel (1935), and Armando (1938).

On December 4, 1912, Florencio Gallego made a homestead entry and on February 12, 1918, he provided five-year proof to establish his official claim to this land with witnesses Antonio Navarro, Casimiro Gallego, Francisco Felix, and Gabino Altamirano, all of Tucson. This property was west of the Santa Cruz Valley where his father's property was located. Florencio settled in the northern foothills of the Sierrita Mountains near other ranches owned by Venturo Maldonado, Rafael Peyron, Jose Maria Quiroz, and Francisco Garcia. His ranch, southwest of the San Xavier Mission near Helmet Peak, was called La Sierra, and later, El Ocotillo. Land records show Florencio homesteading over 792 acres between 1919 and 1959. In addition, he also held a lease to Arizona State Trust land.

The Florencio Gallego ranch property was located in the boundaries of the small Zinc School District where the Gallego children attended school on the mine property. Most of their classmates were children of area mine workers.

In the *Arizona Daily Star*, the "Zinc Zippers" column was penned by young reporter, Concha Coronado. The Gallego family was mentioned a number of times between 1935 and 1937:

"Our Christmas program was held at night on December 20, 1935. We gave a play of five tableaus . . . Third Tableau: Dolores Coronado, tap dancer; Lupe Maldonado, Ernesto Coronado, Cruz Vindiola, Frank Gallego, Romelia Coronodo, Francisco Maldonado, Armida Barredaz, Max Sainz, Concha Coronado, Lorenz Barredaz, dancers in the Virginia Reel. Fourth Tableau: Frank Gallego, janitor." (December 22, 1935)

Florencio and Mercedes Gallego pose for a wedding photo on January 8, 1914. Courtesy of the Gallego family.

Florencio Gallego homestead notice for publication on January 11, 1918, in the Arizona Daily Star.

"We had a Valentine dance Friday, February 14. We had chocolate cake, popcorn, and marshmallows for refreshments. We had a nice time. We had a Valentine box. The 4-H girls decorated it. The following attended the dance: Victoria Parra, Socorro Parra, Lupe Maldonado, Josefina Parra, Romelia Coronado, Concha Coronado, Miss Schneider, Reuben Sainz, Reynaldo Carreraz, Jesus Ortega, Ernesto Coronado, Frank Gallego, Francisco Maldonado, and Max Sainz." (February 16, 1936)

"The little boys from 10 years down, made a little play house. They go and eat their luncheon there. They, too, put up an old mailbox and when the mailman passed by, he stopped there. He took off the mailbox. Ernesto Coronado, one of the school boys, made a pair of stilts. Sometimes the other boys who walk on them fall down. They [have lots] of fun. The height is six feet, six inches. Frank Gallego and Ernesto Coronodo, our two eighth graders, went to the rodeo." (March 1, 1936)

Casimiro, Concepcion, and Francisco Gallego. Courtesy of the Gallego family.

Jesus Celaya and Rosario Gallego. Courtesy of the Gallego family.

"Martiriano Ramirez and Casimiro Gallego, two first graders, entered our school a week ago. The little boys made some stilts for themselves. They copied the big boys. They use any old kind of sticks, a rock for a hammer, and wires to keep their feet in place. They fall off more than they walk." (March 8, 1936)

"Lydia Gallego, a 7th grade pupil, entered our school Monday, March 16th. She came from Safford school. Our meeting was held Monday, March 16th, at 4:30 at Miss Schneider's house . . . Lydia Gallego, a new club member, has started on her dish towel." (March 22, 1936)

"Lydia Gallego has finished her woven square. A cow of Mr. Gallego has twin calves. They are so pretty." (March 19, 1936)

"Cruz Vindiola and Lydia Gallego are patching a stocking. Mr. Gallego gave a tiny puppy to Mr. Coronado. His name is Sandy." (April 6, 1936)

Mercedes Gallego and six of her children pose with their grandmother for a photo. Courtesy of the Gallego family.

"Frank Gallego has been bringing his guitar and we have been singing at recess to amuse ourselves." (April 19, 1936)

"We plan to have a local achievement day on May 20, when we have graduation. The following boys will graduate: Ernesto Coronado and Frank Gallego. This is the first time as far as we know that our school had anyone graduate from the eighth grade. We are going to have a program. We will have refreshments served by the 4-H club girls. Afterwards we will have a dance." (May 4, 1936)

1936 Zinc Zippers 4-H club, with Miss Schneider in the back, pose with their award for garment making. "At the completion of their first year of work, one of their individuals made the highest score made by a single individual in one year's work." Courtesy of University of Arizona Special Collections.

The Zinc Zipper 4-H club exhibit displayed on April 18, 1936. "This small group of only seven members made the second-highest average per member in Pima County and was given second place in publicity." Courtesy of University of Arizona Special Collections.

Maria Carmen, Federico, and Ricardo Gallego. Courtesy of the Gallego family.

"Max Sainz and Lolita Gallego entered our school Monday, May 4. There were in town so they could make their first holy communion." (May 11, 1936)

"Sunday, May 17, Mrs. Coronado and her children went to Mr. and Mrs. Gallego's house. They went horseback riding." (May 25, 1936)

"The Maldonados, Reuben Sainz, Mauro Trejo, and Florencio Gallego are picking cotton at Sahuarita." (September 13, 1936)

Florencio Gallego shared the following memories of El Ocotillo, "As kids we played war in the arroyo and used dry horse-poop balls as ammo to throw at each side. There was a barbed-wire fence between the fox holes on either side of the fence. Panino would drop us younger cousins off at the ranch and leave the older cousins and younger uncles to look after us. Junior Padilla had a scrapbook where he would keep track of lizards, snakes, and other small animals around the ranch. In the late 1940s, I remember Johnny and Joe Badilla, Frankie Gallego, Lalito, and Mike and Armando Gallego being there. There used to be two old Victrolas in the house and we slept on the floor on homemade Levi denim mats. There were saddles hanging from the ceiling. At roundup time, the older uncles would brand the new calves and cook "mountain oysters" on the branding fire. We also got to buck on the calves as little kids.

Florencio Gallego standing with Mercedes Heredia Gallego. Courtesy of the Gallego family.

"Later, when I was about twelve or thirteen, my father would take me and my brother rabbit hunting at El Ocotillo. He would skin and clean the rabbit meat and cook it over a campfire. We also went dove hunting at the ranch. There was a *represo* [reservoir] that held rainwater on the southeast side of the house and birds would fly in. I remember my father would invite his brothers-in-law, uncles on my mother's side, and my cousins, Freddie and Armando Palafox. They would saddle the horses and go hunting on horseback. I remember Tio Gurreito Gallego killing a

Maria Jesus Celaya Gallego sitting by the ranch windmill. Courtesy of the Gallego family.

javelina while hunting on horseback and later I saw him skin it and fix the meat for barbecuing. Picko Blanco is the only horse name I can remember from the ranch. There were a few horses that weren't broken in for riding.

"I remember Panino roping horses when I was about eight years old and he would *amansarlos* [break them in] by himself. He was probably in his mid-fifties then. I also remember a big party that was held at the ranch where there were *tinas* [galvanized tubs] full of ice and beer and sodas. There were many people there. Maybe it was a wedding celebration or birthday."

Working the cattle on the Rosario Gallego family ranch. Courtesy of the Gallego family.

Selina Barajas wrote, "The ranch was known as a place of herding, roping, and branding cattle but also a place for family, roundups, and fiestas." Florencio's daughter, Lydia, recalled that, "Both Florencio and Mercedes loved to dance *rancheras* and *chotis*. In 1935, during the Great Depression era, they moved to South Tucson and had a business selling wood and would go back and forth to the ranch until they sold it in 1959."

Many members of the family remained in the Tucson area. Mercedes passed away on April 9, 1970, and Florencio soon followed on May 1, 1972. Both are buried in Holy Hope Cemetery.

Rosario Gallego portrait. Courtesy of the Gallego family.

Rosario Gallego married Maria Jesus Celaya Bustamonte on June 20, 1919, in Pitiquito, Sonora Mexico, the town of Maria's birth on November 22, 1899. Rosario and Maria had eight children: Casimiro (1920), Concepcion (1921), Rosario (1922), Francisco (1926), Maria Carmen (1928), Jose (1932), Federico (1937), and Ricardo (1940).

Rosario was a lifelong cowboy and worked on ranches in the Sahuarita area. One of the ranchers he worked for was Mike Torrington. Mike's property was in the area west of what was Pima Mine. At that time, pay for cowboys was one dollar per day and they were expected to provide their own horses and equipment.

On February 11, 1935, Rosario, who had on October 24, 1929, made a Stock-Raising Homestead Entry, filed his notice of intention to make final five-year proof to establish claim on his land. Witnesses were Ramon Felix, Roy Brown, Alberto Villa, and Ramon Soto, all residents of Sahuarita.

Rosario often herded cattle to and from Mexico. Cattle were sold or auctioned in Tucson. Rosario's son, Federico, recalls that his dad's herds were as many as five hundred head of cattle at a time. Rosario owned seventy-five acres where the Rancho Casa

Rosario Gallego on horseback. Courtesy of the Gallego family.

Casimiro standing in the doorway of his tent. Courtesy of the Gallego family.

Blanca foundation stands today. He also owned a section of land around where Anamax Park is located in Santo Tomas. Two of Rosario's sons, Casimiro and Francisco, served in World War II.

Casimiro, born May 6, 1920 in Pitiquito, Mexico, was working on the Lee Moor Ranch No. 2 when he registered for the draft. He enlisted as a private in the United States Army on November 16, 1945, at Camp Campbell, Hopkinsville, Kentucky.

When Francisco, born May 22, 1926, in Tucson, registered for the draft, he, like his brother, was also employed on the Lee Moor Ranch No. 2, with his supervisor being Clyde E. Gaines. He enlisted as a private in the United States Army on February 16, 1942, at Fort Bliss in El Paso, Texas, and was discharged on January 2, 1946.

Rosario's son, Federico, still lives on the Casa Blanca Ranch property in a home that was built by his grandfather, Casimiro. He remembers his dad's building a house across Old Nogales Highway, the main road. In his younger years, Nogales Highway, west of the railroad, was wide enough for only one car, but he recalls the expansion and paving. His older brothers worked on the road crew.

Federico and his siblings went to Sahuarita Elementary School. The school bus, a vehicle so small that some students were forced to stand due to lack of seating, picked them up by the house. During and after rains, the bus would often get stuck in the mud or sand, requiring the students to disembark and push out the bus.

In 1943, when Federico started school, he had to walk to the Nogales Highway to meet the school bus. Often he did not want to go to school, so he spent the day hiding under the bridge. Then he would walk home after the school bus passed by in the afternoon.

Erlinda Gastelum Gallego, Frank Gallego, and Lydia Gallego Santa Cruz pose near the water. Courtesy of the Gallego family.

Florencio and Mercedes Heredia Gallego with twelve of their thirteen children. Courtesy of the Gallego family.

Because he started school late, Federico was older than his friends in the same grade. They were Maria Ortega, Eugene Olivas, Margaret Gonzales, Sarah Camacho, and Arturo Gomez.

At that time, Mr. Gregory was principal and he taught a class. Mrs. Burrel, Mrs. Black, Mrs. Irvin (Lee), and Porter Wilson were the other teachers.

Federico did not attend school after the seventh grade. Instead, he went to work to help support the family.

In 1956, Federico was working in the cotton gin in Sahuarita when a terrible accident happened. He was up on the grinding machine when one of the "teeth" got hold of the jacket he was wearing. Slowly the machine started wheeling him in. One of his coworkers noticed what was going on and immediately ran to shut the machine off, but by the time the gears stopped turning, his left hand was stuck in the machine. Three of his fingers, middle, ring, and pinkie, were severed.

The owner rushed him to Tucson to the County Hospital on South 6th Avenue. Upon arrival, Federico was unconscious from the loss of blood. When he woke up, his arm was bandaged and he was told about the loss of his three fingers.

The injury did not stop him from living a full life and taking care of his family. He continued playing his guitar, driving a car, and working the 72 acres of property his father, Rosario, left him.

~ Contributed by Oscar Gomez and Monica Lee Elam Christiansen

Federico Celaya Gallego and Martha Valenzuela Gallego with their dog Bandit and daughters Rosario Gallego and Alejandrina Gallego de Santa Maria. Courtesy of Yolanda Gallego Mariscal.

NOTES

Arizona Daily Star, Tucson, Arizona.

Barajas, Selina. *Gallego Family—Tucson's Original Vaqueros*. Retrieved January 28, 2022, from https://mireinaboutique. wordpress.com/tag/gallego-family

Tucson Citizen, Tucson, Arizona.

Gallego, Florencio. Personal memories shared by the Gallego family.

Oscar Gomez: My Story in Sahuarita

My family moved to the Sahuarita area in the early 1950s. I did not fully realize until recently that the Sahuarita area has quite a history that predates my family's arrival. Some of the "old families" have been living here for a very long time.

I came to Sahuarita at the approximate age of five. Recalling conversations with family members, I know that we came from Texas, southeast of El Paso, along the Rio Grande River, between Clint and Fabens. In researching my family, I learned that my father, Gumercindo Gómez, was born on the January 13, 1901, in San Miguel el Alto, Jalisco, Mexico. He left home during the Mexican Revolution when he was very young. He just started walking north and came to the United States when he was in his late teens or early twenties. The rest of his

Christmas for Oscar at age thirteen. Courtesy of Oscar Gomez.

family stayed in Mexico. I know Antonio Cortezar, his nephew, gave him money to take the train into Mexico to visit his family after World War II. He went, but upon his return, he never spoke of that visit and, to my knowledge, never returned to Mexico again.

My father married his first wife, Bersabe Acuña, around 1927 in Anthony, New Mexico. She had three daughters with a previous husband, Francisco Estrada—Juliana, Elvira, and Virginia, all of whom were born in Durango, Mexico. Juliana married Maximo Madrid. She passed away on June 15, 1937, just fourteen days after giving birth to her daughter, Maria Eva Madrid. Elvira married Juan Duenas Galvan and they had five children together. Juan was killed in an accident on Lee Moor Ranch No. 1 in Fabens, Texas, on May 30, 1950, and in 1969, Elvira remarried to Juan Delgado Medrano. Virginia died in February of 1930 when the family was in Anthony, New Mexico. She was only five years old when her clothing caught fire while the children were playing near open flames.

Gumercindo and Guadalupe Batista Gomez pose for a photo on their wedding day. Courtesy of Oscar Gomez.

Together, my father and Bersabe had four children: Alicia (born in 1928 in Texas), Alfredo (born in 1929 in Anthony, New Mexico), Felipa (born in 1932 in Juarez, Mexico), and Arturo (born in 1939 in Fabens, Texas).

In the late 1930s, Bersabe went to Mexico and returned with three of her sister Francisca's children: Anthony Cortazar who was about fourteen years old, and his half-siblings, Carmen and Manuel Guzman, who were nine and seven. The youngest, Alicia, died as a baby in Mexico. I am not sure why these children came to Lee Moor Ranch No. 1 to live with my family, but my father treated them as his own. Even after Bersabe died, Francisca's children remained a part of our family.

Looking back, my father definitely had a tendency to move quite frequently, but overall, he spent the majority of his years on the Lee Moor Ranch in Fabens. His first wife, Bersabe, died of a heart attack on Lee Moor Ranch No. 1 in April of 1942. She was only forty-two years old.

My father met my mother, Guadalupe Portillo Batista, and they were married in September of 1944. I have no memories of my mother, but from photos, I know she was tall and very beautiful. She was born into the large family of Antonio Barrera Batista and Mercedes Portillo on March 17, 1917, in Sisoguichi, Chihuahua, Mexico. Her brother, Antonio Portillo Batista, worked at Lee Moor Ranch No. 1 in the '30s and '40s before eventually opening his own small grocery store in Fabens. I remember my sister taking me to visit him when I was very small, but, aside from that brief contact, I never was acquainted with my mother's family.

I was born on November 24, 1945, in Clint, Texas. By that time, my sister, Alicia, was married to Roberto Acuna Estrada and they had two daughters, Maria and Olga. I was the only child from my dad's second marriage. My mother died in August of 1947 when she was only thirty years old. I was two years old at the time. Before her death, she begged my sisters to promise to take care of me. They never forgot that promise.

I have no recollection of living on the Lee Moor Ranch in Fabens, but my two older sisters, Alicia and Felipa, met their husbands Ramon Estrada and Juan Lopez there. My brothers-in-law were raised in the same small Mexican town of San Augustine, just across the Rio Grande from Lee Moor Ranch No. 1.

Mr. Massey worked on Lee Moor Ranch No. 1 in Fabens, Texas, at the same time that Roberto and Juan were there. Their children remember being told that Mr. Massey was responsible for their coming to work on the Lee Moor Ranch No. 2 in Sahuarita around 1950.

My sister, Felipa, was sixteen years old when my mother died. Felipa took responsibility for taking care of me and my brother Arturo, who was six years older than me. Felipa married Juan Lopez in 1949. Approximately two years later, they also came to live at Lee Moor Ranch in Sahuarita. Arturo and I had originally stayed in Texas with our father, but in 1951 our sisters took a Greyhound bus trip to Texas and brought us to the farm in Arizona.

Guadalupe Batista Gomez in October of 1945. Courtesy of Oscar Gomez.

When we arrived in Sahuarita, Arturo and I lived with Felipa and Juan. I recall living in a two-room house on the ranch. One room was the kitchen and the other was a bedroom for my sister, her husband, and their daughter, Delia. This was the first time I had my own bed to sleep in. Arturo and I had identical army cots that we unfolded each night in the kitchen.

Felipa would prepare meals on a small two-burner kerosene stove. Every morning I would awake to the smell of that kerosene stove as she was preparing breakfast. I quickly developed an intense dislike of kerosene.

Lee Moor Ranch in Sahuarita was an exciting place for a young boy to live. There were lots of large families with plenty of kids to play with. There were also a lot of adults with widely varying personalities. I also remember that there seemed to be a lot of other families from Texas.

Armando Estrada; Delia Lopez holding Juan Lopez and Javier Lopez; Oscar Gomez with Laura Lopez and Jamie Estrada. This was taken at the west end of the current pecan plant. The house in the background burned down due to children playing with matches and was never rebuilt. The Johnson family lived there for several years. Their daughter, Barbara, was a year ahead of me and was a dwarf. Everyone in her class respected her—she was smarter than most students. The family left the Sahuarita Ranch after their home burned down. Courtesy of Oscar Gomez.

My first two memorable spankings took place at Lee Moor Ranch No. 2. One day, I was having fun on top of the haystack close to our house. I started pushing hay bales off of the top of the towering stack. It was fun to see them burst and spread as they hit the ground. My brother-in-law, Juan, caught me and he didn't think it was nearly as funny as I did. Part of his job was to water, cut, bale, and stack the alfalfa, so I was undoing his hours of hard work.

The second time, I must have found myself with far too much time on my hands and nothing constructive with which to occupy myself. I was wandering around the shop area where the tractors had been lined up for the night. I decided to explore and found that all of them had the keys left in the ignition switches. I went down the row, climbing up onto each tractor, and turning the ignition key to the on position. Of course, when the men got to work the next day, they discovered that none of the tractors would start because all of the batteries were dead. One of the observant adults recalled seeing me in that area the previous evening. I confessed when asked what I had done, not knowing what the consequences would be, but I surely did not mess around on the tractors again.

Juan may have had to discipline me, but he also did many fun things for me during those years. Often he would catch bunnies as he harvested the alfalfa. He would bring them home in his lunch pail. He built a wire cage so I could keep the rabbits for a few days. After that, he insisted the bunnies had to be returned to their natural environment.

Most of the work on Lee Moor Ranch No. 2 was centered around cotton. During harvesting time, my brothers-in-law drove the cotton pickers. Once, my nephew Ramon and I were put into a picker's large cotton basket. We had fun jumping around. As the cotton pickers moved through the fields, cotton was blown in and the baskets filled up. The real treat was at the end of each row when the cotton basket was dumped into the cotton trailer. It was exhilarating for us to roll out with the cotton and land in the back of the cushioned trailer.

While living on Lee Moor Ranch No. 2, I started first grade at the Sahuarita School. The school bus did not come onto the Lee Moor property to pick us up. We had to walk out to the Nogales Highway, at least three-eighths of a mile away. One year geese were being raised in the fields near our house. We had to walk between the two fields where the geese were living. Some of them got into a routine of following us to the bus each morning, honking all the way to the stop. We thought it was fun to have them coming along with us on our walk.

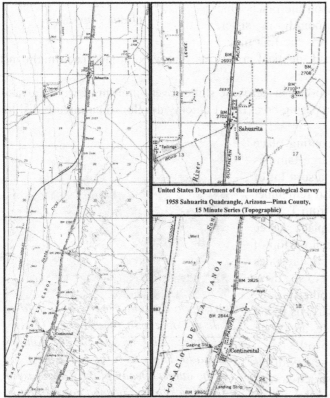

Survey map. Courtesy of U.S. Department of the Interior. Edited by Monica Lee Elam Christiansen.

In the afternoon, on the return trip, the route was different. We would walk by the first three houses on our way home. The lady who lived in the first house, probably Mrs. Massey, would sometimes be outside tending her rose bushes. If she saw us, she would call us over to her and give us each a few roses to take home.

Around Christmas time of the year that I was in third grade, we moved away from the Lee Moor Ranch. Many of the other families were also leaving. Why we moved is still a mystery to me and I never thought to ask why everyone was leaving Lee Moor.

Juan Lopez moved our family to Sahuarita Ranch, then owned by Harris Ranch, in the winter of 1954. The home available for us was on the Old Nogales Highway (now Santa Rita Road), surrounded by huge cottonwood trees. The house was an old adobe building built up off the ground. My sister, Felipa, told me the kitchen floor had many boards missing. Down below, there were imprints of a heavy box or chest. The imprints were two feet by three feet and almost three inches deep. She surmised that the chest must have been full of coins in order to make it heavy enough to leave such a mark. She had heard stories that such treasures were common in Arizona. To me it was a spooky story and I had difficulty believing it. Later I learned that during the depression, people distrusted banks so they buried or hid their money. I guess there probably was some truth to her theory.

The home we moved into was located just east of the old Sahuarita Elementary School, and the first time I had to walk to school, I discovered that the most direct way to get there was through a plowed field. We lived in that house only a short time. By the end of the summer, we had moved to another house and I didn't have to walk through the fields.

At Sahuarita Ranch, I had my first experience picking cotton by hand. It was a family affair on Saturdays. I went with an older sister and her children. We all carried small sacks or we just made mounds of cotton for the older pickers to collect. My sister's cotton sack was at least eight feet long. Picking cotton started in late September when the cotton plants were still too green for mechanical pickers. Hand picking continued through December, even though machines were also picking by that time. I always looked forward to Christmas vacation so I could make a little extra money for myself.

Oscar leans his bike against Arturo's car while little Juanito Lopez looks on in January of 1959. Courtesy of Oscar Gomez.

In later years, my sister suffered from dementia. In one of my many visits with her, I showed her a picture of a cotton field in Marana. Her eyes sparkled with old memories. Her body twitched and, sitting up straight, she asked, "Can we go pick cotton? I will make mounds of cotton for you to put in your cotton sack!" "Whoa!" I said. "We are not reversing roles. I used to make the mounds and you dragged the sack!" "OK," she replied, "but you will have to be there to take the stack up the ladder and empty it into the cotton trailer." "It's a deal," I agreed, and she smiled.

I was a poor, inefficient cotton picker. From the time I started until the age of seventeen, the pay for cotton was three cents a pound. That was the age when I finally picked a hundred pounds for the day. Three dollars! That was plenty for the week! At the time, sodas were ten cents, candy bars cost five cents, hamburgers were five for a dollar, and gas was eighteen cents a gallon.

Cotton trailers after a storm. Courtesy of Oscar Gomez.

My first real paycheck came from Farmers Investment Co. (FICO) when, at the age of thirteen, my nieces and I formed a cotton chopping crew. FICO had just acquired the Sahuarita farm. They felt it best to keep the kids busy working instead of having them running around the farm being mischievous and destructive. We were dropped off at 6:00 a.m. at the cotton fields with hoes, a file to sharpen the hoes, and our lunches. We were told to hoe out weeds growing among the cotton plants, and we worked until 4:30 p.m.

Mr. Booker Musgrove was an African-American who had been made supervisor over the farm's large cotton chopping crew. He provided transportation and water for all individuals, local or from Tucson, who were there to work. Pay for them, as for us, was sixty cents an hour. Mr. Booker, as he was known to us, also supervised the cotton pickers in the fall. Students that I met at Pueblo High School related their tales of coming to Sahuarita to chop or pick cotton. They could not understand how we survived under such horrible working conditions all those years!

Summers were endlessly long and unbearably hot, as we worked six days a week. On one hot July Saturday afternoon, we were complaining and disgruntled about the long week when all of a sudden my nose started bleeding. It would not stop. Maria Estrada suggested I lie down alongside the irrigation ditch so she could splash water on my face. She hoped cooling my body temperature down would stop the bleeding. All of a sudden, Mr. Keith Walden appeared in his car. It was not unusual for him to drive through the farms to check on things when he was home. He asked what was going on and then proceeded to use his two-way radio to contact Roberto Estrada to come and take us home. Roberto arrived quickly and he was very irritated, thinking that Mr. Walden had caught us goofing off! We quickly explained what had happened and he loaded us into the truck. Awesome! We were happy campers getting to go home.

We never could duplicate the nose bleeding incident to get us out of the cotton fields, but we got similar results from July and August monsoons. It was not fun when we realized how cold summer rain could be. Sometimes the storms brought gusting winds and occasionally we were pelted by hail! We found that, once we were wet, it took quite a while to dry off and get warm. Eventually, one of the foremen would come by to check on us and give us a ride home for the day.

Another summer, we were spraying weeds that were growing alongside the irrigation ditches. There were three of us on this crew. One would drive the vehicle holding the pesticide tank while the other two walked alongside with four long hoses to spray weeds. Border patrol agents were common in the Sahuarita area. On that day, as we were parked beside the railroad tracks filling the tank up with weed oil, a border patrol agent approached us.

Oscar, while in Vietnam, poses for a photo in his jeep. Courtesy of Oscar Gomez.

My brother-in-law, Juan, had always told me to be respectful if ever confronted by one of the agents. Remembering his words, I said, "Good morning," before he even had a chance to start talking. The agent started speaking to me in Spanish and I answered all the questions in Spanish. "Are you an American citizen? Where do you live? How about your buddies? Where do they live? Do you go to school?" "Yes," was the simple answer to most of his questions. "Where do you go to school?" he grilled. Again, I politely answered, "Pueblo High School in Tucson." Then he asked, "Why are you speaking in Spanish to me?" I said, "Well, you started in Spanish and so I followed you." He looked irritated but turned away and left.

About nine years later I was approached by border patrol agents again. In April of 1971, I had just returned from Vietnam, having been discharged after two long years of service. I had committed to a teaching job at Eloy Junior High School in Eloy, Arizona. I was living on the farm for the summer and spent most of my time in the welding shop. I was bent forward, with the hood over my face, when I sensed that someone had walked into the shop. I was surprised to feel a tap on my shoulder. Shocked, I pulled the hood up, and, much to my surprise, it was a border patrol agent. Before I could say anything, he blurted out in a terse tone, "Are you an American citizen?" For a moment, my brain spun as I contemplated which language to use to answer his question—English, Spanish, or Army—the latter being a rich barrage of rapid-fire "military words."

I disregarded what Juan had taught me about always presenting a respectful demeanor and I let loose in my wonderfully, descriptive army jargon. "Mister! I just got out of the army and Vietnam. Not one [*obscenity*] time did any [*obscenity*] one ever ask me that [*obscenity*] question! I am a [*obscenity*] American Citizen! Now don't you ever step in this [*obscenity*] shop again! If you do, I am [*obscenity*] going to call my [*obscenity*] senator and complain about you [*obscenity*] guys harassing me!"

He left quickly, but quite a few times after that, I would see agents slowly driving by the shop but never stopping. One day I had to leave the shop for a few hours so I left Tony, the undocumented welder from Guaymas, Mexico, alone to continue working. Upon my return, he was gone. Over the radio, I inquired about Tony's whereabouts and no one had seen him or taken him to a different job site. Two days later, Tony reappeared. In my absence, the border patrol agents had come to the shop. They had picked him up and eventually took him to Nogales where he was released and told not to return. Tony was an excellent, experienced welder and an asset to the company. Some time before Christmas that year, Tony left Sahuarita and never returned again. It was a great loss for FICO.

An aerial view of the FICO pecan trees and the Santa Rita Mountains. Courtesy of the Walden family.

In 1962, FICO decided to build a gin for the next cotton harvest season. It was to be constructed in the same building that Harris Ranch had used for their cotton gin. Toops Culbertson surprised me when he told me I was going to spend the summer working on the gin site. Wow! The gin site was no more than seventy-five yards behind my house. I could come home for lunch! No more getting hot and sweaty! It was also at this time that I met Dick Walden, who was on summer vacation from college. My friendship with him has been a great one since that time.

The following season I was taught to drive a cotton picker, a cotton cultivator, and to work with other farm equipment. The gentleman who taught me to drive a cultivator and picker was an African-American individual—one for whom I had great respect since his earliest days in Sahuarita. His name was Eugene Murray.

When Mr. Murray and I were on the back of the truck together, he would relate stories to me about things he remembered. He shared with me the many times my sister Felipa would drive around the farm with the young 'uns trying to find Juan at lunchtime. Juan insisted he wanted a warm lunchtime meal. Felipa was always asking Mr. Murray, "Where is Juan and his tractor?" I knew that to be the case! When I would come home from school at lunchtime, as did many students who lived close to the school, I ate a plate of food that Felipa had left on the table and then returned to school. I was usually alone because Felipa was out looking for Juan to take him his food.

In the late 1960s, Mr. Murray's wife had a stroke. Mr. Murray asked if he could have Sundays off to help his wife. Juan told him he could, but that he still needed to have his tractor running on Sundays. Mr. Murray asked if I could drive his cultivator on those Sundays. After that season, his wife got worse. They left the farm and moved to Rillito to be close to their sons.

While still in high school, I took welding classes. Toops found out what I was doing and arranged for me to work in the welding shop with Cliff Hammond. Clifford and his family were from Salmon, Idaho. Cliff was tops in his profession. Working for him, I learned many practical techniques, and he was always willing to share. During the school year, the high school bus would get us home before 4 p.m. The shop was across the street from our house so, from 4–7 p.m., Wally, Cliff's son, and I would put in three hours completing any jobs Cliff had left for us.

Cliff and his family left Sahuarita in 1966. During my college years, between school and other jobs on the farm, I spent an enormous amount of time in the welding shop. The year before, 1964–65, FICO started planting pecan trees and made many changes in personnel and equipment. FICO leased farmland throughout the Santa Cruz Valley. Besides the Sahuarita and Continental Farms, the company managed workers at Midvale Farm, Baca Float (Rio Rico), Amado, Sopori, KX Ranch, Maricopa, and Lee Moor Ranch.

Some forty years later, I saw Lorell Clark, a longtime FICO employee, at a function in Tucson. He commented, "Oscar, your shop has been knocked down—demolished! It's gone!" "My shop?" I exclaimed. "When did it become my shop?" He responded, "You spent a lot of time inside that building."

The last job or project I had at FICO occurred just after graduating from the University of Arizona in January of 1969. Toops Culbertson had come up to me and asked about my reporting date for the Army. After confirming that it was April 7, 1969, I asked, "Do you have something you want me to do?" He said, "I want you to run the pecan planting crew 'til the season is completed around the first week of March."

With a crew of fifty people, 3,000 pecan trees were planted each day—six days a week! That was my last major task with FICO. After that season, FICO had 6,000 acres of pecan trees between Sahuarita and Continental farms.

Years later, I occasionally went back to visit Toops Culbertson after he retired and before he passed away. Besides my immediate family, he is on the top of my list of individuals who had a major effect on the person I have become. He was a true and important mentor, and an influential person in my life. I cherished his friendship and sincerity. When we got together, we shared many stories about the farm and different people there. He once asked if I was the only individual from the farm who graduated with a college degree. I told him that I was probably the first, but not the only one. He laughed with a large roar when I told him I was probably the only college graduate whose butt he wore out with all the tasks and jobs he had me do in those short years growing up at FICO.

In 2006, after I was fully retired, I was visiting Toops. As we sat together, he asked, "Do you ever think of coming back to work for FICO?" Surprised, I looked at him and said, "No! I grew up working for FICO and, in my mind, I feel like I never left!" He seemed satisfied with my answer because it left a thoughtful smile on his face.

Thinking back, as I put just a few of my memories on paper, there are so many events and people I know that have been left out. I spent more time with adults at Sahuarita than my peers. I am thankful for this opportunity. I have a lifetime of wonderful relationships and experiences to treasure.

~ Contributed by Oscar A. Gomez; researched and
compiled by Monica Lee Elam Christiansen

The Hernandez Family in Lee Moor and Sahuarita

Melquiades Gastelum, grandfather of Ernesto Hernandez, was born in Navajoa, Sonora, Mexico about 1893. The family frequently traveled back and forth between Mexico and the United States by way of the Nogales port of entry. On August 25, 1914, he had a son, Luis Avila Gastelum with 14-year-old Josefa (Josefina) Avila, a native of Guadalajara, Jalisco, Mexico.

Melquiades was in Southern Arizona prior to October 31, 1916, when Josefa and Luis came to Nogales from Esperanza, Sonora, to join him. For the next ten years, the family moved between Nogales and Continental, during which time, seven more children were born to the family: Luis (1914), Margarito

(1917), Carmen (1919), Francisca (1921), Aurelio (1922), Susie (1924), Romelia (1926), and Melquiades (1927).

On December 22, 1924, the Ivey-Dale-Owens Corporation, a cotton grower with a large scale operation in Fabens, Texas, signed a multiple year lease on 4,100 acres in the Santa Cruz valley where guayule growing had "proved to be a commercial failure."[1] They brought in hundreds of experienced Mexican cotton farmworkers from their Texas operation, and in July of 1925, began the process of constructing a "large six-stand cotton gin at the site of the company's buildings beside the Southern Pacific tracks."[2]

Melquiades got a job working at the Ivey-Dale-Owens gin and on November 17, 1926, tragedy struck. "Melquiades Gastelum, 36, was instantly killed . . . [in the] cotton gin at Continental [when] he was thrown violently against a large tank nearby and his head was crushed by the impact." Testimony given before a coroner's jury called by J. P. Mallory, ex officio coroner, on November 18 at Continental, revealed that, "Gastelum had been only recently employed by the Ivey-Dale-Owen company . . . He was an experienced man . . . There were no eyewitnesses to the accident. Fellow workers [were]

The old cotton gin in Continental with the Santa Rita Mountains in the background. Courtesy of Arizona Historical Society.

attracted to the scene when the gin was stopped by the breaking of a belt and the thud of Gastelum's head as it struck the tank. It was first thought that he was still alive and Gastelum was immediately brought to Tucson where it was learned he was dead. It is believed that Gastelum's jacket was caught in the pulley and he was thrown against the tank and to the floor, his left leg being drawn under the pulley, causing the belt to break."[3]

Clearing the Lee Moor farmland with a 95 H.P. Caterpillar and bulldozer.

Melquiades was buried in the Continental Cemetery. His simple, gray marble headstone in the shape of a cross reads, "Recuerdo de Melquiades Gastelum, Fallecio el 16 de Noviembre de 1926, su esposa y ninos." His sudden, tragic death left Josefa a 26-year-old widow with six young children and a seventh on the way.

In 1930, Josefa Gastelum and her children were living in the Sahuarita cotton farm camp. She was working as a wash woman while her children attended the Sahuarita School. Luis (grade 4) and Margarito (grade 3) were enrolled in R. R. Roberts's class while Carmen (grade 1a), Susie (grade 1b), and Aurelio (grade 1b) were in Helen Green's classroom.

When the 1940 U.S. census taker made her rounds, Josefa and her children were living with Jose Tapia Gonzales and his children in Sahuarita, "off of Highway 89 west of C. E. Gaines Ranch." Jose, Margarito, and Aurelio were working as farm laborers on Lee Moor Ranch No. 2, managed by Clyde E. Gaines, while Aurelio, Susie, Victoria, Frank, and Melquiades continued attending Sahuarita School in Sarah Itzweire's classroom.

Carmen Avila Gastelum, Melquiades and Josefa's daughter, met and married Joaquin Loretto Hernandez on Lee Moor Ranch No. 2 in Sahuarita. Joaquin had been born on September 1, 1910, in El Paso, Texas, to Jose Joaquin Hernandez and Petra Guitron.

On October 16, 1940, when he completed his World War II draft registration card, Joaquin was living on Lee Moor Ranch No. 2 in Sahuarita. His parents were still living on Lee Moor Ranch No. 1 in Fabens, Texas. Clyde Gaines, the Lee Moor Ranch No. 2 foreman, was listed as his employer, but was soon replaced by O'Dell Massey, whom Ernesto remembered as responsible for running the property.

Leveling the land by hand and with a 65 H. P. Caterpillar in January 1940.
Courtesy of University of Arizona Special Collections.

Joaquin was sent to Lee Moor Ranch No. 2 in Sahuarita because of his experience operating heavy equipment. Raw land north of Pima Mine Road and west of the Nogales Highway needed to be prepared for planting cotton. The farmland Joaquin cleared eventually totaled about one thousand acres.

Carlos, Carmen and Joaquin's first child, was born in February of 1941, at home on Lee Moor Ranch. Other children include Ernesto, Carmen, Pat, Joaquin, and Lucy.

In the 1950s, the Hernandez family left Lee Moor Ranch No. 2 after it was sold. They moved on to look for another job and place to live.

Ernesto married Maria Estrada, the daughter of Roberto and Alicia Gomez Estrada, another family that had come to Sahuarita from Lee Moor Ranch No. 1 in Fabens. It seems highly likely that Roberto Estrada and Juan Lopez knew the Joaquin Hernandez family in Texas.

Carmen and Joaquin spent their later years in Casa Grande where Joaquin died on January 17, 1989, and Carmen on January 3, 2008. Both are buried in Casa Grande's Mountain View Cemetery.

~ Contributed by Ernesto Hernandez and Oscar A. Gomez; researched and
compiled by Monica Lee Elam Christiansen

NOTES

1. Mactavishm, Caton. "Cotton Oil Mill to be Built and Water Output Made Larger." *Tucson Citizen*. December 23, 1924, p. 1.
2. "Ivey-Dale-Owen Co. to Build Gin." *Tucson Citizen*. June 30, 1925, p. 10.
3. "Gin Worker Caught in Belting, Killed." *Arizona Daily Star*. November 19, 1926, p. 1.

Itzweire Ranch

Ferdinand (Ferd) I. Itzweire was born December 20, 1893, in Missoula, Montana, and died September 29, 1954, in Tucson, Arizona. He was described as tall (over six feet) with dark brown eyes and black hair.

His father was Ferdinand (Frank) Itzweire, who had been born in 1852 in Canada and was a carpenter by trade. His mother was Julia Giroux, born in 1862 in Clyde, Kansas. They were French Canadians. Julia died in 1909 in Bisbee and is buried in Clyde, Kansas. Frank died in Warren, Arizona, in 1937 and is buried in the cemetery there. Ferd had four sisters: Josephine, Ellen, Alda, and Alma.

In 1898, the family moved to Tombstone, Arizona, and then in 1900 to Bisbee.

Ferd attended school in Bisbee, Arizona, from 1910 to 1912. After finishing school, he worked as a butcher for Welbourne & Dodds in Bisbee in 1914.

Ferd Itzweire on horseback. Courtesy of Sutah Thomas Harris.

Ferd and Sarah Itzweire in front of their home about 1930. Courtesy of Sutah Thomas Harris.

During World War I, Ferd served in the infantry in France. He was in Battery A, 340th Field Artillery 89th Division; his rank was Private. He departed on June 21, 1918, from Brooklyn, New York, on the ship "Shropshire" and was in the battle of Argonne, France, which was known as the largest and last battle of World War I from September 29 to November 11, 1918. Ferd was awarded the German Iron Cross medal for exceptional bravery and courage. That medal is now in my possession. He returned on May 16, 1919, from Brest, France, on the ship Agamemnon.

In 1921, Ferd was manager of the Johnson Meat Company in Bisbee. After the war he married Viola Kimble, who was born in 1897 in Texas and died in 1928. She is buried in Calvary Cemetery in Douglas, Arizona.

In 1930, Ferd was residing in Tucson and worked as manager and head butcher for Peyton Packing Company.

He then married Sarah Wilson, who was born in Pittsburgh, Pennsylvania. She was a graduate in the class of 1926 from the University of Arizona in home economics. They then moved to El Paso, Texas, where Ferd was working in the main office of the Peyton Packing Company. Later, they acquired some land west of Pearce, Arizona, in Cochise County near where the Cochise Stronghold is today. Sarah was teaching school at Empire School No. 37 in 1936 when it had an enrollment of seventeen students. She was also active in 4-H and taught a calf project. They had no children and lived on the Pearce ranch for about ten years.

Ferd and Sarah later bought a ranch near Continental. It was called the Bar TA

Tractor on the Ferd and Sarah Itzweire ranch. Courtesy of Sutah Thomas Harris.

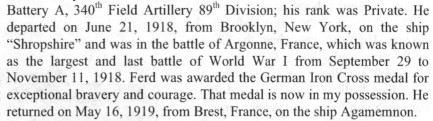

Ferd Itzweire, Francisco Olivas, and Sarah Itzweire. Courtesy of Sutah Thomas Harris.

cattle ranch, west of the Santa Cruz River and the Thomas farm and south of what is now the Walmart in Sahuarita. He was a member of the Arizona Cattle Growers Association, Tucson Elks Club, and Morgan McDermott post of the American Legion.

During the summers, Ferd and Sarah boarded polo ponies for the University of Arizona.

There was a Quonset hut on the Nogales Highway east of the Itzweire Ranch and south of the Thomas farm. According to my brother, John Thomas, it was used by a chemical and fertilizer business to store their supplies.

Jeanne Klingenberg Herman remembers a barbed-wire fence that ran between their property and the Itzweire Ranch. She told me she remembers a gate made of barbed wire and wood spacers. The latch was formed out of a small branch of mesquite and wire. She needed help to open and close it. I remember that gate! When Jeanne and I were in elementary school, our mothers would take us back and forth to play. There weren't many girls our age close by. There was a dirt road that went west from the Nogales Highway and crossed the Santa Cruz River to get to Ferd's house and ranch. Just south of that on the west side of the Nogales Highway was where the German POW camp used to be.

Some summers, Ferd's nephew and my father, William Thomas, would stay at the ranch and help out rounding up cattle and doing other ranch chores when needed.

Sarah taught the 1939–40 school year in Sahuarita. By 1947, she was teaching at

Itzweire home in front of the Santa Rita Mountains. Courtesy of Sutah Thomas Harris.

Continental School and was also helping with the 4-H boys' and girls' projects there.

In 1948, Ferd had eighty acres of peanuts growing on his land. At that time there were 1,505 acres of peanuts growing around the Continental area. Intercontinental Rubber Co. was the largest grower with about a thousand acres. J. B. Bull had about 275 acres. Lee Moor had about fifty acres and R. A. Land had about a hundred acres. This was printed in the *Tucson Daily Citizen* on October 14, 1948.

Sarah Itzweire with her horse and dogs. Courtesy of Sutah Thomas Harris.

There were horses and cattle, and in addition Ferd and Sarah raised Doberman pinscher dogs for quite a while. Pumpkin was the mother dog and we were never allowed to play with her. We could play with the puppies. The breed had a bad reputation for going for the throat when they attacked.

Ferd drilled a nice well on the property to water the field, cattle, and horses. There was also a nice pond of water near the house and there were always ducks and geese around. They raised chickens and had a few roosters.

We had a good time playing in their yard!

Ferd died in 1954 at age sixty-one of a heart condition. His neighbor and friend, Paul Klingenberg, was one of the pall bearers at his funeral. After Ferd died, Sarah sold the ranch and went back to Pearce and at times stayed in Tucson where she died in 1961. She and Ferd are both buried at South Lawn Cemetery in Tucson.

The Itzweire Ranch was sold in March 1955 to Yale and Fern Seminoff.

~ Contributed by Sutah Thomas Harris

Lee Moor Ranch and the Massey Family

The Lee and Beulah Johnson Moor story is definitely a "rags to riches" saga, but by the time the couple became a part of Sahuarita-area history, their legacy was already well established. When the Lee Moor farmland was purchased in Arizona, a very successful farming operation was already up and running in Fabens, Texas, southeast El Paso. Parcel by parcel, the Lee Moor company had accumulated over 3,600 acres along the Rio Grande, which came to be known as Lee Moor Ranch No. 1. It is not clear what influenced Lee Moor's expansion into Southern Arizona, but it was most likely his investments in the railroad and local construction projects that initially brought him to the area.

In the April 7, 1925, issue of the *Arizona Daily Star*, it is reported that Moor was in Tucson on a business trip and that he had recently acquired 160 acres of cotton land which he intended to plant for the upcoming season. Over the next thirty years, he successfully procured almost 1,040 acres along the Nogales Highway, surrounding Pima Mine Road.

In the early 1940s, Lee Moor transferred O'Dell Massey, an employee of the Fabens farm, to become the Lee Moor Ranch No. 2 manager in Sahuarita. It appears that Lee Moor trusted Massey implicitly to make decisions about the property he was managing, and Massey was quick to become involved in the local farming community.

Beatrice and O'Dell Massey. Courtesy of Margaret McGee Elam.

On February 3, 1945, articles of incorporation were filed for the Santa Cruz Valley Producers Association. Per the *Arizona Daily Star*, "Directors of the organization are H. W. Lane, O'Dell Massey, J. B. Bull, George P. Butts, and C. C. Cooper, Jr."

When World War II brought a great labor shortage in September of 1945, Mr. Massey became involved with a program to employ German prisoners of war from Camp Continental. He hired prisoners as cotton pickers in the Lee Moor Ranch fields.

Lee Moor was also very forward-thinking when it came to involvement in testing new and innovative ideas. Mr. Massey was an active participant in soil-enrichment

O'Dell Massey (left) showing off the sprinkler system in the cotton fields of Lee Moor Ranch No. 2. Courtesy of the Massey family.

trials, testing out new varieties of seed, as well as working to find more effective watering methods using sprinkler systems instead of traditional irrigation methods.

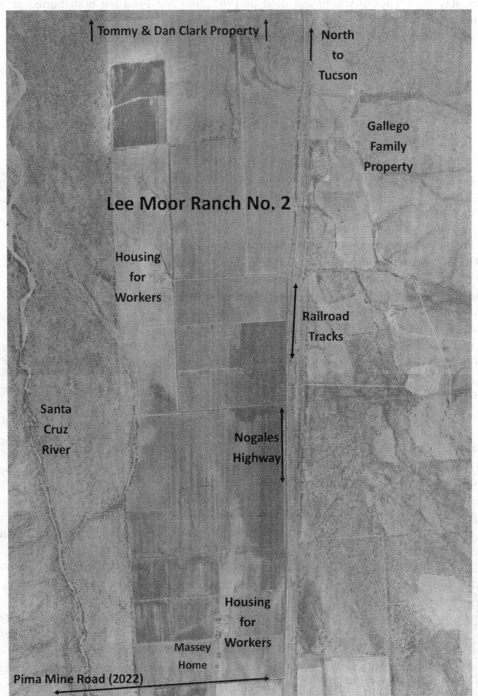

1946 aerial image of Lee Moor Ranch No. 2. Courtesy of the Pima County Department of Transportation.

It is said that Lee Moor was a caring man who treated his workers well, often providing them with homes and food services in addition to secure employment. When lifelong employees retired, he gave them a small pension and allowed them to remain on the farm. Once workers became a part of his "farming family," they typically stayed with him for life.

One such example of Moor's caring nature was shown on May 30, 1950, when Juan Duenas Galvan, a thirty-six-year-old Lee Moor Ranch No. 1 worker, died from injuries sustained when he fell from a truck. He left a wife and five young children, ranging in age from seven months to eight years. Mr. Moor told the family that each child would receive $1,000 when they turned eighteen so that they would have something to start out their lives. The family was able to live on the farm for as long as they wanted. This promise was upheld even though Lee Moor passed away before the children reached their maturity.

After the death of his wife, Beulah, in September of 1951, Lee Moor decided to liquidate some of their assets. This included the acreage in the Sahuarita area. The April 25, 1952,

The Massey family poses near their home in Lee Moor No. 2. From left to right are Billy Fred, William, Milton, O'Dell, and Beatrice. Courtesy of Margaret McGee Elam.

edition of the *Arizona Daily Star*, headlines, "Estate Has Valuable Farm Tract for Sale." Mr. Henry R. Merchant, Jr., was listed as the contact person and the farm manager, O'Dell Massey, was available to answer questions about the property.

Lee Moor passed away on December 15, 1958, in El Paso, Texas. He left their legacy in a trust to the Lee and Beulah Moor Children's Home, an organization that, to this day, provides care for women and children in the El Paso area.

Mr. Massey stayed on at the Lee Moor property until the acreage was sold. Then, in 1953, he and his wife, Beatrice, moved to the Animas Valley of New Mexico where he joined his sons, William and Billy Fred, in a farming venture. He passed away in December of 1994 at the age of eighty-nine.

~ Contributed by Monica Lee Elam Christiansen

William and O'Dell Massey working on the Lee Moor sprinkler system about 1948. Courtesy of the Massey family.

The Juan Lopez Family

Juan Lopez became head foreman of the Sahuarita Ranch that Farmers Investment Co. (FICO) acquired from Harris Ranch in the fall of 1958. Sahuarita Ranch encompassed four thousand acres of farmable land along the Santa Cruz River. Cotton was the main crop for both organizations. Before FICO, barley, sugarcane, sorghum, and field corn were planted to support the feedlot on the property. At one time, before FICO, there was a cotton gin and a crop of potatoes that had been planted. The potato crop was sorted, cleaned, and bagged in the old cotton-gin building that Harris Ranch had left behind.

Juan's background was in agriculture, mostly cotton. He was born in Fabens, Texas, on March 8, 1927. His mother raised him in San Agustín, Mexico, where he went to school. The Rio Grande River separated San Agustín from the Lee Moor 3,400-acre cotton farm.

*Felipa and Juan Lopez portrait. Courtesy
of Oscar Gomez.*

Around the age of seventeen, Juan crossed the river to work on the American side. Thinking that he was not an American citizen, he made attempts to avoid the *federales*. He was caught a few times and on the last apprehension, was beaten badly. His Tio (Uncle) Manuel was shocked and impressed upon Juan that he was an American citizen and could legally cross the border into the United States whenever he wanted.

For a period of five years, Juan worked on the Lee Moor Ranch No. 1, learning basic skills as well as how to operate farming equipment and raise cotton. It was during this time that Juan met his future wife, Felipa. She would fix his lunches and meals, as Juan did not know how to cook for himself. Felipa was the daughter of Gumercindo Gomez and Bersabe Acuna, the latter of whom died in 1942. Felipa had been born on February 5, 1932.

Felipa stayed at home to take care of her two young brothers and her dad. Gumercindo had been remarried to Guadalupe Batista, who passed away in 1947. After her death, Felipa then assumed responsibility for Arturo and Guadalupe's only son, Oscar, who was only two years old.

Juan turned eighteen on March 18, 1945. He and a fellow Lee Moor employee were taken by one of the farm supervisors to the selective service office to register for duty. The supervisor was informed about the probability of both men being called to duty because of World War II. The supervisor told the officer that drafting these two men would be a hardship for the farm as they were the last of the youngest employees left. The officer responded that under the circumstances, only one could be taken, but would not say which one.

Juan was spared and not drafted. Sometimes he wondered that maybe he would have been better off going because his workload and hours increased. He would be awakened before dawn to unload fertilizer or equipment trucks that arrived at Lee Moor and then would have to work the rest of the day. He remarked that maybe his friend was the lucky one, having been drafted. He gave a big smile every time he told someone that the coworker who got drafted was actually his best friend and future brother-in-law, Roberto Estrada.

Juan and Felipa married in Texas on August 29, 1948. Juan continued working at Lee Moor until 1949 or 1950 when he and his wife moved to the city of El Paso. In March of 1950 a daughter, Delia, was born. They soon found that living in the city was not to their liking and, after a short period, a decision was made to move to Arizona to live closer to Felipa's sister, Alicia. In late 1950, Juan and Felipa received word that Roberto and Alicia now lived on Lee Moor Ranch No. 2 near Sahuarita and that plenty of work was available.

*Javier "Rocky" Lopez, Raul Lopez, and
Oscar Gomez on Oscar's new bike while
Juanito Lopez plays in the walker near
the house on the Sahuarita Ranch in
1958. Courtesy of Oscar Gomez.*

Felipa and Juan arrived in Sahuarita without Arturo and Oscar. In the end, the sisters wanted their brothers with them, so the girls took a Greyhound bus to El Paso. Gumercindo was still a single man and it was difficult for him to take care of them. As a result, Oscar and Arturo lived with Juan and Felipa until adulthood.

While living on the Lee Moor Ranch, Juan and Felipa had two more kids, Raul in May of 1952 and Javier "Rocky" in September of 1953. Their house was close to an irrigation ditch. Raul was almost two when he wandered toward the ditch and fell in. One of the workers saw him fall in and ran to his rescue. Raul was pulled out just as he was going into the culvert.

Laura and Juanito Lopez playing in the yard. Courtesy of Oscar Gomez.

Lee Moor Ranch No. 2 was put up for sale and Juan was one of the last to leave. Shortly after Christmas in 1954, Juan moved his family to Sahuarita Ranch. The transition to this farm was facilitated by the fact that many families had moved to Sahuarita from Lee Moor, the latter of which had been primarily a cotton farm. Work done on the Sahuarita farm varied with each season. Skills that Juan possessed were fully utilized. He was a tractor driver who knew how to plant and cultivate cotton. He plowed fields preparing them for cotton, corn, sugarcane, and alfalfa. He cut alfalfa and ran the hay baler with ease. Many years after retiring, he was still called over to help fix the hay baler when it failed to operate.

Juan, at times, worked in the old welding shop servicing and repairing equipment. The shop was not far from Juan and Felipa's house. This must have been the place where he discovered his welding and mechanical skills. One year during the corn and sugarcane harvest, he had to work at night on the corn harvesters. He decided to take his eleven-year-old brother-in-law to help him in the shop. Oscar was sent home at midnight. The next evening, Oscar came out prepared to go to work with Juan. He was dismayed to discover that Juan had left without him. When he asked Felipa why he was not able to go, she told him, "Because you asked too many questions and created disruptions so Juan could not get his work completed."

Juan, Delia, Felipa, Laura, Javier, and Raul Lopez on Easter in 1957. Everyone asks, "Where is Oscar?" "He's taking the picture, dummies!"

Laura and Juan Lopez were born at the Sahuarita farm in 1955 and 1957, respectively, so the family was very busy with the five Lopez children and the two Gomez brothers.

Felipa knew how to drive, but did not have a driver's license, so Juan had to take her to Tucson to buy groceries. Felipa never wanted Juan to go in the store to help her with shopping because he would fill the cart with fruit and treats for the children. Juan always wanted to make sure his children had everything he didn't have as a child. Many nights, after Juan had worked his ten to twelve hours for the day, he would volunteer to drive the grader at night. He never thought twice about taking the night shift and this extra money allowed him and Felipa to purchase shoes for one of their seven children. Although Felipa's two younger brothers were not his sons, Juan accepted them as if they were. Both he and Felipa taught them to be responsible and hard working, just as they did with their own children.

The Juan Lopez family home. Courtesy of University of Arizona Special Collections.

Juan took his job and responsibilities seriously. Some considered him a workaholic. Long hours at work were not unusual or out of the ordinary for him. It was an easy choice for Toops Culbertson to offer Juan the head foreman's job when FICO acquired the Sahuarita Ranch. Foremen were allowed an hour for lunchtime. Juan never took that long. After a half-hour lunch, he was back in his truck driving around the farm. Once he was asked, "Why did you take only a half-hour lunch?" His response was that he had to make sure his workers did not extend their lunchtime past the half hour.

It was not all work on the farm. Juan and Felipa enjoyed going to the Rodeo drive-in theater during the week to watch Spanish-language movies. The kids went along and most of them fell asleep after the first movie. They loved going to the Plaza Theater in downtown Tucson for live appearances of Mexican artists, musicians, and comedians. Juan loved going to the wrestling matches that occasionally came to Tucson. He enjoyed going to Nogales, Sonora, to watch bullfights. On occasional Sundays off, he would take his family on picnic outings. The Desert Museum and Old Tucson were favorite spots. Sabino Canyon was a refreshing delight, totally different from the water in the irrigation ditches on the farm. Even vacations to El Paso included visits to the zoo, movies, theater, amusement park, and drive-ins. Juarez offered entertaining wrestling matches with the noisy crowds and extra antics of the wrestlers.

When the family was visiting Texas, Oscar recalls that Juan would give him two dollars and ask him to run over to the store for a gallon of milk. He would tell him to use the change to buy pastries from the bakery. Milk was only about fifty cents, so he had the remaining amount to buy a huge bag of sweets that cost about five cents for two.

On July 3, 1962, Juan and Felipa's ten-year-old son and their eight-year-old nephew thought it would be exciting to ride on the catwalk of a three-wheeled chemical spray truck. While swerving to avoid hitting another farm vehicle, the brakes failed, causing the vehicle, carrying a 500-gallon chemical tank, to tip over, landing on Raul and Angel. The boys were trapped under the full weight of the load, requiring a crane to extricate them. Angel escaped with a severe concussion, but young Raul did not survive. The death of their son was a tragedy and easily the most difficult thing Juan and Felipa experienced in their lives.

Over the thirty-five years that Juan worked for FICO, he had excellent personal and working relationships with Keith Walden and Toops Culbertson. Mr. Walden had a yearly bet with Juan over the barley harvest. If Juan could guarantee a two-ton-per-acre yield, Mr. Walden would provide Juan with a new Stetson hat. Over the years, Juan was never able to wear out all of his Stetson hats because he wore them only on special

Warren Culbertson and Juan Lopez checking cotton blooms. "Muy bueno," said Lopez. "Best cotton I've seen in nine years." Courtesy of Tucson Citizen.

outings or occasions.

In February 1980, Felipa was cleaning her fireplace when she noticed the face of Jesus Christ on a wall inside the fireplace. She called Juan and asked him to look at the wall and tell her what he saw. Juan also saw the face of Jesus. There were other pictures that appeared, one at a time—an open Bible and San Martín de Porres, the saint. Thousands of people from all over came to see the apparitions. One of these people was the owner of Farmers Investment Co., Keith Walden. Mr. Walden kneeled alongside Felipa as she showed him the wall, and he asked, "Felipa, why do you think this appeared to you?" Felipa responded, "I believe Jesus wants us to build a church in Sahuarita." Mr. Walden told her he would donate the land if Felipa could raise the money to build the church. Felipa was very happy to hear that and, to make the story short, San Martín de Porres Catholic Church sits right in the middle of the pecan fields on the land that Mr. Walden donated.

Felipa G. Lopez sees religious images on the walls of the fireplace in her Sahuarita home. Courtesy of Arizona Daily Star, *February 28, 1980.*

Juan worked and lived on the Sahuarita Ranch for nearly fifty years. Thirty-five years were spent with Farmers Investment Co. He experienced the transition to pecans and eventually to the harvesting of pecan nuts. FICO built a house on the corner of Sahuarita Road and Sahuarita Street in 1962. Juan was able to buy the house and lived there until his death in August of 1997. Felipa stayed in the house until she passed away in January 1999. The house was eventually demolished to accommodate the widening of Sahuarita Road. Their children still live in the Sahuarita and Tucson areas.

~ Contributed by Oscar A. Gomez

The Martin Family

My original story was written some years ago for my kinfolk—my family. I never expected it to be in a book of any kind so no other readership was ever my intention or particular desire. If eventual readers have a different remembrance than mine, so be that. ~ Joe Martin

"Remember what your eyes have seen and tell it to your children . . ." Deuteronomy 4:9

Pay attention to people and events in the lives of others, especially your kinfolk, children, and friends. Pay attention to changes to the places you go in the years to come. You will see things change that won't seem like much right now but thirty years from today you will have seen some history just as I have. Few people can imagine cotton fields where pecan trees are now. Old barns that were cotton gins when I was young. Local grocery stores that were here that are long gone. Canvas tents

Portrait of Warren and Helen Martin taken soon after their marriage. Courtesy of Joe Martin.

The Martin family posing for a photo in Oklahoma about 1925. William is seated on Warren's lap; Helen holds baby Oscar; Rena Mae and Harold stand in between. Courtesy of Joe Martin.

where farm laborers used to live right here in Sahuarita.

My dad, Warren Frank Martin, was born June 9, 1897, in Lamar, Arkansas. He talked most about Coal Hill, around eighteen miles to the west, where he had lived as a boy. He had to drop out of school in the third grade, at nine years of age, due to the death of his father (Thomas Carl Martin). He was the oldest of three boys (Warren, Raymond, and Carl), and it was his place to help his widowed mother as best he could.

The name of my dad's mother was Florence Della Griffin. Her father's name was Franklin Pierce Griffin. I saw both of their graves at the New Hope Garden of Memories Cemetery. Her mother was Mary Ann Stubblefield.

After Thomas died, Florence was briefly married to W. H. Atwell in 1908 before she moved with her kids to the home of her brothers and widowed father in Braden, Oklahoma. My dad had to quit his job due to the move. That job was carrying a bucket of water and a dipper to field workers so they could get a drink on the spot. Dad's uncle, Cullen Griffin, whom most people called "Cully," cut and sold firewood for a living. He told my dad, "I can use some help at the other end of a two-man saw, but you will have to do a man's part or I can't use you." Dad went to work for his uncle and he "did his part." Grandma did not stay at Cully's place long. I know she married a couple more times to William Coer "Dad" Pendleton and Mr. Watson.

My dad and mom had begun courting in 1917. Mom was thirteen years old. Her biological dad was dead at that point. Mom was the third youngest of the Higgins children. It seems her dad died of the flu. Many people died during the years just prior to World War I, and several years after.

Mom's mother was Martha Ida Jones. She had married a Mr. Robert Calvin and had two kids (Rose and Lillie). Then she married Enoch Marion Higgins and had seven kids: Beulah, Myrtle, William, Sanford, Helen, Ida (Tina), and Guy.

My parents married on January 28, 1918, on a cold snowy day in Fort Smith, Arkansas. Mom, born December 13, 1903, was fourteen years and one month old. Mom went to school just one day in her life. She came home excited about the day's events. After telling her parents those things, her dad wasn't impressed, saying, "You'll grow up, get married, and have a bunch of kids. You don't need schooling to do that. You stay home and help your mother." So, that's what she did. She could

Oscar Martin and Leo McNat stand in front of early field-worker tent housing in Sahuarita. Courtesy of Joe Martin.

sew, cook, make clothing and bedcovers called quilts, and can food that was kept in pressure-sealed jars especially for that purpose. She could do anything her mom did. Years later, her daughter, Rena Mae, helped her learn to read, write, and do simple math. She learned a lot on her own after she had the basics to work from. She did really well I think.

During World War I, in 1918, dad was called to serve and was on a train heading to be shipped out when word came that the war was over. He returned home, thank God!

Dad and mom eventually had five children, all born in Braden, Oklahoma. Rena Mae was born in

1919 and lived her life in Oklahoma. Harold was born in 1921; Bill (William) was born in 1923; Oscar was born in 1925; and me, I was born in June of 1936.

Bill was a restless spirit and the reason we came to Arizona. Mom said that in 1939 she found a note on the table which read, "Mom, I've gone to Arizona with Bill Slusher and some other men. Don't worry about me, Bill." He was not yet sixteen. Bill wound up in Sahuarita at W. H. Lane's farm, Oro Verde. Bill lived in a canvas tent along with several other men and worked at whatever was at hand. The tents were in the area north of where FICO's office is. Some tents were south, near where Rocky Lopez lives. Cotton was the main crop and much hard labor was used to grow and harvest it. Remember, that was eighty-two years ago!

Bill eventually married his sweetheart, Mary Bates, in June of 1942, just before the war started—after the bombing of Pearl Harbor, December 7, 1941. Bill went off to war. Mary stayed with my folks, during which time Mary Etta was born. At that time, we were

Brown brothers (Erwin and Finis) with Oscar Martin on the far right. Courtesy of Barbara Brown Bennett.

living in a house just east of the road now heading north to the Catholic church. The house is still there.

Bill was in the army for the duration of the war and he, no doubt, saw much more combat than did Oscar and Harold. His combat was against the Germans. After the war ended in 1945, Bill returned home for a short time before signing a one-year contract to work as a radar tech at a radar station in Greenland. He was trained in radar, but Bill hated the cold. He said they lived in a Quonset hut and, with the wind chill factor below zero, they never went outside. It was good money, but he came back to Arizona instead of renewing the contract.

Bill worked for a short time with FICO, but soon moved to work at Anaconda Mine driving a belly dump. He didn't find that work suited him, so he enlisted in the air force and

Holes drilled for the pecan trees. Courtesy of the University of Arizona Special Collections.

spent twenty years there. After discharge, he worked for a while at a prison for the Texas Department of Corrections, and then worked for the city of San Antonio, maintaining traffic-light switchgear before he finally retired. Will never stayed anywhere for long.

Harold was in the air force during World War II, working as an aircraft mechanic. After the war he worked a short time on the farm at Continental. He then left to work for Selby Lincoln-Mercury. While there, Harold bought a '51 Mercury. He checked cars that were traded in to be sure they were in good shape to sell. He came out from Tucson and told dad there was a '49 Ford that he had checked and found to be like new. Dad bought it and

Oscar Martin drilling holes to plant small pecan trees near Continental. Courtesy of the University of Arizona Special Collections.

Joe Martin in 1941. Courtesy of Joe Martin.

gave me his '35 Ford. I wasn't sixteen yet, but dad let me drive it on farm roads. It was a good old car. Uncle Harold bought me my first bike in 1946 and later he gave me a '39 Ford. When I got the '39, I sold the '35 to a friend, Micky Marstellar, who lived in Continental also. Harold eventually bought a 1954 Ford, kept it several years; then bought a Plymouth station wagon and gave the '54 to dad, who gave the '49 to me.

Harold met his wife-to-be at a wrestling match at the Tucson sports center on West Congress Street, just west of the Santa Cruz River. He married Connie Morales in 1954, and bought a house for $9,000 at 730 East Lester. Harold worked for several years at Marana Airpark as a mechanic. He worked on aircraft there and then later at Fort Huachuca, and finally for Hughes Aircraft until retirement at seventy years old. He was a good brother and a good man.

Oscar got a Model A Ford when he was about sixteen. It was a nice-looking little coupe. He always had a nice car. He went to the old Sahuarita School when we came here in 1939, but only for a short time. He and Manuel Sanchez were in school together for the time Oscar attended. He went to work for W. H. Lane and his son Clyde, the owners of the Oro Verde farm in Sahuarita, where my dad also worked as a blacksmith and mechanic. Oscar worked at whatever there was to do, but soon became a tractor driver.

He, like his two older brothers, went off to war. Oscar was in the navy on a troop ship taking men out to battle. He saw very little actual combat.

Harold, Bill, Oscar, and Rena Mae Martin posing for a photo circa 1928 in Oklahoma. Courtesy of Joe Martin.

After the war, he worked at one or another of the farms—Sahuarita, Continental, or J. B. Bull. Oscar went to work wherever dad was, because he lived with mom and dad, and moved as they did. He had a 1937 Ford convertible in 1946. That was a nice car. He had it while we lived at the old prison camp headquarters. He and dad worked for J. B. Bull for about a year.

Joe Martin stands on the Continental School ball field. Courtesy of Joe Martin.

He eventually went to work for FICO again. He ran a tractor-mounted auger, making holes in which to plant young pecan trees in the mid-'60s. He left FICO in 1970 and came to work for Jim Boyd. I got him the job. He was a good hand. Oscar was a good brother and he was around me most of his life. He could make a person laugh!

When dad and mom married, dad was working for a farmer, John Littlefield, plowing with a team of mules. One day, dad and two other men had been plowing all morning and stopped for lunch. One was a stranger who had just that morning been hired. Mr. Littlefield drove up in his horse-drawn buggy, as he usually did at least once a day. Littlefield stopped, and the new hire asked, "What's the working hours at this place?" Clearly irritated, Littlefield replied, "We're plowing when it's light enough to see, and even a fool knows when it's dark!" Back in that time, the rich treated the poor like dirt.

Mom said dad came in one evening after working the mules all day and said, "I am going to Wichita, Kansas, and going to mechanic school." He boarded a train, was gone for a couple of weeks, came home with a diploma, and opened a shop in Braden. He was doing very well blacksmithing and working on cars. Then the Great Depression hit in 1929. It hurt everyone. Dad said he had as much work as ever but no one had money to pay him. People would offer to trade a pig or a cow or some other thing. My folks had a small field on which mom and the kids gardened and kept animals, so they didn't lack for food, but they needed cash.

Dad had a good friend and drinking buddy, Bill Slusher, who had an old beat-up flatbed truck on which he hauled things for people. At times he needed help and dad would go with Bill. On one particular road, there was a steep hill and Bill's old truck sometimes couldn't make it to the top if the load was especially heavy. When it stalled, the mechanical brakes wouldn't hold.

Rena Mae (age 19), Joe (age 2), and Helen (age 34) sit for a portrait. Courtesy of Joe Martin.

When Bill sensed that the truck would stall, he would say, "Get ready, Warren!" At the last second, my dad would jump off and put a large block of wood behind the wheel. Now, there was the real problem! The truck didn't have enough power to get on over the crest from a dead stop, even though the crest was only thirty to fifty feet away.

Very nearby, there was a house with a porch, on which sat an old man who would be observing all this. He would get up, go very slowly over to a four-horse team of huge work horses, come out, hook onto the truck, not saying a word until all was ready. Then he'd say, "Let out your clutch when the horses lay into the harness." He shouted, the horses dug in, and the truck was on its way. Bill was seventy-five cents poorer and that was a lot of money in those

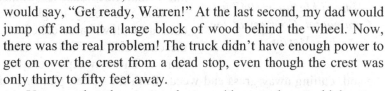

In 1941, Joe (almost 5) and his nephew, Bob (2 years old) stand near a cactus on the south side of Twin Buttes Road. Courtesy of Joe Martin.

days, but there was no other way to get over the crest.

Bill Slusher eventually got a new flatbed. He fixed it up with benches in back and a tarp over the back. He began to hire out to haul men from Arkansas and Oklahoma to Arizona—to Sahuarita in particular. There was a need for farmhands and these men needed work. The men paid Bill what they could and the farmer paid so much per man.

Bill came back from one such trip and told my dad that Mr. W. H. Lane was in need of a blacksmith and mechanic and would pay him well. Bill had moved his family to Sahuarita some months earlier and told dad that he could go with the next bunch Bill took to Arizona and live with Bill and family until he decided if he wanted to move to Sahuarita to work.

Joe on his first new bike, purchased by his brother, Oscar, in 1946 while the family lived at the former POW camp headquarters. Courtesy of Joe Martin.

Harold Martin in 1947 in Continental. Courtesy of Joe Martin.

Dad climbed in the cab with Bill and they were on their way. They pulled into Sahuarita three days later. Dad went to work for Mr. Lane in the old sheet-iron shop. Mr. Lane was impressed with dad's work and made him a good pay offer with a promise of a big house there on the Oro Verde farm as soon as one was available. At the time the only available house was rather small.

Dad went back to Oklahoma, sold the place, and bought a '35 Ford for $300. Mom, dad, Oscar, Harold, me, Rena Mae, Laurence, and their little boy, Bob, all loaded into the car and came west. Surely, someone had to sit on someone else's lap!

Back then, the only fully paved road between Oklahoma and Sahuarita went through Douglas and Bisbee. Texas Canyon wasn't open so it was a long two-and-a-half- to three-day trip, assuming you had no trouble along the way. Dad barely drove over 45 miles an hour back then—that was 1939!

Laurence worked a short time on the farm, but didn't like Arizona so he, Rena Mae, and Bob boarded a Greyhound bus and went back to Oklahoma. Bill moved into the house with the rest of us. As far as I know, that little house is still there, just north of where Julio lives.

Dad was really tough. As a blacksmith, his job was to sharpen cultivator plowshares called sweeps. They were mounted, along with the cultivator beam, to a tractor which was driven down the cotton furrow. These sweeps were lowered to the ground and broke through the sod, cutting away grass and weeds from the cotton plants. In doing this, they would lose their edges and become dull, at which point they were removed so sharp ones could be put on. The dull ones were taken to the shop to dad.

Now came the hard part. In the northwest corner of that old shop was a forge with a blower mounted to the bottom, which forced air up through a steel grate. Coal was placed on the grate, set ablaze, and heated. The air from the blower, flowing through the burning coals, created a fierce flame. Several sweeps were essentially buried in the heap of burning coals. When the sweep was glowing red hot, dad removed it with special tongs, sort of like a large pair of pliers. He laid the sweep on a large anvil and, using a two-

Helen, Joe, and Oscar Martin in 1946 in their Continental home. Courtesy of Joe Martin.

and-a-half-pound hammer, hit the sweep in just the right place, thinning the edge and thus sharpening it. Then he dumped it into a barrel of water to "temper" the metal. You never used a grinder to sharpen a sweep. It had to be done on a forge.

The sharpened sweep was put on a rack, and another dull sweep was put into the forge when another red-hot one was taken to the anvil. This process might go on for most of the day. Late in the afternoon, a pickup truck would bring more dull sweeps and leave with the sharp ones. This lasted all through the summer months.

Once I walked into the shop in mid-summer through a doorway, maybe ten to twelve feet from the roaring furnace. The heat from it was suffocating. Dad would have to approach this inferno to put in and remove a sweep, then take it a few steps to the anvil and pound away. Doing this time and time again, his clothes were soaked with sweat.

You never saw anyone standing around talking to him! I am proud of him. Grandma Higgins once said of my dad when he was in his twenties, "I never saw a better looking man from head to toe, five foot ten, 185 pounds, a perfect man." I have a photo taken of him in 1925, seated with my mom and kids at that time. I look at his hand and imagine it holding a heavy hammer, pounding red-hot steel. This man worked from age nine until age seventy at a time when only a strong arm and back would do the job. I can only imagine the days he endured. The most amazing thing of all was that I never ever heard him complain, not even to my mom. He got up in the early morning to head out for a twelve-hour day as if going on a picnic. He would work all day, come home, get ready, and we would go to a drive-in movie. No wonder the neighboring farms would come and try to hire him away by offering him more money and a better house.

Warren and Helen Martin pose near the road to Madera Canyon. Courtesy of Joe Martin.

Dad was about to enlist in the army at the outset of World War II. Mr. Lane came to see dad and said, "We can't all go to war. Some of us have to stay here to run the country. I can't spare you because men like you are hard to come by. Besides that, if you leave, I'll have to have your house. Where will your wife go?" Dad couldn't answer that so he stayed.

The mechanic work in the '40s was in the company of one Ted Parker and he was liked by dad. They had just finished repair of a Caterpillar RD8. They had started it with the intent to take it out the shop door when up drove Mr. Lane's son, Clyde, in his Cadillac. The Lanes drove Cadillacs or Buicks. Dad and Ted were talking with Clyde. A couple of young girls came into the shop, which wasn't unusual, as they lived nearby. Suddenly the Cat began to move, and began to climb up onto the Cadillac. Someone climbed up on the Cat and disengaged the clutch, but it was too late to save the car!

One of the girls had gotten up on the tractor and engaged the clutch, then jumped off in fear. Dad said the girls were gone in a flash and he never saw them again.

The Lanes got new cars pretty often and rather than trade in the old ones, they would put trailer hitches on them and pull cotton trailers with them. Big cars back in the '40s would outpull the old pickup trucks of that period.

Dad's mechanic helper, Ted Parker, had an older brother, Ira Parker, who had a small farm in the area and

Holiday Market lettuce crate label for Rancho Oro Verde. Courtesy of Medley Crate label archives.

grew love grass, which has a very tiny seed head. In the 1940s, it was just coming into demand by ranchers for cattle grazing. It's very easy to grow and, once established, it's fast at spreading over grassland. To harvest the seed required special machines. Allis-Chalmers had the only combine that would harvest this crop. It wasn't self-propelled, so a tractor was needed to pull the combine. This tractor had to travel very slowly while at a high engine RPM to power the combine to handle the grass cutting and seed threshing. For this job, Ira used U.S.-made Oliver tractors and Cockshutt tractors made in Canada. They had a very low gear which allowed slow travel yet high engine RPM for power to the combine. These are very good tractors. Ira died March 9, 1979. His son-in-law, Jay Pelton, used to drive a school bus for Sahuarita School.

Oscar Martin poses on his horse, circa 1940. Courtesy of Joe Martin.

Two miles north of Sahuarita was Lee Moor Ranch No. 2, a farm back in the '40s. Dad worked there a short while. Nacho Bracamonte's brother, Juan, worked there, too. For the brief time we lived at Lee Moor Ranch, mom and I walked the three-eighths of a mile out to Nogales Highway to get the bus into Tucson. At that time, the bus was a limousine-sized car, usually a Buick. It would stop, the driver would get out, take money for the fare, open a door, let you get seated, close the door, and off he would go. We did this once or twice a month. Later, Citizens Auto Stage, a subsidiary of Greyhound, began a Tucson-to-Nogales run in a larger bus made by Flxible. It had a straight-eight Buick engine in the rear of the bus and a four-speed transmission. It ran just fine.

Long-haul Greyhound buses back then had tandem rear axles under a much bigger bus. These buses were powered by two six-cylinder General Motors diesel engines, two cycle with one engine for each axle. These buses would pass everything on the road, especially trucks. Some singer back then wrote a song for truckers which went, "Lord, just let me pass a Greyhound bus before I die."

As a kid, when we were on the road, those buses passed us like we were tied to a post. They went up mountains like it was level ground. Those engines were supercharged. Years ago, my parents took me to a carnival at night and I could hear an engine running. Eventually we came upon a large flatbed trailer, and there was the engine I'd heard, a 6-71 General Motors diesel powering a big generator for the carnival. What was remarkable was the chrome on that engine and the smoothness of the sound. It was a show in itself. People would stop to admire it, including me and dad.

We moved from Lee Moor back to Sahuarita for a short period, during which Oscar married. We lived in a house at the corner of a cotton field, at the spot where the stoplight is now—just

In 1952, Warren and Helen Martin stand by their '49 Ford, parked on Twin Buttes Road. Courtesy of Joe Martin.

east of the river bridge. The house used to take on water during river flooding. You put your best furniture on the beds. Water would be six inches to a foot deep. It was a real mess to clean up! We didn't stay there long. We were flooded just once. The house eventually burned down.

Around the time we were to move, dad got a job at the Eagle-Picher mill near where Al Engelman lived. I think they were Oklahoma based and the manager was Neal Parker. I knew his son, Eddie Parker. We were both in Sahuarita School

Crews observe a downed drone. Courtesy of the University of Arizona Special Collections.

during the mid-'40s. When dad was hired, he was told he wouldn't have to work nights. After working days welding, they told him to come in for the night shift. He quit on the spot and went to FICO where he stayed, working for them until he retired.

Mom kept chickens for eggs and for meat. She would catch one, cut off its head, dip it in boiling water to loosen the feathers, pluck and cook it. We had chicken about every other week. Mom was an excellent cook. We ate really well. Dad had to have a good meal to do the kinds of work he did. Mom got up at 4 a.m., put breakfast on the table, and called to dad, Oscar, and me at 5 a.m. We were off to work at six.

She was a hard worker. She prepared three big meals a day for dad, Oscar, and me. Oscar and I took our lunches [to work], but dad always drove home for a hot meal. Others got half-hour lunch breaks, but dad always took an hour and no one ever questioned him.

Aside from cooking, mom would sew, make quilts for bedcovers, take care of chickens, clean a large house, and build a fire outside under a cast-iron tub in which to boil water for cleaning my dad's greasy

Crews load a downed drone into a truck. Courtesy of the University of Arizona Special Collections.

work clothes. She put the clothes into the hot water and choused them with an old broom handle to get them clean. This was Monday work and she called it "blue Monday."

Once in a while she would go to the fields to pick a sack of cotton. She was the first person up and the last person to go to bed. As someone said, "A woman's work is never done." I don't know what we men would do without women. She was a good mother. She told me how to conduct myself, told me when to be home when I went out at night, and I pretty much "walked the line."

For a time, FICO had an office on South Stone Avenue in Tucson. They finally moved into the current office. The head bookkeeper was Bob Stuart. When FICO offered my dad a nice pay raise, Stuart told him, "This pay raise will put you into a higher tax bracket and, in your case, with no deductions, you might actually be making less money." Dad refused the pay offer.

Dad was much sought after on these farms. Other men in the shop might be standing around talking, but not dad. I never knew him to even think about cheating anyone.

After dad retired in 1970, and FICO hired a new man, it came time to begin plowing and soon the plow points were worn down. Culbertson came to see dad and asked him to come back to work long enough to fix the plows and show the new man how to get them right. He was making them too flat and they wouldn't "take to the ground." Dad went back long enough to get the plows fixed and train the new man.

In April of 1983, Warren and Helen Martin celebrated their sixty-fifth wedding anniversary at Bull Farms in the home I shared with my wife Pauline. Warren passed away on the first of April in 1989, at almost ninety-two years of age. Helen followed on January 2, 1996, soon after her ninety-second birthday.

Joe's life

I'll tell you about myself in my younger days. When I was a boy, the train that ran between Tucson and Nogales was steam powered. About two miles south of FICO's Continental mechanical repair shop and on the near west side of the railroad tracks, there is a grove of tall salt-cedar trees, which are visible for miles, but best seen from Canoa Road. Among those large trees were some houses where track maintenance men and

Joe walks in front of his parents, Warren and Helen Martin, in Tucson circa 1948. Courtesy of Joe Martin.

their families lived. These men were known as "section hands" because they were charged with maintaining a given section of track. The workers' housing is long gone, but among those trees, you can still see the concrete foundations. This spot was known as Morales Station. I never met any of the people there.

A similar station was, at that same time, located about a mile north of FICO's office, and along the west side of the tracks. Frank Gonzalez's dad lived there, as did his family and other section hands. When I was five years old, I would see Frank walking to school, the old school in Sahuarita. Frank recently died and his widow, Mrs. Gonzalez, and son, Victor, live in Sahuarita. Frank was a special friend to me down through the years, a hard worker and honest man. He has children other than Victor, but their names are lost to me here.

I started school in the old building north of the pecan plant. That was 1942. We lived to the east of there at the time. I walked to school, about three-eighths to a half mile. Eventually a Mr. Blackwell was hired to drive a bus. The Sahuarita building, known as the "old school," and the principal's home, and one other little building about fifty feet south of the main building are all I recall. Some years later, another building near the northeast corner of the main building was built. When we came here in

A few years later, a photographer snapped a photo of Joe and Warren. Courtesy of Joe Martin.

'39, I believe Mr. Dishaw was principal.

Manuel Sanchez and his dad used to load firewood on a donkey and go house-to-house selling the wood, mostly stove wood. Mom bought wood to cook with. In the early '40s, many women cooked on wood-burning stoves. Manuel, soon after that, went to work as a cowboy for Buck Fletcher. Fletcher later sold out to Frank Rees.

Irrigation wells of the '40s weren't very deep. Water was much closer to the surface back then. Most of the farm wells at Sahuarita were powered by big two-cylinder John Deere engines. The cylinders were horizontal and had a very large, heavy flywheel on the side. On the early models, the operator had to manually turn the flywheel in order to start the engine. Once started, the engine had a distinctive sound. People called them "poppin' Johnnies."

During 1942, while dad was working at Sahuarita, the war was underway. We were living in a farmhouse about a half mile east of Sahuarita School. The government installed machine-gun battery stations about a half mile east of said house. They brought to the station site a small radio-controlled plane with a wingspan of perhaps ten feet. It had an engine, too, of course, and a person as a radio controller who would guide the pilotless plane through its maneuvers, as if the plane were "strafing" the machine gunners as its target. This plane was fast and loud and visible clearly from our house, and even from the school for that matter. The gunner would try to hit the plane as it dived at them. If it was hit or if it ran out of gas, a parachute would deploy, affording a "soft landing." These gun batteries were made of cement and were still there some forty years ago.

The site is located west of the 2022 Walden Grove School and very near to the pecan trees. It was just over and near the eastern part of the fence at the end of the road passing in front of our 1942 home. Shooting was directed east from the battery because no one lived in that direction. Few people know there was also a practice bombing range some distance southeast of the gunnery range. Years ago, while hunting, I came across a bunch of whitewashed rocks forming a large circle. I found a couple of old bomb-shaped objects. They were damaged somewhat from impacting the ground after being released from the plane. One bomb had an undetonated twenty-eight-gauge shotgun shell in the nose of the bomb, its purpose being to detonate on impact, making dust to signal a hit to the pilot. There were a fair number of misses as evidenced by the number of bombs found outside of the target circle. Some current Sahuarita residents have found bombs, too.

Dad moved us to Continental in late 1944 to work for Fred Jones. I went to the old original school that was where the clinic is now. The next year I was in the building just across the road to the south. While we were there, Empy McGee and his family lived in Continental in a house that still stands. Empy brought some cattle to graze on Fred Jones's farm. This involved land after crop harvest as well as Fred's holding of considerable desert land known as the Canoa Land Grant, upon which much of Green Valley now rests. They used to have music at the Continental School building during summer nights. I saw Jerry and Keith McGee play there. My parents and I went with others to listen to them.

Shortly after World War II, in 1945, the prisoners left and the POW camp headquarters building was made into living quarters. This was where our family moved on Bull Farms while my dad worked for J. B. Bull for a few months. We were not there long. Soon after Oscar came home from the navy, we left.

As I remember the POW camp, there were several large wooden barracks west of the headquarters. The POWs lived in them. The prisoners were mostly Austrian and some German. There was a large pile of firewood that the POWs used. Just after sundown, hundreds of bats would fly around the woodpile, catching insects that came out of the wood. I don't recall a fence around the camp. Where could the POWs run to? Germany was far away. The POWs worked here and there on local farms in Sahuarita, especially because a good bit of vegetables was growing there—hence the name Oro Verde, or Green Gold.

Back to the POW camp—drinking water came from a well east of the railroad tracks. The water line passed under the truck bed; it was buried of course and continued westward under the existing highway and finally up into the tanks there at the time. The Teso family lived east of the tracks, near the well. I used to play with Joe, Henry, and Lorenzo Teso while at the camp. Lorenzo lives in Continental today. Joe and Henry have passed on.

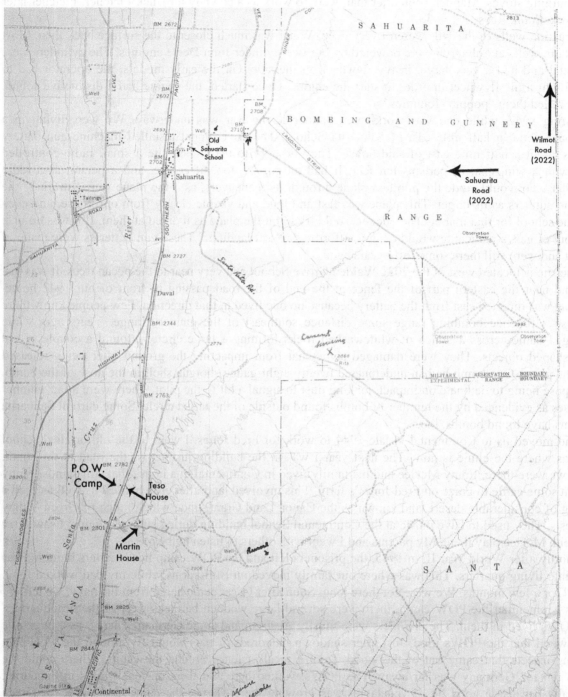

1958 map showing the Sahuarita Bombing and Gunnery Range, as well as the POW camp near Continental. Courtesy of Harold Martin.

During our time at Bull Farms, Mrs. O'Brien picked me up at the POW camp in her Plymouth automobile. There was no school bus. The janitor, Charles Proctor, of Madera Canyon, brought the kids from his area, plus the Brown children from Santa Rita Ranch, all in the covered pickup bed of his Ford truck. He sometimes also brought his nephews from Henry Proctor's Box Canyon Ranch if Henry couldn't bring them.

Dad moved us again in late-1945 when Sahuarita offered him more money. It was then that I went to school with Walt and Martha Spivey at Sahuarita. In late 1946, we moved to Lee Moor Ranch No. 2, a couple of miles north of Sahuarita and about a mile east of where the Desert Diamond Casino is now. Dad worked for Clyde Gaines. We soon moved back to Continental just before the Waldens took over in 1948 or '49, again for more money.

Joe Martin and his '39 Ford in Continental in 1954. Courtesy of Joe Martin.

Dad smoked a lot and drank. He began to cough a lot, especially at night. Our family doctor was an old man, Dr. Thomas, who had an office downtown on Scott Street, near the old Valley National Bank. (Back then, that bank was the tallest building in town.) Anyways, back to dad. His coughing got so bad, and he went to see the old doctor who checked dad and asked, "Do you smoke and drink?" Dad replied, "Yes." Dr. Thomas said, "If you don't quit, you are going to die."

Dad quit cold turkey. He never smoked or drank again, but he said he really missed them both. He lived another forty-eight years. His coughing stopped within a few days. The doctor had told dad, "When you crave a smoke, put a stick of gum in your mouth every time and it will help you quit." Dad chewed a lot of Juicy Fruit gum. It worked. He said smoking was the hardest to give up. All my brothers smoked at one time or another. Bill was the worst. He would quit and go back, quit and go back, right up until he died. I never smoked.

Our time at Bull Farms and right after that is a bit of a mystery to me in many ways. I would describe it as a restless period in my dad's life. He didn't have the "peace" then that he had after he quit drinking and smoking. That event changed him greatly. Then too, he "found his place" when Mr. Walden and FICO came. Mr. Walden had a way about him that suited whatever my dad was looking for. For one thing, dad sensed that the Waldens had come to stay, and they have!

Dad was working for Fred Jones when Walden came. He and Walden got along well. I graduated from Continental, and then went to Tucson to Wakefield Junior High on 44th Street, not far south of where I-10 is now. Next I went to Tucson High, riding the Citizens Auto Stage. The school district gave me and others a book of tickets from which the bus driver would remove a ticket for bus fare. I boarded the bus near the old Continental Store, later the Feedlot Cafe. The bus, driven by Don Morales, picked up Denny Nolen at Sahuarita.

I saw Toops Culbertson (his name was Warren) drive slowly by the old Continental School the day he came here to work for FICO. He and Mary, his wife, hadn't been married for long. This would have been 1949. He worked for FICO until just a few years ago when he retired. He was my first boss. I liked him.

When Toops first came to work at FICO, he knew little about farming, but John and Henry Worthy helped him learn the basics. Toops was a smart man and he learned fast. He was also the bookkeeper before Bob Stuart. Many times I came home at 10–11 p.m. from running around in Tucson, and as I drove in, I could see Toops through his office window, working away at bookkeeping. All that, and he was first on the job the next morning. Call him anything but lazy!

Mr. and Mrs. Walden would take an evening out now and then. They would have me come over to stay with Dick and Tom, being that I'm older. They gave me a book to read to the boys. I also looked after the Culbertson kids from time to time. They lived in the house where Gonzalo lives now.

I was given the job of mowing the lawns and watering the trees for these two families. I mowed with a push mower—not easy if the grass was tall. Both families were nice to me, and they paid me well.

Dad said Walden was good to keep his word. Paychecks were on time and never bounced. Walden and Henry Crown of Crown-Zellerbach founded FICO in 1942. I saw Robert Crown, part of the founding family, as he and Walden toured the Águila Farm in 1953 while I was working there.

Helen and Warren with grandsons Jim and John Martin in Continental. Courtesy of Joe Martin.

As you can tell, we moved a lot during my younger days. My dad never asked for help moving except for the stove and refrigerator. He said, "Whatever you want to move, sit in the living room and I'll load it." He was serious. By evening we were set up in a different house. He was amazing.

Later, while I was in Aguila, mom and dad moved and left behind my old bike, some deer antlers, a train set, and toy cars which were in the attic of the house where Hector Alvarez now lives. These things weren't out in the living room so they didn't get loaded.

Mom and I would sometimes go to the fields and pick a sack of cotton on Saturday mornings. I would put my picking into mom's sack, and, when full, carry it on my shoulder to the scale where I had it weighed and got paid. Then I would go up a ladder and empty the sack of cotton into a big trailer. We would go home in time for mom to fix lunch for dad.

One day mom set in on me to go out to pick cotton by myself since she was too busy to come along. Dad said to her, "Let him be a boy. I never had a chance to be a boy. He will grow up soon enough and work most of his life." Mom never asked me to go out on my own again.

Sure enough, at fifteen, Henry Worthy's sixteen-year-old brother-in-law, Bobby Lynch, and I were given the job of moving four-inch aluminum sprinkler pipes in the cotton fields that were west of where Jack Miller and Rosi live and east of the railroad tracks. We had to move the pipes every six hours and this was at night. We had headlamps so our hands were free to carry the pipe. They were each forty feet long but not heavy.

At the start of school vacation, when we were to work, the cotton was short and the pipe was easy to move. At the end of vacation, the cotton was shoulder high. At this point, we had to carry the pipe above our heads so as to clear the cotton plants. We had to count the rows as we

Joe and Oscar hunting javalina in Continental, circa 1954. Courtesy of Joe Martin.

stepped from one to the other so as to know where to lower the pipe and go make the connection. This was easy to do because it was a quick connector. You had to count rows again to find the next pipe to move. All this was in the dark of night. Just to move through the cotton without the pipe wasn't easy because the plants were big, close together, and wet.

When it was time to move the pipe, we had to go to the pump and shut it down. It was a big sump pump powered by a four-cylinder, air-cooled Wisconsin engine. It had to be hand cranked and that wasn't easy. When the twelve-hour shift ended, we were beat. Bobby drove the old GMC pickup.

John Worthy was a foreman for FICO at Continental for several years and he, his wife, and their two children lived next door to us in the late '40s. One time, John decided to go fishing at a lake near Gila Bend and asked dad if I could go with them. Dad said yes.

We all got into John's '49 Chevy and took off. John drove fast everywhere he went and this was no exception. We were about ten minutes from the lake when the engine developed a knock. We eased on to the campsite and spent the night there. Next morning, John got a toolbox out, got under the car and removed the oil pan after first determining which cylinder was having a rod knock. He then removed the rod and piston, put the oil pan back on and headed out for home at thirty miles an hour. It was summer, there was no AC in the car, and it was a long way from Continental.

It was dark when we got home. I thought John was pretty clever the way he handled the matter. Chevrolets of that period and earlier didn't have oil pumps. They had like a cup on the bearing cap of the connecting rod that dipped oil each revolution of the crankshaft, flinging oil around inside the engine. It wasn't too bad until you had a John Worthy who drove seventy to seventy-five miles an hour. As cars were being driven faster and faster, the splash oiling system just wouldn't cut it so GM began putting oil pumps in their engines.

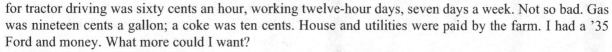

Joe Martin in Continental in 1954. Courtesy of Joe Martin.

I quit Tucson High in 1952 and went to work for FICO, driving a Farmall H tractor cutting down cotton stalks after the pickers had picked the cotton. The pay for tractor driving was sixty cents an hour, working twelve-hour days, seven days a week. Not so bad. Gas was nineteen cents a gallon; a coke was ten cents. House and utilities were paid by the farm. I had a '35 Ford and money. What more could I want?

FICO had a rail siding that the cross ties for the cattle-feed pens came in. Tractors pulled cotton trailers, minus the side racks, alongside the boxcars so as to unload them. The ties were heavily creosoted. Creosote irritates your skin. It was warm weather and it was hot inside those cars. The ties were eight and nine feet long and super heavy. I and three others were sent to unload the boxcars. I was sixteen and weighed about 135 pounds. I was paired with Ray Smith, a big Black guy, who probably weighed 250. We had taken about a dozen ties when the foreman came by. Ray said to him, "I can barely handle my end of these ties and I'm twice as big as this boy. You need to get a bigger man to take his place." The foreman agreed.

About a month after that, I was again teamed with Ray at the feed yard helping him with odd jobs. We were digging a ditch with shovels and I was digging faster than him. He said to me, "We're just getting into a twelve-hour day and you're going strong, but you won't be able to keep it up until quitting time. You need to set a pace now that you can hold up under all day so the boss will think you're as strong at the finish as you were at the start. That's what it takes to make a hand." I took his advice and never forgot it.

Back before big trucks and trailers came on the scene, around 1950, FICO brought in a thousand sheep by train. When they

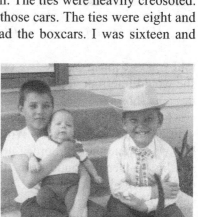

James (10), Harold (3 months), and William (7) Martin on the front steps of the family home. Courtesy of Joe Martin.

sheared the wool, they shipped it out in large burlap sacks that held five hundred pounds of wool and it was loaded into box cars and shipped by rail. They kept the sheep for about two years. They didn't do well—too hot, and predators were a problem. They had sheepherders, of course, but this just isn't sheep country.

The shearing took place in a large tent set up by the shearing contractor, on the spot across from the former Feedlot Cafe where Lorenzo Sanchez's house now sits. There weren't any houses in that area then. The sheep left by train, too.

Ike Doman worked for FICO in the early '50s. He had a '37 Chevy which he drove to work if he was operating a TD-18 plowing at night. Wherever the big tractors were being used, a "trap wagon" was parked. This was a flatbed trailer with a diesel fuel tank, oil, grease, etc. It had everything needed so the operator could service the tractor. There was no service truck.

Joe, Harold, and James stand behind Warren and Helen Martin. Courtesy of Joe Martin.

Ike's old car used lots of oil, so he began using oil off the trap wagon in his car. The oil was made to use in diesel machines and was very high in detergent. It was a Union Oil product called Royal Triton T5X. It was purple in color, and we called it "grape juice." This detergent oil cut the crud away from his engine's piston rings and it began to smoke real bad once it was warmed up good. It looked like it was afire!

Most everyone knew what had happened and Ike even told dad. Dad bought the car to drive the half mile to work. The car would not smoke on so short a drive. Ike sure liked to talk. We called him "Walkie-Talkie." He moved away while I was at Aguila. He was a good worker.

When I worked for FICO, gas was nineteen cents a gallon. A pair of Levi's was three dollars and twenty-five cents. There was a pay phone outside. You turned a crank and an operator came on the line, asked what number you wanted, and told you to deposit twenty-five cents for three minutes. If you were on the line more than three minutes, she would interrupt you and ask for another twenty-five cents. I used to call a girl in Tucson, but I kept the calls short.

In 1953, Culbertson asked me to move to their new farm in Aguila, west of Wickenburg. I was to live with the farm foreman, John Worthy, and his family. John had been a foreman at Continental so I knew him well. I had the '39 Ford, a new engine in it, and a desire to venture out. I agreed to go. Steve Lopez and his brother Fernando were already in Aguila. Steve had just gotten married and wanted his wife to come to Aguila. Toops asked me to take Steve's wife and his mom along when I went. I did. I was seventeen at the time.

John Worthy spent evenings at the Westerner Cafe. He invited me to go along and bought me cokes. One evening, a pretty little redhead came by. She knew John and stopped to talk to him. I continued to go with John and soon the redhead began to talk to me. I started to drive my '39 to the cafe. There weren't many boys in Aguila and none had a Ford with two carbs and dual exhausts. I became pretty popular and that redhead, Helen Southerland, was soon sitting beside me. We would often drive the twenty-eight miles into Wickenburg. I was working twelve-hour days and staying out late. It was killing me!

Asa and Helen Kearns, her step-dad and mom, decided to sell the Westerner Cafe and move to Riverside, California. Helen didn't get along with either of them and did not want to go to California so, one evening, she asked me to marry her. We had been dating about eight months and marriage had never crossed my mind. She needed an answer right away so I said, "Yes." She went on to California with them and the plan was to come back for the wedding on July 14, 1954.

In preparation for the wedding, I had to return to Continental. Back then, if you were under age twenty-one, you had to have your parents sign for you. I was barely eighteen. I also needed a suit. Oscar and a friend, Bobby Brown (Robert Waylon Brown, son of Finis and Nancy Brown), and I went to Wickenburg in Oscar's '53 Ford. The wedding went well. John Worthy was my best man.

Helen at the back door of the old Emmons' house west of Kerley Chemical, built in 1920, with a 1963 Comet car parked out front and Harold's stroller beside her. We lived here from 1960 until 1974. Courtesy of Joe Martin.

Helen and I spent our wedding night at Burro Jim's motel on the outskirts of Aguila. We came back to Aguila and moved into a newly built house on the farm. Ken Ethridge had two D8 bulldozers and was building dikes for FICO. When I married Helen, it was a pleasant surprise to find she was a good cook, even though she was only sixteen. She was always a clean housekeeper and she kept herself and our boys clean.

No sooner did we get back then I got notice to appear in Phoenix for induction into the army to go to Korea. I had registered for the draft when I turned eighteen, as required by law. The officer asked me if anything had changed since my registration. I said, "I got married." He wrote on the draft card saying, "Go home. We're not taking married men right now." I can't tell you how happy I was!

I worked at Aguila until 1956. Then we moved back to Continental into one of the duplexes across from mom and dad. They were paying ninety cents an hour. The worst job was during the winter. It was then that everyone got on a mechanical cotton picker and picked one row at a time. They did a good job. The operator sat up really high and all he had around him was the floorboard and a steering wheel. It was a cold, miserable job. Curt Adams's dad was in charge and he worked on them when they broke down. Nowadays the machines pick four rows.

James was born in 1956. It was probably about that year when I got the tip of my finger smashed. I was making borders, operating a fairly new Farmall 400, a bigger tractor and more powerful than a Super M. It had improved hydraulics. This tractor was just

Skipway at Pima Mine in the late 1950s. Courtesy of Joe Martin.

enough taller than a Super M that you had to pin the hydraulic cylinder in a special hole once in the field in order to make a proper border. You removed the pin by using hydraulics to release pressure so as to

Johnny Martinez stands near a PT-6 dump truck at the Pima Mine. Courtesy of Joe Martin.

manually pull the pin holding the cylinder. Now you had to hold the cylinder and "bump" the hydraulic control lever with your other hand to align the proper holes so as to insert the pin.

The 400 had a hydraulic lever that would toggle over and lock in place until the cylinder ram completed its stroke, then kick back to neutral. It was a long reach from my position up to the lever. I toggled too far and the hydraulic cylinder smashed the first joint of my finger. Even now, I sometimes miss it. I walked about half a mile to the shop. From there, Toops drove me to Saint Mary's Hospital. During that time period, Ken Mathis, who worked at the cattle feed yard, got the end of a finger smashed, too. I used to visit him. He was a neighbor. My finger healed. Ken got blood poisoning. He waited too long to see a doctor and died. He's buried at Continental.

In 1957, Pima Mining Company was hiring. I knew an equipment operator who worked for Ethridge, Clyde Jones, who was a friend of the family. His mother-in-law was a good friend of my mom's. Clyde's brother was Fred Jones, who ran the farm at Continental when dad was there just as Walden took over the operations. Clyde wanted to get on at the mine. I went along and we signed up. That was my first time meeting Ralph Linson. He and Clyde knew one another and Clyde introduced us.

Some months later, on October 4, the mine called FICO. I had listed the FICO number on my application because I didn't have a phone of my own. Toops came to the field where I was on a tractor. He said that the mine had called and wanted me to come to their office by 4 p.m. I got in my car and went to the office, wondering what they wanted. They gave me a hardhat, told me to go to the waiting room, get with the labor crew, and go to my job. I had no idea that I was going to work that evening. I had no lunch and no coat. I about froze after the sun went down. I was sent with a man to train me to be a "skip tender." I was there until 11:30 p.m. What a miserable evening! I was totally unprepared for that cold night.

Helen, baby James, and I got a pickup from the Continental Store keeper, Matt Schuck. Matt had a cabin just below the Madera Canyon Lodge which he rented to us for eighty-five dollars a month. We moved using his new Dodge with a hemi engine in it. We had plenty of power! Two loads and we were done. Santa Rita Mountain had snow on it and the cabin was poorly heated. We were uncomfortable most days and we piled on the covers at night.

A Bucyrus Erie 54-B loads rock into a PT-6 dump truck. Courtesy of Joe Martin.

Madera Canyon Road was dirt then and very rough. We stayed a year. Our car was about shook to pieces and the tires worn out, so we moved into a newly built house on the Thomas place, south of the Felix property. The Thomas family had built two rental homes on their property and the rent was the same, eighty-five dollars. We stayed there about a year, then moved to Tucson to South Veleska, west of Emery Park Drugstore.

In 1960, we moved to the Emmons's place. William was just a baby. At that time, I was operating a DW-21 Carryall at the mine. When I went to work at Pima Mine in 1957, they had a couple of older D-8s that had pony engines and cable dozers, but the newer ones were direct start and had hydraulics. The DW-21 was cable equipped.

Mr. Bull grew peanuts where Quail Creek is now. R. A. Davis grew peanuts where Walmart is today (2022). The Quonset at Bull Farms and the Fitch pasture were used to store hundred-pound bags of peanuts when the market price was too low. When the price was right, trucks were loaded and then the nuts were hauled to market. Mr. Bull and R. A. Davis grew a variety known as Spanish peanuts. Ralph Linson and I bought a hundred-pound sack right out of the field where Walmart is and we divided it evenly. The peanuts were small in size and would give you a bellyache if you ate too many, but they were very tasty.

Joe and James with a Cat twin-engine scraper at Anaconda Mine in 1964. This brand new 666 Model had never been driven. The mining operation had just made the decision to start work above ground. At the time, Anaconda Mine had the largest fleet of Cat equipment in the world working on a single job. Courtesy of Joe Martin.

Jim Boyd came to Emmons's place in August of 1964. He said he had leased land from the mine and was going to run cattle in the area. He had hired a cowboy, Aurelino L. Murrietta, who was living at the rock house on McGee Road. Boyd asked me to come work for him. I was sick of shift work so I said yes. I started September 1, 1964. It wasn't long until he made me foreman. He brought over a Studebaker pickup for me to drive. I drove it until 1971 when he bought me the F100.

While working for Boyd, we built corrals at Spivey's, the 59 Ranch, the Ruby Star, and one on Duval land west of Esperanza Estates. Oscar helped on the one near Esperanza. Murrietta helped with the others.

Murrietta, Marshall Williams, and a Native American family and I put up sixty-five miles of barbed-wire fence in 1964 and 1965. We removed lots of interior fence to reuse along the county roads and to make certain pastures bigger. Lots of hard work!

Boyd used to drive his wife's Cadillac to the Arizona Ranch once in a while "to blow the soot out." She never drove it out of town. On one such trip there was a nice straight road and he got on it. He drove several miles at over a hundred miles per hour. On down the way, he stopped for gas. The attendant called Boyd over and pointed to a "ballooned" out place on one of the tires, and worse, two more were about to blow. This was not a five-star station, but he did have tires, but not cheap. Boyd bought four new tires. It was Boyd's custom to carry five or six hundred dollars in cash on these trips. The tires took most all of it, plus some for gas. He had to get some money from my ranch petty cash just to get back home on. He could have been killed had a tire blown at a hundred miles per hour. He never told Mrs. Boyd. It was funny to have him borrow money from me.

In 1965, we had a pump quit. Arizona Maintenance Company came out and did the job. When Boyd got the bill, he was shook up. He told me, "You are going to do the next one." I made the A-frame rig to go on the '55 Chevy one-ton and took care of the pumps from then on. Oscar helped after 1970. We used the jeep and a "snatch block" to pull the pumps. We had thirteen wells. When someone asks me how long

I've been doing pump work, I tell them, "since 1966."

The toughest ones were Pete Revello's and the Desert Well. The so-called Serasio Well, east of the Ruby Star house, was probably the worst of all. It had a shed over it and a sucker rod inside a two-and-a-half inch pipe. When someone stole the pump jack, we put in a submersible. Bert Walker's was a pain to do on account of Bert messing around in our work with his ideas. Things got much better when we got the crane.

Autocar crane used to take the tank off of the tower. The tank is on a cement pad one-half mile to the west of the house and was still in use as of July 2000. The building is no longer there but the cement and old well still are. Courtesy of Joe Martin.

I was working as foreman when Aurelino Murrieta was dragged to death by his horse in April of 1969. The death occurred at night under very suspicious circumstances. A cowboy working at McGee Ranch, Crecensio Morine, requested a pay advance from his boss, Mr. McVey, saying that his dad was ill in Mexico, and he needed cash to go there. After getting the money, he stopped at Murrietta's house on the way out. Murrieta met Crescensio at the horse barn to say goodbye. When Murrietta did not return to the house, his wife called me to look for him. It was dark and we could not see so early the next morning I went back. We found Aurelino dead, tied to a horse with a strange type of rope. Crecensio never returned to his job at McGee Ranch. He took his wife, kids, and belongs with him when he left.

I worked on my own for almost a year when Boyd hired Oscar. Jimmy and Mark Wyland helped me from time to time until Oscar came on board. In 1974, we moved into Mr. J. B. Bull's former home on Bull Farms. In 1983, I finished my employment with James C. Boyd's cattle operation.

I had a cattle operation for a couple of years, leasing from Calvin Wolfswinkel for a dollar twenty-eight an animal unit. He jumped the rental up to seven dollars and fifty cents a unit, which was too much so I dropped out. We continued the firewood business and some crane work and pump jobs now and then.

I started Green Valley Crane & Pumps in 1986. My son Harold worked with me to build up the business. In 1999, Harold and Julie bought me out and carried on the family business. I left the house on Bull Farms and moved to Andrew McGibbons's Santa Rita Ranch where I worked until I officially retired in 2016, at the age of 80. I still (in 2022) occasionally work with Harold and Julie pulling pumps at the age of eighty-six.

~ Contributed by Joe Martin; condensed by
Monica Lee Elam Christiansen

Rudy Mosley

Rudy Mosley was born to Sidney and Louise Mosley on November 6, 1953. He was one of nine children: Bobby Jean (King); V. L.; Marvis; Rudy; Verlin; Luis Ray; Irma Jean; Robert Sidney; and Kathy Louise.

Rudy stated that his father Sidney most likely moved from Little Rock, Arkansas, to California for better economic opportunities. Like many folks born at the beginning of the twentieth century, Sidney was raised not to discuss his family's struggles; he just dealt with them.

In California, Sidney met and married Louise and moved to Phoenix and then to Continental, Arizona, where, "In 1948, Farmer's Investment Co. [Green Valley Pecan Co.], bought the Continental Farm from Queen Wilhelmina of the Netherlands, who had bought controlling interest of the Intercontinental Rubber Company's Farm, known by locals as the Continental Farm. Queen Wilhelmina leased the land to a local farmer to grow cotton." In turn, "The cotton farm Keith Walden bought had been a plantation during World War I owned by the Intercontinental Rubber Company to grow guayule, a plant that produces latex for rubber, to support the war effort."[1]

Today the old Continental Farm area is part of Green Valley, Arizona, an unincorporated area in Pima County.

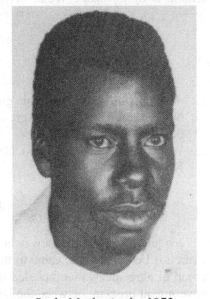

Rudy Mosley in the 1972 Sahuarita High School yearbook.

All of the Mosley children attended Continental Elementary School where Rudy felt that he and his siblings were all afforded a good education with wonderful teachers, both at Continental and later at either Sahuarita High School or Sunnyside High School. The choice of which high school to attend was up to the students and their families. The Sahuarita and Sunnyside high schools varied slightly in their curricula, but Sunnyside was a more blended community, so the Mosley children chose their comfort zones.

As a part of the African-American community in the Green Valley Sahuarita communities, Rudy felt fortunate that the civil strife of the sixties—which included the use of police dogs and fire hoses on the Black population in the southeastern United States—was not part of his formative years. In fact, he felt that folks got along well here. His only negative memory was of one principal at Continental who seemed to be overzealous about preventing minority children from advancing to the next grade: Mexican, African-American, and Native American. Rudy proudly recounted the story of his eldest sister, Bobby Jean, who was an excellent student; she did not submit to the recommendation by this principal and she refused to be held back a year. Bobby Jean attended Sunnyside High School and the University of Arizona, the latter from which she graduated in three years.

Rudy chose Sahuarita High School and he played football and baseball and participated in the Agricultural Studies Internship Program of the Pima Joint Technical Education District (JTED). He graduated in 1973 and promptly was hired by Farmers Investment Co., where he had worked while attending Sahuarita High School. In 1948, Keith Walden discovered that pecans grew well in this climate and between "1965 and 1969, 6,000 acres of pecan trees were planted."[2]

Rudy left Arizona bound for Michigan because his sister, Bobby Jean, had a career, a husband, and was miles away from her family. Rudy accepted a local job to help his sister feel at home as a Michigander. Ironically, while Rudy was headed to Michigan, his future wife, Marsha, was headed from Michigan to Arizona. In Michigan, Rudy worked as a die cast operator, molding metal parts for machines. These parts were made for appliances manufactured by Speed Queen and Eureka.

After ten years in Michigan, Rudy returned home when he received a phone call that his beloved father, Sidney was dying. His father's request was that one of the children look after their mom, Louise. He heeded the call and reconnected with his brother V. L., who knew Marsha's ex-husband, and the rest is history. Marsha Lea Anderson Foster became Mrs. Rudy Mosley and Rudy became the stepdad of her two sons: Michael Roy Foster and Marklin Robert Foster. Rudy returned to work for FICO for three years and then accepted jobs at the Green Valley Janitorial Services and later the Green Valley Country Club for three years.

In 1987, Rudy was promoted to the lead custodian position in which he worked until 1994. That year, Jim Baldwin, a night custodian and colleague, told Rudy that the Sahuarita Unified School District was hiring custodians and they offered a benefits package.

Interviewer's note: Rudy worked as a custodian for a combined twenty-four years at Sahuarita High School and Sahuarita Middle School where he and I were both employed before he retired several years ago. Rudy was a hard worker with an infectious smile and a hearty laugh who kept the classrooms of both schools in tip-top shape. We all are richer because of his contributions to our health and well-being.

~ Interviewed and compiled by Mary A. "Mac" Chernoski

NOTES

1. *Arizona Daily Star.* "Guayule grew town near Tucson." May 21, 2013. Retrieved January 28, 2022: https://tucson.com/guayule-grew-town-near-tucson/article_f6745018-c249-11e2-8cb0-0019bb2963f4.html
2. Walenga, Karen. *The Santa Cruz Valley: a Centennial Celebration.* Sahuarita, AZ: Green Valley News and Sun, 2011.

Joaquin "Jack" Murrieta

Joaquin "Jack" Murrieta was born in Sonora, Mexico, on November 27, 1942. His father, Aureliano (Aurelio) Leon Murrieta, came to the United States under the Mexican farm labor program, which was a group of agreements that included the Bracero (laborer) Program during World War II. The latter was a government program between the United States and Mexico that gave work permits to Mexicans to shore up the United States labor force that was severely depleted due to the war.

"The Bracero Program grew out of a series of bi-lateral agreements between Mexico and the United States that allowed millions of Mexican men to come to the United States to work on short-term, primarily agricultural labor contracts. From 1942 to 1964, 4.6 million contracts were signed, with many individuals returning several times on different contracts, making it the largest U.S. contract labor program. . . . The Bracero Program was created by executive order in 1942 because many growers argued that World War II would bring labor shortages to low-paying agricultural jobs. . . . In 1951, after nearly a decade in existence, concerns about production and the U.S. entry into the Korean conflict led Congress to formalize the Bracero Program with Public Law 78."[1]

It was during one of the cross-border treks that Aurelio would meet his future wife, Magdalena. Magdalena was born in Lochiel, Arizona, a border town between the United States and Mexico. It was an international romance. Aureliano (Aurelio) brought his lovely bride home to live in Sonora, Mexico, where their first son, Jack, was born. Aurelio later brought Magdalena and Jack to Canoa Ranch where he worked as a *vaquero* or cowboy.

Aurelio and Magdalena raised their son Jack and their three daughters in Arizona. In 1944, Marta was born in Nogales, Arizona. Both Irma and Marie were born in Tucson, Arizona. Irma was born in 1946 followed by Marie in 1952. Only Jack, Marta, and Irma were old enough to remember their father's time on Canoa Ranch. Marie was born in 1953 in Tucson after the family moved there—Aurelio had gotten a job at Knox Corbett Lumber Company where he filled orders for lumber and delivered them. Later he went back to his *vaquero* roots and worked at Ruby Star Ranch, which is situated northwest of Twin Buttes near the Sierrita Mountains.

As a result of the move to Tucson from Canoa Ranch, Jack and his sisters attended elementary school and high school in Tucson. Jack attended Sopori Elementary School before there was an English-language learner program. Magdalena realized that Jack, who spoke only Spanish, would need an accelerated English program and so she enrolled him in a "convent program" under the direction of the sisters from Sacred Heart School in Nogales for a year while living with his *Tio* (Uncle) Leoncio and *Tia* (Aunt) Engracia Murrieta Paez. Jack would later attend the University of Arizona and receive a degree in business administration.

Jack was born Joaquin Murrieta. He and other students from the Canoa Ranch area briefly attended Continental Elementary School and then were transferred to Sopori. He does not know why he and others had to change schools. He simply remembers being shuffled from one location to another.

At that time Sopori School was a white adobe building that had concrete steps with a concrete landing all around; Jack recalled that the interior of the building had an elevated wooden floor. It was a large room and each row of desks seated the different grades. A window that faced the southern part of the property overlooked two swings; the children eagerly awaited recess to use them. Jack also fondly remembers the sandbox, toy soldiers, forts, and board games at recess. There were no toys or board games on the ranch. The school day consisted of the three Rs and science and geography, too. Jack remembers reading the Dick and Jane books which were meant to introduce all American children to English and to the American lifestyle at the time.

Two of his teachers were Dorothy Merchant and Pearl L. Feigel, and Jack remembers that one of them came from Illinois. He sadly recalled that one of his teachers could not pronounce Joaquin and called him Walkin'. Jack felt frustrated because that was not his name! Magdalena smoothed his ruffled feathers by telling him to say, "My name is Jack," which is the English translation of Joaquin. In 1950–51, there were

NAME	GRADE	BOY	GIRL	AGE IN YEARS	YEAR	NAME OF PARENT OR GUARDIAN	CITY OR TOWN	STREET, ROUTE, OR TELEPHONE NUMBER	OCCUPATION
BRASFIELD, JACK	7	✓		15	1935	NEWT BRASFIELD	TUCSON	RUBY ST. RT.	RANCHHAND
FEIGEL, STEVEN	5	✓		10	1940	THERAN FEIGEL	"	"	TEACHER
FEDERICO, FRANK	4	✓		10	1940	RUBEN FEDERICO	"	"	RANCH-HAND
GARCIA, RALPH	7	✓		16	1934	RAFAEL GARCIA	"	"	RANCH-HAND
MARTINEZ, JESUS	6	✓		15		CHAPO MARTINEZ	"	"	"
MARTINEZ, PETE	5			10			"	"	
GARCIA, LILA			✓	13	1937	RAFAEL GARCIA	TUCSON	RUBY ST. RT	RANCHHAND
MARTINEZ, DOLLY	7		✓	13		CHAPO MARTINEZ	"	"	"
MORTIMER, BEVERLY	5		✓	10	1939	TED MORTIMER	"	"	"
WHITE, JOAN	4		✓	8	1942	SAM WHITE	TUCSON	RUBY ST. RT	RANCHER
Federico, Arnold	1	✓		6	1943	Ruben Federico	Tucson	Ruby St. Rt. Box 32	Cowboy
Salsido, Ramone	1	✓		6	1944	Ramone Salsido	Nog. St Rt. Canoa Ranch	Cowboy
Camp (Jr.) Chester	1	✓		6	1944	Albert Cox	Kinsley Ranch-Nogales St.	Filling Sta.
Duarte, Olga	1		✓	5	1944	Roberto Duarte	Tucson-Ruby St. Rt. Box 32	Ranch Hand
Murrieta, Martha	1		✓	6	1944	Aureliano Murrieta	Nogales St. Rt. Canoa Ranch	Cowboy
Oros, Carolina	1		✓	7	1943	Manuel Oros	Tucson RR Santa Lucia	Cowboy
Federico, Ruben	2	✓		8	1942	Ruben Federico	Tucson-Ruby St. Rt. Box 32	Cowboy
Murrieta, Jack	2	✓		7	1942	Aureliano Murrieta	Nog. St Rt. Canoa Ranch	Cowboy
Velasquez, Gustavo	2	✓		11	1934	Manerd Gayler	Nog St Rt. Canoa Ranch	Cowboy
Feigel, Linda	2		✓	7	1943	Theran Feigel	Tucson	Ruby Star Rt	Teacher
Gayler, Frances	2		✓	6	1943	Manerd Gayler	Tucson	Nogales Star Rt. Canoa Ranch	Cowboy
Martinez, Gloria	2		✓	8	1942	Manuel Martinez	Tucson RR	Box 5 St Rd	Cowboy

1950–51 school marshal's census for Sopori. Courtesy of Arizona State Archives.

twenty-six students in the one-room classroom and his teacher taught multiple grades. He remembers that Dorothy Merchant lived in several rooms provided for educators in the rear of the building. There was no separate teacherage for her.

Children from Canoa Ranch and elsewhere went to school on the bus and Jack recalled that there were five or six children who took the bus from his location, and the ride was about twenty-five miles to school. His bus driver's name was Bill and he lived on the school property where he cultivated a peach orchard. Bill's peach orchard created a living classroom because students often picked peaches from the orchard, learning about botany and geology along the way. These outdoor adventures encouraged artistic endeavors as well.

When Jack was in third grade at Sopori, the Murrieta family moved to Tucson and he continued his education at C. E. Rose in Tucson. After his graduation from the University of Arizona, Jack utilized his business-administration-degree skills in numerous professional opportunities. First, Jack was a department manager for Sears when Park Place Mall opened in Tucson, and then was a department manager in a Sears store in Costa Mesa, California. After leaving Sears, Jack served as personnel manager for Pacific Mutual Life Insurance Company in Newport Beach, California, but an employment opportunity in Arizona pulled him back. Jack became personnel administrator at the Anamax Mining Company, which operated the Twin Buttes Mine. Coincidentally, Twin Buttes Mine was located near Ruby Star Ranch where Jack's father, Aurelio, worked. Jack had come full circle. He remembers being the designated driver of a fifteen-passenger van that transported employees from their homes to Twin Buttes Mine and back. He drew the short straw because he lived logistically the farthest away. Jack next took the position of director of personnel and assistant superintendent for general services at the Tucson Unified School District.

In the end, Jack retired from Honeywell, which had merged with Garrett AiResearch and a variety of companies including Allied-Signal to emerge as Honeywell Aerospace. Jack worked for twenty years as the human resources director at Honeywell and now lives in California with his wife, Nancy, and children Peter and Danielle.

Lastly, Jack was asked if he was related to the legendary "Mexican Robin Hood," Joaquin Murrieta, who was born in 1829. Various states (*estados*) are listed for his place of birth, but Sonora, Mexico, seems the most likely; possibly in the village (*pueblo*) of Trincheras. Jack's response was that his "grandfather had been born in Trincheras like the legendary Joaquin and his father was born in the neighboring village of Santa Ana, Sonora. His parents told Jack that he was related, but documents substantiating that claim are difficult to find." As a result, it may be true or just family folklore. Regardless, it is fascinating!

~ Interviewed and compiled by Mary A. "Mac" Chernoski

NOTES

1. Bracero History Archive, a project of the Roy Rosenzweig Center for History and New Media, George Mason University, the Smithsonian National Museum of American History, Brown University, and The Institute of Oral History at the University of Texas at El Paso. Funding provided by the National Endowment for the Humanities. Retrieved January 29, 2022 from http://braceroarchive.org/about

Jesus Ortega Family

Juan Ortega was raised in the Sahuarita area and lived there until after he completed eighth grade at Sahuarita Elementary School. Juan's earliest childhood memories are of life on a bustling cotton ranch owned by Lee Moor. Many of the families living on the farm were local to the area, but some were from Texas, and there were also *braceros* (seasonal agricultural workers) from Mexico.

Juan's father was Jesus Ortega. Jesus was born in Juarez, Mexico, in 1917. He and an older brother moved to Tucson early in life. How Jesus met his future wife, Esther Garcia, is unknown to Juan, but they were married in Tucson on April 10, 1931.

Jesus and his family moved to Lee Moor Ranch No. 2 in the early '30s, not long after Lee Moor had acquired the thousand-acre farm in the mid- to late '20s. Jesus worked as a farm laborer and tractor driver. He operated a Caterpillar as well as other kinds of farm equipment. Jesus and his family lived on Lee Moor Ranch for approximately twenty years. Five of the ten children born to Jesus and Esther arrived during that time.

As soon as they were able, the older children started working, chopping down the weeds in the fields and picking cotton. Juan's mother, Esther, was well known for her culinary skills. Many remember her for making very large, thin, and perfectly round tortillas. She would prepare meals and burritos for the *braceros* to buy, charging them twenty-five cents for each meal.

There were many good times on Lee Moor Ranch No. 2, particularly for the large number of kids living there. Some of the older ones were known as the *traviesos*, the mischievous ones, who pulled off some pretty large pranks. Included in this group were children of the Camacho, Estrada, and Gonzales families. Juan recalls the kids going out into the fields at night after the workers

Range sub-soiling demonstration put on by Clyde E. Gaines, manager, at Lee Moor Ranch with a 95 N.P. Caterpillar and 24-inch ripper teeth on April 11, 1944. Courtesy of University of Arizona Special Collections.

had set the irrigation hoses to water the crops and pulling the hoses out of the ditches. Within a few hours, the water would overflow and run down the roads and fields creating a huge mess!

There were enough kids on the farm to be able to play baseball. They would play on the dirt road that ran between two rows of houses. Several of these kids ended up playing ball in school.

Jesus worked nights when they were plowing the fields to prepare for planting. Juan, who was about seven or eight years old, would go with his dad on the tractors. He would take his dog, Shortie, and more often than not they would both fall asleep as Jesus drove up and down the rows.

Juan's dad was the first person at Lee Moor Ranch to buy a car. It was a Model T Ford. Jesus didn't have a driver's license, so he would only drive on the back roads. On weekends he would drive through the fields to go to the Sahuarita Bar. It was on the northwest corner of Nogales Highway and Sahuarita Road, across from the Sahuarita Store on the southwest corner. Juan loved going with his dad because he always got to eat hamburgers and drink sodas.

There were only a few houses on the farm, but the Ortega household was the first to buy a television. It was a large piece of furniture with a ten-inch glass screen. Adults and children alike were anxious to see the TV operate. In the evening the television was scooted into the front doorway and turned on. Kids would sit on the ground and adults would bring chairs over to form rows like a theater so everyone could view the programs. Many adults were not English proficient so there was always a lot of translating going on. They also came to watch Jacinto Orozco, who hosted a Spanish-language variety show. Everyone loved to watch the show and sing along with the music.

In order to combat the growth of weeds and wild grasses as the young cotton plants

Irrigation hoses in a Continental ditch in 1940. Courtesy of University of Arizona Special Collections.

started to grow, geese—hundreds of them—were released into the fields during the late afternoons after the workers were gone for the day. The hope was that they would eat the weeds and not the cotton. At night, the geese wandered all over the fields and a night watchman was assigned to watch over them, protecting them from Arizona's native predators.

Juan was twelve years old when his dad left the farm. Juan's older brother, Arturo, had moved to Tucson to work for a plastering company. Jesus was soon recruited to join that business so the family moved to Sahuarita and, for a short time, lived in a house along La Villita Road just before it became Twin Buttes Road.

Juan and his family heard that their new house was spooked and haunted. Crazy things were rumored to have happened there, but Juan had his doubts. One night, Juan was awakened in the middle of the night. He and Arturo shared a bed. There in the dark, Juan sensed that someone was in bed with him. He reached out and touched something and thought it was Arturo so he went back to sleep. Approximately forty-five minutes later he was jolted awake by Arturo as he walked into the bedroom. "Arturo! What's going on?" Juan asked. "I'm coming to bed," Arturo replied. "But you were already here earlier," Juan responded. "No I was not!" Arturo told him. This incident made Juan a believer that their house truly was haunted!

Jesus Ortega eventually moved his family from Sahuarita and bought a home along the Old Nogales Highway. Juan and his brother Greg went to live with their step-grandfather Rafael Carreras and their grandmother Erlinda. At that time, in the early 1950s, there were three mines operating in the area. His grandfather worked for Banner Mining Company.

Juan recalls that their house in Twin Buttes was very bare. The home was built up against a mountain so the rooms in the back had the mountain rock for walls. The floor had to be wetted down every day before

NAME	GRADE	BOY	GIRL	AGE DE TRANS SEPT. 1 THIS YR.
Saldate, Mack	1	✓		5
Castillo, Louisa	1		✓	6
Sanders, Mary Rose	1		✓	6
Smith, Sharon Lea	1		✓	6
Flores, Jesusita	4		✓	10
Flores, Juanita	4		✓	12
Einboden, Jack	1	✓		6
Saldate, Dick	1	✓		7
Garcia, David	5	✓		13
Garcia, Gabriel	5	✓		12
Kraft, Martha	1		✓	6
Ortiz, Concha	1		✓	6
Ramirez, Norma	1		✓	6
Walker, Shirley	5		✓	12
Montes, Tony	2	✓		7
Kraft, Billy	6	✓		13
Ortez, Rudy	6	✓		12
Sanders, Luis	6	✓		14
Traslavina, Nancy	2		✓	8
Einboden, Joyce	6		✓	
Smith, Emma Lou	6		✓	12
Spivey, Martha	6		✓	12
Einboden, Earnest	3	✓		8
Partrick, Carl	7	✓		14
Spivey, Welton	7	✓		14
Ortega, Arthur	3	✓		10
Ortega, Gregorio	3	✓		7
Smith, Travis	3	✓		8
Bemis, Bobby	3			13
Walker, Beverly	7		✓	14
Montes, Herlinda	3		✓	8
Spivey, Emma Lea	2		✓	9
Ortiz, Nieves	8	✓		15
Ortiz, Rosia	3		✓	8
Labazon, Martin	1	✓		6
Lopez, Carmen	8		✓	15
Ortega, Maria	2		✓	8
Ortega, Juan	1	✓		6

1948–49 school marshal's census for Twin Buttes. Upper grades were with teacher Ruth Barker, and younger grades with Cecelia Stock. Courtesy of Arizona State Archives.

grandmother Erlinda swept the floors. Desert critters, particularly centipedes, were plentiful and all over the place. It was not unusual to wake up and find a scorpion on top of the blankets. Water was brought into the house in five-gallon cans every other day. Clothes were washed in tubs and scrubbed on a washboard.

School was held in a small building in Twin Buttes where only a few students attended. Mr. Spivey was the bus driver and the bus was an old hearse with benches replacing the seats to accommodate students. Juan and his brother Greg attended the school along with the Saldate kids, the Gaylor kids, and Cuate Velasquez, who lived with the Gaylor family.

By the time Juan was in fifth grade, he and his fellow classmates were bused to Sahuarita Elementary School where he started the school year with Miss Lee as his teacher. He met many new students and became good friends with Willie Austin.

Juan finished eighth grade at Sahuarita. Juan and Willie were invited to visit Pueblo and Sunnyside High Schools in an attempt to recruit them into their football and baseball programs. Juan chose Sunnyside because he felt Pueblo was too big and too far away from his home. By that time, his brother Greg had started to attend Sunnyside High, located on the corner of Nogales Highway and Valencia Road. For a short time Juan and Greg drove to school together but when Greg left Sunnyside, Juan moved back in with his parents, who lived in the Sunnyside School District, so he could ride the bus to school.

Juan has many fun memories of Sahuarita Elementary School—in the classroom, on the playing fields with friends, and particularly with Willie Austin. Juan loved to play football! He recalls experiences with Mr. Wilson who was coaching their football and basketball teams.

Juan pursued his interest in sports and played baseball at Sunnyside High School where he became a star pitcher. By that time, Sunnyside had built a new high school on Bilby Road. Juan stayed after school for baseball and football practice. There was no such thing as an "after-school activity bus," so Juan had to walk five or so miles home every day. Sometimes he would hitchhike and, if he got lucky, he would get a ride. After a while, having seen him walking home every day, some people would automatically stop to give him a ride.

One Saturday during baseball season, Juan's coach told him to be sure he was at the game because the Cincinnati Red's scouts were coming in to watch him play. His father, Jesus, refused to allow him to go to the game, telling him it was "just a game" and Juan had to go to work to help the family. Juan missed his big chance that day!

After getting married and settling down, Juan started coaching baseball for Sunnyside Little League. He coached there for almost twenty years and even had the opportunity to coach his own son, Johnny. Juan was known for having a winning team and many parents tried to get their child placed on his team. During this time, he and his coaches won many championships in the city and state. He even had the opportunity to take a team to Colorado to play in the Little League World Series where they won the first two games, but after their shortstop got hit in the face during warm-ups, the team couldn't settle down and lost the next two games.

In about 1972, Juan decided to try training race horses. He bought his first horse, Holiday Hostess, as a baby from a ranch in Sonoita. With his father-in-law Ruben Sainz's help and instruction, he became pretty successful. It was a family effort and everyone got involved in one way or another as they brought home the baby horses and taught them to become runners. Juan's son Johnny learned to ride and helped with the breaking and exercising of the horses. The two of them got really good at handling the horses and

San Martin de Porres Church in Sahuarita.
Courtesy of Monica Lee Elam Christiansen.

won quite a few races. Their family enjoyed traveling all over Arizona taking the horses to events. Juan loved working with the horses, but he finally decided to slow down a little and gave up on training.

When Juan moved his family to Sahuarita in 1989, he then started coaching baseball for Copper Hills Little League. He coached T-ball, minor league and major division, and had the privilege of coaching his grandkids and great-grandkids! He coached girls' softball for a while, but came back to baseball. His team won the city championship and went to Phoenix to compete in the state championship game, but couldn't go any further.

In addition to the years spent coaching young people in the game of baseball, Juan is very proud of his significant contribution to the establishment and development of the San Martin de Porres Catholic Church, an important piece of Sahuarita history. In the early 1960s, Farmers Investment Co. (FICO) and Keith Walden allowed community members to hold mass in the old school building. In the beginning, there were only about three families attending, but as they went around the community telling their neighbors about the local church service, attendance increased. A new building was started in the early 1980s when Keith Walden donated a parcel of FICO land along Santa Rita Road, north of Sahuarita Road, on the old feedlot.

The community pulled together to help get the new church built. Juan was able to get all the fill dirt for the back patio donated and leveled by a local company. Another community connection agreed to pour the cement. Juan's brother, Henry Ortega, built the booths. Juan, his son, and grandson painted the church. Annual fiestas were the church's biggest fund raising activity and for several years, Juan ran them. Juan and Frances still attend mass at San Martin today.

~ Contributed by Juan and Frances Ortega; researched by
Oscar Gomez and Monica Lee Elam Christiansen

Pemberton Family

My grandfather, James Nicholas Pemberton, was born June 7, 1861, west of Fulton, Missouri. He grew up in that area and attended the State Normal School, as teacher preparatory high schools were called, and developed into strong manhood. He attended Westminster College, class of 1884, and was an alumnus of Missouri Beta of the Phi Delta Theta fraternity. He had many letters of recommendation as one of Callaway County's best qualified and most successful teachers. The slogan at that time was "Go West, young man" and he did—to Los Angeles. He taught in Los Angeles city schools for ten years, from 1885 to 1895.

James Pemberton standing on the Arizona-Mexico border. Courtesy of Sandra Jake.

In addition to being a high school teacher, he became a principal and served on the board of education for the city schools in Los Angeles. He was married while in Los Angeles and had two daughters. One died at just a few months old. His wife died shortly thereafter. His other daughter was raised by his wife's family. So he boarded a train for Tucson in the late 1890s.

*Ramona Pemberton.
Courtesy of Sandra Jake.*

He was a man of great intellect. He was a surveyor and worked with a border patrol; he was also a miner—a prospector who founded the Glory Mine, the Vulcan Mine, and the Locomotive Mine among numerous others.

James married my grandmother, Ramona Araiza, in the early 1900s. She was born in 1871 and was seventeen years younger than my grandpa. She was born in Altar, Sonora, Mexico, and moved to Tucson with her sister Julia. Both sisters worked for the old Zeckendorf Hotel. That's where she met my grandpa, James Nicholas Pemberton.

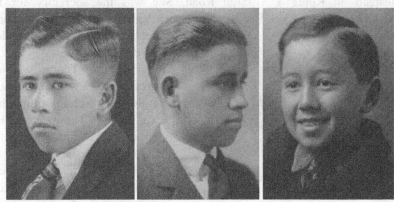

Portraits of James, Joe, and Jack Pemberton. Courtesy of Sandra Jake.

They married and built a house at 912 South 6th Avenue. Together they had five children: James (1905–39), Ramona (1906–93), Joe (1907–75) Tempe (1910–93), and Jack (1912–96). As the children grew they attended Tucson public schools and later, the University of Arizona. James Nicholas and his wife Ramona (along with their children) also homesteaded a little over three sections of land on South Mission Road close to the Mission Mine.

James was a Native American service teacher. Ramona was also a teacher, a member of the WAC (Women's Army Corps) air forces division during World War II, and a secretary at Banner Mine, from which she retired.

Joe owned Pemberton's Lumber Yard on Tucson Boulevard. Tempe was a teacher as well, but just like today, teaching didn't pay a livable wage, so she began working for the Southern Pacific Railroad until her retirement. Jack (who was my dad) worked for the city as well as for ASARCO mines.

My grandparents had a trading post located at the homestead called Las Palmias Ranch. The Native Americans used to trade there. They would park their wagons and get the grasses in the wash for their baskets. A couple that was childless asked my grandpa whether, if they gave him numerous baskets, could they trade them for me as I was still a toddler. Obviously my grandpa said no.

James Nicholas Pemberton passed away in 1951 at the age of ninety. Ramona Araiza Pemberton passed away in 1961 at eighty-two.

Ramona Pemberton DuBose was an outstanding student at the University of Arizona. She was tall, gregarious, and wonderfully enthusiastic. She taught

Ramona and Tempe Pemberton at Las Palmias Ranch. Courtesy of Sandra Jake.

at the Zinc School way before I had memories of her. (Zinc School no longer exists. It was on Mission Road across from the Helmet Peak fire department.) She also taught at the Preventorium for Tubercular Children in the Tucson Mountains in the 1930s.

She was in an unhappy marriage to Julius Dubose and so they soon divorced and she joined the women's army air corps and saw the world during World War II. She returned to Tucson to the old homestead on Route 3 Mission Road. She was the secretary for Banner Mine before it became ASARCO/Grupo Mexico. She lived in Green Valley until her passing on October 12, 1993, and many of her former students attended her funeral. She was eighty-seven years old.

An early photo of the Las Palmias homestead. Courtesy of Sandra Jake.

My aunt Tempe was a petite gal but, oh boy, what a firecracker. I was quite young but I remember her teaching at the Zinc School although I did not know that was what it was called. Tempe grew up in town at the house at 912 South 6th Avenue. She went to the University of Arizona. As time went on she moved to her other career.

When I was four, I went to the one-room schoolhouse with my Aunt Tempe, who was the teacher at the time. It was very quiet, as the students were doing their studies. I went to the front of the elevated part of the room that held the teacher's desk. I stood there on the platform, lifted my dress, and announced to everyone, "I have on new *faldias* (slips)." My Aunt Tempe took me home at lunch and told my grandma, "She's not coming back to school." That was my one and only day at the one-room schoolhouse.

Tempe did not teach for long. The Southern Pacific Railroad was hiring and offered her an enticing salary, so off she went to El Paso to be trained. She was sent to many places in Oregon and Northern California. Oregon is where she flourished. After that we would see her only on vacation when she came to Tucson. She saw a lot of the world traveling on her railroad pass. She was a champion swimmer and won many swim meets. She was proficient in reading and speaking Russian.

She retired in Oregon and later moved to Green Valley to live with her big sister, Ramona. Tempe passed away in February before her sister passed away in October. Tempe was eighty-two. Both sisters were well loved by their students; many of their former students attended the funeral services.

The Pemberton homestead land was sold in the 1950s. The mines were pulling water from the ranches; cattle, horses, and livestock had to be auctioned off. It was a very sad time in the family.

Jack and Tempe at Las Palmias. Courtesy of Sandra Jake.

My mom's horse Sheba was gone. My horse went. The whole property was now someone else's. All we had was memories: watching the summer floods barrel down the arroyo next to the house; walking with grandma to pick *verdolagas* (Mexican parsley) for supper (yum!); feeding the chickens, cats, dogs, and pigs; being careful getting eggs from the under the hens so they wouldn't peck you; riding with grandma in her one-horse buggy; remembering all the family gatherings at Rancho las Palmas—they were no more, just memories.

The actual ranch house is no longer there; the property belongs to Grupo Mexico. The sections of land that were homesteaded are now called Wrangler Ranchettes. It is a quasi subdivision just over the cattle guard at the crossing of the San Xavier Reservation and Pima and Mission Roads. As the mines are still in existence, the property owners who bought ranchettes have to haul water for their cisterns. Due to our droughts, the land is very dry and hard-scrabble looking. No longer is it the proud ranch it once was. Old pictures and our memories are all that remain.

~ Contributed by Sandra Jake

The Revello Family

When I was a little girl, my father and I would take up walking. He would say, "Come on, let's look at the rain. Let's check to see what the rain has uncovered." We held hands and off we went, looking for whatever was on the ground—buttons, marbles, pennies—anything we could find and collect, even if it was just an old, rusted safety pin. Sometimes we did not find anything and then, later on, we would find a nickel or a penny. I later discovered that, so I would not be discouraged, my father sometimes dropped things for me to find—maybe a little old fashioned buckle, small pieces of metal, potage lace, or ornaments. That's the way we would walk through the flats of Twin Buttes, Arizona, our home, an old mining town that was flat and surrounded by small knolls and two majestic buttes.

I was the youngest daughter in a family of one brother and five sisters. My mother, Ysabel Núñez Romo, was born in Baviácora, Mexico, on September 2, 1887. My dad, Domenico Anzavecchia Revello, was born in northwest Italy in a town called Cintano, on May 3, 1875. He left Italy in September of 1903 with his brother Giuseppe (Joe). Several close Italian friends from nearby towns, Basilio Cavaletto, Bartolomeo Bianchetti, Michael Serasio, and Joe Nosetti all came to America as well.

My dad had a girlfriend, Domenica "Minnie" Simonde, who traveled with him. They sailed from Le Havre, France, and came to port in New York City on November 3, 1903. Domenica wanted my dad to go with her to visit relatives in another state. My dad had come to the United States to marry and work in the gold and copper mines so he did not want to go. At that point, she went her way and he headed for San Francisco. He settled there, got busy working, and never sent for her. While in San Francisco, his brother Giuseppe was killed. My dad left California and traveled to the Arizona city of Morenci.

Ysabel Núñez is on the left wearing the white dress (at sixteen to eighteen years old). Rosa Corea is on the right, with her hand resting on her hip. Taken in Baviácora, Mexico. Courtesy of the Revello family.

When rumors of prosperous mines in Cananea, Mexico, caught his attention, Domenico promptly left Morenci. His journey south led him to Baviácora, a remote town in the mountains about sixty miles northeast of Hermosillo—the same town where Ysabel Núñez lived. He quickly fell in love with my light-complected, Spanish mother, the daughter of Domingo Romo Núñez and her mother, Maria Josefa Romo.

Domenico, also called Domingo by speakers of Spanish, married Ysabel at Mineral de las Cabezas, near Baviácora, Sonora, Mexico, on October 19, 1906. They left their wedding pictures with a relative of one of my dad's Italian friends who placed them in a trunk for safekeeping.

While living in Mexico, my brother Pedro was born on October 16, 1907. He was named after my father's half-French and half-Italian father, Pietro Revello, but he always went by "Pete." Seventeen months later, on March 23, 1909, my sister Rosaura (Rose) was born, also in Baviácora, Mexico. (Her baptismal papers mistakenly say 1910 instead of 1909.) She was named after my father's sister, Rosaura. Finally, Josefa (Josephine) was born on January 8, 1912, and was named after my mother's mother.

On April 23, 1914, my mother, traveling alone in a wagon with my three oldest siblings, entered the

Pedro, Rosaura, Domenico, and Concha on the porch circa 1921. Courtesy of the Revello family.

United States through Douglas. She brought only the personal items necessary for survival, leaving many family treasures behind, including the trunk with their wedding photos, which were never to be seen again. They were heading to Tucson, where my dad had gone after walking across the border on April 5th so he could locate a place to live. Maria Elena, or Helen, was born on February 3, 1915, in Tucson.

I also had an adopted Indian brother named Francisco Arguelles. We called him Chico. He lived next door to my mother in Mexico when my brother Pedro was eight or nine months old. When the revolutionaries came through the town, they took the little Indian boy's mother. His grandmother had pushed him up under her many skirts to hide him so they wouldn't hurt or take him, too. My mother helped take care of him. Francisco was about seven years older than Pedro, so he would babysit my brother and take care of him. As he grew, he would do errands for my mother, and she would look after him and his grandmother. When the little old lady died, my mother just kept Francisco with her. He stayed in Mexico with some of our relatives when my family initially moved to Tucson, but about a month later he traveled to be with us again.

Soon after Elena's birth, Francisco was kidnapped in Tucson. We did not know what had happened to him. He just disappeared. He would have been about fifteen years old at the time. He later told me a couple of little old women and a little old man had kidnapped him and they took him to a ranch where he took care of goats. They used him as a handyman so he never went to school because he didn't have the chance.

My mother didn't find him until he was about eighteen. He had run away from the people who took him. He had been kept near where the railroad tracks were being built. The Southern Pacific traveled right by the town, but he did not know what city or state he was in. He could have been anywhere in New Mexico or Arizona.

When he got away, he heard that men were working on the railroad, laying down the track for the Southern Pacific, so he took off with them and worked as a water boy carrying water on a stick across his shoulders with buckets on the end for the working men to drink. He would also slap grease on the wagon's wheels and help take care of the horses. He stayed with the train team and traveled with them until he got to Yuma. From Yuma, they came to Tucson. There were wagons, corrals, fences, and adobe-walled buildings where they would put the wagons, horses, and workmen. While he was working there, he happened to spot my dad in town. He put his

Nana Josefa with Tia Lupe and her children in Marana: Oscar, Francisco, Ramon, Josefa Romo Núñez, Josefita, Lupe Núñez, Hortensia, and Manuel. Courtesy of the Revello family.

hands around my dad from behind, covered his eyes and asked him to guess who it was. My dad positively couldn't figure out who it was, so he turned around and looked at him. There was Francisco, a grown man of about eighteen. My dad ran home, happy as could be, screaming, "Ysabel! Ysabel! Look who's here! Look who's here!" Francisco rejoined our family at that point.

In 1915, soon after Elena had been born and Francisco had been kidnapped, my family moved to Twin Buttes where my dad got a job working in the mines. Thankfully, he worked on the outside, but I understood that he had worked underground somewhere in a gold mine in Mexico. Pedro and Rosaura went to the Twin Buttes country school for the 1915–16 school year and Miss French was their teacher.

In 1916, my grandparents, Domingo and Josefa Núñez, traveled from Baviácora, Mexico, along with my uncles, Juan and Domingo, and my Aunt Ramona. They came to live with my parents in Twin Buttes. My sister, Dionisia (Yolanda), was born in Twin Buttes in June of 1918. Before 1920, my grandparents moved about twenty miles down toward Amado, Arizona. My mother went to stay with them close to my arrival, and that's where I was born in April of 1921. My family continued living at Twin Buttes.

Chico Lopez, Concha, Elena, Rosaura, Dionisia, and Fernando Castillo all dressed up. Courtesy of the Revello family.

In about 1922, my dad got injured and couldn't work in the mine any longer. It was hard for my mother trying to make ends meet. My brother, Pedro, was fifteen and still going to school at the time. He was a tall fellow and was very strong. He decided to quit school and go to work in the mine.

In an *Arizona Daily Star* article published on February 14, 1980, when asked about going to work at fifteen, Pedro is quoted as saying, "If you were man enough to do something, they didn't care about age." It was near that time that he cut through the flesh and bone of his thumb, leaving it permanently crooked. He said, "I ran the hoist with a bunch of rags on my finger the next day."

The Twin Buttes School was a small country school. At the beginning I remember, when I was a little girl in the first grade in 1927, there were three rooms with Catherine Foy as the principal and Mary Maroney as my teacher. The older students were taught by Lucille Titus. There weren't a lot of families living in the mining camp, but there were lots of men there to work in the mines. In April of 1929, Mrs. Foy became the principal and my teacher. We sang a song called, "Six Best Doctors," and I received a health award. In May of 1930, Elena graduated from the eighth grade at Twin Buttes.

In Twin Buttes, on the south side of camp, they used to have a bar up on the hillside, above where all of the

Domenico, Rosaura, Elena, Pedro, Josefa, and Ysabel Revello. Courtesy of the Revello family.

Concha pets a cow while the chickens scratch for food. Courtesy of the Revello family.

men were working. Twin Buttes was called the town of the drunkards. Everybody used to go out and celebrate their birthdays or just go out and get drunk. There was nothing else to do but go to the bar.

I remember that my mother used to say, "Go over there to Mr. and Mrs. Foy's and bring me a dozen eggs." The Foys had a ranch and Mrs. Foy was the full-time teacher. At that time, it was fifteen cents for one dozen eggs and a quarter for two dozen.

In 1930, when Pedro was twenty-three, his appendix ruptured, almost killing him. We rushed him to the hospital but the surgery went wrong, leaving him partially crippled. He could never do heavy lifting again, but he continued working at the mines. He handled the cage that took the miners underground. He was called a hoist man. He was employed in the mining industry until he retired—practically all his life. In the last three years before retirement, he rode a horse around the property edges, checking fence lines and acting as a general watchman.

With my father and brother limited as to what they could do, we women had to do a lot of the hard labor work. We had cattle, goats, chickens, and rabbits. My dad had to have goat milk and cheese for Italian food. When I was nine years old, I had to get up every morning to milk the goats before school. I let the goats loose in the morning with the babies so they could wander and eat all day. In the afternoon,

Twin Buttes School class, May 17, 1929. Standing, from left to right are Rose Vega, Juan Suarez, Frank Mendez, Mary Suarez, Fernando Castillo, Albert Bonillas, Guillermo Castro, Rose Soto, Hector Figueroa, [?], Refugio Castillo, [?], Celia Soto, Lupe Apodaca, Concha Revello, Lydia Bonillas, Jose Valenzuela, Dionisia Revello, Dora Apodaca, Isabel Vega, Alberto Bonillas, Alice Ritchie, [?], and Nellie Vega. Kneeling, from left to right, are Lupe Castro, Margarita Apodaca, [?], Manuel Soto, Reno Zambonini, Eva Castro, Jesus Ruiz, Lydia Castro, Carmen Juarez, [?], Elena Revello, and Joaquine Castillo. Courtesy of the Revello family.

after school, I had to run out to the desert to get the goats and bring them back home. I separated the mothers from the kids and gave them water my dad had hauled from the well. Once the goats were settled, I had to fix the morning's milk and get ready to make cheese. As soon as I had the cheese made, I finished up my other chores before I went to bed. The next morning I would get up and do it all over again.

We were never much as housekeepers because we didn't have the time. We had a lot of hard work to do. We made cheese and butter and tanned leather. We didn't have a refrigerator. I often wondered how we kept all of the food from spoiling.

As little as I was, I had to go with my dad to help carry the wood and load it in the back of the pickup truck. It was a Model T Ford. My dad would have already chopped the tree down and taken the branches off. I would break the sticks off, do some of the axing, and stack it. Later dad would drive home and I would have to unload it into the house, putting it behind the stove so it would be handy for my mother.

There was a little boy in town who decided he was going to make the biggest kite ever. I think he was around eleven or twelve years old. In those days, we used to get our groceries in paper sacks with a string tied around them. We decided to start gathering the paper bags and string. The boy's dad showed him how to whittle sticks and make himself a great big kite frame. It was probably four or five feet wide and long. Then he covered the frame with the paper sacks.

The day came when he was going to fly it. The area he chose was nice and flat, and a lot of teenagers came to help him get it up into the sky. As he started to run with that great big kite, the wind caught it. There was an unforgettable moment when the kite went up, flying high. Sadly, the string was not heavy enough to hold the kite and it broke. The kite wiggled and wiggled as it went down until we couldn't see it anymore.

When I was about nine or ten years old, there was a little boy who was very shy in school. He used to sit outside the door or stand by the building looking sad. He

Francisco holding Concha's daughter, Ysabel. Courtesy of the Revello family.

didn't want to make friends with anybody so I made friends with him. I started to play marbles and tops with him.

The big kid with the big kite started to interfere with me and this other little boy when we were playing marbles. He started running me off. He told me to get away from there and that I wasn't supposed to play around boys. He said I should go play with the girls, but I told him I met my friend first and that he was the one who needed to go away. The little boy wanted to be with the other boys so they decided to chum together. I began to get shoved away more and more.   I

Domenico and Concha with the cattle in 1938. Courtesy of the Revello family.

didn't have much time to be playing marbles and kites anyway. I had all the chores to do with the animals.

Then there were two little boys and their fathers who made a little wagon out of a crate. I wanted to do it, too. I ransacked all the flats left over from deliveries and looked everywhere I could to find wheels, including at the dump. I decided to make the cart my own way by getting two-by-fours and tomato crates to use with the wheels. I went by the country grocery store owned by my godfather, Manuel Figueroa, and we decided to save some tomato crates, orange boxes, egg crates, and whatever else that was there that I could use to make the wagons.

My dad wanted boys. I heard later that when I was born, my dad put his hat on the ground and stomped up and down on it because he wanted boys to carry on the Revello name. I was the sixth child and a girl. Because I

The northwest or "back side" of Twin Buttes School. "We used to carry the wood in that door to store it for our wood heater. Sometimes our teacher donated beans and ham for lunch and we ate strawberry Jell-O served in graham crackers like sandwiches." Courtesy of the Revello family.

Pedro and his first wife, Lydia in 1931. Courtesy of the Revello family.

always knew he wanted boys really badly, I decided I would do everything a man could do. I was going to be tops. I was going to make weapons.

I took the little boy I had made friends with to see my Indian brother Francisco so he could show us how to make slingshots. He told us to get him some leather tongues off of old work shoes. We searched the dump areas and found all kinds of shoes there. We then cut "y" shaped pieces of mesquite tree limbs, cleaned them, and whittled them smooth. We collected old inner tubes from tires to use for rubber.

After our slingshots were finished, we decided we were going to shoot at lizards. We would shoot a rock and flip the lizard right over. How cruel we must have been, but we were kids and it was a sport.

One time my slingshot got misplaced somewhere and I had to have another slingshot. We went around looking for old shoes, but there weren't as many to be found. We decided to sneak into Francisco's room and cut the tongues out of his old work shoes. We brought the tongues over to him and he said, "Oh, where did you find these?" Eventually he figured out that we had cut the tongues out of his old shoes. He never spanked us. He just said, "Oh, so that's where you found them. Now what am I going to do? I don't have tongues for my shoes."

Everyone in town had decided that they had to have slingshots, too. That is why we hadn't been able to find old shoes to use to make a replacement for my lost slingshot. Some of the older boys, the teen boys and bigger boys, would go shooting at the birds. My mother used to get so mad. My family never intended to have slingshots to kill anything.

Francisco was a nice, big, kind fellow. He lived with us but would take off with friends and get drunk. He would be in and out of the ranch, but he did a lot of hard work. He helped my mother.

Pedro and Helen, his second wife. Courtesy of the Revello family.

Juan Núñez with his niece Josefa Revello at Twin Buttes. Courtesy of the Revello family.

Once, he helped my brother and my father dig a fifty- to sixty-foot well by hand. He had worked on the railroad and was really good at dynamiting, which he loved. While they were down in the fifty-foot well, they started getting headaches and feeling nauseated from the dynamite fumes. They could feel a little water and they were trying to trace where the water was coming from, but they had to get out. It turns out that the water actually wasn't very good. It had a lot of copper in it. Occasionally when we would have to use the water, we had to boil it and let the sediment settle before we could use it. My dad converted his 1923 Chevrolet into a flatbed so he could carry four fifty-gallon drums of water for the home to use. He would have to haul water to use in our home and as drinking water because our well water was so terrible.

Elena and I used to wrestle when we were kids. Some of the boys bought boxing gloves. They would bring them over to our house to put on a big show of boxing with each other. Kids sometimes would get bloody noses so they would go home crying. Elena and I decided to get some boxing gloves and started acting up together. My mother didn't allow fighting and she put a stop to that.

We decided we were still going to box so we got Francisco to help. He used to like to get Elena and me to box. He would hold a switch in his hand and then he would say, "Okay, now stand." He would make us stand close together with our elbows bent and our shins together. Then we were supposed to see who could touch each other's cheek. You could dodge your head or "fake" with your hands, but if one of us would start backing up, he would hit us on the behind and if the other one started backing up he would hit the other one on the behind. "That's no way of doing it," he'd say. "Do it this way." Then he would show us again. The idea was that we were boxing, but we were not hitting or slapping. It wasn't allowing brutality and there was no anger because we thought so much of each other. It was more or less for recreation and fun.

In the early 1930s, it was the Depression. Things were not going well with the mines and a lot of people left Twin Buttes. We heard about tungsten mines being worked in Las Guijas, near Arivaca. My brother decided to go check out these mines and discovered that the mine on the hillside was taking applications for workers.

Ysabel Revello in Ruby, Arizona. Courtesy of the Revello family.

In January of 1931, Pedro married Lydia Sanchez. They had two little boys. Pedro, Jr., was born in May of 1931, and died of pneumonia in January of 1935. Julio Cesar was born in July of 1932. When Pedro and Lydia divorced, she went back to Mexico and Julio went to live with his mother's aunt. They raised him in Tucson. Pedro had a horse and wanted to bring Julio out to the ranch. When Julio was not in school, he stayed with Pedro and learned to ride horseback. Julio grew up, went into the service, got married, and went to California to raise a family. He carried on the tradition of the Revello name that my dad had always wanted.

In May of 1933 my sister Elena met Ernesto Garcia. They left Twin Buttes and went to Tucson where they were married. Their daughter Elisa was born in April of 1934. Elena brought Elisa back to the ranch at Twin Buttes.

The Revello family residence on the eastern edge of Ruby. Courtesy of the Revello family.

Pedro eventually left Twin Buttes and settled in Las Guijas, Arizona, about forty miles southeast of Twin Buttes. My mother decided to go out there with Pedro so she could set up a place to sell the food she cooked and take in boarders. She found a location with two big old oak trees that were close together and put a two-by-four from one arch of the tree to the other. Then she put a canvas top up and built walls of mud with wire and ocotillo between the trees. She made windows and tied them up with the

Rosaura Revello Samms laughs behind the counter at the Twin Buttes Store. Cousin El "Tiki" Núñez lounges on the counter while Guillermo Castro and Buddy Jones are on the right. Courtesy of the Revello family.

wires from bales of hay. We had a couple of small buildings that were donated by the person who owned the Las Guijas Mine. We used one for a bedroom with a double bed in it. In the other building, she put a big old wood stove and built herself a big table and benches.

My mom and brother stayed at La Guijas until the price of tungsten came down and the mining camp started losing people. It was decided that they needed to move. They heard of a mine about fifty miles farther south, between Arivaca and Nogales, called the Ruby Mine. My dad went there to work with my brother so some of us girls had to stay at Twin Buttes to take care of the animals, making sure the corrals were holding up and taking care of our house. We would rotate going to Ruby to help my mother. I went to school in Twin Buttes for a while. Then I went to Sopori School, near La Guijas, and had teachers who were sisters, Miss Romo and Mrs. Urquides. In October of 1934, I was elected vice president of the Sopori Willing Workers 4-H Club but by the end of November, I had moved to Ruby School. It wasn't long before I went back to school in Twin Buttes. We were rotated around a lot.

I was about twelve years old when my grandmother fell ill and died. We buried her in the cemetery on our Twin Buttes homestead. Losing her hurt—really hurt. She was such a good person, terrific.

On January 9, 1935, my sister, Rosaura, filed paperwork to homestead 640 acres near Twin Buttes to raise stock. The government told her there wasn't a full 640 acres of land available there, but if she would accept an area of 567.92 acres, they would approve her application. She agreed and the paperwork was processed. The homestead was almost one square mile and gave our family land to raise cattle.

I graduated from eighth grade at the Twin Buttes School on May 22, 1936. There were only three people in the eighth grade. There was Ramona Sanders, Jim Bell, and me. Mrs. Foy was the only teacher and she taught all eight grades. She gave us a high school education. She said if we ever had a chance to go to school in Tucson, she would give us a review before we started at Tucson High School.

There were three different people the teacher recommended that I could stay with to continue to high school. Of course, my mother didn't think I needed to go. We had too much to do—too many chores at home. She said all we would do is go into town and end up married. She wouldn't let us go, even though Elena and I both wanted to go.

Elena and I both liked handling the cattle and

Ysabel and Elena stand by while Rosaura milks the cow. Courtesy of the Revello family.

milking the cows. We'd play, running and throwing weeds, which would get stuck on our backs. We would also throw rocks up into the air and try to hit them with a yucca stick. One time Elena swung and hit me right across the mouth with it.

Elena and I were very close. We both liked the ranch style of life. Dionisia and Josefa liked cooking and working in the kitchen. They became pretty good chefs and worked in restaurants. Elena and I ended up working the cattle roundups.

Rosaura and Elena "clowning" around. Courtesy of the Revello family.

I recall that when I was fifteen and had just graduated from school, I went over to Ruby to see my mother. Most of the time, I stayed at Twin Buttes and took care of the goats and cows. My mother had taken the oldest girls with her and left the three smallest ones—Elena, Dionisia, and me. We rotated to give all of us a chance to stay with my mother, but most of my time was at Twin Buttes with my dad.

At Ruby there was the American side of the mine where the mine bosses lived; they took care of the mine and wrote the checks. The timekeepers lived in the main houses as well. Some of the miners went over to that side of camp to take care of their bosses' horses by bringing them water and hay when they submitted their time. This was way before anything involving machinery was concerned so everything they did involved hard digging in the underground.

We had a country post office run by a man named Mr. Huff. We would go there to get our mail. I don't recall how often the mail ran, whether it came once a week or twice a week, but one of the things I liked to do best was go over and pick up the mail. Mr. Huff used to live in a little building behind the row of houses where the Americans lived. It was between the bar and where the long line of bunk houses was.

The mines had a restaurant with a stove and would supply the American miners with food near where the bosses lived.

Roger Lee and Domenico Revello at Twin Buttes. Courtesy of the Revello family.

We lived on the Mexican side of the camp and we all lived in tents. We had to work awfully hard because there was firewood to chop so that we could make tortillas and food for the miners. I hated cooking and especially hated all of those darned dishes piling up. I had to stand on an empty Cyanamid dynamite box to wash the dishes. I hated the thought of all those dishes. Sometimes someone else would do the dishes while I helped with the tortillas.

My mother had many orders. We had to make lunches because of different shifts at the mine. We worked very hard. My mother put in a wall to divide the kitchen from the two double beds where we slept in the back. She had permission to cut the back out of the tent and she dug out the mountainside to make an additional room back there. She made herself a little hallway in between. There was a shower on the side of the tent. She dug a trench with steps in front of the building and lined it with the rocks had she cut from the mountainside. She built a nice little porch and planted some morning glory vines that she hung along the porch on a string. She also planted a tree and, between the tree and her vines, she had nice shade in the morning. The big boss from the mine even came over and asked if he could have a picture of the front of the tent where she built her trench.

We also had lots of hard work to do helping my mother with the boarders in Ruby. My mother would go to Tucson and take the pay she had received from them. My mother used to sell candy, soda, and food items that she would bring from Tucson. She would buy a big load of food—a hundred pounds each of sugar, flour, corn, and beans. We usually would stop at Twin Buttes. There she would divide the food and take the majority to Ruby where the boarders were.

Dionisia and Domenico Revello stand behind visiting family friends. Courtesy of the Revello family.

My dad and I decided to put up some shelves to start our Twin Buttes store. People would come when they needed coffee, beans, sugar, and whatever else. We could sell it to them and then we would have money to replace the supplies that we were running out of. That's how the little Twin Buttes store got started. Over the years, Rosaura was primarily responsible for running the combination bar and store. It had an old jukebox inside. There was a big metered gas pump with a glass top out front. Children from the McGee Ranch remember what a treat it was to ride their bicycles down the sloped mountain road to visit "Rose's store." They would bring along any money they could scrounge for their great adventure of the day. While they gobbled up their treasures, they would wait at the road for a truck going back up to the ranch. Holding on to the truck bed with one hand and steering their bikes with the other, they quickly found their way back up the steep road to their homes.

My entire family came back to Twin Buttes in the late 1930s. Ruby Mine had been shut down in 1940 and by the end of 1941, the town of Ruby was completely abandoned. By that time, we had more cattle, which meant more work and more water to haul into Twin Buttes. When needed, my mother would sell some of the cattle to have extra money. We were pretty busy.

My dad could not do heavy work so we girls had to do it. It was real men's work—chopping wood, hauling water, and watering cattle. We had to take the cattle and walk over a mile to get water out of the well with a winchless five-gallon bucket. Then we had to walk them another mile back home. Once home, we separated mothers from calves to lock up in separate places so that they would stay apart through the

Frankie Gomez, son of Sally Gomez, near the Twin Buttes Dam. Courtesy of the Revello family.

night. Then, in the morning, the cows would give lots of milk. We had a lot of uses for the milk because, in addition to drinking it, we made cheese, churned butter, and made cottage cheese. We always had good food to eat.

Every so often, we would work with my mother to slaughter a calf. We were not starving, but there were no fancy clothes or fancy furnishings or things like that. We worked hard for everything we had and there was always plenty of food and a happy home.

The only real recreation we had was when people came around to the house in the evenings. My dad used to play the accordion or *fisarmonica*, as he called it in Italian. Occasionally some of us girls would play the guitar. We loved to sing along with the music. The whole neighborhood of kids would come over. My dad loved to tell them all kinds of stories, but his favorite were spooky stories. There were always a bunch of boys and girls hanging out late to listen to him. He got the biggest kick out of watching those kids and how they would have to run home afterward. My mom would always say, "Don't tell those kids those scary stories! Those poor kids are scared to death and they still have to run home." My dad never listened. After they left, they would run up a ways—about thirty or forty yards, and then they would come back and say, "It's awfully dark out there." My dad would chuckle and giggle and then say, "There's nothing out there to get you. Go ahead and run. Run really fast and nobody will be able to take you." Finally, our family would walk together to escort the kids home.

We also used to play games, like bingo, out on our patio in the evening. It wasn't like a recreation center. It was more like a place to sit down and enjoy the company of each other. My mother loved children and loved the neighbors. Occasionally, the ladies would gather at our house to play cards as they were all old friends.

Rosaura and Frank Samms by their car. Courtesy of the Revello family.

Before grandma and grandpa Núñez passed away, they would often come up to Twin Buttes and dance with us. We'd beg and plead with them to come up. My grandfather used to love to dance with me. I was the youngest, but I didn't care. I would dance with anyone—even if it was an older man. I didn't quit dancing until the tune was over and then I went over

Concha's house at 438 West President Street in Tucson. Courtesy of the Revello family.

and complained to my mother until another song started. She didn't seem to understand how much I really loved dancing and why I kept on dancing with everybody.

I remember once when a big, tall fellow asked me to dance. We were dancing and I was barefooted and got a sticker on the bottom of my toe. There was pain from the bottom of my toe to the back part of my foot. It was pretty painful, but didn't seem to faze me at all.

We were not allowed to go out dancing in the neighborhood unless a family would ask us to go. About eighteen miles south of Twin Buttes, between Nogales and Tucson, there was a dance hall called Halfway Station. It was near Kinsley Ranch. We would go to those dances once or twice a year. If we were lucky, we went three or four times a year. We really had so much to do that we couldn't get away from our house very often, but we did have a little bit of time to dance or go out for recreation.

In Amado, about twenty miles south of Twin Buttes, they had a pool hall. It was decided that Twin Buttes needed a big building with pool tables and also room for dancing. My dad and my brother, Pedro, bought a secondhand building for fifty dollars and we transferred it after Rosaura got the homestead. The building had been lying just outside the area of the homestead property line. My dad got the whole community together. We tore it down and took the walls off, leaving nothing but the wooden floor. Then everyone came to start lifting and jacking up the wooden floor. They put two-foot stumps in an area of the floor. My dad backed his little old truck up under the floor and secured it on top of the flatbed. We got back behind him and all the community people gathered around the

The old flatbed truck. Courtesy of the Revello family.

floor to help carry it as the car drove back to Twin Buttes. Then they set it on top of the stumps they had put down. The floor was actually set approximately at the height of a car.

Concha's house at 438 West President Street in Tucson with a second bedroom and porches, circa 1957. Courtesy of the Revello family.

Once the floor was in place, all of the family started building the walls back up and putting a tin roof on it. It was beautiful and you could hear the pounding of rain hitting the tin. My dad built gutters around the edge of the roof and put barrels at the corners. When we had rain, he would fill as many barrels as he could get from the rain running off of the tin roof. It was very nice, soft water. It was always a blessing when it rained because then we had water. When it didn't rain, my dad worked very hard to haul water to our home. In spite of his illness, he would work himself to the bone.

Dances were an outing for the whole community. Of course the older girls started fighting because they wanted a boyfriend. We weren't allowed to date or get married because there was too much work to do. Those things would take us to different places while we were focused on making a living.

We built a dam near our house by hauling rocks, dirt, sacks of sand, and anything else we could find so we would have water for the cows. When it would rain, the small pond would fill up and we could hear the frogs. They croaked all night long. I loved to hear them when it rained. It was also a joy to hear the rain pounding on the tin roof. To us, it was a blessing to know that it would ease our workload of hauling water. We knew we wouldn't have to walk miles with the cattle to take them back and forth to the water hole. In other words, the rain did about half of our work for us.

My mother built a porch off the kitchen. She cut out a big hole in the side of the house and made a window frame covered with wire. She then took the ribs from a saguaro, tied them together with wire, and formed the top of a cage which she attached to the side of the window. She hung crates inside of the cage to set the cheese on and planted vines outside to grow over the porch around this window cage to make shade. She put sliding doors inside the kitchen in front of the saguaro cage to keep the cheese in the shade outside. She used some gunnysacks that were wet to hang around the sides of the cage. When the breeze would blow it

Concha Revello with first husband Eugene Johnson on the street in Tucson. Courtesy of the Revello family.

would cool the area. Twin Buttes was cooler than Tucson, so the vines with the gunnysacks kept the milk and cheese from spoiling. She also used saguaro ribs to form a swing on the porch that she could sit on.

When we made cheese, we would put it in the molds and after it set up, we took it out of the molds to sit in crates so it could dry on the outside. Once or twice a month, my mother drove our 1923 Chevrolet into Tucson where she would sell the cheese, butter, cottage cheese, and gallons of fresh milk. She put everything in a big tub with wet dish towels around it. While in town, she would get new orders for her next trip in. Sometimes people

Ysabel caring for the animals at Twin Buttes. Courtesy of the Revello family.

ordered specialty cheeses like Monterey Jack or one that is made by folding flattened little balls of cheese, similar to mozzarella, in half. Mother would drop them into melted cottage cheese and pack them into little pans with a lid on them. These were made using a little bit of the juice that was secreted from the other cheese that was being cooked. They were very popular and they were very good, too. In fact, as we were making them, it seemed that the whole neighborhood could smell the scent of the cooking cheese. Some of the young fellows would run over to have some of the whey. They

Revello family near the water tank. Back row is Pedro, Robert, Eliza, and Marvin's wife. Middle is Rose. Courtesy of the Revello family.

put pepper in it with little *chiltepins* (chili peppers) and ate it in a hot tortilla. They thought it was pretty fancy that they could sneak up a bowl of the whey broth. It was a nice and creamy whey that came out of the freshly cooked mozzarella cheeses.

Some of my dad's friends would come over to talk with him. They would play guitars and my dad would play his accordion. We had several neighborhood friends and the Ortiz family would come by from the San Xavier mines. They would bring their sister and elderly mother over, but the brother always stayed home. There were several other people who used to visit us. The Coronados came from Silverbell Mine. Everyone would come over to visit in the evenings and we would sit around enjoying their company.

As we got older, we started to get jobs working for people nearby. When I was about seventeen I started doing house cleaning. The wages at that time were two dollars a week. I remember it went from two dollars to four dollars and then six dollars. Then I remember ten dollars going to twelve and twelve to fourteen. They just kept getting higher. I always gave my mother the money from my jobs.

My sister Rosaura got married to Frank Samms on April 22, 1939, and moved to Tucson. Frank was from Chicago; we called him Pancho. At about that same time, I got a job working at the Tanque Verde Guest Ranch with some people by the name of Todd. They used to live on a ranch near Twin Buttes. They

had a big, beautiful home. I got my wages right away. They were two dollars and fourteen cents a week. Those were good wages then and while I was working there, I bought my mother a sofa. It was a nice velvet sofa for eighteen dollars that disappeared when my mother died. I also worked as an assistant cook and cleaned the guest rooms—including the floors and bathrooms. I carried wood in if they had fireplaces and needed to warm up bedrooms.

During World War II, in the 1940s, the people at Tanque Verde decided I needed to have recreation. After all, I was nineteen years old. They said I should go to dances and take a day off to get out of

At the Twin Buttes Dam, Rosaura checks the level of water in the tank. Courtesy of the Revello family.

the house. As I was the youngest in the family, I really had to catch up. They had dances at Emery Park. The soldiers were there and we girls would get in groups. We would be dancing. Mrs. Tartar and my sister, Josefa, would sit up in the balcony and escort us to the dances. It was very enjoyable.

Rosaura Revello Samms, Concha Revello, Monroe Stinnett, and Frank Samms. Courtesy of the Revello family.

Throughout World War II, my mother always said, "Praise the Lord, thank God, my daughters were daughters and not sons. I would have had all of them gone in the service." My brother didn't have to go into the service. He couldn't because of his condition and so he was left to provide for the household because my father could not work. In the meantime, our marriages were broken up. We all started going to work in different places, housekeeping and sending home money for my mother.

In 1940, I bought two lots of land in Tucson with ten dollars down and ten dollars a month. The lots were $150 to $200 each. Between 1940 and 1958, Chico and I built a house made out of adobe—a lot of adobe. Chico would come over and help me. Sometimes my sisters would help and they would bring everybody else to help, too. I built a big home which I was proud of. I felt I didn't want to pay rent. I wanted to work like a man and be strong like a man instead of going into debt for years and years.

I met Eugene Johnson, a taxi driver, in 1943. We had a little girl named Jean the following year. In November of 1949, after we were divorced, I let my sister, Dionisia, take over the lot next to me. She couldn't find a lot for sale and I was happy to have her and her husband beside me. They built a house out of adobe.

Then I married my second husband, James Monroe Stinnett, who was originally from Lawton, Oklahoma. He moved into the house with me. Together we added a second bedroom and built porches on the front and back. We had two more little girls, Ysabel and Mary Etta. Mary Etta lived only one day (September 8–9, 1958). I buried her between my parents at Twin Buttes. During that same time, my husband got sick with leukemia. After only ten years of marriage, he died on January 28, 1959.

Later I met and married my third husband, Dean Parker. We had a little girl, my fourth daughter Virginia Josephine, in February of 1960. We went to live with Dean for a while in Pocatello, Idaho. We also lived in Salt Lake City, Utah, before coming back to Twin Buttes. I rented out my house on President Street, but eventually I decided to move back there to live.

Even after leaving Twin Buttes, and living in Tucson, all of

Rosaura and Elena Revello pose together with a young goat. Courtesy of the Revello family.

us girls would still go to the ranch and help out. I was usually the one taking care of the cattle and Elena was working. She liked to go up and haul hay—she used to haul it by the tons. I would clean the hay barn and stack the hay all up. I'd get up there in the corrals, clean out all the pens, and haul wood. Every chance I had I would run up there and help my mother, going back and forth to the point that she called

me "Churrea," which means "roadrunner" in Spanish. She could recognize the sound of my car coming a quarter of a mile away, and every time I was near, mother would say, "Here comes the roadrunner. I can hear the car coming."

Headstones of Domingo and Josefa Romo Núñez, parents of Ysabel Núñez Revello, in the Twin Buttes Cemetery. Courtesy of the Revello family.

I usually didn't even know for sure if she was out of hay or not. I would just put a couple of bales of hay on the car and take them to her. Many times she was running short and was pleased because I had brought more to her. There was no telephone and sometimes she really needed the stuff I brought to her. Having it made her very happy. I also brought her sugar or coffee or anything that I really thought she would appreciate and might be out of—including chicken feed.

In January of 1943, Dionisia married Robert Jefferson Mixon, from Spiro, Oklahoma. She had a son, Jack Joe Revello, who was born in 1939. In February of 1943, Elena married Carl Nelson Mixon, a brother to Dionisia's husband, Robert. They had a little girl named Mary Helen in May of 1949. Then, in March of 1943, Pedro married his second wife, Helen Acevedo. Pedro and Helen never had children.

In the midst of this, one night my dad took ill just before New Year's. He started having pain and became seriously ill. He was put in the hospital and died the next day—New Year's Day of 1953. My dad was a joker and always a very jolly fellow. He never was a mean man. He never even spanked any of us. On July 5, 1955, my mother joined him in the old private cemetery on our ranch in Twin Buttes. Today, it is beginning to look like weeds. It hasn't been taken care of properly. I've made many trips over there. Francisco and I used to go over there and clean around my grandfather and grandmother's graves; my Aunt Ramona; my Uncle Juan; the little baby boy cousins that belonged to my Tia Theodora from San Diego; my dad; my mother; my sister Rosaura's husband, Frank; and my baby, Mary Etta, buried between my mom and dad. My Indian brother, Francisco, was eventually buried there too.

Concha with two rattlesnakes killed with one shot from her old single-shot .22 rifle in April of 1965. Courtesy of the Revello family.

We've all gotten older. I'm now sixty-seven years old (1988). Pedro is eighty-one and confined to a wheelchair with Alzheimer's. Rosaura is seventy-eight; Josefina seventy-six; Elena seventy-three; and Dionisia seventy. We're all complaining about this and that. None of us has anything serious, at least for the time being, of course. There are still a lot of empty spaces at our cemetery and perhaps, in time, we will each have a place of our own. For now, we will be "hanging in there," as people say. We have our aches, pains, and ailings of one thing or another, but happy we are. I guess it's just another race among us as to who gets to go first.

Over all the years, we were in and out; back and forth; visiting my mom and dad—helping a lot with the animals. We were keeping in touch; going to their house for the holidays; cooking big turkeys and big meals; holding food festivities with everybody in the area. Every

Christmas, every New Year, every holiday—every reason we could find to get together, we would come home and bring bunches and bunches of food and goodies to eat. My mother was very happy. She would always say, "I've got all of my daughters here with me." I tried to be around my family every chance I had. I loved them and I always felt happy when I thought of my mother saying, "Forever my daughters with me."

Colonel Matthew Baird's Tribute to Domingo (Domenico) Revello, written January 12, 1953:

When Domingo passed away, a man went out of my life and left a vacancy which no one else will ever fill. There will never be another "Mayor of Twin Buttes" to me, no matter what the future of that once-thriving mining community may be.

In these days of world chaos and unhappiness, we read daily about great men—the Eisenhowers, the Churchills, and the Stalins—and the great power they wield. But with all their great power, the great wealth and manpower they control, the history they write, tell me how much have they done to bring peace and happiness into the lives of mankind? Very little!

Matthew Baird and Dominico (aka Domingo; Dominick) Revello. Courtesy of the Revello family.

But I know one little old man, whose fame admittedly was not widespread and whose power was not great as the world measures it today, who had one great quality; namely, the ability to impart happiness to others. Domingo Revello was unique in this respect.

All of us seek joy and happiness for ourselves; we work for it, we pay for it and still we don't have it. Old Domingo didn't work for it, and he had very few worldly goods. But he had joy in his heart, and it was this inner joy that he gave so freely to others. People came to Domingo because they needed him; they came to be cheered, and they went away refreshed, with a little part of his happiness as their own.

I loved your father, Rose, and I shall miss him as you and your family will. It is a relief to me that he is buried in Twin Buttes instead of Tucson. He belongs with us who loved him, and not with others who knew him not. He will be nearer this way.

My deepest condolences to your mother, brother, and sisters, Colonel Matt Baird

Memories from Concha's Daughters: Ysabel Stinnett Pannell and Jeanie Johnson Hutchison

Ysabel remembers her mother, Concha Revello, talking about when she purchased a small lot in town at 438 West President Street. She started making her own adobe bricks so she could build a house on her property. She would leave them to dry and every time she went back to town, someone had stolen them. She started building the bricks bigger and bigger and heavier and heavier until they stopped being carried away. Eventually, with

Monroe Stinnett with Ysabel and Jeanie. Courtesy of the Revello family.

Francisco's help, she got the house built. She had her first baby, Jeanie, at the time, and would set her little girl up under a shade tree while they worked on the house.

Ysabel has few memories of her father. She was only six when he died. She remembers that they had a small trailer in Rocky Point, Mexico, where they would stay for a month each year while he went fishing. After his death, her life at Twin Buttes was almost a replica of her mom's, which involved feeding and milking cows before and after school as well as helping her mom gather truckloads of wood and chopping it up with an ax.

Once her dad's brother-in-law gave her a bike. It had a heavy old metal frame with a handmade seating rack on the back for her little

Núñez family making music in 1937. Sisters Teresa Garcia, Guadalupe Ruiz, and Ramona Padilla are seated on the left. Ysabel Revello, on the right, is wearing a leopard-skin coat. Courtesy of the Revello family.

sister to ride in. Ysabel used to ride that bike all over the desert on cow trails with Virginia sitting in the back.

One of grandmother Ysabel's sisters, Ramona, came to live in Twin Buttes for a time. She was pregnant when a mean billy goat caught her off guard and butted her in the stomach. She carried her baby to term, but when he was born, he had severe mental disabilities. They had to let him live at a facility in Phoenix where he could be properly cared for.

Grandmother Ysabel loved bobcats. She would go out into the desert to search for dens. She would find kittens weighing less than a pound and so small their eyes were not open. Once at home, she would bottle feed the kitten, raising it as a pet. At one point, she had one with a beautiful coat that looked almost like a leopard. She had another one that she would put a collar and a leash on, like a pet dog, and take it to Tucson with her. Jeanie remembers playing with the bobcats when she was little.

Most of Jeanie's fondest childhood memories were of events that took place at family gatherings. She loved the summertime holidays when their mothers would pack up all kinds of food and they would go up to the Oaks by McGee Ranch to have a cookout.

Often, when the family gathered, guitars were played and many songs were sung. Extended family members had a mariachi band that played in Tucson. Jeanie remembers all of the kids running and playing in the big sand wash, climbing the oak trees, and gathering acorns that had fallen. It seemed like every weekend would find the family gathered next to a man-made dam at Twin Buttes.

Ysabel had two years of school in Tucson before her father's death. The family then moved back to Twin Buttes

Francisco in Twin Buttes. Courtesy of the Revello family.

and she started school in Sahuarita. Mrs. Irving was her third-grade teacher that year, but before the next school year, her mother had married Percy Dean Parker. They had a daughter, Virginia or "JoJo." Percy "Dean" was a well driller and he traveled a lot. They spent the next year on the road with him. They went to Salt Lake City, Saint George, and wherever the next job appeared, that is where they went next. Ysabel attended at least five schools that year before her mom moved them back to Twin Buttes. They settled back in and Ysabel started third grade in Sahuarita with Mrs. Irvin. Her two favorite teachers were Mr.

Rosaura unloading her old flatbed truck. Courtesy of the Revello family.

Wilson from seventh grade, who invented waist flags for flag football. Their class was his first assembly line for his prototype. He also taught swimming classes. Next was Mr. Thorton, her eighth-grade teacher. He was just awesome—I think it was because he treated us like we were people, not just kids.

Jeanie went to Wakefield Middle School after the sixth grade when the family was living in Tucson and then on to Pueblo High School. When they moved back out to the ranch, Jeanie would have to ride a school bus into Tucson to attend. Ysabel was able to stay in Sahuarita School through graduation in 1971. Virginia attended Sahuarita schools for most of her childhood years, but when Concha moved back to Tucson, Virginia attended Pueblo High School.

In the 1970s, Jeanie and Ysabel's mother, Concha, went on a cattle roundup at the Marley Ranch. She absolutely loved that experience and took hundreds of pictures for slides—from sunup to sundown, it seemed. She used to watch the cattle and would remember that experience as a highlight in her life.

Ysabel recalls that Francisco was always a loner and never really mingled with other people. When he was older, aside from fulfilling his required service during World War II, he stayed in Twin Buttes. Rosaura had a nice house that the McGee Ranch men had helped her build. Francisco had a small house way back behind Rosaura's new one. Francisco maintained the mining claims on the property that Rosaura owned. He told the family that when he died, he wanted to be buried in the Twin Buttes Cemetery—way over in the corner so he could have his own space. They honored that wish.

In more recent years, Twin Buttes Mine partially bulldozed the Twin Buttes cemetery under and destroyed a lot of the graves on the land that had been donated by her aunt, Rosaura Samms, so many years ago. Ysabel remembers her extreme dismay when this happened. Her son, James, had gone to visit

Pedro Revello looks over family graves in 1967. Courtesy of University of Arizona Special Collections.

Grandma Concha's grave and found the destruction. She and her sister met with the mine management team and demanded an explanation. There really wasn't one. A new fence was built and an attempt was made to make repairs, but it will never be the same. Ironically, on November 3, 1967, there was an *Arizona Daily Star* article about the Anaconda Mining Company—one of Freeport's predecessors—entitled, "Anaconda to Preserve Old Revello Graveyard." In the article, Jack B. Knaebel, the Anaconda resident manager, said, "A cemetery must be respected for what it is, and this one will be. It is always open to those with people buried there." At the time that article was published, the oldest legible marker was dated 1910, but much earlier graves were known to be there. Ysabel, Jeanne, and their mother Concha, made a map and detailed record of the cemetery burials. At the time it was made, there were mounds in the dirt and many old markers to use as references. The treasured document even contains notes on the cause of death for any that Concha could recall. A few examples are, "drunk and froze to death" or "he liked a girl, but her family didn't like him so her brothers ran him over." The records contain treasured snippets of history that would be lost if Concha and her girls had not taken the time to document it.

Though it is a registered cemetery, with Jeanie currently listed as the caretaker, in 2015 Freeport McMoRan sent a letter to her informing them that no one else could be buried at the Twin Buttes Cemetery. At the present time, family members and friends must have permission to visit the family resting place. Appointments must be made in advance; mine guards meet visitors at the gate, escort them to and from the cemetery, and wait nearby until they depart. The lonely little space is completely surrounded by mine dumps. Francisco's small grave remains in the corner. Grandfather Domenico lies on one side of the gate and his dear friend, Burt Bianchetti, lies on the other—guarding all of their old friends—just as they had requested. In 2005 Concha, Ysabel and Jeanie's mother, was the last to be buried there—as she requested, right next to her mom, Ysabel.

Rosaura in the Twin Buttes Store. Courtesy of University of Arizona Special Collections.

Rosaura Revello Samms was the very last person to live in Twin Buttes. The mines bought almost all of the property, bulldozing the town and other remaining buildings, but the feisty widow stayed there in the house she had built so many years before, refusing to let "progress" take her from the land she loved. Ysabel remembers fondly that Rosaura absolutely loved New Year's Eve. She would dance through the house with a glass of beer on her head, never spilling a drop. In fact, they used to tease her that she had a flat head. Rosaura loved parties, dancing, and fun times spent with friends and family. It seemed appropriate that she passed away on her favorite day: December 31, 1999, once again proving the tenacity of spirit that was Rosaura.

As Jeanie looks back, thinking of her family, her friends, her life, the stories, and the experiences that shaped her, she shares one final simple, yet profound thought: "Sometimes it was a hard life, but one thing is for sure, we were fed, we were healthy, and we were LOVED."

~ From the life story of Concha "Connie" Revello; edited by Ysabel Stinnett Pannell, Jeanie Johnson Hutchison, and Monica Lee Elam Christiansen

Louis Rumpel and Ike Wilson

The search for instant wealth drew many into the harsh wilderness of the Southern Arizona desert. Many a young man left home, seeking that rumored lucky strike that would ensure a future without cares. For each gambling man who made his dreams come true, hundreds worked tirelessly, coming away with nothing.

It is easy to envision the sea of tents filling small Arizona mining camps; to imagine nomadic workers wandering from one burned out claim to another; to picture the back-breaking work from sunup to sundown. Some came alone, but quickly returned to whence they had come, more than eager to seek new endeavors. Others left their homes and disappeared into the wilderness. "Missing person" ads dotted the pages of early newspapers carrying pleas from families searching for lost loved ones.

Ike and Louis with Matt McGee in the Sierritas. Courtesy of Margaret McGee Elam.

The January 31, 1880, *Tucson Citizen* reported, "Missing Man, John Henry Webber, of St. Louis, Missouri, believed to have gone to Arizona in the early part of 1876, has not been heard of since. Being an only son, his parents are anxious to ascertain whether he is yet alive, and if possible, communicate with him."

The *Citizen* on January 12, 1884, told of "A Missing Man—C. H. Vosburg returned last night from a trip to the Patagonia Mountains. He says that a mining partner of his, Harrison Cline, has been missing from the Patagonia Mountains since last August."

On November 19, 1892, the *Arizona Daily Star* published, "Missing Man. A loving wife mourns his departure. Up in Oakland, California, there is a loving wife, and a family of sons and daughters, who mourn the departure of husband and father. He has been gone for over two years and they have about given him up for dead. He owned mining property several years ago, and needed to come to Tucson frequently and held many friends there. The name of the missing man is W. H. Smith. There is no reason to suppose that he would desert his home, and so it is feared he may have either died of sickness or else met his death at the hands of an enemy."

Some came alone and stayed alone, spending the remainder of their lives searching the dry desert hills. A few brought their wives and children while others completely abandoned their old lives to join local communities, becoming "family" to the people around them. One such pair of lively miners were known to neighbors only as "Ike and Louis."

Ludwig "Louis" Heinrich Friedrich Carl Rumpel was born September 19, 1860, in Bessungen, a district of the city of Darmstadt, in the historical region of Starkenburg, Hessen, Germany. In October of 1878, he left his parents, Johannes Blasius and Apollonis Wagner Rumpel, and siblings to travel to Bremen where he set sail aboard the S. S. Frankfurt. He arrived at the port of New Orleans where he stayed until April of 1885, when he became a naturalized citizen of the United States of America. He was later in San Pedro, New Mexico, near Santa Fe, working at the Black Hawk claim as mine foreman in September of 1889.

Louis was an explorer at heart and records show that, not only did he travel around the United States, he also visited Aspinwall, Panama, in 1885; Barbados in 1896; Stavanger, Norway in 1889; and Bluefields, Nicaragua, in 1900. When he made his trip to Barbados in 1896, he was living in Colorado, but by May 17, 1901, he had filed for three quartz mining claims in the Pima Mining District—Victor No. 1, Victor No. 2, and Victor No. 3.

Isaiah H. "Ike" Wilson was born in 1857 in Middleton Township, Lafayette, Missouri, to English-born immigrant parents, Allen and Ann Harker Wilson. Ike's father, a blacksmith, died in April of 1864 and his mother moved her children to Worth County to live with her widowed father and brothers. In 1850, both of Ike's grandfathers (John

Louis and Ike in a photo with the McGee Ranch kids. Courtesy of Lynn Harris.

Wilson and Simon Harker) were listed as "gold hunters," and it seems that the same restless blood flowed through Ike's veins, as well.

After 1870, Ike's name disappeared from Missouri records and it wasn't until January 31, 1902 that he showed up in Arizona, filing quartz claims to "Victor Nos. 4, 5, and 6" as a partner with Louis Rumpel.

For the next thirty years, Ike and Louis worked their claims, with their names consistently appearing on state voter registration records. Residences listed included 128 West Broadway, Olive Camp, and, eventually, the small home they built in the Sierritas.

Ike and Louie take a ride with James (father), Joe, and James (son) Pemberton. Courtesy of Sandra Jake.

In addition to the small cement headstones located in the McGee Ranch cemetery, only a few scattered photos give faces to the old miners that local families still remember. Each photo shows happily smiling faces posed with local settlers who became their adopted families. We may never know where their travels took them or what they saw along the way. The story of how they met and became partners is lost. We only know that, to someone, they were treasured sons, brothers, grandchildren, or uncles.

In the *Arizona Daily Star*, dated November 21, 1930, Ike is memorialized in a feature entitled, "Partner's goodbye echoes across lonesome Sierritas: Prospectors friends for 30 years." The tribute that followed said:

Louis and Ike stand for a photo. Courtesy of Gary Fox.

Forged in the furnaces of adversity and strife it is welded deep into the heart, outlasting all else, severed only by death.

And so it was that Wednesday [November 19] afternoon, on a bleak rocky hillside in the Sierritas, when Louis Rumpel, 70-year-old miner, stood with silver hair tossed by the wind while the body of Ike Wilson, 73, was lowered into its grave in the little cemetery of the McGee Ranch by kindly ranchers and miners. A rugged journey, sketched in the paths of the desert prospectors for the past 40 years had ended, disclosing for the first time the full extent of the companionship of these two aged men who, for nearly half a century, followed the lure of the precious metals in the hills of the west. For Louis Rumpel has also left the hills, he is now in Tucson, for without Ike Wilson even the Sierritas have lost their lure.

The story of the two aged partners is known as far back as 40 years ago when they came to Arizona from Colorado. For the first 10 years they worked in various mines about the state, prospected in the hills and, when supplies were needed, came to town to work for another grubstake. They established a reputation for sobriety and trustworthiness.

It was 30 years ago that the little cabin on the side of the Sierritas was completed for it was then that the partners believed they had found the mine which was to make them rich. Since then they have lived the life of the desert-mountain miners, until a few days ago [when] death claimed Wilson.

Somewhat of the sturdiness of the friendship that existed between the men is shown in the manner in which they maintained it during the period of the war. The fates had cast their birthplaces in different lands. Wilson was a native of Missouri, Rumpel a native of Germany. Men of the hills as they were, the love of the homeland was deep rooted and in most instances would have caused dissension and strife, but it was Rumpel who faced the situation and solved the puzzling future.

"Ike," he said, "we will not talk about the war. You read the paper and think as you will, then I will read it and keep my thoughts to myself. We will not speak of the war in any manner."

"That suits me," said Wilson, and the agreement was made. All during the war the subject was never mentioned between the two in the little mountain cabin.

There's much more to tell, for the tale of the partners is almost legendary in the Sierritas, but it would not change the motif much.

Forty years ago the trail started that ended on the windswept hill in the Sierritas Wednesday afternoon when Louis Rumpel retraced his steps after starting to leave the newly made grave and, with his hand uplifted, in broken voice said, "Goodbye, partner."

The cabin in the Sierritas stands empty of life, holding only the memories of 30 years of a man's devotion to a [friend].

Lee Harris, Empy McGee, Raymond Kiddoo, Edward Harris, Robert McGee, Ike Wilson, Arthur Lively, and Louis Rumpel get their photo taken at the homestead circa 1934. Courtesy of Margaret McGee Elam.

Louis moved to Tucson, where he spent the last nine years of his life. The September 9, 1939, edition of the *Arizona Daily Star* reported, "Louis Rumpel will be given a permanent resting place Sunday in the hills through which he wandered for almost 40 years.

"Rumpel, veteran prospector, died yesterday morning at the county hospital. Arrangements have been made to bury his body on the McGee Ranch in the Sierrita Foothills, through which he trod many a weary mile in search of gold. He was 80 years old.

"A native of Germany, he came to the United States in the 1890s and after stopping briefly in Colorado, came to Arizona in 1900 to begin the search that occupied him the rest of his days.

"Rumpel had no relatives here, but old friends have arranged that he be buried in the hills of which during his lifetime he had almost become a part."

~ Contributed by Monica Lee Elam Christiansen

Carl Stevenson

Carl Stevenson was born on December 28, 1917, in Hollywood, California.[1] Carl's grandfather, George Stevenson, had traveled to California from the steel town of Pittsburg, Pennsylvania, in search of work. He landed a job in the construction industry and his son, Walter Stevenson (Carl's father) became a well-known and respected attorney who tragically passed away in the pandemic of 1918. His mother, Henrietta (Gill), never remarried and lived with her two sons at her parents' home.[2] Her father, who was in construction, later "dropped a load of wood for a house on the land his daughter had purchased in North Hollywood (formerly called Lankershim), California."[3] This home would house Henrietta and her two sons, Carl and older brother Robert (Bob).

Carl's baby photo taken in 1917. Courtesy of the Stevenson family.

Carl and Bob grew up in San Fernando Valley, California, and attended North Hollywood High School from which Carl graduated in 1935. Even though Carl's family was not in the livestock business, he was drawn to the local horse stables. There he met a horse trader named Gil Traveler from Colorado who brought horses to Hollywood. Gil invited Carl to his ranch in Alamosa. "During the spring of 1936 Carl and Gil delivered horses to Georgia O'Keeffe's Ghost Ranch in New Mexico. Back in California, he and some friends climbed Mt. Whitney that summer."[4] Carl attended the University of California (UC) at Davis along with his future wife, Patricia Fritz. But they were not to meet just yet. Carl graduated in 1940 with a degree in animal husbandry, a major which he nurtured by spending "summers working on the Bliss cattle ranch in Chugwater, Wyoming;"[5] Patricia graduated later with a degree in home economics from the University of California at Los Angeles as UC Davis had been taken over by the army during World War II.

Carl at the track in 1933. Courtesy of the Stevenson family.

"In March of 1941, Carl was drafted into the U.S. Army in Long Beach, California, and in a week was sent to Fort Bliss near El Paso, Texas. His one-year commitment to the army turned into five years after Pearl Harbor was bombed. Due to his husbandry degree, the army sent Carl to veterinary training school to become a veterinary technician. While attending school, Carl requested to be sent to a school for shoeing horses and was sent to the First Cavalry Division at Fort Bliss where he eventually became the horse shoeing instructor."[6] Carl's education in animal husbandry served him well because his military service consisted of being a farrier (a person who shoes horse, trims hooves, and attends to general care of horses' feet). "It was at Fort Bliss that Carl would be put in charge of a trainload of mules to shoe them all and transport them to Fort Carson, Colorado."[7]

Chugwater and Carl in 1937. Courtesy of the Stevenson family.

Carl stands on the FICO feedlot in 1960. Courtesy of the Stevenson family.

"After the war, Carl returned home in 1945. He spent the summer of 1946 visiting friends at the Chugwater Ranch, attending the Cheyenne Frontier Days festivities, and helping a friend in Willits, California, run the Island Mountain Ranch. When he was back at the home in the neighborhood he told a friend he didn't know anybody there anymore. Deke, a childhood and college friend, then introduced him to Patricia (Pat) Fritz, whom he married in 1947. Carl initially worked on the Davis Dam in Kingman, Arizona, but quickly returned to his love of animals and went to work on the Cantua Ranch near Coalinga, California."[8]

"Carl and Pat would be blessed with four children: Tom (1949), Mary Jo (1950), and Dave (1951), who were all born in California. In 1951, Carl was hired by Keith Walden to build the feedlots for Farmers' Investment Co. (FICO). As a result, Carl and Pat relocated their family from California to Continental, Arizona. In Arizona, the youngest child, Barbara, was born in 1955 at Tucson Medical Center."[9] "Continental was a company town and almost everyone worked for FICO."[10]

Carl when he was drafted in 1941. Courtesy of the Stevenson family.

Carl mentioned his gratitude to Keith Walden who entrusted him to design and build the corrals and mills at the Continental feed yard and a second one purchased from Jack Harris. Carl stated, "We pastured a total of 18,000 cattle in Green Valley/Sahuarita"[11] . . . and on a large tract of land in Aguila."[12]

Carl quickly demonstrated that he was a savvy businessman. "He was supplying different meat-packing operations in Los Angeles, California with beef. According to Carl, his biggest packer was a man by the name of Joe Goldstein. One week, Joe declined his usual order of cattle and Carl was not afraid to strike a deal. Carl told Joe he desperately needed to free up space at the feedlot and if Joe could take the usual load of cattle, he could decline the load the following week. Joe replied, 'Oh, send the whole damn lot.' Carl chuckled after recounting this story. Running a feedlot meant cowboys checking the pens daily and veterinarians designing a herd health program with regular immunizations and of course a nutrition plan. This nutrition plan included experimentation."[13]

Carl's induction to the Cattle Feedlot Hall of Fame in 2020.

"Dr. Bill Hale, a nutritionist from the University of Arizona, worked with Carl to increase feed efficiency by steam-cooking corn, milo, and barley and rolling the grain into a flake. This process would be the standard for the industry. Carl also worked with the dean of the College of Agriculture at the University of Arizona, Dr. Bart Cardon, and the Animal Science Department head, Dr. Bruce Taylor, to utilize the unused fat, tallow, a byproduct from harvested animals and combined it into the feed ration."[14] Managing the feedlot was no small task.

In the meantime, the kids attended Continental Elementary School, which had four teachers and a dirt lot. As there was no physical education, Pat Stevenson, who was very athletic, organized for all the schoolchildren to play flag football and baseball in the Tucson city leagues. She was the first woman coach in the Tucson League. The team always stopped at the Lucky Wishbone on South 6th Avenue (across from the rodeo grounds) and her standing rule was that if you hit a double she would buy you a coke; for a triple, a milkshake; and for a home run, a banana split. The Walden's home had an in-ground pool which they opened to the neighborhood for swimming classes that Pat oversaw.

Pat was not the only Stevenson involved with the school. Carl served for years on the Continental School Board and credits himself for being instrumental in pushing for the building of the fourth classroom onto the original adobe schoolhouse. As there was no high school in the area, Tom and Mary Jo attended Sunnyside High School. The county gave them tickets to ride the Greyhound bus that would stop at the Continental Store and transport the older Stevenson children down Old Nogales Highway to the Emery Park Drugstore near South 6th Street in Tucson. There a Sunnyside school bus picked them up and transported them to high school. Barbara attended only grades one through five at Continental Elementary School.

In 1964, Carl and Pat decided to strike out on their own and moved to Red Rock to start their own feedlot. Pat had one request—she wanted a house to be built. She designed a beautiful home. Tragically, Pat died of cancer in 1971.

Carl was widowed for a year when Keith Walden's wife, Dee, introduced him to Betty Schroeder and they were married in 1973. Betty is ninety-eight years young and has a heartwarming smile. Carl Stevenson has been truly blessed with a successful career, a loving family, and two wonderful wives, Patricia and Betty. Visitors likely cannot help noting the handmade cross that prominently adorned his wall and thinking, Carl Stevenson, you pushed through life's difficulties and you succeeded through true grit and perseverance because you never forgot who directs our path.

Carl at his one-hundredth birthday celebration. Courtesy of the Stevenson family.

~ Interviewed by Mary A. "Mac" Chernoski' revisions
by Barbara Jackson and Dayna Burke

NOTES

1. Brandt, Nancy, Joyce Bryson and Julie Murphree. "Meet Arizona Agriculture's Carl Stevenson." *Arizona Farm Bureau,* April 18, 2017. Retrieved January 29, 2022 from https://www.azfb.org/Article/Meet-Arizona-Agricultures-Carl-Stevenson.
2. Ibid.
3. Jackson, Barbara. Timeline.
4. Ibid.
5. Ibid.
6. Brandt, Nancy, et al. "Arizona Agriculture's Carl Stevenson."
7. Ibid.
8. Stevenson, Carl and Barbara Jackson, as told by.
9. Stevenson, Carl and Barbara Jackson, as told by.

10. Tang, Judge Paul (ret.), as told by.
11. Brandt, Nancy, et al. "Arizona Agriculture's Carl Stevenson."
12. Stevenson, Carl and Barbara Jackson, as told by.
13. Ibid.
14. Brandt, Nancy, et al. "Arizona Agriculture's Carl Stevenson."

Spivey Family Story

William "Bill" Walton and Opal Maud Glenn Spivey. Courtesy of Georgia Spivey.

James William Spivey was born in 1879 in Mississippi. He married Effie Lee Flippen in 1907 and became a depot agent in 1910. By 1918 they had moved to Cambray, New Mexico, with their three children, where he worked as a telegraph operator for Southern Pacific (SP) Railroad. In 1930 he was working as the Southern Pacific telegraph operator at the Stockham Railroad Station, which was just north of Tucson. They moved to Buckeye, Arizona, while he was working for SP. Their son, William Walton Spivey, was born in Mississippi in about 1910, but had spent most of his life in the Southwest. He married Maud Opal Glenn in Nogales in 1930. Opal's family had come from Oklahoma to Tucson, via Colorado, to tend to the health of her half-brother, Dalton Langham. Her parents were William M. Glenn and Emma E. Sharp (no relation to Bob Sharp). James and Effie Lee Spivey also had two daughters, Thelma and Dorothy.

William W. Spivey had some trouble finding work but finally got a job in the San Xavier Mine (in the vicinity of the Pima Mine.) Red Hill was a nearby landmark. Georgia

Opal Maud Glenn, Martha Diane, William Glenn, and Walton Grant Spivey in 1937. Courtesy of Georgia Spivey.

Ray Langham, Daniel Langham, William Glen Spivey, Patsy Langham, Emma Sharp Glenn, Walton Grant Spivey, Opal Maud Glenn Spivey, and Martha Diane Spivey in 1937. Courtesy of Georgia Spivey.

Spivey remembered when her father (William W.), and later her brother, worked in the underground San Xavier lead and zinc mine and how dangerous it seemed. That mine is now under the pit of Pima Mine.

William and Opal's children (William Glenn, Walton Grant, Martha Diane, Emma Lee, and Georgia Ann) went to Twin Buttes School at first and then Sahuarita School. The family had no car or electricity or running water. They hauled water in from the San Xavier Mine. They also had no refrigeration but block ice, which they bought three hundred pounds at a time. The mine had a bus that took people to Tucson or brought miners out from town. This bus also transported kids until the bus drivers got tired of it and the school had to get its own bus. William drove the school bus, along with a Mr. Gravely. When living at San Xavier mine, they were close to Mission Road which continued on over to the McGee Ranch. That was their closest place to socialize. On weekends, dances were held at the ranch. Despite the lack of amenities, the family enjoyed their life and friends.

In 1940 they were living in Tucson on Silverlake Road and William was a road foreman. Later they lived at the 59 Ranch on Mission Road. They always lived on the west side in the foothills of the Sierritas. "Bill" Spivey was always a well-liked and helpful person who made an impression on all who met him. Connections with the McGee family bore fruit: Bill's sister, Thelma Spivey, married Numo "Chad" McGee and they raised a large family on the McGee Ranch. Their sister Dorothy married Gilbert Willett of Sasco and they too, remained in Southern Arizona with their family.

William Walton "Bill" Spivey returning to Tucson in the new fire truck purchased by Consolidated Aircraft Corporation. Courtesy of Georgia Spivey.

Besides the McGee Ranch families, the Spivey family became connected through marriage to other prominent pioneer families. William Glenn, son of William W. and Opal, married Roberta (Bobbie) Marinack. Her mother was Jesse Mae Foster, the daughter of Mae Dowdle and Jesse M. Foster. Jesse's sister Elsie had married Ernest Wickersham, who went on to figure in the ranching and banking industries of Southern Arizona. The Dowdles also figured prominently in the early ranching history of Southern Arizona. Along with some of the Proctor boys, the patriarch, David Dowdle, arrived in the late 1870s with his wife Aury, daughter Mary Elizabeth, and sons William, Henry, and John, and found a place in the Santa Rita Mountains, the ruins of which can still be found near Dowdle Canyon.

All of the Dowdles, including Mae's father, Henry "Hank" Dowdle, eventually had homesteads in Graham County. Mae's aunt, Mary Elizabeth, married Frank Proctor who was operating a ranch in

William Walton and Opal Maud Glenn Spivey family Christmas in December of 1969. Courtesy of Georgia Spivey.

Sahuarita, but after a bad drought, ended up working for Col. William Greene of the Greene Cattle Company of Cochise County and Cananea, Sonora. Mary and Frank adopted Mary Benedict, daughter of Albert and Gregoria Alvarez Benedict, early settlers in Sahuarita who had died. For a while, Mary B. Proctor lived an independent life as a typesetter in Tucson, but soon married Colonel Greene and had six children. Frank Proctor's brothers, Charles and Henry, also ranched in the Box Canyon and Madera Canyon areas, as well as at the Sopori and in Graham County. Another Spivey married into the McGee Ranch family: Martha married Frank McGee, who died young in a car accident. Members of the Spivey family are buried in the McGee Ranch cemetery. It is a family connected in many ways to all that is best in Southern Arizona history, reflecting the diligence and hard work that underpins the settlement of the Sahuarita area.

~ Contributed by Mary N. Kasulaitis

NOTES

Bennett, Barbara Brown. Opal Spivey interview. October 24, 1998. Transcribed by Amy Millet.
Dowdle, Andrew. Dowdle family talk at La Frontera Corral of the Westerners meeting in Green Valley, May 6, 2013.
Martin, Georgia Spivey. Interviewed by Mary N. Kasulaitis. August 1, 2021.
Walls, Deborah Spivey. Interviewed by Mary N. Kasulaitis. July 25, 2021.

Paul E. Tang

On Saturday, May 1, 2021, I (Mary A. "Mac" Chernoski) interviewed retired Pima County Superior Court Judge Paul E. Tang in front of his family store, once called the Continental Store and which is Madera Fitness today. The Continental Store was located at one time on Continental Road and it is interesting to note that the road is now called Whitehouse Canyon Road; regardless of the name of the road, the property is still owned by Farmers Investment Co. It was a bliss-filled, impromptu meeting that occurred due to a change of plans by his daughter and included his dog, Precious. Paul Tang had ventured down to Tucson to his old stomping grounds and home in Continental, Arizona.

Don Ling standing in front of the Continental Store. Courtesy of the Tang family.

Paul Tang began by promptly pointing out that at one time the right-hand quadrant of the store's exterior floor was graced with his name. It had obviously been resurfaced. Additionally, Paul pointed out that to our left, by the wrought-iron doors which his father had built at the entrance of the store, had been a phone booth which patrons could use. He began talking about his father's journey as the owner of the Continental Store.

Paul Tang's father, Ah Ling "Don" Tang, ended up in the Southern Arizona area around 1955. He arrived from Chicago, where he had lived after immigrating from China. His port of entry had most likely been Seattle. Paul stated that immigrants from China were rejected due to the Chinese Exclusion Act of 1882, which was the first and only law passed to prevent all members of a specific ethnic or national group—individuals of Chinese ancestry—from immigrating into this county. (The Exclusion Act completely barred Chinese from immigrating into the U.S.) Retired Pima County Superior Court Judge Paul Tang noted the sad history of discrimination that Chinese immigrants faced.

The Supreme Court case *United States v. Wong Kim Ark* posed this question: "Is a child who was born in the United States to Chinese-citizen parents who are lawful permanent residents of the United States a U.S. citizen under the Citizenship Clause of the Fourteenth Amendment?"[1] The majority opinion, handed down by Justice Horace Gray, stated that because Wong was born in the United States and his parents were not "employed in any diplomatic or official capacity under the Emperor of China, the

Citizenship Clause of the Fourteenth Amendment automatically makes him a U.S. citizen."[2] This Supreme Court decision handed down in March of 1898 set a precedent that made life a little easier for the multitude of Chinese immigrants to follow, like Paul Tang's father.

Ah Ling Don Tang was adopted by the Presbyterian family of James (Jim) Ohan, Sr. His education was limited and he had attended school only up to the fifth grade. When World War II broke out, Ah Ling tried to enlist, but was rejected due to his flat feet. He ended up working for the Department of Defense and other agencies for many years. Ah Ling remained a bachelor for many years—due to discrimination, blended marriages were not welcomed and in many cases were illegal, which limited his choices. (The prior Page Act of 1875 had essentially prevented Chinese women from immigrating to the U.S.)

Following his time in Chicago, Ah Ling ended up in a little laundromat in Fort Wayne, Indiana. There he met a gentleman, Bing G. Wong, who was going to Valparaiso College, an institution of higher learning located southeast of Gary, Indiana. Mr. Wong was from Marana, Arizona, and he knew that Ah Ling suffered from arthritis and had some asthma and recommended that he move to the warm climate and drier air of Arizona around 1954. In the meantime, Ah Ling was betrothed through an

Li Pui Ying poses for a photo circa 1954. Courtesy of the Tang family.

arranged marriage (as Paul stated, by a "Chinese yenta") to Paul's mom, Pauline Lee (Li Pui Ying), who was living in Hong Kong. His parents corresponded by mail using the red, white, and blue *par avion* envelopes. Ah Ling returned to Hong Kong for a year to court Pauline and they were married on December 3, 1954, in Hong Kong.

In the spring of 1955, Ah Ling was urgently trying to get his pregnant wife into the United States; Ah Ling's adopted father, Jim, told him to contact Senator Barry Goldwater's office. Senator Goldwater cut through the red tape and the newlywed couple arrived in Tucson in July of 1955. Pauline soon gave birth to their first child, Wei-Liam (William or "Billy"), Paul's eldest brother, on August 14, 1955, at St. Mary's Hospital. As Paul stated, Tucson at this time had a population of about 70,000 people. It was "Little Pueblo" by today's standards.

Ah Ling and Pauline Tang had three children: William, Lorna (Suzie), and Paul. The names William and Lorna were chosen to honor Jim Ohan's siblings. Pauline was supposed to be having a daughter when his parents were delightfully surprised with another son whom they named Paul, to honor Pauline. The kids were raised in the family's general mercantile store which included groceries, dry goods, hardware supplies, and gas from a Union 76 gas pump. Trucks would deliver supplies to the store once a week and Paul's dad would travel to Tucson twice a week for specialty requests. The only other store nearby was the One Stop, which also had a gas station.

The area east of the Santa Cruz River traditionally was

Ah Ling and his bride Li Pui Ying on their wedding day, December 3, 1954. Pauline's mother is standing behind her. Courtesy of the Tang family.

known as Continental, Arizona, after the Continental Farm. The land west of the Santa Cruz River would become Green Valley. Years after Keith Walden purchased the Continental Farm, most folks began to call the area either Green Valley or Sahuarita, the latter of which annexed a large chunk of it into its town. However, the older sages in the community still called this area Continental. The running joke when he was growing up was that Sahuarita, according to Paul Tang, was the bedroom community of Continental. In fact, for Paul Tang and others, Continental School was the building east of his family store over the railroad tracks that now houses the Pima County Community Center. Paul Tang remembers that the main building was a very tall adobe structure and then when he was in junior high, several mobile-wide trailers were purchased to accommodate the seventh and eighth grade classrooms.

Paul also remembers how lucky he and his siblings were to be afforded an education. In fact, Paul used the term "generation skipper." Paul's father's education had been limited; he attended school only up to the fifth grade. His mother was never afforded an education due to her gender. Women did not need an education. The normal process would be elementary education and for the next generation, elementary and high school education. Paul went to elementary school, high school, college, and graduate school. He was thus a generation skipper and Paul remarked, "So are you." I was the lucky daughter of an immigrant family that valued an education for all of their children regardless of gender.

Pauline Tang inside the Continental Store. Courtesy of the Tang family.

Our conversation about Paul's years at Continental School triggered Paul's memory of a painful ordeal faced by the school's kindergarten teacher, Christina Bellios, formerly Christina Henry, at his school and recounted in a book entitled *Deadly Intentions* by William Randolph Stevens, the prosecutor of the case.[3] Paul fondly remembers his middle school teacher, Mr. Holt, who ran an orderly, curriculum-based classroom. In 1969, Mr. Holt allowed his students to watch a New York Mets versus Baltimore Orioles World Series game in his classroom. The New York Mets in 1969 were the underdogs despite their pitching aces Tom Seaver, aka Tom Terrific, and Jerry Koosman.

Like the 1969 underdog Mets, no one expected much greatness would come out of the small communities of Continental, Green Valley, or Sahuarita. Paul, Dick Walden, and others would prove them all wrong. This area was unique because while there might be internal squabbles among folks here, not one person with whom I have spoken with felt that the squabbles were racially or ethnically motivated. As Paul stated, "If something was happening, we addressed it as a neighborhood."

The bottom line is that everyone knew everyone and Paul fondly remembers being welcomed on Christmas Eve at his neighbor's house, the Cordova residence, for holiday green corn tamales. It was sprinkling and cold outside, but Paul vividly remembers the tamale in the husk being placed on his napkin and the warmth of eating the sweet oozing *masa*. He inadvertently touched the chili with his index finger, which he neglected to wash. Later on that evening, Paul discovered that rubbing his eye with his chili-coated finger was not a pleasant experience. Paul's mom and dad were gourmet cooks and Paul proudly stated, "My mom's favorite food to cook was Mexican." Pauline loved green corn tamales, any kind of taco, and especially *sopes*. His mom would fuse her stir-fry technique with a taco recipe and the result was amazing! Culinary exchanges built cultural bridges.

This sense of community carried the Continental neighborhoods through the oil crisis of 1974 when gas prices went through the roof. Paul Tang's father sold Union 76 gas and due to the gas embargo, supplies of fuel were spotty. His father would deny gas to non-locals through a clever signal. This was the time before cell phones. Ah Ling would turn on the Union 76 light so that the neighbors would know that gas was available. It was an ingenious way to allow the neighborhood to fill up. Remember that the Continental Store and the Ora Verde or One Stop were the only gas stations around and Tucson was forty-five minutes away. "This is how we took care of each other," Paul stated, "because we were so far out."

As children growing up and living in the same building that housed the general store, every member of the family pitched in. His father did the bookkeeping. Folks back then paid cash or had a store account. Paul and his siblings cleaned the store and stocked the shelves. Paul remembers being hired out to pick cotton and peanuts. That was grueling work in the hot summer sun.

Paul recounted the tale of his classmate and friend, Ray Mosley, and how the two of them got into a squabble. This squabble included rock throwing and according to Paul Tang, "Ray cleaned my clock."

His mother did not console him or wipe away his tears; instead, she used this as a teachable moment about tolerance. Pauline Tang explained that he could not act this way because their neighbors were not only part of their community, but literally their livelihood. Both Ray and Paul quickly patched up their differences and played on various teams together including Little League and the Continental Mustangs.

Continental Store. Courtesy of the Tang family.

On Sundays, Ah Ling would close the store early to go fishing at Canoa Lake or Parker Lake in Amado. One day, a truckload of folks from out of town arrived. No one seems to know exactly what happened, but there was a loud commotion because fisticuffs had broken out outside the store while Ah Ling was fishing. Paul vividly remembers that there was blood everywhere and the neighbors reacted because it wasn't a fair fight. No police were called. Instead, the neighbors threw rocks at the hooligans, which blew out their back windshield; this served as a reminder to any other troublemakers to stay away from their neighborhood in the future. The bottom line was that the members of the Continental neighborhood did not get into each other's business, but took care of their own. Plus, because many folks were employed by Farmer's Investment Co., a certain comportment was expected by virtue of being a Walden employee.

The immigrant's story is one of making sure that children receive an education.

When Paul completed his studies at Continental Elementary School, he attended Sunnyside High School and Westminster College in Fulton, Missouri—the college where Winston Churchill made his *Iron Curtain* speech. Paul soon became homesick at Westminster and forfeited his scholarship monies to attend the University of Arizona for his undergraduate studies in journalism. "I never did anything the easy way," Paul stated. During the summer before his senior year in college, Paul accepted an internship at the *Tucson Citizen*. The subsequent summer before law school, he accepted an internship at the *Phoenix Gazette*. Paul stated that these two internships were eye-openers because he witnessed seasoned journalists still typing obituaries on old Remington without a writer's guild, which meant minimum wage. He quickly realized that the journalism profession was not for him—especially when he learned that one of his managing editors had gotten himself promoted by going to law school. He later discovered that journalists going to law school is not unique. Indeed, Tucson's own Savannah Guthrie had gone

The Judge Paul Tang family. Courtesy of the Tang family.

from the University of Arizona to Georgetown Law School and eventually landed a job on *The Today Show*.

It was at this juncture that retired Judge Paul Tang really went down memory lane. He mentioned seeing the 1973 movie *Paper Chase* which starred John Houseman, and he commented on the residual effect that this movie had on law school students around the country. He remembers students in Professor Charles "Chuck" Ares's class at the University of Arizona Law School seated in the front rows all wearing bowties. Paul mentioned Professor Chuck Ares because he went to Continental. Professor Ares grew up in Elgin, Arizona, surrounded by cotton and alfalfa fields. He clerked for Supreme Court Justice William O. Douglas. Well-educated and prominent people did come out of the area!

When Paul graduated, he worked as a deputy county attorney. After a few years, he received a call from a large law firm, Bilby & Shoenhair, which later was acquired by Snell & Wilmer. He worked there for about five years to "maintain the firm." In 1994 or 1995, Paul Tang and two friends formed the firm of Quigley, Tang & Whitehill, PLC, where he remained until 2001 when he was appointed to the Pima County Superior bench by Governor Jane Dee Hull. Paul Tang was president of the Pima County Bar Association and chair of the Committee on Character and Fitness of the Supreme Court of Arizona, which oversees attorneys from other states seeking admission to the Arizona bar. He also sat on the board that built the Tucson Chinese Cultural Center.

Interviewer's note: As my interview concluded with retired Judge Paul E. Tang, I extended my heartfelt thanks to him and to his family members: his wife Raquel; their son, Michael, who may follow his parents into law; and their daughter, Selena, who hopes to become a doctor. I am truly indebted to him for journeying down from Tucson for an insightful, informative, and absolutely delightful discussion and to his dog, Precious, who was precious by his side!

~ Interview by Mary A. "Mac" Chernoski; revisions by retired
Pima County Superior Court Judge Paul E. Tang

NOTES

1. Oyez. *United States v. Wong Kim Ark*. Accessed January 29, 2022 from www.oyez.org/cases/1850-1900/169us649
2. Ibid.
3. Stevens, William Randolph. *Deadly Intentions*. Second edition. Signet: 1983.

Teso, Angulo, and Sanchez Families

Alejandro Serrano Sanchez, born on April 10, 1873, came to Arizona from Pitiquito, Sonora, Mexico. He died on November 28, 1958, in Tucson and was buried in Twin Buttes cemetery. For many years, he worked on a cattle ranch called Rancho de Batamote (Desert Willow), which was located in the Sopori area and went south toward Arivaca. He was the grandfather of Mercy Angulo Teso, who has provided this information. He had three wives.

With Francisca Moreno, he had five children: Rosa, Luisa, Mercedes, Victoria, and Rosario. Together with his second wife, Cruz Moreno Ballesteros, he had three children: Francisca, Rafaela, and Lugarda. Rafaela and Lugarda were twins.

His third wife was Maria Jesus Yubeta. They had seven children: Alejandro, Aurora, Amaila, Manuel, Armida, Adela, and Luis.

Francisca Sanchez married Francisco Estrada. They had five children: Enrique, Evangeline, Raul, Efrain "Gaucho," and Virginia. Enrique died at three-and-a-half years of age and was buried on the property that eventually became the baseball field for the Sahuarita Elementary School (the northwest corner of the school yard). Evangeline died at age nine and Raul lived only seven months. They are both buried in Holy Hope Cemetery. Efrain and Virginia lived to adulthood and Efrain is still a member of the Sahuarita Community.

Jose Orozco, Henry Teso, Jose Angulo, Michael Angel Camacho, Pancho Teso pose for a photo in 1961. Courtesy of Mercy Teso.

When Francisco Estrada died, Francisca married Salvador Evaristo Angulo, born August 6, 1901, in Yuma, Arizona. Together they had five children: Clara, Mercedes "Mercy," Rogelio, Jose, and Alex.

Salvador Evaristo claimed membership in the Yuma Indian Tribe. He met Francisca in Sahuarita at the general grocery store and restaurant on the northwest corner of Nogales Highway and what is now Sahuarita Road. At the time, the building was owned by a gentleman named Harry Manelos.

Evaristo worked as a cattle hand and cowboy for a number of ranches in the Sahuarita area. One of Evaristo's friends was Alberto Yescas. Alberto lived on the Continental Ranch for most of his years in the area. According to Mercy's recollection, her father worked at the Sahuarita Ranch when it was owned by a rancher named Mr. Stout, who owned a vast amount of land in the area. He was primarily a cattleman and Evaristo worked the cattle.

Stout sold Sahuarita Ranch to Harris Ranches in the late 1940s. Harris was probably the first to start farming in the area. Another family that was well known to locals was the Camacho family. Alberto Camacho came with Mr. Stout from the Maricopa area in the mid- to late '40s.

Around the time that the Sahuarita Ranch changed ownership, Evaristo sought to buy land and settled in La Villita. The lot he bought was owned by an individual by the name of Merchant. Merchant also sold lots to other families, and their descendants still live on the property. The lots were never surveyed. Merchant just parceled off the acre and staked out four corners. The cost was approximately one hundred dollars and buyers were able to make payments.

Mercy's uncle, Manuel Sanchez, tells the story that when he was young, he and Nacho Bracamonte, his neighbor, would ride their horses to school. They had to cross through the Santa Cruz River because it did not have a bridge. Manuel mentioned that most of the time, there was water flowing in the river. Once at school, they would tie up the horses on school grounds to graze on the grass that was there.

Mercy was born in 1942 at a midwife's house on 1st Street in Tucson. She still lives on the property and in the

Minnie Caño, Mercy Teso, and Clara Angulo. Courtesy of Mercy Teso.

Teddy, Mercy, and Henry Teso stand in the front yard. Courtesy of Mercy Teso.

house her father built in La Villita. Her mother died from uterine cancer on October 18, 1954, and her father from pancreatic cancer on August 29, 1955.

Mercy was left alone at age thirteen to take care of her three younger brothers (Rogelio, age nine; Jose, age six; and Alejandro, age four), but that did not deter her from wanting to keep going to school. Mrs. Burrell, her first-grade teacher, often kept little Alejandro in her classroom during the school day. During early these years, she also gave a lot of credit and appreciation to her neighbors, particularly Cora and Jose Martinez. Mrs. Martinez would watch the boys while she went to school. Trying to go to high school was unbelievably difficult for her. The school bus taking students to Tucson picked them up early and came back late in the day.

Mercy loved school. Her first five years she had to walk to the elementary school because there wasn't a bus available to pick the students up. She remembered fourth grade well because the students could read a lot of biographies. She read about Theodore Roosevelt and loved the name Theodore. Her father-in-law was Teodoro Teso. She was always asked if she named her son after her father-in-law. People were stunned to learn that he was actually named after Theodore Roosevelt.

Mercy did not complete ninth grade. She stayed home to be with her brothers. She helped out making tortillas for Cora Martinez, who used them to make bean burros for her husband who was a labor contractor. He sold them to his employees.

One of the super treats that all of the students looked forward to was movie night on the school grounds. Anyone could attend, but it was mostly intended for students. During the school year, the movies were shown in Mr. Wilson's classroom at night. During the summer, movies were shown outside on the grassy area of the school property. The white wall of the first-grade classroom became the screen. The majority of the kids came from the surrounding area. Many would just walk.

Minnie Cano and Alex Angulo on February 21, 1952. Courtesy of Mercy Teso.

It was at one of those nights in 1955 or '56 that Mercy recalls her future husband attending from Continental. Henry Teso sent her a note and a stick of chewing gum. "Do you want to go to a movie in Tucson?" was on the note. When quizzed about the question, she said, "I was dumbfounded!" I was only fourteen years old and he was nineteen.

They dated for five years and married in February of 1959. Mercy and Henry Teso went on to live in Mercy's home and had four kids together: Diana, Teddy, Frankie, and Debbie.

Mercy kept in communication with Mrs. Irvin, her third

Mercy and Debbie Teso at eighth-grade promotion. Courtesy of Mercy Teso.

grade teacher. Mrs. Irvin's son attended Sahuarita Elementary School for some time before moving to property purchased along the Nogales Highway north toward Tucson. Her son's name was Donald.

Mrs. Irvin died in about 1996. Mr. Irvin remarried and during his second marriage, Mercy was his housekeeper. On March 6, 2021, Mercy received a call from Donald's wife with the sad news that Donald had died from Covid-19.

~ Contributed by Mercy Teso; compiled by Oscar Gomez and Monica Lee Elam Christiansen

Thomas Farm

My grandparents were Carroll Patrick Thomas, who was born in Tempe, Arizona, in 1892, and Josephine Itzweire, born in Missoula, Montana, in 1892. Both of their families later moved into the Tombstone and Bisbee area where they lived and went to school. Carroll and Josephine were married in Bisbee in 1916 and had one son, William Itzweire Thomas, born in 1917. Carroll worked for the Copper Queen Mine as a pipefitter and later for Chicago Pneumatic as a diesel mechanic in one of the mines in Mexico. Josephine worked at the Bisbee post office and her sister, Ella Itzweire, worked at the Warren post office. Bisbee and Warren are right next to each other.

William (Bill) completed elementary school in 1932 at Warren Mining School District No. 2. The family then moved to Tucson in about 1933 when Bill was a freshman in high school. Josephine worked as a bookkeeper for the Peyton Packing Company where her brother Ferd Itzweire was head butcher. During that time, Carroll worked at the power plant between Coolidge and Florence. Bill graduated from Tucson High School in 1936 and went on to the University of Arizona where he graduated with a bachelor of science degree in agriculture in

Thomas gas station and store at Sahuarita about 1945. Courtesy of Sutah Thomas Harris.

1940. He then went to work in Sacaton, Arizona, as a plant breeder at the USDA Experimental Station breeding cotton, mainly long-staple. Bill lived in the bunkhouse there and took his meals in the clubhouse where he met my mother, Katie Lee Barnes. Her stepfather, Orlan Parker was also working at the station and her mother, Ruby, was cooking for the clubhouse. As a side note, Charles Gatterer, who later taught third grade at Sahuarita School (our daughter Ellen was one of his students) also worked at the Experimental Station in Sacaton when he got out of college at the same time.

William and Katie Lee were married in 1941 in Phoenix, Arizona. Bill then joined the navy and attended officer candidate school at St. Mary's College in California and flight school, where he got his wings. He flew blimps out of Moffett Field over Catalina Island during World War II patrolling for submarines off the coast of California. Our government was worried that the Japanese might try to attack our West Coast. I was born in Orange County, California, in April of 1944 while my dad was still in the navy. In 1946, he was medically discharged with the rank of lieutenant junior grade.

Our family then moved to Sahuarita where Bill's parents had some property so that he could help out with the farm. Josephine and Ella Itzweire had acquired property from a Mr. Hummel in about 1939. In

Making adobe bricks on the Thomas Farm. Courtesy of Sutah Thomas Harris.

the spring of 1940, Josephine and Carroll moved to the farm where they built two residences and added a storage structure in 1943. (This was confirmed by a historian in Tucson named Scott Thompson.) It was located about three miles south of the Oro Verde Store on the Nogales Highway. (Their brother, Ferd, had a ranch just southwest of the land they acquired).

They had sixty-seven acres under irrigation in the years 1945–53 according to the Pima County assessor's office. In the spring of 1940, they hired Joe Trujillo, who helped build their house and others that came later.

The front room of their house became a general store and they lived in the back. They carried a small inventory of essential grocery items. They had milk, butter, flour, sugar, and eggs, and would buy canned goods from the grocery warehouse in Tucson. Josephine's brother, Ferd, supplied the meat from Peyton Packing Company in Tucson where he worked. They also put in a gas pump. When the store closed it became the living room of their house. Carroll liked to prospect for minerals in the area when he could. He did quite a bit in the Helvetia area and other places in Southern Arizona.

When we arrived in Sahuarita there was a long house west of my grandparents' house that we moved into. It had been built by workers who had come to Sahuarita to build the bombing range north and east of the old Sahuarita School and needed a place to stay in the area. Grandmother cooked for them and on weekends they used their heavy equipment to help clear some of the farmland which was on the east side of the Nogales Highway and across the railroad from the houses so Carroll could start farming. My brother John was born in November of 1946 while we lived in that house. The grocery store and pump were later closed so that they could concentrate on farming.

Josephine's other sister, Alda, and her husband Pete Mosier, lived in the home on the south side of the property. When they moved to Albuquerque, New Mexico, our family moved into that house after John was born. Dad added on to the house, working in the backyard to make adobes for the walls out of mud and straw, using lumber frames. A patio wall of adobe was also built to enclose the backyard. I do have some memories of adobe making. There was also a windmill and stock tank west of the houses. I remember swimming in that tank.

In July of 1948, Carroll was killed by a hit-and-run driver on the Nogales Highway. After that, Josephine's sister, Ella, came to live with her on the farm. Ella had a green thumb and had a large rose garden in the front yard. She also had zinnias under the mesquite tree in the front yard. There was a greenhouse where she spent a lot of time working with her plants. She raised beautiful violets. We had a well next to the house that dad would open up about once a week and flood the yards so there were nice lawns and flowers. I remember that my mother had a vegetable garden most years. A little southwest of grandmother's house was a shed that was added on to and converted to a two-bedroom house. It was used as a rental until my brother got married and he and his wife, Sue, lived there for a few years while John was going to college.

Bill went back to the University of Arizona in 1948 where he completed a master of science degree. In the 1950s he

The Bonillas place at Sahuarita. Courtesy of Sutah Thomas Harris.

was an associate professor and taught a cotton production class for several years.

All of the farmland was on the east side of the Nogales Highway and railroad tracks. Part of it was acquired around the late 1940s from a Mr. Mitchell, whom I recall as being from California. He gave us our first television set a year or so before television service was available in our area. The Bonillas place was bought from Manny and Cleone Bonillas in 1959. The total land acquired was 360 acres with about 250 acres of that being cultivated, according to my brother, John Thomas. I remember my grandmother walking with me on Bonillas hill.

There was a dirt dam there that helped control the water runoff from rain. I remember her showing me Native American graves and pottery. Dad had plowed up a complete pot in the farmland below the hill and it was later determined to be from the pre-Columbian era. In 2005, the site was excavated by the Archeological Research Services, Southern Arizona Regional Office, so that the gravel pit could be expanded. Lyle M. Stone was the principal investigator. He discovered a pot that was a twin of the one dad had plowed up many years before.

Cotton and some maize were grown on the farm. For a time in the 1950s, dad leased some farmland from Frank Appleton northeast of where the current Sahuarita School is. He and my uncle, Ernest Thomas, worked that as well as the home place for a year or two.

On the south side of the property, where our houses were, farm machinery was stored. I remember an Oliver tractor, several John Deere tractors, plows, cultivators, cotton trailers, and other assorted equipment. One day I remember dad wanted mother to drive one of the tractors to help him move something. She told him she didn't know how to drive a tractor. He said, "It's easy, just do what I tell you." She got it started all right and put it into gear and promptly ran into the back of his pickup. I think that was the end of her tractor driving!

Sutah and Katie Thomas standing by the tractor. Courtesy of Sutah Thomas Harris.

Dad was also very active in the Farm Bureau and other community affairs. The Farm Bureau connected the farmers and ranchers in the area. There was usually a meeting and social event with potluck dinners and sometimes square dancing or other activities about once a month. That was very important in keeping our communities connected.

Dad worked long, hard hours on the farm. He was up and gone before I got up and frequently didn't get home until after I was in bed at night. Occasionally I was allowed to go with him in the pickup to check the fields. This was a special time for us.

Rabbits were pests on the farm, so dad hunted them and mother fried them for dinner. She told us it was chicken. When I found out it wasn't chicken I would no longer eat rabbit and don't to this day! Mother also raised chickens for the meat and eggs. For many years, fried chicken was usually on the menu for Sunday dinner.

One year, dad decided to raise a pig in the back yard for some extra meat. However, it got named and became a pet. When mother cooked it for Christmas dinner with an apple in its mouth, none of us kids would eat it! Another time, he tried ducks and of course we named them. He gave up on putting them on the kitchen table and they were around as pets for a long time.

For a few years, dad helped the University of Arizona track Gila monsters in the area. He would bring them home in the back of his pickup where they would be banded and released back where he found them to track how far they traveled. They had such beautiful markings on their backs.

The Citizen bus to Tucson went by our place and we could take that into Tucson to shop. One day I went out on the road by myself and stopped the bus. The driver honked his horn and mother came out and marched me back into the yard. I didn't do that again!

When it was time to pick cotton, John and I went into the fields with the adults. Mother and dad also picked and dad supervised the workers. Grandmother took care of the scales and the books. The pickers had sacks that would hold fifty to a hundred pounds of cotton. Because I was so small, I had either a gunnysack or a flour sack in which to put the cotton I picked. Grandmother would weigh it and give me ten cents a pound for my feeble efforts. When John and I got tired we were put in the trailer and were allowed to jump up and down to help tamp down the cotton. We thought that was a lot of fun! All of the long-staple cotton was trailered to Marana to the cotton gin there.

There were three cotton gins in the area. The Cotton Producers Association had one several miles south of Sahuarita and west of Highway 89, just east of where the Walmart is now. Joe Ingram was the manager for a time and Jeanne Klingenberg Herman told me that her brother John used to work there also. Producers Cotton Oil was on the south side of Sahuarita Road and just east of the railroad tracks. Jack Collins and Harry Timmons were gin managers there. FICO also had a cotton gin for a time that was across the road from Producers. John Thomas provided me with the details on the gins.

In the 1950s, dad used the Bracero Program to bring in workers from Mexico to help pick the cotton. They were bused to our farm where there were several buildings built with bunkhouses, as well as kitchen and bath facilities, to house them while they were there. At the end of the season, they would be bused back to Mexico.

Dad hired Bart Quihuis to be a foreman on our farm. He and his wife Josephine lived in the Bonillas house on the hill. My brother and I remember that she made wonderful tortillas on a fifty-five-gallon drum made into a grill just outside of the house that was used at times for cooking. Josephine would also take care of us on occasion when our parents had to be away. John remembers that when dad decided to give up farming, he helped to get Bart a job as janitor at Sahuarita School. Bart worked at the school for many years.

On the farm were several wells. One of them had a pond where we used to play and swim. It was nice and cool and we enjoyed being in it as often as possible. It also kept us out of the irrigation ditches.

Mother made a lot of our clothes. She was an accomplished seamstress. In the early 1950s, she used the material from flour and feed sacks to make some of my dresses and John's shirts. They had nice prints on them and there was enough material to make children's clothes. In the early 1960s she and Pila Espino made my wedding dress. She was also very active in community and school affairs such as the PTA.

In 1955 there was a big thunderstorm in Madera Canyon and it flooded the wash behind our houses. Three of the houses were filled with about eighteen inches of water and mud. Our house that had an adobe wall around the back didn't have any water get into it. I remember my parents and grandmother bailing water out of the houses, scrubbing and repainting them. I was old enough to help bail water. I can still remember the mess! After that another house was built on the property between our house and grandmother's. It was built up higher than ground level so hopefully it would not be subject to flooding. This house was used as a rental.

Dad built a dike between the houses and the wash to help protect them from any future floods. In the 1970s, my husband Eiler built it up and made it higher and stronger. Our son, Todd, built it up once more after that. In 1983, Todd was staying at the farm when another flood hit. Luckily the dike held and none of the houses flooded. Todd was stranded on the east side of the river and we had to have the sheriff meet us at the bridge on Highway 89 and walk extra clothes over to him because we were not allowed to drive over the bridge while the water was so high. Todd broadened and raised the dike once more after that.

In the early 1950s, dad decided to see if pecan trees would grow in the area. He brought in seven of them from New Mexico to try. He decided our climate and elevation were about the same as New Mexico. They were planted on the north side of our house. Dad monitored them for several years and counted the crops they produced. Keith Walden and Warren Culbertson were also interested in growing pecans and later they put in the orchards that are all around the valley today.

In the 1960s, dad decided the Bonillas hill would make a great house site so he and mother started planning to do that. He built a swimming pool just down from the hill and put a tall ocotillo fence around it. I remember having friends come over to swim and many parties were held there. Unfortunately, before the house was started, my dad passed away in 1966 and the house was never built. The pool became too much for my mother to keep up and eventually she had it removed. I still hear stories from people in the area who remember the pool.

Josephine died in 1978 in Tucson and is buried at Evergreen Cemetery. After she died, her house became a rental and Jack and Mary Ann Clark lived there for quite a few years. Mary Ann was a clerk for the Sahuarita Schools for a long time.

In 1979, the farmland on the east side of the railroad tracks was sold to Cyprus Pima Mining Company for the water rights.

Katie kept the land the houses were on. She continued to live on the property and rented out the houses. Two of the houses were taken down around 1990, which left three to rent out plus her home. One of the renters, Port Juedes, asked if he could build a shop on the south side of the property as a place to work on cars. He had previously owned a service station on Esperanza Boulevard in Green Valley across from the Arizona Family Restaurant. As a condition of having a mechanic shop, Pima County required there to be a gas pump with it. Port acquired two old Esso pumps to put there. It was called Port's Auto Service. The gas was never advertised to be sold publicly, but if someone had an emergency he would sell to them.

Katie decided to move to Show Low in the 1980s. The houses were then all rentals. Port Juedes had also moved and the shop was vacant. In the early 1990s, our daughter, Ellen, was married and lived on the property with her husband, Tom Rieger. Hickey Industrial was looking for a place for their business and rented the shop for a while during that time. Movie companies from Europe would come by and ask if they could film at the shop. I think they liked the look of the old Esso gas pumps.

William and Katie Lee Thomas pose with the new Ford in 1966. Courtesy of Sutah Thomas Harris.

Sometime around the year 2000 the houses were all rentals again. Tom Rieger then rented the shop and some land around it for his business, Tom's Towing. In the spring of 2013, the remaining land was sold.

~ Contributed by Sutah Thomas Harris

Roberto and Olive Park Traslaviña

Roberto Martinez Traslaviña, son of Joaquin Urias and Anita Ochao Martinez Traslaviña, was born on April 6, 1910, in La Reforma, Sonora, Mexico, a small village about six miles north of Tubutama. The family home had only a partial roof, with a cowhide hung over the doorway, and a packed dirt floor. They raised corn, beans, and fruit on a small plot near their house.

In April of 1919, Joaquin and Anita packed their family into a wagon and moved to the United States. At that time, there were five children: Maria (1907); Carmela (1909); Roberto (1910); Francisco (1912); and Anita (1915). They settled in Sasabe and had four more children—two sets of twins, Pablo and Pastora in 1920, and Jesus and Manuela in 1922. Their first home in the United States was on the Presumido Ranch, located to the west of La Osa.

One of Robert's earliest memories was having four hundred head of cattle to care for. The first rain of the year did not happen until August, so there was very little water. Robert had to water those cows every day with a hand pump. There was no windmill and the old pipeline was patched with rags.

Olive and Roberto Traslaviña pose for a photo. Courtesy of the Revello family.

Roberto also worked as a mailman for his mother's first cousin, Francisco Redondas Rodriguez, who lived on the Presumido Ranch and ran a small store. Roberto made countless trips on a burro, several miles each way, to the nearby ranches to deliver mail. He also baled hay for fifty cents a day on a small farm located to the west of Sasabe. When school was in session, Roberto could work only during summers, but he did not attend school for very long. He liked school, but he never made friends.

Roberto went to work for Joe Ronstadt on the Santa Margarita Ranch when he was only twelve, and it was close to that time that he went on his first cattle drive into Tucson. He drove twenty-five head of cattle for four days to Richard Peyron's slaughterhouse near the base of "A" Mountain. The excitement of that cattle drive solidified his decision to quit school and work full time as a cowboy.

Crisolfo Araiza, Sr., a forty-year-old cowboy on the Santa Margarita Ranch, took Roberto under his wing. Roberto said that over the next five years, Crisolfo taught him "everything necessary to be a *vaquero*." His boss and the owner of the ranch was Joe "Pepi" Ronstadt. Roberto recalls, "The day would begin at 3 a.m. We would shoe our own horses and then start on the roundups. We were responsible for some fifty head of cattle."

In the 1930 Census, Roberto was living in Arivaca with his parents and siblings. His father, Joaquin, was working as a cowboy on a ranch owned by the Garcia family.

On September 22, 1937, he married Olive Aline Park in Las Cruces, New Mexico. Olive, or Ollie, as she was often called, was the daughter of Walker Jack and Hazel Baker Park. She was born on January 2, 1910 in Los Angeles, California, and was raised by her aunt and uncle in Alhambra, California. On June 27, 1927, when Ollie was only seventeen, she married forty-six-year-old Joseph H. Boyd in Nogales. Less than three months later, Mr. Boyd divorced Olive, claiming she "failed to look after his home and had treated him cruelly."

On July 14, 1928, in Florence, Arizona, Olive married a second time to Richard Lee Riggs. On March 2, 1933, the couple homesteaded 640 acres near the base of the Baboquivari Mountains. Richard left her, so Ollie was trying to care for the place by herself. Her responsibilities included a small herd of cattle and approximately a hundred goats. Ollie worked hard to protect her animals from mountain lions, constructing a twenty-by-twenty-foot house from lumber scraps, building corrals for the cattle, and raising turkeys and pigs to sell. When she had animals ready to be sold, Ollie would climb into her old Chevy and drive into Tucson. Aside from these infrequent trips into town, she was very much on her own and, because of the isolation, faced danger on a daily basis. Olive never forgot the daily drudgery of hauling water and food to her animals.

In 1936, while working cattle in the Santa Margarita range, Roberto came across Olive's homestead. Ollie needed help, so she hired Roberto as a cowhand. Ollie habitually carried a "Colt six shooter on her hip and a Remington rifle in her hand." She was a tough woman, and, on February 26, 1981, Ollie told the *Arizona Daily Star*, "I was too mean to cry!"

Roberto added, "She was tough, but she found out I was tougher." He described a ten-dollar bet they made. Ollie insisted that Roberto could not "tie her four-footed like one does to a calf."

"After I did it, I left her there and sat down to smoke a cigarette," Roberto had said with a laugh.

They got married on September 22, 1937, in Lordsburg, New Mexico, after which they moved to Tucson to live with Roberto's oldest sister, Mary Alcaraz, next door to his parents. Roberto worked odd jobs wherever he could find them, typically making only about two dollars a day. Then, in 1938, he was hired to work as a temporary replacement for his brother, Frank, on James McHenry Torrington's Rancho del Rio in Sahuarita. Their daughter, Nancy Ann, was born on August 27, 1939, and the 1940 census showed Roberto and Olive living off of Sahuarita Road next door to Roberto's brother Frank and his wife Isabelle. At that time, both men were working as laborers. The temporary job ended up extending, even after Frank returned, allowing Roberto and Olive to live in Sahuarita for almost three years.

In 1941, the Traslaviñas moved to Ruby Star Ranch, near Twin Buttes. Colonel Matthew Baird III, recipient of a master's degree from Princeton and a bachelor's degree in literature from Oxford, and with eight years of experience as headmaster of the Arizona Desert School for Boys under his belt, had moved to rural Arizona in 1937 to take up cattle ranching. He purchased Ruby Star Ranch but in April of 1942 he entered the air force, leaving his wife, Audrey, and their ranch in the care of the foreman, John Grieves McIlvain, and the crew of cowboys living on the property.

In 1943, Roberto and Ollie decided to become foster parents so that their daughter, Nancy, would have company. Almost immediately, the first of eighty-six foster children came to live with them. The youngsters they brought into their home were "abused, neglected, and homeless children. Some were just bad eggs," Ollie told the *Arizona Daily Star*. The children ranged in age from newborns to teenagers and raising these children was hard work—something not at all new to the Traslaviñas.

Roberto Traslaviña helping the Revello family trim the hooves of a calf at Twin Buttes. Courtesy of the Revello family.

The *Tucson Daily Citizen*, on Valentine's Day of 1953, included an article about Roberto. As a featured piece about the Fiesta de los Vaqueros Rodeo, he was used as an example of a "real cowboy" who, "goes about his day-to-day business hardly aware that he is the person emulated by almost everyone in town during this Fiesta de los Vaqueros." Then, the story goes on to say, "In addition to ranching, Roberto performs an overlooked community service. With his wife, Olive, he takes on the young outcasts of society. They are called welfare children and the next step for them would be Fort Grant. There are few people like Roberto and Olive who will take them. These are homeless children and range in age from seven or eight to fifteen or sixteen. They are children other welfare agencies won't accept. Roberto not only accepts them; he feels it to be his duty.

"Although he has an occasional failure, for the most part, they turn into decent individuals. Roberto, teaching them the ways of the range, makes useful citizens out of them. Olive gives them a home. Together, they have rehabilitated many of Pima County's young 'incorrigibles.' They have had a few failures. Kids who have had a ranch experience with Roberto and Olive find something worthwhile in life.

State and county officials are unanimous in their praise. One of Roberto's principal tools is the annual Tucson Rodeo. He takes all of his 'kids' to it. He pays their way out of his own pocket."

With a great deal of patience, strict rules, and the expectation that each child was to contribute to the household, the Traslaviñas quickly mastered the art of discipline. Aside from infants and toddlers, all of the foster children were expected to work alongside their parents (they called Roberto and Olive "mom" and "dad") on the property. They could choose where they wanted to work—out on the ranch with Roberto or in the house with Olive. Roberto reflected on the fact that some of the girls chose to be outside on the ranch, riding horses and working with the cattle. They had no problem allowing them that option. The children went to Sahuarita School.

In the *Tucson Daily Citizen* on March 31, 1954, Olive was recognized in the "Nominate Your Neighbor" column. The article said:

> *Mrs. Roberto (Olive) Traslaviña has probably been mother to more waifs in the past decade in Pima County than you would believe possible. With her husband, foreman of the vast Ruby Star Ranch, about 30 miles southwest of Tucson, she cares for society's unfortunates—the children who have no other place to go.*
>
> *Mr. and Mrs. Traslaviña have adopted two of these, and are considering a third. With a house full of young ones—at times as many as 15—ranging from toddlers to teenagers, it would seem difficult for Mrs. Traslaviña to find any time for outside activity. Not so. According to neighbor, Mrs. D. G. Chilson, "Everyone knows her out this way for her good-neighbor acts."*
>
> *In addition to being a good neighbor to all for miles around, and keeping the brood fed, clothed, cleaned, and happy, she also finds time for a hobby which sometimes brings in a little extra income 'for the kids.' Mrs. Chilson writes, "At the back of her house is her workshop where she performs miracles with ceramics and textile painting. Olive is always creating her own designs in planters, lamp bases, and plaques, staying up far into the night, long after the rest of the house is fast asleep. It looks so simple the way Olive does it, creating these scenes of the desert flora and mountains, but Olive's gift is a rare one and those of us who have seen her work can appreciate the artistry that is hers. Those of us who have seen the happy, busy youngsters in and out of Olive's house can also appreciate her gift for making a home for all children who come her way."*

Roberto Traslaviña helping the Revello family brand a calf at Twin Buttes. Courtesy of the Revello family.

In 1956, when the welfare department started setting guidelines for foster family homes, the Traslaviñas were forced to retire from the foster parent program. They did not own the ranch home they were living in and they did not have the money to make improvements—specifically, to add additional bathrooms. At about this same time, Ruby Star Ranch changed hands, beginning a trend that continued for many decades, ultimately putting much of the property into the hands of mining companies. The family was able to remain on the Ruby Star property, but Roberto went to work as a night watchman for Banner Mining Company, and, for the first time since he was twelve, was not working with cattle.

In 1958, the family moved to Tucson. Ollie got a job working for the Arizona School for the Deaf and Blind. She was a night supervisor there for about three years. At that same time, she also worked at St. Mary's Hospital providing private-duty care for patients who needed someone with them through the night. She also worked at local nursing homes and for the Commonstock Children's Hospital. Roberto continued commuting to his night job at Banner Mine.

Roberto was not happy working at the mines and decided he wanted to return to the job he knew and loved. In 1960, he was hired by William King on the King 98 Ranch. After three years, he moved to Tortuga Ranch, working for John Donaldson all over Arizona and New Mexico.

After almost eleven years of seeing Ollie only on the weekends, Roberto accepted a job on the twenty-section Robles Ranch. Years before, when he had been working the roundup, he had met Teddy, son of Ralph Wingfield, the Robles Ranch owner. Teddy had told Roberto there was an open job for him if he would ever consider working for them. Roberto was hired immediately, made foreman, and the Traslaviñas moved into a seventeen-room ranch house.

The *Arizona Daily Star*, on February 26, 1981, stated, "As he sat tall in the saddle, Roberto Traslaviña, 70, spoke to the cattle during a roundup at the 34,000 acre Robles Ranch, west of Tucson. His voice was firm, and the cattle seemed to understand the commands of the *vaquero . . .*" Then Roberto proceeded to explain, "You cannot rush them. I sing to them and talk to them. They know me and my horse, so when I call them, they will come to me. I can move all 100 of them by myself just by their listening to my voice." Though obviously referring to the cattle he was watching over, one cannot help but wonder if this same concept saved the lives of countless numbers of children who passed through the doors of the Traslaviña home.

~ Contributed by Monica Lee Elam Christiansen

NOTES

Arizona Daily Star. September 27, 1927, and February 26, 1981.
Tucson Citizen. Colonel Matthew Baird. March 15, 1945.
Tucson Daily Citizen. February 14, 1953.

Tyra Family

Joe "Red" Tyra was born in June of 1921 in Natchitoches, Louisiana, and died in February of 1990 when he was sixty-eight years old. Natchitoches is the oldest permanent European settlement within the borders of the 1803 Louisiana Purchase. It was founded as a French outpost on the Red River for trade with Spanish-controlled Mexico. The inhabitants were primarily of English and Scots-Irish ancestry. He was married to Rita Castillo, who was born in June of 1924 and died in December of 2013. Not much is known about his life in Louisiana but in a census, he is listed as a farmhand. His father was Joseph Tyra who lived from 1866 to 1931, and his mother, Mary Louise, was born in 1881 and lived until 1960. She was listed in a Tucson census as being there in 1945. That is probably when Red came to this area after his military service.

Red enlisted in the military in September of 1940. He was in the army cavalry division in World War II. His first job in the

Lamberto Castillo. Courtesy of Oscar Gomez.

cavalry for a year or more after he enlisted was training horses. When he was sent to the South Pacific, he was disappointed that the horses couldn't go as they would not be of use in the jungle terrain. In October

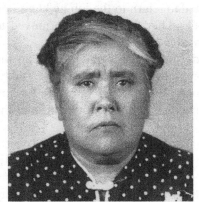

of 1944, as a private first class he was awarded the Silver Star for heroism in action in the South Pacific Admiralty Islands. This was a series of battles in which the United States Army's First Cavalry Division took the Japanese-held Admiralty Islands. In July of 1945, Sergeant Tyra received the Purple Heart for wounds he received in action on Luzon, which is the largest and most populous island in the Philippines. That battle had the highest net U.S. casualties, with 8,000 Americans killed. In February of 1945, the First Cavalry Division captured the bridge across the Tullahan River near the city of Manila. Military casualties there totaled 1,010 Americans. His length of service was four years and seven months.

After the military he went to the Tucson area and settled in Vail. While there he worked for El Paso Natural Gas at the Vail substation. He used to ride his horse from Vail to the Castillo house in Sahuarita to court Rita. Rita used to say "she fell in love

Beatrice Nogales Castillo. Courtesy of Oscar Gomez.

with a cowboy." They married in 1945 and had six children. Kenneth Lee did not survive. The others are Helen (Núñez), Joe Richard, Patricia, Barbara Lee (Delgado), and Kenneth James.

Rita's father was Lamberto Castillo, who was born in 1897 and died in 1968. He married Beatrice Nogales, who died in 1998. They arrived in Sasco, Arizona, in the 1920s. (Sasco is now a ghost town in Pinal County). From there they moved to Red Rock, Marana, and then to Helvetia where he worked for the Helvetia Mine. Wanting his son Lorenzo to attend school, he relocated his family to Sahuarita in the early 1940s. According to Rita's sister, Carmen Castillo, Lamberto purchased about eight acres of land

and his family became the first residents on the property where Sahuarita Village is now. Lamberto sold six acres of that land to Red and Rita, which they divided, giving an acre to each of their children. There are still several of his children and grandchildren who remain on that land in the village.

Red built their house on Castillo Drive, which is in Sahuarita Village. The original house burned but the fireplace chimney still stands. Red and Rita had a very large garden from 1954 to 1960 of between five and seven acres. They grew every kind of vegetable that they could. Every other day when the garden was producing, they would deliver up to twenty crates of produce to Goodman's Market on South 6th Avenue in Tucson and also some to the Chinese market in the same area. They would remove the old produce and replace it with the new. The old was taken back home and used to feed the pigs. Their son, Joe Richard, remembers helping his mother deliver the vegetables. They also had a few milk cows. On occasion they would sell excess milk to some of the people in the community. When their children were small, in the late 1950s, Red built a swimming pool. When they grew up and no longer seemed interested in the swimming pool, he stocked it with fish as he liked to fish. Barbara says it is now a koi pond with lilies and a nice oasis for the family to enjoy.

The Tyra Family (Joe "Red" and Rita with Pat, Joe, and Helen) all rodeo-upped for La Fiesta de los Vaqueros Rodeo and parade. Courtesy of Barbara Tyra Delgado.

At times Red worked as a farmhand. He also worked for both the Banner Mine and the Anaconda Mine. On occasion he held several jobs at once. He also worked for FICO at nights doing security. One of his jobs there was to take the temperature of each of the cotton bales every night to make sure they were not getting hot, which could result in a fire.

Red drove a school bus for many years for the Sahuarita schools. He was one of the drivers who took the students who had graduated from the elementary school to Pueblo High School in Tucson. If any were acting up, all he had to do was look in his mirror and raise his eyebrows (which were red and bushy) and things promptly settled down. He didn't allow any nonsense on his bus. Some of the students liked country music and some liked rock music. He settled that by playing one station in the morning and the other in the afternoon. He was still driving the bus in 1966 when his son, Joe Richard, was a senior at Pueblo High School, but retired shortly after.

After driving the bus, Red worked at the Shell service station and tire shop at the Oro Verde Store when Harold and Mildred Ellis owned it. It was on the east side of the store and had several gas pumps which were well used by the community. The only other gas pumps in the area were at the Continental Store. He wore a Shell uniform while working. Shell had a promotion and gave away collectible glasses with pictures of cacti. He also worked for the Yoder family for a while when they took over from the Ellises. While working at the tire shop one day, a tire blew up and broke his arm. The Yoder's closed down the tire shop and put a feed store in the space that had been the tire shop.

In the 1950s, Red was instrumental in getting Trico Electric Cooperative to put in electricity for Sahuarita Village. In later years he was a meter reader for Trico Electric Cooperative. He told of one not-too-nice encounter with a rooster on someone's property. The rooster attacked him and landed on his head. He wasn't leery of anyone's dogs but he sure didn't like roosters!

Joe "Red" and Kenny Tyra at the Oro Verde Store's Shell gas station circa 1964–65. Courtesy of Barbara Tyra Delgado.

After retiring Red liked to do woodworking and made redwood picnic tables for Sutherland Lumber Company to sell in Tucson. Another hobby was leatherwork. He liked to go deer hunting and often was accompanied by a fellow school bus driver, Jay Pelton.

Rita worked in the cafeteria at Sahuarita School for forty years. One of the ladies she worked with was Martha McGee. During that time the food was exceptional and sometimes folks in the community would have lunch with their children in the cafeteria. The food was all homemade at the time and there were very good cooks working there. After she retired from the school she worked around her house and garden as long as her health held out. Rita died in December of 2013.

~ Contributed by Barbara Tyra Delgado

PART VII: BUSINESSES AND ORGANIZATIONS

Local businesses and community entities share in the fragmented, diverse history that is the foundation of Sahuarita. This assortment of organizations led our communities to survive and thrive.

Who Lives in Arivaca Junction?

Apparently, no one does. Clearly, maps note that Arivaca Junction exists where Arivaca Road meets the old Nogales-Tucson Highway. And yes, that would be the definition of a junction. But this is where it gets confusing. Most of the locals say they live in Amado. The post office sign says Amado. The Amado Mini Market is situated on the corner where you turn to head off to Arivaca. The Amado Food Bank is right there, as well. But according to the U.S. Census, Amado is in Santa Cruz County. The U.S. "Census Designated Place" called Amado is in Santa Cruz County. The old town of Amado is a mile or more away, across the highway to the south. But technically, "Arivaca Junction" is in unincorporated Pima County. This encompasses the whole area from the line north to the post office and west to Honey Lane and includes all the homes in the subdivision known as Lakewood. It could even include the Halfway Station which is a mile or so north of the junction. But as Jeff Smith noted in a 1978 *Tucson Daily Citizen* article, Arivaca Junction exists only on maps printed in Phoenix.

This is what causes the problem. Many tourists, delivery people, and other newcomers think that when they get to Arivaca Junction, they are in Arivaca, not realizing that Arivaca is another twenty-three miles west of there.

This is not a new problem. When researching the history of the name, I found a 1918 military map with "Arivaca" marked right where the junction is, and another "Arivaca" where the town is. Confusing. The official 1893 map of Pima County shows Arivaca Junction located where the road takes off to Arivaca, so we know the designation dates back a while.

This Western Ways *photograph shows Highway 89 passing through Kinsley Ranch on Rodeo Day. Courtesy of* Arizona Highways.

It probably goes back even further, because in 1764, Captain Juan de Anza led an expedition to San Francisco up the road from Tubac, turning off on the road that went to the Sopori Ranch on his way to Arivaca. Father Augustin de Campos took that same road even earlier, in 1722. A road went along the north side of Sopori Wash, a major tributary of the Santa Cruz River, and there is a road to Sopori Ranch on the south side as well. Old roads followed water sources so horses could be watered. To get to the ranches and mines near Arivaca, people have been turning off of the Tucson-Tubac road for eons, so it only made sense to call that area Arivaca Junction. But as a hometown appellation, the name never stuck.

Kinsley Ranch Rodeo circa 1954. Courtesy of Green Valley News.

Up until at least 1980, that area was known as Kinsley's Ranch. Old-timers still call it that. Otho Kinsley bought it in about 1930. Otho was born on a ranch in California in 1899 and moved with his family to Southern Arizona in 1915. During the Depression he built highways on a work gang and made enough money to make a down payment on the land, which he knew he could make into a profitable property even at the height of the Depression. There was a small grocery store there at the time, and Kinsley expanded it to include a gas station, restaurant, bar, dance hall, and grocery store. He (and his brother) constructed a roping arena. Later on he dug two adjoining lakes east of the road and added a swimming pool. Water was pumped from an artesian well (courtesy of the Sopori Wash watershed) into the swimming pool and from thence across the road to the lakes. The pool water changed over twice a day and was icy cold! The lakes were surrounded by lovely weeping willow trees and people could fish and boat there.

Otho loved the rodeo. He had horses and raised livestock for the rodeos in Tucson and elsewhere. He had one bucking Brahman bull that no one could ride, until eventually Dick Griffith, the world champion at the time, actually stuck on for the requisite seconds. This went on throughout the 1930s to 1950s. Kinsley's Ranch became famous and people came from all over to dance the night away to live music. At one point there was a wild animal show featuring an African lion that wasn't too wild. Otho was larger than life, both in physique and personality. He loved flying and built a landing strip up on the hill behind the arena, because his property had at least six hundred acres. For fun and profit, he witched wells. He drove fast and rode hard, as they say. And his name was synonymous with that area for over thirty years, until he sold the ranch. It was after his time that the area began to be called Amado.

Developers came in and created Lakewood Estates in the 1960s. Unfortunately, they also drained the lakes. Then the Longhorn Bar and Restaurant went in and provided an interesting landmark for the area.

We can't talk about the Arivaca

Kinsley's Lake with the Santa Rita Mountains in the background. Courtesy of Arizona Daily Star.

Junction area without mentioning the Halfway Station. At least as early as the 1880s it was a stage stop owned by Lyman Smith and known as "Smith's" or "Junction," and travelers between Tucson and Nogales or Arivaca could get a meal, rest their horses, and even stay there, since it was about halfway between those towns on the Nogales Highway. If you were on horseback or in a wagon, you'd need to stop at about that point. Then Basilio Caranzano bought it in 1914 and made it into a nice restaurant and dance hall, with a gas station, continued in about 1950 by Felipe Jaurequi and his wife Angelina, whose Mexican food was to die for. This competed successfully with Kinsley's operations for many years, but its downfall came with the construction of I-19 in 1978. Exit 48 was situated right by Kinsley's place, with the Halfway Station relegated to an inconvenient spot a mile north.

The old town of Amado was started by the Amado family and was called "Amadoville" for a few years. Everyone from miles around drove their cattle to be shipped at a railroad siding there. In 1910, Manuel H. Amado established a store and post office on the Tucson-Nogales Road. The name of the town was changed to Amado in 1920. He and his sons Antonio and Gustavo had ranches in the area, and the family still does to this day. Other family members continued the store. A school was established at Amado, as well. After 1899, when Santa Cruz County seceded from Pima County, the town of Amado went with it, but Arivaca Junction remained in Pima County. Children at the Junction had to go west to Sopori School and now Sahuarita Middle and High School. Also in old Amado is the Catholic church, Assumption Chapel, a mission of St. Ann's Church in Tubac. Luna's Auto Repair Service is on the corner of the east side frontage road and Amado-Montosa Road.

So when did the Arivaca Junction area become an extension of Amado? Or become even more Amado than Amado is? They were separate communities for many years, but evidently, the name followed the post office. It seems that one can bid on a post office contract location and so it might move around. The Amado post office is a contract station under the Tumacacori post office. In the 1950s, Rancher's Mercantile store (just south of Kinsley's operations but in Santa Cruz County) was established by

Otho Kinsley in Arivaca Junction. Courtesy of University of Arizona Special Collections.

Ernesto and Flora Salazar. The Amado post office was moved there and away from old Amado. Some years went by and it moved a few hundred yards north to Kinsley's area, and significantly, across the county line into Pima County! Joann Stupy, the postmaster at Tumacacori, said this was due to the need for an adequate location, which they didn't have in Santa Cruz County. When zip codes were established in the mid-'60s, the Amado zip code area spanned both counties. This encouraged the name Amado to be applied to street addresses as well as other businesses in the Arivaca Junction area, such as the Amado Mini Market, Amado Feeds, Amado Territory, and now the Amado Food Bank and Amado Self Storage. So now Amado truly extends all the way from Honey Lane to old Amado! Manuel Amado would be proud. But to the dismay of residents who have to deal with address issues, library cards, insurance companies, and government agencies, the map still says Arivaca Junction.

~ Contributed by Mary N. Kasulaitis; originally
published in the *Arivaca Connection*
(Arivaca, Arizona, June 2013)

CORE Construction

CORE Construction has been closely connected to the Sahuarita community for the past fifteen years. In that time, CORE has had the opportunity to work with the local Sahuarita Unified School District on thirty-five projects totaling over $80 million in construction value. These projects have ranged in size from a $3,000 sidewalk replacement to a $20-million high school. At CORE, we take great pride in building schools for our nation's future leaders, we believe that education is one of the most important building blocks in life, and we value the sense of community that schools promote while preparing students for their future. We also understand how important it is to foster a connection between a school district and its local community. To that end, CORE has been involved with numerous groups within the local community, including the Sahuarita Navy JROTC, Verde Valley Rotary Club, and Sahuarita High School JTED, as well as supporting local sports teams and participating in career fairs throughout the district.

Peter MacDonald, Sr. with a local veteran.
Courtesy of CORE Construction.

To highlight one specific example of effective community investment, CORE helped provide funding for a program that brought local World War II veterans to speak to Sahuarita students and our local community. The opportunity for these priceless living historians, including Navajo Code Talker Peter MacDonald, Sr., to meet the community and share their experiences was a once-in-a-lifetime experience for the attendees.

~ Contributed by Seth Beer, LEED AP

Felix Family Businesses: Felix Landscaping Maintenance and MCF Concrete

Around the time that the children were growing up, the new town of Green Valley was prospering, which provided opportunities to Frank L. and Celia's children.

Manuel Felix was the first Felix brother to start a landscaping business. Manuel was twenty-two years old when he started his business, and it thrived in the new town. He soon contracted to landscape newly constructed model homes and more work came from a bank, Continental School, homeowner associations, and other housing developments. As Manuel's business grew, his brothers came to help him. At the request of management, Manuel planted over three thousand trees on the east tailings at Anamax Mine, facing Sahuarita and Green Valley. Those trees stand to this day.

Eventually, each brother would start his own landscaping business. At one time, there were a total of five brothers working on landscaping (Francisco "Panchito," Manuel, Armando, Henry, and Jose). Today, two sons of Armando Felix, Armando Jr. and Gabriel, continue the landscaping business with over thirty employees under the name of Felix Landscape Maintenance.

Miguel Felix, or Mike as everyone called him, ventured out on a different path. He worked in the concrete business and started very young working for Richard Jensen, who showed him the ins and outs of the business. Eventually, Mike would form MCF Concrete, which became one of the biggest concrete contractors in Green Valley. Mike continues the business today under the name Mikey's Concrete. Ever the clown, Mike Felix has blossomed into the guy whom everyone knows in Sahuarita. He is a beloved community member.

Manuel C. Felix standing near his work truck in 1965. Courtesy of Manuel C. Felix.

~ Contributed by Mark Felix

Green Valley Chamber of Commerce

"Unite and Promote!"—The original Green Valley Chamber of Commerce motto is still true today.

Green Valley News, March 28, 1979: Green Valley Board of Realtors calls for Chamber of Commerce!

July, 1979: The Green Valley Chamber of Commerce is formed!

Betty Plank was the first board president with Louis P. Black, James D. Hathaway, John H. Burke, Alan K. Piper, Loretta E. Koppen, Steven M. Myers, Jerry M. Pulliam, and Carl A. Bosse making up the rest of the first board of directors.

Originally housed in the Continental Shopping Plaza, in 1999 the Green Valley Chamber of Commerce moved to the space now occupied by Access Wisdom Care in the M&I Bank building at 270 West Continental Road, Green Valley. In 2004, the Green Valley Chamber of Commerce submitted a DBA (doing business as) application to become the Green Valley Sahuarita Chamber of Commerce & Visitor Center. In 2009, needing more space, the Chamber moved across the street to its current location in Presidio Point Plaza at 275 West Continental Road.

For many visitors to the area, the Chamber of Commerce is the first stop they make to get information. In the early 1990s, it was recognized by the Arizona Office of Tourism as a "visitor center." In 2019, the visitor center had more than 8,000 visitors! The *embajadores* (ambassadors) have been part of the Chamber since the beginning and are volunteers who welcome visitors and assist them with everything from tourism to meeting their business needs. If they want to know about hiking trails, there are maps. Need a plumber or the phone number of an elected official? Call on the Chamber!

Over the years, the Chamber has played a significant role in the community. When the Chamber was formed in 1979, Green Valley was

The Green Valley Chamber of Commerce by-laws were adopted on July 19, 1979. The Articles of Incorporation were received by the Arizona Corporation Commission on July 20, 1979, and all was formally announced in Green Valley News *on August 8, 1979. Courtesy of Randy Graf.*

a community of ten thousand. In the 1980s, town hall meetings with the Chamber and coordinating council were tackling the issue of how business growth was not maintaining pace with the population increase and what role the Chamber of Commerce should have, if any, in the development of Green Valley's business community. From goods to services to jobs, Green Valley needed to be more self-sustaining. On everything from incorporation to economic development, the Chamber of Commerce has been at the table conducting surveys, hosting town hall meetings, and speaking for local businesses.

A chamber of commerce represents and supports a strong business community. The mission statement, "Champion opportunities for business and our community to prosper," is what guides the Green Valley Chamber of Commerce. Its membership of four hundred organizations represents "solopreneurs," not-for-profits, retail and service businesses, and Fortune 500 companies. The Chamber

provides advocacy, networking, marketing, education, and support for every member. It is a resource to its membership in many ways and the first best use of a business's marketing dollars.

The Green Valley Chamber of Commerce is proud of the fact that in its forty-second year there are sixteen charter members that have been with the Chamber from day one. The community is growing and the Chamber is growing with it!

Green Valley Chamber of Commerce lobby. Courtesy of Randy Graf.

~ Contributed by Randy Graf

Halfway Station

From the 1950s through the 1970s, the place to eat Mexican food in the Santa Cruz Valley was the Halfway Station. Angelina Jaurequi cooked, her children waited tables, and husband Felipe (Phil) tended bar and welcomed the guests. The food was so memorable, especially the red chili con carne, that many people remember it to this day. Janie Harris went to great lengths to get the recipe (but by trial and error, not from Angelina herself). Sutah Harris's parents ate there several times a week while the kids did their homework at their own table. Felipe was made for this business—hosting parties and dances. He knew everyone; he had so many friends that even people who weren't inclined to go to bars or dances would patronize his place. Tourists loved to come there. Celebrities like Elizabeth Taylor, Robert Mitchum, Robert Wagner, and Arnold Palmer were a few of the big-name visitors. Felipe would close the place down when they came so no one would bother them. *Pablo and the Dancing Chihuahua* is a 1968 telefilm produced by Walt Disney Productions that was made at Halfway Station. But the Jaurequis were not the first to own this station.

Back in the 1800s, Arivaca Junction was the place where a road left the Nogales Highway and went west twenty-three miles over the hills to the village of Arivaca. Lyman Smith brought his family here in about 1871. He homesteaded a site that bordered the Canoa Land Grant on its southwest corner. He had some cattle, a small farm, and of course, mining claims in the nearby Santa Rita Mountains. Lyman was from Kentucky, born in 1830. He caught the gold bug and went to California. On the way out he went through Yuma in about 1865 and met his wife, Isabel Ballesteros, who was from Altar, Sonora. Then it was on to the Santa Cruz Valley, where he could do some mining.

Lyman referred to his stage stop as "the Junction." It appears on maps as "Smith's" or just "Junction." It was a waypoint on the road from Tucson to Nogales, but it didn't become the "Halfway Station" until after he died. Among other things, Lyman was appointed road overseer in 1905 by the County for the whole road between there and San Xavier Mission. Lyman died in 1908 and Isabel began cooking for people, serving up good Mexican food. She might have cooked when it was still a stage stop. After it was sold, she moved to Tucson.

When Basilio Caranzano (sometimes spelled Carranzano) bought it in 1914, he dubbed it "Halfway Station," and began providing gas, food, and a bar. Basilio was born in 1887 in Italy and immigrated to the U.S. in 1912. In 1920 he married Anita Ybarra who was originally from Sonora, but whose family had moved to the U.S. At the Halfway Station they provided Mexican food and Italian as well. According to Gus Amado, Basilio originally was hoping to serve the Fifth Cavalry soldiers who were stationed at the Junction in 1913 to stop ammunition smuggling by various factions during the Mexican Revolution. Apparently arms and ammo had been regularly smuggled by automobile from Tucson through Arivaca Junction, Arivaca, and Sasabe for some time. (*Tucson Citizen*, June 22, 1913) This was a profitable location for many reasons! How long the soldiers were there is not known.

Basilio built the big white building that we can still see on the I-19 west frontage road (Old Nogales Highway). The restaurant was on the south side and a dance floor was on the north side of the building. He later built the adobe home next door. Angelina's father made the tiles used on the floor of the bar. Basilio had also established a farm and sold vegetables wherever he could. Later on, he sold vegetables in Arivaca and Ruby. Because he owned the 160-acre Smith homestead, he had land up on the ridge above Halfway and also land north of it on the flat where they raced horses and which eventually became a trailer park. In 1957, Basilio sold some of this land to Kemper Marley who was building up his vast ranch holdings.

The Halfway Station on October 1, 1980. Courtesy of Arizona Daily Star.

Halfway Station was conveniently close to the railroad station at Amado and a good distance from Sahuarita, besides being halfway between Tucson and Nogales. And the food was good! Rene Perez, future owner of Papagayo Mexican restaurant in Tucson, shared with Alva Torres that when he went to work for Anita and Basilio around 1950, "I had the best teachers. They made that place famous. *Tres mujeres* [three women], including Doña Micaela, a sweet *indita* [indigenous woman], would come and at 2 a.m. we would begin making the tamales and work all night to have fresh tamales for the day." (*Arizona Daily Star*, July 25, 1989) Angelina also learned how to make the famous red chili sauce from Anita. Basilio held horse races from time to time, bringing in a large crowd of patrons, sponsored dance programs and of course, quinceañeras and parties of all kinds. Local bands were brought in to provide music.

Felipe Jaurequi had moved when he was young from the Jerome area to Tumacacori, where he met Angelina Alegria. He served in World War II and when he got out he came back, married Angie, and went to work for Basilio. They had five children. Felipe soon proved to be invaluable to Basilio. In fact, he was like a son in some ways, as Basilio and Anita had no children. Soon he was running the Halfway Station himself and Basilio could retire. Anita passed away in 1956. Basilio continued to hang out there until he died in 1966.

Felipe put the Halfway Station up for sale in 1972, having put in twenty good years. That was also when I-19 was being constructed, meaning that business would be dropping. He didn't sell it right away, however, and finally retired in 1978 shortly after it was mentioned as the "legendary" Halfway Station in a café-hopping article in the *Tucson Daily Citizen*. Halfway Station was being operated by Elizabeth Caryl in 1984. There were other owners, but from then on it went into a state of decay. Jessie Jaurequi thought to preserve it as a historic building but to no avail. Jessie still owns the house to the south of Halfway Station.

Big excitement interrupted its quietude in 1986 when Paul McCartney, of all people, decided to use it as a venue for a music video! The song is "Stranglehold" on the *Press to Play* album. He had planned to do it in Mexico and changed his mind. Looking around for a location, he came across the Halfway Station, which needed some work. Trevor Jones, Paul's aide, said, "The ceiling was knocked out to get the lights up near the roof, and holes were knocked in the walls to get the best camera angles. (All fixed before we left!) . . . Anyway, the flavour is discreet, onstage at least: a neon cactus, vaguely cowboy clothes, an Indian clasp at Paul's neck instead of a gent's necktie as worn. . . . The audience of 180 extras can't help being a shade Mexican, of course, living so near the border." The boy in the video is not local, but came from Los Angeles. Also in the video is Linda McCartney and their nine-year-old son.

Special thanks to Terry, Delia, and Elvia Jaurequi for their memories.

~ Contributed by Mary N. Kasulaitis, with
memories of Sutah Thomas Harris

NOTES

Resources

Arizona Daily Star
Paul McCartney Project: https://www.the-paulmccartney-project.com/concert/1986-11-04. Video:
    https://www.youtube.com/watch?app=desktop&v=wE41epNvdY4
Tucson Citizen

An Abbreviated History of La Posada
Mission: "To maximize the well-being of seniors"

The La Posada story is one of vision, leadership, a desire to serve seniors and community partnerships, and envisioning possibilities to enhance the lives of others.

For over three decades, La Posada has given seniors a community in which they can live an active and healthy lifestyle without the stresses of home ownership. In this small-town setting of over one hundred acres, friendships form easily and measures of satisfaction have been consistently greater than 95%. Quality assisted-living and memory-care neighborhoods can address needs should they ever arise, giving La Posada residents and their families additional peace of mind.

Donald Shopshire. Courtesy of La Posada staff.

La Posada's initial sponsorship was by Tucson Medical Center (TMC), Southern Arizona's largest not-for-profit hospital, led by Donald Shropshire, President and CEO, in an effort to meet the current and future needs of the Green Valley community and surrounding area.

In the early 1980s, some Green Valley community leaders approached Tucson Medical Center to build a hospital in Green Valley. It was considered not to be feasible, but the conversations resulted in the discussion of what might be brought to the community to meet its needs instead. One of the key issues was that, as residents of Green Valley aged or became ill, they moved out of the community to find needed housing and health care services. The question was asked, "How can we stop this exodus?" Thus, the idea of an "extended care" facility was born that evolved into having a La Posada-type continuum of care.

In 1985, TMC and Farmers Investment Co. (FICO) began work together on a joint venture to develop the La Posada campus. Initial financing of $21.7 million was raised through the sale of bonds. For reasons primarily related to the financing, FICO sold the land to TMC at fair market value, which was then $13,000 per acre for 116 acres. TMC then also put in an additional $45,000 per acre for necessary improvements.

La Posada. Courtesy of La Posada staff.

Jerry Gilmore, then a senior vice president at TMC and head of TMC Health Enterprises, a separate business entity of TMC's health care system, was given the responsibility of the development of La Posada. He was in charge of building La Posada and led the early years of operation, becoming its first official president and CEO after a mutually acceptable separation from TMC at the end of 1996.

Gilmore put together the initial executive team, and members of this team have stayed in place, enhanced over the years by a group of talented others, and together they have served La Posada over its thirty-four-year history. Those members include Lisa Israel, who was the executive director from 1985 through 1996, senior vice president and chief operating officer from 1996 to 2004, and president and chief executive officer from 2004 to 2019; Joni Condit, who was senior vice president from 1999 to 2004 and senior vice president and chief operating officer from 2004 through 2019 and is currently president and chief executive officer; Paul Ide, who was controller and information director from 1986 to 1996 and senior vice president and chief financial officer from 1996 to the present.

Jerry Gilmore. Courtesy of La Posada staff.

The first phase of La Posada was building 174 apartments (with twenty-six different floor plans to give a maximum amount of options) and a skilled nursing home, considered to be an extended-care setting of sixty beds. The first residents moved into La Posada in May, 1987. From that day on, for the past thirty-four years, La Posada has been growing and evolving to better serve seniors and the community at large through both new buildings and new programs.

One initial challenge was La Posada's unique hybrid refundable deposit program. The public was not educated to understand the distinction between a life-lease program and a strict rental program, let alone the difference and advantages of a not-for-profit organization over a for-profit one. This, along with a collapse in the housing market, slowed initial fill-up.

In 1992, as La Vista Apartments (then called La Posada) filled up, it was clear that for some, there was a need for more care than could be offered in an independent living setting. La Posada then developed its assisted living program, the essential bridge between independent living and skilled nursing.

La Posada considered various ways to raise the two million construction dollars needed, and was surprised and delighted when its own residents, Harry and Frances Holmlund, offered to donate one million dollars if TMC would match it. This is how the Holmlund La Joya Assisted Living Suites came to be. This is also how La Posada created its unique charitable gift annuity program—one of La Posada Foundation's most popular giving programs. La Joya opened in 1994 and has been expanded over the

La Posada fountain. Courtesy of La Posada staff.

years with specially designed apartments for couples as well.

In 1992, Park Centre Medical Offices were built to provide room for physicians and specialists on site. TMC, through La Posada management, controlled all the time-share specialists. This was an attempt to meet the medical needs of the community at large, and have now been converted to private physicians' offices.

As residents moved in, La Posada also listened to those who wanted to join La Posada, but decided not to move in. These people in the community wanted to reside in a house with services but not an apartment. This led to the creation of the Garden Home program. This program pushed La Posada into a position of financial stability and met yet another need of the larger community.

Over the years of 1996–2007, the design of the garden homes continued to be refined based upon resident comments and were built to meet market demand. Also, the La Vista dining room was enlarged by enclosing the outdoor balcony and creating the copper design you see today.

By 1996, La Joya's assisted living facilities were bursting at the seams, so a second phase was under construction, later followed by a third phase, funded through gift annuities and a small land donation by FICO. Also, in 1996, due to a need for more social activity and meeting space, a recreation center was constructed north of La Vista. Bocce ball courts and an outdoor fitness park were added later due to resident interest and financial support.

The end of 1996 was a major turning point when it was determined, for a variety of reasons, that La Posada should stand separately from TMC. La Posada refinanced itself through a bond issue to pay back its debt to TMC and became a free-standing not-for-profit organization in charge of its own destiny.

Sally Burbank, who was a board member from 2001 to 2007. Courtesy of La Posada staff.

An administration building, located an equal distance between La Vista and the future La Perla, was built in 1999. At this time, La Vista needed space for more activities, and the new administration building allowed La Vista to use the former administration space and create a lounge and galleria area, a TV studio, and offices for case management and activities. The small building near the administration building, once the La Perla apartment model, became the first Treasure Shoppe (later converted into classrooms for a learning center).

In 2000, the La Perla apartments were developed to address the changing market, with different floor plans (only five this time) and with larger two-bedroom apartment homes because La Vista had so few. Together, they would offer a perfect mix of one- and two-bedroom homes. La Perla opened in 2003 with 153 apartments and assorted community spaces.

The changing marketplace also was demanding more fitness opportunities, so the fitness pavilion was built, along with La Perla, to serve the entire campus, and opened a year prior to La Perla in 2002.

In 2001, Armstrong La Via Memory Care was developed—a uniquely designed building created to accommodate residents with dementia. The building has twenty-nine residential suites, most of which open into a common area used for activities and dining.

The following year, La Posada became first in the state of Arizona to receive CCAC/CARF (Continuing Care Accreditation Commission; Commission on Accreditation of Rehabilitation Facilities) national accreditation for its campus continuum, which furthered its national reputation for excellence.

In 2005, a commitment was made to change the "medical" model nursing home of La Hacienda to a "person-centered care" model that involved changes to the building as well as changes to the training and culture of employees. The philosophy of being driven by rules, regulations, and staff efficiency was significantly altered by the new philosophy of centering all decisions around each resident. Attention to regulations was still required, but La Posada stretched itself to find new ways to operate. This included eliminating institutional noises, like call lights and buzzers, and using technology to replace these. Nursing staff members now wear beepers that are linked to call lights. The nurses' station in the middle of the building was eliminated and replaced with a living room and fireplace. Others followed this model and eventually (in 2014) the licensure was changed from skilled nursing to enhanced assisted living. This was forward-thinking and nationally many others followed this model of care and licensure.

Bill Kephart was a board member from 1996 to 2000. Courtesy of La Posada staff.

In 2006, the outpatient facilities at La Hacienda (now named Sonderegger Outpatient Therapies) were expanded through donor support to include more space and an indoor therapy pool to serve our residents as well as the community at large.

Always keeping its eye on changing trends and demographics, La Posada wanted to create the concept of a main street into its campus, providing a connection for residents to commercial and retail activity and a strong welcome to the external community. The Shoppes at La Posada were developed to serve this purpose; its promotion of community engagement, volunteerism, and socialization through Posada Java and the Vensel Treasure Shoppe exceeded all expectations.

La Posada's merger/acquisition with Casa de Esperanza in 2011 created Casa Community Services and was a key piece of history as well. By combining Casa's programs into La Posada, La Posada further expanded its spectrum of services and outreach with adult day health and behavioral health services while supporting Los Niños preschool, which benefited area employees with trusted care and education for their children. In exchange, Casa, previously a free-standing community nonprofit organization, became part of a larger organization that could provide financial and long-term stability to continue serving those in the community with low financial resources.

La Posada entrance. Courtesy of La Posada staff.

As the campus continued to utilize its space and create new programs, residents were concerned that the campus beauty of open spaces and nature would be lost or compromised. Thus came about the five-and-a-half-acre development of Central Park in the center of the campus, which was designated to be used to promote open-space activity, the spirit of nature, and opportunities for reflection. Central Park now consists of a series of gardens, ranging from a meditation garden with a labyrinth to a prose garden to a chess garden. The latest phase, currently underway, includes a recently built outdoor amphitheater called Center Stage. The vast majority of the expense of Central Park has been underwritten by generous resident philanthropy.

The Park Centre Homes (free-standing homes with smart technology) came along in mid-2011 as market demand grew for even larger homes with more open floor plans and with environmentally conscious building materials. Thirty-four homes were built, and to support the increase in residents on campus, the Continental Restaurant was added to La Perla with its new five-star fine dining program as another option for all. Eventually, a special membership was open to the larger community under the Club Continental program.

The annexation of La Posada into Sahuarita in 2018 was a positive strategic decision that positioned La Posada for its future. Proud of its ties to the community of Green Valley, La Posada's desire is to provide community benefit and partnership with both communities.

The seventeen Pavilion Homes, constructed in 2020–21, offer a contemporary home model as a new addition to the La Posada campus. These homes meet the wishes of another part of the community La Posada serves, complementing the current offerings.

While the continual building development over the past thirty-five years is an obvious sign of La Posada's growth to meet community needs, the development of its partnership and support of the community increased as well.

Today, the La Posada campus serves over 740 residents, employs approximately 550 employees, and provides community services to the thousands of individuals who do not live on the campus itself, ranging from outpatient therapies to adult education to community meals and beyond.

To expand the reach of the mission, La Posada has purchased additional land around its current borders for future growth in the Sahuarita and Green Valley area, as well as eighty acres in Oro Valley to diversify its services to meet the needs of another community and its seniors.

Board member John Riley, who served from 1999 to 2009. Courtesy of La Posada staff.

La Posada has had several advantages that have been part of its success and that have led to its local and national reputation. Its leadership team has been a group of long-term individuals dedicated to La Posada's culture, purpose, people, and programs. Internal leadership transitions have helped strengthen commitment to the mission and culture over time. The transitions have been smooth, due to the strength of the executive team, the commitment of the dedicated employees and the disciplined focus and vision of the board of trustees. Generous donors and volunteers have also played crucial roles.

The Board policy governance manner of functioning provides the disciplined approach that has supported accountability and oversight, while allowing management initiative, creativity, and responsibility.

At La Posada, the not-for-profit philosophy and the initial connection to TMC under Don Shropshire's guidance left leadership with a shared understanding of the desired culture to serve others, as well as the nonprofit commitment to service for the long term in support of the community.

~ Contributed by the La Posada Staff

The Longhorn Grill

"Exiting the Cow Palace, after a quick rainstorm in the desert, I saw this fantastic sight," wrote artist Michael John Cavanagh about his oil painting *Longhorn Grill Amado AZ*. At the time of his inspiration, the Longhorn was likely empty, "victim of a poor economy," as stated by previous owner Ed Madril.[1] The painting, described as impressionistic, shows at a distance the distinctive longhorn cow skull that covers the entire front of the building, its horn tips forty feet apart and reaching thirty feet high.[2] According to Danny West, who was a teen helping build the skull one summer in the 1970s, the workers used cement, stucco wire, and rebar, and followed sketches the artist had made.[3] That artist was Michael Kautza, whose Tucson works included a 4,000 pound concrete monkey[4]; an Easter Island-type head at the old Magic Carpet Miniature Golf course; the huge boot that stood outside the late and famous Tack Room restaurant;

and the huge wine bottle outside the Boondocks Lounge.

The Longhorn was built on Kinsley Ranch. The building, adobe, is from the 1950s and is a bit over 6,000 square feet.[5] Originally, it sat next to one of Kinsley's man-made lakes. Over time, it has housed a remarkable variety of businesses besides restaurants: a Western clothing store, a feed and tackle barn, a roofing company, and a graphic design firm. At one time, it served as headquarters for a volunteer law enforcement organization named the Arizona Rangers. Once Kautza's cow skull was erected, the Longhorn became

Longhorn Grill, statuesque against the summer sky.
Courtesy of Arizona Daily Star.

iconic, one of *Time Magazine*'s top fifty roadside attractions in July 2010.[6] Otho Kinsley had courted celebrities of the 1930s to 1950s, and the Longhorn became a setting for new movies such as *Alice Doesn't Live Here Anymore* in 1974 and *Boys on the Side* in 1995.

Madril and Al Reynolds bought the building, which was an Italian restaurant at the time, in 1993.[7] Al Reynolds died in 2005. Madril employed local residents and felt committed to the community. When the bank foreclosed as the restaurant business lost money, the interior of the building was emptied in 2012. In 2013, Arivaca resident and artist John Gourley purchased the building, the price of which had dropped from $319,000 to $130,000. Gourley, a sculptor, intended to use the building as an event center and gallery for his and other artists' works. Two of his works were on display in Tucson: one outside the Tucson Museum of Art and another inside the Viscount Suites Hotel.[8] While he hoped to book functions such as quinceañeras and dances, Gourley did not plan to apply for a liquor or restaurant license. Gourley died on December 22, 2015. The restaurant went to auction.

Amy and Greg Hansen, experienced restaurateurs, purchased the building in September of 2018 and opened it in 2019. The Hansens own two other restaurants, both in Green Valley: the Longhorn Outpost and Barbeque Company, which will replace the Twist and Shout '50s Diner,[9] and the 19th Hole Bar and Grille, which has been successfully operating for years. As for the original and iconic Longhorn, the Hansens have renovated the building and chosen décor reminiscent of mining towns; they have even washed and repainted the skull that draws tourists from far away for the thrill of walking beneath it.

~ Contributed by Lori Punske

NOTES

References

Longhorn Grill at sunrise. Courtesy of Kaitlynn Christiansen.

1. Ford, Regina. "Longhorn Grill closes down, is up for sale."

442   Friends of Sahuarita

Sahuaritasun.com. July 7, 2012.

2. Villarreal, Philip. "Famed landmark in Amado is now a victim of foreclosure." *Tucson.com.* October 10, 2014.
3. Ford, Regina. Longhorn Grill closes.
4. Ford, Regina. Longhorn Grill closes.
5. Richardson, Jaime. "Amado's Longhorn Grill Stands Test of Time." *Gvnews.com.* September 13, 2007.
6. Ford, Regina. Longhorn Grill closes.
7. Villarreal, Philip. Famed landmark in Amado.
8. Franchine, Philip. "Preserving a landmark: Arivaca man buys Longhorn Grill." *Gvnews.com.* August 27, 2013.
9. "John Alfred Gourley." Obituary. Johnson City Press. March 25, 2016. Retrieved November 26, 2022 from https://www.johnsoncitypress.com/obituary/john-alfred-gourley/article_566dbb19-af2d-5934-9eb5-eaf4c52d61d1.html
10. Bottemiller, Kitty. "Out with the old, in with the . . . old." *Green Valley News*. June 27, 2021.

Additional resources

Cavanagh, Michael John. "Longhorn Grill, Amado, AZ (2012)." Painting. *Artfinder.com.*
Gay, Gerald. "Longhorn Grill in Amado, South of Tucson, will soon see new life." *Arizona Star.* February 28, 2020.

Brown Store in Sahuarito prior to 1918. Harriett "Tootsie" is standing in front of the counter. Courtesy of Susan Strong-Dowd.

Brown's Store, Oro Verde Store, and One Stop Market

The early history, Brown's Store

The earliest mention of "Brown's Store" was in the May 1, 1915, *Nogales Border Vidette*. It merely announces the arrival time for the *Tucson Citizen* newspaper in Sahuarita. On September 9 of that same year, the *Arizona Daily Star* listed it as a "voting place" with J. S. Brown (John Stephenson Brown), inspector, and S. E. Brown (Seward Ellis Brown), judge. On August 10, 1918, it was still being used for this purpose.

It is not clear if this store was the site of the James Kilroy "Roy" Brown, Jr., store that opened in June of 1930 or if it was the site of the James Kilroy Brown, Sr., store from years previous. In the June 11, 1917, edition of the *Tucson Citizen* it says, "J. S. Brown allows that he hasn't kept store at the Sahuarita crossroad for nigh on two years," indicating that the 1915 store was not in operation.

Roy Brown and his wife were living with Roy's parents in Tucson when the 1920 census was taken. Roy purchased Tucson's American Hotel in May of 1923, and posted an ad in the May 19 edition of the *Star*. "For Rent—170 acres in the fertile Santa Cruz Valley, Sahuarita. Large frame house, fine storeroom, well, windmill, outhouses. Good pasture. J. K. Brown, Jr., American Hotel." He was still living in Tucson when his wife, Elsie Siewert Brown, died on May 16, 1926.

On June 13, 1930, the *Arizona Daily Star* reported that, "J. K. Brown Jr. (Roy) had a formal opening of his new mercantile store at Sahuarito a few nights ago, which was largely attended by all the people in that community. It was in the nature of an old-fashioned housewarming, preparatory to opening for business. A dance culminated the evening."

Much later, in the *Arizona Daily Star* on February 15, 1942, it was learned that, "James Kilroy 'Roy' Brown, 60, a resident of Pima County all his life, died unexpectedly yesterday afternoon in the general store he had operated for many years at Sahuarita. Better known as 'Roy' Brown, he had been a figure in the small locality on the banks of the Santa Cruz River, some 17 miles south of here since boyhood. His father before him operated a store almost on the site of the one owned by his son. Most of his regular customers were those who attended school with Roy in earlier days. Surviving are his mother, Mrs. James K. Brown; two sisters, Mrs. M. Windsor of Yuma and Mrs. M. B. Strong of Tucson; and a brother, John S. Brown of Ajo. Funeral arrangements in charge of the Arizona Mortuary, have not yet been determined."

Roy and Elsie Seward Brown. Courtesy of Arizona Historical Society.

Additional details were given in the *Tucson Citizen* for the same date. "Called during the middle of the night by cries of James Kilroy Brown, 60, proprietor of the general store at Sahuarita, James Hopper, employee, first phoned the family physician for aid and then notified the sheriff's office that his employer had died unexpectedly. Undersheriff Herb Wood, with C. W. Gardner, acting as coroner, answered the call but took no action since they were advised death was due to natural causes. Mr. Brown had been a colorful character in that community. In fact, his family had founded the town, Gargner said. Brown, he said, died within 20 feet of the spot on which he was born."

Less than a month after Roy Brown's death, on March 7, the *Arizona Daily Star* reported that William H. and Mary E. Lane had sold the Sahuarita Ranch to Green Gold Ranchos, Inc., led by J. P. Corcoran, President. On November 10, the *Star* tells of an incident at the "Sahuarita General Store" that was taken care of by Stanley Cruze, Green Gold Foreman. On November 13, 1944, Corcoran legally changed the name from Green Gold Ranchos to Rancho Oro Verde, thus setting the stage for the "Oro Verde Store."

Significant Dates

March 16, 1948	Elwood Johnson operates Oro Verde Store and post office (*Citizen*)
December 3, 1948	J. P. Corcoran applies for Oro Verde Store liquor license (*Citizen*)
May 10, 1950	Oro Verde Rancho, Inc. sold to Kemper Marley's United Liquor Co. (*Star*); United Liquor leases to Sahuarita Ranches, Inc. (*Star*)
December 5, 1950	Oro Verde liquor license transferred from J. P. Corcoran to Harry W. Foster (*Star*)
June 16, 1951	Advertisement: "Butcher wanted. Good pay plus percentage." Oro Verde (*Star*)
June 16, 1952	Oro Verde liquor license from Harry Foster to Levi Harris (*Citizen*)
August 16, 1952	Levi and Roy Harris request liquor license for Oro Verde Store (*Star*)
April 10, 1953	Partners, Levi and Roy Harris post "Notice of Intention to Sell in Bulk" (*Star*)
June 12, 1953	Oro Verde liquor license from Levi and Roy Harris to William L. Dean (*Republic*)
October 13, 1953	William L. and Katherine Dean post "Notice of Intention to Sell in Bulk" (*Star*)
October 22, 1954	Deans transfer Oro Verde liquor license to Harold and Mildred Ellis (*Citizen*)
March 29, 1963	Application of Harold Ellis of Oro Verde Store for liquor license (*Star*)
May 22, 1967	Referred to as the Oro Verde General Store in Sahuarita (*Citizen*)

June 13, 1975	Name changed to One-Stop Market; no owner listed (*Citizen*)
October 11, 1977	References to flooding in Lee Yoder's One-Stop Market (*Citizen*)
1982	Richard Jensen bought the store from Lee Yoder
2009	Jensen closed doors for good

Courtesy of Medley Crate label archives.

Fond Memories of Oro Verde

According to Joe Martin, "The store you know as One Stop used to be the Oro Verde Store and was owned by Oro Verde Farm. When FICO bought the Sahuarita Farm from Californian Jack Harris, the store became theirs. Dick Jensen simply leased from FICO. Curt Adams's dad and stepmom, Ruth, rented the northwest corner of the store for a bar. They weren't there long, finally moving back to California.

"In the '40s, some older people called it Brown's Store. It's said the store dates back to 1915. Whether it was Brown's, I don't know, but even my brothers used the name."

According to Lynn Harris, from 1950 to 1952, the store was owned or managed by Harry W. Foster. Brothers Levi and Slim Harris were partners in the building. Per the *Arizona Daily Star*, Foster applied for a liquor store license on December 5, 1950. The *Star*, on August 16, 1952, reported that Levi and Roy Harris applied for a wine and beer license for the Oro Verde Store.

In the *Arizona Daily Star* for October 13, 1954, it is reported that William and Katherine Dean sold all of their business, equipment, fixtures, supplies and inventory. The October 24 edition indicates that Harold Ellis was the purchaser and the November 30th *Star* reports that a liquor license was transferred from William H. Dean to Harold and Mildred Ellis.

Sutah Harris reflects, "My first memories of the Sahuarita Store were in the late 1940s and 1950s. It was on the south side of Sahuarita Road and west side of the Nogales Highway. It had a pay phone outside on the north side of the building and, as far as I know, it was the only public telephone in the area at that time. I remember our family driving up there to make calls.

"Most of my memories of the Oro Verde Store are from the mid- to late 1950s, when it was owned and operated by Harold and Mildred Ellis. Their son, David, was a year ahead of me at Sahuarita School. He graduated from the old school, went to Pueblo High, and graduated from there in 1961.

"The main entrance to the store was on the northeast corner of the building. In the back of the store, in the southwest corner, was the butcher shop. Fred had the best meat. Most of the families in the area bought their meat from him. I remember as a child, when my mother would get meat, Fred would always give my brother John and me either a piece of cheese or a hot dog. There was sawdust on the floor behind the butcher counter.

"When I was in high school I recall Fred having a gallon jug of whole dill pickles on the counter and they were ten cents each. He would wrap them in a piece of waxed paper and we thought that was a great treat. During this same time, in each case of bubble gum there would be a frosted green or orange mug with a wooden handle. Mildred would set them aside for me and I collected a whole set. Like most youngsters, it was a place for us to buy a coke or a piece of candy, things we usually did not have at home.

"Adjacent to the butcher shop on the north was the post office. Josephine Jungen was the postmistress at the time. On the east side was the door to the service station. Joe "Red" Tyra worked there. He always wore a Shell uniform. According to Red's daughter, Barbara, the Shell Company gave out promotional cactus glasses for a time. In the area where Red worked, there were gasoline pumps and, I believe, a tire shop.

"The store gave credit to some of the families on a monthly basis for those that needed it. It was well stocked with all the necessities and had fresh milk and bread. There was an ice cream freezer chest with assorted goodies and room for some frozen food items. It also had assorted sundries. With large grocery stores only in Tucson, those were visited just once a month for major supplies. Between those trips, our family shopped at the Oro Verde Store or the Tang market in Continental.

"The Oro Verde Store could easily be considered the hub of the community. People from all around the area got their mail, meat, and groceries; made phone calls; and visited with one another to catch up on the local "goings on" while there. It seems like mid-morning was a busy time when quite a few would gather there for their mail and to visit for a bit with one another.

"The Ellis family owned the store from 1954 until sometime after the 1960s. According to Mildred Ellis's obituary in the *Tucson Citizen* on March 17, 1993, they owned the Oro Verde Store for over twenty years. The Ellis family bought some land north of the Pima Mine Road and south of the gap on the Old Nogales Highway. They built a nice brick home on it and surrounded it with nice trailer spaces. It was called the Cadillac Mobile Home Park. They had it very nicely landscaped. Harold died in 1982 and Mildred died in 1993."

The One Stop Market on the southwest corner of Old Nogales Highway and Sahuarita Road. Courtesy of the Gorian family.

One Stop Market

A community meeting place, a local news hub, a tiny one-room grocery store, a quick two-pump stop for gas: Sahuarita's One Stop Market served many purposes for its rural population. The small building on the corner of Sahuarita Road and Old Nogales Highway allowed local workers to build up a tab for groceries (Ellis as quoted in Franchine) and visitors on their way to or from Nogales to fuel up. Family members and friends worked behind the counter and knew their town and its people well.

But then Sahuarita's population exploded in the new millennium—a 731% increase that led to a bigger town and bigger, newer stores. According to owner Dick Jenson, the market building dated to around 1915, and its early uses included a produce-packing operation and the area's first post office. (Portillo) From 1982 to 2009, Jenson's whole family, including children and grandchildren, worked there and served a mainly working-class clientele even as the town continued to grow. (Portillo) Jenson, who died in 2016, was an air force veteran and previous owner of RDJ Concrete. Interstate 19 delivered people directly to the burgeoning competition, such as the Shell Super Stop and the emerging businesses on Duval Mine and Sahuarita Roads. (Franchine)

When the building was demolished to broaden Sahuarita Road and the intersection, former employee David Ellis watched, as the building had been a major part of his and his family's lives. (Franchine) What had been a stalwart touchstone in so many Sahuarita lives gave way as the town's population numbers, jobs, and needs changed.

~ Contributed by Sutah Harris, Joe Martin, Lori Punske and Oscar Gomez; compiled and researched by Monica Lee Elam Christiansen

NOTES

Franchine, Philip. "Historic One-Stop Market, nearby bar come down in Sahuarita." *Green Valley News*. August 25, 2013.
Portillo, Ernesto. "Old Sahuarita Store Closed Forever." *Arizona Daily Star*, January 15, 2009.
"Richard (Dick) Jenkins." Obituary. *Sahuarita Sun*. August 21, 2016
Arizona Daily Star, Tucson, Arizona
Tucson Daily Citizen, Tucson, Arizona
Arizona Republic, Phoenix, Arizona

Sahuarita Post Office

The first memories of the post office were in the early fifties. It was inside of the Oro Verde Store on the west side of the store next to Fred the Butcher. It must have had an outside entrance or a door on the north side of its opening into the store, so that the postmistress could get in and out as it was always locked. The boxes had dial combination locks to access one's mail. Some people used general delivery instead of a box. Josephine Jungen was made the head postmistress in April of 1947 and I believe Ethel Stout also worked there.

The Sahuarita Post Office. Courtesy of Susan Dowd-Strong.

Around 1960, a redbrick building was constructed just south of the Oro Verde Store for a new post office, because the community had outgrown the one in the Oro Verde Store. In the September 20, 1960, edition of the *Arizona Daily Star* it was announced that, "Ground-breaking ceremonies for the new post office at Sahuarita will be held at 10 a.m. today, Mrs. Josephine Jungen, postmistress, has announced. The new building will be ready for occupancy Nov. 1. The contractor is the Cleveland Construction Co., Tucson. Owner of the site is Mrs. Marguerite Strong of Tucson, who will be represented at the ground-breaking by Mrs. L. B. Strong. The site was formerly occupied by a residence. The Sahuarita post office currently occupies a corner of the Oro Verde Store and takes up about 88 square feet of floor space. The new building will provide a working area of 905 square feet, and will permit an increase in the number of lock boxes from 130 to about 200. The new facilities will be modern in every respect."

Josephine Jungen was still postmistress in the new building. Rachel Davis was a clerk for many years in this building, as was Pat Graham (whose husband was a bookkeeper for FICO).

Shortly thereafter an addition was built onto the north side of that building for more boxes to accommodate a growing community. In 2002, after Rancho Sahuarita started up, another building was constructed for the

Postmasters of Sahuarita. Courtesy of National Archives.

post office several miles west of the old one on Sahuarita Road on the west side of the river across from the Sahuarita schools.

~ Contributed by Sutah Thomas Harris

NOTES

Record of Appointment of Postmasters, 1832–1971. Records of the Post Office Department, 1773–1971, Record Group 28. Microfilm publication M841; NAID: 596306 and 17027522. Washington, D.C.: National Archives.

History of Quail Creek, a Robson Resort Community

In the summer of 1999, Robson Ranch Quail Creek, LLC, a Robson Company, acquired the existing 2,500-acre Quail Creek community in Green Valley, which had sold fewer than one hundred homes in ten years. Ed Robson saw the potential of this exceptional location with high Sonoran desert terrain and the Santa Rita Mountains providing a panoramic backdrop.

As part of the expanding growth and development of Quail Creek, an all-new model home complex and information and design center was opened in January 2001. The home design collection offered three distinctive series, with twenty floor-plan options and more than fifty exterior design choices, ranging in size from 1,280 to more than 3,400 square feet. In addition to the existing recreation facilities of golf, tennis, bocce ball, and swimming, new amenities were opened including a restaurant, pro shop, and bar and lounge.

Over the years, the developer continued to expand and add to the multi-million dollar amenities that now comprise the Quail Creek community. The resort-like facilities are built campus-style and are designed to support an active adult lifestyle for residents with a wide range of interests.

- Completed in 2005, the Madera Clubhouse is the hub for social interaction and activities within the community. This luxurious facility includes a ballroom for special events, a lending library, multi-purpose rooms, a coffee bar and lounge, a billiards room, and a covered patio with an outdoor fireplace and golf course views.
- The Anza Fitness Center hosted a grand opening in 2012, showcasing state-of-the-art cardio and weight machines; multipurpose rooms for dance, aerobics, and yoga; and a wellness area.
- A new sixteen-court pickleball complex with a ramada and parking was opened in 2014, much to the delight of the residents.
- Residents welcomed a new creative arts and technology center in 2015. This popular facility, covering approximately 12,348 square feet, features well-equipped rooms to accommodate a variety of classes, workshops, and more.
- A newly renovated and expanded grill, lounge, and sports bar was introduced in 2018. The renovations added approximately 4,000 square feet of space between indoor seating and the patio area. Some of the highlights include a boardroom, a private dining room, a U-shaped bar with lots of seating, two large wall-mounted TVs, and an expanded outdoor covered patio.
- A new multi-million-dollar facility, the Canyon Club, was announced in September 2020. Upon completion, this exciting new amenity is planned to feature an indoor pool, state-of-the-art fitness center, game room, bistro with a coffee and wine bar, a multi-purpose room, a spa lounge, massage and locker rooms, and a barbershop. Current plans for the outdoor space includes a

resort-style pool with shade sails, a whirlpool, an event lawn, and a terrace with a barbeque and pizza oven.

Other amenity expansions have included the addition of nine holes of golf, a dog park, and the Kino Conference Center. The Madera Clubhouse was revitalized in 2020, and is a popular gathering place for residents.

Many organizations and clubs come together to connect with the Sahuarita and Green Valley community through service and volunteering. Just a few include:

- Adopt-A-Highway
- Blanket Brigade
- Women of Quail Creek—Offering military baby showers that provide everything families may need to welcome their newest patriot into the world
- Unit 22—Food and other necessities for dogs and cats at the Animal League of Green Valley
- Miscellaneous food drives

Over the years, Quail Creek and Robson Resort Communities have garnered many prestigious awards from a variety of professional organizations, peers, and industry experts, including the National Association of Home Builders (NAHB) and Eliant Homebuyers' Choice Awards. The town of Sahuarita has grown substantially, providing Quail Creek residents an abundance of choices for retail, professional, and medical services.

To further expand the community, a 614-acre section was purchased from the state of Arizona in 2019. Today, more than 2,700 homes have been sold at Quail Creek with more than a hundred clubs, classes, organizations, and activities available to the residents. Quail Creek has come a long way since Ed Robson recognized the potential of this development in 1999 and created a flourishing community filled with homeowners living fulfilling and rewarding lifestyles.

~ Contributed by Murphy Kulasa

Rancho Sahuarita

From the very beginning, the developer and founder of Rancho Sahuarita, Bob Sharpe, had it in his mind to someday create an incredible place for families to call home.

Born in Minnesota in 1952, Bob was delighted by building and creating things, even as a young child. He often reflected on his younger years playing with Lincoln Logs and Tinker Toys, all the while developing a keen sense of vision and a love for placemaking that would one day lead him to a successful career in land development.

Bringing life to Rancho Sahuarita

After a series of land partnerships and weathering the economic cycles of the 1980s, Bob eventually acquired the land that would one day become the master-planned community of Rancho Sahuarita in 1993. Where most saw vacant land, he saw something that would one day be much greater. He saw a place where families could come together and experience a good quality of life at an affordable price; one that would be the most affordable, highly amenitized community in Southern Arizona. Rancho Sahuarita would grow to offer residents a life filled with opportunities to enjoy the things that matter most—family, friends, and fun, and a community in which everything could be found "right in your backyard."

Rancho Resort, the active adult community within the master plan, first opened in 2000. The Rancho

Sahuarita community followed, opening in the summer of 2001 with thirteen neighborhoods boasting new homes constructed by six different builders. Rancho Sahuarita's main recreation center, Club Rancho Sahuarita and nearby Sahuarita Lake opened to the earliest residents that same year. Other amenities, including the Bark Park and two larger neighborhood amenities, Parque Del Rio and Parque Del Presidio, opened later to residents in 2007.

Over the years, the Rancho Sahuarita team has continued to expand and add to the community's offering of resort-style amenities and recreation spaces, and increase the offerings of events, classes, and special programs. More amenities are planned as the community continues to grow in the future.

Current amenity highlights (as of March 2021)

Rancho Sahuarita

- Club Rancho Sahuarita, designed with a full fitness center, multi-use spaces, an activities lawn, mini putt-putt course, sports courts, a kids' club facility, demonstration kitchen, and splash park and pools; located directly adjacent to the stunning Sahuarita Lake Park
- Over seventeen miles of paved walking and biking trails
- Pocket parks and green spaces throughout the neighborhoods
- Parque Del Rio and Parque Del Presidio neighborhood amenities complete with pools, basketball courts, and more
- Flamingo Splash Pad and Armed Forces Tribute (at Parque Del Rio)

Rancho Resort

- The community is centered around Rancho Resort's own resort-styled Clubhouse
- It includes a ballroom, library, lounge, multiple activity rooms, computer center, full fitness center, and nine-acre village green
- Outdoors, residents have access to a heated swimming pool and spa, picnic areas, bicycles, and courts for tennis, pickleball, and volleyball

The community's proximity to jobs, shopping, health care, and good schools, coupled with its offering of affordable housing and amenities, has made it attractive to home buyers of all ages. At full build-out, the community will include nearly ten thousand homes and hundreds of acres of commercial, educational, and mixed-use space in the Sahuarita Town Center.

Rancho Sahuarita today

All that the community has become would not have been possible without leveraging the many opportunities for partnerships that make the greater Sahuarita region so unique. Knowing the effect that good schools have on creating a great place for families to live, Rancho Sahuarita holds a long history of working with the Sahuarita Unified School District (SUSD).

To date, over 120 acres of land have been donated to SUSD for the development of educational spaces. Rancho Sahuarita team members work closely with district leaders and other community stakeholders to find new avenues and mutually beneficial partnerships that result in innovative educational opportunities for students. Various resident groups and events throughout the year also allow the community to come together to give back and raise funds, resources, and awareness for important causes.

In the early 1990s, Bob met with area residents to explore their desires for the future and the need to incorporate the area of Sahuarita, which formally became a town in 1994. Together they foresaw an opportunity to create a family-oriented community that would offer a lifestyle unique to Southern Arizona. Later in 1996, Bob and a group of key pioneers in Sahuarita created "Sahuarita 2020." This document contains ideas and designs for what the team envisioned for development in the coming years. Now, twenty years later, many of the ideas contained in "Sahuarita 2020" regarding items such as education, sustainability, and community building have been brought to fruition.

Key partnerships with the town and other community members have led to countless additional development and growth opportunities in Sahuarita, such as the Sahuarita Town Center, which provides residents access to important services and will continue to serve as key economic drivers to the growing town in coming years.

Rancho Sahuarita has received many prestigious awards since its inception. Having historically led the local market in new home sales, it has been named one of the top-selling master-planned communities in the country; in 2008, it was recognized as the best-selling community in Arizona, and the fifth best-selling nationwide. In 2013, the Urban Land Institute recognized Rancho Sahuarita as one of thirteen communities around the world that demonstrate best practices in building healthy places to live. Regionally, the community has received honors as well, including the Project of the Decade Award in 2014 by the Metropolitan Pima Alliance (MPA) and as a partner recipient of various Common Ground Awards from the MPA.

Bob Sharpe. Courtesy of Rancho Sahuarita.

Laying a promising foundation for others

In March of 2015, Bob was diagnosed with glioblastoma, an aggressive form of brain cancer. Despite being given only fifteen months to live, he turned that time into four-and-a-half years by battling the disease head-on with the same tenacity, determination, and positivity that helped to make the development of Rancho Sahuarita possible. Through efforts such as the Rancho Sahuarita Cancer Walk, personal appeals to those he knew, and with the support of residents in the greater community, over one million dollars have been successfully raised to benefit the National Brain Tumor Society.

With a personal motto that quickly became the rallying force behind Bob, as well as his family and friends, he moved through each day to the credo of "Today is a good day." On August 28, 2019, Bob lost his fight to cancer, but his sense of perseverance and vision in creating an incredible place for families to call home continues to drive the team at Rancho Sahuarita and see the development of the master plan through.

Looking to the future, Jeremy Sharpe, Bob's son and now managing partner for Rancho Sahuarita, shares that the greatest parts of Rancho Sahuarita are in the small moments—in watching a family kick a soccer ball in the green spaces or parks; observing a retired couple take a relaxing stroll along the trail system; seeing a veteran quietly reflect at the Armed Forces Tribute. It is these moments that make the community a special place, and the moments that will define its future in the years to come.

~ Contributed by the Rancho Sahuarita Team

Ruby Star Ranch and 59 Ranch

Ruby Star Ranch

The area of Ruby Star was often lumped in as a part of the Twin Buttes settlement; Ruby Star Route was the name of the United States postal route for rural deliveries along Mission Road. It is hard to pinpoint the exact year that the "Ruby Star Ranch" came to be or who was responsible for the original name, but several homestead entries over the years account for property ownership in what would eventually be included in the ranch boundaries.

Individuals tied to the property included Clarence F. "Gus" Altfillisch (claimed February 27, 1929); William W. "Bill" Choate (claimed November 3, 1932); Fred Mitchell (claimed October 22, 1934, with claim overridden by William Choate on July 10, 1936); James R. Hopkins (claimed July 17, 1934); and Richard A. Morse (claimed June 14, 1932).

Ruby Star Ranch home. Courtesy of Architectural Forum.

Well-known Tucson architect Richard A. Morse filed his notice of intention to make his three-year proof to establish claim to his homestead on July 19, 1935. He was known to have been living on his homestead acreage on November 22, 1934, when the *Arizona Daily Star* reported his giving a party to honor his fiancée, Miss Ann Houle. By 1939, Richard had designed and built a home on his acreage. It was featured in several Tucson displays, as well as in the April 1940 edition of *Architectural Forum* magazine where the house is described as, "A ranch house of conventional design, its long lines reflecting the need for free circulation of air. The porch is a required part of the general scheme for living and is used as a passageway between various parts of the house. In harmony with the house and its surroundings is the living room, an attractive informal room broken up into two units for greater flexibility of use. Cost: about 44 cents per cu. ft." The *Star* on the 28th of that month explained that the house had been sold to Mr. and Mrs. Matthew Baird, who were planning to make additions to the home.

For the next twelve years, Matthew Baird III became the main face of the Ruby Star Ranch. He was

Matt Baird of Ruby Star Ranch is conducting experiments in raising Brahmans. He came to Arizona via Princeton, Oxford.

A Western Ways *photo of Matt Baird posing by his jeep and the Ruby Star Ranch sign. Courtesy of* Arizona Highways.

born on December 28, 1902, in Ardmore, Pennsylvania, the first of two children born to Matthew Baird Jr. and Mary Louise Register. His sister, Marie-Louise Baird (married first to Thomas Graham and then to Frank Adams Keen), was born in April of 1905. Matthew's young life was spent entwined in the "high society" of old Pennsylvania families. As was expected of him, he attended Princeton where he received a bachelor's degree in 1924 and a master's degree in 1925. His time at Princeton was followed up with extensive travel abroad, culminating in 1928 with a doctor of literature degree from Balliol College at Oxford University.

In June of 1923, then a student residing in Princeton, New Jersey, Matthew had completed a passport application stating his intent to spend the next year visiting France, Italy, Switzerland, and then touring England before starting school at Oxford. He renewed this passport for travel and education in June of 1924 with the stated intent of visiting France and Norway, and then returning to Great Britain to continue his education.

In the midst of his time in England, on January 22, 1926, in Manhattan's St. Thomas Church, Matthew married Mary Stuard Stevens. The *Philadelphia Inquirer*, on February 7, 1926, touts a bit of the family history involved in the Baird–Stevens union. "Young Matthew Baird, 3d., recently married a daughter of the old Stevens family, of Castle Point, Hoboken. He is a grandson of the late Matthew Baird who was president of the Baldwin Locomotive Works. He is also a cousin of Byron and A. King Dickson, two famous athletes of Penn in the '90s. Their mother was a sister of the first Mrs. Matthew Baird."

In Brooklyn's *Standard Union* on December 3, 1930, it is reported that, "Paris, Dec. 3 (UP). — Divorces granted to-day by the Paris Court included the following: Mrs. Mary Stuard Stevens Baird from Matthew Baird of New York. They were married in January, 1926." Several months prior to this announcement, the 1930 census showed Matthew living with his mother and sister back in Marion Township, Pennsylvania, with his occupation listed as schoolteacher, so it is assumed the couple had already separated.

This overseas divorce apparently created quite an uproar, as the January 23 edition of the *Camden Morning Post* included the following feature: "Baird-Stevens Divorce Distresses Relatives at Home. Mary Stuart Stevens, five years back was so madly in love with Matthew Baird 3d, that she defied the jinx and became Mrs. Baird on a Friday. Today, the importantly born Mary is quietly letting it be known that she is adopting the usual, unoriginal hyphenated divorce cognomen and will be addressed as Mrs. M. Stevens-Baird. Between these two paragraphs lies the tale of a young couple blessed with position, wealth, and good looks, and whose great romance waned almost from the minute they walked away from the altar. Mary had divorced 'Matt,' a Princetonian who has social connections in his native Quaker City that vie with those of his ex-wife here on Manhattan Isle and bother Mrs. Robert Livingston Stevens, Mary's mater, and Mrs. Matthew Baird, Sr. (born a Pennsylvania Register). Both are very distressed over the decree handed down in Paris a few weeks back.

"If there is a more patrician lady in all of New York than Mrs. Robert Livingston Stevens, I have not met her. It is easy to realize how the divorce has distressed Mrs. Stevens, who entered this vale of tears a daughter of the celebrated Stephen Whitney and a direct descendant of the Stephen Whitney who occupied a great mansion facing Bowling Green and was one of the richest dandies of his Colonial Era. But Mary and 'Matt' could not make a go of it—their frequent marital outbursts at Oxford, England, where they made their home following their wedding, bear testimony to the now established fact that theirs was not one of those unions manufactured in the celestial regions. Mary and 'Matt were married at St. Thomas' on Fifth Avenue, with the flower of Mayfair in attendance."

Near the time of the aforementioned divorce, Matthew left Pennsylvania for Arizona where he became headmaster of the Arizona Desert School for Boys. The Tucson newspapers frequently mentioned activities he was involved with, including starting and running an extensive intramural polo program (*Star*, Oct 7, 1932); Christmas activities and a correspondence program with the children from the Arizona Children's Home and St. Joseph's Orphanage (*Citizen*, Dec 12 and 19, 1970); field trips to Mexico (*Star*, Jan 29, 1933); summer camps (*Star*, May 28, 1935); and a free annual rodeo with the boys performing (*Star*, Jan 18, 1934). On October 5, 1934, the *Arizona Daily Star* reported, "With an enrollment of 35 boys from the east, the Arizona Desert School will begin its eighth year. Matthew Baird will continue as the headmaster of the school, this being his fifth year. According to the announcement, the enrollment of the popular school for boys has doubled in attendance since its beginning."

Matthew resigned his position at the Arizona School for Boys in 1937 and, that same year, in Kensington, England, on November 11, he married Audrey Lewisohn, the daughter of wealthy New York banker Frederick Lewisohn.

During his time at the Arizona Desert School, Matthew had become acquainted with Richard A. Morse, William W. Choate, and James R. Hopkins, so the connections were in place for Matthew and Audrey to be the owners of what would become the Ruby Star Ranch, located in southern Pima County between San Xavier and Twin Buttes. In addition to the spotlight focused on the well-known couple, there was a great deal of interest in the ranch itself, the people who worked there, and the guests who visited.

On September 14, 1941, the *Star* reported England's Marchioness of Queensberry, also known as artist Cathleen Mann, accompanied by her children, [Lord David Douglas, 12th Marquess of Queensbury] and Lady Jane Douglas, making an overnight stop to visit the Bairds.

In April of 1942, when the Japanese were making large pushes toward Australia, Matt entered active duty service at Duncan Army Field, Texas, and "was assigned to an air depot group, which went overseas in November of the same year and was part of the nucleus from which the 13th Army Air Forces (AAF) was formed on January 13, 1943. As executive and later commanding officer of the group, he was one of the administrative ground officers who had to meet the hectic problems of supply and maintenance for the 13th AAF bomber and fighter planes which were striking daily in the battles for Guadalcanal, Russell islands, and New Georgia in the South Pacific. He was advanced to plans officer of the 13th AAF service command in June of 1944, later being promoted to chief of staff and then commanding officer. Throughout this, soldiers in his aircraft repair squadrons were just one jump behind the 13th AAF engineers who were building the air strips on newly taken bases in New Guinea and the Dutch East Indies." His soldiers also prepared heavy bombers to blast Japanese strongholds in the Philippines, Borneo, and Formosa. (*Arizona Daily Star*, Mar 11, 1945)

In late 1941 or early 1942, John Grieves McIlvain had come to Ruby Star Ranch to take over management while Matt Baird was in the service. Born in Philadelphia on March 14,1881, John had spent a large part of his life around Sheridan, Wyoming, as either owner or manager of several well-known ranches. His specialty was "ranch planning management." (*Arizona Daily Star*, Sept 16, 1953)

At about this same time, Roberto Traslaviña came to Ruby Star to act as foreman for the Bairds. In addition to caring for the ranch animals, he and his wife, Olive, would enable a countless number of foster children to also make Ruby Star their home.

On July 7, 1942, the *Star* reported that, "Death yesterday tracked down William Pate "Billy" Chester, game hunter and guide, former government scout and deputy sheriff and one of the few remaining authentic figures of the old west. Born March 10, 1872, in Texas to cattle and racehorse owners, Billy participated in races from a very young age and left home when he was 12. He was a Sonoran ranch foreman prior to becoming scout for government forces in 1916. Later, he used his scouting knowledge to guide hunting parties. He was a deputy sheriff and prison guard who retired to guide and work as a cowboy. Last winter before his illness brought him down, Chester worked for Matt Baird, Twin Buttes rancher, living alone and taking care of a herd of steers."

On February 10, 1944, the *Star* announced that Matthew Baird had been made a full colonel. "In the informality of a pyramidal tent and surrounded by enlisted men who had campaigned with him in the south and southwest Pacific, the recently promoted commanding officer of the 13th AAF air service

A Christmas card from Audrey and Matt Baird. Courtesy of the Revello family.

command, Colonel Matthew Baird, of Tucson Arizona, had his new rank insignia pinned upon him by a sergeant major with whom he had served through more than two years of foreign duty. At the officer's own request, the enlisted men witnessed the ceremony of his promotion from lieutenant colonel. The soldiers all were men who saw duty with him in an air depot which departed overseas in November of 1942. 'I know that my start in the army and my subsequent boost up the ladder can be attributed directly to the non-coms and other enlisted men who broke me in, and who did the work with me,' Colonel Baird said."

The April 19, 1945, edition of the *Star* reported, "Colonel Matthew Baird has joined Mrs. Baird at the Ruby Star Ranch on a 21 day leave," and the June 10 edition told that, "Colonel Matthew Baird, husband of Mrs. Audrey L Baird, Ruby Star Ranch, was recently awarded the Legion of Merit for 'exceptionally meritorious conduct in the performance of outstanding services in the South Pacific area from November 22, 1943 to June 16, 1944.'" Finally, word was received via the September 3rd *Citizen* that, "Col. Matthew Baird, Tucson resident and veteran of the Pacific War, is returning to civilian life and his home in Tucson at the Ruby Star Ranch. Effective September 1, all mail addressed to Col. Matthew Baird, at the Pentagon building in Washington, D. C., will be forwarded to Matt Baird, Ruby Star Ranch."

Colonel Baird returned to Ruby Star with gusto and immediately got involved in the local community. The May 15, 1946, *Citizen* published articles of incorporation for the Vulcan Copper and Zinc Mining Company, a joint venture with Edward N. Foy of Twin Buttes. The *Star* reported on August 13 that Matt Baird had become a member of the Twin Buttes School Board. The August 14th *Citizen* named him as director of aviation for Greater Arizona, Inc. Over the next few years, Matt was the vice president of the Tucson Airport Authority, a thirty-second-degree Mason, director of the Tucson Kiwanis Club, and president of the Tucson Chapter of the Air Force Association. (*Citizen*, Oct 4, 1972)

Matt Baird with his Brahmans at Ruby Star Ranch.
Courtesy of the Gayler family.

Matt began an exciting new cattle "restocking program." The January 17, 1947 *Arizona Daily Star* reported that, "The last of a registered Hereford herd which included at its peak 250 breeding cows, is being shipped as of today by Matt Baird of Ruby Star Ranch, Twin Buttes, Arizona. The cattle have been purchased by S. L. Narramore, of Gila Bend, Arizona. Baird is restocking the Ruby Star Ranch with purebred registered Brahman bulls and some registered heifers, while the remainder of his new stocker herd will be crossbred Brahman cows, the result of breeding Hereford, Shorthorns, and Angus cows to purebred Brahman sires. Baird's Brahman bulls are from the American Brahman Breeders Association, in Houston, Texas. The bulls are already at the ranch and the heifers are in route."

The February 7, 1949, *Tucson Citizen* reported that, "India's sacred cattle, the world renowned Brahman breed, may one day soon become the sacred cattle of Arizona. If so, no small share of the credit will be due Matt Baird, founder, immediate past president, and current secretary of the Brahman Breeders Association of Arizona. Baird, who is owner and manager of the Ruby Star Ranch, 32 miles south of Tucson, is anxious to develop a breed of hybrid cows which will boost the milk and butter fat yields on his ranch and throughout the ranches and farms of Arizona." Baird, along with other ranchers throughout the nation, was working to substantiate the theory that crossing European and Brahman stocks will produce a strain of dairy cattle better suited to environmental conditions of the southern areas of the United States.

The July 29, 1949, *Citizen* told of the death of Merritt White Rundle, a horse trainer who had operated a polo arena at Ruby Star before his retirement.

On October 20, 1949, the *Star* reported that Prince Ferdinand "Andy" of Liechtenstein was traveling through the Southwest and, at the time, was staying at Ruby Star Ranch with Matt Baird. The jovial prince, visiting his brother John, whose occupation is to "put meat into bins and take it out when it looks like frozen bricks," in Phoenix, gave quite a speech in a Tucson hotel prior to his time at the ranch. "The prince stated that he would like to live in Arizona. 'Since I am so far away from the throne—my distant cousin Francis Joseph is now the ruler—I think my country can do without me, and I can quite probably do without my country.' He hopes to return to Arizona, leaving princes and principalities to the writers of light opera."

In July of 1950, *Western Ways* photographers visited the ranch and took pictures of the Brahman cattle. On August 28th of that same year, the *Citizen* told of a "cattle tour," originating in Los Angeles, with plans to spend a day visiting Matt Baird's ranch.

The spotlight continued to shine in the September 29th *Star* that carried the headline, "Brahmans Set For TV Debut: Ruby Star Ranch's Cattle Will Be Seen Sunday on Eastern Video Programming." Tom Galvin, a film editor with Fox and Paramount News, visited Tucson's Charles Herbert of *Western Ways*. "When he went back to New York, NBC called him in to ask about some educational features. It seems that TV was getting in bad with parents because there was way too much 'blood and thunder' and not enough educational stuff." Galvin contacted Herbert about creating a program featuring the Brahman crossbreeding experiments and Herbert knew "the easiest place to get photos of Brahmans was at Col. Matt Baird's Ruby Star Ranch" where the cattle have "been photographed so much they know their best camera angles."

On December 9, 1950, the *Arizona Daily Star* made a headline announcement that, "Col. Matt Baird, veteran World War II air force officer and prominent in business and civic affairs in Arizona, has been recalled to active duty, and will leave December 26 for Washington D.C. He has been assigned to a post in the Central Intelligence Agency under Lt. Gen. Walter Bedell Smith. What his new duties with central intelligence will be he was unable to disclose. He has remained active in the air force reserve, and more recently has been in charge of mobilization day assignees at Davis-Monthan Air Force Base."

A *People Today* magazine article on September 26, 1951, explains further that, "For the first time in history, the U.S. government is training professional spies—and picking the brightest college youngsters to make espionage their career. By December, some 250 men and 50 women will be learning the spy business from the bottom up, at schools they mustn't even admit exist.

Matt Baird with one of his Brahmans at Ruby Star Ranch.
Courtesy of the Gayler family.

"Repeated intelligence failures (from Pearl Harbor to Red China's offensive in Korea) jolted Washington into awareness that a sound intelligence system can't grow on a catch-as-catch-can basis. Result: A training program looking 20 years ahead to staff the CIA with dedicated espionage experts and reward them with a career as other nations have done for ages. Until recently, U.S. Intelligence was a dumping ground for mediocre officers and playboys picking up cocktail gossip abroad. CIA boss, Lt. Gen. Walter B. Smith, recalls how he sought a G-2 post after WWI, and was asked only, 'What's your private income?'

"Today's CIA recruits need brains, not money. They were quietly approached on campus, after undercover scouts (mostly ex-professors) watched them at work and play. Thus hand-picked from the class of '51, they'll cram languages (especially Russian, from records), then concentrate on basic intelligence elements—research, economic analysis, report writing. Next, they'll train on the job in CIA offices, fan out to armed services and the State Department, do more university work or travel. Throughout, they'll study top-secret U.S. operations behind the Iron Curtain, and later may take part in them. CIA's Director of Training is studious, dynamic Col. Matthew Baird, Princeton and Oxford grad who became a cattle breeder and school headmaster in Arizona. The first 80 boys and girls of the CIA's career corps are already at work. Among the top 10% of their classes, they were carefully FBI-screened, start at $2,800 a year for BAs, to $4,600 for PhDs. The best of them are expected to reach the top of the espionage ladder in 15 years."

Alice Parker and Manerd Gayler.
Courtesy of Georgia Spivey.

While Matt Baird was setting up the new CIA training program, the *New York Daily News* announced on March 24, 1951, "Audrey Lewisohn Baird, of the Lewisohn banking clan, quietly divorced Matthew Baird 3d in Tucson, Ariz."

At the end of that year, his dear friend, Dory Dublin, passed away. "Famed Arizona Cowboy, Swings Last Loop," was the byline in the Tucson *Daily Citizen* on December 6, 1951, as yet another character associated with the Ruby Star Ranch was lost. Forty-year cowboy Thomas C. Dublin, known as Dory, worked on many ranches throughout the Southwest. For the four years prior to his death, Dory had lived in semi-retirement on the Ruby Star Ranch. Matt and Dory had developed a "firm and lasting friendship."

John G. McIlvain, the Ruby Star Ranch manager, passed away September 13, 1953, and soon after that, Roberto Translaviña, the foreman, departed. By March 7, 1954, the Manerd Gayler family was living on Ruby Star Ranch. Gayler was interviewed by the *Star* as one of the Southern Arizona ranchers who was "becoming more mechanized, more up-to-date" with a mobile telephone in his car. Manerd told the reporter that he was "kind of scared to use it. He's got it rigged to his car horn and whenever somebody calls him, that horn blasts away without any warning in the most lonesome country and gives him a lively case of the jumps."

According to John Gayler, his father, Manerd Gayler, had come from Claremore, Oklahoma, and had worked around Texas before coming to Arizona. (Elmer Kelton's *Good Old Boys* book carried a dedication to him.) Prior to Manerd's arrival in Arizona, he was what would today be called a "pro rodeo" man, who made the papers nationwide with his success. He eventually met and married Alice Parker, the daughter of C. C. "Bud" Parker, "The man who introduced the Brahman breed of cattle to Mexico, and who helped introduce the Fiesta de los Vaqueros to Tucson." Parker, a cattleman, expert rider, and championship steer roper had worked for ten years in Chihuahua as a cowboy for the San Domingo Land and Cattle Company where he was charged with keeping the cattle safe during the Mexican Revolution. (*Tucson Citizen*, Sept 26, 1946)

John Gayler shares that his mother, Alice, traveled with her father, Bud. At that time, there were no horse trailers so the rodeo cattle and horses were shipped on the rail lines and the rodeo participants traveled the roads in their vehicles, camping along the way. Alice was a good rider but at the time, women weren't involved in the rodeo, so she traveled with her dad to cook and help out as needed. A friend of Manerd's introduced him to Alice.

After their marriage, Gayler owned several Arizona ranch properties over the years, but by the late 1940s, he was settled in the Canoa area and was an associate of Howell Manning's. While working with Brahman cattle near Canoa, he became acquainted with Matt Baird, the founder and past president of the Brahman Breeders Association of Arizona. When Baird went back east, the Gayler family (Manerd, Alice, Frances, and John) left Canoa and bought Ruby Star.

The Santiago and Olga Gallardo family was working at Canoa, moved to Ruby Star, and eventually to T-4 Ranch. They were like family to the Gaylers. All said and done, the Gallardos worked for Manerd Gayler for over forty years.

John Gayler was born in 1949 while the family lived at Canoa and was about five years old when the family moved to Ruby Star. He remembers the old house, which he says is probably long gone. It was a wood-frame house with lots of paneling and was unique in that almost every room had a screened porch. It was the home the Bairds had owned and was very nice for that time period.

In November of 1954, Baird made a quick Thanksgiving visit to the ranch. On the 24th, the *Star* quotes him as saying, "I just wanted to get back for a while and see the old familiar places. The ranch looks great. Never saw the grass so high in this area, everything looked just perfect."

John remembers Matt's visits to Ruby Star. He could come and stay for a week or two during the spring and summer. Matt was very worldly—probably because of the secret service stuff he was involved in. His expertise was Iran and Iraq and Matt brought him coins back from his travels, which John played with and lost. At one time, Matt gave him a dagger from the Middle East.

John said Matt was a wonderful gentleman—"very well versed, but down to earth." The most unique thing he remembers about Matt was that he often wore shorts—khakis with no shirt—and men just didn't wear shorts in those days. He was very tanned and weathered. When John got married, Matt heard about it and asked if they wanted to use his beach house in Delaware for a honeymoon. John declined and is still in trouble for it fifty-two years later.

Gayler's Ruby Star longhorns. Courtesy of the Gayler family.

John doesn't remember how big the Ruby Star Ranch was when they bought it, but he knows they bought Baird's cattle along with the ranch. They had some pure Brahman bloodlines, but mostly used them to cross Brahmans with English breeds.

In March of 1956, Gayler introduced Texas Longhorns to Ruby Star. Mr. Yates, an acquaintance from Texas, had spent over thirty-five years working on a Longhorn breeding program. When the old rancher got ill, Gayler purchased his friend's cattle and had them shipped to the ranch in Arizona. In an article about the new cattle, on March 21st, the *Citizen* quoted Gayler as saying, "I don't know what I'm going to do with them. I guess you can just say I'm crazy. Maybe they'll be used in enough movies to help pay for their keep. But even if they never earn a nickel, they're not going to be slaughtered as beef."

Over the years, Manerd did as he said and used the Longhorns in the filming of Western movies. His son, John Gayler, was recently watching an old Audie Murphy (decorated war hero and TV star) movie and saw some of their cattle. According to John, they made out okay with the Longhorns, but the stories in the newspapers were completely exaggerated. In total, they probably had only about fifty to sixty Longhorns (compared to the two to three hundred mentioned in the papers).

According to the *Star* on January 31, 1957, Gayler was making plans to take some of his Longhorns to the Rodeo Parade on February 21st. Said to be one of the biggest single herds of Longhorns left in the Southwest, Gayler was breaking sixteen of his animals to the yoke so they could pull wagons in the parade. John Gayler remembers this event and said the animals were quite gentle, but difficult to transport. When loading for travel, they would have to carefully turn the heads of the cattle sideways to fit them safely in the trailers.

John went to school in Sahuarita and remembers Rose's little store at Twin Buttes. It was a big deal to go get a soda pop there. Old town buildings were still there at the time. They would go east to Mission, which was one of the few paved roads, and then over to Twin Buttes.

The Gaylers were good friends with the McGee Ranch families and often went up to the community building for dances. Frances went to school with all of them. Kathy Bell was the same age as John. Shelly and Kelly Fox were a year or two older. Years later, when the Gaylers were at Rosemont, Sierrita Mining and Ranching came with their big equipment to do assessment work for them.

In the late 1950s, Manerd Gayler purchased the neighboring 59 Ranch, across McGee Ranch Road to the south of the Ruby Star, from the Kiddoo and Harris families. From that time on, the 59 Ranch would be considered a part of Ruby Star holdings.

An announcement in the April 3, 1959 *Citizen* provided notification that the Gaylers had sold over 3,800 acres to Montclair Investment Company, made up of four businessmen from Danville, Illinois, for

$686,000. "Included in the sale is land that was formerly part of Gayler's old Kiddoo Ranch and part of the Ruby Star Ranch. The Gaylers plan to remain and continue the cattle operations on the Ruby Star, which formerly was owned by Matt Baird, a pioneer Brahman cattle breeder in

Gayler home at Ruby Star Ranch. Courtesy of Georgia Spivey.

this country. Gayler has been ranching in the area for approximately 25 years." Montclair representatives claimed there were no plans to develop the property.

According to John Gayler, his family finally left the Ruby Star Ranch in about 1963 when the land was deeded to Anaconda Mining Company. In the deal, Manerd chose land in the Nogales area which Anaconda bought and built a house on. Anaconda then "traded" him that property for the Ruby Star Ranch. The new Gayler Ranch was called the T-4.

On October 4, 1972, the Tucson *Citizen* reported the death of Matthew Baird III, at his home in Bethany Beach, Delaware. Survived by only one nephew and two nieces, there were no longer any ties to Arizona or the Ruby Star.

In the Arizona *Daily Star* on June 29, 1990, an article announced that Ruby Star was going on the auction block. At the time, the ranch consisted of 7,914 acres of deeded land and an additional 4,360 acres of assumable federal and state lease land. The current owner, Calvin Wolfswinkel, had purportedly purchased the ranch property from Anamax Mining Company (which had been affiliated with Anaconda) in 1986, but was being forced to sell as a condition of his Chapter 11 bankruptcy reorganization.

By April 26, 1993, the *Star* reported that Ruby Star Ranch, now consisting of 5,388 deedable acres, adjacent to 4,360 acres of leaseland, was again on the market, but this time, through the Federal Resolution Trust Corporation (RTC), representing the interest of Lakeland Savings Bank of Detroit Lakes, Minnesota, which had acquired title in a trustee sale. It was learned that developer, Calvin Wolfswinkle, had ties to Charles H. Keating, Jr. The sale was delayed, but the land was ultimately sold for $1,303,000 to Larry Holmes of Las Vegas, who immediately flipped the property to the Sombrero Land and Cattle Company. (*Star*, Oct 21, 1996)

That deal sealed the fate of the Ruby Star Ranch. A systematic division of the property completely dismantled the abandoned ranch and with each additional sale, the segments were chopped into smaller parcels. Cyprus Minerals Corporation bought 910 acres of the property in October of 1997 for $1.7 million to create a "buffer" between the mine operations and the subdivisions being built on the properties. At that same time, it was revealed that Gilbert Aguirre, a part-time Tucsonan, was a major player in the Sombrero Land and Cattle Company operation. (*Star*, Oct 30, 1997)

In 2010, Gilbert Aguirre donated over 750 acres of the remaining Ruby Star to the Reid Park Zoological Society to be used for conservation. At the time of donation, it was valued at over $5.4 million and the ranch land was being leased for grazing. (*Star*, Jan 15, 2011). The Zoological Society held the property for only a short time before completing a quiet sale of the Sierrita foothill property, once designated for "conservation," to Freeport McMoRan Copper and Gold for $3 million in November of 2014. (*Star*, Jan 5, 2014). Aguirre expressed his frustration to the Arizona *Daily Star* on January 5, 2014. "I'm very disturbed. They gave me a song and dance

Playing music at the McGee Ranch community building by Henry Hibbetts, Jerry McGee, Leander Harris, and Keith McGee. Courtesy of Lynn Harris.

about how they were working with the San Diego Zoo. The board came out and looked at the property and they talked about having a great breeding program for some of their animals. Then, all of a sudden, recently, the next thing I know is that I heard they had sold it to a mining company. I think as a common courtesy, they should have contacted me first and said we got the land under one pretense, and it didn't work and at the least try to sell it back to me. I would have bought it back." Schlegel, the zoo's representative admitted that, "In hindsight, it might have been best to at least notify Aguirre of the sale just after it was done." Freeport said, "The land purchase helps ensure the company will have enough space to keep mining operations going over the long term." Local environmentalist, Nancy Freeman, "criticized the society for selling the land intended for conservation. 'They made $3 million profit when they did nothing there but talk about what they might do.'"

The legacy of the Ruby Star ended, in many ways, similar to the way it began—small pieces of sloping rangeland surrounded on all sides by miners looking to make their fortune. The lifetime of stories, known only to the people who lived on these rolling, cactus-covered hills, may remain untold, but the songs of dusty cowboys, sung in echoing harmony to the lows of restless cattle, will forever be carried by the wind.

~ Contributed by Monica Lee Elam Christiansen

NOTES

Architectural Forum magazine, April 1940
Arizona Daily Star, Tucson, Arizona
Brooklyn Standard Union, Brooklyn, New York
Camden Morning Post, Camden, New Jersey
Daily News, New York, New York
Elam, Margaret Norton McGee. Interviewed by Monica Lee Elam Christiansen. May 2021.
Gayler, John R. Interviewed by Monica Lee Elam Christiansen. July 12, 2021.
Harris, Lynn. Interviewed by Monica Lee Elam Christiansen. 2021.
Trowbridge, Dianne McGee. Interviewed by Monica Lee Elam Christiansen. 2021.
People Today (magazine). September 26, 1951
Philadelphia Inquirer, Philadelphia, Pennsylvania
Tucson Citizen, Tucson, Arizona

59 Ranch

The earliest recorded homestead claim on what would become known as 59 Ranch was that of Juan V. Mendoza, who initiated his first 160 acre homestead application in August of 1915. Over the next ten years, he and his wife Rosa filed for a total of almost 800 acres, witnessed by Ramon, Ronaldo, Roberto, and Rudolfo Soto.

It appears that Juan was active in the local community. The *Arizona Daily Star*, on September 3, 1932, said, "The Sahuaro Ranch of Juan V. Mendoza, on the Mission Road between Twin Buttes and San Xavier Mine, will be the scene of a barbecue Sunday afternoon, to which all [general election] candidates are welcome. The party is being given for the purpose of permitting the people of that district to gather and hear the candidates present their cause."

The next mention of Juan V. Mendoza was his death notice in the April 18, 1938, edition of the *Arizona Daily Star*. "Juan V. Mendoza, 58 year old Twin Buttes cattlemen and Arizona Pioneer, was found dead yesterday morning in the house on his Homestead, 23 miles south of Tucson. He was found by his son, Juan Jr., who had gone there to visit him. Death was from natural causes, his son said. Mr. Mendoza had lived in Tucson and surrounding territory for 50 years, coming here as a child from Hermosillo, Sonora."

A second set of players in the early history of the 59 Ranch were Charles Johnson and Annie Beatrice Syverson Cunningham who married on January 28, 1933 in Tucson. The *Arizona Daily Star*, dated February 19, 1935, offers a sad summary of their story:

> *Charles J. Cunningham, 73, veteran prospector and Tucson saloon and Café owner, was killed early yesterday afternoon when a scaffolding collapsed and plunged him and Charles B. Marcus, 31 W. Kelso St., into the shaft of the old Port Arthur mine, 4 miles west of Twin Buttes and some 25 miles southwest of Tucson. Hope for his life was abandoned with the failure of rescue efforts later in the day. It was only the possibility of recovering his body from a welter of timbers and water, 85 feet below the surface, that led Sheriff John Belton, Deputy mine inspector Jim Malley of Bisbee, and their assistants to leave here with mine rescue equipment at 8 o'clock last night.*
>
> *Returning to Tucson shortly before midnight, Sheriff Belton reported last night that inspector Malley had found the mineshaft in such dangerous condition that he refused to permit any work in it before daylight. Marcus owed his miraculous escape to the fact that he broke his fall by clutching a stringer, momentarily interrupting his fall. After floating in the icy water for some*

time, badly bruised, he climbed to the surface and was driven here in search of aid by Mrs. Cunningham.

The accident was reported at the sheriff's office, and Marcus was taken to Saint Mary's Hospital. Sheriff Belton and deputies sped to the mouth of the mineshaft, but could see only a floating mass of wreckage on the surface of the water, which is believed to be about 200 feet deep. Marcus had seen no sign of Cunningham during his stay in the water, and under the circumstances, Belton refused to allow his deputies to descend into the shaft, where further cave-ins of rotting timber were feared. He sent at once for Jim Malley, Deputy State Mine Inspector, who arrived from Bisbee early in the evening with mine rescue equipment. Meanwhile, preliminary preparations for a dissent were supervised by Belton.

Mr. Cunningham, who had lived with his 27-year-old pregnant wife and an eight-month-old baby on his Homestead property at the Port Arthur group of mining claims, was 73 years old last Thanksgiving day.

His mining ventures had been various. He had reportedly started the Klondike mining rush, and was proud of having "returned with more gold than he took into the North country." He had also mined in the Black Hills and at Leadville and Butte, and at San Xavier, and the Lincoln camp in Southern Arizona.

He came to Tucson in 1903, and was best known here as former proprietor of the Cabinet Café, which had one of the largest bars and the largest gambling layout in Tucson's earlier history. In later years, the Cabinet was reduced by prohibition and the passage of years to a pool hall and near the end, a beer parlor. Several years ago, it was removed to permit widening of Church Street.

It took almost a week to finally recover the body of Charles Cunningham and he was laid to rest in the Evergreen Memorial Park on February 26, 1935.

May 16, 1935, found Mrs. Annie B. Cunningham, widow of Charles J. Cunningham, filing notice to establish a five-year claim for the stock raising homestead entry initiated May 7, 1930. On August 3, 1936, Earl J. Barnhard, 48, and Annie B. Cunningham, 32, were married in Tucson. Soon thereafter, on September 24th, the *Tucson Citizen* published notice that Annie B. and E. J. Barnhard were selling their 640 acres, lying between Twin Buttes and the Tinaja Hills, to William Nicholson for $2,000.

William and Bertha Benson Nicholson had once owned extensive ranch property in the Santa Rita Mountains. In 1928, the August 29th edition of the *Arizona Daily Star* announced that Dink Parker had purchased all of that property.

In the May 8, 1935, edition of the *Arizona Daily Star*, Billy Nicholson was listed as one of several individuals looking for homestead property. The Nicholson purchase from Annie Barnhard in 1936 gave them the property they sought and brought them across the valley to the Sierrita foothills.

According to William's obituary posted in the *Tucson Citizen* on April 23, 1940, the fifty-six-year-old owner of the 59 Ranch near Twin Buttes was a "longtime resident of Southern Arizona and once a Tucson Police Detective. Mr. Nicholson came to this country from England when he was 14 years old. He first lived for some time in Tombstone and later

Ed Harris on horseback. Courtesy of Lynn Harris.

came to Tucson, where he became a detective on the police force. He worked in Tucson as a detective for six years and later became a rancher. He was a member of the school board of Twin Buttes School

District and a member of Tucson Lodge number 385 of the Elks." William was buried in the Evergreen Cemetery on April 26, 1940. Pallbearers included Wallace Blackwell, Greg Baxter, Jesus Camacho, Elliot Dunseath, William Irwin, Nick Hall, Dr. Edward Gotthelf, Jr., Bud Parker, and William Schultz.

The Hibbetts family moved to the ranch to run it for Bertha Nicholson after Bill passed away. Henry Everett and Bessie Anita Shults Hibbetts were married on September 11, 1939, at Patagonia. Their first child, Jimmy Everett, was born on July 17, 1940, and his birth certificate indicated that his father was the

Ed and Flora Harris.
Courtesy of Lynn Harris.

ranch foreman on Nicholson's 59 Ranch. When Martin Henry came along on April 7, 1942, Henry was still working there, but they had moved to the Continental School District by the spring of 1943. The family's third child, Jerry Lee Hibbetts, was born on April 10, 1944, while the family was living at the Santa Rita Experimental Station. They were there a while and then wandered a bit through Arkansas and Texas before returning to build a home at Madera Canyon where their last child, Linda Mia Hibbetts, was born in 1952.

The following article appeared in the *Arizona Daily Star* on December 6, 1944: "If you think the wild and woolly west has disappeared, you are mistaken—at least that's the opinion of Mr. and Mrs. R. J. McMahon of 59 Ranch at Twin Buttes. A couple of rattlers, a Gila monster, and a few scorpions were all the McMahon's had to show for their days as Westerners until early this week. Then the Zane Grey climax came in the form of a 40-pound wildcat which invaded their yard late one night bent on destruction. The cat had made two visits and the destruction had reached five roosters before McMahon succeeded in shooting the animal. The family's satisfied—the west is wild, the country is primitive. Mrs. McMahon keeps a sharp eye out now when she's doing her landscape painting, and her husband has a rifle handy when he concentrates on his writing. Their two daughters? Well, they have a wildcat skin to remind them of Arizona."

It is unknown how the McMahon family came to be visiting the ranch, but it is obvious that they had quite an adventure. Irish-born author Robert James McMahon, Jr., and his wife, Ena Beatrice McClain, lived there for only one year. Their daughters Sandra and Sharon were born near Kansas City and spent the 1944–45 school year in Twin Buttes with Mrs. Foy.

Edward Royal "Ed" and Florence Sidney "Flora" Lyon McGee Harris sold their homestead at McGee Ranch and used the proceeds of that sale to purchase the 59 Ranch property from Bertha Nicholson. Family stories indicate that there was quite a drought in the area. Ed was moving cattle east from McGee

Longhorns on the road from Twin Buttes to 59 Ranch in 1956.
Courtesy of the Revello family.

Ranch and came across the nice house with a productive well. He immediately took steps to buy it.

Ed and Flora soon moved into their new ranch house with their son-in-law Raymond Plummer Kiddoo, daughter Janet Florence Harris Kiddoo, and grandson Edward Raymond Kiddoo. In 1926, 1927, and 1928, Janet had given birth to three infants, all of whom died within a few hours of birth. On November 10, 1944, while living at McGee Ranch, the couple was blessed with twin boys, born in a Tucson hospital. Sadly, little Eugene Plummer Kiddoo passed away only five days after his birth, leaving Edward, who weighed only three pounds, to come home from the hospital in a shoebox. His mother and grandmother kept him close to the stove through the winter months and, with love and prayers, kept the tiny baby alive.

Only a few months after Edward's third birthday was celebrated at the 59 Ranch, Grandma Flora passed away on March 24, 1947. A year and a half later, Arnold Bradley Kiddoo was born on September 11, 1948, in Tucson and came home to the ranch for his early years during which Raymond Kiddoo was a member and president of the Sahuarita PTA (1951–52). Sometime after 1954, the Kiddoo family moved to Los Angeles, where Grandpa Ed Harris died on December 27, 1956.

The Gaylers, owners of Ruby Star Ranch, directly north of 59 Ranch, purchased the property from the Kiddoos. From there, a number of families rented the home on the property. The *Star*, on April 20, 1957, published an obituary for William W. Spivey's mother-in-law, Emma E. Glenn, who at eighty-one years of age had passed away in her home at the 59 Ranch. The Gayler and Spivey families were friends. Eventually, the Spiveys moved to another house on the Ruby Star where Opal lived out her life.

Mr. Gayler may have merged the 59 Ranch holdings with the Ruby Star property, but, to those who have lived here for generations, more than McGee Ranch Road separates the two. The old 59 Ranch will forever tell a story of its own.

~ Contributed by Monica Lee Elam Christiansen

Emma Sharp Glenn and her granddaughter, Georgia Ann Spivey, taken about 1941. Courtesy of Georgia Spivey Martin.

NOTES

Arizona Daily Star, Tucson, Arizona

Elam, Margaret Norton McGee. Interviewed by Monica Lee Elam Christiansen. May 2021.

Gayler, John R. Interviewed by Monica Lee Elam Christiansen. July 12, 2021.

Harris, Lynn. Interviewed by Monica Lee Elam Christiansen. 2021.

Trowbridge, Dianne McGee. Interviewed by Monica Lee Elam Christiansen. 2021.

Personal information from Sutah Thomas Harris.

Tucson Citizen, Tucson, Arizona

Manelos Sahuarita Mercantile and Sahuarita Bar and Grill

Harry B. Manelos (Haralambos Basilis Manelos) was born on February 23, 1884, in Argolis, Greece. It is believed that Harry came to the United States on a boat when he was only twelve years old, in about 1896. He came into New York and lived pretty much on the streets, doing whatever jobs he could find to survive. It was a very difficult life and he eventually decided to go to Los Angeles, California. In the 1910 census, the first official record of Harry in the United States, he had moved down to San Diego and was working as a janitor in an office building. Soon after this, payroll records of the Southern Pacific Railroad in 1916 and 1917 show him as a supply man in the Tucson area.

Maria Toribia Páez Alcalá, born on April 16, 1883, was the third of at least thirteen children born to Ramón Páez Rodriguez and Maria Concepción Alcalá Villegas. The family lived for many years in the La

Paz area of Baja California Sur, Mexico, before moving to Lampazos, Tepache, Sonora, Mexico, where their youngest son, Martin, was born in 1904. On March 5, 1908, Toribia's mother, Concepción, died in Minas Nuevas, Alamos, Sonora, Mexico, and soon after, in September of 1913, her father Ramón died as well.

Border crossing records indicate that on December 18, 1913, Rufina (age 29), Teodora (age 24), Simon (age 16), and Martin (age 10) left Navajoa, where they were living, and headed to Tucson via

Nogales, seeking their maternal aunt, Maria Dolores Alcalá Villegas Acuña. By that time, Toribia had been briefly married to German immigrant, Adolfo Meyer, but indicated she was single when she crossed into the United States.

It is unknown whether the siblings actually went to their aunt in Tucson, but on January 8, 1918, Toribia was in Nogales, Arizona, where she married Harry Manelos. In March of 1918, Harry was working as a waiter for the Southern Pacific in the dining cars and when he filled out his draft registration card for World War I on September 12th of that same year, he and Toribia were living in Hotel Blanco's room 13, running a cafe they owned on Grand Avenue.

Harry and Toribia were living in Nogales when their son, William Manelos was born. Billie Manelos transferred into the Sahuarita School for first grade during the 1925–26 school year, with teacher Ethel A. Taylor. William Manelos stated, "I was born in Nogales, Arizona, on January 19, 1919. At the time, based on information from my parents, my father owned and operated restaurants in Nogales, Arizona, and Deming, New Mexico. My first recollection of my life with my parents was when I was five years old (1924) when we lived in Sahuarita, Arizona, where my parents owned and operated a general store in a rented facility. A year or so later my parents were able to build a large facility across the road to serve as a general store and living quarters. I attended Sahuarita School, grades one through eight."

*Maria Toribia Páez Alcalá.
Courtesy of the Manelos family.*

William Manelos stated, "My sister Mary was born in Tucson, Arizona, on January 24, 1926, in a private residence. I do not recall the address but I recall riding my bike up and down the street waiting for Mary's birth. This date, January 24, 1926, is etched in my memory as we celebrated Mary's first birthday on January 24, 1927, after a death [sic] threatening illness. Shortly after her birth (I do not recall the period of time), Mary was struck down with an extremely serious case of spinal meningitis and hovered on the brink of death for many days. As I recall, she was hospitalized at St. Mary's Hospital in Tucson for several weeks. Miraculously, she recovered without any aftereffects."

Toribia maintained a very close relationship with her siblings. When the Manelos family moved to Sahuarita, it was to join Rufina, who had become the second wife of Canadian-born Louis Curtis, a Southern Pacific Railroad engineer. The couple was married on February 20, 1916, in Tucson, Arizona. Rufina became a

*Harry Manelos with a customer in his store circa 1940.
Courtesy of the Manelos family.*

stepmother to Julia, Lewis, Katherine, and Richard, the children of Louis and his deceased wife, Mary M. Spofford. Additionally, the couple had four children of their own, Raymond (born in 1917 in Nogales, Arizona), Emilia (born in 1920 in Nogales, Arizona), Nelson (born in 1922 in Nogales, Sonora), and John (born in 1924 in Nogales, Sonora).

In 1920, Louis Curtis was living in the Southern Pacific section housing in Sahuarita with Julia, Richard, and Raymond. Rufina was living on Grand Avenue in Nogales with her brother, a restaurant waiter, Martin Páez, and their sister, a restaurant manager, Teodora Páez. Rufina listed Katherine and Raymond as living with her so it appears that little Ramón, (enumerated as Raymond), was counted twice. It is likely they were keeping the Nogales cafe open because Harry and Toribia had moved to Sahuarita to run the store there.

Records place Louis in the Sahuarita area much earlier than 1920. In 1910, railroad pump man Louis Curtis and his first wife, Mary, were living in Helvetia. An article in the *Tucson Citizen* on September 8, 1911, states, "The school district of Sahuarita has been created and there will be a new school this year where none has been before, according to Louis Curtis, a resident of the district. Mr. Curtis came to Tucson today to have the appointment of himself and A. W. Roberts as school directors certified by the district attorney, subject to a school election to be held in the fall. The new school will open with 68 pupils, most of whose parents are employed in the construction of the Pioneer smelter, which is located in the immediate vicinity of Sahuarita."

Louis was quite involved in the business of the Sahuarita School District and as of 1925, the Curtis children were attending there, along with Billie Manelos. When the 1930 census was taken in Sahuarita, Louis and Rufina were living right next door to Henry and Manuela Lundquist, Toribia and Rufina's sister and brother-in-law, and the Lundquists lived beside the Manelos family. At the time, Swedish-born Henry Lundquist was working as a railroad mechanic and Louis was employed as a railroad pump man. Isabel Páez, brother of the three sisters, was living with the Lundquists, working as a garage mechanic. Harry Manelos was employed as a merchant in his grocery store.

Soon after the 1930 census was taken, the Lundquist family appears to have returned to Mexico. The marriages of their three daughters, Enriqueta, Agnes, and Carolina, took place in Sonora, Mexico. (Their youngest daughter died when she was only four years old.) Manuela Páez Lundquist died in Navojoa on May 19, 1970.

Louis Curtis died in Tucson on August 21, 1935, and at the time of his passing, he was working as the postmaster of the Sahuarita post office. He had assumed charge of the post office on July 24, 1931 and, upon his death, his position was assigned to Mrs. Clara V. Luker. Louis's obituary in the August 22, 1935, *Citizen* shared that he had come to Arizona forty years prior, from Michigan, and that his funeral would be the

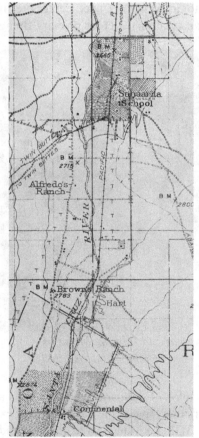

1926 Corps of Engineers, U.S. Army Tactical Map, Arizona, Helvetia Quadrangle, Grid Zone "F."

following day. U.S. Post Office Department records indicate that Louis had also been the Sahuarita postmaster from February 1919 to July 1921 and again in July of 1923 until it was briefly discontinued in October of 1923 when mail was routed to Twin Buttes.

Rufina and her children stayed in Sahuarita through at least 1935. By 1940, she had moved to Tucson and was living on 8th Street. She died in November of 1968. Teodora spent some time in California, but eventually returned to Tucson where she died in September of 1973.

The Manelos family stayed in Sahuarita and ran the family's store and restaurant. William "Bill," Harry and Toribia's only son, started out early with an interest in the military. William shared that he attended "grade nine at Roskruge Junior High School, Tucson; grades ten through twelve at Tucson Senior High School." The November 6, 1937, *Arizona Daily Star* told of his becoming a platoon sergeant in his Tucson High School ROTC Company B. He graduated from Tucson High School in the spring of 1938—quite an accomplishment for a young man who had to hitchhike to class each day.

William continues, "Following graduation from high school I attended a business college for a brief period. In 1939, I enrolled at the University of Arizona at Tucson and worked with the Southern Pacific Railroad. On July 16, 1942, after passing all the physical, academic, and psychological tests for acceptance into flight training, I enlisted as a private in the then U.S. Army Air Corps, pending assignment to flight training."

The January 14, 1943, *Arizona Daily Star* told of Cadet William Manelos graduating from the San Antonio Aviation Cadet Center preflight school. On the 23rd, it was announced that he had been admitted as an aviation cadet for primary flying training at Hicks Field, Ft. Worth, Texas. William tells, "I received my flight training in Texas where I also met my wife-to-be, whom I married on April 24, 1943, at San Antonio, Texas, after a three-month whirlwind romance."

Newspaper ads published when Harry Manelos made an attempt to sell out in July of 1943 reveal that the official store name was Sahuarita Mercantile. The *Star* and the *Citizen* both carried the ads in their "Business Opportunities" section, stating, "FOR SALE-Sahuarita Mercantile, general merchandise store and restaurant. Guaranteed good business of $100 per day. H. B. Manelos." The sale obviously did not take place.

The *Tucson Daily Citizen*, on August 21, 1943, proudly announced that, "Navigation Cadet William Manelos, 24, has reported to the world's largest aerial navigation school at the San Marcos Army airfield for an advanced course. Upon completion of the work in 18 weeks, he will receive a commission as second lieutenant or flight officer and be awarded the silver wings of an Army Air Force navigator." Then, the *Star*, on Christmas day, followed up by reporting that, "Second Lieutenant, William Manelos, 24, son of Mr. and Mrs. Harry B. Manelos of Sahuarita, Arizona, was among those who received his silver wings at the Army Air Forces Christmas Eve at the San Marcos, Texas, Training School."

Gloria and William Manelos. Courtesy of the Manelos family.

William Manelos recalled, "I graduated from flight school and was commissioned a second lieutenant in the U.S. Army Air Corps on December 23, 1943. After completing crew training, I was assigned to the Pacific Theater of Operations as a member of the B-29 air crew on Saipan, Mariana Islands, from where we flew air strikes on Japan, including the low-level firebombing of Tokyo when over sixteen square miles of the city center were totally destroyed."

The *Arizona Daily Star* closely followed the advancement of hometown Billie Manelos. They reported his bombardier training in Roswell, New Mexico, in January of 1944, and his advancement to the Lead B-29 Bombardier-Navigator of his unit making flights over Tokyo from its base in Saipan in

January of 1945.

In the May 31, 1947, edition of the *Tucson Daily Citizen*, it was announced that, "After a 15-month tour of duty at Kelly Field as a budget and fiscal officer, William Manelos of 1034 E. 5th St., left this week for separation from the service. Lieutenant Manelos spent eight months on Saipan during the war, where he received the Distinguished Flying Cross with two Oak Leaf Clusters, the Air Medal with four Oak Leaf Clusters, the Presidential Unit Citation with one Oak Leaf Cluster, and the Asiatic-Pacific theater ribbon."

Mary Manelos. Courtesy of the Manelos family.

While Bill had gone off to school and eventually into service, Mary Margaret "Maria" Manelos remained in the Sahuarita area. William Manelos tells that "Mary attended grade school (grades one through eight) at Sahuarita School; grade nine at Wakefield Junior High School, Tucson, and grades ten through twelve at Tucson Senior High School. She also attended the University of Arizona." Unlike her brother, Bill, she didn't leave to travel the world. Mary instead returned to Sahuarita where she focused on the family's business, cared for her aging parents, and raised her own three children (Richard McDaniel, Randy Gahart, and Carolyne Robinson).

William's story continues, "After completion of the combat tour of duty I was reassigned to the United States. In June, 1947, while assigned to a new career field as budget and fiscal officer (I continued to maintain my flying proficiency) for the San Antonio Air Material Command, Kelly Field, San Antonio, Texas, I requested relief from active duty to continue my education at the University of Arizona at Tucson."

William and his wife, Gloria, returned briefly to Sahuarita to help the Manelos family business and for Bill to attend college. As reported in the June 21, 1947, edition of the *Arizona Daily Star*, William Manelos, recently returned from military service overseas, submitted an application for a wine and beer license for Sahuarita Mercantile. The July 8th edition reported that a hearing had been set for the application because a petition of protest had been received in response to William's request for licensure. The July 15th *Tucson Citizen* provided additional detail. "The Pima County board of supervisors Monday approved the application of William Manelos for a beer and wine license at the Sahuarita Mercantile Company. . . . Several protests were filed with the supervisors. They stated that most of the patrons of the store are migratory farm workers who are unable to spend their money for intoxicants. The applicant asserted, however, that he has a demand for the liquor from nearby ranchers. There is no other beer and wine license in the vicinity."

In August of 1947, Bill and Gloria's son, Aaron, was born in Tucson. William tells, "I went back on active duty in October, 1948, and was assigned to Germany during the Berlin Conflict."

He flew U.S. planes through a narrow corridor into West Berlin's Tempelhof Airport to supply humanitarian aid to the people being strangled by the Soviet blockade. The family was in Germany until 1964 when they moved briefly to Langley Air Force Base in Tidewater, Virginia. Soon after, Bill was called to the Pentagon by Robert S. McNamara.

The *Arizona Daily Star* and *Tucson Citizen* ran yet another series of "Business Opportunity" classified ads in July of 1958 that provide a list of changes after 1943. "GOING business and property, grocery store, bar, and service station. Contact owner, Sahuarita Mercantile, Sahuarita, Ariz. Must sell!"

As Harry, the Greek personality behind the store, aged, more and more of the responsibility fell on the shoulders of Toribia and Mary. Toribia, always behind the scenes, worked day in and day out to keep the store running and her family cared for. Her fluency in Spanish and her family connections with local community members enabled them to create rapport—making a secure place for them in the close-knit

Sahuarita area. Mary was there beside her, placing orders, stocking shelves, waiting tables, and helping customers, all while making sure her children were safe and cared for. The back room of a store is a difficult place to raise a family.

On March 7, 1963, the *Tucson Citizen* printed that, "Harry B. Manelos, 79, born in Greece, longtime resident of Sahuarita, died March 3ʳᵈ. Owner and operator of the Sahuarita Mercantile & Bar. Survived by wife Toribia, son, Lt. Col. William Manelos, stationed in Germany, daughter Mrs. Mary Gahart, 5 grandchildren."

By the time Harry passed away, Toribia was almost completely blind and unable to leave the store and residence. Her early-onset blindness left most of the business decisions to Mary, who elected to slowly close down the mercantile portion of the business to enable her to focus on the bar and grill. With the Oro Verde Store (later One Stop Market) right across the intersection, there wasn't enough business to support both stores. Mary capitalized on her location, right beside the Old Nogales Highway, to bring in tired mine workers who elected to stop in on their way home from long work shifts.

The November 16, 1971, *Star* reported, "Toribia P. Manelos, 87, of Sahuarita, entered into rest November 12, 1971. Widow of Harry B. Manelos." With the loss of her mother, who had been mostly bedridden, Mary was left to continue the business. Her oldest son, Richard, was nineteen and had graduated from Sahuarita High School in 1970. Randy was twelve and little Carolyne was only seven. Mary's husband, William "Bill" Robinson was a huge help to her over the next number of years. At one point, Mary and Bill sold the bar and moved to Amado, but the buyer could not keep up the payments so, within a very short period of time, they bought it back.

Several community members shared their memories of the Sahuarita Mercantile and the Manelos family.

According to Joe Martin's recollection, "Harry Manelos was the owner of the oldest store in Sahuarita. The store, including the building, belonged to 'the old Greek,' and everyone called it 'Greek's store.' He had a pretty good stock of groceries and had a gas pump which had a handle you used to put gas up into a glass reservoir that would hold ten gallons and was marked one gallon up to ten. You put what you wanted in it, then put the gas in your car by gravity feed. There was no electric pump.

"My brother, Bill, knew 'the old Greek' very well. He was married to a Mexican woman who was also old and was quite blind when we came here in 1939. Harry didn't see well either, being very old. Bill said he saw people come in, pick up something, and leave without paying. Same with the gasoline. It upset him because Harry was a good man who extended credit to people he knew, but, unfortunately, people took advantage of that, too.

William Manelos outside the Sahuarita Bar and Grill. Courtesy of the Manelos family.

"Harry had a son named Billie, who was a close friend of my brothers', especially Bill. Billie went off to war and never came back to Sahuarita to live. He lived his life in San Antonio, Texas. Mary, Harry's daughter, got a liquor license along with her dad. She stayed around and took over the store and bar. When her dad passed, Mary dropped the grocery and opened the Sahuarita Bar and Grill. She eventually married Bill Robinson, Joe Robinson's brother. While a boy, I saw her now and then. She was very pretty! I think my brother, Bill, was sweet on Mary, but the war cooled that."

Oscar Gomez remembers that the Spanish-speaking population referred to Harry Manelos as "El Griego," and the grocery store he owned served the area for many years. Part of the building was a bar run by the family. The store closed around 1963 and that part of the building became a dance hall. The building existed until the Nogales Highway was rerouted to the west and then it was torn down.

Oscar knew that Maria operated the bar for a number of years and there were times that she closed the bar around 9 p.m. when customers dwindled. She would re-open around 11 p.m. when the night shift from the mine ended. Miners on their way home to Tucson would frequent the bar until 1 a.m. when beer couldn't be sold anymore. Oscar has a treasured photo of his father, Gumercindo Gomez, visiting with Bill Robinson inside the old bar.

Gumercindo Gomez at the Sahuarita Bar and Grill. Courtesy of Oscar Gomez.

William's personal affidavit in 1992 stated, "I decided to make the air force my career and I remained on continuous active duty until February 1, 1975, when I retired, with the rank of colonel, with over thirty years of active military service. One of the most challenging, rewarding, interesting, and satisfying tours of duty was with headquarters, U.S. Air Force, the Pentagon, Washington, D.C., as a budget officer overseeing allocation of billions of dollars of operation and maintenance appropriation funds. I served four years there from 1963–67, during which service I was promoted to the rank of colonel. I retired on February 1, 1975. At the time of my retirement I was serving as chief of staff, U.S. Air Force Security Service command (now the U.S. Air Force Intelligence Command), Kelly Air Force Base, San Antonio, Texas. I am proud to have served my country and enjoyed every assignment from unit level to headquarters, U.S. Air Force, and every rank from private through colonel. I have no regrets.

"After retirement I continued to work. On the Monday following retirement I went to work as assistant manager of the USAA Federal Credit Union in San Antonio, Texas. In January, 1980, at the age of sixty-one, I had the opportunity of establishing a credit union from scratch for a new energy corporation, Valero Energy Corporation, in San Antonio. I retired as president (chief operating officer) in January, 1987. I continued to do volunteer work in the San Antonio Community."

The November 28, 2003, *San Antonio Express-News* published a final tribute to Colonel William Manolos. "Bill served 33 years in the United States Air Force. Duty included service in World War II on Saipan where he flew B-29s over Japan as lead navigator/bombardier. After retiring as Chief of Staff at Security Service, Bill briefly served as the assistant manager at USAA Federal Credit Union. He later organized Valero Federal Credit Union and spent nine years as its manager. Bill served as president of the Alamo Chapter of Credit Unions and was president of the Knife and Fork Club. Bill spent many years as a volunteer financial advisor

William and Mary Manelos at the Sahuarita Bar and Grill in 1996. Courtesy of the Manelos family.

for the San Antonio Council on Alcoholism and Drug Abuse as well as numerous other organizations."

Mary Manelos Robinson passed away on April 19, 2020. She maintained ownership of the Sahuarita Bar and Grill under the umbrella of Sahuarita Mercantile LLC. On March 17, 2009, the *Arizona Daily Star* listed the following in its "Tucson Real Estate" section: "Farmers Investment Co. has purchased commercial property at 1197 E. Sahuarita Road from Sahuarita Mercantile LLC. The property sold earlier this month for $790,000 with $200,000 down." Sadly, soon after this, the historic piece of history was leveled, but the building and the family who owned it will forever have a place in the history of the Sahuarita community.

Her obituary on the Evergreen Mortuary website says, "Mary was a successful business woman and well-known pioneer resident of Sahuarita, Arizona. The Manelos family owned a tiny general store and gas station; sold meat, supplies, and groceries. After the war, Mary worked the store and cared for her aging parents, and soon a young family. A tiny grill, and beer and wine license led to the liquor license, and the area boom led to good times. The Sahuarita Bar and Grill was a meeting place for families and friends. Great memories and friendships remain."

~Contributed by Monica Lee Elam Christiansen

NOTES

Arizona Daily Star, Tucson, Arizona
Evergreenmortuary-cemetery.com
Manelos, Aaron. Interview by Monica Lee Elam Christiansen.
Gomez, Oscar. Personal recollections.
Harris, Sutah. Personal recollections.
Martin, Joe. Personal recollections.
Manelos, William. Personal affidavit dated January 31, 1992.
Records of the Post Office Department, 1773-1971. National Archives, Washington D.C.
San Antonio Express-News, San Antonio, Texas
Tucson Daily Citizen, Tucson, Arizona

Sahuarita Tortilla Factory and Cafe

On that same stretch of Old Nogales Highway where the Felix family farm lies, sister Celia Felix, known to the family as Durongi, and her husband Roberto Orozco, known as Guero, started the Sahuarita Tortilla Factory in 1982 after Roberto was laid off after fourteen years with the Anamax Mining Company. Roberto's mother had run a tortilla factory in California for ten years and had kept the equipment after it closed, so she brought it to her son in Sahuarita.

Per the *Arizona Daily Star* on June 7, 1984, "For the Orozcos, the day starts at 4 a.m. when Roberto, his 71-year-old mother, Dolores, and his wife, Celia, walk the few paces down the dirt path from their homes to the small building they use as their factory.

"Cousin Elodia Alvarez and friend Rogelio Pacheco lend a hand during the process that starts with Roberto kneading the flour and water into dough. The dough is then cut into round balls by a special biscuit-making machine, flattened by another, and finally patted by hand, like pizza dough, before it is laid on a hot, flat stove top and heated.

"On a recent day, the factory had churned out 140 dozen tortillas by 10 a.m. The phone had started ringing before 9 a.m. with customers ordering everything from tamales, tacos, and enchiladas to "mini" beef chimichangas and peach or cherry fruit burros.

"By noon, Roberto had left the factory practically empty of fresh-baked food, taking the tortillas and 'gorditas' with him to deliver to restaurants from Arivaca and Tubac-Tumacacori to Green Valley.

"'We have no closing hours," Roberto said, noting they work Monday through Saturday. In addition, they cater parties and will deliver orders of more than ten dollars.

Celia's sisters Maria Elena and Martha also worked at the factory for many years. Guero was an excellent cook, allowing them to open a small cafe selling authentic Mexican food in addition to just making tortillas. The Sahuarita Tortilla Factory and Cafe was so popular that Union Pacific trains would stop so passengers could dine there. Many residents of Sahuarita and Green Valley came to the cafe regularly. On Sundays, Guero would prepare a huge pot of menudo to sell early mornings to families hungry after attending mass.

~ Contributed by Monica Lee Elam Christiansen

Santo Tomas and Anamax Park

It's extraordinary that two of Sahuarita's early ranchers and developers were single women. Frances Emmons and Betty Hazen were not afraid to work hard to make their dreams appear out of the dry desert dust.

To attract settlement to Arizona, there were several homesteading acts that made public lands private if they were improved. One of them was the Dry Homesteading Act of 1909, which helped people see the need for growing drought-tolerant crops.[1] Twenty-five percent of Arizona's privately owned land was obtained through homesteading. The Stock Raising Homestead Act of 1916 made it possible for a rancher to obtain 640 acres, or one square mile of land. The government still had the mineral rights to anything underneath, but the settlers owned the surface that was valued only at the grazing level and needed to be improved upon.[2]

Frances Emmons claimed her land on west Twin Buttes Road in 1937, and for the first three years lived in a small shack hauling water from Tucson in barrels. She was told that the "shack" had to be built within six months and had to be lived in for seven months of the year for at least the first three years. Also, she had to add a corral, dig a well, and run a mile of barbed wire fence on it with improvements costing at least $800.[3] The daughter of an army colonel, she had been born in Georgia and raised abroad in Paris, the Philippines, Hawaii, and New York. Her father was also stationed at Fort Huachuca and was on campaigns to chase Pancho Villa down to Mexico.[4] She was heavily involved with

Mrs. Frances G. Emmons at the Orval Brown home on Twin Buttes Road in 1960. Courtesy of Barbara Brown Bennett.

the University of Arizona Boosters and in politics as an adult. She had multiple luncheons at her ranch for the Republican Party,[5] including for Barry Goldwater, during which 150 Tucsonans drove the eighteen miles to be entertained there.[6] She later married Lawrence Emmons, but remained on the property to fulfill the time requirement before living in Tucson for a time.

Orval and Richadeen Brown were the caretakers who lived in a house by the front gate on the land with her for eighteen years. Their daughter, Barbara, and her three brothers loved Frances like a grandmother and she spoiled them with gifts, sending them to summer camp and funding a trip to Disneyland. Frances was very active dancing, riding horses, and going on walks with her dogs.[7] She had two stepchildren from her marriage, but no children of her own. Frances was very generous with her

Front patio of Frances Graves Emmons home taken in August of 1953. Furniture is "pre-plastic" redwood and metal. This is not her original homestead house on Twin Buttes Road. The interior had red concrete floors. Courtesy of Barbara Brown Bennett.

funds in Tucson and Sahuarita, helping others and serving as a board member for various groups in both towns. She received the Distinguished Citizen Award from the University of Arizona in 1982. Her ashes lie on her land that she named the Roadrunner Ranch, dying at the age of ninety-one.[8]

Another single woman pioneered the development of Sahuarita west of I-19 from between what are now Sahuarita Road and Duval Mine Road. Betty Press Hazen had a dream of making custom homes for people who wanted to get out in the country, away from Tucson city life, similar to what Scottsdale was to Phoenix. She had grown up in Evanston, Illinois, and came to the University of Arizona to attend college. She loved horses and soon met, fell in love with, and married a cowboy in the Tucson rodeo circuit, James Hazen. She was the arena secretary, keeping records and paying the

cowboys as her husband rode broncos. It was the fashion for the wives to tailor Western shirts and pants and make leather belts for their husbands in the rodeo.[9] She and Jimmie bought forty acres of land in 1939 near the Twin Buttes area, twenty-three miles southwest of Tucson, for fifteen dollars down. They started homesteading it themselves, naming it the Lazy JB Ranch. They built fences, lived in a tent while building adobe walls for their home, cooked on an open fire, and gathered abandoned railroad ties, saguaro ribs, and ocotillo branches for building supplies to make ramada roofs and chicken fences. The only hired help they had was a Mexican adobe brick maker who made bricks on-site.

Betty had to haul water and get her mail three to four miles away but enjoyed the frontier lifestyle, even with the coyotes eating her chickens and howling every night and the many rattlesnakes that she had to kill. They had cows, horses, and chickens to sustain them and to keep them company. Her experiences on the ranch helped her make it on her own after she became divorced in 1947. She went off to see the world, going from Alaska to Chile to Hawaii, gaining experience along the way, seeing how far she could stretch her dollar, working when she had to, and enjoying the art she saw in each new place.

In 1958, she bought 640 acres (one square mile), half a mile wide east to west and one-and-a-half miles long north to south, bulldozing and grading the main road, Camino de Las Quintas,

Another view of the front patio. Courtesy of Barbara Brown Bennett.

herself. She formed two housing-development entities called Las Quintas Serenas Development Co. and Santo Tomas Development Co. She loved the word "Quintas," meaning country estate, which she had heard while in South America. The county accepted her route and she put in the Las Quintas Serenas Water Company by drilling two wells. The land was divided up into five- to nineteen-acre lots.

She began by building a home for herself that her parents later lived in and experimenting with materials. She brought in metal craftsmen and adobe makers from Nogales, Mexico. It looked like her dreams were coming true when a Hughes engineer and the television star Jane Wyatt were her first two buyers. She envisioned a town center with shops on Calle De La Plaza alongside her blacksmith shop. Betty Hazen had a theory that she could do anything she set her mind to and not to wait on others to make it happen. She had practice from when she had built her ranch out of nothing, and now she was going to do it for a living. There was not a task she was afraid to tackle. She could be seen laying brick, doing ironwork, sawing lumber, running electrical wiring, putting down plumbing, building fireplaces, doing woodworking, and whatever else needed to be done. She often outworked the others with her thirteen-hour days. She was something of a nonconformist who didn't fit the mold of the 1960s housewife, always preferring to do things herself with her own two hands.

Betty literally blazed her own trail. She envisioned a place outside the busy city where life was more tranquil and could be enjoyed through beautiful mountain scenery, desert landscape, wildlife, individualized custom adobe homes, and furniture influenced by Spanish, Filipino, South American, and Mexican artistry. She traveled the world bringing back ideas on architecture and furnishings from every country. Betty Hazen had the vision, grit, work ethic, and determination to carve beauty out of the dry desert and make it a comfortable place to live. Without her, this part of the town would not have been developed for many years. She built artistic custom homes from the ground up, establishing a community along with it.

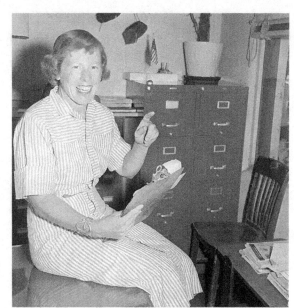

Little did Hazen know that the mine would buy up all of the land around for water rights and halt most of the development of Sahuarita for the next twenty years. This turned her high-end neighborhood into a subdivision to house workers

Elizabeth Hazen in August of 1960. Courtesy of University of Arizona Special Collections.

from the mine. By 1965, she had sold the Santo Tomas neighborhood to Anaconda Copper Co., which then sold it to the Holbert Development Co., which had Estes Construction Co. begin building the homes. She began another development south of Green Valley in Amado, called Quinta San Ignacio. She had eleven acres of the 240 for herself and built her twelfth custom home there.[10] After that she lived for a time in Green Valley in the Desert Hills area.

Hazen liked the simple life despite her fortune and ended up in the Iron Hills area of the Tucson Mountains. Thirty years after she started her neighborhood, Tony Marrs from A. W. Marrs Inc. sought her out to find out what her vision was and finished her dream of developing beautiful homes in Sahuarita.[11] It was at that time considered a prime location off La Canada, being close to the interstate where people could commute to Tucson or Nogales to work. He built Colonias La Canada and was surprised at the demand for more housing.[12] Sahuarita and Green Valley experienced a development boom over the subsequent few years.

The stables Betty Hazen built on what became Anamax Park were used to house horses for 4-H after she left the area. The 4-H program is a positive youth development organization for head, heart, hands, and health that is run by mentors in the community. The park was first named Anaconda Park when Anaconda Mining Co. bought the land. Oscar Kelly remembers making the sign. He remembers the 4-H fun days during which kids would have to catch goats and dress them in clothes. There was also a horse-roping shoot and arena put in later where the kids would practice roping. Kelly's wife, Sheila, helped with the horse projects, chickens, rabbits, and small stock.[13] After training locally, the families would go camp at the Pima Fair grounds for two weeks during the county fair and take turns caring for the animals and enjoying the events they participated in. Barry Callaway, a school counselor, lived close to the park and helped Lee Parish run the 4-H program there.[14]

Other people in the new Santo Tomas neighborhood helped build a much-needed park, volunteering time and materials. The parents wanted a Little League baseball field for their kids. Nancy Bessett took a tractor down to the park and filled in the wash. She and her family picked up garbage, glass, and baling wire to clean up the area. Her husband, John Bessett, helped her build a snack shack and put electricity in

Elizabeth "Betty" Hazen portrait by Amy Millet.

it.[15] He tore down the old mesquite piles that were used as fencing for the horses. Nancy got some sponsors for the field and got in touch with a contractor to level the ground. She bought the plates and John helped put up the new baseball fence. He and some others organized the Little League program and Nancy helped the kids run the snack shack nightly from three o'clock until the last game ended.

Anaconda Mining Co. merged with American Metals Climax Inc. (Amax), first called the Amax-Anaconda Agreement.[16] The two organizations together were now Anamax Mining Co. and had a 50/50 partnership in the Twin Buttes Mine, which had undergone an expansion in 1975.[17] They donated fifteen acres for the park in January of 1975, and work started in July of the following year.[18] In 1984, Anamax Mining Co. donated the park to the Sahuarita School District, but the funding, staffing, and operations were done through Pima County Parks and Recreation.[19] It wasn't until 2001 that the Town of Sahuarita took over the park and its operations.[20]

The park went up in phases—the first involving the clearing of land, the paving of a parking lot, growing turf, adding playground equipment, putting up ramadas, and constructing the Joan Swetland Recreation Center.[21] The octagon-shaped building was finished and opened for use in 1977; a senior citizen center was opened to the public in 1978. Finally, the community had a place for young and old to gather to play games and learn new skills. They offered classes in crafts, had organized sports, did field trips, showed movies, and held arts and crafts fairs.[22] The teens in Sahuarita could now do more than hunting, hiking, and school sports. Some parents were afraid there were still not enough things to keep teens busy and away from underage drinking and off of the couch watching TV.[23] Anamax Recreation Center offered billiards, football, baseball, basketball, ping-pong, and horseback riding six days a week. The park piloted a mentoring program for juvenile offenders doing community service to interact positively with the elderly.[24] In 1988, it was announced that the park would double in size.[25] The park continued to evolve over the years with two new lighted ball fields and a dog "bark park" in 2006.[26] The Town of Sahuarita Parks and Recreation Department continues to offer activities for people of all ages: art, dance and karate classes for children, exercise and dance classes for adults and seniors, and festivals and programs for the whole community. The Sahuarita Teen Advisory Council plans activities throughout the year for teens. Anamax Park has been a place to build memories and support the community through programs, people, and places to meet and interact.

The residents in the Santo Tomas neighborhood cared about the community and before there was a town council, they organized the Santo Tomas Awareness Group (STAG) to stop unwanted things from happening in Sahuarita. Barbara Bennett, president of STAG, along with others were worried that their neighborhood was looking too much like a road going to the dump with all of the garbage strewn around La Canada. The landfill on La Canada had no rules about using tarps to cover loads of garbage yet. A forty-person cleanup project was organized and the area was thoroughly picked up. A group member saw on TV that the City of Tucson had picked their landfill as the site to get rid of food and supplies contaminated with radioactive tritium. They quickly rallied together, opposing it and bringing it to a stop.[27]

In 1984, STAG organized seventy-five people to protest the "noxious chemical stench" coming from Kerley Mining Chemicals Inc. They complained of headaches and unpleasant "dead carcass" odors coming in waves for two minutes to two hours. Residents of Santo Tomas could not easily go for a walk, garden, or open their windows, and children could not ride bikes or play outside.[28] The company voluntarily stopped manufacturing the chemicals after the Pima County Air Quality Control Board refused to give them a permit.[29] The residents wanted more clout, so the Sahuarita Area Council was formed in 1988. Now, Sahuarita had an entity looking out for the area as development boomed. They opposed Tucson in building more landfills, got traffic lights put in, pushed back Green Valley from encroaching on boundary lines, made sure things were zoned properly before development, and acted as guardians of the town pushing for its incorporation in 1994. After incorporation, the town had the power to make laws and have its own law enforcement and town council. Development could be done much faster through the town rather than Pima County.

The people in the Santo Tomas and surrounding neighborhoods had helped build a community they were proud of and united themselves into a town that others were attracted to. These people were much like Betty Hazen and Frances Emmons in that they were not afraid to get their hands dirty to get things done and make their dreams come true as to what Sahuarita could become.

~ Contributed by Amy Millet

NOTES

References

1. Stein, Pat. "Homesteading in Arizona 1870–1942." A Component of the Arizona Historic Preservation Plan. Phoenix, AZ: Arizona State Historic Preservation Office. August 1990: 6. PDF available from http://www.ansac.az.gov/UserFiles/PDF/10162014/X017_ASLDSupplement2/105%20-%20Homesteading%20in%20Arizona%201870-1942.pdf.

2. Featherstone, Roger. "The Stock Raising Act of 1916 and Mining Claims." Earthworks. PDF available from https://earthworks.org/assets/uploads/archive/files/publications/SHRA_FS.PDF.

3. Cardon, Charlotte. "Sahuarita Homesteader May Well Take Pride in Charming Home." *Arizona Daily Star*, June 19, 1960: 27.

4. Bennett, Barbara Brown. Interviewed by Amy Millet. October 21, 2020.
5. "Tomorrow," *Tucson Daily Citizen*. October 25, 1958: 4.
6. "Homestead Luncheon." *Arizona Daily Star*, April 30, 1957: 12.
7. Bennett, Barbara Brown. Interviewed by Amy Millet. October 21, 2020.
8. "Frances Emmons, UA Booster Dies." *Tucson Citizen*, September 22, 1989: 33.
9. Eubank, Johanna. "Tales from the morgue: Elizabeth Hazen went from rodeo professional to contractor." August 1, 2018. Accessed January 30, 2022 from https://tucson.com/morguetales/tales-from-the-morgue-elizabeth-hazen-went-from-rodeo-professional-to-contractor/article_38ff8614-95d0-11e8-9de6-531edf70fb4c.html
10. Brown, Mary. "Hazen Houses by the Dozen." *Tucson Daily Citizen*, June 27, 1970: 38–40.
11. Richer, Dave. "She Had a Dream: Founder of Santo Tomas is Remembered." *Green Valley News and Sun*, May 15, 1996: B1.
12. Macario, Juarez Jr. "Development Boom Hit Green Valley, Sahuarita." *Arizona Daily Star*, August 22, 1999: 45.
13. Kelly, Oscar. Interviewed by Amy Millet. November 16, 2020.
14. "Sahuarita 4-H Finding Sheep a Shear Joy." *Arizona Daily Star*, December 8, 1983: 29.
15. Bessett, Nancy. Interviewed by Amy Millet. September 12, 2018.
16. Wilbur, Richard E. "Banner-Amax Mine Merger Would Boost Copper Here." *Tucson Daily Citizen*, April 13, 1973: 5.
17. "Arizona Copper Mining Has its Roots On Ancient Cyprus." *Arizona Daily Star*, November 30, 1976: 32.
18. "Green Valley History—Where We've Been: January 1964 to January 2000." *Green Valley News*, January 1, 2000.
19. Bailey, Rob. "Pima County Seeks to Transfer Anamax Park Reins to Sahuarita." *Arizona Daily Star*, July 9, 2001: 4.
20. Mustapha, Gael. "Sahuarita Gains a Park." *Arizona Daily Star*, October 1, 2001: 5.
21. Leigh Duyn, Daisy. "Green Valley Vetoes Rezoning Plea Again." *Arizona Daily Star*, November 27, 1975: 3.
22. "Anamax Arts and Fun." *Tucson Citizen*, October 24, 1984: 2.
23. "Teens Aren't Grinning." *Tucson Citizen*, December 14, 1978: 86.
24. Vandeveire, Mary and Gael Mustapha. "Second Chance for Youths: Sahuarita Helps Keep Their Records Clean and Channel Their Energies." *Arizona Daily Star*, October 22, 2001: 3.
25. "Green Valley History—Where We've Been: January 1964 to January 2000." *Green Valley News*, January 1, 2000.
26. "Sahuarita 2 Lighted Ball Fields OK'd for Anamax Park." *Arizona Daily Star*, May 4, 2006: 177.
27. Sowell, Carol. "Tackling Tritium, Trash Unearths Santo Tomas' Clout." *Arizona Daily Star*, May 15, 1980: 58.
28. Kay, Jane. "Sahuarita residents organize rally to protest 'noxious chemical stench.'" *Arizona Daily Star*, October 18, 1984: 19.
29. Fischer, Howard and Jane Kay. "Kerley Halts Manufacturing in Sahuarita." *Arizona Daily Star*, November 15, 1984: 1.

Additional resources

Bennett, Barbara Brown. Interviewed by Amy Millet. October 21, 2020.
Cardon, Charlotte. "Sahuarita Homesteader May Well Take Pride in Charming Home," *Arizona Daily Star*. June 19, 1960: 27.
"Five-Acre Lot Purchased By Jane Wyatt." *Arizona Daily Star*, February 13, 1958: B1.

"Frances Emmons, UA Booster, Dies." *Tucson Citizen*, September 22, 1989, p. 33.

Missing, Noel. "In and About Tucson." *Arizona Daily Star*, April 30, 1957: A12.

Riddick, John. " Do-It-Yourself Town Grows on Arizona Desert." *Tucson Daily Citizen*, late ed., August 2, 1958: 5.

"Supervisors Okay Yaqui Village Zoning." *Tucson Daily Citizen*, August 17, 1965: 7.

"Water Franchise Granted-Las Quintas Serenas Water Company." *Arizona Daily Star*, May 6, 1958: 8.

"Water Utilities OK'd for 3 Subdivisions." *Tucson Citizen*, April 10, 1958: 28.

Sierrita Mining and Ranching Company

There was never a time that the McGee, Harris, and Lively families did not contract out their services to earn money. In the late 1800s, records show them using wagons and teams to run freight throughout New Mexico and Arizona. Even after the families had settled at the base of the Sierrita Mountains to pursue mining, farming, and ranching, some family members still hired out to do "odd jobs" to bring in the money they needed to survive. They hauled ore for local mining operations, transported all kinds of goods across the state, and even helped with grading and bridge-building when the Twin Buttes Railroad was being built.

Two teams of horses pull a huge hay wagon. Courtesy of Gary Fox.

The Great Depression took its toll on the hard-working ranch families, just as it did on all other hard-working people across the United States. Survival was a struggle for the families living at McGee Ranch. Many had to work part-time at the ranch while supplementing income with jobs at nearby mines, for the railroad, and in area construction projects.

Jerry McGee, Elmer McVey, and Leander Harris working on machinery. Courtesy of Lynn Harris.

It was during this time that five families and five single people, some of whom were very young, decided to pool their resources and work as a group. These determined people wanted to live on the ranch they loved and somehow find a way to "make do" with the money their hard work would provide.

In 1943, a legal partnership was formed to create Sierrita Mining and Ranching Company (SM&R). The group members dry-farmed corn and pink beans in the summer, with beans being the main cash crop. During cooler weather, the men mined for gold and tended a few cattle. They started keeping bees, another very lucrative venture, to harvest honey and wax. Whenever one or more could get a job, they took it, building fences, working at the mines, driving trucks, etc. During World War II, they hauled potatoes from the farms at Sahuarita and loaded the sacks onto box cars.

At the end of the war, army surplus items were widely available for private purchase. The partnership

Building the road up Mount Hopkins. Courtesy of Lynn Harris.

acquired clothing, shoes, blankets, tents, a bulldozer with a scraper, a dump truck, etc. The pieces of heavy equipment enabled them to take on bigger and more productive jobs, which resulted in more capital to support additional family members who had moved home to the ranch to work. It also provided them the money to reinvest in the company itself. Funds were used to purchase additional trucks and other machinery.

In addition to road building and ore hauling, SM&R began bidding on construction jobs, and was involved in erecting quite a few Tucson-area buildings, as well as a dude ranch and restaurant. The men hauled ore from the New Year's (now Duval), Pima, and Helvetia mines to the railhead at Sahuarita. Some of the men drove ore trucks for Mr. Hubble, taking ore from the San Xavier Mine to the Sahuarita Eagle-Picher mill. Work continued on family mining claims, some of which were on Native American reservation land with others located on property that eventually became a part of the Duval mining operation. Ore in these mines was not rich enough to support small-scale mining.

In the '50s, when work was scarce, they built several houses. One was located in Casas Adobes and another in Santo Tomas. During the '60s they acquired additional bulldozers and worked building roads and drill sites for the big mining companies throughout Arizona. SM&R was contracted to build the road to Mount Hopkins for the Smithsonian Institution in 1967. At that time, this contract was the largest they had ever received.

The United States Forest Service was the company's main source of contracts through much of the '70s and '80s. They built roads and campgrounds; blasted rock for riprap; and capped, graded, and improved existing roads in the Arizona forests.

Men at "the shop," Shelly Fox, Jerry McGee, Eiler Harris, Kenny Lively, Mac McVey, Gary Fox, Lynn Harris, and Lee Harris. Courtesy of Gary Fox.

Hauling the giant telescope mirror to Mount Hopkins. Courtesy of Lynn Harris.

For many years SM&R specialized in building and improving "difficult" mountain roads, building power lines, and pouring concrete foundations for communication towers and other mountaintop projects. They happily accepted projects that no other company would dare to consider and took great pride in "figuring out how to get it done" using unconventional methods and "thinking outside the box." Several of these projects involved structures embedded in the rock at the top of the Tucson Mountains, power lines requiring helicopters to set the poles in place, and the transportation of mirrors up to the Mount Hopkins Observatory in the Santa Ritas.

Since 2000, the company has acquired six auger trucks which keep workers busy drilling holes for towers, utility poles, solar structures, gas stations, billboards, trolley lines, and many other projects throughout Arizona and neighboring states.

Over the years, many Sierrita Mining and Ranching family members have come and gone. Technology, building regulations, equipment designs, and job dynamics have evolved with the times, but through the generations, what has not changed is the determined pioneer spirit that drives SM&R's success.

~ Contributed by Lynn Harris and Monica Lee Elam Christiansen

Early Faith Communities in Sahuarita

In the Sahuarita area, faith communities grew out of missionary activities of many Christian denominations. First was the Roman Catholic faith, which was brought into the area in the 1690s by Jesuit missionaries, headed up by Father Eusebio Francisco Kino. He established missions at San Xavier del Bac, Guevavi, and Tumacacori to extend Catholicism to the O'odham people. Missionary priests made trips through the Native American and Spanish/Mexican communities to teach, baptize, and marry couples on a periodic basis over the years. Catholics might have attended mass at the churches in Tubac, Tumacacori, San Xavier, or later the cathedral in Tucson, but mainly kept their faith going in their families. This tradition held sway for the next three hundred years.

For some Catholics, faith practices included visiting or building shrines where they could go to pray in lieu of attending services at a church building that might be far away. The most prominent of these is the Shrine of Santa Rita on the rocky outcrop overlooking the Sopori Ranch on Arivaca Road, built in 1929 by owner Grace Lee. It was frequently patronized by travelers from Arivaca. where there was no church, from the 1920s until 1970. By mid-century churches were being built in many of the smaller towns. It was not until the 1960s that the mission San Martin de Porres was established in Sahuarita.

At first, priests came from San Xavier, Saint John's, or Saint Monica's churches in Tucson to hold masses at the old brick schoolhouse in Sahuarita. Eventually, Sahuarita grew large enough to have its own church building. A similar process was happening in neighboring Green Valley. Our Lady of the Valley Catholic Church was founded in 1970, and by 1983 they were raising money to help build the church/hall building for San Martin de Porres on property donated by Keith Walden in the FICO pecan groves. Walden wanted to support the migrant farm workers, most of whom were Catholic. The current building was finished in 1983. Bishop Manuel Moreno raised the San Martin de Porres mission to the level of parish church on December 12, 2002.

Members of Protestant denominations such as Baptists often went to Tucson to attend church. There was a Union Baptist community in Sahuarita for a short time in the 1950s but the pastor died quite young. They didn't have a building, and it was not until the 1960s that Baptist congregations such as Cornerstone began to be established. As early as 1964, the Green Valley Community Church welcomed members of nearly two dozen denominations to a meeting led by a Methodist minister. Missionaries like those of the American Sunday School Union would hold worship services and classes in school buildings or even homes. As the area population grew, so did communities of the other Protestant denominations, many of them along La Cañada Drive. Sahuarita residents could go next door in Green Valley to find their own choice of faith community, as diverse as Lutheran, Assembly of God, Jewish Beth Shalom Temple, Bahai, Jehovah's Witnesses and Unitarian. The Church of Jesus Christ of Latter Day Saints community met in the McGee Ranch schoolhouse, and also the Continental School, for years before they finally built a church in Sahuarita. Now, since Rancho Sahuarita was developed, the Latter-day Saint population has grown to need two church buildings. Today there is a wealth of communities of all faiths that can provide spiritual support for the residents of Sahuarita.

~ Contributed by Mary N. Kasulaitis

NOTES

Arizona Daily Star, October 17, 1955.

Barber, Natalie. *God's Heart—Our Hands*, commemorating the fiftieth anniversary of Green Valley Community Church.

Our Lady of the Valley. Accessed November 26, 2022 from http://olvgv.org

Polzer, Charles W. S. J. *Kino Guide II: his missions – his monuments*. Tucson, AZ: Southwestern Mission Research Center, 1982.

San Martin de Porres Church. Accessed November 26, 2022 from http://sanmartinsahuarita.org/parish-history.html

Shearer, Dan. *Green Valley News*

Walls, Deborah. March 28, 2022, interview. Special thanks to Rita Quihuis Simonton.

The Church of Jesus Christ of Latter-day Saints

Napoleon "Empy" and his wife Mildred Hopwood "Mamie" Norton McGee, residents of McGee Ranch, became members of the Church of Jesus Christ of Latter-day Saints in 1946. They and their eleven-year-old daughter Dianne drove to Tucson to attend church at a meetinghouse located at 6th Street and Park Avenue.

As the years went by, Dianne married and lived at McGee Ranch close to her parents and they together made the long trip to Tucson each week for church meetings. Over the next few years, Empy and Mamie's son Norman, daughter Margaret (Elam), and daughter JoAnn (Tate) returned to the ranch with their spouses and young children. It was impossible for these young families to attend their church meetings, having to travel into Tucson and spend most of the day there with many young children.

Napoleon "Empy" McGee. Courtesy of Margaret McGee Elam.

Under the direction of Bishop Wayne Goodman of the Tucson Arizona Third Ward, a weekly home Primary was organized to provide religious instruction for the children. From that beginning, a dependent branch, called the McGee Branch, was organized on September 18, 1966.

Mildred "Mamie" McGee. Courtesy of Margaret McGee Elam.

Empy McGee presided as the Branch president. Members continued to travel to Tucson for Sunday meetings, but other meetings—Sunday school, Primary, and women's Relief Society meetings—were held in different homes on the ranch. Mamie McGee served as the first Relief Society president for McGee Branch.

As more families joined the McGee Branch, there soon was no home

large enough to hold all the members. On June
6, 1968, an independent branch was organized
with Norman McGee as Branch president. The
name was changed from the McGee Branch to
the Sahuarita Branch.

Empy McGee owned property and an old
schoolhouse on a hill at McGee Ranch. He said
the branch could use it for a meetinghouse for
as long as they wished. Branch members went
to work fixing up the building. They took out
partitions, plastered and painted, and put on a
new roof. The end results gave these members
a "chapel" measuring fourteen by twenty-four

*Early church members standing beside the building
at McGee Ranch. Courtesy of Kerry Lynn Elam.*

feet, along with two other rooms—one ten feet by ten feet and the other ten feet by six feet. Tucson Third
Ward donated some old wooden folding benches (that loved to shred nylon stockings). Empy bought
clothesline wire and some white fabric to be made into curtains. He strung the wire across the big room
and hung curtains in two places so the "chapel" could be partitioned into three classrooms. Later, Third
Ward donated an old green stage curtain, which the women of the branch nailed to the walls.

*Dick and Marva Sanders pose
for a photo. Courtesy of Kerry
Lynn Elam.*

Long-time Sahuarita resident Marva Sanders recalled her
family's first experience attending a meeting in the Sahuarita
Branch. She said: "We lived at Continental and also had to drive to
Tucson to attend our meetings. When I heard that Primary was
being held at McGee Ranch, I decided to start taking my children
there. It was a hot summer day. I drove for over an hour up the
rough, dry, dusty road to the ranch. My children were hot, thirsty,
and tired, and I didn't know where I was going. Kevin was bawling
every breath. After giving up, we finally found the place, only to
discover that Primary had been canceled that day! My kids took a
look at the little building and said, 'Is this where we have to go to
church? We want to go to the Third Ward!' But when Sunday came
and we went inside that little
church, we really had a pleasant
surprise. Everyone was so
friendly and made us feel so good
and so welcome that we felt like
we were family and we really

belonged. We were few in number, but there was a wonderful spirit
there in the Branch. The size and the look of the building were not that
important. It was the spirit and the people that made it a special place."

In 1971, Dick and Marva's oldest son Craig became the first
missionary to serve from the Sahuarita Branch.

There was one very dedicated and special member of the branch
that never missed a single meeting. He belonged to Tom and Dianne
McGee Black's family and his name was Josh. He was a German short-
hair pointer who loved to chase rocks and sticks, and he always
accompanied his family to church.

As more members joined the Sahuarita Branch, the old
schoolhouse became very crowded, so three rooms were added to the

*Craig Sanders, the first
missionary from the
Sahuarita Branch. Courtesy
of Kerry Lynn Elam.*

Tom Elam, Bruce Elam, and Craig Sanders stacking wood for the barbeque. Courtesy of Kerry Lynn Elam.

old building. Archie Romney bought a small trailer and donated it to the branch. It was parked alongside the building and used as the branch media center and library and as a classroom.

Earning money to eventually build a new meetinghouse was an important goal for Sahuarita Branch members. The Relief Society women began making oatmeal cookies for a coffee shop in Green Valley. Every week they made up to fifteen dozen cookies, a very popular item on the restaurant menu. After the cookies, they began making delicious spudnut doughnuts. Each Saturday morning the women of the branch would make and sell 200 dozen doughnuts. Dick Sanders complained (jokingly) that with all the thousands of cookies and doughnuts Marva made, he never did get to eat a good one. He always had to settle for burnt cookies and misshapen doughnuts.

With the money they raised, the women bought a piano for the branch. Next they purchased silverware service for 144 people and went into the catering business, serving lunches and dinners for various organizations in Green Valley. These projects prepared branch members for a really major undertaking—serving barbecue dinners to over 2,700 people at the Green Valley Country Fair.

On June 4, 1972, approval came from Church headquarters in Salt Lake City for the construction of a new ward building. Empy McGee had offered to donate land at McGee Ranch for a building site, but Church leaders felt the meetinghouse needed to be more centrally located. The Church purchased seven acres of land just north of Green Valley, between Interstate 19 and Camino De Las Quintas, from Anaconda Mine.

In June of 1974, J. M. Bird, father of local resident Bill Bird, replaced Norman McGee as branch president. By this time the old school building at McGee Ranch was much

Cutting wood for the barbeque. Courtesy of Kerry Lynn Elam.

too small to hold the growing congregation. Arrangements were made to rent the old Continental School building for Branch meetings. The Continental building had plenty of room, but meeting there only made Branch members more eager to have a building of their own. Each Sunday the men of the Branch arrived early to sweep out debris left by other community organizations and to rearrange chairs to get ready for church.

On May 7, 1975, three years after approval came from Church headquarters, groundbreaking ceremonies were held for the new Sahuarita Branch building on Camino De Las Quintas. During construction, the branch had continued to meet at Continental, but scheduling meetings there became more and more difficult. Then the Continental building was leased to another organization, and for several weeks branch meetings were again held in members' homes. The Sacrament meeting was conducted in the home of J. M. and Margaret Bird in Santo Tomas. The bedrooms of the Loren

Men watching over barbeque pits full of cooking meat. Courtesy of Kerry Lynn Elam.

Shumway home on Twin Buttes Road served as classrooms for the Primary. Finally, permission was granted for the branch to use the south wing of the new building before the chapel was completed. Branch members were very happy to have a place to call their own, even though construction was still underway.

J. M. and Margaret Bird stayed in Sahuarita long enough to see the building completed. During construction, the only thing ever stolen from the building site was the top spire for the steeple. A new one had to be ordered and when it was finally installed, it was a big event for branch members.

Women serving community members at the barbeque. Courtesy of Kerry Lynn Elam.

When the organ arrived for the chapel, President Bird was excited. He called Sandy Shumway and asked her to come to play the organ for him so he could be sure it had arrived in good condition. Sandy remembered playing a favorite hymn, *The Spirit of God Like a Fire is Burning*, on the new instrument before it was hardly out of the packing crate.

Groundbreaking ceremony for the new building. Courtesy of Kerry Lynn Elam.

In February of 1976, the Sahuarita Branch was dissolved, and Sahuarita Ward was created. Gerald C. Brooks became the first bishop of the new ward. Work on the chapel was completed, and the new building was dedicated on December 19, 1976.

The Relief Society women continued catering dinners in Green Valley to raise money to finish paying for the new building. Raymond N. Larsen replaced Gerald C. Brooks as the Sahuarita Ward bishop on October 15, 1978.

The ward continued to grow and soon there was not enough room for all the needed classes in the new building. Some classes began meeting in Steve Gay's home across the street from the

church. Ward members once again started catering dinners for organizations in Green Valley to raise money for an addition to the building.

This second phase included a large cultural hall or gym, a larger kitchen, a Relief Society room and baptismal font, and additional classrooms. The new section of the building was first used for meetings on Sunday, March 13, 1983, and an open house was held March 25, 1983, to show the new addition to community members. Ward members put the new kitchen to use right away and enjoyed holding parties and activities in the spacious new cultural hall.

Church membership in the Sahuarita area continued to grow. Longtime resident Archie

Metal framework completed for the new chapel. Courtesy of Kerry Lynn Elam.

Romney served as bishop for a number of years, followed by Tom Elam, son of Margaret McGee and Bob Elam. Tom served for over six years. When his service ended in November of 2000, the Sahuarita Ward was divided into Sahuarita First and Second Wards. Thayne Hardy became bishop of the First Ward. Wayne Housley was the first bishop in Sahuarita Second Ward.

It became necessary to split the Sahuarita Wards again early in 2007, when Sahuarita Third Ward was formed. Just over a year later, on May 18, 2008, Sahuarita Second Ward was divided again to form

Placing the steeple. Courtesy of Kerry Lynn Elam.

Sahuarita Fourth Ward. Robert Bruce Elam, another son of Bob and Margaret McGee Elam, became bishop of the new ward.

The Sahuarita Ward building, first used in 1976, began to bulge at the seams again, and it underwent its fourth phase of construction to help accommodate the membership of four wards.

In 2009 a Stake was organized in Sahuarita to provide local leadership for the growing number of Church members and wards. Thayne Hardy served as the first stake president, and a fifth ward, Madera Ward, was formed in the Sahuarita area.

As of 2021, there were six wards in Sahuarita: Pecan Grove, Olivero, Anamax, Ranch, Madera, and one still retaining the original name of Sahuarita. A larger meetinghouse, called a "stake center," was constructed in Rancho Sahuarita, just south of the Sahuarita school complex behind the Sahuarita government center. The building was completed in late 2013. The stake center accommodates three wards, and the original building on Camino De Las Quintas provides a meeting place for the other three. Two wards in Nogales—Nogales Ward and Valle Verde Ward (Spanish speaking)—are also part of the Sahuarita Stake.

The Church in Sahuarita started out in a small, dilapidated schoolhouse on a hill at McGee Ranch. Empy McGee, who made that building available for the tiny McGee Branch, passed away in December 1973, before ground was broken for construction of the first phase of the spacious building in Santo Tomas. That building was once again bulging at the seams before the new stake center was constructed to help accommodate the

Cooking breakfast at the father and son overnight campout at McGee Ranch—David Nelson and Bob Elam cooking. Courtesy of Kerry Elam.

(then) five wards with perhaps 2,000 members in the area. For Church members who have lived in the area since the humble beginnings, the growth of the Church of Jesus Christ of Latter-day Saints is beyond anything they could have imagined back when everyone fit comfortably in the tiny school building at McGee Ranch.

~ Contributed by Kerry L. Elam

R. Keith Walden Story: Early Years in California

R. Keith Walden was born July 4, 1913, in Santa Paula, California, the oldest of five children of Arthur Frisbie and Eva Walden. Keith's father was a banker who owned a citrus farm of his own and partnered with this brother on a fruit and vegetable farm in the rich San Fernando Valley. Keith helped on the farm from a young age. When he was twelve years old, his uncle sent him to the Los Angeles central produce market to sell a truckload of melons and vegetables. Concerned that the older buyers might take advantage of his youth, his uncle told him not to "budge on the price," and to "bring anything back that he did not sell back to feed the hogs." Keith made no sales from Monday to Wednesday and sold one-half the truckload on Thursday. By Friday the buyers realized the boy could not be had, and he sold everything.

From these humble beginnings, Keith grew into an innovative and entrepreneurial agriculturalist. Young Keith developed his own ten-acre nursery, and also worked on the Limoneira Ranch, one of the largest citrus and avocado farms in

Portrait of R. Keith Walden. Courtesy of the Walden family.

California, which was a customer of his. When Limoneira's pathologist was accidently killed, the ranch manager gave Keith a crash course in plant diseases, and a crew of forty men to supervise. Later Keith moved to manage the Ford-Craig Ranch, a thousand-acre citrus and vegetable operation in San Fernando, California, when Bill Craig was called into service.

Keith saved his money and purchased 960 acres in Tulare Lake Bed in California. He correctly surmised that the land had excellent soil and quickly sold half the land to pay off his debt. He was able to

Harvesting pecans in the FICO Fields. Courtesy of the Walden family.

leverage this equity into 800 acres south of Bakersfield. Refusing to borrow money from his father's bank, he submitted a proposal to Security First National, now part of Wells Fargo Bank, which agreed to finance the farm if Keith found water. He did.

Keith began to farm cotton in California, and was one of the first farmers to use anhydrous ammonia (NH_3) that had been developed during World War II for use as fertilizer. Formerly, sodium nitrate and manure had been used on cotton. He also rotated sugar beets, potatoes, and grains with cotton, improving soil conditions and therefore the yield per acre. Keith was always looking for better equipment or ways to modify existing equipment to make it more productive. He was soon a recognized leader in the cotton industry.

In the 1940s, Keith became concerned that land was becoming too expensive to farm profitably in

California. Sterling Hebbard, an Arizona realtor and investor, tried to interest him in buying land in Yuma where irrigated vegetable farming was just getting underway. Keith also sought help from Kemper Marley, a native Arizonan, who was a well-known businessman with extensive agricultural holdings. In 1946, in order to supervise his dispersed and growing holdings, Keith bought a Cessna 140 airplane, subject to the seller getting him certified to fly. He flew his own planes until 1970, as he traveled to buy cattle and to oversee the farms in Oklahoma, Florida, and Georgia that he acquired later.

Aerial photograph of the feed lot at Continental. Courtesy of the Walden family.

Keith formed Farmers Investment Co. (FICO) in 1946, joking that he wouldn't put his name on the company in case things didn't work out! With additional capital from Colonel Henry Crown of Chicago, Keith purchased the 10,000-acre Continental Farm in the Santa Cruz Valley south of Tucson in 1949. The close working relationship with the Crown family has now entered its sixth decade and third generation with the Waldens.

Continental Farm has a colorful history. Bernard Baruch, Joseph Kennedy, and J. P. Morgan had founded Continental in 1914 with the plan of growing guayule—a plant that can be a source of rubber. There were fears at the time that the Germans might cut off the sea lanes, blocking rubber imports. When World War I ended, the project was abandoned. In 1922, the farm was sold to Queen Wilhelmina of the Netherlands, who rented it to cotton farmers. Sometime in 1948, the farm came on the market. In 1949 Keith moved his wife and two young sons to Continental. At that time, Continental consisted of a general store and the machine shop, along with a three-room schoolhouse on what is now White House Canyon Road. Their "supper neighbors," the Browns, lived twelve miles away on the ranch now owned by former State Senate Candidate Bill McGibbon. Everyone knew each other and pitched in to help at harvesting and roundup times.

Between 1950 and 1960, Keith acquired additional farms for FICO in Eloy and Picacho—both in Pinal County; a farm in Aguila, Arizona, in western Maricopa County; and bought the Sahuarita Farm which adjoined the Continental Farm. During this time FICO grew many crops including alfalfa, corn, wheat, barley, milo, maize, higira (a type of sorghum), lettuce, watermelons, and the principal crop, cotton. At one time FICO was the largest grower and shipper of lettuce in the United States. Keith also ran as many as nine thousand sheep and, in 1953 opened a cattle feedlot that grew to twenty thousand

R. Keith Walden examining cotton blossoms. Courtesy of the Walden family.

head. FICO closed the feedlot in 1976 when its operations became incompatible with the growing town of Green Valley.

His son Dick remembers how they got into the pecan business from cotton. "Dad was concerned that names like Dupont and Union Carbide were heavily invested in developing synthetic fibers which might replace much of the market for cotton. So he began to experiment methodically with different crops. He tried all the stone fruits, all the tree nuts, and a dozen varieties of grapes. The crops that thrived best were grapes and pecans. Dad chose pecans over grapes because they have a longer window of harvest and can be harvested by machine.

In 1965, Keith began planting pecans in the Santa Cruz Valley and in Maricopa, Arizona. Today FICO operates one of the largest irrigated pecan orchards in the United States, growing and processing about ten percent of the nation's crop. FICO operates a pecan farm in Albany, Georgia, as well. FICO employs nearly three hundred people, many of whom are second- or third-generation employees. In the 1970s, FICO cooperated with the federal government by donating land so that employees could own their own homes. FICO also provided land for the La Posada retirement home, a medical clinic, and a hospital to serve Green Valley. Keith always believed that "people are the company's greatest asset." For much of FICO's history, Warren "Toops" Culbertson, Keith's brother-in-law, was a partner and confidant to Keith.

Richard S. and R. Keith Walden standing amidst pecan trees. Courtesy of the Walden family.

Both Keith and his son Richard (Dick), the latter of whom has been president of FICO since 1983, were featured in Professor Hiram Drache's book, *Creating Abundance: Visionary Entrepreneurs of Agriculture*. At a conference introducing the book at Concordia College, Hiram stressed that only innovative, creative entrepreneurs who take educated risks can succeed in agriculture today, especially in family enterprises. Dick agrees with Drache's assessment and adds, "Dad's commitment to agriculture came from his recognition that there were three basic human needs: food, clothing, and shelter. He took seriously his objective to provide those basic needs to make life better. In his view, land was a resource to be put to its best use, growing food and fiber for people. Under good stewardship farmland was a renewable resource that could be productive forever. Dad saw opportunities where no one else did. He worked closely with the University of Arizona and others to stay on the cutting edge of agricultural research and technology, offering the opportunity for cooperative research to the University of Arizona faculty. He had the strongest courage of his convictions about the proper use of land, and never doubted his ability to produce from the land for the marketplace. He was an advocate of a free and fair market in agriculture and even spoke against federal subsidies for cotton. He pursued all his endeavors with unwavering dedication and shared his knowledge generously with other farmers at home and abroad."

Keith was the past president of Cotton Council International, which took him to seventeen countries to promote cotton. He was a trustee of the national Cotton Council of America, the Cotton Producers' Institute, and a founding board member of Cotton Incorporated, one of the earliest and most successful marketing organizations in the U.S. He was a trustee of Pomona College and a member of the Advisory Committee on Agriculture for Stanford Research Institute. He served as a consultant to the Ford Foundation in Pakistan. For many years he was a trustee and president of the school board in Continental, Arizona. He served as a director of the First Interstate Bank of Arizona, was a past chair of the Arizona Oil and Gas Commission, director of Arizonans for Jobs and Energy, and a panelist for several sessions of the Arizona Town Hall. He was a director of the Arizona Cattle Growers Association and the National Pecan Council.

The University of Arizona gave Keith its Distinguished Citizens Award in 1973, and the university awarded him an honorary Doctorate of Law in 1998 for his leadership in agriculture, education, and the Arizona economy.

Like his parents, Keith graduated from Pomona College, earning a degree in economics in 1936. He felt that Pomona offered him an excellent education, which was one of the reasons he later served as a trustee of Pomona. His first wife, Barbara Eldridge Culbertson (Burkholder), whom he married in 1938, graduated with the Pomona class of 1935. Keith and Barbara had two sons, Richard and Thomas. Since 1983, Richard has been president of Farmers Investment Co. (FICO), the holding company for Green Valley Pecan Company. Thomas died in 1973 in an aviation accident.

Keith is survived by his son, Richard S. Walden, current chairman and CEO of FICO; his daughter-in-law, Nan Stockholm Walden; his granddaughter Deborah Walden Ralls who is married to David Ralls; his grandson Richard Thomas Walden; and his wife Caroline Daly. Others are his sister, Eileen Walden Hardison, and his brother, A. F. "Bud" Walden, Jr. Surviving family members of his second wife are stepson Jonathan D. Beck and his wife Jean, the latter of whom is an artist in Tucson; and step-grandchildren Amy Beck Gallo, Jeff Beck, Michael Beck, and Christina Beck Stanley.

His son Dick remembers Keith as a good father, especially to two young boys, as well as a role model. Keith spent an entire year in bed with polio as a sixteen-year-old, an experience which gave him time to read, think, and dream. His grandchildren remember him as "Poppa," a doting grandfather who loved to tell stories about the early days in California and Arizona. FICO employees in the front office remember him as an employer who came around and said good-bye to each of them individually before he went home for the weekend. Keith drove around the farm daily, and came to the office every day, even at age eighty-eight.

~ Article reprinted with permission of
K. Richard Walden and Dan Shearer

White Elephant historian Nola Scott. Courtesy of Regina Ford.

Brief History of the Country Fair White Elephant

The Country Fair White Elephant had humble beginnings. Green Valley's popular thrift store began as a community-wide sale in October 1964 at what is now Green Valley Recreation's East Social Center. The sale was organized by a group of volunteers with the goal of raising money to be given back to the community for local projects. Sales from that first fair totaled $146.20.

In 1965, the sale was so successful that a fifteen-minute parade was held afterwards with Will Rogers, Jr., named as grand marshal.

Then, in 1972, the Green Valley Country Fair (GVCF) was formally established as a nonprofit with a fifteen-member board of directors, all volunteers. The sale was a three-day event with a parade held on the last day of the sale.

In 1980, the GVCF Board leased a parcel of land from Pima

County in the government complex in Green Valley for one dollar per year. A 3,000-square-foot building was erected on the site to serve as a year-round thrift shop as well as storage for donated goods.

Store volunteers sorted, priced, and sold donated goods, and proceeds were donated back to the community.

In 1990, Pima County allocated additional land south of the White Elephant building for another expansion. The White Elephant subsequently occupied a 9,800-square-foot building. That same year, a scholarship program was initiated with $10,000 for scholarships and another $127,000 distributed to community nonprofits. In 1991, distributions to the community were $286,500, which included $30,000 in scholarships.

In 1992, the J. C. Penney Volunteer Center recognized the Country Fair White Elephant as one of the outstanding volunteer organizations in the United States. At that time, the White Elephant operation included the board members and about seventy-three volunteers.

In the early 1990s, the Country Fair board had changed the name of the annual parade to the Green Valley Country Fair White Elephant Parade. Although it had had various names during the course of its life, Country Fair White Elephant Inc. was adopted as its official name in 1993.

2018 Country Fair White Elephant Parade. Courtesy of Green Valley News.

Since the beginning, its thrift store prices were kept purposely low; however, it is interesting to note that in 1984, men's ties were fifty cents, socks were twenty-five cents, and *Arizona Highways* magazines were twenty-five cents. In 2000, men's ties were ten cents, socks ten cents, and *Arizona Highways* cost ten cents.

By 1998, the White Elephant had again outgrown its facilities and plans were made to build a 7,500-square-foot addition on the west side of the building.

In 2000, a major expansion project got underway. The expansion was broken down into three phases which included building a new parking lot on the west side of the building as well as the construction of a new addition. Also in 2000, the Country Fair White Elephant was honored by the National Society of Fund Raising Executives for the outstanding work of its volunteers in raising money for area social and health services.

In early July, 2001, Phase III was completed. Two new staff restrooms had been added, receiving and pricing areas had been expanded, the kitchen and coffee break area had been improved, and patio sales were moved indoors. Three cashier stations had been added at the front of the new addition, with an additional cashier station at the back door in the patio area.

In 2001, the White Elephant organization consisted of a twenty-one-member board of directors that oversaw the thrift store. The executive committee consisted of the president, vice president, secretary, treasurer, and assistant treasurer. A parade committee planned, organized, and conducted the annual Country Fair Parade. The contributions committee received, investigated, and reviewed requests for funds and the committee's recommendations were presented to the board for approval. Additional committees included social, long-range planning, nominating, and public relations. Each board member served on two committees.

Sales for 2001 were a record $1,040,640. The White Elephant had become a year-round million-dollar operation with a modern 17,000-square-foot facility and 260 volunteers. Donated items were picked up and deliveries made with a new Ford 250 three-quarter-ton pickup. After the new building and all expenses were paid, the White Elephant was still able to provide a record $620,000 to area nonprofits.

After months of often acrimonious debate, in the fall of 2001 the CFWE Board voted to hire a general manager. At the annual distribution day held in December 2002, a record $1 million was distributed to worthy organizations and charities in the area.

The White Elephant celebrated its fiftieth anniversary in October 2014. More than 380 students in the Sahuarita Unified School District held a Variety Appreciation Show in the district auditorium in honor of the Country Fair White Elephant volunteers. A White Elephant Game Changer grant of $100,000 was presented to the Elephant Head Volunteer Fire Department and $1.4 million was distributed back to the community. That year posted 635 volunteers and four paid staff.

Midnight Madness Green Valley Style, a special three-hour sale from 3 p.m. to 6 p.m. on one afternoon during Country Fair Days, brought in $27,240.05.

In 2017, General Manager Karen Lavo accepted the Arizona Retailers Association Award for District 2 on behalf of the thrift store. On check distribution day, the White Elephant donated $1.5 million to schools, social service agencies, arts support groups, and other nonprofit entities as well as another $150,000 in student scholarships.

For the past fifty-seven years, net proceeds from the thrift store, including profits from eBay sales, total more than $32 million given back to the community. The Covid-19 pandemic closed the White Elephant for more than six months in 2020 and again for nearly three months in 2021 as the store followed the Centers for Disease Control and Prevention Covid-19 guidelines. The store currently has five paid staff members and more than six hundred volunteers who work in two shifts to keep the operation running smoothly in the 34,400-square-foot building.

Although Covid-19 restrictions prevented an in-person check distribution day in 2020, the Country Fair White Elephant gave away $590,000 in December of that year. The number paled in comparison to the $1.7 million distributed in 2019, but was still impressive given that the thrift store had been closed for months during the pandemic.

~ Contributed by Regina Ford; made possible by
longtime White Elephant Historian Nola Scott

ACKNOWLEDGMENTS

Heartfelt thanks go to the many sages of our communities, their families, and our local businesses leaders who either contributed their individual stories or worked with an interviewer to preserve their stories for posterity: Barbara Bennett, historical writer and contributor; Amy Millet and Alaura Millet, researchers, writers, editors, and digital media masters; Steve Brown, an Ivy League graduate, published author, and contributor; Monica Christiansen, our team leader, technology guru, researcher, and writer; Oscar Gomez, researcher, writer, and a retired educator with an encyclopedic memory; Lynn Harris, wise elder and contributor; Sutah Harris, local historical writer and contributor; Mary Kasulaitis, a retired librarian, researcher, published author, and contributor; Jeanne Klingenberg Herrman, an invaluable team member who somehow fit six years of writing into six months and her dear husband, Tom, who spent countless hours scanning the treasure trove of photos in the Bull/Klingenberg family collection; Bill McNarie, retired principal, school board member, and contributor; Charles Oldham, retired principal, interim superintendent, and contributor; Lori Punske, retired educator, text editor, and writer; Kay Richardson, administrative assistant and contributor; Dr. Jay St. John, retired superintendent of SUSD No. 30 and contributor; Emily Tingle, writer; Barbara Tingle, award-winning SUSD No. 30 educator and writer; Burton Tingle, SUSD No. 30 retired, football coach, award-winning and legendary educator, and contributor; and Rachel Wear, retired educator, historical writer, and contributor.

Monica, Mary, Oscar, Amy and Alaura Millet, and Barb and Emily Tingle spent countless hours meeting and consulting with individuals online and in person—all in the name of ensuring everyone's stories were captured and documented for the future. Dayna Burke and Debbie Kutina graciously edited and blended stories together. An extra special thanks goes to our team researchers Monica Christiansen and Mary Kasulaitis, who not only researched their own work, but assisted others with their research. Their exceptional interpersonal and organizational skills have been absolutely invaluable to the completion of this project. They kept us laughing and sane!

This six-year project had many professional hands contributing their research skills and expertise: Dan Shearer, editor of the *Green Valley News*; Rick Wiley of the *Arizona Daily Star* and Tucson.com; Jeff Kida of *Arizona Highways* magazine; Perri Pyle of the Arizona Historical Society; Wendi Goen and Jane Cadwalader at Arizona State Archives and Public Records; and Patricia Ballesteros and Bob Diaz from University of Arizona and Special Collections.

The Sahuarita Unified School District Educational Enrichment Foundation (SEEF) board members Jane Lateer, president; Jan Spooner, vice president; Jana Turner, secretary; and most especially its treasurer, Fran Jaeger, guided us through the nuts and bolts of publishing along with our editor Kay Jones and our publishing consultant Debora Lewis. Other friends at SEEF who gave of their time and talents include Jane and Tom Burns, Tim Campbell, Cheryl Schaefer, Debbie Kutina, Jeff Herndon, Sara Mora, and Lora Nastase.

We would also like to thank the Sahuarita Unified School District's administrators and staff, especially Dr. Manuel O. Valenzuela; Scott Downs, assistant superintendent; Brett Bonner, assistant superintendent; Betsy Palacios, executive assistant to the superintendent; Lizette Huie, chief financial officer; Amber Woods, director of community outreach; Yolanda Mariscal, human resource specialist—support personnel; and Lorena Gastelum, customer service specialist. Likewise, the support of the Sahuarita town council is much appreciated—Tom Murphy, mayor; Kara Egbert, vice mayor; Gil Lusk, former town council member; and town council members Bill Bracco and Deborah Morales.

To Ellen Allgaier Fountain of the National Watercolor Society, who taught art at Sahuarita Junior High School between 1974 and 1980, we express sincere gratitude for your contribution of the beautiful watercolor paintings used on our book covers. The painting on the front, *End of the Road*, was done in 1978 and depicts a rural scene along Mission Road. *Through Rolling*, on the back cover, was created from a photo of the rusted old wheels that were used to relocate the Sierrita (McGee Ranch) schoolhouse.

When the idea of a Sahuarita history project was first broached, Mary "Mac" Chernoski, a dedicated teacher with a lifelong love of history, did not hesitate to step forward as a volunteer. In fact, she was one-hundred-and-fifty percent on board. Her tenacity and dogged determination are contagious and we were all gladly infected. She constantly reminds us that we are a team and this project was made possible through divine providence. We are all grateful for each other's dedicated efforts and for our family members (John and Steve Chernoski; James Christiansen and Kerry L. Elam; Rob Kasulaitis; Daniel Millet) and our friends who encouraged and motivated us along the way.

CREDITS—REFERENCE INFORMATION

Arizona Historical Society

Arizona State Archives

Made in the USA
Monee, IL
16 October 2024